School-Age Language Intervention: Evidence-Based Practices

School-Age Language Intervention:

Evidence-Based Practices

edited by

Teresa A. Ukrainetz

8700 Shoal Creek Boulevard
Austin, Texas 78757-6897
800/897-3202 Fax 800/397-7633
www.proedinc.com

8700 Shoal Creek Boulevard
Austin, Texas 78757-6897
800/897-3202 Fax 800/397-7633
www.proedinc.com

Library of Congress Cataloging-in-Publication Data

School-Age Language Intervention : evidence-based practices/edited by Teresa A. Ukrainetz.
p. cm.
ISBN 978-1-4164-0595-5 (Print)
ISBN 978-1-4164-0610-5 (e-book PDF)
1. Language arts—Remedial teaching. 2. Language disorders—Treatment. I. Ukrainetz, Teresa A., 1962- II. Ukrainetz, Teresa A.
LB1576. S3257 2015
372.6—dc23

2014025315

Art Director: Jason Crosier
Designer: Bookbright Media
This book is designed in Minion Pro and Myriad Pro.

Printed in the United States of America

3 4 5 6 7 8 9 10 23 22 21 20 19 18 17

This book is dedicated to

Jerry L. Starr

For his patient listening and enduring support

Contents

Foreword

What This Book Is About

This book is about how to teach students with language impairments the skills, strategies, and underlying processes needed for educational success. It is primarily directed at speech–language pathologists (SLPs), but both regular and special education teachers should find helpful ideas for addressing language skills in their instructional settings.

This book continues a journey begun in the late 1980s when I worked as an SLP in a school district in British Columbia, Canada (or perhaps even before then, as a graduate student, when I was assigned to present the seminal chapter by Carol Westby, 1985, on narrative as a bridge between oral and written language). I was fortunate to be an SLP in a time and place that allowed and encouraged freedom and innovation. Our school districts were experimenting with inclusive service delivery, noncategorical service, continuous progress in ungraded primary classes, and anecdotal reporting. Teachers were provided release time for collaborative planning. There was no high-stakes testing or standardized curricula. Speech–language services were not yet part of Individualized Education Programs (IEPs). We set our own eligibility requirements, caseload size, and waiting lists. We could vary between pull-out and inclusive intervention, individual and group, as many times a week as we each saw fit, so long as we could satisfy principals, teachers, and parents in our assigned six-to-eight schools. All this freedom meant there were occasional poor practices, but it also allowed some of us to soar.

Connecting to teachers, classrooms, and classwork helped me make sense of what I was doing and made me feel part of a team. I heard Margaret Lahey speak on narrative development (Lahey, 1988), which inspired me to develop narrative intervention units employing children's literature and pictography to target story grammar skills in a developmental order. I co-taught these units with regular and resource teachers. These experiences taught me a lot about classroom management, working with teachers, and linking between the speech room and the classroom. However, they also revealed significant challenges to providing explicit, systematic, supportive attention to specific language skills for my caseload students amid the busyness of the regular classroom.

During my doctorate at the University of Texas at Austin, I sought out experiences in developmental psychology, speech–language pathology, speech communication, and literacy education to better understand how to combine explicit skill instruction with contexts that provided meaning and purpose. In 1995, I made by way back to snow and mountains, and found a home at the University of Wyoming. There, in my graduate school-age language intervention course, students worked through a stack of readings, largely from *Language, Speech, and Hearing Services in Schools.* These articles set the foundations but often lacked the "end of the story" of the details of intervention. As a result, I invited some of these like-minded scholars to share in creating a theoretically driven but practical text on school-age language intervention for SLPs (Ukrainetz, 2006). In addition to an emphasis on teaching skills within purposeful contexts, I introduced the critical treatment elements of RISE: Repeated opportunities for Intensive, Systematically supported, Explicit instruction.

That book has served students and clinicians well, but with time and use, I judged more was needed. I invited a different array of top scholars and researchers to contribute chapters. This new book extends attention to history, legislation, and other approaches to intervention. It includes explanations of major categories of language learners and intervention guidance for reading, spelling, phonological processing, and older students. This book has a distinctly different tack from Ukrainetz (2006); staying more theoretically neutral and letting the empirical evidence lead to the answers. It turns out that, across language, and even cognitive areas, the answers again converge around contextualized skill intervention and RISE. There is still a lot to learn about how to conduct this challenging combination of explicit skill instruction and meaningful contexts. However, the broad outline continues to be what Judith Johnston called for so many years ago:

> The challenge of intervention with the language-disordered child is to simplify the language learning task without changing its basic character. Language learning must remain integrated with intellect, motivated by communication, actively inductive, and self-directed. . . . But language learning must also be facilitated in specific, well-calculated ways. The challenge for educators is to manage this tension between the common and the extraordinary. What sort of intervention programme can maintain the essence of language learning and yet accelerate it? (Johnston, 1985, p. 128)

Overview of the Book

The first four chapters of this book explain the fundamentals of SLP practice in the schools. Chapter 1 introduces the roles, service delivery options, and practices in the schools, the *who works on what where* part of the business, with enough of a historical context to show the widening road that school SLPs travel. Chapter 2 addresses the foundations of language intervention: how language intervention is organized and the level at which it is aimed to intercept the problems—underlying neuropsychology, language skills, or classroom transactions. This chapter examines what the research evidence indicates overall about school-age language intervention. Chapter 3 explains how to provide contextualized skill intervention with RISE in a whole-part framework. In this chapter I have tried to take the best of the popular Gillam and Ukrainetz (2006) chapter on literature-based intervention and combine it with interventions that reference standardized academic outcomes, specifically those of the *Common Core State Standards* (National Governors Association Center for Best Practices and the Council of Chief State School Officers, 2010). Chapter 4 is what I call the "rules of the road": the federal laws and regulations that govern special education and SLP services. There is even a very brief look at how special education is delivered in my home country of Canada. Two chapters (5 and 6) sort out the major categories of language learners on an SLP's caseload in the schools: specific language impairment, reading disability, and bilingual learners. Trina Spencer and I explain what those labels mean, the terminology used in the schools, how the categories differ (and overlap), and what the research says about how these children fare over the school years.

The next chapters address best practices for spoken and written language intervention. In Chapter 7, Karla McGregor and Dawna Duff guide assessment and intervention for the diverse and deep vocabulary knowledge important in school. Catherine Balthazar and Cheryl Scott provide a primer on the grammar needed to understand and produce academic texts (Chapter 8). In Chapter 9, I discuss how to teach episodic structure, cohesion, and artful storytelling of narrative structure intervention. Carol Westby, Barb Culatta, and Kendra Hall-Kenyon explore facilitating the many dimensions of informational discourse (Chapter 10). In Chapter 11, Celeste Roseberry-McKibbin discusses how to help children with backgrounds that put them at environmental risk to cope with the language of the classroom.

Three chapters address the written code and the cognitive underpinnings of communication and learning. Chapter 12 explains the very teachable skill of phonemic awareness and the emerging areas of phonological memory and retrieval intervention. Pamela Hook and Elizabeth Crawford-Brooke hit the highlights of assessment and instruction for word identification and fluency (Chapter 13). In Chapter 14, Julie Wolter attends to spelling and its connections to language knowledge. Chapter 15 deals with reading comprehension: I attempt to provide coherent and manageable guidance for SLP intervention in this extensive and diverse domain. The book ends with a chapter in which Lauren Katz and Karen Fallon explore "the final frontier" of SLP services to high school and college students with reading disorders.

I hope this book serves students, instructors, and clinicians well. It is certainly still not the entire story, but is a research-based, comprehensive step toward effective intervention across the many aspects of what is called "school-age language" for the school SLP. I would like to thank Doug Petersen, Melissa Allen, and Mark Guiberson for many thought-provoking conversations about the nature of language learning and facilitation. I would also like to acknowledge the graduate students in my school-age language intervention course who perpetually lead me to new insights about language learning and teaching. Catherine Ross, my colleague, collaborator, and critic, continues to be my touchstone, helping me make sense to those on the front lines of speech–language pathology in the schools.

References

Johnston, J. (1985). Fit, focus, and functionality: An essay on early language intervention. *Child Language Teaching and Therapy, 1*(2), 125–134.

Lahey, M. (1988). *Language Development and Language Disorders.* New York, NY: Macmillan.

National Governors Association Center for Best Practices and Council of Chief State School Officers (2010). *Common Core State Standards for English Language Arts & Literacy in History/Social Studies, Science, and Technical Subjects.* Washington, DC: Author. Retrieved from http://www.corestandards.org

Ukrainetz, T. A. (2006). *Contextualized language intervention: Scaffolding preK–12 literacy achievement.* Austin, TX: PRO-ED.

Westby, C. E. (1985). Learning to talk—talking to learn: Oral-literate language differences. In C.S. Simon (Ed.), *Communication skills and classroom success: Therapy methodologies for language-learning disabled students* (pp. 181–213). San Diego, CA: College-Hill Press.

Contributors

Teresa A. Ukrainetz
Professor, Division of Communication Disorders
University of Wyoming
Laramie, WY

Catherine H. Balthazar
Professor
Governers State University
Chicago, IL

Elizabeth C. Crawford-Brooke
Vice President of Education and Research
Lexia Learning Systems
Medford, MA

Barbara Culatta
Professor
Brigham Young University
Provo, UT

Dawna Duff
Doctoral Candidate
University of Iowa
Iowa City, IA

Karen A. Fallon
Associate Professor
Towson University
Towson, MD

Kendra M. Hall-Kenyon
Associate Professor
Brigham Young University
Provo, UT

Pamela E. Hook
Professor *Emerita*
MGH Institute of Health Professions
Boston, MA

Lauren A. Katz
Founding Partner
Literacy, Language, and Learning Institute
Ann Arbor, MI

Karla McGregor
Professor
University of Iowa
Iowa City, IA

Celeste Roseberry-McKibbin
Professor
California State University, Sacramento
Sacramento, CA

Cheryl M. Scott
Professor Emerita
Rush University
Chicago, IL

Trina D. Spencer
Research Director
Northern Arizona University
Flagstaff, AZ

Carol Westby
Affiliate appointment
Brigham Young University
Provo, UT

Julie A. Wolter
Associate Professor
Utah State University
Logan, UT

Chapter 1

The Groundwork of Practice: Speech–Language Pathology in the Schools

Teresa A. Ukrainetz

This chapter presents the practice and roles of speech–language pathologists (SLPs) within the school system. SLPs have been present in the schools since the early 1900s, but the services provided have expanded considerably, from a narrow focus on speech correction to a comprehensive attention to speech, language, and cognition related to school success. SLPs work in a variety of service delivery models with other educators to provide prevention, assessment, and treatment services for spoken and written language.

The Evolution of Speech–Language Pathology Services in the Schools

In the Beginning

Sometimes there is the impression that our profession is new on the scene. In fact, SLPs have been part of public education since the early 1900s (Duchan, 2010, 2011). Speech therapy arose out of the multiple forces of compulsory education, widespread expansion of educational opportunities, and efforts to provide comprehensive education to most children.

Speech services were provided initially by existing teaching staff whose training was supplemented by continuing education courses available from a few medical schools, universities, and private clinics (Duchan, 2010). The first degree program in speech correction was offered at the University of Wisconsin–Madison in 1921. By 1952, even the very rural state of Wyoming offered a Bachelor's degree in speech correction.

In the 1950s, speech correction services were common in metropolitan schools (Gravani, 2007). Services were generally limited to the primary grades, through itinerant correctionists and self-contained classes. Although the shorter title of *speech pathologist,* along with the Master's degree requirement for certification, has existed since 1965 (Malone, 1999), neither existed in the public schools until 1975. In 1975, with P.L. 94-142, *speech or language impairment* became a disability category in the newly created system of special education. Speech correctionists became *speech–language pathologists* within special education and the master's degree became the terminal professional requirement. However, it still took many years for school districts to shift to Master's-level SLPs. Even now, schools struggle to find sufficient Master's-level clinicians and the title of *speech–language pathologist* continues to be poorly recognized (Box 1.1).

SLP workloads are generally described by caseload, which is the number of children receiving some type of intervention, including indirect service, from the SLP (American Speech-Language-Hearing Association [ASHA], 2002). Prior to the 1970s, caseloads were often over 100 students: In 1960, SLPs reported working with an average of 111 students per week (Peters-Johnson, 1992). After speech services became part of special education in 1975, caseloads began to drop. By 1981, Peters-Johnson (1992) reported that caseloads had dropped to an average of 43 students. Between then and 1995, median caseload increased to 50, which is where it has held since (ASHA, 2010a)—but more on this later.

Box 1.1. ***What's in a Name?***

The label of *speech–language pathologist* is embedded in our line of work and educational legislation. It is intended to reflect the wide scope of the profession. However, this label still lacks ease of use and "brand recognition." Instead, in informal parlance, *speech therapist* and *speech teacher* have persisted.

Speech–language pathologist is a mouthful for any child to say but especially for one with a speech impairment. It also has clear medical connotations that do not suit SLP practice in the schools (Simon, 1995). Even beyond "pathologist," there is a clear dispreference for *language* as a distinctive identifier. Teachers judged that, while SLPs have particular expertise in the spoken modality, all educators work on language all the time. As a resource teacher said, "What *isn't* language?" (Ukrainetz & Fresquez, 2003, p. 288). In 2000, the Canadian Association of Speech–Language Pathologists and Audiologists (now called Speech–Language and Audiology Canada) sought a name that was more meaningful to the general public. A focus group was given background information on the profession and asked to generate alternate names, which resulted in four variations on speech and hearing (e.g., Speech and Hearing Canada). These names, the existing name, and background information were shown to a cross section of Canadians who identified their first and second choices. Of the 350 respondents, 90% preferred the labels that did *not* include "language" or "pathologist."

Merriam-Webster (1993) defines *speech* as the communication or expression of thoughts in spoken words, which includes oral language. Even the U.S. Constitution considers any expression of ideas, including writing, as speech. There is no question that SLPs should address language—this book is all about language. However, the distinction between *speech* and *language* is important only to this profession. For non-SLPs, *speech* is inclusive of all manners of communication, while *language* only complicates matters.

The Emergence of Language Intervention

Historically, speech correctionists dealt fairly exclusively with what was called speech impediments. Duchan (2010) described the various early typologies of speech impediments, which included stammering (stuttering and cluttering), lisping (/s/ and /z/ distortions), lalling (immature pronunciation or /r/ distortion), nasality (cleft palate), mutism, and thick speech (by children with intellectual disabilities). In 1960, SLPs reported caseloads of 81% articulation compared to 5% language (Peters-Johnson, 1992). By 1981, the percentage of language disorders and articulation were each at 47%. The range of ages increased over that time span, with students beyond fourth grade constituting only 6% of caseloads in 1960 and 33% in 1981.

The roots of language intervention date from the 1930s, but services were delivered primarily by clinical psychologists and teachers of students with disabilities (Duchan, 2011). Samuel Orton and Mildred McGinnis treated "word deafness" of children with specific language impairment (then called congenital or childhood aphasia). These children were viewed as having difficulty in recalling speech sounds in proper temporal sequence (somewhat like the phonological processing difficulties of today). Orton focused on reading and spelling and McGinnis focused on speech, teaching precise articulatory productions based on principles of deaf education (Duchan, 2011). Both taught students to produce phonemes, blend and sequence phonemes, and associate phonemes with letters, using sensory-motor association methods.

After the Second World War, approaches began to shift from peripheral and mechanistic treatments to more holistic views of cognitive and linguistic processing (Duchan, 2011). For example, Kurt Goldstein's 1948 "organismic theory" held that language symptoms must be examined in the context of occurrence and that children needed to be taught "inner speech." Specific abilities involved in the internal processing of visual and auditory information were identified and treated. Alfred Strauss treated visual discrimination and figure-ground differentiation, while Helmur Myklebust emphasized auditory awareness, discrimination, and localization. Mykelbust's inner speech activities sound familiar: symbolic play, acting out daily events, matching words to objects, completing sentences, associating word meanings, and unscrambling mixed-up sentences. Myklebust was a pioneer in linking phonological processing to reading disabilities and bringing language intervention professionals into reading instruction (e.g., Johnson & Myklebust, 1967).

In the 1960s, attention began to focus on linguistic accounts of language difficulties (Duchan, 2011). Mildred Templin in 1957 reported the articulation of sounds, speech-sound discrimination, vocabulary, and sentence structure for 480 children from 3 to 8 years old. Templin conducted one of the earliest language sample analyses, obtaining 50 utterances and calculating mean length of response, number of different words, and types of words and sentences (Duchan, 2011). Emphasis moved to syntax with Chomsky's (1957) concept of an abstract, generative underlying language system. Children's language was seen as rule-ordered and systematically related to that of adults. Gleason, Brown, Bellugi, and others provided detailed descriptions of morphosyntax acquisition that still guide preschool intervention.

By the late 1960s, simple accounts of behaviors as stimulus-response associations were proving insufficient for the complexity of language development (Duchan, 2011). Grammatical evaluation tools and linguistic targets (e.g., is-verbing, wh-questions, and regular past tense) for language intervention began appearing (Rees, 1983). Processing-oriented models were also employed. A popular model was Charles Osgood's psycholinguistic depiction of language as multileveled and modality-based chains of mental associations, which led to the popular *Illinois Test of Psycholinguistic Abilities* (ITPA). The ITPA assessed automatic and language-mediated levels of auditory and visual processing and set the basis for treatment programs designed around the profiles identified on this test.

Speech correctionists of the early 1960s did not generally teach language, and the bit they did address was not viewed as "language intervention." Rees (1983) recalled the simplicity of the period:

> We had no tests and very few materials. We cut pictures out of magazines and bought Golden Books and toys and board games that stimulated talking and

> helped to teach vocabulary. In fact, vocabulary teaching was pretty much the major activity; color names were very big, as were animals, vehicles and "community helpers." (p. 310)

By the close of the 1960s, speech correctionists were specifically attending to language and beginning to use specific procedures for teaching it. A few individuals, such as Laura Lee, espoused a naturalistic conversational approach to teaching grammar (Duchan, 2011). However, the predominant intervention theory was behaviorism (Skinner, 1957): the imitation of observable verbal behaviors with external reinforcement of correct productions in drill or game formats. Fey (1986) described programs in which language productions were built from single-word to multiword productions in reinforced additive sequences with little consideration for syntactic rules, meanings, or developmental progressions (e.g., *is* → *is baby* → *is baby happy?*). This was a period that Rees (1983) described as "exciting for the language professional but still simple" (p. 310). There were relatively few aspects of language that SLPs addressed, and they taught these using clear instructional procedures. This would change quickly: "Things started getting rough for the language professional when it became apparent that morphology plus syntax plus semantics does not equal language" (p. 310).

In the 1970s, new understandings of semantics, phonology, and pragmatics complicated the picture of children's language and how to support its development. Communicative intention and context of use mattered when explaining a young child's language performance. SLP training programs addressed many language areas, including Brown's five stages, Brown's 14 morphemes, semantic relations, new word in an old function versus old word in a new function, competence-performance distinctions, performatives, and individual language-learning strategies (Rees, 1983). Naturalistic interventions, such as milieu teaching and focused stimulation, appeared that highlighted language structures within communicatively motivated learning opportunities (Fey, 1986). Even behavioral programs incorporated more meaningful and developmentally based goal sequences (e.g., *happy?* → *baby happy?* → *is baby happy?*).

For older children, language development was less obvious, reading was often a concern, and auditory processing was examined as a source of both areas of difficulty. Researchers investigated memory for auditory span and sequence as well as for discrimination of rapidly changing acoustic components of the speech signal (e.g., Tallal & Piercy, 1973). Findings were translated into training programs for auditory memory (e.g., digit repetition drills), auditory discrimination (e.g., identifying bird tweets versus doorbells), and phoneme discrimination (e.g., judging *time* and *dime* as same or different). Tasks that tapped phonemic awareness were judged to reflect difficulties perceiving differences between sounds: The current *Lindamood Phoneme Sequencing Program* (Lindamood & Lindamood, 2011) was originally called *Auditory Discrimination in Depth*.

By the close of the 1970s, there was a substantial body of scholarship on the nature of language, language development, language ability impairment, and how to remediate language impairments. Processing and linguistic approaches of language impairment existed concurrently, with more emphasis on developmental-linguistic models for preschoolers and more emphasis on cognitive-processing models for school-age children.

Curriculum-Based Language Intervention

In the 1980s and 1990s, school-age intervention turned to *communicative competence* and the academic language needed for success in school (Simon, 1985). *Specific language impairment* became preferred over terms that implied brain damage. Specific language impairment in school-age children was also referred to as *language learning disability.* Inclusive formats of service delivery were strongly supported (Westby, Watson, & Murphy, 1994).

Language concerns expanded to literate vocabulary and later to morphosyntactic structures, conversational pragmatics, discourse cohesion, narrative structure, cultural considerations, and being "meta" about language. Word-finding, which is the ease with which known words are retrieved, mattered for both fluent reading and fluent spoken communication. Resources for school-age language intervention that went beyond the traditional drill books and picture cards appeared. Simon's (1984) *Evaluating Communicative Competence* described a host of activities for evaluating and teaching within conversational, narrative, and expository discourse. Literature-based resources appeared, such as *The Magic of Stories* (Strong & North, 1996). Miller and Chapman (1985) developed the Systematic Analysis of Language Transcripts (SALT), a computerized clinician-friendly language sample analysis program with age-reference data that has continued to be revised and expanded.

Teaching language within communicative interactions also came from education. The 1980s was a time of a whole language model of reading development. With this view, in a literate society, children learn to read and write without direct instruction, through engaging with print in meaningful, motivating, purposeful contexts where component skills are taught in an integrated manner (Goodman, 1986). Phonics, which is systematic instruction in the correspondence between phonemes and spelling, was embedded in interactions with print (Dahl, Scharer, Lawson, & Grogan, 1999). Whole language was controversial for the acquisition of the decoding aspect of reading (Vellutino, 1991), but it certainly helped students discover the pleasure of reading (Sawyer, 2007). Current reading instruction attempts to maintain a balance between explicit, systematic skill activities and pleasurable, meaningful reading opportunities.

Written composition was taught through a process that was modeled on how professional writers write. Process writing, originally called Writers' Workshop, broke writing composition into manageable parts. Children composed works on personally selected topics at an individualized pace with guidance and feedback from teachers and peers (Graves, 1983; Calkins, 1983). This soon evolved into more manageable steps through which students moved together: generate, outline or map, draft, peer conference, revise, teacher conference, edit, illustrate, publish, and share (Gillam, 1995). The process of writing is still taught, but there is more emphasis on the quality of writing than on personal expression.

SLPs borrowed from whole language and process writing approaches in designing language interventions for syntactic, semantic, and pragmatic skills (Gillam, 1995; Gillam, McFadden, & van Kleeck, 1995). Meanwhile, the traditional approach of addressing skills one at a time in an isolated manner also continued. For narratives of students with language impairments, Gillam et al. found that both approaches resulted in gains, but in differing ways. Processing approaches to intervention split into general auditory or sound processing and specific phonological or speech processing. SLPs taught students the awareness of the phonological structure of speech needed for reading and spelling (e.g., Ball & Blachman, 1988). A proprietary software program, called FastForword (Scientific Learning Corporation, 1996) caused considerable excitement for its possibility of "curing" auditory processing disorders through exercises involving systematically modified acoustic elements of speech (e.g., Merzenich et al., 1996).

Accountability and Achievement Standards

In the first decade of the 21st century, all past possibilities of language intervention still existed. While in-class interventions continue to be recommended, questions began to arise concerning whether the services provided were sufficiently therapeutic to make significant changes for students with language impairments (Ehren, 2000). Pull-out and skill-based approaches became appropriate alternatives again as educational policy and practice emphasized measurable results and research showed the importance of explicit, systematic skill instruction. Use of scientifically based evidence in practice became much more heavily emphasized (ASHA, 2007, 2010b). Evidence-based practice involves making decisions about the care of individual patients by integrating the best available research evidence with clinical expertise and the values and preferences of the patient (Dollaghan, 2007). ASHA and other professional organizations began providing practice guidelines and resources (Justice & Fey, 2004; see http://asha.org).

In this decade, SLPs became increasingly and more visibly involved in the high-value area of reading. ASHA (2001) put forth a position paper elucidating SLPs' knowledge and skills in reading and writing instruction in terms of both language and decoding. SLP roles included preventing written language problems by fostering language acquisition and emergent literacy, identifying children at risk for reading and writing problems, and assessing, intervening, and documenting outcomes for reading and writing. SLPs needed to learn more about classroom practices and expectations as well as ways of collaborating with teachers to provide services. As standardized academic goals and benchmarks were mandated by states, it became easier to design treatments around these skill expectations. The decade closed with the introduction of a single set of K–12 academic expectations developed by the National Governors Association Center for Best Practices and the Council of Chief State School Officers in 2010. These rigorous and carefully sequenced *Common Core State Standards for English Language Arts & Literacy in History/Social Studies, Science, and Technical Subjects* (and an equivalent set of standards for mathematics) culminate in students graduating with globally competitive college and career readiness preparation. Adoption of a single set of standards was intended improve coordination of instructional aims across the grades, educational settings, and geographic locations. These standards were quickly adopted by most state educational agencies across the United States. However, as this book went to print, some resistance was emerging with criticisms that the standards were too rigorous, too uniform, and too prescriptive (see Chapter 3 for more on the standards).

The Current Practice of Speech–Language Pathology in Schools

School SLPs provide therapeutic services to students with communication (and occasionally swallowing) difficulties. They serve many children over long periods of time, generally outside the classroom. They teach underlying skills and processes rather than curricular content, but tight links to the classroom and subject-area achievement are emphasized. Service delivery has an increased emphasis on reading proficiency, academic standards, accountability of results, pre-referral intervention, and research evidence (ASHA, 2010b).

Caseload Size

School SLPs typically work in one or two schools with a caseload of 50 that spans multiple grade groups, disability categories, and communication characteristics (ASHA, 2010a; Katz, Maag, Fallon, Blenkarn, & Smith, 2010). However, there is considerable variation. ASHA reported median monthly caseloads ranging from 76 in Indiana to 33 in North Dakota. For 98% of the 634 public school SLP respondents in Katz et al.'s survey, caseloads ranged from 13 to 85. ASHA (1993) recommended a maximum caseload size of 40, but few states follow that guideline.

In terms of the features of caseloads, 30% of SLPs travel to three or more schools (ASHA, 2010a). Elementary school was a responsibility for 90% of the respondents. Half served preschoolers, over 40% served middle or junior high schools, and 30% served senior high schools (the total is greater than 100% because many SLPs serve more than one school). ASHA's survey results were compiled into mean monthly numbers across disability categories (e.g., autism, developmental disability), characteristics (e.g., auditory processing, selective mutism), and treatment areas (e.g., pragmatics, reading). The highest categories forming the greatest proportion of SLP caseloads were language impaired or learning disabled; the next, speech sound disorders; and the third, cognitive impairments, including autism. Since many children would fit into several of the groupings, these numbers are difficult to interpret.

There are factors beyond caseload size that affect the job: frequency of service, caseload diversity, evaluation services, planning time, documentation requirements, and meetings with teachers and parents. Having multiple schools means more travel time, more work spaces to find, more carting around supplies, and more personnel to know. ASHA (2002) proposed moving to a workload reporting system that considers these features. However, as of ASHA's 2010 report (2010a), 80% of SLPs still reported caseload was used to determine the amount of effort required from the job.

Katz et al. (2010) analyzed the factors that contributed to making a caseload seem unmanageable. A clear relation to caseload size was found: 20% of SLPs reported feelings of unmanageability with caseloads of 41–45, almost 40% reported these feelings with 46–50 students, and 60% reported these feelings with 56–60 students. For SLPs with caseloads of over 47, experience mattered: Those with more years of experience were less distressed. The perceptions of lack of manageability of large caseloads were not related to whether the SLPs considered they were adequately prepared to teach written language or to the presence of literacy preparation in their university programs. For SLPs with caseloads over 47, collaborative service was less favored. Despite the theoretical satisfactions of sharing responsibilities with other educators, it appeared that, with large caseloads, there were more drawbacks than benefits in negotiating shared territories.

Service Delivery

SLPs typically conduct the full process of screening, evaluating, determining goals, and conducting intervention for each referred student in their assigned schools. In some districts, SLPs may specialize in particular services, such as augmentative/alternative communication or communication skills classes. Links to the curriculum and achievement standards are now emphasized, but SLPs are notable for their relative freedom and independence from the curriculum compared to teachers.

SLPs employ a variety of service delivery models, including consultation, in-class intervention, and pull-out individual and small group services. Typically, direct services are provided several times a week in approximately half-hour sessions. While speech cases may "graduate" in a year, language students are often on an SLP caseload for 3 or more years. This can lead to motivational issues for the student. As one experienced SLP said, "Many of the students will remain in my program for many years and I need them to think of this as a positive thing and not a prison sentence" (Ukrainetz & Fresquez, 2003, p. 293).

Brandel and Loeb (2011) surveyed almost 2,000 school SLPs on the factors considered when deciding on service delivery models and treatment schedules. The SLPs reported that characteristics of their students were the main factors, not the SLP or workplace characteristics. However, these SLPs reported little variation in what was provided: small group pull-out sessions of 20–30 minutes. Students with severe to moderate disabilities received treatment 2–3 times per week, while those with milder disabilities received treatment once per week. Some decisions were associated with caseload size and clinical experience: Larger caseloads in preschool settings were associated with lower service intensity, and SLPs with university training in shared teaching were more likely to provide intervention in resource rooms. Brandel and Loeb's results suggest that the service delivery format is not as individualized as many SLPs may believe.

Roles and Responsibilities

SLPs are responsible for service delivery to children with speech and language impairments. The domain of speech has maintained a constant scope since inception: articulation, phonology, voice, fluency, and swallowing concerns. In contrast, that which constitutes language changed and expanded considerably over time. Language is "a code whereby ideas about the world are expressed through a conventional system of arbitrary signals for communication" (Lahey, 1988, p. 3). Lahey goes on to consider language in terms of the triad of form, content, and use and its alignment with the classical linguistic divisions. However, that is only the beginning of what is addressed within language intervention. In efforts to effect functional change for students, SLPs also deal with the

Box 1.2. ***What Is the "Language" Part of Language Intervention?***

Language intervention addresses the phonology, morphology, syntax, semantics, pragmatics, prelinguistic communication, and paralinguistic communication of speaking, listening, reading, writing, and manual modalities. Language intervention also addresses the cognitive aspects (e.g., attention, memory, sequencing, problem solving, and executive functioning) and the social aspects of communication (e.g., behavioral and social skills affecting communication).

Note: From the "Standards for Accreditation of Graduate Education in Audiology and Speech–Language Pathology" (updated January, 1, 2013). Retrieved from http://www.asha.org/academic/accreditation/accredmanual/section3

cognitive, behavioral, and social aspects of communicative competence (Box 1.2). Discourse, metalinguistics, print decoding, spelling, attention, memory, social skills, learning behaviors, and even curricular content all fall under the aegis of language intervention.

In addition to the many possible targets of intervention, the school SLP has diverse roles and responsibilities (Box 1.3). The ASHA (2010b) policy statement emphasized academic performance standards, pre-referral services, subject-area intervention, and evidence-based practice. Specific attention was devoted to the need for SLPs to attend to maintaining their position in schools, explaining and demonstrating to other stakeholders the distinctive and important contributions of SLPs to the academic success of students.

The ASHA (2010b) statement does not specifically explain SLP involvement in reading and writing but rather assumes it. Students must be competent readers and writers to succeed academically, but how SLPs approach academic competence varies. Fallon and Katz (2011) conducted a survey of the provision of written language services by SLPs. From responses of 645 school SLPs, 35% reported not providing any services in the area of written language to students, while 20% reported providing written language services to all their students with written language weaknesses. Whether or not they believed they had the expertise varied by area: phonological awareness (about 90%), phonics (80%), morphological analysis (70%), reading comprehension (65%), spelling (40%), narrative writing (50%), and expository writing (45%). Although about 50% thought the SLP scope of practice should include it, most of the SLPs (70%) thought others were better equipped to work with written language. However, even SLPs who think that they should not deal with written language likely use print materials in their interventions.

Service Delivery Formats

Speech–language services fall broadly into three formats: pull-out, in-class, and self-contained classroom (Box 1.4). Speech correction service delivery includes individual

Box 1.3. ***Roles and Responsibilities of SLPs in the Schools***

A. Critical Roles

1. Work Across All Levels – From pre-K to high school with no school level underserved
2. Serving the Range of Disorders – Serve the full range of language, speech sounds, fluency, voice, and swallowing disorders
3. Ensure Educational Relevance – Address personal, social, academic, and vocational needs that have an impact on attainment of educational goals
4. Provide Unique Contributions to Curriculum – Use expertise in the linguistic and metalinguistic foundations of curriculum learning for students with disabilities and other struggling learners
5. Highlight Language-Literacy Connections – Use and demonstrate the interrelationships of listening, speaking, reading, and writing to obtain significant improvements in literacy achievement
6. Provide Culturally Competent Services – Distinguish a language disorder from "something else," including cultural and linguistic differences, socioeconomic factors, and lack of adequate instruction; address the impact of language differences on student learning and assist teachers in promoting educational growth

B. Range of Responsibilities

1. Prevention – Participate in evidence-based school initiatives to prevent academic failure, such as Response to Intervention
2. Assessment – Conduct evidence-based, collaborative assessments to identify students and to inform instruction and intervention
3. Intervention – Provide evidence-based intervention appropriate to each student's needs in service delivery models that include therapeutic techniques
4. Program Design – Configure a continuum of service delivery models in the least restrictive environment appropriate to the needs of students served
5. Data Collection and Analysis – Use data-based decision making for individual students and overall program evaluation
6. Compliance – Meet federal and state mandates and local policies, including IEPs, Medicaid billing, reports, treatment plans, and progress logs

C. Collaborative Roles

1. School Professionals – Support the instructional program at schools and the general education teachers who are primarily responsible for curriculum and instruction; complement and augment services of reading specialists, special education teachers, and other professionals and administrators

Box 1.3. ***Roles and Responsibilities of SLPs in the Schools*** *(continued)*

C. Collaborative Roles *(continued)*

2. Universities – Form relationships with universities for mutual benefit in resources, knowledge, and perspectives
3. Community – Work with individuals, such as private practitioners, as well as agencies, such as vocational rehabilitation, that serve students with disabilities
4. Families – For students of all ages, engage families in planning, decision making, and program implementation
5. Students – Engage students in participating in their own goal planning, intervention, progress monitoring, and self-advocacy appropriate to age and ability

D. Leadership

1. Advocacy – Advocate for appropriate programs and services, including reasonable workloads and professional development; articulate SLP roles and responsibilities to stakeholders; influence the development and interpretation of laws, regulations, and policies to promote best practices
2. Supervision and Mentorship – Supervise SLP students and mentor new SLPs; supervise paraprofessionals
3. Professional Development – Design and conduct professional development for educators and administrators
4. Parent Training – Educate parents on communication development and disorders; guide parents in providing rich language and literacy environments
5. Research – Federal law requires use of scientific research evidence. Participate in research to improve clinical practice and promote clinical use of research evidence

Note: From *Roles and Responsibilities of Speech–Language Pathologists in Schools* [Professional issues statement], by the American Speech-Language-Hearing Association, 2010b, Baltimore, MD: Author. Adapted with permission.

and small groups seen outside the classroom, inclusive services, classes dedicated to communication skills, consultation services, and a variety of prevention activities.

Pull-Out Intervention

Within the pull-out model, children can be seen individually or in small groups. Although for teachers small group may mean half a class, for SLPs a small group numbers two to four children. Small groups provide less individual attention, but compensate with social energy and peer models. Large groups require classroom techniques to provide sufficient learning opportunities, such as choral responding of the whole group or the SLP moving among students engaged in independent learning activities.

Box 1.4. ***Types of Service Delivery Formats***

Pull-Out

- Individual
- Small group

In-Class

- One teach, one observe
- One teach, one drift
- Half-class stations
- Independent and guided centers

Self-Contained Classroom

- Lessons with a self-contained resource room
- Teaching a self-contained language class
- Communication skills class for credit

Supervision of SLP Aides

- Assisting with the SLP caseload
- Conducting independent caseloads

Prevention

- Professional education
- Pre-referral intervention

Consultation

- Recommending new activities and behaviors
- Coaching new activities and behaviors

Group composition may be based on age, disorder, or severity. Child attributes may be considered, such as grouping a distractible child with two more attentive children or a passive child with a socially engaged child. Alternately, scheduling issues may result in undesirable groupings that take effort to make work.

Traditionally, pull-out services operated largely without reference to the classroom. However, this has changed. State standards and benchmarks can guide treatment goals and activities. Classroom topics and curricular materials can be used. SLPs can be in close contact with teachers through formal meetings, informal conversations, and classroom visits. Open spots and cancellations in the schedule can be used to drop in on classrooms as long as the visiting SLP checks with the teacher first. The SLP can assist caseload children or circulate to observe and assist where needed, providing both contact and help to the teacher.

In-Class Intervention

The regular classroom is the least restrictive environment for all students. It promotes delivery of educationally relevant services and functional outcomes. For in-class or inclusive intervention, treatment is embedded within the regular classroom lesson, using the class activities and materials. The treatment goal may align with the goal of the lesson (e.g., composing a description), be a subgoal of the lesson (e.g., using adjectives in a description), or may be additional to it (e.g., segmenting phonemes of words involved in the descriptive essay). If the regular classroom can be set up as an appropriate environment for language intervention, this is the preferred option. While an extra pair of hands in the room is helpful, the SLP should be cautious that her or his expertise is being used appropriately and the student is benefiting from it.

In-class intervention can take several formats that vary on who is taking the instructional lead and how the students are grouped. One arrangement is where one educator is teaching and the other is observing or moving around the room assisting students. The SLP may take the secondary role to learn what is happening in the classroom, to monitor how caseload students are doing with their target skills, or to provide specific support to achieve skills in this busy context. The SLP may present the lesson because the two educators have deemed the SLP is better qualified to teach this phase of a particular unit they are coteaching. The teacher may take the secondary role temporarily to learn about and take over some previously overlooked language aspect of classroom instruction. Half-class stations involve both teacher and SLP teaching parallel lessons to large groups of children. This provides twice as many response opportunities per child and half as many behavioral challenges for each instructor.

Learning centers or cooperative group projects are other alternatives. In these arrangements, a small number of children work at a table on one topic. They may each work on their own assignments or they may work cooperatively to create a single product. There may be a "speech" table presided at by the SLP where the goals and activities will benefit typical peers but are built around caseload children. The SLP may move around tables or groups, providing additional support to caseload children or other children in need. Group projects are most successful if the assignment involves cooperative learning principles, such as positive interdependence and individual accountability (Putnam, 1993). Students are taught to use cooperative interaction skills, such as sharing and listening, as well as cooperative roles, such as encourager, scribe, materials person, and presenter.

As a school SLP, supplemental to my regular pull-out services, I provided in-class narrative units to teachers who had several of my caseload children in their classrooms. The format was a 6-week unit which began with me teaching a lesson to the whole class: introducing a story grammar chart, sharing a piece of children's literature, and identifying story grammar parts in the story. I then created a parallel story with the class using a quick sketch method called pictography. After that, the class broke into cooperative learning groups to create shared parallel stories. The teacher and I each took responsibility for half the class, sometimes taking our half to another room. We circulated among the groups to observe, listen, and facilitate. The groups would come together as half-classes to present their stories with the respective educator guiding the process. During the week, the teacher had each student individually write the story then revise and edit it with attention to the targeted story grammar skills.

In-class services require a close partnership between teacher and SLP. A single recipe cannot be used with all teachers (Ehren, 2000). Effective and satisfying in-class service delivery can take time to establish. It can begin with a substantial proportion of service delivery occurring collaboratively in the classroom. Or it can begin more cautiously, as a supplement to pull-out or as traditional treatment given in the corner of a classroom and gradually integrated into classroom activities. Regardless, from the start, the SLP should be mindful of her or his role, and not settle with "sorting it out later."

Curriculum Modification

Another service format is curriculum modification. This involves the SLP evaluating curricular materials for linguistic complexity and clarity, either incidentally to other activities or as a formal curriculum review. For example, students may not be fully completing spelling assignments. The SLP may observe that the directions in their spelling books are too syntactically complex. The SLP can demonstrate to the teacher how to simplify instructions.

Curriculum modification decisions should not occur in a vacuum, but should always consider the larger classroom context. Written work may appear complicated, but the teacher may have orally presented simpler instructions or there may be typical routines for doing those tasks. There may be subtle cues about what is expected from the students. I observed a fifth-grade teacher who, in introducing a personal narrative unit, said she would "tell a story," but told only a five-sentence summary of a story. She then asked for students to give examples of their own stories, and they each gave a 1–2 sentence story idea. The teacher's brief model, plus the typical practice of giving short answers to teacher questions, led the students to appropriately understand that an actual story was not called for in this introductory part of the lesson.

Self-Contained Class

Students with the same or mixed disabilities may be grouped together as a self-contained group of 8–12 students taught by a teacher with special training and sometimes assisted by an aide. Usually the regular classroom is the home room, with students visiting this *resource room* for one to three hours a day for reading and math support. For students with intellectual disabilities, *life skills classes* may be the home classroom as well as provide the academic instruction. Life skills students attend the regular classroom only for specified nonacademic subjects, such as physical education, music, and art.

Self-contained classes fall between pull-out and in-class service for the SLP. The students are taught their academic curriculum together for some or all of the day, so the SLP can be curriculum based and collaborative with the teacher of the self-contained class. These classes provide a more homogeneous skill and behavior grouping than the regular classroom, so therapeutic instruction to a group of students can more easily be provided. In addition, scheduling is less of a concern because the students are already grouped together. When I taught language units with a learning disabilities teacher in her class, our partnership was very effective.

Sometimes, students with speech or language impairments are grouped together for part of the day in a language class. Students receive the language arts and reading curriculum in these settings along with language treatment. The SLPs teaching these classes usually have regular teaching endorsements. A version of this for older students is a communication skills or study skills class. Older students may be resistant to being taken out of their subject area classes because of the material missed. They may also not like in-class service because it clearly identifies them to other students as special needs. An alternative is a for-credit class that is part of their daily schedule like their other classes (e.g., Buttrill, Nizawa, Biemer, Takahashi, & Hearn, 1989). A communication skills class works on language skills and helps students become better learners. Effective study, note-taking, and exam-taking practices are taught. The SLP serves as an advocate for the students and consultant to subject area teachers. The SLP may arrange accommodations, such as untimed exams and modified assignments. Students are graded on their effort and progress toward meeting the goals of their Individualized Education Program (IEP[1]).

Buttrill, Nizawa, Biemer, Takahashi, and Hearn (1989) emphasized the importance of considering both learner characteristics and demands of the school setting. Citing several survey and observation studies, Buttrill et al. noted that students are required to listen and work independently far more than participate in communicative interactions. Teachers ranked in importance independent work habits, socialization skills, and study skills before subject matter knowledge. In terms of time, independent seat work, lectures, and audiovisual presentations occupied 80% of class periods, while expressive language use (discussions, group work, and oral reports) occurred only a small portion of the time. While the studies reported by Buttrill et al. are dated now, classroom interactions have not changed a lot.

Supervision

An SLP may supervise one or several aides (also known as SLP assistants and paraprofessionals) in pull-out or in-class service. The supervising SLP may share in the direct services or may only supervise the aide and have no direct knowledge of the students involved beyond eligibility or annual evaluations. This format allows school districts to hire fewer SLPs. Depending on how this type of program is instituted, it may be effective as well as economical.

SLP aides are not regulated by ASHA. Their duties, training, and independence varies considerably (ASHA, 2004). Aides may have on-the-job training, a community college preparatory program certificate, a Bachelor's degree in speech and hearing science, or a Bachelor's degree with clinical coursework and training. SLP aides may work closely with the SLP, assisting with a portion of the caseload or with different students as needed, or may essentially manage their own caseloads, with periodic checks by the supervising SLP. The only constants are that there is a supervising SLP and that aides do not conduct evaluations (ASHA, 2004).

1. Plan required for all students qualifying for special education services

Supervision introduces an authority relationship. It mandates the Master's level SLP to tell the aide "what to do." However, the aide is an educator with work experience, knowledge of the student, and his or her own individual qualities. This service format will work best if both educators respect each others' expertise and work as a team to provide the best service possible to their students.

Consultant

Consultation is an indirect service, in which the SLP guides the teacher to provide intervention. It can occur in combination with direct services or it can be the sole service. It may occur as the primary service delivery format in a school district.

Consultation occurs on a continuum of structure, frequency, and knowledge of the student. At the lowest end of contact, consultation may involve no direct contact with the student, such as informally advising a teacher on resolving a classroom issue without a referral to special education. It may occur as a single meeting following a diagnostic evaluation for a student who does not meet eligibility criteria but the IEP team judge that some guidance is needed. Some students may be on a "monitor" status, where the SLP periodically checks on the student's performance and the teacher's management strategies. At the highest end of contact, consultation may involve a performance plan, regular contact across the school year with teachers, and aids to review progress data and modify intervention plans.

Consultation can focus on the student—what the student needs to do in the classroom and how the teacher can enforce or monitor this. Or it can address systemic or interactional difficulties of the classroom: difficulties in the space between teacher and student, student and student, or student and curriculum. The teacher may be guided to modify her or his general teaching style, such as using a slower rate of speech, particular visual supports, or more small group activities. The teacher may be shown how to embed more therapeutic interactions in her or his instruction, such as eliciting a more complete answer from a caseload student or prompting a student to use pictographic planning for story creation. The teacher may bring particular issues to the SLP for shared problem solving. There are many ways the SLP can help a teacher, but the key aspect is that the SLP is not providing services directly to the caseload children.

A consultation format may be necessary in areas with low populations and large distances between inhabitants. Yukon in northern Canada is larger than California but has a population of only 31,000. In 2011, there were four SLPs in the Department of Education for the entire territory. They provide consultative services to teachers and aides for 5,000 children in 28 schools across the remote region.

Consultation is the least expensive and most inclusive service delivery format because the SLP can manage a large caseload simply by periodically talking to teachers while students remain in their regular classrooms with no disruptions or intrusions. However, this format should be applied cautiously because it can easily be ineffective.

Prevention

Prevention involves the SLP conducting activities that avoid or minimize the onset or development of communication disorders and their causes (ASHA, 1988). SLPs work with children at risk for future difficulties or with parents and educators of these children. In ASHA's report (2010b), prevention includes averting academic failure, which makes prevention and intervention essentially indistinguishable.

Prevention can entail provision of formal continuing education activities, brief in-services, written information, or informal conversations about the causes, characteristics, maintaining factors, and services for speech and language disorders. Prevention can be educating teachers about what SLPs offer or about what teachers themselves can offer. When I was a school SLP, the district SLPs provided an evening in-service for teachers in their school district on identifying students for referral based on oral language behaviors. The presentation involved videos of caseload children demonstrating immature morphosyntax, limited vocabulary, word-finding, and pragmatic difficulties. The presentation was intended to improve referrals of children in need, but it also addressed general awareness of spoken-language difficulties.

Prevention includes pre-referral services aimed at reducing or eliminating future need for special education (ASHA, 2010b). Prevention does not involve a particular service delivery format: It can be conducted within a regular classroom with all the students or in small groups of at-risk students or even individually with a child suspected of having some kind of language impairment. Typically the service provided is of short duration with regular progress monitoring so that a judgment can be made concerning referral for special education.

RTI: Prevention, Intervention, and Diagnosis

Prevention is present within the Response to Intervention (RTI) model of reading instruction occurring in schools across the nation. Within RTI, students are provided tiers of successively increasing intensity of quality, standardized intervention delivered with high fidelity (Fuchs & Fuchs, 2006). Tier II is the most distinctive tier, consisting of short-term intense small group intervention without the requirement for eligibility for special education. Data are collected regularly and systematically on student progress, and instructional decisions are made based on the amount and nature of progress. RTI is intended to redirect at-risk learners to an acceptable growth trajectory without requiring special education services. It is also useful for determining experientially based deficits versus inherent learning disabilities, although the accuracy of different methods is still under investigation (Fuchs, Fuchs, & Compton, 2004; Swanson & Howard, 2005). RTI is based on the same conceptual foundation as stimulability, diagnostic intervention, and dynamic assessment: Readiness for learning and instructional needs are determined through students' responses to instruction rather than through static measures of independent performance.

The role of the SLP in RTI is still emerging (Ukrainetz, 2006; ASHA, 2010b). ASHA says only that SLPs may participate in RTI in whatever way needed. Troia (2005), Staskowski and Rivera (2005), and others have seen the SLP role as primarily additive, doing everything they have been doing and more. SLPs can be consultants, trainers, and auditors for Tier I, assessors and instructors in Tier II, and clinicians in Tier III. This does not seem like the best use of a limited resource. One promising option is to offer Speech RTI, which is short-term intensive intervention to remediate mild speech impairments without the need for a special education referral. A needed option is a Language RTI to complement the current decoding emphasis of Reading RTI, which might be designed or overseen by SLPs, but delivered by other educators.

Making Teamwork Work

Coordinating, Collaborating, and Consulting

Service delivery formats vary in their connection to the physical classroom and daily lessons. All versions should be tied to the skills and knowledge of the curriculum and achievement standards. SLP services should be coordinated and preferably collaboratively delivered with regular and special educators.

Classroom-based intervention typically refers to in-class service delivery. However, one could consider pull-out as classroom based if the therapeutic activity was closely aligned with what was happening at that time in the classroom. For example, a pull-out session may involve verbal fluency in show-and-tell, using the script followed in the classroom.

Curriculum-based intervention refers to basing goals, procedures, activities, or materials on the regular education curriculum. Any service delivery format can be curriculum based. Links to the curriculum are usually considered to be ties to the *official* curriculum, which is the state or district outline of material that is to be learned for each subject at each grade level (Nelson, 1989). States have official achievement standards and benchmarks that specify not only what should be learned but expected achievement levels. Unofficial curricula, such as the curricula of the dominant culture and student peer curriculum, affect teacher expectations and peer relations, then in turn affect students' competence in the official curriculum (Box 1.5). Each classroom has individual student personalities that can come together to create a class personality (e.g., the go-getter class, the complainer class), further complicating matters.

Individual styles of the teachers affect the classroom behavior and self-regulation (Westby, 1997, 2006). For example, Westby reported how a second-grade teacher guided the children's behavior and participation through modeling, explicit instructions, subtle cues, group activities, and individualized support. Students were allowed to move around the room and engage in quiet talk. The teacher provided learning support in a warm, responsive manner. In contrast, a third-grade teacher used explicit, highly structured academic and social scripts in her room. Behavioral expectations were posted and students were publically penalized for infractions. Students were expected to complete academic assignments independently, get permission to talk, and request help as needed. Both teachers provided structure and support, but in very different ways, reflecting both the age of the students and the style of each teacher.

SLPs and teachers *coordinate* their instructional efforts to avoid gaps and redundancies. This may be as simple as listing the knowledge and skills to be acquired and determining who will teach what. Even such limited interaction still has the major challenge of coordinating teaching schedules. Patient, polite persistence and creative flexibility are

Box 1.5. *The Many Curricula of School*

1. The *cultural* curriculum is the world knowledge needed to be competent members of society, involves history, literature, science, and religion. It also includes functioning in daily experiences, such as knowing when to be competitive versus cooperative as well as knowing how to display knowledge without appearing boastful.
2. The *de facto* curriculum is the specifics of academic knowledge required as a result of textbook or material choices made by the school or the teacher.
3. The *school or classroom* curriculum is the set of implicit and explicit rules that students must acquire to act appropriately in particular classrooms, such as the length and detail expected in answers to teacher's questions.
4. The *hidden* curriculum is the set of expectations teachers have for categorizing which students are considered the "good" or "problem" students in their classrooms, such as considering messy work a sign of not caring.
5. The *underground* curriculum is the peer rules for social interaction that determine other students' attitudes and acceptance, such as considering students who show eagerness to learn as wanting to be "teacher's pets."

Note: Summarized from Nelson (1989).

needed to organize a reasonable working schedule for the SLP, all her or his students, and all the teachers involved.

SLPs and teachers may work more closely together in *collaboration*. Collaboration refers to two or more educators with different areas of expertise working together to design and deliver support to students (Hoskins, 1996). Collaboration is a reciprocal relationship where each professional contributes expertise and resources to create a whole greater than the sum of two individually designed and delivered parts. Teachers and SLPs may work together extensively over time with groups of students, just for a particular student, or just for a particular situation or issue. Degree of collaboration will vary with the needs of the student, the resources and skills of the educators, the personalities and preferences of the educators, and the culture of the school.

The most challenging service format is *consultation*. Consultation is a "second order" approach to language intervention (Fey, 1986). It involves changing the teacher to change the child. The SLP, who holds no particular authority, must be skilled in the interpersonal dynamics of one educator advising another educator on how to teach. The SLP is likely to meet with resistance if the SLP is seen as an occasional visiting expert who tells the teacher of 25 heterogeneous learners what should be done differently for one particular student. Instead of taking the role of *expert consultant*, the SLP should present as a *collaborative consultant*. This role involves the SLP working in a partnership with the teacher and recognizes the teacher's perspective, strengths, and challenges (Hoskins, 1996).

As a collaborative consultant, the SLP arrives in the spirit of being there first to listen. The SLP may find that the classroom issues are not what would be suggested by the student's testing results and the recommendations quite different from the initial ideas. In general, the better the SLP knows the student, the teacher, and the school and the more open the SLP is to others' input, the better the guidance and the more enduring the effects of consultation. Hoskins (1996) suggested that the SLP should even think of the consultation as a business transaction: The teacher is the client who has hired the SLP to help resolve self-identified difficulties. If the SLP has a mental image of "earning a fee," then he or she is likely to be more motivated to give the service needed for "customer satisfaction." Box 1.6 presents a list of practices that contribute to effective collaborative consultation. There are two role-play scenarios that contrast expertive and collaborative consultative stances in the Appendix for this chapter. Take the time to role play these experiences to feel how they unfold.

Even collaborative consultation can involve resistance to recommendations. Hoskins (1996) recommended observing the interaction on three levels: (a) identify the behaviors that might be cover-ups for fears or concerns (e.g., rebuffing all suggestions); (b) identify suspected underlying fears and concerns (e.g., fear of looking like a bad teacher); and (c) identify what is really wanted (e.g., acknowledgement of the teacher's efforts in a difficult situation). By recognizing fears and concerns, the SLP can better respond to both the underlying factors and the presenting situation so he or she can help the teacher help the student.

Collaborative consulting may also involve *coaching*. A congenial coach can assist a teacher in changing his or her ways of communicating with or teaching students. SLPs should resist the temptation of simply giving the teacher a handout. Just as for improving diet, increasing exercise, or learning a new skill, the coaching plan should include explanation, demonstration, practice, and supportive feedback. The SLP should be open to modifying recommendations. Observing the teacher in action may reveal that he or she is already doing what was planned, that the plan will not address the issues, or that the plan is not workable in the classroom setting.

Teaming and Multiskilling

In the schools, teachers and other educators with diverse areas of expertise and strengths operate as teams to develop a comprehensive education for each student. Teams may be legislatively required, such as IEP teams, or may be formulated within the school, such as a team-taught classroom.

Special education teams are intended to be *interdisciplinary*, meaning that educators with different areas of expertise come together collaboratively to evaluate, plan, and teach a single student across a range of needs (Patterson & Gillam, 1995). A less integrated version of teaming is *multidisciplinary*. Multidisciplinary teams involve several professionals providing a comprehensive picture of a child but each staying separate and autonomous in evaluations and recommendations. The most integrated team model is *transdisciplinary*. This model involves professionals crossing disciplinary boundaries. In toddler assessments, one evaluator interacts with the child in a systematic, play-based manner while others assess across developmental domains (Linder, 1993).

Box 1.6. *Effective Collaboration and Consultation Practices*

A. Know the Players

1. *Know the student.* Know the student beyond performance in the speech room. Observe the student in class, talk to the student, look at the student's work, and talk to the parents.
2. *Know the classroom as a system.* What is the teacher's style of classroom management and teaching? What is the mix of easy and challenging students?
3. *Know the school.* Is the school a "back to basics" school or an inquiry-based learning school? Is it a relaxed or a worried environment?

B. Establish Mutual Concerns

1. *Listen to the teacher.* What does he or she say are the concerns (e.g., poor language comprehension), and what else may be implied (e.g., difficulty managing the behaviors within the classroom)? Imagine what it is like to be in the teacher's situation.
2. *Translate concerns.* How do behaviors and competencies in the classroom relate to test score and language sample results? Are there aspects of the concerns that are not revealed by the formal evaluation?

C. Develop a Partnership

1. *Recognize the teacher as another expert.* The teacher has an array of knowledge and skills that are both similar (e.g., using semantic webs) and different (e.g., keeping an entire class involved in a lesson) from yours as an SLP.
2. *Recognize the teacher's expertise on the student.* The teacher knows the student in different ways and perhaps better than you.
3. *Develop a sense of trust.* By recognizing the teacher's concerns and expertise and being available with your expertise and resources, establish the mutual trust needed.

D. Plan Together

1. *Establish common goals.* Based on the mutual concerns and working partnership, establish goals that will make real, noticeable changes in student performance. Goals may be first order, such as addressing the student directly, or second order, such as addressing the system of the classroom.
2. *Develop realistic plans.* What can be done in this classroom by this teacher for this student? Keep plans simple and manageable. It is better to aim too low initially and have success, then raise the aim later.
3. *Take progress data.* Plan for how the teacher can reasonably collect data on the first order and second order goals. Systematically collected data can reveal surprisingly different findings from impressionistic memories.
4. *Revisit and revise the plan as necessary.* Whatever you establish may work for a little while or not at all. Plan future meetings to revisit and revise the plans.
5. *Be open to possibilities.* What works with one teacher or classroom or in one year may not work with another. Generate creative solutions.

Motor, sensory, cognitive, social, and communicative intervention is embedded in the home or preschool setting and delivered by all caregivers. Transdisciplinary evaluation for school-age children is difficult to accomplish within the requirements of norm-referenced testing, but teams may engage in descriptive assessment and intervention across functional or academic domains (Patterson & Gillam, 1995).

Multiskilling relates to transdisciplinary expertise. It is a term more commonly used in health care settings. Multiskilling refers to a single technician who is trained in functions from outside the standard areas of expertise. An example is an x-ray technician who is trained in phlebotomy (drawing blood). Multiskilling is difficult to apply to school professionals whose scopes of practice are already large and overlapping. An SLP who is specially trained in delivering a math program or coaching volleyball might be considered multiskilled.

Selecting a Service Delivery Format

The foregoing spectrum of service delivery formats allows SLPs to select the most appropriate service delivery option for each child and situation. School resources, conventional practices, and SLP preference all play a role in service format selection. Professionals may support particular approaches, but there is little research evidence to guide format selection.

Cirrin et al. (2010) conducted a systematic review of the effect of service delivery formats. Cirrin and colleagues examined controlled randomized, nonrandomized, and single subject design studies for elementary grade children published in peer-reviewed English-language journals after 1975. The studies could vary only the service delivery format or dosage. They had to involve an SLP and provide objective measures of treatment outcomes. Only five studies met these criteria. These revealed no clear effects of service delivery model. Vocabulary outcomes did not differ for services delivered by SLPs versus highly trained SLP aides or for individual versus small group delivery. For language and literacy, in-class and pull-out methods did not differ. One study reviewed appeared to find differences in favor of a collaborative classroom model on curricular vocabulary. Throneburg, Calvert, Sturm, Paramboukas, and Paul (2000) compared the collaborative model to parallel classroom lessons by the SLP and teacher and to a pull-out model in which the SLP taught the same vocabulary as the teacher. However, the collaborative format actually provided a lot more resources than the other two 40-minute-per-week conditions: four educators (teacher, SLP, and two graduate students), 40 minutes of in-class instruction, 40 minutes of planning time, and 15 minutes of pull-out treatment each week.

Classroom intervention is recommended when it can be provided appropriately, both to fulfill the legal requirement of the least restrictive environment and to link with the curriculum and communicative demands of the classroom. The starting point should always be the regular classroom, with educators justifying why a student's needs will be better met outside the room rather than starting outside the room and justifying why the student should be taught in the regular classroom. In addition, there is always the issue of missed class time and a disjointed day. Classroom teachers often find that, with all the special events that individual and groups of students leave their room to attend, there is rarely the full roster for an entire lesson.

Despite the benefits of keeping a student in the classroom, quality speech and language intervention often requires the focus and freedom of separate space. Considerations include whether the treatment goals and procedures can be incorporated into the classroom lessons, how distractible the student is, the activity level of the classroom, and what is being taught in the classroom at the scheduled treatment time. For a very academic goal of summarizing main ideas, an SLP could sit by a student guiding him to find the main idea of a paragraph while the student completes assigned chapter questions in a reading lesson, but it is likely that both aims will suffer. Students with language disorders or learning disabilities are certainly not candidates for doing more than other students, having more points of attention, or having fewer opportunities for learning and practice. Westby et al. (1994) reported on a fifth-grade classroom, which included students with learning disabilities, students with limited English proficiency, and typical students. Even with a regular educator and a special educator teaming up in a classroom, it proved to be too difficult to provide instruction to such diverse learners, so the students with learning disabilities were pulled out for reading and math instruction. Pull-out may be the most appropriate option, but it needs to be delivered in a functional manner where it is integrated with meaningful educational activities and related to curriculum expectations (Whitmire, 2002).

Fundamentally, SLPs need to have flexibility to adjust service delivery format to provide the most appropriate format for a student as needed. IEPs should allow for being responsive to student needs. For example, for one student working on complex syntax within narratives, the SLP might ideally provide in the following order: (a) a classroom visit in which the SLP listens to the assignment instructions and observes the student; (b) individual pull-out to work on particular sentence structures in a drill format for one session; (c) small group pull-out to compose those sentences into a cooperatively authored story in the next session; (d) an in-class opportunity for the students to participate in oral story presentations with the rest of their class; and (e) a return to the small group setting to review performance.

Teaming Over an IEP

Collaboration is especially important for the IEP process. The IEP is developed by educators and parents as a team. However, teamwork can be challenging. Typically, the IEP is developed in a 2-hour meeting following an evaluation. Sometimes, what should be minor or resolvable disagreements can escalate into serious issues and adversarial stances that can even end in litigation. The following are some helpful hints for successful IEP teaming.

A starting point in avoiding and resolving conflict is to "know thyself" (Schraeder, 2008). Recognize your own biases and how you handle conflict. Be aware of when you are tired, distracted, or impatient. Be aware of how you view your own competence as well as challenges from others. Do you see other perspectives easily? Do you engage easily in self-doubt? After considering yourself, turn your awareness to the other participants. Are there others who may feel their competence is under question or who are just having a bad day? Notice the physical features of a meeting: whether it is in a neutral location, how the furniture is arranged, and even the height of the chairs (be the confident one who sits in the kid chair). When interacting in difficult situations, use active listening, stay in control of your emotions, be respectful of all participants, and stay focused on the topic (Schraeder, 2008). All this sounds obvious but can be difficult to remember in the heat of the moment. I often remind myself to "listen, not wait to talk." Sometimes, educators think of it as "just one more meeting," forgetting how emotionally fraught these discussions can be for parents. Sometimes, parents forget that educators are trying to do the best they can for each student with limited resources.

I gleaned a valuable perspective on IEP meetings from an unexpected source: small claims courts, where litigants present their own cases. In their ethnographic analysis of legal discourse, Conley and O'Barr (1990) found that a person's orientation toward disputes tends to lean toward either *rules* or *relationships*. Rules-oriented individuals provided factual, chronological, topic-sequenced accounts divested of emotional content. These individuals focused on issues of interest to the court and answered the judge's questions concisely. In contrast, individuals who held a relationships orientation moved in a topic-associated fashion, with lengthy digressions about the history and relationships of the event. They meandered through time and place, with assumed background knowledge. Not surprisingly, judges were more sympathetic to the rules than the relationships style. Conley and O'Barr found that people could shift from one orientation to another depending on how others interacted with them (e.g., giving a rules-oriented account in response to cues from the judge).

Like judges, educators are likely to take a rules orientation, moving quickly and efficiently through the meeting, but it is important to let parents participate in their own way. A relationships orientation may result in a deeper picture of the child than an efficient but sparse rules orientation, and parents can be gently guided toward the information needed for the planning process. Rules-oriented parents may be prompted to provide more background on relationships and situations that can lead to better understandings of their children.

Conley and O'Barr (1990) also observed the importance of "telling one's story." In small claims court, there is considerable variation in how a case is presented. In one example, a plaintiff brought a case of owed fees for a work assignment. The judge, in a desire to be efficient, did not let the plaintiff present her case, but rather rendered the judgment in her favor based on the defendant's failure to show up and based on the documentary evidence. This plaintiff won, but in her later interview, said it was unfair that she could not present her case. Conley and O'Barr found that "losers report that the chance to tell their story to the judge made the whole effort worthwhile, whereas some winners . . . go away dissatisfied because their story went untold" (p. 130).

In the same way, during an IEP process, each parent needs to feel his or her story was told. Struggles, successes, and views of the complexity and uniqueness of each son or daughter do matter. Although educators may have encountered many children with similar profiles or may disagree with the parent's view of the situation, the account needs to be honored. If stories and interactional styles are honored, along with the recognition that everyone is doing their best, then escalation into formal disputes may be avoided, even if it is on a basis of "agree to disagree."

Who Works on What?

The section on service delivery format ended with a recommendation for flexibility. This section opens with the same. Almost three decades ago, in relation to management of reading disabilities, Cirrin (1989) asked, "Who does what to whom?" That question is with us now, more than ever.

Factors Affecting Cooperation

Cirrin (1989) called for cooperative planning among professionals and recognition of each professional's particular expertise. However, cooperation can be affected by regulation, resources, and philosophies. Funding limitations affect the number of SLPs hired, and thus the number of schools and students for whom each are responsible. These limitations affect class size and planning time for teachers. Programs may be merged or separated, and collaboration encouraged or discouraged. States or school districts may change eligibility criteria. Categorical labels, which are intended to be used for funding, not for programming, affect decisions about who does what. For example, a label of *speech or language impairment* will involve SLPs rather than resource or reading teachers. Workload demands affect who chooses to attend meetings. Meetings may focus more on presenting data by discipline than on integrating findings across disciplines.

Professional territoriality is another factor that affects educator roles, especially because role boundaries in education are not clear: "Not only is everyone involved because of the multidisciplinary nature of the disorder, but everyone claims to be able to perform teaching functions that everyone else can" (Cirrin, 1989, p. 354). Teaming can be affected by desires or pressures to operate in visible, high-value but common arenas, such as that of reading, versus hidden, lower-value but distinctive arenas, such as speech. Each profession comes with its own educational track, theoretical perspectives, and jargon, resulting sometimes in differences that are more apparent than real. For example, teachers may have trouble defining the term "language" but still clearly teach it (Ukrainetz & Fresquez, 2003). There can also be real differences: Language evaluations by school psychologists are typically limited to norm-referenced tests while SLPs also employ descriptive measures. Cirrin (1989) notes that special education teachers typically operate within a behaviorist model of child learning, while SLPs are usually educated more within a social-cognitive interactionist model.

Despite these differences, as with students, colleagues should not be viewed categorically. Rather, each should be approached as an individual operating within a dynamic, layered system, with differences related to individual preferences and complementary practices as well as institutional or professional customs and prescriptions.

SLP Versus Classroom Teacher

Teachers and SLPs are both professionals working within their domains of expertise and job requirements. Officially, the SLP manages language and caseload students, and the teacher manages curriculum and the whole class. But what does that mean in practice?

Teaming with a teacher does not mean that the SLP operates as a teaching aide. Teaching aides provide assistance to students under the direction and supervision of teachers. They may prepare materials, keep children on task, help children complete assignments, or teach small groups following instructional scripts. In contrast, SLPs are independent professionals who design, deliver, and analyze the data from their own interventions for their own caseloads. Their professional judgments and demands must take precedence over classroom assistance.

SLPs focus on developing language skills, such as increasing syntactic complexity or improving discourse organization. They teach learning strategies that cut across content areas, such as the use of graphic organizers, previewing textbook structure, or identifying main ideas. While teachers also attend to underlying skills and strategies, they primarily need to cover the curriculum. A federal report on teaching reading comprehension by the RAND Reading Study Group (2002) concluded that there is strong evidence indicating that weak readers can be taught to use reading strategies that improve their reading comprehension, but that classroom teachers do not effectively teach these strategies.

In addition to a focus on skill over content, the SLP needs to maintain a therapeutic focus (Ehren, 2000). This therapeutic focus, more than attention to language or caseload children, is what distinguishes the SLP from the classroom teacher. Teachers sometimes deliver instruction in small groups and even individually by setting up the class with independent seat or group work. Even during whole class instruction, the teacher moves around the classroom as she speaks to check on individual student understanding and provide additional prompts or explanations. However, teachers cannot provide the sustained, systematic individual attention to accelerate learning or compensate for deficits that is the primary responsibility of the SLP.

Commonalities Between SLPs and Other Remedial Educators

SLPs are not the only providers of therapeutic instruction. Both resource teachers and SLPs provide individualized functional and educational services to students with identified disabilities. Both services are governed by IEPs and other special education regulation. Reading teachers provide remedial individual and small group reading instruction within regular education. With RTI, SLPs are now being called on to provide short-term pre-referral intervention, thus increasing similarity to reading teachers.

There is little available to guide SLP practice in relation to other special educators. Potentially, almost anything in school could be included in some aspect of a broad definition of language, and an SLP could do anything done by a teacher of students with learning disabilities or a reading teacher. Although position statements, such as that of ASHA (2010b), refer to the "unique" expertise of SLPs, it is not clear how actual practice differs from other educational interventionists.

To gain insight into this question, Ukrainetz and Fresquez (2003) conducted a qualitative study that examined the practices of five experienced school SLPs and their teacher colleagues. In this study, SLPs and teachers were interviewed and observed, and IEPs and treatment records were examined. Key issues, recurrent events, common perceptions, and notable exceptions were identified and synthesized into major themes. The findings revealed more commonalities than differences in treatment goals, activities, and methods of instruction. As one resource teacher said, "The lines don't exist almost between any of our jobs anymore" (Ukrainetz & Fresquez, 2003, p. 294). Resource teachers taught semantics, syntax, discourse, and pragmatics. SLPs employed print material, reading, and writing in their interventions. Treatment goals were similar, such as following directions, identifying main ideas and supporting details, sequencing story events, presenting a well-organized report with complex grammar and vocabulary, and composing stories with certain story structure, grammar, spelling, and punctuation. Both professionals used discrete skill mastery, contextualized skill intervention, and unfocused enrichment and assistance activities.

At times, the SLPs and resource teachers provided the same service to the same student, such as individualized assistance in completing a science report, with no observed difference in interactions and emphases. More often, within a school, an SLP and a resource teacher had different, complementary instructional foci, resulting in comprehensive attention to student needs. In one school, the SLP worked more on word decoding and spelling, while the resource teacher worked on text comprehension and composition, while the roles were reversed in another school. Whether overlapping or complementary, both the SLPs and teachers judged that educators needed to be flexible enough to do whatever the children needed.

Distinctive Practices of SLPs

SLPs certainly have distinctive features of practice. Ukrainetz and Fresquez (2003) found that "speech" was unique to SLPs. The SLPs observed that they could make noticeable changes in speech and discharge children in less than an academic year. None of the teachers considered they had the expertise to teach articulation, fluency, or voice. Oral language instruction was another specialty domain of SLPs. Instruction in vocabulary, story structure, and text comprehension occurred more often and more systematically through the spoken modality for the SLPs than for the resource or reading teachers. For curricular spoken language activities, SLPs were notably direct in their instruction. One taught eye contact and pausing in oral presentations. Another had daily show-and-tell speeches in which she and the other students gave oral feedback on specific skill performance, such as clear articulation. One SLP formalized this with a grading rubric and taught her students to score each other on the many impromptu speeches they gave in therapy. In contrast, teachers reported mainly correcting errors as they heard them.

Ukrainetz and Fresquez (2003) observed that the SLPs attended to written language indirectly. Print materials, reading, and writing were used by the SLPs as tools for developing speaking and listening skills. Language taught through speaking and listening was expected to transfer to print domains. These qualitative observations were consistent with the lack of direct attention to written language reported in Fallon and Katz's (2011) survey.

The service delivery formats observed in Ukrainetz and Fresquez (2003) distinguished SLPs from resource and reading teachers. Resource services involved low numbers of children taught daily for long sessions, in a simultaneous, heterogeneous manner. Resource teachers provided a sheltered learning environment where students felt liked and safe. Resource teachers commented on how, with the heterogeneity of skills and ages, the presence of emotional disabilities, and the fragmented scheduling, there was more behavior management than teaching. Both of these contrasted with the remedial reading service, which involved brief daily individual sessions for less than a year. The reading teachers were notable for their enthusiasm, possibly because they provided short-term help that often resulted in students achieving grade-level expectations. SLP services involved high numbers of children taught individually and in small groups in sequential sessions. The SLPs emphasized teaching underlying skills and strategies. While one SLP might focus on phonological processing and another on text comprehension, all emphasized working on critical skills that would improve academic performance across subjects:

> What I see happen in the resource room is that they're not taught any strategies, they're just taught how to maintain. You've got a test coming up, let's all study.... But as far as a strategy to help them on the next test, I don't see that the resource teachers have any time for that. They're doing all they can do to just to help the kids pass. Whereas I can have time to teach them the strategy that they may eventually use. Nobody else is doing that. (Ukrainetz & Fresquez, 2003, p. 293)

A happy finding was that the teachers considered the SLPs knowledgeable, scientific, and flexible problem solvers who were willing to come into the classroom, find out what teachers were doing, and help problem solve. A reading teacher described an SLP as: "great because we can go in there and ask her things, she figures out things, she can analyze something" (Ukrainetz & Fresquez, 2003, p. 293).

Conclusion

This chapter covers a lot of ground, beginning with the evolution of speech correctionists and language intervention in the schools to the current roles and responsibilities of the speech–language pathologist. The continuum of service delivery formats from pull-out to consultation, were reviewed. While in-class varieties are most inclusive, curriculum-based and collaborative intervention can be provided even with pull-out services. A critical examination of the roles of different educators was presented. The wide domains of language and literacy, along with the broad responsibilities of all educators, result in many commonalities, but SLPs have distinctive and complementary roles to play in supporting student learning.

References

American Speech-Language-Hearing Association. (1988). *Prevention of communication disorders*. Rockville, MD: Author.

American Speech-Language-Hearing Association. (1993). Guidelines for caseload size and speech–language pathology delivery in the schools. *Asha, 35* (Suppl. 10), 33–39.

American Speech-Language-Hearing Association. (2001). *Roles and responsibilities of speech–language pathologists with respect to reading and writing in children and adolescents.* Rockville, MD: Author.

American Speech-Language-Hearing Association. (2002). *A workload analysis approach for establishing speech–language caseload standards in the schools* [Position statement]. Baltimore, MD: Author.

American Speech-Language-Hearing Association. (2004). *Support personnel* [Issues in ethics]. Rockville, MD: Author.

American Speech-Language-Hearing Association. (2007). *Scope of practice in speech–language pathology.* Rockville, MD: Author.

American Speech-Language-Hearing Association (2010a). *Schools survey report: SLP caseload characteristics.* Baltimore, MD: Author.

American Speech-Language-Hearing Association (2010b). *Roles and responsibilities of speech–language pathologists in schools* [Professional issues statement]. Baltimore, MD: Author.

Ball, E. W., & Blachman, B. A. (1988). Phoneme segmentation training: Effect on reading readiness. *Annals of Dyslexia, 38,* 208–225.

Brandel, J., & Loeb, D. F. (2011). Program intensity and service delivery models in the schools: SLP survey results. *Language, Speech, and Hearing Services in Schools, 42,* 461–490.

Buttrill, J., Nizawa, J., Biemer, C., Takahashi, C. & Hearn, S. (1989). Serving the language learning disabled adolescent: A strategies-based model. *Language, Speech, and Hearing Services in Schools, 20,* 185–204.

Calkins, L.M. (1983). *Lessons from a child: On the teaching and learning of writing.* Portsmouth, NH: Heinemann.

Canadian Association of Speech–Language Pathologists and Audiologists. (2000, July). What's in a name project on hold. *Communiqué,* 4–5.

Chomsky, N. (1957). *Syntactic structures.* The Hague: Mouton.

Cirrin, F. M., Schooling, T. L., Nelson, N. W., Diehl, S. F., Flynn, P. F., Staskowski, M., Torrey, T. Z., & Adamczyk, D. F. (2010). Evidence-based systematic review: Effects of different service delivery models on communication outcomes for elementary school-age children. *Language, Speech, and Hearing Services in Schools, 41,* 233–264.

Cirrin, F. M. (1989). Issues in determining eligibility for service: Who does what to whom? In A. G. Kamhi & H. W. Catts (Eds.), *Reading disabilities: A developmental language perspective* (pp. 345–368). Boston, MA: College-Hill.

Conley, J. M., & O'Barr, W. M. (1990). *Rules versus relationships: The ethnography of legal discourse.* Chicago, IL: The University of Chicago Press.

Dahl, K. L., Scharer, P. L., Lawson, L. L., & Grogan, P. R. (1999). Phonics instruction and student achievement in whole language first-grade classrooms. *Reading Research Quarterly, 34,* 312–341.

Dollaghan, C. (2007). *The handbook for evidenced-based practice in communication disorders.* Baltimore, MD: Brookes.

Duchan, J. F. (2010). The early years of language, speech, and hearing services in U.S. schools. *Language, Speech, and Hearing Services in Schools, 41,* 152–160.

Duchan, J. F. (2011). *Getting here: A history of speech–language pathology*. Retrieved from http://www.acsu.buffalo.edu/~duchan/new_history/overview.html

Ehren, B. J. (2000). Maintaining a therapeutic focus and sharing responsibility for student success: Keys to in-classroom speech–language services. *Language, Speech, and Hearing Services in Schools, 31*, 219–229.

Fallon, K. A., & Katz, L. A. (2011). Providing written language services in the schools: The time is now. *Language, Speech, and Hearing Services in Schools, 42*, 3–17.

Fey, M. E. (1986). *Language intervention with young children*. Boston, MA: College-Hill.

Fuchs, D., & Fuchs, L. S., (2006). Introduction to response to intervention: What, why and how valid is it? *New Directions in Research, 41*(1), 93–99.

Fuchs, D., Fuchs, L. S., & Compton, D. L. (2004). Identifying reading disability by responsiveness-to-instruction: Specifying measures and criteria. *Learning Disability Quarterly, 27*, 216–227.

Gillam, R. B. (1995). Whole language principles at work in language intervention. In D. F. Tibbits (Ed.), *Language intervention beyond the primary grades* (pp. 219–255). Austin, TX: PRO-ED.

Gillam, R. B., McFadden, T. U., & van Kleeck, A. (1995). Improving the narrative abilities of children with language disorders: Whole language and language skills approaches. In M. Fey, J. Windsor, & J. Reichle (Eds.), *Communication intervention for school-age children* (pp. 145–182). Baltimore, MD: Brookes.

Goodman, K. (1986). *What's whole in whole language?* Portsmouth, NH: Heinneman.

Gravani, E. H. (2007). Individualized educational program. In E. H. Gravani & J. Meyer (Ed.), *Speech, language, and hearing programs in schools* (pp. 199–244). Austin, TX: PRO-ED.

Graves, D. (1983). *Writing: Teachers and children at work*. Portsmouth, NH: Heinemann.

Hoskins, B. (1996). *Developing inclusive schools*. Bloomington, IN: CASE Research Committee.

Johnson, D. & Myklebust, H. (1967). *Learning disabilities: Educational principles and practice*. New York: Grune & Stratton.

Justice, L. M., & Fey, M. E. (2004, September). Evidence-based practice in schools: Integrating craft and theory with science and data. *The ASHA Leader*. Retrieved from http://www.asha.org/Publications/leader/2004/040921/f040921a.htm

Katz, L., Maag, A., Fallon, K. A., Blenkarn, K., Smith, M. K. (2010). What makes a caseload (un)manageable? School-based speech–language pathologists speak. *Language, Speech, and Hearing Services in Schools, 41*, 139–151.

Lahey, M. (1988). *Language disorders and language development*. New York, NY: Macmillan.

Lindamood, P., & Lindamood, P. (2011). *The Lindamood Phoneme Sequencing Program for Reading, Spelling, and Speech* (4th ed.). Austin, TX: PRO-ED.

Linder, T. (1993). *Transdisciplinary play-based intervention*. Baltimore, MD: Brookes.

Malone, R. (1999). *The first 75 years: An oral history of the American Speech-Language-Hearing Association*. Rockville, MD: ASHA.

Merriam-Webster. (2002). *Merriam-Webster's Collegiate Dictionary* (10th ed.). Springfield, MA: Author.

Merzenich, M. M., Jenkins, W. M., Johnston, P., Schreiner, C., Miller, S. L., & Tallal, P. (1996). Temporal processing devices of language-learning impaired children ameliorated by training. *Science, 271*, 77–81.

Miller, J. F., & Chapman, R. S. (1985). *Systematic Analysis of Language Transcripts* [Computer software]. Madison: University of Wisconsin-Madison, Waisman Center, Language Analysis Laboratory.

National Governors Association Center for Best Practices and Council of Chief State School Officers (2010). *Common core state standards for English language arts & literacy in history/social studies, science, and technical subjects.* Washington, DC: Author. Retrieved from http://www.corestandards.org/

Nelson, N. W. (1989). Curriculum-based language assessment and intervention. *Language, Speech, and Hearing Services in Schools, 20*, 170–184.

Patterson, S. S., & Gillam, R. B. (1995). Team collaboration in the evaluation of language in students above the primary grades. In D. F. Tibbits (Ed.), *Language intervention beyond the primary grades* (pp. 137–182). Austin, TX: PRO-ED.

Peters-Johnson, C. (1992). Professional practices perspective on caseloads in schools. *ASHA, 34*(Nov), 12.

Putnam, J. W. (1993). *Cooperative learning and strategies for inclusion.* Baltimore, MD: Brookes.

RAND Reading Study Group (2002). *Reading for understanding: Toward an R&D program in reading comprehension.* Santa Monica, CA: RAND. Retrieved from http://www.rand.org/pubs/monograph_reports/MR1465/index.html

Rees, N. S. (1983). Language intervention with children. In J. Miller, D. Yoder, & R. Schiefelbusch (Eds.), *Contemporary issues in language intervention* (pp. 309–317). Rockville, MD: ASHA.

Sawyer, M. T. (2007). All I remember is that it was fun. In M. Taylor (Ed.), *Whole language teaching, whole-hearted practice* (pp. 116–135). New York, NY: Peter Lang.

Schraeder, T. (2008). *A guide to school services in speech–language pathology.* San Diego, CA: Plural.

Scientific Learning Corporation. (1996). *FastForword* [Computer software]. Berkeley, CA: Author.

Simon, C. (1995). School-based SLP services in 2001: A career odyssey. In D. F. Tibbits (Ed.), *Language intervention beyond the primary grades* (pp. 3–60). Austin, TX: PRO-ED.

Simon, C. S. (1984). *Evaluating communicative competence: A functional-pragmatic approach.* Tucson, AZ: Communication Skill Builders.

Simon, C. S. (1985). *Communication skills and classroom success: Therapy methodologies for language-learning disabled students.* San Diego, CA: College-Hill Press.

Skinner, B. F. (1957/1992). *Verbal behavior.* Cambridge, MA: B. F. Skinner Foundation.

Staskowski, M., & Rivera, E. A. (2005). Speech–language pathologists' involvement in responsiveness to intervention activities: A complement to curriculum-relevant practice. *Topics in Language Disorders, 25*, 132–147.

Strong, C. J., & North, K. H. (1996). *The magic of stories: Literature-based language intervention.* Eau Claire, WI: Thinking Publications.

Swanson, H. L., & Howard, C. B. (2005). Children with reading disabilities: Does dynamic assessment help in classification? *Learning Disability Quarterly, 28*(1), 17–34.

Tallal, P., & Piercy, M. (1973). Defects of non-verbal auditory perception in children with developmental aphasia. *Nature, 241*, 468–469.

Throneburg, R., Calvert., L., Sturm, J., Paramboukas, A., & Paul, P. (2000). A comparison of service delivery models: Effects on curricular vocabulary skills in the school setting. *American Journal of Speech–Language Pathology, 9*, 10–20.

Troia, G. A. (2005). Responsiveness to intervention: Roles for speech–language pathologists in the prevention and identification of learning disabilities. *Topics in Language Disorders, 25*, 106–119.

Ukrainetz, T. A. (2006). EBP, RTI, and the implications for SLPs: Commentary on L. M. Justice. *Language, Speech, and Hearing Services in Schools, 37*, 298–303.

Ukrainetz, T. A., & Fresquez, E. F. (2003). "What isn't language?": A qualitative study of the role of the school speech–language pathologist. *Language, Speech, and Hearing Services in Schools, 34*, 284–298.

Vellutino, F. R. (1991). Introduction to three studies on reading acquisition: Convergent findings on theoretical foundations of code-oriented versus whole-language approaches to reading instruction. *Journal of Educational Psychology, 83*, 437–443.

Westby, C. E. (1997). There's more to passing than knowing the answers. *Language, Speech, Hearing Services in Schools, 28*, 274–287.

Westby, C. E. (2006). There's more to passing than knowing the answers: Learning to do school. In T. A. Ukrainetz (Ed.), *Contextualized language intervention: Scaffolding preK–12 literacy achievement* (pp. 319–388). Austin, TX: PRO-ED.

Westby, C. E., Watson, S., & Murphy, M. (1994). The vision of full inclusion: Don't exclude kids by including them. *Journal of Childhood Communication Disorders, 16*, 13–22.

Whitmire, K. (2002). The evolution of school-based speech–language services. *Communication Disorders Quarterly, 23*, 68–76.

Appendix: Trying Out Collaborative Consultation

Consultation is much more than telling a teacher what to do or even working with a teacher. These two role play scenarios are based from Hoskins (1996).[2] Keep your role play material in front of you to refer to as you interact. Each role play should take 5 minutes.

I. First Scenario – Expert Consultation

#1 Role Play – Teacher Material

As the teacher, imagine you have a 10-year-old student, James, in your class. The SLP, who has completed an evaluation of James, has asked you to meet with her over your break. You are not sure how you are going to be able to deal with this new student. You have 28 students in your class, including two other students with disabilities and five

2. From *Developing inclusive schools: A guide*, by B. Hoskins, 1996, Bloomington, IN: CASE Research Committee. Adapted with permission.

students with limited English proficiency. You are an experienced teacher but are feeling a bit overwhelmed. You have given up your break time for the meeting this SLP consultant has set up.

You have not had time to read the student's file, but what you have seen so far leads you to suspect that James does not know what is going on. James seems like a bit of a troublemaker and is often doing something other than what you have told the class to do. You are wondering, but know you shouldn't ask, whether he really belongs in your class. Your observations of James are as follows:

- Not able to keep up with the rest of the class
- Is disrupting the class, talks to other students, doesn't follow directions
- Seems to be smart in some ways, such as doing math worksheets
- Doesn't complete the reading assignments properly
- Handwriting is slow and sloppy
- Doesn't hand in assignments, even completed ones

#1 Role Play – SLP Consultant Material

You are going to consult with a classroom teacher regarding a student who is having difficulty in her class. This is the first time you have met with this teacher. You have 5 minutes to meet, so you are going into this first meeting prepared. You have read the student's file. Your findings on James are as follows:

- Average cognitive potential
- Has been in a resource self-contained class for academics
- Adequate reading decoding but poor reading comprehension
- Poor spoken language comprehension
- Good vocabulary and syntax but disorganized in expression in speaking and writing
- Poor visual-motor integration
- Difficulty following lengthy or complex directions
- Acting out behavior
- Possible attention deficit

You have looked over the curriculum used in the class. You have some specific suggestions and have brought along an article on language-learning disabilities. Review the student's profile and the recommendations listed below. Then introduce yourself to the teacher and go on to your recommendations:

- Use only known vocabulary when giving James directions
- Break directions down into individual steps
- Encourage him to use an assignment book to track assignment due dates and progress
- Provide him with an example of what you want and help him get started
- Help him develop outlines before speaking or writing longer answers

- Cue him to stay on topic and in sequence when he speaks or writes
- Encourage him to ask questions when he does not understand

P.S. Remember to give the teacher the article.

Teacher and SLP Consultant Reflection

After conducting the role play, reflect on the process. Have the consultant ask the teacher: What specific aspects in the role play triggered resistance in you as the teacher? What triggered an experience of openness in you as the teacher? Then ask yourself: As the consultant, how did you react to resistance?

II. Second Scenario – Collaborative Consultation

In this second role play, the same person should play the teacher again. The other person or another plays the new consultant. In this role play, the classroom teacher has become more resistant. This is the second time you have tried meeting with a consultant. The last time, the person came across as an "expert" who was not understanding or actually helpful. You have not heard from that person since.

#2 Role Play – Teacher Material

You are still not sure how you are going to deal with James along with your 27 other students. You still feel a bit overwhelmed. You still have not had time to read his file. A second SLP consultant has made an appointment with you to talk about James. You have given up your much-needed break for yet another meeting. You have the same concerns about James as before.

#2 Role Play – SLP Consultant Material

You are going to consult with a classroom teacher regarding a student in her class. You are taking over someone else's caseload. You are following up on a situation that you expect may be difficult. You have looked over some of the work in the student's classroom portfolio and have briefly observed in the classroom. Now you would like to meet with the teacher to find out her concerns and see how the two of you might work together. You recognize that the teacher has 28 students in the class and that she has given up a break to talk to you. You are going to do your best to be collaborative. You have the same information on James as the previous SLP. Review the student's profile and the recommendations listed below. Then introduce yourself to the teacher and begin the conversation. Introduce yourself and proceed to the following actions:

- Thank the teacher for taking the time to meet
- Mention that you enjoyed observing the class
- Point out something that went particularly well during the observation
- Find out what concerns the teacher has about James
- Find out what has been tried and acknowledge why that was tried

- Generate ways you may be able to work together
- Set up a next step or next time to get together

Teacher and SLP Consultant Reflection

After conducting the role play, reflect on the process. Have the consultant ask the teacher: Even though initially resistant, what did I say that made you more open to the interaction? What made you feel even more resistant? Then ask yourself: As the consultant, how did you react to resistance?

Chapter 2

The Foundations of Language Intervention: Theory and Research

Teresa A. Ukrainetz

This chapter lays out the foundations of language intervention aimed at the social and academic competence needed for success in school and later life. The many ways of language intervention can be organized and analyzed by the level at which it intercepts the disorder and by the structure of intervention. Grouping treatments by underlying common elements, along with a basic understanding of research design, helps the SLP sort through research studies to make sense of the evidence and integrate it into clinical expertise to fit each student's needs and resources.

Defining Language Intervention

Communication is aided by defining terms. The *language* part of school-age language intervention addresses semantics, syntax, morphology, discourse, and pragmatics. However, language intervention goes far beyond these classical linguistic areas to the cognitive, behavioral, and social aspects of oral and written communicative competence. (And does not include the linguistic component of phonology, which in clinical practice, is grouped within the *speech* part of speech–language pathology.)

The term *intervention* refers to intentional actions taken to accelerate, modify, or compensate for inadequate performance (Fey, 1986; Johnston, 1983; Paul, 2007). It may also be called *treatment* or *therapeutic instruction*. Intervention or treatment involves both direct interactions with the affected individual, and more indirect, systemically-focused actions, such as consulting with teachers on classroom structure and interactions, providing educational materials for parents, or providing supplementary instruction for children at risk for educational difficulties. While the term treatment is used only for the amelioration activities, intervention can include the assessment component of the process. In the schools, with response to intervention (RTI) tiered models of instruction, the term intervention is used for both special education individualized instruction and for noncategorical supplementary remedial assistance. Intervention is expected to follow a systematic progression of assessment, selection of treatment goals, execution of treatment procedures, collection of outcome data, judgment of attainment of goals, and ongoing modifications of procedures (Roth & Worthington, 2011). The aim of intervention is not just to improve particular skills or behaviors but to improve performance within the varying conditions of daily life.

Intervention by Level of Interception

A language disorder affects a person from the physiological makeup through to the social world. One way to make sense of the many ways of intervening with language is to organize interventions by the level of interception with the disorder (Box 2.1). Intervention directed at changing the neuropsychological underpinnings of functions should reduce the need for higher level behavioral and environmental interventions. These are "bottom-up" interventions. Intervention that intercepts the problem at higher

Box 2.1. ***Interventions Organized by Level of Focus***

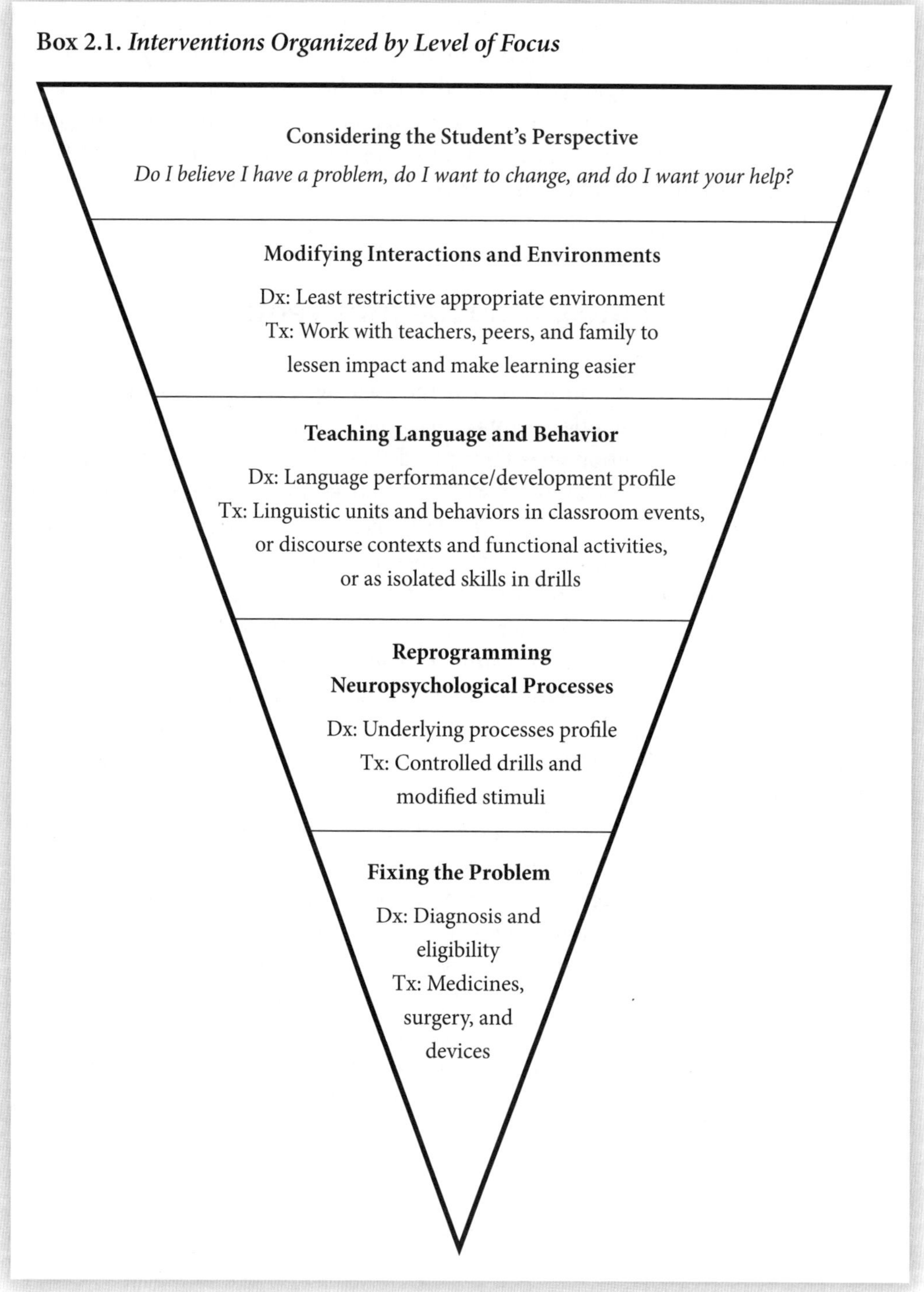
Considering the Student's Perspective
Do I believe I have a problem, do I want to change, and do I want your help?
Modifying Interactions and Environments
Dx: Least restrictive appropriate environment
Tx: Work with teachers, peers, and family to lessen impact and make learning easier
Teaching Language and Behavior
Dx: Language performance/development profile
Tx: Linguistic units and behaviors in classroom events, or discourse contexts and functional activities, or as isolated skills in drills
Reprogramming Neuropsychological Processes
Dx: Underlying processes profile
Tx: Controlled drills and modified stimuli
Fixing the Problem
Dx: Diagnosis and eligibility
Tx: Medicines, surgery, and devices

levels centers around improving presenting behaviors and their ease of use in daily life situations. They may even address the larger social and physical conditions affecting the individual's performance. Changes in interactions at this level can spread "top-down" to neuropsychological processes, as individuals more competently and efficiently engage their cognitive and linguistic resources.

There is no single correct choice of level at which to intercept language disorders and difficulties. An SLP needs to consider the disorder, the skill targets, the situation, and the individual. Each SLP selects the level of focus that is most appropriate for the student. SLPs may use procedures from multiple levels to provide a comprehensive treatment plan. For example, the SLP may primarily engage in addressing morphosyntax and discourse goals through a literature-based intervention but give the student some ownership by allowing him to prioritize his treatment goals. The SLP may include some computer-based treatment each session to drill verbal working memory and work with the teacher to modify curricular materials in the classroom. Each of these actions intercept the language impairment at different levels but in complementary ways that increase the impact of treatment.

Fixing the Problem at the Source

Interventions can be directed at fixing the underlying problem. In the categorical or medical orientation to disabilities, language disorders are identified and categorized on the basis of known or presumed causes or etiologies (Lahey, 1988; Paul, 2007). The Individuals with Disabilities Education Act (IDEA) reflects this model in its eligibility categories, such as autism, mental retardation, and traumatic brain injury. The categorical orientation and its labels give children, families, and service providers a sense of why the person is having difficulties and what to expect. These labels are used for eligibility for services. A child labeled with attention deficit disorder is likely to have a different pattern of strengths and weaknesses and different intervention needs from a child labeled specific reading disabled.

The categorical orientation does not account well for patterns of performance because within a single category children's behaviors and skills can vary considerably, and between categories there is often considerable overlap in patterns of performance. One child's specific reading disability may be manifest primarily as word recognition difficulties while another struggles with text comprehension. Text comprehension difficulties may look the same in a child with specific reading disability and a child with attention deficit disorder. The heterogeneity within and overlaps among categories of developmental disorders make it difficult to find a single best label for each child and result in limited treatment guidance.

Interventions at this bottom level are expected to spread upward, so that less (or no) intervention is needed at higher levels of function. These are typically medical treatments, such as drugs (e.g., Ritalin) or surgeries (e.g., cochlear implant). However, medication and surgery are not within the scope of practice of SLPs (American Speech-Language-Hearing Association [ASHA], 2007), so whatever is available at this level will occur through other professionals. Even so, the SLP should know the etiological category assigned to the student because of its role in eligibility determination and because it is a starting point in selecting and crafting interventions.

Reprogramming Neuropsychological Processing

The specific disabilities orientation focuses on the pathology—what has gone wrong with specific neuropsychological abilities or processes thought to underlie language, literacy, and school success (Lahey, 1988; Paul, 2007). The word "processing" is often used for this level of dysfunction. The problems may be localized to particular processes, such as auditory temporal resolution, working memory, or selective attention. Some categories of disorders have characteristic difficulties with particular processes, such as phonological code retrieval for specific reading disability. Other types of processing difficulties have become categories of disorders themselves with familiar acronyms, such as central auditory processing disorder (CAPD) or attention deficit disorder (ADD). Assessment involves carefully structured testing to isolate and evaluate contributions of particular neuropsychological abilities or processes. It is challenging to separate out the effects of auditory memory versus attention while also controlling for the effects of higher level skills, such as vocabulary (e.g., in the memory task of recalling geometric shapes, labels will aid recall). Often the testing procedures are not suitable for young or distractible students.

Treatment at this level involves a tight control of task complexity. Treatment may consist of simple drills, such as repeating increasing spans of digits to improve working memory. It may involve sophisticated computer programs that systematically modify acoustic elements of the speech signal to improve auditory discrimination. Intervention at this level is expected to spread upward, improving children's skills and behaviors in contexts of use. Regardless of whether treatment at this level is effective, it is important to take into consideration a student's neuropsychological resources and how they affect language learning in planning treatment. Attention and memory can be addressed directly, as a components of a broader treatment, or incidentally, such as reducing distractions or controlling task demands.

Teaching Language and Learning Skills and Behaviors

The third level involves what might be considered traditional language intervention, targeting the communicative and behavioral manifestations or symptoms of underlying pathology. It is based on a descriptive-developmental perspective, in which a child's language function is assessed through sampling communicative behaviors in daily life activities and structured tasks (Lahey, 1988; Naremore, 1980; Paul, 2007). Treatment goals are referenced to developmental sequences and situational expectations. Detailed profiles are made of children's language and language-related skills to determine strengths, weaknesses, and priorities for treatment. A label like specific language impairment reflects this descriptive orientation because it does not imply a cause for the difficulties or a specific new psychological deficiency.

In this functional orientation, there are diverse language intervention possibilities, from discrete skill training in hierarchical formats that falls just above the prior "processing" level to skill instruction embedded in meaningful contexts that falls just below the "systems" level described next. Treatment may focus on word, sentence, or discourse level skills. Metalinguistics (e.g., phonemic awareness) and strategy instruction (e.g., skimming textbook headings) may occur at this level. Interventions may result in a downward spread of improvement to neuropsychological processes. For example, an older student who is distractible but motivated may learn strategies to select and sustain attention during class lectures. The language level is likely to be the main arena for intervention. It is best conducted functionally, in reference to the classroom, the curriculum, and the student's individual perspective.

Modifying the Social and Physical Environment

The systems or environmental approach takes a wider view than direct intervention perspectives. Rather than focusing solely on problems in the child, this approach involves examining problems in "the space between" participants or between the child and the curriculum. Observation, examination of work products, and interview will reveal areas of mismatch, such as the teacher's style of lecture, peer interactions, classroom seating, visual learning supports (and distractions) posted on classroom walls, textbook language, and assignment instructions. In a systems approach, compensations may be provided, such as teaching a student to use a communication picture board. Interventions may involve changing the social environment by modifying how teachers or peers interact with the student. The physical environment may be modified through seating adjustments, changing materials, or modifying the curriculum to increase communicative motivations, decrease distractions, or reduce language demands. Supports may be gradually reduced either as the student learns to cope on his own or as other treatment improves the child's abilities. This approach can work top-down: If a student is less frustrated and confused in the classroom, he can improve skills as well as content, thus improving his language and processing performance.

Individual Perspective: In the Eye of the Beholder

One final overarching perspective on disability and intervention is the individual perspective or sociopolitical model (Smart & Smart, 2006). This model promotes the idea that a disability is only a disability if the individual believes it to be so. Society may call it a disability, but that is an imposed state of being. This model is embraced by many *capital D Deaf* individuals who consider that hearing level is simply one of the ways in which humans vary. Another example is reading. In the past, when society did not value reading proficiency, an inability to read was not considered a disability. That is clearly not the case today.

Language intervention within the sociopolitical perspective includes the acknowledgment that no one has the right to label another as having a disability or to prescribe treatment for them. This freedom is difficult to apply within the legal prescriptions of education and expectations of society. It could take the form of seeking to understand a student's perspective on his own disability or giving an older student the option of not receiving intervention. Regardless of the degree of ownership that is allowed to students, SLPs should understand that students' perceptions of themselves will affect the outcome of intervention. Motivation and engagement in learning are critical to immediate gains in learning but even more so to students taking ownership of their new knowledge and skills and continuing to use them beyond the treatment context.

The Structure of Language Intervention

Language intervention procedures vary in structure, explicitness, and organization. All aim at children's competence in daily life activities, but take different routes to achieve

Box 2.2. *Five Different Ways of Selecting and Teaching Vocabulary*

Basic concept vocabulary: Basic concept words, such as spatial and directional taught in following direction tasks as well as semantic knowledge, such as same/different, categories, and functions taught in word-sorting tasks.

High frequency words: A school-wide list of high frequency vocabulary, unrelated to each other or any larger context co-taught with the resource teacher through definitions, sentence use, illustration, and weekly written quizzes.

Thematic vocabulary: Difficult or interesting words were selected from SLP-designed thematic units based on topics from the curriculum taught through crossword puzzles, board games, story comprehension questions, and story retells.

Curricular vocabulary: Difficult or interesting words were selected from children's literature or expository passages from classroom textbooks taught through retellings, making definitions, using the words in sentences and figuring out the meanings from passages.

Incidental vocabulary: Technical words needed to explain story structure, such as episode or complication, and new words arising from storybook sharing and chapter book discussions taught through story grammar analysis, story discussion, and oral reports.

Note: Observed from the practices of five school SLPs. From Ukrainetz (2005).

it. These routes are typically grouped along a continuum of structure and naturalness from clinician-directed to child-centered interventions (Fey, 1986; Paul, 2007). However, the SLP interventions that occur in school settings, even those that focus on the level of teaching language skills and behavior, vary in more ways than can be captured by that single continuum.

For example, a case study report on the practices of five experienced school SLPs showed considerable variation among this small number of clinicians (Ukrainetz, 2005). For vocabulary alone, the five SLPs were observed to use five different specific treatment procedures (Box 2.2). For overall approaches to treatment, two of the SLPs favored teaching isolated skills in a hierarchical format. One did this primarily with basic concepts, moving in a hierarchy from receptive to expressive and simple to complex with directional prepositions. Another did it with phonemic awareness and word spelling, moving from representing single phonemes with blocks to representing multiple phonemes in progressively longer words and then to spelling those words. Three SLPs favored teaching skills embedded in meaningful contexts: One used a unit approach, with word and sentence activities thematically linked to a curricular topic while two taught discourse skills through lessons around books, one using children's literature and the other classroom texts. Assistance in classroom assignments and rich language activities with no specific skill focus and drill-play on skills disconnected from a larger skill progression were also sometimes used. These practices all exemplify variations present in the field and reflect systematically different ways of ordering skills in treatment that go beyond a smiple continuum of structure (Box 2.3).

Box 2.3. ***Interventions Organized by Skill and Task Structure***

Hierarchical Skill Intervention	One skill at a time in tasks on a hierarchy of simple contrived tasks to natural activities with minimal prompting and correction
Skill Stimulation	Skill practice in contrived simple tasks with minimal prompting and correction
Enrichment and Task Assistance	Participating in naturalistic and life activities with prompts and corrections on any skills, as required
Contextualized Skill Intervention	Several skills at time in mix of naturalistic activities and simple contrived tasks with prompting and correction on those target skills

Hierarchical Skill Intervention

The classic approach to intervention is *hierarchical skill intervention*, also known as discrete skill, skill mastery, or clinician-directed intervention. In the reading arena, this approach is called direct instruction (e.g., Berninger et al., 2003), but in speech–language pathology, *direct intervention* simply means working on a treatment goal with the child rather than through another person or through incidental gains from working on another skill. Such intervention is extremely structured, with the SLP predetermining how materials will be used, what responses are acceptable, and how responses will be facilitated (Fey, 1986; Berninger et al., 2003). One skill is addressed at a time in tasks that are hierarchically ordered with increasing skill or activity complexity as well as skill mastery at each level (Roth & Worthington, 2011).

In this approach, treatment activities through most of the hierarchy are contrived to provide practice and feedback solely on the target skill, with no larger communicative purpose. They may involve entertaining games or artificial reinforcers to maintain motivation. The difficulty level is designed to match the student's competence so that the student can work largely independently at a level that is challenging but not frustrating. If error levels are too high, the child is returned to the simpler activity for more practice or an intervening step is inserted into the progression. Meaningful daily life activities occur only after the component skills have been established in simpler activities. Systematic variations in materials, locations, and participants are employed to encourage independent, flexible use of skills.

Hierarchical skill intervention is used across the field, such as with articulation treatment for isolated speech errors (Bernthal, Bankson, & Flipsen, 2009) and discrete-trial training for autism (Goldstein, 2002). Generally, language intervention that takes this approach has successfully trained simple language forms, but there is less success with more complex forms and generalization to daily life communicative contexts (Goldstein, 2002). The *Lindamood Phoneme Sequencing Program* (LiPS) (Lindamood &

Lindamood, 2011) is an example of hierarchical skill intervention for teaching phonemic awareness and word decoding.

Skill Stimulation

Another discrete skill treatment approach is one termed here as *skill stimulation.* Although not generally addressed in the child language literature, this occurs widely in practice. Sohlberg and Mateer (1989) noted the popularity of a cognitive version of this within rehabilitation settings: The expectation is that "any stimulation of cognitive processing will result in improved mental faculties" (p. 20). Skill stimulation involves addressing a variety of language skills during simple entertaining activities. Students respond to prompts while they progress around a game board, advance in a computer game, or earn a reward for completing a workbook assignment. The skills are not an inherent part of the activity and there is no framework for how the skills combine or for moving the skills into daily life communicative contexts.

This approach is attractive because students enjoy playing the games, and they are easy to set up, administer, and score. There is a cornucopia of games and materials available from commercial vendors in conferences and catalogs. The drill-play activities provide practice of isolated skills and some instruction through models and prompts of correct answers. For this approach to work, repeated practice of isolated skills with support of correct answers in an entertaining but arbitrary task must be sufficient to teach language. Students should then be able to independently apply the skills to communicative contexts in which the skills belong. For example, repeated practice at conjoining two sentences with *however* at each shake of the dice in a board game that results in 90% independent correct sentence production in the game and in a test that uses the same item form is then expected to translate to independent, appropriate use of *however* sentences in narrative and expository compositions in the classroom.

Enrichment and Task Assistance

Another approach emphasizes teaching language within contexts of use. The child-oriented or language *enrichment* approach involves following the child's lead within daily life communicative activities while providing rich language models and interactions (Fey, 1986; Paul, 2007). For older students, the SLP may help the child participate in a school event or complete an assignment, and thus the additional label of *task assistance.* This approach includes what Berninger et al. (2003) called *constructivist instruction* to teaching reading: "The teacher offers instructional activities that encourage student reflection but does not transmit instructional cues—the student must construct his or her own knowledge from the activities—and instructional feedback is incidental rather than systematic." (p. 103).

In this approach, skills are addressed in the complex, meaningful activities in which they are communicatively needed right from the beginning of intervention. The communicative environment and the conversational partner's interactions are subtly modified to highlight the language goals and support the student's responses. Only general goals are targeted, and there is flexibility to address teachable moments for a variety of language skills. Because language skills are taught within the daily life activities in which they are needed, generalization of skills is not a major concern.

In the schools, language may be taught using literature, thematic units, or classroom activities. A large number of language and literacy skills may be targeted in these rich, meaningful contexts, but there is little explicit attention to facilitating learning. The instruction may be essentially what is already provided in language-rich activities in the regular classroom. For instance, Merritt and Culatta (1998) outlined a thematic treatment unit for the primary grades which simultaneously addresses 39 treatment objectives. Expectations for students of differing levels and scaffolds for individual responses were presented but there was no larger plan for systematically addressing the many objectives. Other examples could be when the SLP assists the teacher in a classroom lesson or assists a student in a classroom assignment (Ehren, 2000; Ukrainetz, 2005). The SLP may model advanced language and correct student responses, but, even if the activity is quite structured and skill focused (e.g., a phonics lesson), there is no particular attention to the student gaining competence in specific language goals.

Contextualized Skill Intervention

The final approach is one that is intended to combine the best elements of clinician-directed and child-oriented interventions called hybrid (Fey, 1986) or *contextualized skill intervention* (Ukrainetz, 2006a). Berninger et al. (2003) might fit *explicit instruction* for reading here: "In the middle of the continuum, the teacher provides clear and systematic instructional cues explicitly stated in lesson plans but the student is given opportunity for open-ended responding and receives instructional feedback" (p. 103).

Contextualized skill intervention involves treatment goals that are targeted in a systematic, explicit manner embedded within simplified but communicative contexts. This can mean delivery within the regular classroom in an inclusive format, or in pull-out using activities and materials based on those from the classroom. Considerable learning support is provided initially and then is reduced as the student gains competence over repetitions or variations of the activity. A familiar form for early language is milieu teaching for which there is considerable research support (Hancock & Kaiser, 2006).

Contextualized skill intervention can involve a combination of whole communicative activities and contrived single skill activities. The process of composing and sharing a research presentation or a personal narrative is carefully designed to provide repeated opportunities for the targeted skills. Instruction is embedded as microlesson moments within these whole activities and as longer minilessons during breaks from the larger communicative activity (Eisenberg, 2006). Short drill and drill-play activities that employ the skill communicatively (e.g., for relative clause practice, *I spy with my little eye something that is red*) or arbitrarily (e.g., saying a relative clause sentence for each move around a game board) can be used for additional focused skill practice. Micro, mini, and drill-play activities combine with integrated use of the targeted skills in whole, communicative events in a whole-part framework (see Chapter 3).

Evidence-Based Practice

Research has always been a source of information for SLPs but is emphasized more than ever now (ASHA, 2007, 2010). A 2011 survey of 2,762 responding school SLPs showed that the majority of SLPs had graduate or continuing education in evidence-based practice (Hoffman, Ireland, Hall-Mills, & Flynn, 2013). Few of the responding SLPs sought out research evidence on questions that arose in their work, but most reported a high interest in obtaining additional expertise and resources to guide them in using scientifically based practices. In education, the term "scientifically based instruction" is limited to use of research evidence of experimental and quasi-experimental designs (U.S. Department of Education, 2007). In speech–language pathology, a more comprehensive and integrated approach is taken with *evidence-based practice*. Evidence-based practice involves making decisions about the care of individual patients by integrating the *best available research evidence* with *clinical expertise* and *patient values and preferences* (Dollaghan, 2007; Robey & Schultz, 1998).

Attitudes to Research Evidence

Evidence-based practice requires a basic understanding of research methods, critical thinking skills, and perseverance in sorting out the evidence. It requires SLPs to be open to honest doubt, aware of preferences and biases, willing to let strong evidence guide actions, and mindful of ethical responsibilities (Dollaghan, 2007). If a clinician is not open-minded, then he or she will selectively attend only to supporting evidence. If a preferred treatment is shown to be ineffective, the SLP may judge that he or she does it better than the researchers (Siegel, 1987). The SLP may be correct because research standards rarely allow flexible, mixed-method treatments that respond dynamically to individual children's needs. However, the SLP must also be open to the possibility that her or his own practices need to change.

SLPs should also be aware of whether particular questions are amenable to scientific answers (Siegel, 1987). Some questions involve social values, such as whether adequacy of public financial resources should determine which children receive treatment. As Siegel explains, child language treatment is provided in schools now not so much due to research evidence but because society has shifted from thinking that treatment should be given only individuals who can contribute economically to viewing intervention as part of a right to quality of life and equal educational opportunities. Other questions require more logical reasoning, such as whether language treatment will improve cognition, which depends on how you define *language*, *treatment*, and *cognition*. Research data inform discussions, but ultimately these questions go beyond empirical evidence.

Research Questions and Designs

Research studies involve systematic collection and reporting of empirical (measurable) data. Research designs vary in how much control is exerted over the variables being tested, from experiments in laboratory conditions to unobtrusive observations of lived events. Studies that answer treatment *efficacy* questions require a high degree of control and randomized participant assignment to treatment conditions (Robey & Schultz,

1998). The term *effectiveness* is used for designs that suggest cause-effect relations but have lower levels of control. *Efficiency* is a term used for comparing the relative benefits and costs of different treatments.

Descriptive design research provides systematic pictures of individual situations (e.g., *case studies* or *program evaluations*) or populations (e.g., *group observational studies* or *surveys*). They answer questions such as: "What is the nature of this disorder?" "What is the nature of client response to this treatment?" "How can this research treatment be implemented clinically?" "What is the prevalence of this disorder?" and "How much improvement is obtained with this treatment?" These studies contribute to the clinical knowledge needed for evidence-based practice. However, these designs are not suited to answering cause-effect questions and thus can offer only a low level of evidence for such questions.

Some research designs provide more systematic control of the treatment and other variables. *Correlational* studies can determine relations among variables, such as what aspects of narratives are related to high teacher ratings of overall quality. The strength and direction of relationships among variables along with unique and overlapping contributions of multiple factors can be determined, but this design does not provide cause-effect answers (except in a very complicated version called *path analysis*). *Comparative* studies show that the treated children improved compared to norm-referenced expectations or to other children who did not receive the treatment. The amount of change is analyzed statistically to determine if it is large enough to be reliable and not due to chance. These studies are quite common. However, these designs lack enough control to confidently judge that it was the treatment, and not life or situational factors, that was responsible for the greater improvement.

Group experimental studies are required to confidently answer efficacy questions. These designs determine the effect of manipulating a treatment variable on an outcome variable with extraneous variables held as constant as possible. Participants are randomly assigned to a treatment condition and a control or an alternate treatment condition (*between group*) or one group undergoes all the conditions with treatment order controlled (*within group*). Individual researchers can conduct small randomized experiments that provide preliminary efficacy evidence and information about optimal treatment procedures, treatment intensity, and testing measures. When treatments are understood quite well, then large-scale, highly controlled (and very expensive) treatment experiments, called *randomized clinical trials* (RCTs), can be conducted. Not surprisingly, RCTs are rare in speech–language pathology.

Often for communication disorders it is difficult to even conduct small-scale group treatment experiments. Fortunately, there is an alternate class of research design called single-subject experiments. In these, the participant serves as his or her own control: Instead of just one pretest and one posttest data points (so the participant could happen to have a bad pretest day and a good posttest day), performance is repeatedly tested during baseline and treatment phases (akin to having data points from many participants in each condition in a group design). In a single-subject experimental design, the judgment of treatment efficacy is made primarily on visual-graphical analysis rather than statistical analysis. The pattern of data points is examined for whether performance changes noticeably when—and only when—the treatment is in force. Box 2.4 shows the

Box 2.4. ***An Example of a Single-Subject Experimental Research Design***

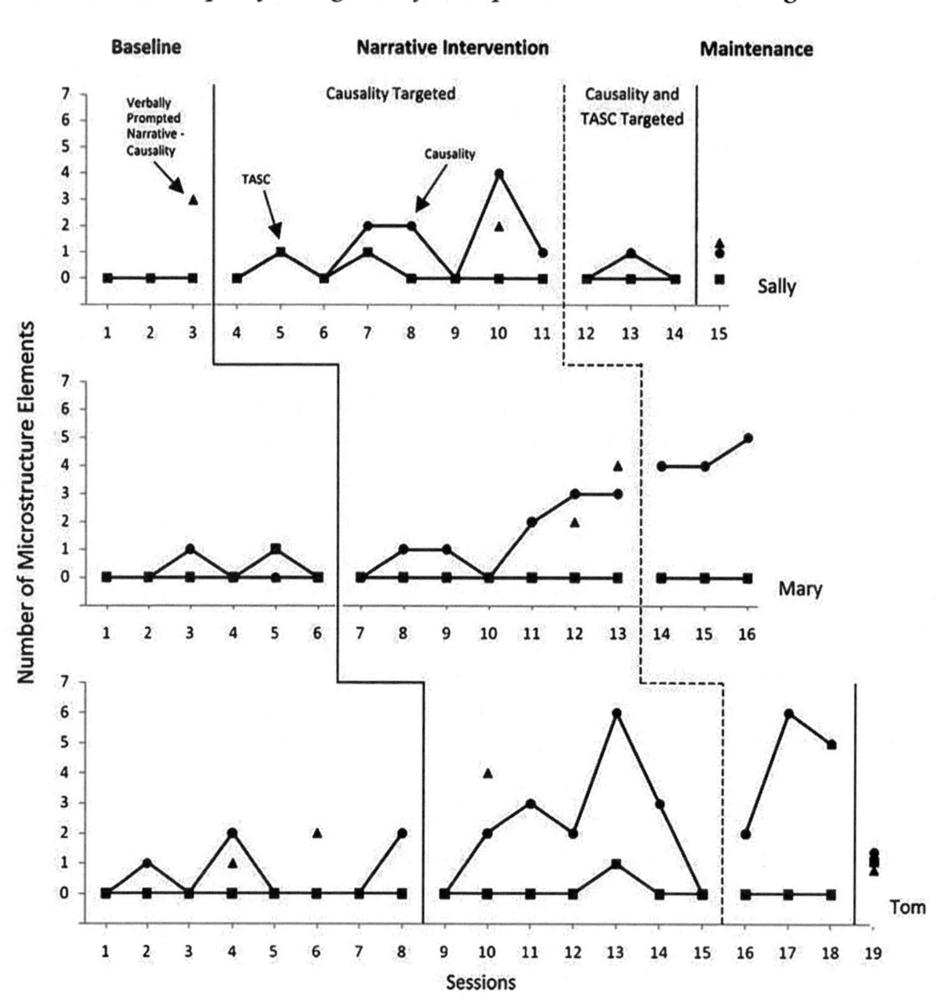

A design with multiple baselines across behaviors and participants shows results for a narrative intervention study teaching causal words with temporal adverbials as a control behavior for three 6- to 8-year-old children with neurological impairments.

Note: From "The Effects of Literate Narrative Intervention on Children With Neurologically Based Language Impairments: An Early Stage Study," by D. Petersen, S. L. Gillam, T. Spencer, & R. B. Gillam, 2010, *Journal of Speech, Language, and Hearing Research, 53*, p. 972. Copyright 2010 by the American Speech-Language-Hearing Association. Reprinted with permission.

graphical results of a single-subject experiment by Petersen, Gillam, Spencer, and Gillam (2010) that investigated the efficacy of a narrative intervention for three 6- to 8-year-old children with neurodevelopmental impairments. The pattern of data points for each of the children and each behavior indicated that the treatment was responsible for the change. Added confidence comes from the pattern of data across multiple behaviors and subjects with differing baseline durations (see Byiers, Reichle, & Symons, 2012 for more on single-subject experimental designs and evidence-based practice).

Like group experimental designs, these single-subject experimental designs require a high level of control to have confidence that the only reasons for change in the outcome (the dependent variable) was the treatment (the independent variable), rather than other features of the person's life or the clinical situation (extraneous or confounding variables). This degree of control is difficult to exert in daily clinical practice and can even be undesirable. Most clinicians continuously individualize, adjust, and mix treatments based on their judgment of what is needed for each client at each moment in time. They also extend and vary treatments to obtain maintenance and generalization. Furthermore, clinicians do not generally need to answer specific cause-effect questions. Instead, it is enough that a clinician keeps systematic, reliable data to show that sizeable and functional improvement resulted from whatever combination of interventions and life factors occurred for each client.

Evaluating the Big Picture

Decisions about treatment should be informed by research evidence. However, individual studies can be found that report "statistically significant" treatment effects for almost any treatment approach or procedure. This research varies in how well it is designed, conducted, and reported. Fortunately, standards for treatment research design in our field have increased over the years. One improvement is requiring measures of treatment fidelity (how well the instructors followed the treatment plan). Another improvement is moving from no-treatment control conditions to "active" control conditions in which the participants at least receive special attention and practice with listening and responding. Studies that compare different treatments are more helpful than comparing something to nothing, but at least one of the treatments should have established validity so it is not a matter of comparing two ineffective treatments that both show improvement because of maturation or practice effects. In addition, treatment comparisons must be very carefully structured to provide equivalent quality and intensity so valid comparisons can be made (Warren, Fey, & Yoder, 2007). Another improvement is reporting outcomes in terms of practical or clinical significance (whether the change is big enough to matter) in addition to statistical significance (whether the change is bigger than chance). A statistic called an *effect size* allows comparisons of the magnitude of outcomes across different studies (see Meline & Schmitt, 1997).

It is important to look at many studies on a particular question and determine where the strongest evidence lies. However, it can be difficult for individual clinicians to locate, review, and synthesize a body of research to answer their treatment questions (Brackenbury, Burroughs, & Hewitt, 2008). Fortunately, guidelines on searching for and evaluating research can be found (e.g., Gillam & Gillam, 2006) and systematic reviews and meta-analyses composed by experts in an area are appearing more frequently (see http://asha.org/research). These reports differ from traditional literature reviews because of the explicit procedures used to search, select, evaluate, and report studies. These standards help prevent authors from reporting only studies that support their hypotheses and making claims that go beyond the evidence.

Even if systematic reviews do much of the work, the SLP must still read critically. For example, authors may state that there is no evidence on a particular question because only group experimental studies were examined but single-subject experimental studies exist. In addition, due to lack of research in the field, a conclusion may be made only on two or three studies that clump different ages or treatment approaches together. For example, a meta-analysis of treatment outcomes by Law, Garrett, and Nye (2004) judged that language intervention had only mixed and tentative evidence of effectiveness, but Johnston (2005) challenged the report, saying that many successful outcomes were missed by the way that the authors selected and grouped studies.

The other two parts of the triad of evidence-based practice are clinical expertise and client preferences (Dollaghan, 2007). Clinical expertise comes through education, observation, experience, and reasoning. SLPs must think about whether the treatment makes sense based on what is known about typical and atypical language development (Johnston, 1983). They must decide whether the treatment and the outcomes fit their own intervention setting. Even if a treatment has a strong research base, makes sense, and fits the setting, the characteristics of each student and his or her own specific situation must be considered. The best treatment will not work if the client rejects it. Evidence-based practice involves having available a variety of approaches and procedures; fitting the treatments to students, settings, and resources; and adjusting treatments along the way as needed. From all this, it should be clear that conducting evidence-based practice is an art as much as a science!

Research Evidence on School-Age Language Intervention

There is often little research, especially controlled studies, investigating and comparing particular treatments for particular aspects of language for particular types of language impairments at particular ages. However, overall, there is a lot of research addressing treatment of the linguistic, cognitive, and social skills involved in school success. Evaluating the full spectrum of possibilities is beyond the scope of this chapter, but some systematic reviews and studies comparing treatments are considered in evaluating the evidence for treatment approaches.

Cirrin and Gillam (2008) conducted a systematic review to determine the efficacy (well-controlled) and effectiveness (use in more natural situations) of language intervention for school-age children with spoken language disorders by area of language. The studies involved randomized assignment, nonrandomized assignment, and single-subject experimental designs, published in peer-reviewed journals since 1985. For the 21 studies located, Cirrin and Gillam found immediate gains (moderate to large effect sizes) compared to no-treatment controls across language areas, but maintenance and application in daily life situations were often not examined.

Cirrin and Gillam's (2008) results did not indicate any single preferred service delivery format or treatment procedure. The learning supports of modeling and elicited or imitated productions were helpful for syntax and pragmatics. Explicit instruction and feedback were also helpful for pragmatics. Vocabulary could be taught through interactive reading strategies and analogies. Semantic elaboration, semantic cueing, and phonological cueing were all helpful for word-finding. Phonological awareness improved with any type of explicit instruction. Software programs that modified the speech signal showed the same improvement in auditory processing and language measures as conventional treatments. Cirrin and Gillam did not locate any studies on narrative or exposition. A systematic review by Petersen (2011) with the same search criteria, but going back to 1980 and including preschoolers with language impairments, reported treatment effects for vocabulary, grammar, and narrative structure through generating and retelling imaginative and personal narratives using children's literature, picture supports, with interactive scaffolding, such as prompting, modeling, and recasting.

Reviews of the literature for early language show that discrete skill interventions are effective in increasing the presence and rate of gains of skills in the contexts in which they were taught (e.g., Abbeduto & Boudreau, 2004; Goldstein, 2002; Peterson, 2004). More contextualized interventions, such as milieu teaching, focused stimulation, and conversational recasting, show significant gains in more natural contexts (Peterson, 2004; Warren et al., 2007; Weismer & Robertson, 2006).

For reading, better gains have been shown for word recognition skills with explicit, systematic phonics instruction than with whole word "look and say" instruction (National Reading Panel [NRP], 2000). Berninger et al. (2003) found for reading that explicit instruction had greater benefits than implicit, constructivist procedures. Berninger et al. also demonstrated that combining instruction in comprehending meaningful texts with word recognition instruction increased word recognition skills over word-level instruction alone. Phonics-based instruction can be effectively delivered in both hierarchical and more contextualized systematic approaches, with large and maintained gains in phonemic awareness, word recognition, and reading comprehension (e.g., Torgesen et al., 2001; Torgesen, Wagner, Rashotte, Herron, & Lindamood, 2010). Text comprehension instruction is most effective when it includes contextualized features of invoking background knowledge, providing motivated student choices, modeling comprehension strategies, setting up peer tutoring and cooperative work, giving opportunities to read connected text, and using authentic text genres (NRP, 2000; RAND Reading Study Group, 2002). In sum, the research indicates that reading can be taught in a variety of ways, but instruction needs to be explicit, intensive, and systematic, with links made to contexts of use.

For spoken language, both discrete skill and contextualized skill treatments can be effective, but in different ways. For two classes of 9- to 12-year-old students with language impairment, word and sentence worksheets and contrived activities resulted in more improvement in form measures (e.g., morphemes and connectives per T-unit), whereas listening to and creating whole stories resulted in more improvement in content (e.g., more ideas per T-unit and more episodes) and better overall quality of spoken and written narratives (Gillam, McFadden, & van Kleeck, 1995; McFadden & Gillam, 1996). Gillam, Gillam, and Reece (2012) randomly assigned 16 6- to 9-year-olds with language impairment to discrete skill and contextualized skill interventions for multiple linguistic targets. Significant changes were obtained for both approaches in both sentence-level and discourse-level language, but effect sizes for all the outcomes were larger for the more natural approach.

Gillam et al. (2008) conducted a large scale randomized controlled clinical trial comparing the language and auditory processing outcomes for: (a) a computer-based language intervention with modified speech intended to improve auditory processing; (b) a computer-based language intervention with no modified speech; (c) an SLP-delivered individualized language intervention; and (d) nonspecific mathematics, social studies, and science computer games. The 216 children between the ages of 6 and 9 years with language impairments were randomly assigned to each condition for 100 minutes of individual treatment 5 days per week for 6 weeks. The children participated in noninstructional group activities while waiting their time to attend the individual sessions. Language and auditory processing measures were applied immediately after and several months after treatment.

Gillam et al. (2008) found that all four conditions showed significant and maintained improvement with similar effect sizes on a global spoken language test and on a backward masking task. Another analysis of the data by Loeb et al. (2009) found that phonological awareness and reading improved significantly in that time, but the three treatment conditions significantly improved more compared to the academic enrichment condition only on phonological awareness. These results showed that all three treatments were beneficial for language, reading, and auditory processing skills, resulting in changes that would not have been obtained in just six weeks of normal schooling. However, the performance of the academic enrichment condition was unexpected because the computer games did not explicitly and supportively teach particular language skills. Nevertheless, they did at least focus attention and give extensive corrective practice opportunities. Gillam and colleagues (2008) concluded that:

> It is possible that similar improvements may be obtained from a variety of interventions: that are presented on an intensive schedule, that focus the child's auditory and visual attention, that present multiple trials, that vary task complexity as a function of response accuracy, and that reward progress. (p. 273)

The processing approach to treatment that targets specific neuropsychological processes considered to underlie language function has received some investigation. For auditory processing, the Gillam et al. (2008) study and others have shown that auditory processing treatment does not result in gains in auditory processing greater than those gained with other linguistic and academic interventions (Cirrin & Gillam, 2008; Strong, Torgerson, Torgerson, & Hulme, 2011). However, research on working memory treatment has shown some positive effects. The treatments typically involve daily sessions over several weeks of exercises involving repeating sequences of digits backward or identifying visual patterns, with computer algorithms that keep the exercises at each child's maximum working memory capacity (see Chapter 12). Compared to no-treatment controls, several studies have shown improvements in standardized neuropsychological test performance (Gillam & Gillam, 2012), with one study showing improved reading comprehension (Dahlin, 2011). However, methodological features have allowed other explanations, such as the effect of the additional monitoring and encouragement at school and home. Holmes, Gathercole, and Dunning (2009) suggested changes in their study may have been due not to capacity improvement, but to improved control of voluntary attention and strategy use: A majority of their 8- to 11-year-old participants reported concentrating harder to improve performance by closing their eyes, rehearsing items, and tracing visual patterns with their eyes.

A reasonable conclusion from this brief look at the treatment literature is that school-age language and its related areas should be taught with some type of explicit, systematic instruction that engages children's active attention on skills and in activities that are relevant to the demands of the classroom (Nippold, 2012; Ukrainetz, 2006a). Supplemental training in working memory may be beneficial, especially if the increased capacity or learned strategies are applied to school activities. In addition, the amount of treatment appears to matter. Although optimal intensities are generally not known and likely vary with the number and nature of skills treated and the features of treatment (Warren et al., 2007), explicit systematic treatments of 1 to 2 hours per day for two or more months can produce impressive and lasting changes in a variety of oral language and reading skills (e.g., Gillam et al., 2008; Torgesen et al., 2001). Thus, there is reseaerch guidance for the general conduct of language intervention. This evidence must be used in judicious combination with theoretical knowledge, logical reasoning, and clinical experience to make good evidence-based decisions about service for each student.

Critical Features of Treatment: RISE+

The foregoing research indicates that a small array of treatment elements is important for effective intervention. These critical features or quality indicators cut across treatment approaches, procedures, skills, modalities, and disorders. They can be reduced to the simple mnemonic of RISE: *repeated opportunities* for practice and learning, at an adequate *intensity*, with *systematic support* and an *explicit* skill focus (Ukrainetz, 2006a).

There are no absolute levels for RISE. In general, regular classroom instruction is marked by lower levels of each feature. Remedial assistance provides mid-level support, while treatment provides maximal support (Box 2.5). The amount and nature of each feature will vary with the characteristics of the student, the skill being taught, and the larger context. A child with a language impairment requires more instruction than a child with an intact learning mechanism. Skills that are addressed only in the treatment room will require more intensity than skills that are also addressed in the classroom. Spelling and expository structure will take more instruction than the more predictable areas of phonemic awareness and narrative structure. In addition, RISE features interact. If the support is provided exactly how it is needed, fewer learning opportunities are likely to be necessary. If opportunities are densely provided in a session, then similar gains may be achieved as for more frequent sessions where less is happening in each. In fact, in a retrospective analysis of a series of investigations of language treatments with apparently only small differences in procedures, Gillam and Gillam (2014) found quite variable outcomes. They emphasized the need to determine carefully observe, document, and match the "amount" of RISE to the treatment goal, the client, and the conditions of intervention.

Box 2.5. *The Continuum of RISE+ From Instruction to Intervention*

Feature	Regular, Supportive, and Intervention Contexts
Repeated Opportunities	Few ⇒ Some ⇒ Many
Intensity of Scheduling	Class ⇒ Group ⇒ Individual; Occasional ⇒ Regular ⇒ Frequent; Short ⇒ Middling ⇒ Long
Systematic Support	Little ⇒ Some ⇒ Lots
Explicit Skill Focus	Implicit ⇒ Explicit ⇒ Meta
+ The Learner Factor	Passive attention and minimal engagement ⇒ Motivated attentive engagement ⇒ Motivated self-directed and sustained engagement (*being in the flow*)

Note: The amount and nature for each level depend on the skill, the learner, the context, and the interaction of the RISE and learner features.

Repeated Opportunities

Skilled performance typically requires repeated opportunities for learning and practice. The number of opportunities required varies by skill, context, and learner characteristics, but some amount of repetition is needed for learning. To become a skilled practitioner a lot of deliberate practice is needed. It has been estimated that, to become a master in music, sports, computers, and other skilled endeavors, as many as 10,000 hours (20 hours per week for 10 years) of intentional practice are required (Gladwell, 2008). SLPs are aiming for competence not mastery on the part of their students. Regardless, practice really matters.

Repeated opportunities should be present within a single activity. The close succession of learning opportunities with modeling, guidance, and explanation is important for students to internalize a new behavior or strategy. For example, for teaching expanded noun phrases, a whole activity that presents repeated opportunities is listening to the introduction of an adventure tale and identifying the expanded noun phrases as the explorers are described in many ways (e.g., "Now that we have heard this story once, let's listen to the beginning for the phrases that include a modifier and a noun. *The intrepid explorers* started out on *their great adventure. All the men* were *truly men of stout heart. These first men* to brave *the rigors of the South Pole* would come back to tell *a tale never equaled . . .*"). Repeated opportunities should also occur across activities. There can be a mix of purposeful and drill activities, but the sum should allow the students to observe the targeted structure or behavior in use, try the skill out with feedback, practice it, and use it in communicative contexts where it can be integrated with other skills and automated.

Repeated opportunities are easy to program and track in discrete skill instruction. The number of opportunities for responses are predetermined or counted as they occur. Responses are typically short and easy to score as correct, incorrect, or assisted. The amount and variety of assistance is usually fairly limited. Twenty picture cards on regular present tense versus past tense can be scored as percent correct independently or with assistance. A computer program can quickly present and score a student on 100 trials of backward digit repetition.

In whole communicative activities, many skills may be modeled and elicited, but there will be fewer occurrences of each skill than in drill-play activities. These activities may need to be somewhat engineered to ensure sufficient learning opportunities, resulting in them being "naturalistic" rather than fully natural. The number of learning opportunities in whole communicative activities is facilitated by loosely scripting an activity sequence. For example, for story structure, the number of opportunities to construct a complete episode can be estimated in the following sequence: brainstorm story plot ideas, draft story with three conjoined episodes, compose story, revise story structure, tell the story to an audience, and evaluate the storytelling.

The use of whole contexts spreads the learning opportunities over a longer time period with more distracters. For example, embedding ten phoneme segmentation comments in reading aloud a verse book will take 15 minutes, whereas ten drill items on phoneme segmentation may only take 5 minutes. The trade-off is that the meaningfulness and active engagement in the learning is expected to improve internalization, spontaneous use, and generalization. Although the number of opportunities may be fewer than in discrete skill instruction, the activities should "make sense" for the child, possibly resulting in fewer opportunities required or longer spans of attention (Warren et al., 2007). In addition, whole activities allow for multiple objectives to be addressed in an integrated, functional manner, bridging between treatment and daily life uses.

Intensity

Intensity is considered here to be the frequency of encounters between a student and the therapeutic experience. Repeated opportunities are part of intensity, but intensity also refers more globally to session length and frequency. Interventions that produce significant, lasting improvements in reading or oral language provide one or more hours of daily individual instruction for two or more months (e.g., Gillam et al., 2008; Torgesen et al., 2001).

There is an almost complete lack of systematic research on the effects of different treatment intensities (Warren et al., 2007). When treatment research is conducted, often little is reported on the details of learning opportunities or treatment schedules. Treatment time is typically reported only in terms of general figures (e.g., 30 to 60 minutes per week) and lacks fidelity information on whether the planned intensities actually occurred (cancellations and absences occur frequently in school practice). Operational definitions of intensity also differ. Intensity estimations have included the quantity of services delivered in a given period of time, the number of hours of intervention over a specific time period, the ratio of adults to children, and the number of specific teaching episodes per unit of time. This lack of information on optimal treatment intensities limits understanding of effective treatments. We cannot say how best to provide treatment or which treatments are better when treatment intensities are not equated. Even equating intensities is problematic: Discrete skill treatments benefit from a high frequency of practice opportunities, whereas naturalistic interventions benefit from the salience of the learning opportunities occurring in a meaningful context.

Warren et al. (2007) proposed that to systematically program intensity (scheduling and repeated opportunities) we use a medical *dosage* framework. This framework starts with specifying the active ingredients of treatment, which for language intervention is at the level of the teaching (or learning) episode. A teaching episode "contains one or more interventionist (or confederate) acts hypothesized to lead a child toward a given intervention goal" (Warren et al., 2007, p. 71). This broad definition allows considerable latitude to customize teaching episodes. A basic episode is an instructor initiation, a child response, and an evaluation (e.g., *What are the sounds in dog? /d-aw-g/. Yes, three sounds, /d-aw-g/*). The teaching episode may be longer if it involves prompts, repeated attempts, or simple skills built into more complex ones (Ukrainetz, 2009). Group intervention will involve listening to peers and choral responding.

Teaching episodes are grouped into the larger unit of a *dose*. A dose is usually a session, but could be a school day if treatment is embedded explicitly and systematically throughout the curriculum. A dense presence of teaching episodes within a session constitutes a high-strength dose while few teaching episodes within the same length session constitute a low-strength dose (like morphine versus aspirin). Doses must be specified in terms of the form, frequency, and duration of delivery. The cumulative or total intervention intensity is the number of doses (i.e., sessions) multiplied by the dose strength (i.e., teaching episodes). Box 2.6 provides an example of how to calculate dosage intensity for teaching relative clause subordination in a small group setting with a mix of intervention activities over the school year.

The distribution of dose delivery may also matter. Two common schedules are massed practice, in which the teaching episodes are concentrated in a short time, and distributed practice, in which the same number of opportunities is spaced over a longer period of time. Massed versus distributed learning has been examined for a range of verbal learning skills for typical language learners, such as Janiszewski, Noel, and Sawyer's (2003) meta-analysis of 93 studies. Comparisons in very controlled settings over a short time span (e.g., one dense session versus five light sessions in a week) indicate distributed practice is generally superior to massed practice.

Scheduling is likely the intervention feature that is least under the individual SLP's control. The SLP can try to densely program teaching episodes within a session, but session length and frequency are dependent on other factors. School settings typically provide 30 to 60 minutes of intervention per week on multiple skills in groups of children with diverse needs (Brandel & Loeb, 2011). Estimates of treatment intensity need to consider what is being provided in the regular classroom and any supplementary instruction, although those may be less effective for the unit of time if the instruction does not meet the needs of the target student. Special events such as field trips, programs, and achievement testing as well as student absences cut significantly into scheduled time, as Ukrainetz, Ross, and Harm (2009) discovered in attempting to investigate the effects of treatment scheduling in a school context.

Intensity appears to matter a lot. If so, SLPs must work toward caseload sizes and school cultures that allow more intense service delivery (Ukrainetz, 2006b). Possibilities that do not demand more resources include redefining eligibility standards, reducing the range of SLP responsibilities, increasing collaboration with resource and classroom teachers, and providing alternate schedules, such as periodic cycles of short-term intensive intervention.

Systematic Support

Daily life interactions facilitate children's learning about the world and their place in it. Teaching involves intentionally facilitating learning. Intervention involves facilitating beyond that which occurs in classroom instruction. Extraordinary facilitation is the systematic support feature of quality intervention. Extraordinary facilitation involves

Box 2.6. ***Applying a Dosage Intensity Framework to Teaching Subordinate Clauses***

Term	Explanation	Example
Teaching Episode	Act intended to move child toward an intervention goal; typically an instructor elicitation, a child response, and an evaluation	For relative clause subordination, each time a student identifies, composes, and uses in a description and receives feedback
Dose	A specified number of teaching episodes; typically a session with several skill goals	Dose = One 25-minute session for 2 students involving 1 drill and 1 whole relative clause activity
Dose Form	Nature of the activities in which the learning episodes are presented; includes type, order, and structure of activities	Activity 1 = Sentence combining drill; Activity 2 = Identify relative clauses in passage; Activity 3 = Compose and insert sentences in a description; Activity 4 = Compose a description with relative clause sentences
Dose Strength	Number of teaching episodes in the session	Activity 1 = Seven items; Activity 2, 3, or 4 = Three items each; Dose = Ten shared learning episodes
Dose Frequency	How often the sessions occur; usually per week	2 sessions per week
Treatment Duration	Total time during which sessions are provided	180-day school year, 72 possible sessions − (cancellations + absences) = 50 sessions
Total Intensity	Total number of doses multiplied by dose strength	50 × 10 = 500 total shared teaching episodes

Note: Based on Warren, Fey, and Yoder (2007).

close attention to managing task complexity so the learner can be successful in the immediate task, more able and independent in subsequent applications of the task, and, most importantly, more able and independent in related daily life tasks. This facilitation is directed not simply at helping with the task, but at facilitating the learning. For example, Wood, Bruner, and Ross (1976), in observing adults helping young children learn to build puzzles, reported the adults strategically supported learning by recruiting the children's attention to task requirements, reducing the task to a manageable level, maintaining direction in problem solving, encouraging attempts at harder moves, controlling frustration, and demonstrating solutions in ways the learner can follow.

Systematic supports that aid learning can be grouped into static, structural adjustments and dynamic, interactive facilitations. Structural adjustments involve modifying the environment to reduce complexity and highlight target skills. Environmental modifications are usually done in advance of the treatment session. Interactive supports involve intentional, strategic moves on the part of the SLP during the intervention activity. Although they sometimes overlap, it can be helpful to group interactive scaffolds by their main aim: (a) to regulate behavior (e.g., waiting expectantly for a child to respond; signaling the child to think before responding) or (b) to provide information that helps the child create a better response (e.g., expanding a child's utterance into an adult form). The varieties of structural and interactive learning supports and ways of incorporating them into intervention will be discussed further in Chapter 3.

Explicit Skill Focus

The final feature is the explicit skill focus of therapeutic instruction. An explicit skill focus involves the intentional actions of the SLP to highlight and facilitate the learning of a particular skill, strategy, behavior, or process. Explicitness is simple to achieve in single skill activities: A drill on using elaborated noun phrases cannot be confused with any other skill instruction. In whole communicative activities, the SLP must strategically highlight a small number of skills among the myriad present. Composing a sea life poster and discussing what is depicted is simply an enriching language interaction. For intervention, the skill focus should be apparent throughout the session. The SLP and student's talk should make explicit the treatment target: *We will be learning about how to use describing phrases so listeners have pictures of fish in their minds . . . What did we learn about today? How to build describing phrases so listeners have pictures in their minds.* There should be repeated opportunities to talk about the variously textured, colored, and shaped fish. There should be clinician modeling, prompting, and expanding of noun phrases and a distinct lack of attention to other language and literacy skills.

Plus the Learner Factor

Whether through discrete or contextualized procedures, RISE assists in planning clinician-devised interventions or aids in evaluating intervention procedures. However, RISE is incomplete. A fifth complex element could be called *involvement* or possibly *the learner factor.* If children are fully engaged in what they are learning, they can sometimes make surprising leaps of understanding with few repeated opportunities for explicit skills with systematic support. And the inverse is also true: Students may learn very little if what is being taught does not matter to them despite the best efforts of the clinician.

Involvement turns out to be a complex construct, comprising attention, motivation, and engagement. While children can be required to attend (*mouth closed and eyes over here!*), enticed to participate (*we will make this fun*), and rewarded for performing (*a prize for the most correct answers!*), learning proceeds best if it derives from self-directed interest. Children can learn astoundingly easily if they are captivated by what they are doing. They can be captivated—and learning—even while they are squirming and chattering in a noisy classroom. Students who are engaged in mastering what matters to them learn without and almost despite adults: witness the prowess of young skateboarders and gamers, and the almost single-trial learning from overheard private adult conversations or discoveries of loopholes in disciplinary systems.

Estimations of how much intervention is needed or the degree of benefit that children accrue from specific therapeutic moves are fundamentally affected by children's attention and interest in what they are being taught (Hoffman, 2009; Warren et al., 2007). In Gillam et al.'s (2008) carefully designed efficacy study, an academic enrichment group was provided an equal amount of time on interesting activities with repeated opportunities and feedback as three treatment groups. This control group made the same overall gains in language and reading skills as the three treatment groups. While it remains unclear what exactly was operating, these students were absorbed in these language activities and learning a lot from them.

Attention is the most elemental and organismic aspect of involvement yet is a surprisingly complicated phenomenon. The construct of attention encompasses arousal and alertness; orienting and responding; searching and spotlighting; and selecting, sustaining, and dividing attention (Ashcraft & Radvansky, 2010). Attentional processes can be extremely rapid and reflexive, or slow and deliberate. Some attentional acts take a lot of perceptual and cognitive resources and some take very little. Initial, reflexive, automatic attention occurs more to familiar events (i.e., we notice important stuff immediately), while subsequent intentional orienting and focusing occur more to novel events (i.e., we try to make sense of novel stuff) (Hogarth, Dickenson, & Duka, 2010). Hogarth et al. distinguish these two mechanisms of attention as "looking for action" and "looking for learning." In addition, Hogarth noted an emotional component: If we like what we notice, we will keep attending to it or "looking for liking."

Motivations are reasons and attitudes toward the skill, the activity in which it is being learned, and the effort involved in learning. Students may have intrinsic positive or affirming motivations, such as interest and enjoyment of the activity, confidence in likelihood of success, valuing the activity, or desire to be prosocial (e.g., wanting to please the teacher) (Guthrie, Klauda, & Ho, 2013). Alternately, motivations may be negative or undermining, such as feeling incompetent, devaluing the activity, and having antisocial goals (e. g., desire to denigrate others' performance). Engagement is involvement with learning, which is sometimes called being *in the flow*. Guthrie et al. separate motivation to do the learning activity, measured through attitudinal reports, from being engaged in it, measured by behaviors during the activity and judgments of effort afterward. Measures of behavioral engagement include self-reported effort, amount of time spent, observed concentration, and persistence of effort when the activity becomes difficult.

While artificial, extrinsic awards can create temporary interest in an activity, children need more permanent intrinsic motivations to maintain interest and effort. For example, Lepper, Greene, and Nisbett (1973) gave one group of preschoolers a prize for drawing pictures, one group drew and received a prize but the prize was not contingent on drawing, and a third group drew with no prize. Two weeks later, classroom observations showed that the children who had received the reward had decreased their levels of spontaneous drawing, while the other two groups maintained their interest in drawing. Deci, Koestner, and Ryan (1999) conducted a meta-analysis of 128 studies examining the effects of external reward systems. Results showed that temporary tangible rewards, from marshmallows to money, for preschoolers to college students, had a significant negative effect on returning to and persisting at tasks, such as word games and construction puzzles, that participants had previously identified as interesting.

Involvement comes from the child, but can be mediated by the activities, procedures, and interactions of the SLP. To promote attention, motivation, and engagement with learning, students should know what they are learning and why it should matter to them. Students can be given choices of activities, topics, or materials in treatment. They can share in reviewing and planning their own learning, not just in terms of whether they are well-behaved or get a lot done but how they are progressing on treatment goals, how they can learn to apply the skills in classroom work, and what they need to do to "graduate" from speech. Especially as students get older, learned helplessness and being tuned out of school can undermine learning. Partnerships with students in their learning, making goals functional and attainable, and treating skills through curricular activities all promote buy-in for the older student (see Chapter 16).

Guthrie et al. (2013) statistically modeled the relationships among reading instruction, motivation, engagement, and achievement for seventh graders in experiential science-based reading instruction that taught comprehension strategies and provided choices of texts matched to reader level. The statistical path analysis revealed a cascading and reciprocal positive effect between student interest and educational achievement. Not only were more motivated and confident students more successful, but even low-achieving students had greater confidence in their capacity to succeed and increased interest in science reading, even when they found it hard. This perseverance improved their performance, which further promoted positive attitudes toward academic learning.

The challenge for SLPs is to make prescribed academic learning in treatment, if not captivating, at least interesting, to their students. The SLP needs to arouse students' automatic attention and sustain their conscious, directed attention. Students need to be guided on how to regulate their attentional resources: selecting, sustaining, and dividing attention as needed. And students need to like what they are attending to so they keep on attending and become involved in and push ahead their own learning. Students enter the therapeutic situation with their own set of motivations. Some of these are affirming, and some are undermining. Language intervention is not rocket science, but sometimes it can feel that way!

Conclusion

This chapter laid the foundations for the conduct of language intervention that helps students be successful in school. There are many ways of conducting language intervention. It can be layered by the level at which the intervention intercepts the language impairment within the individual, from underlying neuropsychological abilities, such as attention, memory, and auditory processing to higher level language and learning behaviors and beyond the individual to the social and physical environment. Alternately, interventions can be grouped by how the teaching-learning process is structured. Hierarchical skill and contextualized skill approaches explicitly and systematically teach specific language goals in ways that simplify language learning and support application in daily life activities. Enrichment/assistance and skill stimulation approaches lack a systematic progression from simple to complex, using either (but not both) meaningful contexts or explicit, simple practice opportunities.

Clinicians must make choices of interventions and then craft the interventions to suit the particulars of their own situations and students. Evidence-based practice was explained and guidance was provided on evaluating research evidence. Research evidence on the areas and structure of language intervention indicated treatment has beneficial effects across areas of language and that both discrete skill and contextualized skill approaches are supported by the evidence. The research evidence indicates that a small set of features are important across approaches: *repeated opportunities* for learning with *intense scheduling* and *systematic support* of *explicit skills* (RISE+). A fifth important element for effective intervention is *the learner factor*—the degree to which the learner is actively involved in his or her own learning process. The skillful SLP weaves RISE+ into interventions that capitalize on students' attention and engagement with learning to make significant, lasting changes in students' daily lives. From these intervention fundamentals, SLPs can select and construct effective interventions that fit with their students' needs and their own resources and instructional styles.

References

Abbeduto, L., & Boudreau, D. (2004). Theoretical influences on research on language development and intervention in individuals with mental retardation. *Mental Retardation and Developmental Disabilities Research Reviews, 10*, 184–192.

American Speech-Language-Hearing Association. (2007). *Scope of practice in speech–language pathology*. Rockville, MD: Author.

American Speech-Language-Hearing Association. (2010). *Roles and responsibilities of speech–language pathologists in schools* [Professional issues statement]. Baltimore, MD: Author.

Ashcraft, M. H., & Radvansky, G. A. (2010). *Cognition* (5th ed.). Boston, MA: Prentice-Hall.

Berninger, V. W., Vermeulen, K., Abbott, R. D., McCutchen, D., Cotton, S., Cude, J., Dorn, S., & Sharon, T. (2003). Comparison of three approaches to supplementary reading instruction for low-achieving second-grade readers. *Language, Speech, and Hearing Services in Schools, 34*, 101–116.

Bernthal, J. E., Bankson, N. W., & Flipsen, P. (2009). *Articulation and phonological disorders* (6th ed.). Boston, MA: Allyn & Bacon.

Brackenbury, T., Burroughs, E., & Hewitt, L. E. (2008). A qualitative examination of current guidelines for evidence-based practice in child language intervention. *Language, Speech, and Hearing Services in the Schools, 39*, 78–88.

Brandel, J., & Loeb, D. F. (2011). Program intensity and service delivery models in the schools: SLP survey results. *Language, Speech, and Hearing Services in Schools, 42*, 461–490.

Byiers, B. J., Reichle, J., & Symons, F. J. (2012). Single-subject experimental design for evidence-based practice. *American Journal of Speech–Language Pathology, 21*, 397–414.

Cirrin, F. M., & Gillam, R. B. (2008). Language intervention practices for school-age children with spoken language disorders: A systematic review. *Language, Speech, and Hearing Services in Schools, 39*, S110–S137.

Dahlin, K. I. E. (2011). Effects of working memory training on reading in children with special needs. *Reading and Writing, 24*, 479–491.

Deci, E., Koestner, R., & Ryan, R. (1999). A meta-analytic review of experiments examining the effects of extrinsic rewards on intrinsic motivation. *Psychological Bulletin, 125*, 627–668.

Dollaghan, C. (2007). *The handbook for evidenced-based practice in communication disorders.* Baltimore, MD: Brookes.

Ehren, B. J. (2000). Maintaining a therapeutic focus and sharing responsibility for student success: Keys to in-classroom speech–language services. *Language, Speech, and Hearing Services in Schools, 31*, 219–229.

Eisenberg, S. L. (2006). Grammar: How can I say that better? In T. A. Ukrainetz (Ed.), *Contextualized language intervention: Scaffolding preK–12 literacy achievement*, (pp. 145–194). Austin, TX: PRO-ED.

Fey, M. (1986). *Language intervention with young children*. Boston, MA: College-Hill.

Gillam, R., McFadden, T. U., & van Kleeck, A. (1995). Improving narrative abilities: Whole language and language skills approaches. In M. E. Fey, J. Windsor, & S. F. Warren (Eds.), *Language intervention: Preschool through the elementary years* (pp. 145–181). Baltimore, MD: Brookes.

Gillam, R. B., & Gillam, S. L. (2012). N-Back and CogMed working memory training: Proceed with caution. *Perspectives on Language Learning and Education, 19*, 108–116.

Gillam, R. B., Loeb, D. F., Hoffman, L. M., Bohman, T., Champlin, C., Thibodeau, L., . . . & Friel-Patti, S. (2008). The efficacy of Fast ForWord language intervention in school-age children with language impairment: A randomized controlled trial. *Journal of Speech, Language, and Hearing Research, 51*, 97–119.

Gillam, S. L., & Gillam, R. B. (2006). Making evidence-based decisions about child language intervention in schools. *Language, Speech, and Hearing Services in Schools, 37*, 304–315

Gillam, S. L., & Gillam, R. B. (2014). Improving clinical services: Be aware of fuzzy connections between principles and strategies. *Language, Speech, and Hearing Services in Schools, 45*, 137–144.

Gillam, S. L., Gillam, R. B., & Reece, K. (2012). Language outcomes of contextualized and decontextualized language intervention: Results of an early efficacy study. *Language, Speech, and Hearing Services in Schools, 43*, 276–291.

Girolametto, L., & Weitzman, E. (2006). It takes two to talk – the Hanen program for parents. In R. J. McCauley & M. E. Fey (Eds.), *Treatment of language disorders in children* (pp. 77–104). Baltimore, MD: Brookes.

Gladwell, M. (2008). *Outliers: The story of success*. New York, NY: Little, Brown.

Goldstein, H. (2002). Communication intervention for children with autism: A review of treatment efficacy. *Journal of Autism and Developmental Disorders, 32*, 373–396.

Guthrie, J. T., Klauda, S. L., & Ho, A. N. (2013). Modeling the relationships among reading instruction, motivation, engagement, and achievement for adolescents. *Reading Research Quarterly, 48*, 9–26.

Hancock, T. B., & Kaiser, A. P. (2006). Enhanced milieu teaching. In R. J. McCauley & M. E. Fey (Eds.), *Treatment of language disorders in children* (pp. 203–236). Baltimore, MD: Brookes.

Hoffman, L. M. (2009). Narrative language intervention intensity and dosage: Telling the whole story. *Topics in Language Disorders, 29*, 329–343.

Hoffman, L. M., Ireland, M., Hall-Mills, S., & Flynn, P. (2013). Evidence-based speech–language pathology practices in schools: Findings from a national survey. *Language, Speech, and Hearing Services in Schools, 44*, 266–280.

Hogarth, L., Dickinson, A., & Duka, T. (2010). Selective attention to conditioned stimuli in human discrimination learning: Untangling the effects of outcome prediction, valence, arousal, and uncertainty. In C. J. Mitchell & M. E. Le Pelley (Eds.), *Attention and associative learning from brain to behaviour* (pp. 71–98). Oxford, UK: Oxford University.

Holmes, J., Gathercole, S. E., & Dunning, D. L. (2009). Adaptive training leads to sustained enhancement of poor working memory in children. *Developmental Science, 12* (4), F9–F15.

Janiszewski, C., Noel, H., & Sawyer, A. (2003). A meta-analysis of distribution effect in verbal learning: Implications for research on advertising repetition and consumer memory. *Journal of Consumer Research, 30*, 138–149.

Johnston, J. R. (1983). What is language intervention? The role of theory. In J. Miller, D. Yoder, & R. Schiefelbusch (Eds.), *Contemporary issues in language intervention* (pp. 52–57). Rockville, MD: American Speech-Language-Hearing Association.

Johnston, J. R. (2005). Re: Law, Garrett, and Nye (2004a). "The efficacy of treatment for children with developmental speech and language delay/disorder: A meta-analysis" [Letter to editor] *Journal of Speech, Language, and Hearing Research, 48*, 1114–1120.

Lahey, M. (1988). *Language disorders and language development*. New York, NY: Macmillan.

Law, J., Garrett, Z, & Nye, C. (2004). The efficacy of treatment for children with developmental speech and language delay/disorder: A meta-analysis. *Journal of Speech, Language, and Hearing Research, 47*, 924–943.

Leontiev, A. N. (1981). The problem of activity in psychology. In J. V. Wertsch (Ed.), *The concept of activity in Soviet psychology* (pp. 37–71). New York, NY: Sharpe.

Lepper, M. R., Greene, D., & Nisbett, R. E. (1973). Undermining children's intrinsic interest with extrinsic reward. *Journal of Personality and Social Psychology, 28*, 129–137.

Lindamood, P., & Lindamood, P. (2011). *The Lindamood phoneme sequencing program for reading, spelling, and speech* (4th ed.). Austin, TX: PRO-ED.

Loeb, D. F., Gillam, R. B., Hoffman, L., Brandel, J., & Marquis, J. (2009). The effects of Fast ForWord Language on the phonemic awareness and reading skills of school-age children with language impairments and poor reading skills. *American Journal of Speech–Language Pathology, 18*, 376–387.

McFadden, T. U., & Gillam, R. (1996). An examination of the quality of narratives produced by children with language disorders. *Language, Speech, and Hearing Services in the Schools, 27*, 48-57.

Meline, T., & Schmitt, J. F., (1997). Case studies for evaluating statistical significance in group designs. *American Journal of Speech–Language Pathology, 6*, 33–41.

Merritt, D. D., & Culatta, B. (1998). *Language intervention in the classroom.* San Diego, CA: Singular.

Naremore, R. (1980). Language disorders in children. In T. Hixon, L. Shriberg, & J. Saxman (Eds.), *Introduction to communication disorders* (pp. 137–176). Englewood Cliffs, NJ: Prentice-Hall.

National Reading Panel. (2000). *Teaching children to read: An evidence-based assessment of the scientific research literature on reading and its implications for reading instruction: Reports of the subgroups* (NIH Publication No. 00-4754). Washington, DC: U.S. Department of Health and Human Services, National Institute of Child Health and Human Development. Available at http://www.nationalreadingpanel.org/

Nippold, M. (2012). Different service delivery models for different communication disorders. *Language, Speech, and Hearing Services in the Schools, 43*, 117–120.

Paul, R. (2007). *Language disorders from infancy through adolescence* (3rd ed.). St. Louis, MO: Mosby.

Petersen, D. (2011). A systematic review of narrative-based language intervention with children who have language impairment. *Communication Disorders Quarterly, 32*, 207–220.

Petersen, D., Gillam, S. L., Spencer, T., & Gillam, R. B. (2010). Effects of literate narrative intervention on children with neurologically based language impairments: An early stage study. *Journal of Speech, Language, and Hearing Research, 53*, 961–981.

Peterson, P. (2004). Naturalistic language teaching procedures for children at risk for language delays. *The Behavior Analyst Today, 5*, 404–424.

RAND Reading Study Group. (2002). *Reading for understanding: Toward a research and development program in reading comprehension.* Santa Monica, CA: RAND. Retrieved from http://www.rand.org/pubs/monograph_reports/MR1465/index.html

Robey, R. R., & Schultz, M. C. (1998). A model for conducting clinical-outcome research: An adaptation of the standard protocol for use in aphasiology. *Aphasiology, 12*, 787–810.

Roth, F. P., & Worthington, C. K. (2011). *Treatment resource manual for speech–language pathology*. Clifton Park, NY: Delmar.

Siegel, G. M. (1987). The limits of science in communication disorders. *Journal of Speech and Hearing Disorders, 52*, 306–312.

Smart, J. F., & Smart, D. W. (2006). Models of disability: Implications for the counseling profession. *Journal of Counseling and Development, 84*, Winter, 29–40.

Sohlberg, M. M., & Mateer, C. A. (1989). *Introduction to cognitive rehabilitation: Theory and practice*. New York, NY: Guilford Press.

Strong, G. K., Torgerson, C. J., Torgerson, D., & Hulme, C. (2011). A systematic meta-analytic review of evidence for the effectiveness of the "Fast ForWord" language intervention program. *Journal of Child Psychology and Psychiatry, 52*, 224–235.

Torgesen, J. K., Alexander, A. W., Wagner, R. K., Rashotte, C. A., Voeller, K. K. S., & Conway, T. (2001). Intensive remedial instruction for children with severe reading disabilities: Immediate and long-term outcomes from two instructional approaches. *Journal of Learning Disabilities, 34*, 33–58.

Torgesen, J. K., Wagner, R., & Rashotte, C., Herron, J., & Lindamood, P. (2010). Computer-assisted instruction to prevent early reading difficulties in students at risk for dyslexia: Outcomes from two instructional approaches. *Annals of Dyslexia, 60*, 40–56.

U.S. Department of Education, Office of Special Education Programs. (2007). *IDEA Regulations: Alignment with No Child Left Behind*. Retrieved from http://idea.ed.gov/explore/view/p/%2Croot%2Cdynamic%2CTopicalBrief%2C3%2C

Ukrainetz, T. A. (1998). Beyond Vygotsky: What Soviet activity theory offers naturalistic language intervention. *Journal of Speech–Language Pathology and Audiology, 22*, 122–133.

Ukrainetz, T. A. (2005). What to work on how: An examination of the practice of school-age language intervention. *Contemporary Issues in Communication Sciences and Disorders, 32*, 108–119.

Ukrainetz, T. A. (2006a). Assessment and intervention within a contextualized skill framework. In T.A. Ukrainetz (Ed.), *Contextualized language intervention: scaffolding preK-12 literacy achievement* (pp. 59–94). Austin, TX: PRO-ED.

Ukrainetz, T. A. (2006b). EBP, RTI, and the implications for SLPs: Commentary on L.M. Justice. *Language, Speech, and Hearing Services in Schools, 37*, 298–303.

Ukrainetz, T. A. (2009). Phonemic awareness: How much is enough within a changing picture of reading instruction? *Topics in Language Disorders, 29*, 344–359.

Ukrainetz, T. A., Ross, C. L., & Harm, H. M. (2009). An investigation of treatment scheduling for phonemic awareness with kindergartners at risk for reading difficulties. *Language, Speech, and Hearing Services in Schools, 40*, 86–100.

Warren, S. F., Fey, M. E., & Yoder, P. J. (2007). Differential treatment intensity research: A missing link to creating optimally effective communication interventions. *Mental Retardation and Developmental Disabilities Research Reviews, 13*, 70–77.

Weismer, S. E., & Robertson, S. (2006). Focused stimulation approach to language intervention. In R. J. McCauley & M. E. Fey (Eds.), *Treatment of language disorders in children* (pp. 175–202). Baltimore, MD: Brookes.

Wood, D., Bruner, J. S., & Ross, G. (1976). The role of tutoring in problem solving. *Journal of Child Psychology and Psychiatry, 17*, 89–100.

Chapter 3

Contextualized Skill Intervention Framework: The Whole and the Parts

Teresa A. Ukrainetz

This chapter presents a framework for language intervention based on the practices, prescriptions, and research evidence set out in the previous chapters. The aim is to increase the trajectory and rate of language learning and enable children to use their improved knowledge and skills in daily life situations. This framework responds to Johnston's (1985) challenge to simplify the language learning task without changing its basic character:

> Language learning must remain integrated with intellect, motivated by communication, actively inductive, and self-directed. . . . But language learning must also be facilitated in specific, well-calculated ways. . . . The challenge for educators is to manage this tension between the common and the extraordinary. What sort of intervention programme can maintain the essence of language learning and yet accelerate it? (Johnston, 1985, p. 128)

The framework is set up as a metaphor of getting students "into the game" of academic and functional communication. Like athletes, students must learn both specific skills and how to bring those skills into the complex communication "games" of life. To accomplish this, a whole-part contextualized skill framework with interactive and structural learning supports is explained that addresses the acquisition and application of skills in activities that matter for school success. Intervention goals and activities are linked to a set of nationwide academic standards. These standards are set up as contextualized endeavors in which significant communicative activities drive the expectations for the knowledge and skills that comprise them.

The Game Is the Aim

Start With the Game

Basketball is just a game. But basketball can illustrate how other, more significant games of life are constituted, learned, and taught. Like with basketball, we want our students to be skillful, motivated players in the communication games of life (Wolter, Ukrainetz, Ross & Andrus, 2011). In basketball and in communication, skills matter, not in how they are performed in practice drills, but rather in how they contribute to the real game. The game is the aim—of basketball and language intervention.

SLPs are skilled at working on communication skills. However, we sometimes confuse the means with the end: Skills are important only insofar as they apply to communicative effectiveness. Like a basketball coach, the SLP should start with the end: telling a story, reporting on a science experiment, or learning about a historical event. Skills should be taught with a clear view of how they fit into a larger academic communicative activity *and* a clear plan for not only improving individual skills but making those skills do their jobs in functional communication activities.

The key is keeping the game as the aim: instead of teaching a skill like "explaining relations between words" because a student scored poorly on that in a norm-referenced test and it is a part of academic language, the SLP should "reverse engineer" communicative activities to find the skills that matter. The SLP analyzes activities for their components and how these components fit together, and then systematically works on the components in constant relation to the larger activities. Work happens in parts and wholes, until progress data shows that the skills, and, more importantly, the whole activities, are performed noticeably better. Noticeably better means apparent to those involved: the SLP, the students, their teachers, and their families. This contextualized skill approach to intervention is hard, and the changes that can be made are few, but these are real changes that matter in the lives of our students.

Going Inside the Game

What I am calling a game here is not a board or video game. Communication games are complicated events with purposes beyond teaching skills or display of knowledge (Harris-Schmidt & McNamee, 1986; Pretti-Frontczak & Bricker, 2004). These significant life activities consist of five components that orchestrate into functional wholes (see Box 3.1).

The first component of a significant life activity is *purpose*. The purpose of the activity affects who participates and how they participate. For basketball, the primary purpose of a game is to win. For a recreational game, other purposes might be exercise and friendship. The purpose of schooling, in sum, is to educate students into contributing, satisfied citizens of a society with grades and test scores as indicators of progress. To achieve that overall purpose, students engage in diverse communicative academic activities, such as history essays, civics presentations, literature discussions, poetry composition, and science projects. These have the dual purposes of acquiring and transmit-

Box 3.1. ***Components of an Activity, Whether Basketball or Communication***

Component	Definition
Activity	Purposeful event or task
Motive	Basic underlying force driving engagement
Purpose	Aim or reason for conducting the activity
Condition	Facilitating and constraining features of the immediate and wider contexts
Skill	Unconscious, automatic execution of actions or behaviors
Strategy	Conscious, deliberate execution of actions or behaviors

Note: Based on Leontiev (1981) and Ukrainetz (1998).

ting ideas and experiences and getting better at that acquisition and transmission. More structured, simple activities, such as reading and spelling exercises, are intended for learning and practice of the skills involved in the larger communicative activities.

In significant life activities, the purpose should align with the *motivation*. Motivations are the basic human needs that drive participation in life. Basketball players are motivated by common human desires, such as personal accomplishment, public acclaim, being part of a team, and fear of failure. In school, students are motivated by those same forces. Even when players or students have positive motivations, these must be managed to optimize performance and achieve the purpose of the game. If playing well individually is more important than the team winning, the game will suffer. Players and students are more likely to work hard if their efforts consistently lead to better scores. If the score matters more than the performance, then the temptation will be to go for the score with whatever shortcuts that requires.

What happens in and around the game are the *conditions* of play. One condition in basketball is that no one plays alone. Each player skillfully and strategically works in concert or in opposition with other players, the coach, referee, and the crowds. Temperature, humidity, and even the altitude (the University of Wyoming is at 7,200 feet!) affect play. Larger personal issues, such as breaking up with a girlfriend or a parent's unemployment, can affect game performance. Likewise, and perhaps more so, school activities have many layers and interacting forces of home, classroom, building, district, and community that affect a student's performance.

The purpose, motivation, and conditions all affect the *skills* involved in significant life activities. Skills are mental and physical operations applied "unconsciously for many reasons including expertise, repeated practice, compliance with directions, luck, and naïve use" (Paris, Wasik, & Turner, 1991, p. 611). Good basketball players engage in the fundamentals of ball handling, moving around the court, and interacting with other players without conscious thought.

While being skillful, players are strategic about the game. *Strategies* are the conscious use of physical actions or mental operations to achieve particular purposes in a particular situation: knowing how and when to apply what (Paris et al., 1991). The same thought or action can be performed skillfully or strategically, depending on the conditions. We want our students to be both skillful and strategic: Students should operate unconsciously with little effort for most academic tasks but be able to turn their attention on and act strategically when the going gets tough.

Skills (and their conscious deployment as strategies) matter in how they function, not how they look. In basketball, two very different-appearing moves may have similar functions: dribbling and passing both move the ball down the court. Players move fluidly between these two skills to achieve the same purpose. Two similar movements may function very differently: tipping the ball to start the game versus tipping the ball into the net. In school, the different-appearing actions of subvocal rehearsal and writing can achieve the same purpose of memorization. Typing on a smartphone can function very differently: setting a task reminder or texting gossip. Whether for sport or school, it is the activity and all its components operating together that matter, not isolated skills.

Assessment for Intervention

Language assessment is intended for diagnosis, determining eligibility for services, intervention planning, and progress monitoring. While diagnosis and eligibility often rely primarily on norm-referenced test scores obtained in a few hours, evaluation for intervention has much more freedom in method, sources, and time.

Assessing Motivation and Purpose of School Activities

When a clinician asks me about treatment ideas, I always start by asking about the student: what he or she can do well, where he or she struggles, and what motivates him or her. I then ask about a few activities that matter in the classroom for this student. I try to classify the activities by discourse genre: narrative, expository, or conversation. We then conduct an "activity analysis" to understand the student's strengths and weaknesses in carrying out that discourse activity. The focus is mainly on the student's skills and strategies. However, all five activity components matter. Progress will suffer if there are problematic motivations, discordant purposes between student and teacher, or conditions that amplify skill weaknesses.

First is the purpose of the activity. The SLP should examine whether the student recognizes the purpose of what he or she is required to do. If the student considers the activity as make-work, then he is likely to expend less effort or take shortcuts. If the purpose of a school-wide book reading competition is to increase student vocabulary and text comprehension, but the student perceives the goal simply as winning, then his strategy of skimming many short, easy books will compromise the school goal. Happily, sometimes the student's purpose differs but does not conflict with those of his teacher, such as if students see a book club primarily as a social center, but it achieves the purpose of students seeking out challenging books to talk about.

Student motivation needs to be considered. Before higher motivations, such as desire for self-improvement or academic learning can be invoked, fundamental needs of hunger, safety, belonging, and self-respect must be fulfilled (Maslow, 1954). Box 3.2 shows the fundamental human needs that will affect higher order learning accomplishments. While it is not the responsibility of the SLP to feed or clothe a student, it is important to know if these needs are being met and, if not, to let others know. The atmosphere of the classroom affects a student's sense of belonging and interest in learning (Westby, Watson, & Murphy, 1994). The resource room, with its multiyear, individualized relationship with students, may be a sheltered learning environment where students feel particularly liked and safe (Ukrainetz & Fresquez, 2003).

After checking on whether basic needs are being met, then assessment of motivation involves considering what is impeding desires to learn. Most students with language disorders are motivated by the same forces as typical learners: competence, self-esteem, and a sense of autonomy. Giving our students the same opportunities for these motivators is often enough. However, older students with histories of academic failure may have perceptions of helplessness or fear of failure (Apel & Swank, 1999; Bashir & Singer, 2006). These students need to see themselves as capable of success and see errors as part of the path to learning. A major motivator for most students is positive social interac-

Box 3.2. ***Hierarchy of Human Motivations That Affect Success in School***

Internal locus of control (Self-direction and responsibility for others)

⇧

Esteem (Feelings of success and self-respect)

⇧

Improved academics (Knowledge and skills competencies, test performance)

⇧

Belongingness (Sense of trust, validation, acceptance, care)

⇧

Safety (School structure and discipline)

⇧

Physiology (Hunger, thirst, attention)

Note: From "The Vision of Full Inclusion: Don't Exclude Kids by Including Them," by C. E. Westby, S. Watson, and M. Murphy, 1994, *Communication Disorders Quarterly, 16*, p. 10. Copyright 1994 by Hammill Institute on Disabilities. Reprinted with permission.

tion. Simply having two students work together on project can change the tone from "work" to "fun." While this is recognized for young students, it is arguably even more important for adolescents for whom academics might be considered rest periods in the main game of negotiating social relations.

Assessing Conditions of Activities

Assessment for intervention must consider the conditions of activities in the classroom, the school, and beyond. Many aspects of a student's educational life are beyond the SLP's control, but the SLP should be aware of how these forces affect performance, both negatively and positively. In addition to formal measures, just being part of the life of the school provides a valuable interpretive framework (e.g., knowing that the third-grade teacher is a rapid, disorganized speaker with inconsistent classroom routines and expectations or that the new second-grade teacher has a high number of students with special needs).

A multiple lens approach to observation ensures a comprehensive view of a student's functioning (Silliman & Wilkinson, 1991). These lenses examine (a) the overall context of the lesson, (b) the structure or organization of the lesson, (c) the interactional patterns used to get the lessons done, and (d) communication breakdowns. Silliman and Wilkinson use a wide angle lens to view the backgrounds of the teachers and students and the physical features of the classroom: who is teaching, who is assisting, adequacy of space, level of noise, and the number of needy students in a class. The regular lens involves a specific activity. Observations and interviews reveal the components and sequence of a lesson or activity.

The close-up lens examines the interactions among participants in an activity at a specific point in time. This includes how students are directed to participate, the degree of explicitness or complexity of the questions, the nature of the students' responses, and how teachers react to those responses. Even reading and writing can be analyzed with this participant-level lens: Is the chapter disjointed and hard to understand or is the reader focusing so much on individual sentence comprehension that the main points are missed? The view narrows in the microscopic lens, which involves the moment-by-moment breakdowns a student exhibits during communicative interactions. What are the sentences that are leading the reader astray and what is the problem with those sentences for this reader? Structured testing and language sampling help answer how the linguistic conditions of the reading activity affect the student.

Spoken and written language conditions can intersect within an activity. A student with good comprehension but word-finding and utterance formulation difficulties will not show her or his reading competence if the teacher asks questions too quickly. A student may underperform if he or she understands the material immediately, but then must wait while the teacher accommodates other students who require multiple repetitions of instructions and comprehension checks.

In sum, the wide- and regular-angle lenses provide the background information needed to interpret the interactional patterns and the breakdowns observed in the close-up and microscopic lens. The SLP integrates the information from each lens to construct a full view of a student's communicative strengths and weaknesses within the school context.

Assessing the Skills and Strategies of Activities

Once the purpose, motivation, and conditions involved in activities have been evaluated, the SLP arrives at the heart of the matter: the student's skills and strategic control of those skills. Both standardized and descriptive measures are important windows into communication skills.

Norm-referenced, standardized tests are intended to reveal "pure" skills, relatively independent of other skills and context. A picture-pointing task with carefully constructed foils is intended to examine receptive syntax with minimal influence of vocabulary, memory, and pragmatics. The score on the test is intended to indicate how the student will perform on that language skill across varied contexts and activities of the classroom. While there is some truth to this, the sum of test scores certainly does not equal a student's performance in school.

Descriptive measures are intended to sample a student's performance in the context of a communicative activity. Performance is compared to criteria such as developmental expectations (e.g., grammatical complexity for that age across activities), peer performance (e.g., five typically achieving peers on that activity), or individual capacity (i.e., what the student's "best" can be). Classroom observation, teacher and student interview, language sampling, and work analysis are all ways of understanding a student's strengths and weaknesses in communicative activities. Unlike with norm-referenced tests, these measures reveal how the student deploys that skill orchestrated with other skills, the effort it takes him to do this, and what conditions make it easier or harder for him.

It is important to know what effort it takes for a student to be successful. A student's actions may result from automatic, unconscious skills or may require conscious, deliberate strategies. Skillful execution of an activity is done easily, with little mental energy. In contrast, strategies take work: strategic operators can only focus on a few strategies at a time and tire quickly. Learning new skills, modifying old skills, or applying skills in challenging conditions are all strategic and energy consuming. For example, when reading for pleasure, fluent readers can enjoy a book for hours, without conscious attention to the act of reading. However, when dealing with challenging text, even fluent readers must deliberately attend to their reading. In a strategic mode of reading, they may even need to attend to basic skills, such as word decoding: reflect on what it takes you to read this word aloud: *iodopropynyl butylcarbamate* (an ingredient in my moisturizing lotion). After the reader has decoded the difficult word, decoding can drop away from awareness, letting the reader return to deliberate text comprehension (while perhaps wondering when she or he can return to skilled, unconscious pleasure reading).

Dynamic assessment is useful for exploring a student's capacity and readiness for learning (Vygotsky, 1978; Lidz & Pena, 1996). By teaching a student a task and noting his learning behaviors, his responsiveness to instruction, and the effort it takes him to learn, rich information emerges for intervention. For example, in an early study, Wood, Bruner, and Ross (1976) compared the performance of 3- and 5-year-old children, both of whom "failed" a puzzle construction task. In teaching the two ages, the younger children required step-by-step assistance and many repetitions, whereas the older children made leaps in understanding with only a few prompts. Dynamic assessment has been conducted on many aspects of language, including labeling, categorization, narration, and phonemic awareness, but what matters is not so much the skill taught, but what is revealed about the student as a learner. Dynamic assessment is particularly helpful for determining whether a child has an inherent learning difficulty or is a good learner but has missed out on learning experiences (Ukrainetz, Harpell, Walsh & Coyle, 2000; Pena, Quinn, & Iglesias, 1992; Pena et al., 2006).

From these assessments, an SLP may find that a student is not only lacking in skills and strategies, but that these deficits are leading to lack of attention or motivation. For our students, most of the school day involves the hard work of strategic engagement, often with little success. No one has the energy for that. Students may avoid tasks, attend for only a few minutes, or just stop trying. Being aware of the effort required helps the SLP plan for a manageable challenge.

A Problem-Solving Stance to Assessment

School SLPs have standard assessment measures and procedures, but assessment should not be a standard routine. Each student should be approached with a problem-solving stance in which the SLP seeks to understand why and when the student has difficulties (Kratcoski, 1998). Kratcoski calls this hypothesis testing. For example, a teacher reports that a student has difficulty with X. The SLP theorizes and hypothesizes about possible explanations for X and generates testable hypotheses. The SLP systematically collects and analyzes data related to the hypotheses. The SLP determines which hypothesis is best supported by the data. Then the SLP makes his or her recommendation about services and the direction of intervention. Often, there is little time between a referral and setting intervention goals, but further problem solving during treatment can modify or refine earlier assessment findings.

For example, a teacher reports that a first grader has difficulty asking *wh-* questions in storybook discussions. The SLP investigates. She has two hypotheses: that the student has weak interrogative grammar or that he is a passive communicator who avoids asking questions. Norm-referenced testing shows age-appropriate comprehension, but odd word order in a sentence formulation task (e.g., SLP: *Make a sentence using "where."* Child: *Where the boy is going to the store?*). In a language sample, the student answers questions and talks willingly, but when the SLP tries to elicit interrogative syntax (e.g., *I am going to the store soon. Ask me why in a full sentence.*), the student does not respond. Observation reveals the student asks other students and even the teacher questions, such as, "Where does our group sit?" and "Why are you acting like the boss of our group?" In the storybook discussion activity, the student asks the teacher, "Why did Jack trade his nice cow for yucky beans?" However, when the teacher tells the students to each ask a question about the story starting with *Who*, *Where*, or *When*, the student again mixes up his word order. The SLP decided that neither of the two original hypotheses was correct. This student's difficulty lies in asking questions when there was no real need to know. Through this problem-solving stance, the SLP determined that the student needed to learn how to formulate question statements on request, leading to clear direction for intervention.

Setting Intervention Goals

Selecting Goals

Assessment leads into intervention by way of goals. While IEPs require only broad goals, the SLP needs to know his or her own specific treatment objectives, how to measure progress on them, and how to translate the progress data into documentation for the IEP goal.

Significant life activities involve many language and cognitive skills and strategic decisions, as well as motivations and learning conditions. Students with language disorders usually demonstrate far more weaknesses than can be effectively addressed within intervention. Only one to two significant life activities can be addressed effectively in a school year. Within an activity, only three to four component skills can be effectively addressed.

In addition to language skills, language-related skills can be addressed. These include pragmatics, such as raising a hand to respond and displaying knowledge when called upon. Metalinguistic skills (e.g., how to segment words into phonemes or how to formulate definitions) are possible treatment goals as are metacognitive skills (e.g., self-monitoring comprehension or inhibiting impulsive responding). Underlying cognitive processes, such as working memory and word retrieval, are potential targets. Attitudes to learning, such as persevering in challenging situations, are critical to academic success. These language-related skills and learning behaviors can often be addressed incidentally during treatment of language goals.

Even within a single domain or level of language, there will be many skills that could be addressed. In addition to presence in the curriculum, considerations include: skills that can be remediated fairly quickly (e.g., episodic structure so basic stories can be composed); skills that contribute to the student becoming a better, more independent learner (e.g., comprehension-monitoring strategies); skills that can come together to make a noticeable change in a significant activity (e.g., temporal words and event sequencing for science procedure reports); and skills that bother the teacher or the student the most (e.g., understanding what the teacher wants). Box 3.3 gives examples of arrays of intervention targets from across language areas that come together to build competence in whole communicative activities. Improving performance across multiple aspects of a significant academic activity is more likely to result in noticeable improvement than if each is involved in a different activity. Having one significant whole activity as the source of data also simplifies progress reporting. Selecting goals that come together in

Box 3.3. ***Language Targets That Come Together in Whole Communicative Activities***

Activity	Skill	Example
Conduct a science experiment	1. Measurement lexicon 2. Expanded noun phrase 3. Procedure sequence 4. Follow instructions	• *Rams, millimeters, weigh scale* • *A glass beaker with a measurement scale* • *First, set out the materials, next...* • *Pay attention to exactly what is said*
Understand a history book	1. Suffix analysis 2. Conditional tense 3. Main ideas 4. Note taking	• *Deregulation, investigation, expectation* • *Ought to do it, would avoid* • *Explicit and implicit idea statements* • *Words and phrases in outline format*
Write an imaginative narrative	1. Pronoun reference 2. Causal and adversative conjunctions 3. Elaborated episode 4. Self-regulation	• *Justin wanted to win the race, so he tried to go his fastest. He ran, but there was a cliff, so he jumped, causing his ankle to sprain, so he found a stick for a cane. Justin was the slowest, but he was the toughest!* • *Don't get upset, identify what you did wrong, figure out how to fix it, and try it again.*
Give a science presentation	1. Definitions 2. Relative clauses 3. Description 4. Verbal fluency	• *My report is on penguins, which are flightless fish-eating birds that live in Antarctica.* • *A description organized by habitat, diet, appearance, and behavior* • *Adhere to list of good speaker features*

a single whole purposeful activity reflects Nelson and Van Meter's (2006) analogy of words being the bricks of language, shaped through morphological variation, mortared together with syntax, and framed by discourse structure into a functional building.

Intervention goals and progress data should come from criterion-referenced, not norm-referenced, measures. Norm-referenced tests are designed to be stable, global estimates of performance. They can provide general guidance, such as whether language is below age expectation or that grammar is more of a concern than vocabulary, but test scores should not direct intervention. In addition to the gap between test scores and communicative performance, such scores do not reveal the particular structures with which the student struggles.

Item analysis is often used, but it has caveats. In most norm-referenced tests, especially those that provide a comprehensive picture for eligibility purposes, there are too few items of one type for a reliable estimate of performance. In addition, despite an overall low score, correct responses on those particular items might not be expected for that age. Extension testing can help with this. More items like the failed items can be devised to provide a reliable estimate of performance. To determine if that age of student should pass those particular items, the SLP can administer the extension test to average peers (not high achievers) and make their average score the criterion. Such tests can then serve for goal setting and progress monitoring although they still do not reveal a student's competence in actual communicative activities.

Setting Context and Criteria for Goals

Intervention goals are intended to be clear, measurable, attainable, and functional. The typical components of an intervention goal are a behavior, a context, and a criterion. Level of support, time frame, baseline level, or data source may also be required. Expressing all those attributes in a single, understandable, measurable statement can be an achievement in itself. Box 3.4 presents a goal template and examples of specific skill goals. The two goal statements contrast a single-skill statement and a multiple-skill statement. The criterion can be derived from a minimum or an average expectation across the multiple skills. A vague criterion such as "80% correct" allows the SLP to fit the data collection to the student's situation. The progress statement example shows how variation can occur in the actual along-the-way performance.

Standard statements of support and performance are "independent" and "90% correct." However, context, support, and accuracy interact. Progress will vary depending on whether data are reported from a simple drill activity or from a communicative activity. With their complexity and variability, classroom data will likely show lower performance. Activities similar to those of the curriculum, but designed and conducted by the SLP, often work well. Generally, the activity should be simple enough to allow low support and high accuracy in year-end measures. Skills may be required by rule or regulation that are beyond what can be achieved in a year. If so, the activity can be simplified, the support increased, or the criterion lowered.

Some skills require other criteria. For example, for word decoding accuracy of a 100-word reading passage, 90% is actually a frustration level. The instructional level is 95%, and the independent level is 99% (Johnson, Kress, & Pikulski, 1987). For skills that occur

Box 3.4. ***Treatment Goals and a Progress Report***

1. By S date, T student will improve U behavior in V context from W baseline to X level with Y support as measured by Z.
2. By 05/20/2013, Tyson will summarize main ideas and details from expository paragraphs read aloud, improving from 40% accuracy with high support to 90% accuracy with low support, as measured by SLP data.
3. By 05/20/2013, when participating in a story retell, Tyson will independently provide clear pronoun reference, relative clauses, and elaborated episodes with accurate self-review in generated oral narratives, improving from under 50% to 80% accuracy, based on SLP report.

Progress Statement: At the first reporting period, Tyson is 80% correct on independently combining simple sentences into relative clause sentences in worksheet drills, is using 3 of 6 episodic elements with maximal support in story retells, and is 50% correct on independent pronoun reference in generating his own imaginative narratives.

infrequently, a percentage does not work. This is a common issue for discourse structure (e.g., only one elaborated episode may occur in a story retell). Instead, a number of occurrences can be stated (e.g., three elaborated episodes in three consecutive story generations). Alternately, opportunities can be increased by counting elements of the whole, thus allowing a percentage. For example, counting presence of the story grammar elements of place, time, character, problem, motivation, plan, attempt, resolution, and reaction allows a 90% accuracy criterion.

Finally, performance reports should not be based on one data point but rather on enough data to present a reliable picture of current achievement, such as performance across three samples. For quarterly progress reports, performance may be averaged across the entire learning period. It should be noted if the overtime average does not reflect the student's current status.

Linking Goals and Progress Monitoring to Achievement Standards

Common Core State Academic Standards

Treatment goals should reflect school demands. They can be referenced to the classroom curriculum, but a more convincing link is to academic standards. *Common Core State Standards for English Language Arts & Literacy in History/Social Studies, Science, and Technical Subjects* (often abbreviated to CCSS, but more pronounceable as "Common Core") were issued in 2010 by the National Governors Association Center for Best Practices and the Council of Chief State School Officers (NGA-CSSO). As this book went to print, Common Core had been adopted by all but six states as of 2014 (see http://www.corestandards.org/standards-in-your-state/).

The Common Core standards for language arts specify sets of overall anchor standards within four categories: reading, writing, speaking and listening, and language (Box 3.5). Within each anchor standard are grade-specific knowledge and skill standards. The grade standards are organized around understanding, producing, and evaluating literary and informational texts to achieve the communicative purposes of persuasion, explanation, and conveying experience. The emphasis of the standards is on higher levels of critical comprehension and expression, rather than on basic reading skills and links to personal experience (Calkins, Ehrenworth, & Lehman, 2012). As Calkins and colleagues note, "Even young children are asked to analyze multiple accounts of an event, noting similarities and differences in the points of view presented, assessing the warrant behind people's ideas" (p. 9). Students are expected to become self-directed learners who ask questions, request clarification, and seek out resources. A theme is "staying on topic" (NGA-CSSO, 2010, p. 33), which means that teachers are encouraged to delve deeply into a topic within and across grades, developing rich interconnections of knowledge and skills rather than more superficial teaching of a wide array of isolated topics. The Common Core standards were developed through reverse engineering: setting the significant life activity competencies needed for international competitiveness and for college and workforce training programs, and then working backward to establish the knowledge and skills required for each grade (Calkins et al., 2012).

A single set of achievement standards greatly improves coordination of instructional aims and performance expectations across grades, settings, and locations. However, as this book went to press, concerns were emerging about the rigor, uniformity, and prescriptiveness of the standards. The gap between current performance and Common Core expectations are particularly large in the secondary grades (differences between the U.S. and other countries are also largest there; Adams, 2011). However, these stan-

Box 3.5. ***Categories of Common Core State Standards for Language Arts***

Reading Standards: Foundational Skills	**Reading Standards for Literature and Informational Text**
Print Concepts Phonological Awareness Phonics and Word Recognition Fluency	Key Ideas and Details Craft and Structure Integration of Knowledge and Ideas Range of Reading and Level of Text Complexity
Writing Standards Text Types and Purposes Production and Distribution of Writing Research to Build and Present Knowledge Range of Writing	**Speaking and Listening Standards** Comprehension and Collaboration Presentation of Knowledge and Ideas **Language Standards** Conventions of Standard English Knowledge of Language Vocabulary Acquisition and Use

dards are attainable if changes start in the early grades and are built upon in subsequent grades (Calkins et al., 2012). Regardless of what happens with Common Core, some kind of state academic standards will exist. SLPs should reference whatever the state is using for setting academically relevant treatment goals.

Goals for language intervention can be drawn from any of the Common Core categories; some reading and writing goals could even be formulated as spoken language goals. For example, the third-grade reading standard to "determine the main idea of a text, recount key details, and explain how they support the main idea" (NGA-CSSO, 2010, p. 14) could be taught and measured through spoken language interactions. Grade standards that come together in a single communicative activity can be selected. Box 3.6 shows third-grade standards that contribute to competence in narrative generation.

The standards within a grade or category vary on their specificity. For example, for third-grade language, one standard is the broad statement of "produce simple, compound, and complex sentences" while another is a very specific statement of "ensure subject-verb and pronoun-antecedent agreement." The former is far too broad to be a meaningful goal, instead a particular structure, like relative clauses, would need to be specified. The latter could be used as is.

Box 3.6. ***An Example of Tying Language Goals to Common Core Academic Standards***

Skills for IEP Goals	Common Core Identifier	Common Core Third-Grade Standard
Pronoun reference in narrative generation	Speak & Listen 4	Report on a topic or text, tell a story, or recount an experience with appropriate facts and relevant descriptive details, speaking clearly at an understandable pace
Clausal conjunctions in narrative generation	Language 1.h	Use coordinating and subordinating conjunctions
	Writing 1.c	Use linking words and phrases (e.g., *because, therefore, since, for example*) to connect opinion and reasons
	Writing 3.c	Use temporal words and phrases to signal event order
Elaborated episodes in narrative generation	Writing 3.a	Write narratives to develop real or imagined experiences or events using effective technique, descriptive details, and clear event sequences

Note: Based on National Governors Association Center for Best Practices and Council of Chief State School Officers (2010).

Some of the language goals are developmentally late, such as the prior example of simple sentences in third grade or, for fourth grade, the preschool expectation of "form and use prepositional phrases" (NGA-CSSO, 2010, p. 28). This late appearance can be helpful for our students for whom even spoken language may be considerably below the standard. It is also helpful for instruction when the language structure is difficult to explain. For example, relative pronouns (*who, whose, which, that*) are listed as a fourth-grade standard. First graders may use relative pronouns in conversation (e.g., *the students who yelled got detentions*), but teaching even a fourth grader to intentionally use them in formal English requires considerable metalinguistic awareness (from the student and the clinician), as exemplified by this lesson introduction:

> This new type of sentence has a relative clause in it: "The cup that is green is my favorite." This part that starts with "that" is the relative clause and it gives extra information about this noun, the cup. Let's practice making up relative clause sentences and then we can try them out in your paper. (Eisenberg, 2006, p. 164)

Quantitative performance criteria for a skill or activity, such as 90% correct, is not specified on Common Core because that requires a particular assessment task. However, there is a sense of increasing expectations across grades. Tasks increase in difficulty, such as the increasing number of rules for participating in discussions from kindergarten to third grade. Tasks also change, such as moving writing from picture-and-print to written composition across this period. Some standards move from supported to independent performance. For example, third graders should "with guidance and support from adults, produce writing in which the development and organization are appropriate to task and purpose" (NGA-CSSO, 2010, p. 21).

Academically Relevant Progress

SLPs are trained to take progress data. They are accustomed to counting opportunities, rating accuracy and level of support, and adjusting treatment as needed. However, often there is only a vague connection between the data reported and performance in the classroom. There is increasing pressure for all educators, including SLPs, to show empirically that what they are doing matters for students' educational success. For example, SLPs may be asked to report data from state achievement tests or standardized unit reading tests to show their treatment effectiveness. This will be less of a problem if skills have been chosen and taught with a clear idea of how they operate in communicative activities rather than because they were sampled in a norm-referenced test.

Intervention should have academically relevant effects and the SLP needs to be mindful of connecting the speech room and the classroom. However, progress data must be chosen carefully. Performance on such broad achievement measures is affected by much more than weekly language sessions with the SLP. The SLP needs to select data that is likely to be sensitive to what is taught in treatment. In addition, pressure to show immediate change in curricular tests should not lead to content tutoring or test training; the SLP's job is to improve the underlying language skills and learning behaviors that will help the student become a better and more independent learner.

Box 3.7. ***Grade 3 Performance Level Descriptors for Writing***

ADVANCED PERFORMANCE

Third-grade writers performing at the advanced level write with a clearly intended purpose and audience, successfully integrating voice and format. Their writing shows logical and sophisticated organization. Ideas are presented clearly and supported by specific and precise details. Sentence structure is varied and complex; language is effective throughout. Advanced writers demonstrate control of conventions. They exhibit appropriate organizational and delivery skills when speaking.

PROFICIENT PERFORMANCE

Third-grade writers performing at the proficient level write with an intended purpose and audience with evidence of voice and format. Their writing shows logical organization. Ideas are supported with sufficient, relevant details. Sentence structure is varied and correct. Proficient writers demonstrate reasonable control of conventions.

BASIC PERFORMANCE

Third-grade writers performing at the basic level need support to write with evidence of intended purpose and audience. Their writing shows some organization with minimal awareness of voice. Ideas are evident but supporting details may be minimal or irrelevant. Sentences have some variety with few errors in structure. Word choice is generally correct and there is some control of conventions.

BELOW BASIC PERFORMANCE

Third-grade writers performing at the below basic level require extensive support or provide little or no evidence in meeting the standard.

Note: Based on Wyoming State Board of Education (2008).

Many states have holistic rubrics for writing proficiency levels (see Box 3.7). It will be difficult to show the impact of language intervention on such broad standards. An alternative is to report proficiency in a more restricted manner, such as "shows logical organization" in a descriptive essay, without attending to details, sentence structure, and all the other aspects measured. Even for a single skill, our students will mostly start out at the Below Basic level. Box 3.8 shows a clinician-designed progress monitoring scale that holistically rates a combination of degree of independence and accuracy level (Wolter et al., 2011). This rubric uses the more attainable descriptors of *competent, functional, emerging,* and *full support.* It can be customized to a particular skill or activity by detailing what counts as correct and partially correct responses. This rating scale can be used to examine performance on a classroom activity or standardized test but with the more restricted focus that is more sensitive to small improvements.

In addition to standardized achievement tests, some states require students to pass standardized curriculum-specific unit tests. The tests take a variety of forms, such as a multiple-choice memorization test on "history of the U.S. in the 1920s and 1930s," an

Box 3.8. ***Level of Support Rubric for Intervention Goals***

Skill	*State the intervention goal or skill component of the goal being rated*
Activity	*State the activity in which rating is conducted*
	Level of Support
4 = Competent (≈ Basic)	Requires little to no prompting; independently self-regulates and strategizes to fully correct basic responses
3 = Functional	Requires some clinician reminders and prompts; may be multiple attempts but student self-cues and repairs to almost correct responses
2 = Emerging (≈ Below Basic)	Requires clinician multiple choice, partial answers, expansions, cues, prompts but student shows some partially correct responses
1= Full Support	Requires maximal clinical models and scaffolds; student mainly imitating with successes dependent on the clinician's actions

Note: Based on Wolter, Ukrainetz, Ross, and Andrus (2011).

analysis of the outcome of a heredity experiment, or a group experiment followed by an individual lab report on genetic variation. This uniformity certainly has its drawbacks, but it is easier to plan for than teacher-specific evaluations. To use these to show progress, right and wrong answers are not enough. The SLP needs to engage the student in "think-alouds" in which the student reflects on how he or she arrived at the answers. What caused the student to err: lack of content knowledge, struggle with sentence meaning, or failing to systematically evaluate each response choice? Fixing the deficits might involve practice taking tests in addition to going back to the unit materials and activities, or even topically different activities, to work on comprehension skills and effective strategies for making the most of the student's limited skills.

The Game Plan

Start With the Game

From language goals, we move to the conduct of intervention. Treatment is built around whole activities, so individual language skills can be learned and applied in their contexts of use. Children play card and board games for the pleasure of the play, upon which SLPs have long capitalized. But there are other activities that matter more in school and life. Reading a story, composing a dinosaur report, creating a magazine article, writing a play, and reporting on a field trip are all whole activities that make sense in and out of school. Execution of these activities is affected by the motivations of the student, the purpose of the activity, and the conditions existing in and around the activity. Moving skills into the classroom is always a challenge, but if the speech and classroom activities are similar in purpose and skills, then transfer is less of an issue.

For older students, activities should also be linked to life beyond the classroom. For example, in our clinic a graduate student worked with a 19-year-old deaf student. He used American Sign Language (ASL) to communicate. His writing often lacked English grammatical morphology and followed ASL word order. He hoped to enter the local automotive training program after leaving school. For this student, a beneficial activity was composing a minimanual on hotrod modification. The aim was to improve English morphosyntax and procedural discourse within a functional activity similar to what this student would encounter within his vocational interests.

The Common Core standards show the relevance of teaching through whole activities. The standards are organized into narrative and exposition with the communicative purposes of persuasion, explanation, and conveyance of experience. Audience and purpose are considered, such as requiring third graders to speak in complete sentences "when appropriate to task and situation in order to provide requested detail or clarification" (NGA-CSSO, 2010, p. 5). Even standards that address particular skills are intended to be taught through "a single rich task" (p. 5). Single rich tasks, despite surface differences, can link functionally between the classroom and speech room. For example, if a student knows that the imaginative narratives composed in the classroom and the personal narratives retold in speech time are both intended to convey experience, she is likely to think about what an audience needs to know in both settings. If the teacher knows the SLP is working on clausal conjunctions and elaborated episodes, and comments on presence of those in classroom work, the student is more likely to transfer her new skills to the classroom.

The Dimensions of Treatment Activities

Activities are devised, selected, and combined to fit different intervention approaches, language goals, student characteristics, and clinician preferences. The dimensions include where the activity takes place, who is involved, the unit of language, the degree of student choice, and the source of the materials. The activity can involve highly structured steps, a fairly predictable routine, or a variable composition of actions. In terms of "wholeness" an activity can exist only to teach the target skill, such as a picture-labeling drill, or the skill can be only a minor aspect of the activity, such as telling an entertaining story that includes a few elaborated noun phrases. The activity can be in between, such as retelling stories designed with many elaborated noun phrases.

These dimensions are presented on a continuum of control in Box 3.9. The more typical continuum is one of communicative naturalness (e.g., Fey, 1986). However, in school, educational success and not social communication is the aim, so the situation

Box 3.9. ***The Dimensions of Control for School-Age Intervention Activities***

Dimension	High	Mid	Low
Location	speech room	resource room	classroom
Social	individual	speech group	classmates
Unit	words and sentences	paragraphs and passages	stories, poems, reports
Choice	assigned	this or that	inquiry based
Materials	designed for treatment	classroom textbooks	children's literature
Procedure	scripted	predictable	variable
Wholeness	drill play	structured discourse	communicative
Source	speech programs	class lessons	district curriculum

is complicated. Although education prepares a student for life beyond school, the classroom is daily life. Depending on the style of the individual teacher or the reigning education philosophy, a student's daily life may be structured and drill based instead of experiential and inquiry based. For a student from a back-to-basics classroom, a storybook intervention activity may not be "natural." Thus, there is no simple continuum of naturalness for school-age intervention.

The SLP does not need to copy the classroom approach but does need to know and work within the nature of instruction in the school. The SLP may even be able to promote alternate ways of instruction. For example, Palincsar (1998) commented that, in her research on teaching writing to students with learning disabilities, transfer of skills to the classroom was weak because the regular education teachers used writing for low-level skills, such as matching and copying. Palincsar guided teachers to include a class newspaper, a class handbook, and letters to family and book authors, so the students had communicative reasons to write.

Intervention activities are usually a mix of positions on the continuum of control. For example, an SLP might teach phonemic awareness in the speech room (High) to a small group (Mid) using a children's rhyming storybook (Low), chosen by the child from three possible books (Mid). The SLP reads a few pages of verses but not the whole book (Mid). The students isolate, segment, and blend phonemes of whatever rhyming words appear in the story (Low), but there is a predictable teaching sequence for each rhyming pair (Mid). The dimensions of this systematic, explicit, but naturalistic treatment activity include all levels of control.

Teaching Skills Through Conscious Attention

SLPs teach students new skills, modify undesirable skills, or accelerate emerging skills. The degree of student awareness varies with age. Preschoolers may know only that they are learning to "talk better." Kindergartners can a have general sense of what they are working on in "Speech" and how they performed that day. As students move through the grades, they should be increasingly aware of their IEP goals, the reasons for therapeutic activities, and their learning progress. Awareness of one's own cognition and language (metacognition and metalinguistics) are critical parts of this process (e.g., *Let's think about how to do this. I am going to talk aloud to show what I think about when I do this. Then I want you to talk aloud as you do it. Then we will look at how you can do it better.*).

The process of change is not a smooth trajectory. Skills that used to be done automatically must be raised into consciousness for modification and improvement. A student must plan in advance, monitor execution, and review afterward. This is not easy, particularly if the activity is a complex, functional event. In the process of improving the skill, execution will temporarily become awkward. Only one skill should be raised to conscious attention at a time. To return to basketball, the player may focus on his dribbling within the game, but not his dribbling, his passing, and his shooting simultaneously. Once a skill has been acquired or improved, treatment turns to other targets, but the skill needs continued practice so it becomes a fluent, unconscious process. Achieving automaticity is important. Students cannot move on to new learning challenges if recent acquisitions use up their attentional resources.

Once some competence is achieved with a single skill within a communicative activity, several skills can be worked on in functional clusters. Activities involve arrays of skills that are flexibly employed to achieve a purpose within reigning conditions. This means that a student should have more than one option for carrying out an activity. If a student is learning to use a graphic organizer, he or she should know why the organizer is helpful and when he or she can employ it, along with alternative skills, such as mental rehearsal or writing key words.

Along with the skill targets, there will be other skills that are weak or deficient. The temptation is to address these too, directing the student's attention to all his errors. However, a learner has only limited attentional resources and a weak learner even more so. Choices have to be made. Very simple activities avoid nontarget weaknesses. In more functional activities, nontarget weaknesses should be ignored (e.g., *Use your best guess for spelling*) or assisted (e.g., *This word is difficult, so I will spell it for you*). An example of this is an eighth grader's one-paragraph biography of the historical figure in Box 3.10. The student's work contains many errors and weaknesses that call out for red ink. However, the SLP should resist pointing out all the errors and focus only on the treatment goals.

So long as the aim is to improve performance, the interplay between conscious attention and automatic execution will coexist. A skill is worked on, then it is dropped from attention and another is worked on, cycling among skills over time. Basketball players constantly move among ball drills, skill focus in practice games, and real game play. For the player who strives to be the best, conscious practice goes on and on. When the time

Box 3.10. ***Potential Instructional Targets in a Student's Short Biography***

(Robert E. Lee, 1863, Photgrapher: Julian Vannerson)

He was born in 1807. He graduated from west point in 1829. He became the superintendent for a academy in 1852 it was military academy. In 1857 the death of his father in law he ask for a series of leaves to settle the estate. The north ask he to still be there general he said no this was in 1861. Early in 1862 he was recalled to Richmond and made an advisor to the president. He gradually became "Uncle Robert" and "Marse Robert."

comes that a player judges his skills to be "good enough" and switches from a competitive to a recreational league, play becomes automatic: The player stops getting better (but maybe enjoys it more). Students should also have the opportunity to just enjoy academic activities, such as reading high-interest, low-difficulty materials for pleasure and self-directed learning rather than constantly being faced with tasks that require continual conscious attention and energy-devouring strategies.

Systematic Learning Supports

Structural Learning Support

Learning is supported by simplifying activities. Environmental, physical, and social arrangements are set up in advance of the session and are fairly static. These are *structural* supports or scaffolds (Ukrainetz, 2006a). A bare speech room with few distractions, visual support from picture cards, and the communicative temptation of an appealing storybook are all ways of engineering the environment to provide structural support.

Activities can be structurally simplified in two very different ways. One is to contrive an activity that consists of only practice opportunities for the target skill at a difficulty level that can be done almost independently. Drill-play activities are so simplified that they have no communicative function, such as describing 50 picture cards using particular grammatical structures. To maintain motivation, the drills often earn points or are embedded in games (e.g., describing the picture each time the player lands on a certain square). These *part* activities provide a high rate of practice with few distractions.

Alternately, the environmental modifications can be more subtle. A daily life activity may be simplified but still retain its communicative purpose and some of the orchestration of skills needed to accomplish that purpose. Such activities are called purposeful, functional, communicative, meaningful, or naturalistic. For example, a high number of a particular grammatical structure may be embedded in a short story. Such customized *whole* activities lessen the leap required to daily life application.

Oral and print modalities provide structural support for each other. On one hand, speaking avoids the slow and laborious act of writing that robs attention from language goals. The dynamic process of speaking allows the SLP to view and scaffold student attempts. On the other hand, many spoken language goals are aided by a sketch, a printed word, or a text passage. It is easier to see a language target, analyze errors, revise work, and review performance in print.

Computers and hand-held devices are flexible and appealing structural supports. These provide entertaining drill-play activities in which language goals can be inserted. Some have been created especially for language instruction, such as vocabulary or sentence-maker applications. Whole communicative activities can be built through word processing, presentation, and reference software. There are ready-made whole communicative activities, such as e-books. Device time can be used as an enrichment activity or as a reward for working hard in other activities. The constant evolution of software allows ever more options.

Interactive Learning Support

The other major class of learning support is *interactive* scaffolding or facilitation. Interactive scaffolding involves intentional, dynamic, responsive moves on the part of the SLP during the intervention activity. There are many moves an SLP can make that help a student learn. They can be grouped into *linguistic* or *regulatory* scaffolds (Box 3.11).

Linguistic scaffolds provide new information to assist the child in producing a better response. They are contingent on the child's previous utterance and improve its content

Box 3.11. ***Types of Interactive Learning Support***

Linguistic Scaffolds	Regulatory Scaffolds
• Model the desired structure • Emphasize the key part of the structure • Provide part of the answer with a Cloze procedure • Provide the answer • Expand on the child's response (add linguistic elements) • Extend the child's response (add to topic) • Recast the child's response (change the structure) • Vertical structure (combine two responses into one structure) • Focused contrast (pair the error and correct structure) • Redirect (model by having child ask a peer using the structure)	• Wait expectantly for a response • Ask an indirect question • Ask a direct question • Repeat the directive or request • Use a physical signal to cue a response • Require an imitation • Use student name to recruit attention • Maintain awareness of the goal • Highlight importance of content • Relate content to past knowledge • Comment on child performance • Inhibit impulsive responses • Aid selective and sustained attention • Help child manage challenges • Review cumulative performance • Comment on task similarities

or form (Box 3.12). Linguistic scaffolding is most often associated with syntactic goals in conversational play treatments, such as focused stimulation (e.g., Camarata & Nelson, 2006; Weismer & Robertson, 2006). However, any linguistic target can be expanded or recast into a better response. For example, for episodic structure if a child fails to provide the consequence of the attempt to resolve a complication, and the SLP does so, that is a linguistic facilitation. For phoneme segmentation, if a child segments *sleep* into onset and rime (e.g., */sl-ip/*), the SLP may execute a focused contrast (e.g., *not /sl-ip/ but /s-l-i-p/*). For a semantic categorization goal, the student might say, "The bananas go in the vegetable group," and the SLP can respond by emphasizing the correct category, "Here, I will put the bananas in the *fruit* group." The SLP may incorporate the linguistic information into a scaffold that also elicits a better answer (e.g., Student: *The boy runned down the hill.* SLP: *Should that be runned or ran?*).

Behavioral or *regulatory* scaffolds help the student do what he needs to do: listen to the SLP, give a response, take a turn, think before answering, or identify the skill he is learning. Waiting expectantly or prompting with a hand signal does not introduce new information, but rather works toward obtaining a response. Such scaffolds are seen in milieu teaching (e.g., Hancock & Kaiser, 2006). Scaffolds that help a student learn, such as recruiting attention by using a student's name or asking a student to reflect on his performance, are parts of the mediated learning involved in dynamic assessment (e.g., Lidz & Pena, 1996). Regulatory scaffolds are aimed, not only at obtaining desired behaviors, but also at helping the student become a better learner. The student needs to regulate his own behavior, attention, and thinking, but initially, the SLP provides the regula-

Box 3.12. *Examples of Linguistic Scaffolds*

1. Syntactic Expansion – Makes the child's utterance grammatical.

   Child: That bird gonna ask him come in.

   Adult: Yes, the bird is gonna ask him to come in.

2. Semantic Expansion – Adds new but relevant information to the child's utterance.

   Child: Then him fell all over that.

   Adult: Yea, the kangaroo fell into the bear's swimming pool.

3. Syntactic Recast – Retains the semantic information but alters the syntactic structure.

   Child: That board picture was from Jason.

   Adult: Yeah, Jason drew that picture on the board.

4. Syntactic Prompt – Induces the child to modify an ungrammatical utterance.

   Child: Hims going to run back home.

   Adult: Who's going to run back home?

   Child: He's going to run back home.

5. Elaboration Question – Induces the child to expand on what he or she has said.

   Child: He was scared of that dinosaur.

   Adult: Why was he scared?

   Child: He thought the dinosaur might chase him and bite him.

6. Vertical Structure – Combine two child utterances into a more complex utterance.

   Child: That moose holding up a hammer.

   Adult: What would happen if he dropped it now?

   Child: It would hit his toe.

   Adult: If the moose dropped the hammer, it would hit his toe.

Note: From *Contextualized Language Intervention: Scaffolding PreK–12 Literacy Achievement* (p. 69), by R. B. Gillam and T. A. Ukrainetz, 2007, Austin, TX: PRO-ED. Copyright 2007 by PRO-ED, Inc. Reprinted with permission.

tory controls and then gradually transfers them to the student. Children who can self-regulate will learn better and be more successful in educational and vocational pursuits.

The mediation lessons in dynamic assessment explicitly include regulatory scaffolding (Pena et al., 1992). For example, in teaching categorization, the session begins by giving the students the learning goal (e.g., *We're going to learn about how to put things together in a group*) and a general principle for learning (e.g., *What if you told the teacher to be in the parent group? Will the teacher understand? No, because she is in a different group*). The SLP elicits student perspectives and experiences to link new to known information (*In this school, what group are you in?*). The task is kept challenging but possible, with praise and encouragement to persevere. Throughout the activity, the focus is kept on the skills the student is learning, with repeated opportunities for practice and feedback. The SLP monitors the student's behaviors and responses in an atmosphere of caring and enjoyment. To close the activity, the SLP reviews the purpose of the activity and the student's performance on the targeted skills.

Peers as Learning Support

Peer models are both structural and interactive supports. The SLP designs the group in advance, so group composition is a structural support. However, they are also part of the social interactive process of a treatment session. Depending on the situation, the SLP may prefer to see a student individually for increased control or in a group for peer models and social interaction.

SLPs can employ peers as informal models or as formal parts of the teaching process. Peer models involve more capable others demonstrating responses at a level slightly above that of the student. They can also involve less skilled students demonstrating, with support, the desired skill. Peer models show the student how others like him enact the activity. For example, in McGregor (2000), African American preschoolers learned from each other in story narration activities. Children who were paired to perform story retells showed more similar content and form in their retells than children who told their stories individually. Children with more advanced narrative skills were also assigned to be "tutors" to their less able peers. Clinicians scaffolded the tutors' retellings to their tutees to ensure good models of targeted narrative skills. Tutees had an expanded repertoire and greater number of story elements in both trained and untrained stories compared to their classmates who did not receive the scaffolded tutoring.

For older students, a reading comprehension program called Reciprocal Teaching formally involves the learner as teacher (Palincsar & Brown, 1984). Students learn to ask themselves to summarize, seek details, clarify, and predict what they have read or heard through being "teacher" to other students. By asking peers the questions they need to learn to ask themselves as they read, Reciprocal Teaching provides "learning through teaching" and a real, communicative reason for "thinking aloud" that the SLP can scaffold. The combination of strategy instruction and student-as-teacher has been effective in improving reading comprehension (e.g., Lederer, 2000; Palincsar & Brown, 1984; see Chapter 15).

Student Ownership of Learning

The learning support provided in intervention allows a student to achieve a whole, complex activity. However, the aim of this support is not just to complete the task, but rather

Box 3.13. ***Progression of Skill Handover Across Repeated Opportunities***

Steps	Clinician	Student
Story 1	• Leads discussion of what and how • Pictographic sketching of key events • Prompts a lot • Reviews performance	• Looks to clinician for support throughout • Mainly imitative in contributions
Story 2	• Guides advance discussion • Guides student pictography • Prompts a lot • Reviews performance	• Conducts advance practice aloud • Sketches with prompting • Is responsive to prompts • Contributes to review
Story 3	• Is responsive to student's lead • Prompts pictography and story-telling a little • Assists student's review of performance	• Leads advance discussion • Sketches story • Tells story mainly independently • Reviews own performance largely accurately
Story 4	• Asks student what needs to be done for a successful story • Is an attentive listener • Requests performance review	• Prepares independently • Tells story with desired skill accuracy and independence • Reviews own performance accurately

Note: Based on Ukrainetz (2006a).

to give the student ownership of the skill. This is a critical distinction. The focus is on the student's active acquisition of the targeted skills with the long-term aim of better and more independent learning. For example, for the skill of summarization, the support should result not just in correct responses (e.g., *I will say half of the main idea sentence and you finish it.*), but rather in the student gaining the self-talk needed to help himself (e.g., *How do I find the main idea in this long paragraph? I will see if the first sentence tells a bigger idea than the next two sentences. Maybe I will have to put together the main idea from several sentences*). Box 3.13 illustrates this transfer of responsibility across repeated opportunities for story retellings.

Treatment involves the SLP knowing how much is needed when. Too much help leads to boredom and lack of learning, while too little leads to frustration and, again, lack of learning. When graduate student clinicians taught children to compose stories, Schneider and Watkins (1996) reported that "there is a tendency to retain responsibility and to keep the child's role at a low level, at which he or she attains consistent success" (p. 161). While consistent success is pleasant, it can mean the student is not being challenged toward higher levels of competence. Students need to struggle a bit, make some errors, learn from the errors, and try again.

Intervention is not just the SLP handing over skills, but also the student reaching out to grasp those skills. The teaching-learning process is a reciprocal endeavor in which a learner cues a responsive teacher about what makes sense, what does not, and what is needed to make it so. An active learner will succeed faster, with much less clinician effort, than one who is being dragged along. The SLP needs to examine what it takes for the student to have "buy-in" to what he is learning and why he is learning it, so he is willing to grasp control.

Grasping control should be an explicit part of intervention for older students. Secondary grade students should know why they are doing what they are doing and should have some ownership in the process and goals: a partnership rather than a prescription. One way to do this is to shift from developing language skills, which can feel like a Sisyphean endeavor, to teaching the student a small set of learning strategies (e.g., for reading comprehension, what context cues, background knowledge, and reference tools they can use to figure out unfamiliar vocabulary). These strategies should be measurable, attainable, and important to the student. The SLP hands over control to the student (e.g., *So that isn't working, what else can you do?*) so that students can strategically use the same tools that SLPs find so helpful. Older students need to see that, despite their persistent language-learning deficits, they can be more reasonably capable learners on their own.

The Game Plan for Organizing Intervention—Whole and Part

All the foregoing comes together in RISE: *Repeated opportunities* in an *Intense schedule* with *Systematic support* of *Explicit learning goals.* This should happen in activities that encourage engagement with learning, in a mix of whole and part activities. Whole activities provide contexts for motivating, meaningful use while part activities provide simple, focused practice opportunities.

As explained in Chapter 2, approaches to intervention can be grouped in four ways: (a) enrichment and assistance, (b) skill stimulation, (c) hierarchical discrete skill, and (d) contextualized skill. Each has a different way of using whole and part activities to teach language skills, as illustrated one final time with the basketball analogy (Box 3.14). In a beginner league, how will a novice be taught to play? Will the coach immediately let him loose on the court with a ball and other players and periodically call out weaknesses from the sidelines, like the language enrichment approach? Will the coach put him in a corner and have him learn to dribble a ball for months and then expect him to play in a game competently, like the skill stimulation approach? For basketball, the most likely choice is the contextualized skill approach. The player is given the pleasure of lively games with the structural support of a small court and low baskets. Some practice games are just for fun and some focus on specific skills. At the same time, the players are assigned practice drills to work on dribbling or shooting. The players move back and forth between games and drills, getting better at both, but knowing that what really matters is performance in the tournament games. For both game and drill, the coach is

Box 3.14. *A Basketball View of Four Approaches to Language Intervention*

Just Play the Game – Enrichment and Assistance Approach

Play the game over and over with coach comments about any aspect of performance, which are expected to eventually result in being a better player.

Just Drill Skills – Skill Stimulation Approach

A set of dribble, shoot, and pass drills that the player practices over and over, which are expected to eventually result in being a better player.

Progression from Skill to Game – Hierarchical Discrete Skill Approach

1. Dribble a ball
2. Dribble and shoot
3. Dribble, move, and shoot
4. Dribble, move, and pass
5. Dribble, move, and pass with an opposing player
6. Dribble, move, and pass with three on each side
7. Play the game—uh-oh, too late, the year is over, maybe next year

Cycling Between Skill and Game – Contextualized Skill Approach

1. Play a chaotic but fun basketball game with a low net, small teams, with the coach modeling, calling out moves, and helping game play
2. Work on a dribbling drill, a passing drill, a shooting drill
3. Play a less chaotic but still fun basketball game with less coaching
4. Work on skill drills a bit more
5. Work on dribbling in the game, passing in the next game, shooting in the next game, with the coach on the sidelines
6. Take a break and just play the game
7. Back to skill drills, but no worries, another game is coming up

there, strategically guiding the novice player, with just enough help to keep him in his zone of challenging but manageable learning.

The contextualized skill approach of mixing whole and part activities along the path to competence makes sense and has the strongest evidential base. However, for some situations, SLPs may prefer a hierarchy of discrete skill drills that move systematically from very simple exercises to complicated communicative events. The difference between the two approaches is not so much the particular treatment activities and therapeutic procedures within those activities, but how the wholes and parts are put together in an overarching treatment plan. Contextualized skill plans will move beween whole communicative activies that allow integrated use of multiple target skills and part focused skill activities that highlight a single skill for learning and practice. Discrete skill hierarchical plans will start with very simple focused skill activities and gradually make them more complicated, with whole communicative activities not occurring until the end of the treatment progression.

Whole communicative activities are usually intrinsically engaging for students and require little external reinforcement beyond social recognition. Focused skill part activities usually need points, stickers, and other extrinsic motivators to keep the student on task. It is better to use intrinsic motivation, but both contextualized and hierarchical approaches employ intrinsic and extrinsic motivators.

Approaches that involve decreasing support in whole activities versus increasing complexity of part activities differ in the nature of the responses to student errors. For example, I observed an SLP teaching phonemic awareness through a strict task hierarchy with nonsense syllables and manipulatives, and another SLP teaching episodic structure through literature units (Ukrainetz, 2005). In both sessions, the students had significant difficulties. During the phoneme segmenting lesson, the first SLP provided about six prompts. After the session, she commented that she had provided too much help and that she would use an easier task in the next session. In the story grammar lesson, the SLP had provided more than a dozen prompts. She commented that she had provided a lot of help, but the student would do better as he became more familiar with the lesson. These two skilled SLPs took very different approaches to intervention that were reflected in how they responded to student errors and supported student learning.

Contextualized Skill Intervention Using Narrative and Exposition

Programs and procedures for contextualized skill intervention, with varying combinations of wholes and parts, have been emerging. Using RISE, these language programs are organized around the whole discourse unit of a narrative or exposition. They typically consist of a recursive pattern of a whole discourse event that introduces integrated use of several target skills, followed by a series of focused skill part activities, culminating in a discourse event that again integrates the skills within the whole. This whole-part-part-whole pattern may be a brief "treatment unit" that lasts only 3 to 4 sessions but is repeated several times. Alternately, it may be a more extended unit of 8 to 10 weeks that involves many repetitions or variations on the part and whole activities. The larger units may culminate in a fairly complex project that takes multiple activities and sessions to accomplish. The longer treatment units may provide enough RISE to allow a student to achieve the treatment goals within a single presentation of the unit. A close look at how to develop a basic whole-part treatment unit with RISE is provided in Appendix A.

Customized Narrative Intervention

An example of a very systematic narrative intervention is that of *Story Champs* by Petersen and Spencer (Spencer & Slocum, 2010; Petersen et al., 2014). The procedure can

Box 3.15. ***Steps for Teaching Language Skills in a Narrative Intervention***

Steps	Clinician	Child
1. Story model with visual supports	Models story while placing story grammar icons by each of five sequenced pictures	Listens attentively
2. Story retell with full support	Provides verbal scaffolds of episode sequence, visual supports, and language targets	Retells story with pictures and icons
3. Story retell with partial support	Provides fewer prompts and scaffolds	Retells story only with icons
4. Independent story retell	Listens attentively	Retells story without visual or verbal supports
5. Child tells a thematically related personal narrative	Sketches pictography on sticky notes	Generates a personal narrative
6. Retell of generation with full support	Provides verbal scaffolds of plot, support use, and targets	Retells narrative with pictographic notes and icons
7. Retell of generation with partial support	Provides fewer scaffolds of plot, support use, and targets	Retells narrative with icons
8. Independent personal narrative retell	Listens attentively	Retells narrative without visual or verbal supports

Note: The eight steps are repeated every session with a different customized narrative. The child must produce the targeted story structure, grammatical structure, and vocabulary in each step. Based on Petersen et al. (2014).

be used for dynamic assessment, for tiered instruction for groups, or for individualized language treatment. Procedures and materials are available at http://www.languagedynamicsgroup.com.

In every *Story Champs* session a student is cycled through eight steps that teach retelling and generating of personal narratives (Box 3.15). Sets of model narratives about plausible child experiences have been created that are controlled for length, story structure, grammatical structure, and vocabulary. To aid in retelling and generation, three types of structural scaffolds aid the telling of main events and episodic elements: picture sequences, story grammar icons, and pictographic sketching. Four levels of hierarchical prompts are used to obtain correct productions: from imitation to Cloze sentences (e.g., *He fell and hurt his knee. Now he feels* ____.) to direct prompts (e.g., *Tell about the*

Box 3.16. ***Customized Story for Narrative Structure and Complex Syntax Treatment***

Once, *when it was bedtime* Joseph was playing a video game with his sister in her **bedroom**. *When Joseph's mom saw him,* she told him to go to sleep in his **bedroom** ***because*** it was late. *When he heard his mom,* he was sad ***because*** he wanted to play the game with his sister in her **bedroom** ***because*** they were having fun. Joseph thought about what to do. He needed an idea. Joseph decided to ask his mom if he could finish the game then go to his **bedroom**. Joseph thought, "***When*** I ask my mom, she might let me finish the game with my sister." This was Joseph's plan. So Joseph said, "Mom, *when I finish the game* with my sister can I go to my **bedroom** ***because*** we are playing together?" Joseph's mom said, "*When you finish the game* you can go to bed ***because*** you are playing together, but remember *when you finish the game* you have to go to bed ***because*** it is late." *When Joseph and his sister finished playing the game,* he went to bed ***because*** he listened to his mom. He was happy ***because*** he did what his mom asked.

Note: Targets: Plan, **Location**, *Temporal Subordinate Clauses,* ***Causality***. Based on Petersen et al. (2014).

problem) to indirect prompts (e.g., *What's next?*). Narrative language measures for retell, generation, and comprehension score children's responses for presence and quality of story grammar and linguistic complexity.

For language treatment (or dynamic assessment), the model stories are further individualized by omitting or adding elements for an individual student based on baseline performance. For example, Box 3.16 shows the customized model story used for a child with high-functioning autism in Petersen et al. (2014). The student's performance was sampled in baseline and then the narrative targets of plan and location. The syntactic target of temporal subordinate clause and a subordinating conjunction were embedded five to eight times in the story. The student had to retell and generate narratives based on this story. The child was scaffolded into using the language targets within his narrative. To keep the focus on these language targets, later targets of adverbs and adjectival subordination were omitted from this story, and then appeared in subsequent stories when they were being addressed.

Story Champs is a very structured treatment that teaches language use within a constrained context of customized story retells and personal narrative generations. This manualized program is easy to set up, can be delivered with high treatment fidelity, and allows reliable progress monitoring. There is also research evidence supporting it for language intervention (Petersen et al., 2010; Petersen et al., 2014; Spencer & Slocum, 2010).

Literature-Based Intervention Units

Another format is literature-based intervention. Intervention units organized thematically around children's literature and SLP-generated customized stories facilitate both SLP planning and student learning (Box 3.17). Units provide a common fund of knowledge that links among whole and part treatment activities. A single unit can be used for many students, with modifications for different skills and learning supports. Literature selections can come from students, the SLP, or the classroom. Common Core standards list literature and informational books that exemplify the range and complexity of reading expectations across grades. Examples of science books for teaching the human body from kindergarten to the fifth grade are presented in the Common Core language arts document, from *My Five Senses* (Aliki, 1989) in kindergarten through to *The Amazing Circulatory System* (Burstein, 2009) for third and fourth grade. This is called "staying on topic" (NGA-CSSO, 2010, p. 33), which means to engage deeply and repeatedly in a single subject so that elaborated networks of knowledge can support acquisition of new conceptual knowledge and skills. This can be done in a miniature version by building an intervention unit of whole and part activities that repeatedly tap the language and concepts introduced in a single informational book.

An example of a classroom unit program is *Text Talk* (Beck & McKeown, 2005). *Text Talk* is a compendium of vocabulary and comprehension lessons based on children's literature. For each unit, six vocabulary words and story structure are taught in five

Box 3.17. ***Benefits of Thematic Treatment Units***

Benefits	Explanation
Ease of Planning	The structure of a unit, particularly one with a culminating product, makes activity selection easier than planning a dozen separate short activities. With a unit structure, skills, content, activities, and difficulty levels can be easily modified.
Predictability	The unit provides structure and predictability for the student and clinician. Complex activities can have elements of the familiar, allowing student and clinician to perform the old easily and focus on the new.
Coherence	Learning is facilitated when an item to be learned fits into a larger, meaningful whole. Ten thematically or semantically linked words will be learned more easily, with greater depth of meaning, than ten assorted words.
Extended Learning	A larger purposeful activity can be erected over multiple short sessions, allowing motivating projects, such as composing a written narrative, reading a chapter book, or developing a science presentation.
Whole and Part	Purposeful, complex activities where multiple skills are integrated and simple activities with a single focus can both be employed; the simple activities can make sense in how they contribute skill practice toward the whole of a game of communication.

Note: Adapted from "Language Intervention Through Literature-Based Units" (p. 67), by R. B. Gillam and T. A. Ukrainetz, in *Contextualized Language Intervention: Scaffolding PreK–12 Literacy Achievement*, by T. A. Ukrainetz (Ed.), 2006, Austin, TX: PRO-ED. Copyright 2006 by PRO-ED, Inc. Adapted with permission.

lessons around a storybook. The storybooks are even included in the program. SLPs can incorporate other language goals into the units and make the instruction more therapeutic by teaching students strategies such as determining meaning from context and noticing familiar parts of words.

Gillam and Ukrainetz (2006) describe a language unit organized around the storybook *Mushroom in the Rain* (Ginsburg, 1974). It involves a sequence of related whole and part activities for teaching vocabulary, syntax, discourse, and pragmatics skills. The example in Box 3.18 targets more language goals than a single treatment unit typically addresses, but it shows the types of activities that can be used in each language area. Thematic unity across the whole and part activities provides additional "staying on topic" support for concept and vocabulary development promoted in the Common Core document (NGA-CSSO, 2010).

Literature-based intervention flexibly employs whole and part activities to match a variety of needs and situations. The literature used is part of the child's daily life. The intervention can be metalinguistic and strategic as SLP and students talk about why, when, and where to use their new skills. This approach takes more effort to set up than scripted programs, and the quality depends a lot more on the individual SLP, but generalization of skills to the classroom will be less of a concern. There is research evidence to support this approach for vocabulary (e.g., Goerss, Beck, & McKeown, 1999; McKeown, Beck, Omanson, & Pople, 1985) and for grammar and story structure (Gillam, McFadden, & van Kleeck, 1995; Gillam, Gillam, & Reese, 2012).

Expository Intervention Units

One major advantage with a thematic unit is that, in contrast to activities with disconnected topics, concepts and vocabulary are linked across intervention activities (Adams, 2011). Knowledge is progressively built through the unit: dinosaur vocabulary and concepts are introduced in an introductory science book (or story) then are revisited repeatedly, building semantic depth and networks in subsequent focused skill and whole activities, until the student becomes a mini-expert in paleontology along with his intervention goal achievements.

A thematic unit can culminate in a project, such as a formal science presentation or a visitor brochure. Projects should have a minimum of writing, such as series of short descriptions or bulleted notes with graphics. Intervention goals need to be explicitly and repeatedly addressed throughout the project. To provide more skill practice, part activities targeting individual skills are interspersed along the way. Over the course of the unit, students are directed to review their progress on intervention goals and their performance on the whole activity. In examining both the process and product of learning, they consider the quality of their work and the amount of help they needed.

In Ukrainetz (2006b), I explain an intervention unit organized around developing a visitor brochure. This is a simple format with a minimum of writing and repeated opportunities for learning and practice of the skills involved. A brochure about the student's school could involve taking pictures of notable features and individuals, and then composing short descriptions and lists about each picture. Descriptive structure, predicate

Box 3.18. *A Literature-Based Treatment Unit*

A. Whole Activity: Pre-Story Enrichment Discussion

1. Discuss the pictures on the cover and each page.
2. Ask questions to help guide the child through the main storyline.
3. Use contingent linguistic facilitations (e.g., semantic expansion) to make the child's language more complete and complex.

B. Whole Activity: Enrichment Reading

1. Read the book aloud.
2. Stop occasionally to comment or discuss concepts, sentence structures, or plot elements.

C. Whole Activity: Post-Story Comprehension and Awareness Questions

1. Ask questions about the main events of the story.
2. Ask what made the story appealing.
3. Show on a chart the vocabulary, syntax, narrative, and pragmatic skills that will be learned in this story unit.

D-1. Part Activities for Targeted Semantic Skills

1. Select about five vocabulary items from or related to the story.
2. Make a "New Word Book" that lists words from the story.
3. Define, discuss, and use the words in sentences with child-friendly language.
4. Create a wall chart and encourage use of the target words in other activities.
5. Use the words yourself and emphasize them in your talk about the book.

D-2. Part Activities for Targeted Syntax Skills

1. Using a sentence pattern that is repeated throughout the book, read the sentences aloud.
2. Place the noun and verb phrases onto sentence strips that children can manipulate.
3. Have children sketch pictographs to represent the sentences.
4. Match the sentence strips to the pictographs.
5. Retell the story with an added focus on using the target sentence pattern.

D-3. Part Activities for Targeted Narrative Skills

1. Analyze the story by filling in the elements of a story grammar chart.
2. Use the story grammar terminology when identifying the story parts.

(continues)

Box 3.18. *(continued)*

D-3. Part Activities for Targeted Narrative Skills (*continued*)

3. Retell the story using pictographic sketching.
4. Create a "retold" booklet with sentences or pictography and key words.
5. Create a parallel story with different characters and setting but a similar theme or storyline.

D-4. Part Activities for Targeted Pragmatics Skills

1. Discuss how the characters used targeted language to handle a situation in the story.
2. Create parallel situations and discuss the language involved.
3. Verbally act out the situations, using the targeted language.
4. Have students identify each others' use of the targeted language.
5. Apply one of the created situations and the pragmatic usage in the parallel stories.

E. Whole Activity: Returning to the Book

1. Review the vocabulary in the child's "New Word Book."
2. Find the target vocabulary in the original book and read those sentences.
3. Review the syntactic structure sentence strips.
4. Find the target sentence structures in the original book and read those sentences.
5. Review the filled-in story grammar chart.
6. Find the story grammar elements in the original book and share those parts of the story.
7. Review the pragmatic language behaviors practiced.
8. Find those pragmatic behaviors in the book and reshare those parts of the story.
9. Have the students retell the storybook with the targeted vocabulary, sentence structure, story grammar, and pragmatic language.
10. Have the students retell their parallel stories with the targeted vocabulary, sentence structure, story grammar, and pragmatic language.

F. Whole Activity: Carrying the Target Skills Beyond the Unit

1. Review the target skills and each student's performance on each skill.
2. Discuss where and when they will next use these language skills.
3. Help students decide how they will show that they have applied the skill elsewhere.

Note: Based on Gillam and Ukrainetz (2006).

structure, and key vocabulary are addressed in the unit. Each student can compose a complete brochure or several students can compose pieces with the best selected for the final shared product. The clinician interactively scaffolds the students by showing models, discussing possibilities, and having the students reflect on the language targets. At the end of the unit, students enjoy sharing the product with an audience, such as guiding parents around the school with the brochure.

Ukrainetz and Ross (2006) detail a library research project that addresses text comprehension skills within a theme of "Animals of the Yellowstone Ecosystem." Each student's culminating project was a poster presentation on an animal of his or her choice. Ukrainetz and Ross found that middle school students, often resistant to speech services, could be motivated and engaged in learning through these mini research projects. The students showed impressive self-directed learning with questions to the SLP, such as:

- Can I start my Boolean search on the Internet today because I finished identifying my keywords last session?
- I have highlighted the answers to my research questions, so today do I get to start note taking?
- You said we would present our posters to each other here in Speech, but I was wondering if I could present mine in reading class because I think Mrs. Smith and the other students would like to see what I've been working on. (p. 547).

The students reminded each other of next steps, made sense of source material together, and showed interest in their peers' work. They guided each other, such as asking why a student had highlighted a sentence and which research question it answered. To keep attention on the treatment goal, Ross employed self-evaluations that asked students to reflect on their performance of both the activity and their individual treatment objectives (see Appendix B). Over the course of the unit, the students became quite competent in rating their own behaviors (e.g., *Mrs. Ross, you should give me a 3 today on summarizing because I only needed to ask for help one time, and then I worked independently without stopping during the whole session*, p. 547).

Expository language intervention is newer on the scene than narrative, but it follows the same structure. Expository units can be built around classroom topics, academic standards, or individual interests. Some students enjoy the physical world of exposition more than the social world of narration. There is evidence in the learning disabilities literature that written language skills can be improved through expository units that include explicit instruction in self-regulation (e.g., Sexton, Harris, & Graham, 1998; Wong, Butler, Ficzere, & Kuperis, 1996, 1997).

Conclusion

This chapter set out a framework for language intervention. Teaching the communication games of life is not so different from coaching the game of basketball. Student performance is evaluated in light of motivations, purposes, and learning conditions. The leagues in which the student must succeed are his classroom and state academic standards. Intervention goals are determined and progress is measured in relation to these standards. The SLP engineers structural scaffolds to simplify activities and motivate performance. Within these activities, the SLP provides interactive moves that dynamically scaffold student language skills and self-regulatory behaviors. Whole and part activities are combined to provide systematic attention to skill performance in and out of the game of communication. Thematic units or projects linked to the classroom build language skills on a coherent foundation.

References

Aliki. (1989). *My five senses.* New York, NY: Crowell.

Adams, M. J. (2011). Advancing our students' language and literacy: The challenge of complex texts. *American Educator, 34*(4), 3–11, 53.

Apel, K., & Swank, L. K. (1999). Second chances: Improving decoding skills in the older student. *Language, Speech, and Hearing Services in Schools, 30,* 231–242.

Bashir, A. S., & Singer, B. D. (2006). Assisting students in becoming self-regulated writers. In T. A. Ukrainetz (Ed.), *Contextualized language intervention: Scaffolding preK–12 literacy achievement* (pp. 565–598). Austin, TX: PRO-ED.

Beck, I. L., & McKeown, M. G. (2005). *Text talk.* New York, NY: Scholastic.

Burstein, J. (2009). *The amazing circulatory system: How does my heart work?* New York, NY: Crabtree.

Calkins, L., Ehrenworth, M., Lehman, C. (2012). *Pathways to the Common Core: Accelerating achievement.* Portsmouth, NH: Heinemann.

Camarata, S. M., & Nelson, K. E. (2006). Conversational recast intervention with preschool and older children. In R.J. McCauley & M.E. Fey (Eds.), *Treatment of language disorders in children* (pp. 237–266). Baltimore, MD: Brookes.

Eisenberg, S. L. (2006). Grammar: How can I say that better? In T. A. Ukrainetz (Ed.), *Contexualized language intervention: Scaffolding preK–12 literacy achievement* (pp. 145–194). Austin, TX: PRO-ED.

Fey, M. (1986). *Language intervention with young children.* Boston, MA: College-Hill.

Gillam, S. L., Gillam, R. B., & Reece, K. (2012). Language outcomes of contextualized and decontex \tualized language intervention: Results of an early efficacy study. *Language, Speech, and Hearing Services in Schools, 43,* 276–291.

Gillam, R., McFadden, T. U., & van Kleeck, A. (1995). Improving narrative abilities: Whole language and language skills approaches. In M. E. Fey, J. Windsor, & S. F. Warren (Eds.), *Language intervention: Preschool through the elementary years* (pp. 145–181). Baltimore, MD: Brookes.

Gillam, R. B., & Ukrainetz, T. A. (2006). Language intervention through literature-based units. In T. A. Ukrainetz (Ed.), *Contextualized language intervention: Scaffolding preK–12 literacy achievement* (pp. 59–94). Austin, TX: PRO-ED.

Ginsburg, M. (1974). *Mushroom in the rain.* New York, NY: Aladdin.

Goerss, B. L., Beck, I. L., & McKeown, M. G. (1999). Increasing remedial students' ability to derive word meaning from context. *Journal of Reading Psychology, 20,* 151–175.

Hancock, T. B., & Kaiser, A. P. (2006). Enhanced milieu teaching. In R. J. McCauley & M. E. Fey (Eds.), *Treatment of language disorders in children* (pp. 203–236). Baltimore, MD: Brookes.

Harris-Schmidt, G., & McNamee, G. D. (1986). Children as authors and actors: Literacy development through "basic activities." *Child Language Teaching and Therapy, 2,* 63–73.

Johnson, M. S., Kress, R. A., & Pikulski, J. J. (1987). *Informal reading inventories.* Newark, DE: International Reading Association.

Johnston, J. (1985). Fit, focus, and functionality: An essay on early language intervention. *Child Language Teaching and Therapy, 1*(2), 125–134.

Kratcoski, A. M. (1998). Guidelines for using portfolios in assessment and evaluation. *Language, Speech, and Hearing Services in Schools, 29,* 3–10.

Lederer, J. M. (2000). Reciprocal teaching of social studies in inclusive elementary classrooms. *Journal of Learning Disabilities, 33,* 91–106.

Leontiev, A. N. (1981). The problem of activity in psychology. In J. V. Wertsch (Ed.), *The concept of activity in Soviet psychology* (pp. 37–71). New York, NY: Sharpe.

Lidz, C., & Pena, E. (1996). Dynamic assessment: The model, its relevance as a nonbiased approach, and its application to Latino American preschool children. *Language, Speech, and Hearing Services in Schools, 27,* 367–372.

Maslow, A. H. (1954). *Motivation and personality.* New York, NY: Harper & Row.

McGregor, K. K. (2000). The development and enhancement of narrative skills in a preschool classroom: Towards a solution to clinician-client mismatch. *American Journal of Speech-Language Pathology, 9,* 55–71.

McKeown, M. G., Beck, I. L., Omanson, R. C., & Pople, M. T. (1985). Some effects of the nature and frequency of vocabulary instruction on the knowledge and use of words. *Reading Research Quarterly, 20,* 522–535.

National Governors Association Center for Best Practices and Council of Chief State School Officers (2010). *Common Core State Standards for English Language Arts & Literacy in History/Social Studies, Science, and Technical Subjects.* Washington, DC: Author. Retrieved from http://www.corestandards.org

Nelson, N. W., & Van Meter, A. M. (2006). Finding the words: Vocabulary development for young authors. In T.A. Ukrainetz (Ed.), *Contexualized language intervention: Scaffolding preK–12 literacy achievement* (pp. 95–145). Austin, TX: PRO-ED.

Palincsar, A. S. (1998). Keeping the metaphor of scaffolding fresh. *Journal of Learning Disabilities, 21,* 370–373.

Palincsar, A. S., & Brown, A. L. (1984). Reciprocal teaching of comprehension-fostering and comprehension-monitoring activities. *Cognition and Instruction, 1,* 117–175.

Paris, S. G., Wasik, B. A., & Turner, J. C. (1991). The development of strategic readers. In R. Barr, M. L. Kamil, P. B. Mosenthal, & P. D. Pearson (Eds.), *Handbook of Reading Research, Vol. II* (pp. 609–640). New York, NY: Longman.

Pena, E. D., Gillam, R. B., Malek, M., Ruiz-Felter, R., Resendiz, M., Fiestas, C., & Sabel, T. (2006). Dynamic assessment of school-age children's narrative ability: An experimental investigation of classification accuracy. *Journal of Speech, Language, and Hearing Research, 49,* 1037–1057.

Pena, E. D., Quinn, R., & Iglesias, A. (1992). The application of dynamic assessment procedures to language assessment: A nonbiased procedure. *Journal of Special Education, 26,* 269–280.

Petersen, D., Gillam, S. L., Spencer, T., & Gillam, R. B. (2010). Effects of literate narrative intervention on children with neurologically based language impairments. *Journal of Speech, Language, and Hearing Research, 53,* 961–981.

Petersen, D. B., Brown, C. L., Ukrainetz, T. A., Wise, C., Spencer, T. D., & Zebre, J. (2014). Systematic individualized language intervention on the personal narratives of children with autism. *Language, Speech, and Hearing Services in Schools,* 45, 67–86.

Pretti-Frontczak, K., & Bricker, D. (2004). *An activity-based approach to early intervention* (3rd ed.). Baltimore, MD: Brookes.

Schneider, P., & Watkins, R. V. (1996). Applying Vygotskian developmental theory to language intervention. *Language, Speech, and Hearing Services in Schools, 27,* 157–170.

Sexton, M., Harris, K. R., & Graham, S. (1998). Self-regulated strategy development and the writing process. *Exceptional Children, 64,* 295–311.

Silliman, E. & Wilkinson, L. C. (1991). *Communicating for learning: Classroom observation and collaboration.* Gaithersburg, MD: Aspen.

Spencer, T. D., & Slocum, T. A. (2010). The effect of narrative intervention on story retelling and personal story generation of preschoolers with risk factors and narrative language delays. *Journal of Early Intervention, 32,* 178–199.

Ukrainetz, T. A. (1998). Beyond Vygotsky: What Soviet activity theory offers naturalistic language intervention. *Journal of Speech–Language Pathology and Audiology, 22,* 122–133.

Ukrainetz, T. A. (2005). What to work on how: An examination of the practice of school-age language intervention. *Contemporary Issues in Communication Sciences and Disorders, 32,* 108–119.

Ukrainetz, T. A. (2006a). Assessment and intervention within a contextualized skill framework. In T.A. Ukrainetz (Ed.), *Contextualized language intervention: Scaffolding preK–12 literacy achievement* (pp. 59–94). Austin, TX: PRO-ED.

Ukrainetz, T. A. (2006b). The many ways of exposition: A focus on discourse structure. In T.A. Ukrainetz (Ed.), *Contextualized language intervention: Scaffolding preK–12 literacy achievement* (pp. 247–288). Austin, TX: PRO-ED.

Ukrainetz, T. A., & Fresquez, E. F. (2003). "What isn't language?": A qualitative study of the role of the school speech–language pathologist. *Language, Speech, and Hearing Services in Schools, 34,* 284–298.

Ukrainetz, T. A., Harpell, S., Walsh, C., & Coyle, C. (2000). A preliminary investigation of dynamic assessment with Native American kindergartners. *Language, Speech, and Hearing Services in Schools, 31,* 142–153.

Ukrainetz, T. A., & Ross, C. L. (2006). Text comprehension: Facilitating active and strategic engagement. In T. A. Ukrainetz (Ed.), *Contextualized language intervention: Scaffolding preK–12 literacy achievement* (pp. 503–563). Austin, TX: PRO-ED.

Vygotsky, L. (1978). *Mind in society: The development of higher psychological processes.* Cambridge, MA: Harvard University Press.

Weismer, S. E., & Robertson, S. (2006). Focused stimulation approach to language intervention. In R.J. McCauley & M.E. Fey (Eds.), *Treatment of language disorders in children* (pp. 175–202). Baltimore, MD: Brookes.

Westby, C. E., Watson, S., & Murphy, M. (1994). The vision of full inclusion: Don't exclude kids by including them. *Journal of Childhood Communication Disorders, 16,* 13–22.

Wolter, J., Ukrainetz, T. A., Ross, C. L., & Andrus, J. (2011, November). *Writing meaningful goals and monitoring progress in school-age language intervention.* Presentation at the annual ASHA Convention, San Diego, CA.

Wong, B. Y. L., Butler, D. L., Ficzere, S. A., & Kuperis, S. (1996). Teaching low achievers and students with learning disabilities to plan, write, and revise opinion essays. *Journal of Learning Disabilities, 29,* 197–212.

Wong, B. Y. L., Butler, D. L., Ficzere, S. A., & Kuperis, S. (1997). Teaching adolescents with learning disabilities and low achievers to plan, write, and revise compare-and-contrast essays. *Learning Disabilities Research and Practice, 12,* 2–15.

Wood, D., Bruner, J. S., & Ross, G. (1976). The role of tutoring in problem solving. *Journal of Child Psychology and Psychiatry, 17,* 89–100.

Wyoming State Board of Education. (2008). *Wyoming language arts content and performance standards.* Cheyenne, WY: Author.

Appendix A: Thematic Treatment Unit Guide

This is intended as an assignment for graduate students but is a useful guide even for experienced SLPs. It creates a basic whole-part-whole treatment unit for two language skills and one self-regulation skill. The theme provides a common set of concepts and vocabulary across the treatment activities. The component activities or entire unit are repeated with variations (or the unit is expanded with additional activities for each skill) until the target skills are achieved.

A. Introduction

1. Specify *two skill targets and their respective* language areas that will be addressed. Link the two language goals to a Common Core standard for that grade level. Identify one ancillary goal that involves an executive function (e.g., self-review, peer interaction, persistence) that will be treated alongside the language skills within the treatment activities (e.g., practice self-review by analyzing your own progress in producing subordinated relative clauses in information passages).
2. Provide an overview of your small group (2 to 3 students) treatment unit with its approximate grade level, thematic foundation, whole-part-whole and RISE+ structure.
3. Report three measurable treatment objectives for one student. Explain created baseline data for each objective for that student. All activities, performance examples, and expectations should be consistent with the these objectives and baseline

levels as well as with the grade level of the group (e.g., do not address second-grade students like they are middle school students and vice-versa).

B. Opening

Provide an opening skills preview for the students you will teach in words appropriate to them. Keep the learning focus on skills, not specific activities.

C. First Whole Activity

1. Summarize how you will use a piece of literature to begin the unit, with explicit attention to the two treatment targets.
2. Briefly summarize the narrative or expository literature. Provide the book reference, a copy of the cover picture, and a copy of one relevant page.
3. Explain why this book is suited to teach these two skills or how it could be modified to be suitable, with a focus on repeated opportunities for learning and practice.
4. Briefly explain how you will interactively present these two skills while you share the book and how you will scaffold learning for a child who is deficient in these skills.
5. Provide two mini imaginary dialogue transcripts that demonstrate the SLP eliciting a target response, a student's partially correct response, and the SLP's scaffolding that improves the response at some point during the book sharing (about 5 to 8 student turns long each). Each dialogue should demonstrate at least one linguistic and one regulatory scaffold that assist the student to learn those two skills.

D. Middle Part Activities

1. Explain a focused skill activity for each of the two targets. Detail the materials and expected progression of the two 15-minute activities (i.e., beginning, middle, end).
2. Make the activities maximize the number of learning opportunities. Report how many opportunities will occur in a single presentation of each activity.
3. Each activity will be carried out several times, providing additional learning opportunities. Explain how the learning support will change as the student's performance improves across repetitions of the activity.

E. Last Whole Activity

1. End the unit with a whole, integrative activity that brings together all three skill targets. Describe the progression (i.e., beginning, middle, end) of this activity.
2. Explain how this final activity will provide explicit skill attention, repeated opportunities, and systematic learning support for both skills.
3. Report how data will be collected in this final project for all three treatment targets.
4. Explain how one deficient nontarget skill would be avoided, assisted, or ignored at this time.

F. Ending

1. Detail a self-evaluation activity in which the students evaluate their progress on the three target skills with specific examples reported.
2. Report what you and your students need to consider these skills satisfactorily achieved with specific examples from the classroom.

Appendix B: Final Student Self-Evaluation

Name ______________________________ Grade ______ Date ________________

My topic was ____.

This is my ______ first ______ second ______ third research project in Speech.

A. RATE YOUR PROCESS

Amount of Help Needed / Task	1 A Lot	2 Quite a Bit	3 A Little	4 Independent
Identify topic				
Identify research questions				
Identify keywords				
Locate good sources				
Read information and find answers				
Take notes from sources				
Organize info for poster				
Construct bibliography				
Speak and use visuals in presentation				

B. RATE YOUR PRODUCT

1. My learning objectives for this project were:

a) ____

b) ____

c) ____

2. I improved on my objectives in the following ways:

a) ____

b) ____

c) ____

I also learned ____

3. I still need to improve ____

____

____

Note: From "Text comprehension: Facilitating Active and Strategic Engagement," by T. A. Ukrainetz and C. L. Ross, in *Contextualized Language Intervention: Scaffolding PreK–12 Literacy Achievement,* by T. A. Ukrainetz (Ed.), 2006, Austin, TX: PRO-ED. Copyright 2006 by PRO-ED, Inc. Reprinted with permission.

Chapter 4

Speech–Language Services in the Schools: Rules of the Road

Teresa A. Ukrainetz

Speech–language pathology services are legally mandated and closely regulated. The laws and regulations assure a minimum level of service delivery and comparability across the country. This chapter reviews the history and current status of significant federal laws and regulations affecting speech–language pathology services in the schools.

The Legislative Basis of Education

In the United States, education is considered a "state right," but the federal government plays a dominant and an increasing role. In addition to assuring constitutionally guaranteed rights to equal education, the federal government has taken on the task of setting detailed accountability and performance expectations for both regular and special education. The federal government also provides significant funding to states toward the costs of federal mandates. Regardless of funding, states must enact federal mandates. However, there is freedom to determine the specifics of programs and procedures. States themselves vary as to the degree of control allowed to school districts. Within a district, schools (and individual teachers) vary in their operations. As a result, school speech–language pathologists (SLPs) must become familiar with conduct in their local areas in addition to broader prescriptions.

The focus of this chapter is on major legislated laws. Rules of conduct passed by local, state, and federal governments are *legislated* statutes or laws. Laws can be individual rules or large, complex collections of rules. At the federal levels, these collections are called *public laws.* A new public law may be an amendment to a prior law or a new law that supersedes prior laws. Public laws are periodically reviewed and reauthorized. Reauthorizations may involve substantial changes and new names, but they are intended to build on each other in coherent and complementary ways to optimally regulate the conduct of education.

Federal laws are translated into codes of federal regulation (CFRs). Codes of regulation are the operational rules. For education, each state also develops its own codes of regulation to interpret and apply federal and state laws. Codes of regulation must consider the current law and whatever preceded it that is still in force. As a result, codes of regulation may be better guides to current practices than the source laws (see http://ecfr.gpoaccess.gov/ for locating specific CFRs).

Court cases brought by parents, school districts, or other stakeholders test the applications of laws, regulations, and practices. These can occur in trial, appellate, and supreme courts at local, state, and federal levels. Judicial decisions of legal cases are called *case law.* Case law results in new interpretations of legal statutes and contributes to future amendments to legislated laws. There have been many Supreme Court cases that have tested interpretations and applications of federal law (see Gravani [2007] for more detail than will be provided here).

History of Special Education Law

The history of special education can be divided at 1975, when Public Law (P.L.) 94-142 (Education for All Handicapped Children Act), which created special education, was passed. This law identified the disability category of *speech or language impairment* and shifted SLPs from regular to special education.

Special Education Before 1975

The late 1800s to the early 1900s was a period of rapid expansion of educational opportunities across the country. Public education began in New York in 1874 and, by 1918, had spread to all 48 states (Duchan, 2010). Most states had compulsory attendance laws, along with child labor laws, but attendance was not systematically enforced until it became tied to school funding (Katz, 1976). Katz reports that the number of children attending high school burgeoned from less than 1% in 1880 to 47% in 1930.

Public schooling largely excluded children with significant disabilities. These children were cared for at home or in residential institutions, such as the Columbia Institution for the Instruction of the Deaf and Dumb and Blind (which later became Gallaudet University) and Massachusetts School for Idiotic Children and Youth. However, the idea that public schools were responsible for more than academics was emerging with the employment of nurses, dentists, and visiting teachers (Duchan, 2010). In large, metropolitan school districts, there were specialized "day" classes in the public schools for children who were blind or "feeble minded."

Efforts to measure variation in student intellectual capacity began in the early 1900s. Intelligence tests, such as the 1916 Stanford-Binet, were developed and applied widely (Robinson & Robinson, 1976). The early IQ tests were efficient, objective tests that could sort the large number of World War I inductees into appropriate training programs. In addition, with the rapid expansion of public schools, IQ tests were considered fairer methods than family background to sort children into academic programs. The standard for attending public school was often a minimum mental age of 5 years (Schraeder, 2008).

Physical and sensory impairments also resulted in exclusion of children from public school. For example, Gravani (2007) describes the 1919 case of *Beattie v. State Board of Education* in Wisconsin. In this case, a child with normal intelligence and cerebral palsy had attended public school for several years. The child had been making adequate academic progress, but the local school board claimed that the child's body movements, voice prosody, drooling, and facial behaviors were depressing to teachers and other students. The board reported that the student took teachers' time away from other students. The board recommended the child attend the only special program available, a school for the deaf. The judge supported the child's removal from public school. Hints of awareness of civil rights were apparent in the minority opinion that there was no evidence that the boy's presence had a harmful influence on the rest of the class and that every child had a fundamental right to attend school. However, this case reflected the predominant view that children with disabilities did not belong in public schools.

Changes in attitudes to students with disabilities began in the 1950s with the civil rights era. The 14th and the fifth amendments to the U.S. Constitution, which deal with citizenship and due process, were the basis of many of the judgments that advanced public education for children with disabilities (Gravani, 2007). The 1954 U.S. Supreme Court case that ushered in this era was *Brown v. Board of Education*. This historic case, dealing with the requirement of segregated schooling for white and black students, resulted in the judgment that "separate but equal" was inherently unequal. The Civil Rights Act of 1964 required the federal government withhold funding from institutions that discriminated on the basis of race, color, or national origin. These two foundations for the right to equal public education for all children implicitly included those with disabilities.

The earliest federal law specifically targeting individuals with disabilities was in 1958, with P.L. 85-926, the Education of Mentally Retarded Children Act (Box 4.1). This bill provided funds to colleges to educate teachers of children with intellectual disabilities. In 1961, President John F. Kennedy called for a presidential panel to examine schooling of children with intellectual disabilities. From 1965 to 1968, three education acts were passed. These acts and subsequent judicial actions affirmed the right to public education for children regardless of disability and disallowed the defense of insufficient resources. The acts provided funds for special education services, including the operation of state institutions, local school district needs, model demonstration programs, and regional resource centers. In addition, the Elementary and Secondary Amendments of 1966 established Title 1, which provided funds for enrichment programs for poor students.

Changes in special education requirements continued in the 1970s, with a combination of legislation and court cases. In 1970, the Education of the Handicapped Act (P.L. 91-230) established minimum standards for what the states had to provide to access federal funds. The Rehabilitation Act of 1973 (P.L. 93-112) established civil rights of individuals with disabilities. Section 504 of this act continues to be an important way of accommodating children in need who do not qualify as educationally disabled.

P.L. 94-142 of 1975

The legislation that issued in the modern era of education of children with disabilities was the Education for All Handicapped Children Act of 1975. P.L. 94-142 and its subsequent amendments set forth an important array of educational mandates based on the premise of equal access to education for all children, regardless of disability.

P.L. 94-142 specified and defined a set of disability categories, including blindness, deafness, mental retardation, emotional disturbance, orthopedic impairment, health problems, communication disability, and specific learning disability. The latter two categories reflected an expansion of attention from severe mental, physical, and sensory disabilities to more subtle difficulties within the scope of specialized educational services. These children, who have difficulty with educational achievement but may appear "typical" in casual interactions and nonschool situations, would come to form the largest number of children in special education.

P.L. 94-142 required states to have "child find" programs to identify potential children with disabilities. Identified children had to be evaluated and, if eligible, provided educational plans and services customized to each individual child. The plans were intended to emulate as closely as possible the educational opportunities of nondisabled students. Parents (any reference to parent in this chapter also pertains to legal guardians and caregivers) had the right to be involved in identification, eligibility, placement, and service decisions. States had to provide a system of dispute resolution called due process so issues might be resolved within the educational system without going to the expensive process of litigation.

(text continues on p. 123)

Box 4.1. ***Major Federal Legislation Affecting Special Education***

Year	Law	Title	Primary Intents
1954	—	*Brown v. Board of Education*	Judgment that determined "separate but equal" is inherently unequal
1958	P.L. 85-926	Education of Mentally Retarded Children Act	Financial assistance to colleges educating teachers of children with mental retardation
1964	P.L. 88-352	Civil Rights Act of 1964	Federal funds withheld from institutions excluding individuals based on race, color, or national origin; Federal responsibility to judge whether a school was desegregated
1965	P.L. 89-10, P.L. 89-313	Elementary and Secondary Education Act (ESEA) and Amendment	Provided states with funds to evaluate and educate some students with disabilities in state institutions
1966	P.L. 89-750	ESEA Amendments of 1966	Provided federal grant money to local school districts for the education of students with disabilities; Established Title 1 funding for disadvantaged students
1968	P.L. 90-247	ESEA Amendments of 1968	Expanded special education services and established regional resource centers; Established centers for students who were deaf and blind
1970	P.L. 91-230	Education of the Handicapped Act (EHA)	Established minimum requirements that states must follow in order to receive federal assistance
1971	—	*Pennsylvania Assoc. for Retarded Children v. Commonwealth of Pennsylvania*	All children can benefit from education; Not legal to refuse to educate children with mental ages of less than 5 years
1972	—	*Mills v. D.C. Board of Education*	Public schools could not use the excuse of inadequate resources as a reason to deny students with disabilities an education
1973	P.L. 93-112	Rehabilitation Act of 1973 (Section 504)	Prohibited discrimination based on disability; Persons with disabilities had the right to vote, to be educated, to be employed, and to have access to public environments

Box 4.1. *(continued)*

1974	P.L. 93-380	ESEA Amendments of 1974	Identified and evaluated all handicapped children; Due process rights; Procedural safeguards for evaluation and placement of students
1975	P.L. 94-142	Education of All Handicapped Children Act	Access to a free, appropriate public education in a least restrictive environment guided by an individualized education plan; Set eligibility categories including speech or language impairment
1984	P.L. 98-524	Vocational Educational Act of 1984	Federal funds to support vocational education programs for disabled, disadvantaged, or limited English proficient
1986	P.L. 99-457	EHA Amendments of 1986	Extended public education for children with disabilities down to 3 years; Assisted states in disability program development for 0–2 years
1987	P.L. 100-407	Technology Related Assistance for Individuals With Disabilities Act	Authorized funding to allow states to create statewide systems to promote awareness and access to a broad array of technological assistance
1990	P.L. 101-476	EHA Amendments of 1990 or Individuals With Disabilities Education Act (IDEA)	Renamed act as IDEA; Expanded services for children with disabilities; Mandated transition and assistive technology services in IEPs; Added autism and traumatic brain injury categories
1990	P.L. 101-336	Americans With Disabilities Act (ADA)	Prohibited discrimination against individuals with disabilities for employment, public accommodations and services, and telecommunications
1991	P.L. 102-119	IDEA Amendments of 1991	Added assistive technology, vision services, and transportation to early intervention; Allowed age 3–5 either IEPs or IFSPs (Individualized Family Service Plans).
1989	—	*Daniel R.R. v. State Board of Education*	Placement in the regular classroom with supplementary services must be considered before alternative special education classrooms; Established criteria for school district obligations to least restrictive settings

(continues)

Box 4.1. (*continued*)

1997	P.L. 105-17	IDEA Amendments of 1997	Reauthorized IDEA with emphasis on access to general curriculum and least restrictive environment; Required participation in state and district-wide assessments; Streamlined evaluation requirements; Increased parent participation in eligibility and placement decisions; Required mediation option for dispute resolution
2001	P.L. 107-110	No Child Left Behind Act of 2001 (NCLB)	Reauthorization of ESEA; Aim to improve academic performance through increased testing, prescribed performance improvements, highly qualified teachers, supplemental education services (especially for early literacy), and use of scientifically based instruction
2004	P.L. 108-446	Individuals With Disabilities Education Improvement Act of 2004	Reauthorized and revised IDEA; Highly qualified providers for special education; No short-term objectives in IEPs unless on alternate assessment; Demonstration 3-year IEPs for paperwork reduction; Early intervention for ages 3 to 5 years must include literacy; Must have response to instruction in determination of specific learning disability
2008	P.L. 110-325	ADA Amendments Act of 2008	Reinstated intent of broad protection: An impairment that substantially limits one major life activity need not limit other major life activities in order to be a disability; The determination of whether an impairment substantially limits a major life activity is made without regard to the ameliorative effects of mitigating measures such as medication, prosthetics, hearing aids, and cochlear implants
2009	P.L. 111-5	American Recovery and Reinvestment Act of 2009 (ARRA)	Included $12.2 billion in additional funds toward implementation of IDEA; ARRA required that recipients separately account for, and report on, how those funds are spent

The federal legislative actions of the 1960s and 1970s occurred in a context of supportive economic and societal conditions. The economy was strong, employment rates were high, and federal and state deficits were low. The building of America was in full force, with major public and private investments in public infrastructure and services. Society was moving from viewing the individual in terms of economic contributions (i.e., Will education enable a person to hold a job or raise a family?) to rights to quality of life (i.e., Will education enable a person to have a better quality life?) (Siegel, 1987). Educational concerns broadened from academics to the full continuum of individual well-being. Terminology changes reflected efforts to foreground students rather than their disabilities and use socially neutral labels for disabilities (Box 4.2).

Box 4.2. ***Societal Attitude to Disability as Reflected in Terminology***

The terminology used in the titles of special education laws and the changes in this terminology over time reveal changing societal attitudes to people who have low abilities. The preference for person-first language is the most familiar example of this, but there are at least two other conventions that are reflected in the evolution from *the handicapped* terminology of the 1960s to *handicapped children* in the 1970s to *individuals with disabilities* in the 1990s.

An early shift in terminology was away from reporting the person solely by the disability as a single noun (e.g., Retardates and dyslexics need special accommodations.). The preferred term was to include a person-status noun (e.g., retarded child or dyslexic student). The next shift was from premodification to postmodification. This is called *person-first language* and is intended to foreground the person rather than the disability (Moore-Brown & Montgomery, 2001). Positive or neutral descriptors can be pre-modified (e.g., a tall child, a bright student) but negative descriptors follow the noun (e.g., a child with language impairment, a child with attention deficit disorder). This can make for awkward phrasing, but the convention is followed even for scientific writing (American Psychological Association, 2009).

Another change in terminology was from *handicap* to *disability* to describe a person's condition. The World Health Organization (WHO) terminology framework of 1980 specified that handicap reflected modifiable environmental and social barriers (e.g., regular curriculum without supports, peoples' attitudes) rather than functional disabilities that arose from organic impairments. Subsequently, WHO (2002) moved away entirely from *handicap* to *disability* as the umbrella term for all impairments, activity limitations, and participation restrictions.

This quest for socially neutral language is particularly persistent for intellectual disabilities. Robinson and Robinson (1976) describe how the original terms for levels of intellectual disability were *idiot*, *imbecile*, and *moron*, denoting IQs of 0–30, 31–50, and 51–70, respectively. These terms were replaced by *trainable* and *educable* or *profound*, *severe*, *moderate*, and *mild mental retardation*. In some regions, *retardation* was replaced by *handicap*. Currently, reference to specific level of cognitive function is avoided. While the federal category is still called mental retardation, the acceptable term is *intellectual disability* or the broader term of *developmental disability*. In addition, there are many local labels, such as *mentally challenged*, *cognitively disordered*, and *cognitively impaired*.

P.L. 94-142 authorized the federal government to pay up to 40% of each state's "excess cost" of educating children with disabilities (Council for Exceptional Children [CEC], 2007). The intent was to phase in over 5 years this "full funding" amount. However, the mandated educational services proved to be an expensive endeavor. The category of specific learning disability saw large annual increases in number of children over the following decade, from both better identification processes and movement away from the category of mental retardation (Frankenberger & Harper, 1988). President Gerald Ford, at the time of signing the legislation, expressed concern about whether the federal government would be able to deliver on promises made (Weiner, 1985). Ten years later, the concern would prove to be well-grounded: "Money: Federal policymakers groan when you ask them about it, but it's the special education problem that just won't go away" (Weiner, 1985, p. 53). Weiner reported that, while special education funding increased or held stable in the face of large budget cuts in general education, the funding simply kept the program at the 12% level, forcing local and state sources to make up the gap, thus putting more pressure on funding for other education programs. This scenario has continued: Since 1975 and P.L. 94-142, annual federal funding has covered less than 20% of state and local costs of special education (CEC, 2007; Schraeder, 2008).

Despite state concerns over control of education and funding issues, special education became firmly established in the years following P.L. 94-142. Federal regulatory interpretations and legislative amendments continued to strengthen and refine interpretations of the law, such as requiring schools to provide every identified student with an Individualized Education Program (IEP) and needed services regardless of whether the district had the funding or the school had the service (Weiner, 1985). Deregulatory revisions that would have weakened guarantees were proposed by the Ronald Reagan administration in 1982. However, Weiner reported that strong bipartisan and public reaction resulted in the proposals being dropped.

The next major legislative initiative was in 1986, with P.L. 99-457. This legislation extended the requirement for educational services for children with disabilities downward in age to 3 years and assisted states in development of programs for children from birth to 2 years. Family-oriented intervention was provided through an Individualized Family Service Plan. Preschoolers were not required to have a specific disability category to be served, but all services had to be provided by "qualified" personnel. The standard for qualified provider status was left to states to specify.

IDEA of 1990

The Individuals with Disabilities Education Act of 1990 (IDEA, P.L. 101-476) reauthorized and expanded P.L. 94-142. IDEA mandated consideration of transition and assistive technology services in IEPs, incorporated the 99-457 infants and toddler requirements as Part H, improved services for children with serious emotional disturbance, and added a research and information program on attention deficit disorder. Autism and traumatic brain injury were added as federal eligibility categories. The following year, the IDEA Amendments of 1991 required transition services from preschool to kindergarten and allowed children reaching 3 years to stay in their early intervention setting so long as a literacy and numeracy component was provided. This amendment also added vision services, assistive technology and services, and transportation to early intervention services.

In 1997, IDEA was reauthorized as P.L. 105-17. IDEA '97 emphasized greater access to the general education classroom and curriculum and participation in state- and districtwide assessments. The concept of *least restrictive environment* (LRE) was more strongly enforced with IDEA '97. LRE did not demand full inclusion but required only as much removal as was necessary to provide an appropriate education for each child. The crucial criteria for applying LRE were whether significant beneficial learning could be obtained in the general education classroom with supplementary aids and services, and if not, whether the student was with his regular education peers to the maximum extent possible (Gravani, 2007). Students with disabilities, like their nondisabled peers, were to have access to challenging curriculum and quality instruction consistent with state and local standards. However, like for their nondisabled peers, there was no assurance that their educational programs are optimal or will maximize their potential. Achieving LRE involved having a variety of assessment methods and a continuum of services to identify and match each child's strengths and needs.

Finally, IDEA '97 required that IEPs be developed jointly with parents. Parents were given the option of mediation whenever a due process hearing was requested. This was an additional cost-saving and less adversarial step prior to due process that had been brought in with P.L. 94-142 (which itself had been brought in to avoid the costs of court hearings).

Americans With Disabilities and Section 504

The Americans With Disabilities Act (ADA, P.L. 101-336) was a civil rights law that addressed the full life sphere of individuals with disabilities. ADA assured full civil rights of all individuals with disabilities, guaranteeing equal opportunity in employment, public accommodation, transportation, state and local government services, telecommunications, and higher education. ADA strengthened Section 504 of the 1973 Rehabilitation Act, extending access to all public domains. After several Supreme Court decisions with stringent interpretations of disability determination, a 2008 amendment of ADA (ADA, P.L. 110-325) specified the intent of liberal determinations, such as allowing someone to be considered disabled even if an impairment only limited some but not all major life activities.

ADA provisions are not supported with federal monies, requiring instead local funding for compliance. Educational qualifications for 504 are less stringent than for IDEA. For example, students with spina bifida who are succeeding academically may be "504ed" to allow extra time to travel between class periods. Efforts are made to accommodate 504 children within regular education or move them into an IDEA disability category rather than providing unfunded resources from special education.

No Child Left Behind: Accountability and Results

The next major federal legislation to affect special education practices was the No Child Left Behind Act of 2001 (NCLB), which aimed to improve educational performance across the nation. This act reauthorized the Elementary and Secondary Education Act. NCLB was quickly followed by the reauthorization and revision of IDEA. IDEA '04 aligned with NCLB around "four pillars" of "stronger accountability for results, more freedom for states and communities, proven education methods, and more choices for parents" (http://www2.ed.gov/nclb/overview/intro/, para. 1). These translated into requirements such as more frequent standardized achievement testing, prescribed performance goals, supplementary education services, increased teacher training requirements, the use of scientifically based instructional methods, and increased charter school opportunities. A summary of NCLB and IDEA changes can be found at http://idea.ed.gov/explore/home.

The President's Commission on Excellence in Special Education

The reauthorization and revision of IDEA in 2004 emerged from the President's Commission on Excellence in Special Education (United States Department of Education [USDE], 2002). The commission report acknowledged that IDEA provided basic legal safeguards and access for children with disabilities. However, the report expressed overall dissatisfaction with performance outcomes. It cited the high dropout rate of youth with disabilities, the lack of confidence of teachers to address the needs of students with disabilities, the over-representation of minority children in special education, and the continuing gap in achievement for children in special education.

Of particular concern was the high proportion of students with a learning disability (half of special education) and the rapid growth of this group since inception of the category (by more than 300% since 1976). The commission report said that 80% of learning disabilities were solely reading problems. It attributed up to half of the reading difficulties of children with learning disabilities to poor reading instruction. Many methods widely used to identify children with disabilities had a high number of false and missed identifications. The existing "wait to fail" model had too little emphasis on prevention and lacked early, accurate, and aggressive identification along with pre-referral attention to learning and behavior problems. The commission report called for more qualified teachers, which involved preprofessional education, ongoing support, and professional development. Research conducted in special education needed better rigor and long-term coordination, and then, once good scientific evidence existed, wider implementation.

The commission report cited complex regulations, excessive paperwork, and administrative demands that placed process and compliance above effective instruction and student achievement. The pressures of litigation added to this culture of compliance. There was concern that special and general education were treated financially as two separate systems, not as a single system with additional services and expenses, contributing to misidentification and academic isolation.

The new aim for special education was to move "from a culture of compliance to a culture of accountability for results" (USDE, 2002, p. 4). The main recommendations were prescribed performance goals, decreased emphasis on procedural compliance, increased local funding flexibility, and pre-referral scientifically based instruction, with better teacher preparation and support.

Funding and Procedural Changes

Federal funding was increased with NCLB and IDEA 2004. A 6-year schedule of incremental increases in funding of IDEA was planned. If honored, the original 40% per student commitment made in 1975 with PL 94-142 would be achieved. As of 2007, IDEA funding was at only 17% of the national average per pupil expenditure in special education (CEC, 2007). Additional funding was provided for programs outside of special education, such as Reading First, Early Reading First, and Even Start Migrant Education Program. School districts were allowed more spending flexibility for federal funding special education and supportive services (e.g., Title 1) allocations, especially for pre-referral interventions for reading in kindergarten to third grade. Related service providers, such as SLPs, could be employed in the development and delivery of pre-referral supplemental instruction. A highly qualified teacher requirement specified that, for special education, teachers were required to have at least a Bachelor's degree and to meet state standards for special education and subject area instruction.

An important change was in the requirements for identifying specific learning disability. The standard approach since 1975 for identifying specific learning disabilities was a significant, unexplained gap between academic achievement and some aspect of intellect. Considerable evidence against the validity of this approach had accumulated by the time of IDEA '04 (Catts, Kamhi, & Adloff, 2012; see Chapter 5). Under NCLB and IDEA '04, school districts could opt to use the discrepancy formula but were also required to consider other findings that showed that the student had an inadequate response to regular and supplemental scientifically based instruction.

Performance Expectations in Special Education

Students with disabilities had been required to participate in state- and district-wide assessments since IDEA 1997. A major change was that NCLB/IDEA required that their performance be included in state, school district, and school achievement expectations and performance reports. Results had to be reported despite the recognition that performance reports from such heterogeneous collections of students tested with a range of accommodations would be difficult to interpret (USDE, 2007).

To allow valid participation, state-sanctioned accommodations that did not affect the difficulty or nature of the test items continued to be allowed with NCLB/IDEA. Allowable accommodations had to be specified on the IEP or Section 504 plan. Accommodations typically involve scheduling (e.g., frequent breaks), location (e.g., a study carrel), format (e.g., listening to rather than reading a question), and manner of response (e.g., pointing to an answer). To ensure that students could access required classroom instructional materials in addition to testing materials, a national instructional accessibility standard demanded that Braille, audio, digital, or large-print text alternatives were made available as needed.

In addition to accommodations, NCLB/IDEA allowed a small percentage of students with disabilities to take evaluations based on different academic achievement standards. Up to 1% of students, those with the most severe disabilities, could take alternate achievement evaluations fitted to their functional level. Alternate evaluation procedures and achievement standards had to be set by the state. They could include work samples, teacher observations, or standardized tasks. In 2005, in response to state concerns, a third option of modified achievement standards was introduced for an additional 2% of students with disabilities. These were more extensive than the timing and modality accommodations already allowed (USDE, 2007). However, the difficulties of setting these standards led to few states implementing them.

Part of NCLB is a goal of having all children proficient in reading and math by 2014. In 2011, in response to widespread concern that states would be unable to meet this requirement, the federal government allowed states to apply for elementary and secondary education flexibility in exchange for rigorous and comprehensive state-developed plans that would improve the educational outcomes for all students, close achievement gaps, increase equity, and improve the quality of instruction (USDE, 2012). By 2013, 46 states, the District of Columbia, and the Bureau of Indian Education had ESEA flexibility requests approved or in review (USDE, n.d.).

In addition to state legislative actions to promote educational achievement, states moved toward a common set of academic standards for language arts and mathematics (National Governors Association Center for Best Practices and the Council of Chief State School Officers, 2010). As of 2012, these voluntary standards had been adopted by all but five states (Ehren, Erickson, Hatch, & Ukrainetz, 2012).

Speech–Language Pathology Within NCLB and IDEA

Highly Qualified SLPs

The highly qualified provision of IDEA 2004 had implications for SLPs. Most states recognize the Master's degree as the appropriate level of educational preparation for a speech–language pathologist. However, federal regulation required only a Bachelor's degree and compliance with state standards for area preparation. This federal change opened up the possibility of clinicians with Bachelor's degrees independently providing speech–language services. In a *Federal Register* public hearing report (U.S. National Archives and Records Administration, 2006), the review panel concluded that the highest degree requirement of a Master's degree had set an unreasonable standard, leading to a shortage of SLPs in the schools. The final regulations left it to the states to determine the qualifications of SLPs.

Speech or Language Impairment as a Disability Category

Speech–language pathology services moved from the aegis of regular education to special education in 1975 with P.L. 94-142. *Speech or language impairment* was one of the eight original categories of special education. Like the other categories of special education, numbers have increased greatly since 1975. However, the way of counting children who qualify for speech–language services and the ways services can be provided are complicated.

Under federal regulation, a speech or language impairment is defined as "a communication disorder such as stuttering, impaired articulation, a language impairment, or a voice impairment that adversely affects a child's educational performance" (34 CFR 300.8.b.11 available through the electronic code of federal regulations, www.ecfr.gov).

Educational performance is composed of both academic achievement and functional performance. Adverse effect is not limited to discrepancies in age and grade performance in academic subject-matter areas but also includes oral communication (Whitmire & Eger, 2003). The presence of speaking and listening skills in state achievement standards also supports speech–language services.

What specifically constitutes a speech or language impairment falls to state jurisdiction. There is considerable variation from state to state in this matter, both in criteria and in what speech conditions are considered to adversely impact education. Apel presented a compilation of state criteria present in 1993 (Moore-Brown & Montgomery, 2001). Criteria were based on classical linguistic divisions, form-content-use divisions, or modality divisions. Severity judgments included specific error requirements, cutoff scores on norm-referenced tests, or functional ratings. Some states required particular measures, such as a norm-referenced test and a language sample, two norm-referenced tests, or locally normed measures. Some states required lower language than cognitive performance, which is called cognitive referencing.

A cognitive referencing requirement persists in some jurisdictions despite the lack of theoretical basis, empirical evidence, and federal requirements (American Speech-Language-Hearing Association [ASHA], 2002; Casby, 1992; Notari, Cole, & Mills, 1992). Barring the provision of service based on IQ-language discrepancy is based on the ideas that language is not disordered if it is similar to IQ and that IQ serves as a ceiling for language growth. This theory involves the expectation that children with greater cognitive capacity will benefit more from language intervention than children with depressed cognitive skills and that resources should not be dispensed on children with poor prognoses for improvement. This restriction serves more as a way to reduce the number of children qualifying for services than as a valid argument about treatment prognosis for developmental or compensatory intervention. Box 4.3 sets out some of the reasons and evidence against the denial of speech–language services based on cognitive referencing.

Language Impairment as a Specific Learning Disability

Difficulties with language fall under the federal disability category of *speech or language impairment*. However, there is a redundancy in that at least the language difficulties also fall within the category of *specific learning disability*, which, in the Code of Federal Regulations, involves:

> a disorder in one or more of the basic psychological processes involved in understanding or in using language, spoken or written, that may manifest itself in the imperfect ability to listen, think, speak, read, write, spell, or to do mathematical calculations. (34 C.F.R. 300.8.b.10)

Distinguishing the two categories is more a matter of conventional practice and professional territory than conceptual consistency: Reading difficulties are addressed primarily by reading or resource teachers, and spoken language difficulties are addressed primarily by SLPs. However, neither of the professionals is limited by modality, and often children are dually qualified.

Box 4.3. ***Arguments Against Cognitive Referencing for Speech–Language Services***

1. **The size of the discrepancy varies with the measures paired.** Cole, Mills, and Kelley (1994) found from 23 to 3 out of 26 children with language impairments having adequate discrepancies, depending on which language and cognitive measures were paired. This variation is due the multifaceted nature of language and cognition, along with the many ways of testing each. In addition, test construction can produce significant differences in scores, such as by having a normative sample representative of the population versus one including only typically developing children (McFadden, 1996).
2. **IQ is not a very stable indicator of intelligence in childhood.** Krassowski and Plante (1997) reviewed 75 cases of monolingual children with primary language disorders receiving language services whose records showed IQ testing three years apart. The mean performance IQ score increased significantly from the first to the second testing. Individual case analysis revealed that over 30% of the children increased 10 or more points in the full, verbal, and performance scales. These increases were far larger than the standard test error of 3 points or what would be expected as ancillary gains from language treatment.
3. **Language intervention may improve IQ scores.** IQ scores reflect how well individuals listen to questions, analyze information, and choose or formulate answers. These are modifiable abilities. For example, Kaniel, Tzuriel, Feuerstin, Ben-Shacher, and Eitan (1991) found that Ethiopian immigrants to Israel showed significantly lower intelligence test scores as compared to Israeli citizens. With brief mediations focusing on test-taking behaviors, the immigrants improved their IQ scores to levels comparable to Israeli citizens. Extended time in language intervention, where students get individualized, intensive attention, can help young children learn to learn and do better on tests.
4. **The relationship between IQ and language varies by language area.** The semantics aspects of vocabulary and information are sampled in verbal IQ tests. Syntax, pragmatics, and phonemic awareness are not. These areas of language for individuals with developmental delay may develop in advance of cognitive abilities (e.g., Curtiss, 1981). Furthermore, even if progress is slower, language development extends into adolescence for individuals with intellectual disabilities (McDuffie, Chapman, & Abbeduto, 2008).
5. **SLP intervention is about communication.** IDEA requires that all individuals be supported in developing adequate communicative means (ASHA, 2002). In addition to improving language and learning, speech–language services address compensating for or finding ways around problems, such as being a more active communicator or using sign language or AAC (augmentative and alternative communication) devices (e.g., Kangas & Lloyd, 1988). Older students with language and reading performance that has plateaued may be taught how to strategically approach difficult reading material or supplement content with audiovisual materials.

Box 4.3. (*continued*)

6. **IQ does not predict learning potential.** Children with lower IQs can make similar gains in their language and word reading development as those with higher IQs. Cole, Dale, and Mills (1990) found, for both preschoolers with cognitive skills at or below their language skills and those with cognitive skills above language, that language development accelerated compared to prior to intervention. After one year of intervention, the two groups made similar progress. For poor readers, IQ is not a good predictor of who makes the most improvement from early reading intervention (Vellutino, Scanlon, & Lyon, 2000). Nor does IQ even predict who learns the most about electricity when the science curriculum makes minimal verbal demands (Budoff, Meskin, & Harrison, 1971).

The overlap between the two eligibility categories is beneficial for children with low-average IQ scores. These children often do not have sufficient discrepancy between IQ and achievement scores to be eligible for specific learning disability. However, they can qualify for speech–language eligibility based simply on low language scores. This speech–language eligibility then allows academic support. The IDEA '04 abandonment of the discrepancy requirement for specific reading disability should reduce this need, but speech–language eligibility may still remain easier to obtain than specific learning disability given the federal emphasis on reducing numbers in the latter category and the complexity of using response to intervention (RTI) criteria.

Special Education or Related Service

Speech–language impairment can fall under one of two types of federal eligibility: as a core *special education service* or as an ancillary *related service*. Special education services deal with "specially designed instruction, at no cost to the parents, to meet the unique needs of a child with a disability" (34 CFR 300.39.a). These are the core teaching services that deliver curriculum and usually are provided by teachers with specialized qualifications. Ancillary related services are defined as those "required to assist a child with a disability to benefit from special education" (34 CFR 300.34.a). Related services include audiology, interpreting, physical therapy, occupational therapy, recreation, and counseling. The distinction is important: If a student qualifies only for a related service, he or she is not disabled under IDEA and thus is not eligible for IDEA funds.

Speech–language pathology falls under both service types. Giangreco, Prelock, and Turnbull (2010) commented that determination of which category services fall is "an aspect of IDEA that remained unclear to even some of the most knowledgeable and well-informed professionals" (p. 532). Basically, IDEA '04 only allows a child to qualify for one special education eligibility category, and speech or language impairment is the core category only if eligibility for another special education category is not present. If a child qualifies for another special education category, the speech–language category automatically becomes secondary or related regardless of the type of support provided. Since most federal disability categories include speech or language needs (e.g., autism, specific learning disability, mental retardation, hearing impairment, and traumatic brain injury), this is a common occurrence. Whitmire and Eger (2003) reported that almost all school SLPs regularly serve dual-eligible students: For example, more SLPs regularly served children with learning disabilities (92%), mental retardation (90%), and autism (83%) than stuttering (80%).

State regulations have generally followed the dual assignment provision for speech–language services. However, some states have their own specifications. Giangreco et al. (2010) report that for Rhode Island, speech–language services are only related service after age 9 years. Colorado and Indiana consider speech–language services as special education only.

For some children who could qualify for a second category, eligibility may only be solicited for speech or language impairment. For example, a child with autism may only be labeled speech–language eligible in the early grades because the SLP is fully meeting the child's specialized educational needs or because another category, such as mental retardation, is too stigmatizing. Alternately, the child may not meet score requirements for another category, such as specific learning disability. Parental wishes or local programming resources may affect decisions.

These eligibility complexities mean that federal statistics significantly undercount the number of children with speech or language impairments. Specific language impairment occurs at a rate of approximately 7% (Tomblin et al., 1997). Articulation, stuttering, and voice disorders take the numbers higher. In addition, SLP caseloads will include students with nonspecific language impairment (i.e., low-average nonverbal IQs) and communication difficulties secondary to other conditions, resulting in at least 10% of elementary grade students served. However, in 2009, for ages 6 through 11 years, the percentage of children reported for speech–language services was only 3.8% (based on IDEA Part B 2009 count of 943,689 speech–language children and 2009 federal census data of 24.3 million total children).

Other Ways of Obtaining Speech–Language Services

Children may receive speech–language services in ways other than IDEA-funded services. One possibility is through Section 504 of the Rehabilitation Act. However, services must be paid for through state or local resources. One cost-efficient way of dealing with minor speech difficulties is *speech improvement classes*. However, if class size is large, needs are heterogeneous, or service is infrequent, this service delivery approach may not be effective. With emphasis on pre-referral intervention, some states or school districts provide short-term intensive speech–language service. Such intervention may resolve minor difficulties without a referral to special education.

Individualized Education Programs: Process and Product

The IEP has been central to provision of special education and related services since 1975 through P.L. 94-142. The IEP helps ensure that students with educationally significant disabilities from ages 3 to 21 years are provided an education customized to their particular constellations of strengths and needs. The IEP is most commonly thought of as a document, but it is also the process to achieve the written product.

Remediation Prior to Referral

The first step in the IEP process is pre-referral. For a child with concerns, educators must make and document their best efforts to remediate difficulties within general education before referring for special education services. This occurs through collaborative meetings of regular and special education teachers within the school, which may be called student study teams or building intervention teams.

Pre-referral options are those that are potentially available within general education, such as changing classroom seating, increasing visual supports, developing a homework monitoring system, installing a classroom FM system, modifying the teacher's instructional style, and providing tutoring or peer study buddies. Quick and simple screenings of a number of children, conducted by a teacher or even a specialist, provide information toward determining appropriate teaching strategies. This level of assessment is considered part of regular education, so it can be conducted without parental consent.

Supportive services outside of special education, such as response to intervention (RTI), have been implemented widely. RTI typically involves administration of short periods of intense quality standardized instruction with close progress monitoring. It has the dual intention of improving overall student performance and better identifying inherent learning disabilities. There has been some increase in funding and more flexibility in fund diversion from federal special education and remedial programs (e.g., Title 1) toward RTI.

Evaluation Process

A referral for an educational evaluation can be initiated by a parent, an educator, or an outside related professional, such as a social worker or a physician. Once the referral is received, the process must move forward speedily. IDEA '04 allows a maximum of 60 days between receipt of referral by the school district and a notice of eligibility determination.

Parents are informed of their legal rights to due process at the time of the initial referral. On receipt of the referral, an IEP team is composed. At minimum, the IEP team involves the parents, one general education teacher who has been involved with the child, one relevant special education teacher, and a representative of the school district (usually the school principal). One of these or another member must be qualified to interpret the evaluation results. One team member is the *case manager* who organizes the process and ensures all proper actions are taken. If appropriate, the student can also be present. At parent and school district discretion, other individuals with knowledge or special expertise concerning the child, such as related service personnel, can be part of the team.

The educators on the IEP team review the data available before the formal evaluation is conducted. This includes the reason for referral, parental concerns as well as the results of screening, observation, and pre-referral remediation. The team is required to consider how the child's behavior may affect other children and what positive behavioral supports can be employed to alleviate this. Other considerations include English proficiency and the physical, visual, or hearing supports that may benefit the child, including Braille and American Sign Language.

The formal evaluation is then conducted. It must include multiple data sources, types of data, and environments. More than one measure must be used per area of suspected disability. Measures must be valid and reliable, administered by trained and knowledgeable personnel, and performed following the stated procedures of the measure.

Following the evaluation, an IEP meeting is set. The parents must be invited but may choose not to attend. Attempts to contact the parents or reschedule the meeting must be documented. At the meeting, each evaluator provides a summary of findings that is understandable to the parents. Recommendations are discussed and agreed upon. The recommendations come from the whole team based on the totality of the findings.

If an agreement between parents and the rest of the IEP team cannot be reached on some part of the IEP, there is a process to come to a resolution. The first step is mediation, which is a formal process aimed at achieving understanding, reconciliation, compromise, and agreement between the parties. If mediation does not result in an agreement or if parents refuse mediation, the next step is a due process hearing. All this must occur within 45 days of the initial complaint. Appeals go to the state educational agency and then, if still unresolved, to civil state or federal district court. There is a statute of limitations of two years for requesting a hearing from when the parents knew or should have known about the alleged action or situation unless the school district either misrepresented or withheld information.

The Individualized Education Program

Following the evaluation report, a written IEP document is developed. The Appendix presents a sample IEP based on the Wyoming format. Details and format vary by state. The IEP must include the evaluation elements listed in Box 4.4.

The IEP must be reviewed at least annually. It can be amended during the year without a meeting but with parental consent. Amendments can occur due to lack of progress on the stated goals, re-evaluation results, new information provided by the parents, the child's anticipated needs, or other matters. Annual goals and conditions of delivery are revised based on formal and informal progress data from the educator and parent team members. The child's eligibility status and IEP are re-evaluated at least every three years (called a *triennial*). There is more flexibility in the triennial standards and process than in the initial eligibility evaluation.

The *Present Level of Performance* is the first element of the IEP. It is a collaborative statement of the student's level of educational and functional performance, including how the child's disability affects the child's involvement and progress in the general education curriculum. This statement should address strengths, weaknesses, and learning needs. Helpful teaching information such as stimulability, learning rate, attentiveness, and behavior are included. Each need listed is translated into an instructional goal.

Functional performance relates to nonacademic routine activities of daily living appropriate to the age of the child. Functional strengths and needs are considered in the realms of social, physical, and daily living. Educational performance is typically re-

Box 4.4. ***Required Components of an Individualized Education Program***

1. The child's present level of academic achievement and functional performance
2. Measurable academic and functional annual goals
3. How progress toward meeting the goals will be measured
4. When periodic progress reports will be provided, which is at least as often as regular education parent reports
5. Special education, related services, and supplementary aids to the child or to school personnel
6. Extent to which the child will not participate with nondisabled children in regular class activities
7. Accommodations on statewide and district-wide assessments or an explanation of why the child cannot participate in regular assessments and the alternate assessment selected
8. Projected date for the beginning of the services and modifications and the anticipated frequency, location, and duration of those services and modifications

Note: Based on 34 C.F.R. 300.320.

ported across the areas of reading, math, writing, and speech–language. Emotional and behavioral needs are also considered. The needs are described in terms of current skills and performance levels and expected levels based on state standards and benchmarks.

The Present Level of Performance statement should not repeat the evaluation report but rather be a summary of what is directly relevant to the child's educational plan. This is primarily descriptive data that can be used as baseline referents for learning goals. Test scores may be included if they are directly linked to academic or functional learning needs and goals.

The heart of the IEP is the *Annual Goals* section. Each goal must be linked to a need stated in the Present Level of Performance section. Each goal is stated in a measurable manner, but the format is not specified in federal regulation. Typical components are listed in Box 4.5. In addition, the goal may be linked to a particular achievement standard by number or code. The context in which the behavior is demonstrated should be the least restrictive possible. Ideally, this is within the regular classroom and curriculum. However, the stated context should match where performance will actually be measured. For example, if performance will be measured in the speech room, the least restrictive version of this would be in naturalistic activities, such as in peer-peer conversation, retelling a storybook, or presenting an oral report.

The SLP is primarily responsible for the speech–language goals but could be responsible for reading or writing goals. One goal may involve multiple skills with criteria, conditions, and contexts, or multiple goals may each address individual skills (see the speech–language and math goals in the Appendix IEP). A change with IDEA '04 was the

Box 4.5. ***Typical Components of an IEP Annual Goal***

1. Time frame to achieve the goal, not exceeding one academic year
2. Conditions required to achieve the goal, such as within a structured task or with support
3. Target behavior stated in observable terms
4. Baseline data for the target behavior
5. Criteria that the student must demonstrate to show goal achievement
6. Context in which the student will demonstrate the behavior

abandonment of short-term objectives for most IEPs. Short-term objectives continue to be required for children with severe disabilities taking alternate assessments aligned to alternate achievement standards.

The IEP must list the special education, related services, supplementary aids and procedures, assistive technology, and supports for school personnel. These include the *least restrictive environment* in which the services are deemed appropriate (regular classroom, resource room, special classroom, special school, or home instruction). Classroom modifications are stated. In addition to instructional changes, these include specialized items such as Braille machines, large print books, or interpreters. *Testing modifications*, such as increased testing time, verbally presented questions, or pointing to responses, are noted. These modifications should be present for daily classroom teaching and evaluation activities as well as formal testing situations. If the child will not participate in statewide and district-wide assessments, the *alternate assessment plan* is stated.

The date of initiation of services, transportation needs, duration, and frequency of the services are listed. The IEP may be in force over the entire 12-month year, with summer services provided (called *Extended Service Year* or ESY). Typically, service frequency is stated per week, but other more flexible periods (e.g., total time per month) can be used.

There must be an explanation of the time not spent in regular education. This may be stated as a percentage or as specific classes not attended. IDEA '04 reversed the IDEA '90 requirement of listing the amount of contact with regular education peers. This is an important distinction, reflecting the philosophy that all children belong in the regular classroom and are only removed as far as necessary to provide an appropriate education rather than children with disabilities belonging in a separated condition unless their fitness for the regular classroom is demonstrated.

Finally, the IEP must provide transition plans between preschool and elementary as well as between elementary and secondary grades. At 16 years of age, the IEP must include measurable postsecondary goals related to training, education, employment, and independent living. For students with intellectual disabilities, this could include taking public transportation, ordering in a restaurant, and completing tasks in a supportive workplace. For students with specific learning disabilities, this could include completing job applications, following procedure manuals, and explaining policies to customers. Transition services needed to reach those goals, such as remedial community college classes, are also included.

A Peek at Our Neighbor to the North

This section provides a brief overview of legislative requirements in Canada. Readers may find themselves working north of the border or may simply learn from the contrast of two sovereign systems. The preparation for and practice of speech–language pathology is similar in Canada and the United States. The two national associations, Speech–Language and Audiology Canada (SAC) and ASHA, have agreements that recognize each entity's professional certification standards.

The System of Authority and Funding

Canada and the United States have similar educational systems. In both countries, there are constitutional, legislative, and regulatory requirements for the assurance and conduct of free and universal public primary and secondary education. Speech and language impairments qualify children for special education and SLPs serve school-age children. Like with individual states, the 10 individual provinces and three territories (collectively known as *jurisdictions*) vary in how education is conducted and funded. However, there are some notable distinctions between the two countries.

A significant difference is in the organization of authority for education. In the United States, education is considered to be a state right, but the federal government maintains centralized power and a strong guiding hand. In contrast, in Canada there is no federal department of education. Instead, Canada's Constitution Act of 1867 assigned authority and responsibility exclusively to the provinces. The only federal requirements are that educational practices minimally confirm to the human rights (called civil rights in the U.S.) specified in the Constitution Act of 1867 and the 1985 Canadian Charter of Rights and Freedoms (Bowlby, Peters, & Mackinnon, 2010). In addition to fundamental rights, these documents provide certain linguistic and religious guarantees. As a result, there are significant differences in curriculum, assessment, and accountability policies among provinces and territories in regular and special education (to explore education patterns across Canada, see http://www.cmec.ca).

Financial support of education comes from local property taxes and provincial funding. Provincial and territorial regulations set the level of funding for each school board, based on factors such as the number of students, special needs, and location. Special education is provincially funded, but some additional support comes through federal equalization payments.

Equalization is the system by which the Government of Canada remediates fiscal disparities among provinces (see http://www.fin.gc.ca/fedprov/eqp-eng.asp). Equalization payments enable less prosperous provincial governments to provide public services at reasonably comparable levels to those in other provinces, with comparable levels of taxation. More prosperous provinces contribute funds to support these equalization payments. Equalization payments are unconditional, allowing provinces and territories to determine how best to use the funds.

Canada is constitutionally bilingual in French and English. Constitutional guarantees address public provision of minority language instruction where numbers render it reasonable. As a result, French schools operate in English-speaking parts of Canada and English schools in French-speaking parts. French schools are offered primarily as "immersion" schools, where francophone children maintain their native tongue and other children gain conversational and academic fluency in French. The major French-speaking area of Canada is the province of Quebec. In Quebec, English immersion is not encouraged. Rather, in an effort to maintain the dominance of French in the province, there are restrictions on who can attend the English system schools.

Constitutional guarantees also allow denominational or religion-based education, resulting in dual publicly funded educational systems in three provinces and a territory. In these jurisdictions, in addition to a nondenominational "public" school board, there are Catholic or Protestant "separate" school boards in areas where sizeable minorities desire their own system of education. These separate systems are supported by property taxes and provincial funds.

Speech–Language Pathology in Canadian Schools

Although all Canadian children have the right to free and appropriate education, SLP services are not viewed as central to the educational mission or mandated in the schools. Where they are present, there may not be comprehensive procedures for identifying children nor strict eligibility requirements. IEP teams may use judgment in determining student need and prioritizing students for services. All of this results in considerable variation in presence and density of SLP services.

SLPs are typically assigned on a population basis, with one SLP per 1,500–2,000 students. Many Canadian SLPs deal with caseloads of 100 or more, spread across eight or more schools. A caseload report by Canadian Association of Speech–Language Pathologists and Audiologists (2003) showed a median monthly caseload of 58 and a mean monthly caseload of 65. Caseloads of 75 or more were reported by 39% of school SLPs, often with additional waitlists.

SLP services can fall under provincial ministry of health or ministry of education. For example, in British Columbia, SLPs are employed by school boards under the Ministry of Education. In Alberta, SLPs are employed by community health centers under the Ministry of Health. Services in Alberta are provided in the centers or by the SLPs traveling to schools and homes. Referrals for speech–language evaluation require input from a teacher for a language issue, but the service is considered essentially a health rather than an educational issue. Ontario has a combined approach, where language issues fall under the Ministry of Education and school board responsibility, voice and resonance fall under the Ministry of Health, and articulation, fluency, and nonspeech communication fall under both. There is a preference for only one SLP to work with a child, so mixed conditions are assigned to one Ontario ministry.

Canadian Special Education Law

Each province and territory has its own special education laws and mandates, but the basic structures and requirements are similar (Bowlby et al., 2010). Ontario, the most populous province and site of the national capital, is presented as an example of special education. Bowlby et al. and the website of the Ministry of Education of Ontario (http://www.edu.gov.on.ca/eng/) are the sources for this brief description. Ontario is located north of the Great Lakes. It has nondenominational and denominational public education systems and many French-English bilingual speakers.

Canadian legal provisions for special education are more recent than in the United States: For Ontario, the landmark legislation was Bill 82 in 1980. This law amended the Education Act to incorporate requirements that exceptional students (i.e., students with disabilities) be identified and provided special education placements for appropriate programs and services. Funding for special education comes from the provincial Ministry of Education.

Eligibility categories for disabilities are similar to those in the United States. However, speech or language impairment is split into two separate eligibility categories in Ontario. This might provide greater clarity concerning services needed but seems not to: The language category includes dysfluency, voice, and articulation, while the speech category is "a disorder in language formulation" (Bowlby et al., 2010, p. 51), as well as an impairment in articulation, rhythm, and stress. The learning disability category in Ontario, like in the United States, is inclusive of oral language. It involves difficulties in the "proper use of spoken language or the symbols of communication" in academic and social situations (Bowlby et al., 2010, p. 51). It includes developmental aphasia, which is an old term for specific language impairment.

Each school board must have a ministry-approved special education plan and a Special Education Advisory Committee (SEAC), consisting of representatives of parent advocate groups, interests of First Nation students (called Native Americans in the U.S.), and board trustees. School boards are required to have at least one Identification, Placement, and Review Committee (IPRC). School boards may choose to have multiple IPRCs responsible for groupings of schools or particular disabilities, but unlike IEP teams, these are not based in each school. The IPRC is made up of three or more members: a principal, a supervisory officer from that school board, and a supervisory officer from another school board. Teachers and other special education professionals may be present, but there is no requirement that any IPRC member have direct knowledge of the student in question. The IPRC, in consultation with parents, determines whether a student is exceptional, provides a placement decision, and reviews the placement at least annually. The IPRC recommends special education programs and services to the child's school to assist in development of the IEP. Parental consent is required for the eligibility and placement decision. Appeals result in a second IPRC meeting, and then they go on to a special education appeal board then to a provincial tribunal before moving into the courts.

Educational placements are provided on a continuum from regular classrooms with resource support to self-contained classrooms to provincially operated residential schools. Similar to the United States, a movement toward inclusive services occurred in the 1980s. However, tribunal and judicial decisions heavily favored segregated over integrated placements as the most appropriate settings, particularly for children with severe disabilities (Bowlby et al., 2010). Bill 82 specifically required the option of segregated classes for students with intellectual disabilities.

Children with disabilities necessitating special education are provided IEPs (or Individual Program Plan, IPP in some jurisdictions). IEPs are developed at the school level. The principal is the named authority, responsible for developing the IEP in consultation with the parent. The principal oversees a Development Team who, collectively, has knowledge of the provincial curriculum, the student, and special education strategies and resources. The components of an IEP or IPP are similar to those in the United States. Some differences for Ontario IEPs are that, if the student is aiming for grade-level curricular expectations, specific annual goals are not required, report card grades (noting any testing modifications) can be used to measure achievement, and short-term objectives are listed in addition to annual goals.

In contrast to the United States, Ontario IEPs are not closely tied to disability status. IEPs are always issued following an IPRC statement of eligibility and placement. However, they may also be issued for children who are awaiting IPRC decisions. IEPs may be formulated without going through the IPRC process. Many Ontario school boards provide such non-IPRC IEPs, despite having to meet the cost of these special services locally.

Conclusion

This chapter reviewed the history of special education law. The civil rights movement contributed to recognition of the rights of children with disabilities to free, appropriate public education. Special education and the requirement of the IEP came into force with the federal legislation of the Education for All Handicapped Children Act (P.L. 94-142) in 1975. IEPs currently have a strong emphasis on the provision of a least restrictive environment for services and the accommodations or modifications needed for students to accomplish statewide and district-wide achievement assessments. With P.L. 94-142, SLPs moved from regular to special education to serve the eligibility category of speech or language impairment. Speech or language impairment is a complicated eligibility category with overlap with other eligibility categories and multiple avenues of service. The 1990 laws of IDEA and ADA were other important legislative actions that further assured the rights of all individuals with disabilities in their schooling and elsewhere. NCLB of 2001 and IDEA '04 were intended to improve the education of all children through strict accountability and performance requirements, along with supplementary scientifically based instructional support. In Canada, similar protective educational legislation is present, but special education is fully a provincial responsibility. There is much more variability in requirements for SLP services, but in sum, the systems in the two countries are more similar than different.

References

Americans With Disabilities Act of 1990, 42 U.S.C. § 12101 *et seq.* (1990) (P.L. 101-336)

Americans With Disabilities Act of 1990, 42 U.S.C. § 12101 *et seq.* (amended 2008) (P.L. 110-325)

American Psychological Association. (2009). *Publication manual of the American Psychological Association* (6th ed.). Washington, DC: Author.

American Speech-Language-Hearing Association (2002). *Access to communication services and supports: Concerns regarding the application of restrictive "eligibility" policies* [Technical report]. Rockville, MD: Author. Retrieved from www.asha.org/policy

Bowlby, B., Peters, C., & Mackinnon, M. (2010). *An educator's guide to special education law* (2nd ed.). Aurora, Ontario: Canada Law Book.

Budoff, M., Meskin, J., & Harrison, R. G. (1971). An educational test of the learning potential hypothesis. *American Journal of Mental Deficiency, 76*, 159–169.

Canadian Association of Speech–Language Pathologists and Audiologists (2003). *2003 caseload guidelines survey: Final report.* Ottawa, Ontario, Canada: Author.

Casby, M. W. (1992). Cognitive hypothesis and its influence on speech–language services in schools. *Language, Speech, and Hearing Services in Schools, 23*, 198–202.

Catts, H. W., Kamhi, A. G., & Adloff, S. (2012). Defining and classifying reading disabilities. In H. W. Catts & A. G. Kamhi (Eds.), *Language and reading disabilities* (3rd ed., pp. 45–76). Boston, MA: Allyn & Bacon.

Council for Exceptional Children (2007). *Full funding for IDEA: It's a guarantee, not just a promise.* Arlington, VA: Author.

Code of Federal Regulations. Title 34 Education, 300–399 Office of Special Education and Rehabilitative Services, Department of Education. Retrieved from http://www.ecfr.gov/cgi-bin/ECFR?page=browse

Cole, K. N., Dale, P. S., & Mills, P. E. (1990). Defining language delay in young children by cognitive referencing: Are we saying more than we know? *Applied Psycholinguistics, 11*, 291–302.

Cole, K. N., Mills, P. E., & Kelley, D. (1994). Agreement of assessment profiles used in cognitive referencing. *Language, Speech, and Hearing Services in Schools, 25*, 25–31.

Curtiss, S. (1981). Dissociations between language and cognition: Cases and implications. *Journal of Autism and Developmental Disorders, 11*, 15–30.

Duchan, J. F. (2010). The early years of language, speech, and hearing services in U.S. schools. *Language, Speech, and Hearing Services in Schools, 41*, 152–160.

Education for All Handicapped Children Act of 1975, 20 U.S.C. § 1400 *et seq.* (1975) (P.L. 94-142)

Education for All Handicapped Children Act of 1975, 20 U.S.C. § 1400 *et seq.* (amended 1986) (P.L. 99-457)

Ehren, B., Erickson, K., Hatch, P., & Ukrainetz, T. A. (2012, November). *SLPs—At the core of the Common Core State Standards.* Panel Presentation, ASHA Convention, Atlanta, GA.

Frankenberger. W., & Harper, J. (1988). States' definitions and procedures for identifying children with mental retardation: Comparison of 1981–1982 and 1985–1986 guidelines. *Mental Retardation, 26*, 133–136.

Giangreco, M. F., Prelock, P. A., & Turnbull, H. R. (2010). An issue hiding in plain sight: When are speech–language pathologists special educators rather than related services providers? *Language, Speech, and Hearing Services in Schools, 41*, 531–538.

Gravani, E. H. (2007). Educational history and legal landmarks. In E. H. Gravani & J. Meyer, J. (Eds.), *Speech, language, and hearing programs in schools: A guide for students and practitioners* (pp. 3–22). Austin, TX: PRO-ED.

Individuals With Disabilities Education Act of 1990, 20 U.S.C. § 1400 *et seq.* (1990) (P.L. 101-476)

Kangas, K., & Lloyd, L. (1988). Early cognitive skills prerequisites to augmentative and alternative communication use: What are we waiting for? *Augmentative and Alternative Communication, 4*, 211–221.

Kaniel, S., Tzuriel, D., Feuerstein, R., Ben-Shacher, N., & Eitan, T. (1991). Dynamic assessment: Learning and transfer abilities of Ethiopian immigrants to Israel. In R. Feuerstein, P. Klein, & A. Tannenbaum (Eds.), *Mediated learning experience* (pp. 179–209). London, England: Freund.

Katz, M. S. (1976). *A history of compulsory education laws.* Bloomington, IA: Phi Delta Kappa Educational Foundation.

Krassowski, E., & Plante, E. (1997). IQ variability of children with SLI: Implications for use of cognitive referencing in determining SLI. *Journal of Communication Disorders, 30*, 1–9.

McDuffie, A., Chapman, R. S., Abbeduto, L. (2008). Language profiles of adolescents and young adults with Down syndrome and Fragile X syndrome. In J. E. Roberts, R. S. Chapman, & S. F. Warren (Eds.), *Speech and language development and intervention in Down syndrome and Fragile X syndrome* (pp. 117–142). Baltimore, MD: Brookes.

McFadden, T. U. (1996). Creating language impairments in typically achieving children: The pitfalls of "normal" normative sampling. *Language, Speech, and Hearing Services in Schools, 27*, 3–9.

Moore-Brown, B. J., & Montgomery, J. K. (2001). *Making a difference for America's children: Speech–language pathologists in public schools.* Austin, TX: PRO-ED.

National Governors Association Center for Best Practices and Council of Chief State School Officers (2010). *Common core state standards for English language arts & literacy in history/social studies, science, and technical subjects.* Washington, DC: Author. Retrieved from http://www.corestandards.org/

No Child Left Behind Act of 2001, 20 U.S.C. 70 § 6301 *et seq.* (2002) (P.L. 97-110)

Notari, A. R., Cole, K. N., & Mills, P. E. (1992). Cognitive referencing: The (non)relationship between theory and application. *Topics in Early Childhood Special Education, 11*, 22–38.

Robinson, N. M., & Robinson, H. B. (1976). *The mentally retarded child* (2nd ed.). New York, NY: McGraw-Hill.

Schraeder, T. (2008). *A guide to school services in speech–language pathology.* San Diego, CA: Plural.

Siegel, G. M. (1987). The limits of science in communication disorders. *Journal of Speech and Hearing Disorders, 52,* 306–312.

Tomblin, J. B., Records, N. L., Buckwalter, P., Zhang, X., Smith, E., & O'Brien, M. (1997). Prevalence of specific language impairment in kindergarten children. *Journal of Speech, Language, and Hearing Research, 40,* 1245–1260.

U.S. Department of Education. (n.d.). *ESEA flexibility state-by-state implementation timeline chart.* Retrieved from http://www2.ed.gov/policy/elsec/guid/esea-flexibility

U.S. Department of Education. (2012). *ESEA flexibility.* Retrieved from http://www2.ed.gov/policy/elsec/guid/esea-flexibility

U.S. Department of Education Office of Special Education and Rehabilitative Services. (2002). *A new era: Revitalizing special education for children and their families.* Washington, DC: Author. Retrieved from http: www.ed.gov/pubs/edpubs.html

U.S. Department of Education Office of Special Education and Rehabilitative Services. (2007). *Final regulations on modified academic achievement summary.* Retrieved from http://www2.ed.gov/print/policy/speced/guid/modachieve-summary.html

U.S. National Archives and Records Administration. (2006). Part II: Dept. of Education, 34 CFR Parts 300 and 301, Assistance to states for the education of children with disabilities and preschool grants for children with disabilities: Final rule. *Federal Register, 71* (155).

Vellutino, F. R., Scanlon, D. M., Lyon, G. R. (2000). Differentiating between difficult-to-remediate and readily remediated poor readers: More evidence against the IQ-achievement discrepancy definition of reading disability. *Journal of Learning Disabilities, 33,* 223–238.

Weiner, R. (1985). *P.L. 94-142: Impact on the schools.* Arlington, VA: Capitol.

Whitmire, K. A., & Eger, D. L. (June, 2003). *Issue brief on personnel preparation and credentialing in speech–language pathology.* Gainseville: University of Florida, Center on Personnel Studies in Special Education.

World Health Organization. (1980). *International classification of impairments, disabilities, and handicaps.* Geneva, Switzerland: Author.

World Health Organization. (2002). *World health report 2002: Reducing risks, promoting health life.* Geneva, Switzerland: Author.

Appendix: Sample IEP

Individualized Education Program
34 C.F.R. 300.320–300.324

School District / Public Agency: Wyoming County School District 1
Name of Student: Jane Doe
WISER ID: 12341234 **DOB:** 01/01/2000 **GRADE:** 04
Date of IEP Meeting: 01/01/2010
Date of last IEP Meeting: 01/01/2009 **Due Date of 3-Year Reevaluation:** 01/01/2012
Disability Category: Learning Disability

STRENGTHS, EDUCATIONAL CONCERNS, and PREFERENCES/INTERESTS

Student's Perspective

Strengths/Interests:

Jane told Ms. White that she's good at (in this order): reading (said with a big smile), math, being creative in writing, Exploration because she helps her group, music, P.E., and shark research. Jane is happy about how she is doing in school. She really likes anything with horses.

Parent's Perspective

Strengths:

Jane is taking ownership for her behavior. Her mother has her read every night. Jane is seeing progress in herself.

Educational Concerns:

Basic math facts are hard, as is being organized. Her mother wanted to know if she had more homework than Jane was remembering to tell her.

School's Perspective

Strengths:

Jane is very positive and has a sunny outlook. She is improving a lot. Jane tries really hard and doesn't give up easily. She is taking responsibility for her behavior. She is kind and wants to help others. She is reading now at grade level.

Educational Concerns:

Writing is difficult for Jane—she can get her thoughts down on paper, but not in an organized manner. Math facts are difficult—she relies on manipulatives to work problems. Jane needs a lot of 1:1 support to complete a task, especially in writing. Jane has a hard time letting go when social situations get tense. She still needs adult attention.

CONSIDERATION OF SPECIAL FACTORS

34 C.F.R. 300.324(a)(2). Any item checked "YES" must be addressed in the IEP.

	YES	NO
Does the student's behavior impede his/her learning or the learning of others?		X
Does the student have communication needs, or is the student deaf or hard of hearing?		X
Does the student need instruction in an alternate communication mode?		X
Is the student blind or visually impaired?		X
Does the student require orientation and mobility training?		X
Does the student require instruction in the use of Braille?		X
Does the student require assistive technology devices or services?		X
Has the student been determined to be Limited English Proficient?		X

PRESENT LEVELS OF ACADEMIC ACHIEVEMENT AND FUNCTIONAL PERFORMANCE

Describe the child's present levels of academic achievement and functional performance across services and settings, including special education, regular education, and interventions.

____ **Preschool Student:** In relation to participation in appropriate activities engaged in by nondisabled students.

_X_ **School-Age Student:** In relation to involvement and progress in the general education curriculum engaged in by nondisabled students.

Special Education, March White, Reading:
For oral reading fluency (rate), using Aimsweb
Fall: 57 wcpm
Winter: 107 wcpm/1 error
For comprehension, using MAZE
Fall: 9 words correct
Winter: 15 words correct
Developmental Reading Assessment (DRA)
Fall: Level 34, mid-3rd grade reading level
Winter: Level 40, 4th grade reading level
Since the fall, Jane has been in a 1:1 reading group. Due to her improvements she recently moved to a 1:3 reading group. The new reading group uses both guided literature and Read Naturally to increase comprehension and fluency at the student's instructional level. Jane volunteers to read in small groups and class. Her extra practice at home is helping her at school.

Special Education, March White, Math:
Since the fall, with parent permission, Jane has been in the regular classroom with pull-out for special education support. Math is not easy for her and she often has misconceptions but she is making progress. Jane was assessed with Add-Vantage in the fall and the winter. This helped match instruction to just where she is in math.

Special Education, March White, Writing:
Jane receives special education support in the classroom for writing. This year Jane has learned keyboarding. This allows her to compose stories on the computer and edit them in a more efficient manner than writing/composing on paper. Learning to compose a story with a beginning, middle, end and supporting details has been difficult for Jane. She is improving but still needs adult support for composing and editing.

Speech/Language, April Black, CCC-SLP:
Jane has been working on improving narrative discourse and vocabulary skills. After a story has been read aloud to her, she has retold the story using story grammar elements with 78% accuracy and targeted vocabulary with 55% accuracy. She has defined targeted vocabulary with 55% accuracy and used these words in sentences with 84% accuracy. These accuracy levels reflect some cueing and prompting by the clinician.

Regular Education, May Blue, 4/5th Grade Teacher:
I'm pleased to say we're seeing a lot of growth in Jane's academic work this year. Her reading continues to get better and she always has her hand up in class when I ask for volunteers to read. I think that a great part of her growth is due to her reading at home.

Jane has been a real champ in learning to keyboard this fall. She got so excited when she passed test after test. Now her keyboarding is quite independent. In math she tries hard and is making good gains, but she still struggles with some of the concepts.

The area I am most concerned about is Jane's writing. She tends to write whatever comes to mind and she needs 1:1 guidance to help her stick to the topic. Her shark story, for which the whole class received a lot of direction, and that she worked diligently on, in the end did not follow the assignment criteria. Jane's attention wanders when we are teaching whole class. I will be sure she understands the criteria before she begins working on writing assignments.

Socially, Jane is doing well with other students. She worked well with her Exploration group and was on task and tried her best on assignments. When she notices someone is sad, she is the first one there. If she has difficulty with another student, she will talk to them or write them a note to try to work things out. She doesn't get stuck on issues, but instead moves on in a positive way.

One marvelous attribute is Jane's willingness to work hard at whatever she takes on. She approaches everything with enthusiasm and a "can do" attitude. I am very pleased with Jane's progress. With her family support, she has come a long way and will continue to grow.

Counseling Report, June Green, Outside Counselor:
Jane has had support as an anxiety-related student. The aim is to reduce the anxiety that arises when she is working with other students through a reflective approach, with models and practice. Continued counseling at a reduced amount of time is recommended.

Jane has progressed a lot. She likes people and wants to interact with other students. Jane has a good family and teacher support system that has helped her to work through her anxiety. She is improving at seeing other people's feelings and dealing with the other students. She still needs to improve on how she reacts to what is said to her at the time. Once Jane is able to put the event into words, she can deal with it better.

EXTENDED SCHOOL YEAR

34 C.F.R. 300.106
Are Extended School Year (ESY) services necessary for the student to receive FAPE, considering the student's rate of progress and the effect an interruption in programming will have on that rate of progress, or the degree of regression in current levels of functioning that may occur as a result of an interruption in programming?

YES _____ NO __X__ If yes, indicate the goals to be implemented during ESY and the amount, frequency, location, and duration of services in the services section.

ESY services must be addressed at least annually. Will ESY be addressed at a future meeting?

YES _____ NO __X__ If yes, specify date: __________

If necessary in order to receive FAPE as determined by the IEP team, ESY services must be available beyond regular school hours and during any school breaks.

MEASURABLE ANNUAL GOALS

- A statement of measurable annual goals, including academic and functional goals, designed to: meet the student's needs that result from the student's disability to enable the student to be involved in and make progress in the general education curriculum; and to meet each of the student's other educational needs that result from the student's disability
- Each goal must include a baseline, target, and method of measurement
- Benchmarks or short-term objectives and time frames are required only for students that will take alternate statewide or district-wide assessment(s)

MEASURABLE ANNUAL GOAL NUMBER __1__

SPEECH-LANGUAGE: ESY implementation? N

By 2/8/2011, when discussing a narrative or expository book, Jane will improve narrative, expository, and vocabulary skills by: (a) defining and using targeted vocabulary words and story grammar elements while retelling a story, improving from 57% accuracy to 80% accuracy, and (b) summarizing main ideas and details from expository texts, improving from 0% accuracy to 80% accuracy, as measured by SLP data collection sheets.

Periodic Reports of Progress Toward Meeting the Annual Goal*

**Same progress report present for each annual goal, but not included in this sample IEP.* Progress must be quantified by the method of measurement specified in the goal. Periodic reports must coincide with the district or public agency regular reporting schedule.

DATE	02/19/10	06/02/10	11/12/10
DATA TO SUPPORT MEASURABLE PROGRESS	68% accuracy to 90% accuracy	Defines target vocabulary—87%, includes story grammar elements—78%, identifies details—90%, main idea—63%	Vocabulary—80%, story grammar elements in retell—80%, main ideas—55%, details—70%

DATE	02/19/10	06/02/10	11/12/10
NARRATIVE TO DESCRIBE PROGRESS	Jane used story grammar elements and targeted vocabulary in her story retells with 68% accuracy, defined targeted vocabulary words with 69% accuracy, used them in sentences with 81% accuracy, identified main ideas with 63% accuracy, identified details with 9% accuracy.	Jane is successful in identifying details in expository texts. She is improving in integrating details into one coherent main idea but needs more practice. She improved with vocabulary definitions and story retelling. She needs more practice with organizing her thoughts and including all ideas.	Jane's narrative and vocabulary skills have improved to the point that maintenance will become the focus. She continues to need support with expository activities. She is enthusiastic and uses good work effort.
STAFF NAME	AB	AB	AB

MEASURABLE ANNUAL GOAL NUMBER 2

MATH, Multiplication: ESY implementation? N

By 2/8/2011, when given a sheet of multiplication facts and one minute to work, Jane will correctly solve the problems increasing from 40% accuracy to 90% accuracy as measured by classroom-based assessments.

MEASURABLE ANNUAL GOAL NUMBER 3

MATH, Subtraction: ESY implementation? N

By 2/8/2011, when given a sheet of subtraction problems and two minutes to work, Jane will use math facts to 30 to solve them, improving from 20% accuracy to 50% accuracy as measured by curriculum-based data.

MEASURABLE ANNUAL GOAL NUMBER 4

MATH, Addition: ESY implementation? N

By 2/8/2011, when given an additional sheet of problems to 30 and two minutes to work, Jane will use math facts to solve them, improving from 30% accuracy to 90% accuracy, as measured by curriculum-based data.

MEASURABLE ANNUAL GOAL NUMBER 5

WRITING: ESY implementation? N

By 2/8/2011, when given a writing prompt, Jane will write a 4-sentence paragraph that includes a topic sentence, 2 detail sentences, a conclusion sentence; and will use proper conventions increasing from a rubric score of 1 to a rubric score of 2, as measured by classroom writing rubrics.

MEASURABLE ANNUAL GOAL NUMBER 6

READING, Rate: ESY implementation? N

By 2/8/2011, when given a reading passage at her instructional level, beginning fifth grade, Jane will increase her words per minute from 115 to 120 words correct per minute, as measured by curriculum-based measurements.

MEASURABLE ANNUAL GOAL NUMBER 7

READING, Comprehension: ESY implementation? N

By 2/8/2011, when given reading materials at her instructional level—beginning fifth grade—Jane will answer comprehension questions maintaining at least 8/10 correct, as measured by classroom assessments.

MEASURABLE ANNUAL GOAL NUMBER 8

COUNSELING: ESY implementation? N

By 2/8/11, Jane will independently respond with appropriate strategies to social situations with peers and adults, improving from 10% of the time to 50% of the time, as based on counselor reports and teacher reports.

PROGRAMS AND SERVICES

A. SPECIAL EDUCATION SERVICES

34 CFR 300.39 A statement of the special education, related services, supplementary aids and services, based on peer-reviewed research to the extent practicable, to be provided to the student, or on behalf of the student, and a statement of the program modifications or supports for school personnel that will be provided to enable the student:

- To advance appropriately toward attaining the annual goals.
- To be involved in and make progress in the general education curriculum and to participate in extracurricular and other nonacademic activities.
- To be educated and participate with other students with disabilities and non-disabled students

Special Education	Frequency	Duration (Amount)	Location	Projected Start Date
Area of Specialized Instruction: Math	4x/week	240 min/ week	Reg Ed Rm/Sp Ed Rm	1/1/10
Area of Specialized Instruction: Reading	5x/week	250 min/ week	Reg Ed Rm/Sp Ed Rm	1/1/10
Area of Specialized Instruction:				
Postsecondary Transition Services:				
ESY Services:				
Speech–Language Pathology (Primary disability)				
Physical Education				
Vocational Education				
Travel Training				

B. RELATED SERVICES

Necessary to benefit from special education

Related Service ___N/A	Frequency	Duration (Amount)	Location	Projected Start Date
Audiology (hearing aid checks and external checks of surgically implanted devices)				
Counseling Services				
Educational Interpreting Services				
Occupational Therapy				
Orientation and Mobility				
Parent Counseling and Training				
Physical Therapy				
Psychological Services				
Recreation				
School Health Services				
School Nurse Services				
School Social Work Services				
Speech–Language Pathology (For students with other primary disability)	2x/week	60 min/ week	Speech Room	1/1/2010
Transportation				
Other (specify) Outside Counselor	1x/week	30 min/ week	Outside School	1/1/2010

C. SUPPLEMENTARY AIDS AND SERVICES

Accommodations, aids, services, assistive technology, and other supports that are provided to avoid removing the student from regular education classes, other education-related settings, and extracurricular and nonacademic settings.

Supplementary Aids and Services ___N/A	Frequency	Duration	Location	Start Date
Repetition of directions Scaffolding of assignments	Daily	All sub areas	All locations	1/1/10
Clarification of directions Adult support	Daily 5x/week	All sub areas 300 min/week	All locations	1/1/10
Explain materials in a variety of ways Adult support for organization	Daily	All sub areas	All locations	1/1/10
Self-talk through various academic strategies to complete assignments and tests	Daily	All sub areas	All locations	1/1/10
Directions, assignments, tests broken into smaller steps	Daily	All sub areas	All locations	1/1/10
Reduce math homework (length and assignment)	Daily	All sub areas	All locations	1/1/10

D. PROGRAM MODIFICATIONS AND SUPPORTS FOR SCHOOL PERSONNEL

Modifications to enable the student to advance appropriately toward attaining the annual goals, be involved and make progress in the general education curriculum, and participate in extracurricular and nonacademic activities.

Program Modifications: N/A

LEAST RESTRICTIVE ENVIRONMENT

A student with a disability shall be removed from the regular education environment only if the nature or severity of the disability is such that education in regular classes with the use of supplementary aids and services cannot be achieved satisfactorily.
34 CFR 300.114 through 300.117

	YES	NO
Educational placement is based on the student's IEP.	X	
Removal from regular environment is necessary based on nature or severity of disability, not needed for modifications in general curriculum.	X	
Educational placement is as close as possible to the student's home.	X	
Educational placement is in the school that the student would attend if he/she did not have a disability.	X	
IEP team considered any potential harmful effect of the educational placement on the student or the quality of needed services.	X	
Student has the opportunity to participate in extracurricular and nonacademic activities with nondisabled students.	X	

Considering Sections A through D and the questions above, justify removal of the student from the regular education environment: Jane is removed from the regular education environment for speech therapy. This will allow her to receive intensive instruction and master her goals.

PARTICIPATION IN STATE- AND DISTRICT-WIDE ASSESSMENTS

Determine how the student will participate in state and district-wide assessments consistent with 34 CFR 300.320(a)(6).

____ N/A (check if student is in preschool)
____ Student is in a grade where state assessments are not given.
____ Student is in a grade where district-wide assessments are not given.

Participation Without Accommodations ____ N/A

____ The IEP team has determined the student will participate in the following assessments without test accommodations. (check all that apply)
____ PAWS State General Assessment
____ District-wide Assessment(s)________________________

Participation With Accommodations ____ **N/A**

_X_ The IEP team has determined the student will participate in the following assessments with test accommodations. Selection of test accommodations for the student must be made in accordance with the identified standard accommodations for each assessment given. (check all that apply) Attach a list of allowable accommodations.

_X_ PAWS State General Assessment

____ District-wide Assessment(s)________________

Participation in Alternate Assessments _X_ **N/A**

____ The IEP team has determined the student will take an alternate assessment consistent with 34 C.F.R. 300.320(a)(6)(ii). The student will participate in:

____ PAWS Alternate State Assessment

____ Alternate District-wide Assessment(s) ____________________________

If alternate assessment participation checked, explain why. Guidelines for Participation in Wyoming's Alternate Assessment for Students with Significant Cognitive Disabilities must be utilized for this determination.

State- and District-Wide Assessment Test Accommodations

Selected for this student from a list of approved accommodations.

PRESENTATION ACCOMMODATIONS

#10. A certified staff member access assistant reads directions word-for-word exactly as written in Reading, Writing, Mathematics, and Science Tests. It is recommended that one reader be provided for each individual student.

#11. A certified staff member or access assistant reads and can re-read test questions word-for-word exactly as written in Writing, Mathematics, and Science Tests. Readers may not clarify, interpret, define word meanings, elaborate, or provide assistance to students. Readers need to be familiar with the terminology and symbols specific to the content. It is recommended that one reader be provided for each individual student. Reading of test questions and reading passages is not allowed on the Reading test.

#12. Student may ask for clarification of directions (not test questions or answer choices).

RESPONSE ACCOMMODATIONS

#25. A certified staff member or access assistant monitors the placement of student responses on the Student Test and Answer Book.

#26. Student uses visual organizers including graph paper, highlighters, place markers, and templates.

SETTING ACCOMMODATIONS

#27. Student takes the test in a different location in the building, in a small group, or in an individual location, monitored by a certified staff member or access assistant. Changes may also be made to a student's location within a room to reduce distractions to the student or to other students.

TIMING AND SCHEDULING ACCOMMODATIONS

#29. Student is provided with extended time to complete the assessment.

#30. Student is provided with multiple, individual breaks as needed, monitored by a teacher or access assistant.

#31. Student takes the tests at the time of day when he or she is most likely to demonstrate peak performance. A test must be completed in single testing session.

IEP TEAM MEMBER PARTICIPATION

Names and signatures of IEP team members attending or participating by alternate means in the IEP meeting.

Parent	**Student**
Jill Doe	Jane Doe
Special education teacher of the student	**Regular education teacher of the student**
March White	May Blue
School district representative	**An individual who can interpret evaluation results**
July Red, Principal or Admin. Designee	August Yellow, Case Manager/Admin. Designee
Agency representative	**Agency representative**
N/A	N/A
Other	**Other**
April Black, SLP	June Green, Counselor

COPY OF IEP PROVIDED TO PARENT

34 CFR 300.322(f)

Copy to Parent:	Date Provided:	Staff Initials:

Chapter 5

Sorting the Learning Disorders: Language Impairment and Reading Disability

Teresa A. Ukrainetz & Trina D. Spencer

Children who struggle with language, reading, and learning come with diverse constellations of strengths and weaknesses, as exemplified by Casey, Judith, and Antonio in Box 5.1. Instruction should be matched to each learner's needs, but instruction is also informed by consideration of distinctive features of types of learning disorders. The purpose of this chapter is to explain the two types of learning disorders that compose the large majority of special education students: specific language impairment and reading disability. These two disorders form the bulk of the school speech–language pathologist's (SLP) caseload. There are particular challenges in sorting out who is what and why for these two related disorders which "belong" to the different disciplines of speech–language pathology and education. This chaper will critically consider the features of and relationship between these two very common developmental disorders.

Specific Language Impairment

Specific language impairment (SLI) refers to a disorder of language production, comprehension, or both, in the absence of hearing impairment, intellectual disability, neurological damage (e.g., from perinatal bleeds or seizure disorders), and autism (Leonard, 1998; Schwartz, 2009). The descriptor "specific" reflects the presenting picture of a child who is developing typically in all major developmental domains but is failing to achieve the developmental milestones of language. Most of the research and clinical guidance for SLI deals with the preschool population and spoken language development. As will

Box 5.1. ***The Language Caseload—Who Is What?***

Casey's primary speech and language issues were remediated in preschool. Now in the first grade, his classroom teacher is concerned that he's struggling to read proficiently. She refers Casey for a special education evaluation, believing he could have a learning disability. Results of the evaluation indicate that Casey has intellectual performance below the average range and reading scores a full 1.5 standard deviations below the mean. Casey's receptive and expressive language scores are low-average. Casey is having reading problems, but is he learning disabled?

Judith has received language intervention from an SLP since she was in kindergarten. She has never read as proficiently as her peers. Each year an eligibility evaluation was completed and her reading scores were low but not low enough to qualify for reading services. Judith is now in the fourth grade. She still shows low expressive and receptive spoken language performance. Her reading scores are finally low enough to warrant a specific learning disability classification. Is Judith reading disabled or language impaired?

Antonio, a Latino second grader, has been at his school since kindergarten. He speaks a mixture of Spanish and English at home but scores as proficient in spoken English. Antonio has been receiving supplementary reading intervention since kindergarten. His reading comprehension is low-average but his word decoding, spelling, and phonemic awareness are much lower than his Latino peers. Is Antonio reading disabled or just growing into his English capabilities?

become clear from this chapter, once a child begins school, with its focus on written language and academic achievement and the wide variety of children being educated, the distinctiveness of the category of SLI largely disappears, and most SLPs resort simply to considering this very large group of low-language-with-no-good-reason students as "language kids."

Identification of SLI

SLI is a *developmental disorder.* Developmental disorders appear in childhood and typically have no known etiology: The children were not dropped on their heads as babies, did not suffer from a particular disease, nor did they have a distinct genetic abnormality. There is also no clear neuropsychological pathology for SLI. The language deficits of SLI have been attributed to a variety of sources, such as specific linguistic deficits, including a faulty "grammar gene;" underlying speech-specific cognitive processes; auditory processing; or general processing capacity (Leonard, 1998; Schwartz, 2009). An emergentist perspective posits that language performance is the product of dynamic interactions among levels of processing, the language input, and the child's active engagement with the input (Poll, 2011; Tomblin, 1991). Some children emerge as language impaired due to unfortunate intersections among weak skills, processes, and environmental conditions. The particular manifestations of SLI for each child are dependent on where weaknesses or strengths lie and how they combine.

Although the label and the surrounding concern are about an abnormal condition, SLI can also be viewed as the low end of the normal distribution of verbal ability. In this view, SLI is caused by the same factors that cause variation in language function among normal learners (Leonard, 1991; Tomblin, 1991). As with other human skills, such as music or mathematics, there is variation in aptitude, with some people endowed with extraordinary ability and other people struggling through with marginal ability. While being a tone-deaf and inept pianist has little implication for life success, verbal skills in modern society have obvious and significant negative implications. While everyone needs to be able to communicate socially, in cultures where cultivating early development and a high level of verbal skill are less emphasized, SLI will be much less noticeable.

Since the term came into use, it has become clear that SLI is not very specific. Children with SLI show limitations in auditory and speech perception, memory, attention, executive function, problem solving, number skills, motor function, and nonverbal social abilities (Bishop & Snowling, 2004; Leonard, 1998; Schwartz, 2009). In addition, questions have been raised about the theoretical requirement for IQ to be "normal," and some researchers require only that it is above the level considered to reflect a significant intellectual disability (Tomblin, Zhang, Buckwalter, & O'Brien, 2003). Because of these nonspecific features, some researchers prefer *primary language impairment* or *primary language disorder* (e.g., Edwards & Munson, 2009; Kohnert, Windsor, & Ebert, 2009; Tomblin et al., 2003). If IQ levels are uncertain, many researchers avoid the issue by using the generic label of *language disorder.* For older students, *language-learning disabled* connects the disorder to learning disabilities and difficulties with academic language (e.g., Butler & Wallach, 1982; Berninger, 2008). One consistent feature across this variation in terms is that all of them are descriptive rather than reflecting presumed etiology or pathology like old terms for SLI, such as *developmental aphasia*, *word deafness*, and *auditory processing disorder*.

There is no single diagnostic marker for SLI. Like many other developmental disorders, it is defined by a set of behaviors that range in severity. Typically, a judgment of SLI involves evaluation of spoken expressive or receptive grammar and vocabulary. The operational distinction between impaired and normal is typically somewhere between 1.5 and 1 standard deviations below the mean on a norm-referenced measure. A widely accepted research criterion for SLI comes from a large-scale, longitudinal epidemiological project by Tomblin and colleagues (e.g., Tomblin, Records, & Zhang, 1996; Tomblin et al., 1997). The project, called Epi-SLI, identified population-sampled (rather than clinically referred) kindergartners as SLI if they had two or more composite scores 1.25 standard deviations (12th percentile) or more below the mean on an omnibus language test of vocabulary, grammar, and narration. To exclude other causes, the Epi-SLI project required: (a) absence of hearing impairment on a pure tone screening due to reasons other than otitis media; (b) parent report of absence of intellectual disability, autism, neurological problems; and (c) a nonverbal IQ score greater than 85. Children were also required to be monolingual to provide a more homogeneous research sample, but multilingualism is not excluded in the concept of SLI.

The condition of SLI is most evident in preschoolers, when children lag in achieving developmental milestones in spoken language but are amenable to structured testing. Late first words and small expressive vocabularies are apparent for many toddlers, but the less prescriptive term of *slow expressive language development* or SELD is used at this age. Most of these children will turn out to be late talkers who largely catch up and achieve within the average range in the school years (Rescorla, 2005). Those whose difficulties persist become SLI. In the later elementary grades and beyond, children with SLI manifested in reading and academic problems may acquire labels of *specific learning disability* or *reading disability*.

Spoken language deficits are overlooked by families and teachers surprisingly often (at least surprising to an SLP). Unintelligible or lisping speech causes concern. Reading difficulties are noticed because students are closely graded and compared on written language performance. However, smaller-than-typical vocabularies, more-than-usual grammatical errors, and sparser-than-expected narratives, particularly in the spoken modality, are not obvious. In fact, unlike more popular conditions and despite the large caseloads of school SLPs, SLI is under-referred; researchers often detect many cases of children who have never been identified (e.g., Nation, Clarke, Marshall, & Durand, 2004; Tomblin et al., 1997). In the Epi-SLI project, Tomblin et al. reported that 71% of the research-identified kindergartners had *not* been flagged previously to parents as having speech or language problems. Even for those with more severe deficits (−2 SD), 51% of parents reported not having been notified. Furthermore, at second and fourth grade, only 25% of the children identified as having a primary language disorder were receiving language intervention (Tomblin et al., 2003).

Prevalence and Persistence

Estimates of the prevalence of SLI have varied from 3% to 10% (Tomblin et al., 1996). Differences arise from how the sample participants were located, at what ages, and the measures and criteria used. The Epi-SLI project found, for kindergartners, a prevalence of 7.4% with a 1.3 to 1 ratio of boys to girls (Tomblin et al., 1997).

SLI is a highly persistent condition, with many children identified as having deficient language as preschoolers continuing to have language problems into adolescence (e.g., Aram, Ekelman, & Nation, 1984; Catts, Bridges, Little, & Tomblin, 1998; Stothard, Snowling, Bishop, Chipchase, & Kaplan, 1998; Scarborough, 1990; Tomblin et al., 2003). For example, Aram et al. reported a 10-year follow-up of 20 children diagnosed with speech and language difficulties prior to first grade. At 13 to 16 years, of the 16 children whose IQs were above the level of intellectual disability, 70% had required tutoring, grade retention, or learning disability placement. The majority showed continuing deficits in language and academic achievement. Parents rated the adolescents as less socially competent and having more behavioral problems than their peers.

In another longitudinal project, Bishop and Edmundson (1987) identified 68 4-year-olds with SLI. By 5.5 years, 56% of the children scored below the 10th percentile in expressive language. The children with poor performance as 5-year-olds continued to show difficulties at 8.5 years on language and reading measures (Bishop & Adams, 1990). At 15 to 16 years, these children continued to show significant impairments in spoken and written language (Stothard et al., 1998). Their vocabulary growth rate had slowed over time and the gap between them and their typical peers had widened. Even the adolescents whose spoken language performance had resolved before first grade continued to perform significantly worse than peers on phonological processing and a composite of word reading, spelling, and passage comprehension.

The picture of SLI persistence may be even more pessimistic than these studies indicate. Tomblin et al. (2003) followed 196 of the Epi-SLI children identified with language impairment into third grade. In this report, the nonverbal intelligence requirement was lowered to 70 because a number of children's IQ scores had dropped since entering the study in kindergarten. As a result, the impaired group was then termed with Primary Language Disorder (PLD). Results showed about 40% of the children with PLD moved out of the diagnostic category 4 years later, with most of the change occurring between kindergarten and second grade. However, a procedure that controlled for regression to the mean (the likelihood that extreme scores will be closer to the mean on a second testing) showed no significant change in language status across the 4-year time period for children with PLD. There was slightly better improvement for the SLI and expressive-only subgroups. Tomblin et al. concluded that prior judgments of a substantial proportion of SLI cases resolving may have been affected by initial false positive identifications and regression to the mean, and that SLI is even more stable over time than thought.

Adding further concern is the possibility of what Scarborough and Dobrich (1990) call *illusory recovery*. Scarborough and Dobrich followed four children with severe and broad impairments in syntactic, phonological, and lexical production from 2.5 years old to the end of second grade. Performance was compared to a control group of 12 children.

Over time, the children's deficits became milder until falling within the average range at 5 years. However, when followed up 3 years later, three of the four children had been identified as reading disabled. This illusory recovery has also been detected, at a milder level, for toddlers identified as slow expressive language development (SELD), with 75% to 85% showing language skills within the average range at 5 years old but at 13 years old showing language, reading, and writing skills below their peers (Rescorla, 2005).

SLI in the Schools

For school service delivery, students are not identified as SLI but only as meeting the requirements for the federal eligibility category of *speech or language impairment*. This broad eligibility category includes impaired articulation, voice, and fluency and students with other primary disorders, such as autism or specific learning disability. The specific eligibility requirements are determined by each state. As discussed in Chapter 4, this category is more about eligibility and who delivers services than type of disorder and learning needs.

SLPs and other educators do not use the term "specific language impairment." Rather they refer to students who appear as typically developing across developmental domains other than language and have no other label as *language impaired* or *language disordered*. When speaking to parents, SLPs may avoid a pathological implication and just refer to students as having "weak language" or "language problems." For young children, SLPs may use the more hopeful term of *language delayed*, although this implies a catch-up that often does not occur. For older students, SLPs may use *language-learning disabled*. A single child's language difficulties may be subjected to multiple labels over the years of schooling.

Linguistic Characteristics of SLI

For children with SLI, language acquisition follows a typical developmental sequence, but the rate of development is slower. Language deficits are seen across syntax, semantics, discourse, and pragmatics, but the hallmark of SLI is considered to be deficits in syntax.

Young children with SLI have notable difficulties with understanding and use of syntax and grammatical morphology (Leonard, 1998; Schwartz, 2009). Most research has concentrated on expressive difficulties with grammatical morphology. In preschoolers, verb morphology errors involving bare stems that lack tense and agreement markers (e.g., *Yesterday, I jump; She jump*) are highly reliable indicators of SLI even compared to younger language-matched controls (Bedore & Leonard, 1998; Leonard, Miller, & Gerber, 1999). Past-tense difficulties distinguish children with SLI even for those speaking British English, Southern White English, and African American English (Conti-Ramsden, 2003; Oetting & McDonald, 2001). For children with SLI, grammatical morphology appears to be particularly challenging in English compared to more heavily but regularly inflected languages, such as Icelandic, Italian, French, and German (e.g., Thordardottir, 2008). For older children speaking English, although morphosyntactic errors may persist, they are no longer reliable indicators of SLI (Conti-Ramsden, Botting, & Faragher, 2001).

For children with SLI even up to 8 years of age, there are notable difficulties with finite verb morphology in complex sentences (e.g., Owen & Leonard, 2002; Rice & Wexler, 1996; Schuele & Tolbert, 2001). Schuele and Tolbert found 3- to 5-year-old typical children rarely left out "that" in subject relative clauses, but 5- to 7-year-old children with SLI left it out in than half the obligatory contexts. In simple finite and nonfinite complement clauses (e.g., *The Count decided that Ernie should eat the cookies; Cookie Monster decided to eat the cookies*) and those with additional arguments (e.g., *Ernie told Elmo that Oscar picked up the box; Ernie told Elmo to pick up the box*), Owen and Leonard found more omission of finiteness markers, the nonfinite particle *to*, arguments in finite complement clauses, and the optional complementizer *that*.

Relative clause sentences and passive sentences, with their long-distance dependencies, are a consistent source of difficulty (e.g., Friedmann & Novodgrodsky, 2004; van der Lely, 1996). Sentences like *The zebra that the hippo kissed on the nose ran far way*, and *Zebra says Hippo is tickling him*, confuse children with SLI about who did what to whom. Across ages and discourse contexts, findings include shorter average sentence length, less complex syntax, more grammatical errors, and poor comprehension of complex sentences for children with SLI (Schwartz, 2009; Scott & Windsor, 2000).

In the area of semantics, children with SLI show a late onset of first words and a small vocabulary as toddlers, and continue to show receptive and expressive delays as preschoolers (Schwartz, 2009). Children with SLI are poorer word learners than their age peers. They need more repetitions to learn new words and show less maintenance and generalization (e.g., Rice, Oetting, Marquis, & Bode, 1994; Schwartz, Leonard, Messick, & Chapman, 1987). In the school years, in addition to overall lower vocabulary scores compared to age peers, children with SLI do not know a lot about the words they know (McGregor, Newman, Reilly, & Capone, 2002). Verbs, especially mental state verbs (e.g., *think, know*), are a particular problem (Johnston, Miller, & Tallal, 2001).

Some children with SLI have trouble accurately and quickly accessing the words they know (Messer & Dockrell, 2006). In conversation, they may stumble and pause, trying to find the word, with hesitations, pauses, and fillers (e.g., *um, you know*), or may travel around the word with substitutions and circumlocutions. They may be unaware of their conversational gaps or say that the word is on "the tip of their tongues." In reading, they may be slower to "recognize" the meaning of a printed word they have sounded out. However, word-finding difficulties are not consistently present in SLI and can occur for anyone in stressful verbal tasks. MacLachlan and Chapman (1988) found that verbal mazes distinguished children with SLI from typical learners for narratives but not conversation. Scott and Windsor (2000) found no differences in maze frequency in narrative or expository discourse between children with SLI and typical learners. It turns out, contrary to intuition, that although word-retrieval difficulties are partly about lack of depth of word meaning (McGregor & Waxman, 1998), they are fundamentally about phonological processing: difficulty retrieving and mapping the phonological code onto the sensed meaning (e.g., *Oh, what is that word, it means couch, not chesterfield, a shorter word, two syllables, starts with /s/, sofa, that's it*).

Discourse involves organized units of language larger than a sentence. Children with SLI show difficulties in dealing with the macrostructure of discourse. In young children with SLI, there are deficits in contingency between conversational utterances and coherence of the overall message (e.g., Craig & Evans, 1993). For school-age children, narratives are less structurally complex and less cohesive, with omitted information and poor event sequencing (e.g., Fey, Catts, Proctor-Williams, Tomblin, & Zhang, 2004; Gillam & Johnston, 1992; Liles, 1985, 1987; McFadden & Gillam, 1996; Newman & McGregor, 2006; Ukrainetz & Gillam, 2009). Narrative elicitation tasks tax the language system, revealing weaknesses not apparent in word and sentence tasks (Bishop & Edmundson, 1987; Fazio, Naremore, & Connell, 1996; Wetherell, Botting, & Conti-Ramsden, 2007).

There is very little research on expository structure for SLI. Koutsoftas and Gray (2012) found that fourth and fifth graders with SLI showed lower performance on a six-trait holistic rating of quality that considered expository structure, productivity, vocabulary diversity, and grammar. Scott and Windsor (2000) investigated expository and narrative summaries of films by 9- to 12-year-olds. For both language impaired and typically developing students, expository summaries were shorter and less fluent, with more errors, than narrative summaries. The students with SLI did particularly poorly on the expository writing task.

It should be noted that children with SLI typically say less than their typically developing peers. Because lack of productivity affects presence of other language features, researchers and clinicians need to consider that a student may simply be saying less rather than have a deficit in a particular language structure compared to peers. Likewise, for treatment outcomes, checks should be made on whether the student is simply saying more or whether there is also improvement in the complexity, organization, or accuracy.

Pragmatics, or use of language, is a challenging area to sort out. Deficits can be due to lack of linguistic knowledge, lack of social knowledge, or lack of knowledge of how to achieve social aims with language (Schwartz, 2009). Children with poor receptive abilities show greater difficulties managing conversational turns and coherently linking their contributions (Craig & Evans, 1993). Preschool and school-age children with SLI show greater passivity and social withdrawal in communicative interactions with peers in both social and academic contexts, even in nonverbal interactions (e.g., Brinton, Fujiki, & Higbee, 1998; Craig & Washington, 1993; Fujiki, Brinton, Isaacson, & Summers, 2001). Hart, Fujiki, Brinton, and Hart (2004) found that teachers rated children with SLI as more reticent, solitary, and passive, with lower levels of prosocial and impulse control behaviors. These lower levels of emotional regulation do not reach clinical levels, but they contribute to the same degree as do language deficits to the reticent behaviors observed (Fujiki, Spackman, Brinton, & Hall, 2004). Fujiki et al. found that, while better receptive language abilities were associated with more prosocial behaviors and better impulse control or likability, children with more severe expressive deficits had no worse impulse control or likability than children with less severe deficits.

Phonology and Motor Coordination of SLI

Phonology is one of the classical linguistic divisions of language. Phonology involves the mental rules and patterns that organize speech and the resultant speech production, minus the contribution of motor planning and execution. However, the output inescapably involves sensory-motor components. *Speech sound disorder* is being increasingly used so as to avoid having to distinguish the source of the difficulty.

Many children with significant speech sound disorders have concomitant language deficits: with one third having comprehension deficits and three-quarters having production deficits (Shriberg & Kwiatkowski, 1994). However, the inverse does not hold: The rate of clinical levels of speech sound problems in children with language as the primary disorder is low (Beitchman, Nair, Clegg, & Patel, 1986; Shriberg, Tomblin, & McSweeny, 1999). From the Epi-SLI project, Shriberg et al. reported prevalence in 6-year-olds of 3.8%, but for those with SLI or PLD, the comorbidity rate was less than 2%.

Despite the lack of clinical levels of speech sound problems, there are subtle difficulties present (Edwards & Munson, 2009). These may intersect with linguistic difficulties, such as omissions of morphological elements related to more difficult phonological features of words (Leonard, Davis, & Deevy, 2007; Marshall & van der Lely, 2007). There are differences at the motor level: Children with SLI have less organized and less stable productions (Goffman, 2004), more variability in lip kinematics (Gallon, Harris, & van der Lely, 2007), and less accurate productions of multisyllabic and low-probability phoneme sequences (e.g., Catts, 1986; Munson, Kurtz, & Windsor, 2005). Hand and limb control investigations suggest that these speech incoordinations may reflect weakness in overall motor planning or execution abilities (e.g., Zelaznik & Goffman, 2010).

Accurate discrimination of speech sounds is not a particular problem for children with SLI. Unlike the years it takes to develop expressive control, children discriminate the phonemes of their native language before their first year (Menn & Stoel-Gammon, 2009). Children with SLI do not show difficulties discriminating words that differ by a phoneme (Gathercole & Baddley, 1990). The auditory perception task of identifying whether minimal pair words are the same or different (e.g., Are *dog* and *dock* the same or different?) is more about phonemic awareness and word concepts than sound discrimination.

Reading and Writing of SLI

One would expect children with SLI to have reading and writing problems. Reading can be basically divided into recognition of printed words and comprehending the discourse formed from those individual words (Gough & Tunmer, 1986). Both involve language.

Fluent printed word recognition involves language. It is accomplished through phonological decoding, orthographic recognition, and syllabic or morphological analysis, followed by retrieval of the word meaning, and then confirmation or revision based on what the reader has comprehended from the larger text information (Catts, Kamhi, & Adlof, 2012a). Small vocabulary and poor phonemic awareness affect the speed and accuracy of word recognition. Reduced depth and elaboration of vocabulary, along with deficient grammar and discourse, further affect ability to confirm or revise word recognition choices.

One cannot understand what one reads without adequate vocabulary, grammar, and discourse. The content, structure, and style of spoken and written language differ, due to different uses (e.g., speaking is typically informal) and presentation features (e.g., the printed text can be read at a rate chosen by the reader), but regardless of modality, they are both language (Catts, Kamhi, & Adlof, 2012b). Abilities other than language are involved in reading comprehension, such as topic expertise, motivation, inferential abilities, and cognitive strategies like skimming and identifying main ideas, but these are also involved in challenging spoken language tasks.

Writing is also largely about language. Writing has been described as a juggling act among the many components of composition (Flower & Hayes, 1980). Rarely is writing an automatic and easy process, and it is particularly hard when a person is trying to transmit difficult ideas clearly. An additional challenge is spelling, which must be generated exactly for writing. Handwriting or keyboarding skills must also be present. It is little wonder that many people, not only those with diagnosed learning disabilities, struggle with writing (Hooper & Montgomery, 1993).

Results of longitudinal studies have consistently shown that half or more of children with SLI in preschool or kindergarten show concomitant poor early reading skills and go on to be reading disabled or at least poor readers (Conti-Ramsden, St. Clair, Pickles, & Durkin, 2012; Scarborough & Dobrich, 1990; Stothard et al., 1998; Tomblin et al., 2003). They also show poor written compositions, with lower quality, simpler structures, and more errors in vocabulary, syntax, and discourse (Fey et al., 2004; Gillam & Johnston, 1992; McFadden & Gillam, 1996; Scott & Windsor, 2000). Dockrell, Lindsay, and Connelly (2009) found poor writing for students with SLI longitudinally between 8 and 16 years old. The writing evidenced short texts, with poor vocabulary, sentence structure, and difficulties with ideas and organization.

Goulandris, Snowling, and Walker (2000) compared the reading of adolescents with SLI to those with identified reading disability. Adolescents who had childhood histories of language impairment but whose spoken language had resolved by school entry showed better word reading and spelling than adolescents with reading disability, but the same difficulties with phonological awareness and nonword spelling. The adolescents with persistent spoken language deficits showed the same word reading and spelling and worse reading comprehension than the adolescents with reading disabilities.

Subtypes of SLI

In an effort to understand the variety of manifestations of SLI, more homogeneous subtypes have been proposed by modality and language domain. However, variations appear to be more related to severity than to distinctly different profiles of linguistic strengths and weaknesses (Schwartz, 2009).

Expressive-only versus expressive-receptive has been a common distinction (e.g., Craig & Evans, 1993; Edwards & Lahey, 1996). Tomblin and Zhang (2006) analyzed whether performance of the Epi-SLI participants reflected different dimensions of language and if it changed with development from kindergarten to eighth grade. Results indicated that the standardized language measures, regardless of the subtest labels, sample a single common trait, rather than receptive versus expressive abilities. Tomblin and Zhang found only one distinction, between grammatical and vocabulary abilities, that emerged in middle childhood.

A syntax SLI has been proposed (Bishop, Bright, James, Bishop, & van der Lely, 2000; van der Lely, 1997; van der Lely & Stollwerck, 1997). These children rely on nonsyntactic cues to interpret meaning in passive sentences, relative clauses, and other complex sentences. While many children with SLI have trouble with these kinds of sentences, a distinctive subtype appears to be very rare: Bishop and colleagues found, out of 144 children with SLI, only 11 met the criteria, and all these children had deficits in other areas.

Lexical SLI involves particular difficulty with word finding (Schwartz, 2009). However, many children with SLI do not show word-finding difficulties (Newman & McGregor, 2000), and many children with word-finding difficulties do not show general language deficits (German & Simon, 1991; German & Newman, 2004). As previously mentioned, this may not even represent a semantic deficit, but rather one of phonological representations and processing speed (Messer & Dockrell, 2006).

A pragmatic SLI has been proposed (Bishop, 2000; Botting & Conti-Ramsden, 2003). These children have, along with linguistic deficits, atypical social behaviors, irrelevant utterances, and poor nonverbal cue awareness. These are considered to be different from Asperger's Syndrome. However, Botting and Conti-Ramsden also identified a fourth subgroup with features of both pragmatic SLI and autistic noncommunicative behaviors, such as obsessive behavior and rigidity of thought, suggesting, rather than subtypes, a continuum between SLI and autism.

Finally, phonological versus nonphonological SLI has been distinguished (Bishop & Snowling, 2004). Children with SLI and phonological processing deficits have a much greater likelihood of comprehensive reading problems. Children with language problems only are likely to show adequate decoding but poor reading comprehension (Nation & Snowling, 1998). Again, this may be more a case of severity than qualitative differences.

Reading Disability

The other type of disorder that school SLPs frequently encounter is reading disability. Reading disability involves problems more severe than expected given the person's other abilities and environmental conditions. The reading disability may be primarily at the word recognition level, primarily at the text comprehension level, or both. Unlike SLI, reading disability is a widely recognized (though often misunderstood) condition.

Learning Disability

Reading disability is a type of learning disability. *Learning disability* refers to an unexplained underachievement in listening, speaking, thinking, reading, writing, or mathematic skills. Children who experience significant difficulties in any of these areas not primarily due to intellectual, sensory, or emotional impairments, cultural differences, or environmental disadvantages fall within the IDEA category of *specific learning disability* (Box 5.2). The modifier *specific* is intended to differentiate underachievement in isolated domains from more pervasive learning problems due to low cognitive ability. The IDEA definition excludes other conditions as primary causes, but a hearing impaired, poor, English language learner with intellectual disability and poor school attendance could potentially have an intrinsic learning disability that is causing additional academic difficulties. The challenge would be to identify it.

The category of learning disability, despite its stated heterogeneity, is largely about reading. Approximately 80% of students who are identified with specific learning disability present with primary deficits in basic reading skills or reading comprehension (Shaywitz, Gruen, Mody, & Shaywitz, 2009). Most of the remaining 20% will have difficulties

Box 5.2. ***Definitions of Specific Learning Disability and Reading Disability***

Learning disability is a disorder in one or more of the basic psychological processes involved in understanding or in using language, spoken or written, that may manifest itself in the imperfect ability to listen, think, speak, read, write, spell, or to do mathematical calculations, including conditions such as perceptual disabilities, brain injury, minimal brain dysfunction, dyslexia, and developmental aphasia. The term does not include learning problems that are primarily the result of visual, hearing, or motor disabilities, of mental retardation, of emotional disturbance, or of environmental, cultural, or economic disadvantage (Federal Educational Eligibility Regulations, n.d.)

Dyslexia is a specific learning disability that is neurobiological in origin. It is characterized by difficulties with accurate and/or fluent word recognition and by poor spelling and decoding abilities. These difficulties typically result from a deficit in the phonological component of language that is often unexpected in relation to other cognitive abilities and the provision of effective classroom instruction. Secondary consequences may include problems in reading comprehension and reduced reading experience that can impede growth of vocabulary and background knowledge (Lyon, Shaywitz, & Shaywitz, 2003, p. 2).

in reading accompanying their qualifying weaknesses. Although listening and speaking are included in the definition of learning disability, children with primary difficulties in spoken language fall in the eligibility category of *speech or language impairment.*

Identification of Reading Disability

The conceptual definition of reading disability—a weak reader for no apparent reason—must be operationalized. There is considerable variation in the criteria used to identify reading disability in research and practice. The many disciplines involved in different aspects of reading disability further complicate matters: special educators, reading specialists, physicians, optometrists, psychologists, and SLPs (Catts et al., 2012a).

There is some agreement on what reading disability is not. It is not about all individuals who are poor readers (Catts et al., 2012a). The *reading disability* label is intended for those who have a significant intrinsic difficulty learning to read. There is the same list of exclusionary factors as for learning disability and SLI on general intellect, hearing, and vision. Individuals should have had adequate opportunities to learn to read, meaning sufficiently good instruction and sufficiently good attendance in a sufficiently good frame of mind for learning. The instructional element is different from the requirements for SLI because learning to read, unlike learning to speak, generally requires formal, explicit instruction. Some newer definitions of dyslexia include deficits in phonological processing, but a deficiency in those underlying cognitive skills is not a requirement. For resource reasons, students must have below-grade-level proficiency to qualify for federally funded services, but a student with a high IQ and good effort who reads only at grade level would still fit the concept of reading disability.

A cornerstone in the operational identification criteria has been a significant difference between IQ and reading achievement (Catts et al., 2012a). This was based on the idea that IQ scores, which are highly predictive of school achievement, reflect learning potential for all academic skills, including reading. Normal learners were expected to show similar IQ and reading standard scores. A large gap, such as more than 1.5 standard deviations, between these scores was considered to reflect untapped learning potential. Students with such a score discrepancy could achieve their potential with specialized instruction and students who did not would not. This latter group, called "backward readers," "slow learners," or "garden-variety poor readers," was considered to have too little learning potential to be worth the investment of specialized instruction.

Considerable evidence against the validity of the discrepancy theory has accumulated (Box 5.3). Problems include that the procedure is biased toward higher IQs (explaining the popular but inaccurate image of children with dyslexia being more intelligent than average), that it unfairly works against language deficits and cultural differences, that it does not predict learning potential for decoding nor comprehension, and that it excludes many poor readers from beneficial specialized instruction (Catts et al., 2012a). The Commission on Special Education (USDE, 2002) was especially critical of the reliance on IQ scores for identifying learning disabilities and recommended as a key part of identification for special education, evaluation and documentation of a student's response to instruction and instructional facilitations within general education. The commission claimed that the discrepancy method led to too many of the wrong children being identified and served within special education and called these children "instructional casualties" (USDE, 2002, p. 26). However, the real casualties seem to be the children with inherent learning problems who were not eligible for reading intervention.

Federal legislation has not removed the discrepancy requirement, but now prevents school districts from requiring it and allows alternative procedures, such as response to intervention (RTI) or phonological processing performance (C.F.R. 300.307 Specific learning disabilities, from http://ecfr.gpoaccess.gov/). RTI is commonly present in the schools to improve general reading performance, but procedures and criteria for using it to identify reading disability are still emerging (e.g., Fuchs & Fuchs, 2006). Dynamic assessment, which has the same conceptual basis as RTI, shows considerable promise as a faster and more uniform way of identifying children with inherent learning impairments affecting reading (Bridges & Catts, 2011; Grigorenko, 2009; Spector, 1992; Wagner & Compton, 2011).

An Exceedingly Brief History of Reading Disability

Reading disability has a long history: at the turn of the twentieth century, physicians noted a puzzling type of pupil, one who was apparently bright and able, but had inordinate difficulty learning to read (Catts et al., 2012a; Shaywitz et al., 2009). Morgan (1896) reported on a 14-year-old English pupil who was unable to learn to read despite strong intellect, vision, and motor skills, and seven years of instruction. The student was described by his schoolmaster as the smartest lad in the school if only the instruction were entirely oral. The condition was called *congenital word-blindness*, based on the similarity to the acquired loss of reading ability in an adult with intact vision reported

Box 5.3. ***Problems With the Reading-IQ Discrepancy Criterion***

1. **The size of the gap is not stable:** Different sizes of gaps occur depending on which IQ tests and subscales and which reading tests and subscales are used.
2. **A large gap is not significant for decoding:** There is little relationship between the basic reading skills of sounding out and visually recognizing letter patterns and the vocabulary, information, pattern recognition, and analytic skills examined in IQ tests.
3. **Lack of a gap is not significant for comprehension:** There is a close relationship between reading comprehension and IQ tests; language and knowledge deficits can lower both scores.
4. **A gap may be late appearing:** A sufficiently large difference between IQ and reading is often not obtained until third grade because reading is a new skill for all the students, resulting in less difference between typical and low achievers.
5. **A gap is affected by other factors:** Gaps are smaller and take longer to become sufficiently large for students with low-average IQ scores, including those whose scores might be lowered by linguistic or cultural differences.
6. **A gap does not predict responsiveness to instruction:** Poor readers with lower IQs benefit as much as dyslexic readers with average IQs from intensive word quality reading instruction. They can even "learn how to learn" and improve their IQ scores a little.

Note: Based on Catts et al. (2012a).

by a Scottish ophthalmologist, Hinshelwood. Hinshelwood (1905) reported on several of these puzzling children. He emphasized the specificity of the deficit in otherwise capable children. Although most eventually learned to read, they were slow readers later in life. Hinshelwood speculated that there was likely neurological damage and recommended intensive multisensory phonics instruction (Hinshelwood, 1912). As Shaywitz et al. (2009) note, these early reports demonstrated that severe cases of this disability are diagnosable simply from clinical observation and history.

A prominent subsequent researcher and clinician was Orton (1937), who directed a private clinic in Iowa. Orton viewed congenital word-blindness as a kind of developmental language disorder, paralleling the old "word deafness" of congenital aphasia (SLI). Word-blind children had reading problems with concomitant or prior difficulties with spoken language. Orton proposed that word-blind children had failed to develop a left cerebral dominance for language and that reversal and sequencing letter errors resulted from confusion between mirror images of words represented in each hemisphere (Catts et al., 2012a). Both the neural representation and the significance of reversal and sequencing errors proved to be incorrect, but much else of what Orton (and Hinshelwood) reported is consistent with what is known today (Catts et al., 2012a; Shaywitz et al., 2009). Orton developed a multisensory program of explicit phoneme-grapheme association that later became the popular Orton-Gillingham approach.

A final notable historical contribution was Johnson and Myklebust's (1967) observations that children with *auditory dyslexia* had problems perceiving the similarities in the initial and final sounds in words, breaking words into syllables and phonemes, retrieving the names of letters and words, remembering verbal information, and pronouncing multisyllabic words (e.g., saying *enemy* as *emeny*). Their work laid the foundation for moving away from visual-perceptual explanations to underlying phonological processes and linguistic skills (Catts et al., 2012a).

The term *dyslexia* is confusing. Dyslexia has been used both synonymously with reading disability and as a subtype of reading disability (Catts et al., 2012a). Traditionally, dyslexia has been employed mainly by medically related professionals and the popular press. *Reading disability* carries fewer preconceptions and misconceptions and is preferred in the educational system. Catts et al. noted efforts to have mainstream educators use the word *dyslexia* more in reference to specific difficulties with printed word recognition but intact reading comprehension.

Prevalence of Reading Disability

Shaywitz et al. (2009) reported, across studies, prevalence rates in school-age children between 5% and 18%, depending on criteria used. Research studies that claim to be about reading disability or dyslexia may not be limited to severe reading problems, but simply lower quartile readers, thus inflating the prevalence rate.

If learning disability, or any other disorder, is due to a particular pathology, (which tend to cause more low than high performers) there should be a hump at the lower end of the normal curve. There is such a hump for intellectual disability, which is often caused by neurological pathologies and genetic anomalies so that far more individuals with profound disabilities are present than would be predicted statistically (Robinson & Robinson, 1976). Early prevalence studies for reading disability suggested this, but subsequent work revealed that the apparent hump was a testing artifact and that there was no excess at the low end of the distribution for reading (Shaywitz, Escobar, Shaywitz, Fletcher, & Makuch, 1992). Thus, reading disability, like SLI, is a socially defined rather than organic pathology.

Most children with reading disabilities are identified in second grade on word recognition and fluency issues. A sizeable additional number are identified around fourth grade, when comprehension demands jump, in what has been called the *fourth-grade slump* (Chall, 1983). There are also late-appearing problems with word recognition as students who previously read adequately start to struggle with the challenging phonotactics and orthography of more advanced reading materials (Lipka, Lesaux, & Siegel, 2006). The difficulties seem to be issues of late emergence rather than simply being missed in early identification (Catts, Compton, Tomblin, & Bridges, 2012). Using data from the Epi-SLI project, Catts et al. reported that 13% of children could be expected to emerge late as poor readers. Most problems appeared at fourth grade in their study, but a few were fine until the testing sessions in eighth and tenth grade. Problems involved reading comprehension (52%), word reading (36%), or both (12%). Kindergarten measures of the late emergers showed early weaknesses in phonological processing, spoken language, and nonverbal intellect for those with word-reading problems, and across the latter two for comprehension problems.

It is commonly thought that there are more boys than girls with reading disabilities. Early studies showed 3 to 5 times as many boys as girls (e.g., Naidoo, 1972). However, later studies failed to find such large differences (e.g., Prior, Sanson, Smart, & Oberklaid, 1995; Shaywitz, Shaywitz, Fletcher, & Escobar, 1990). The conflicting results appear to be due to whether the sample selected for study was identified by schools and clinics or by researchers (Catts et al., 2012a). Attention, activity level, and classroom behavior are more likely to be problematic for boys and can impinge on decisions made by practitioners (Willcutt & Pennington, 2000). Shaywitz et al. (1990) demonstrated this by directly comparing a school-identified sample to a research-identified sample: The ratio was 4:1 in favor of boys for the former and 1.3:1 for the latter. However, the gender question is not closed: An international report of four longitudinal, epidemiological studies using only objective measures found 3 times as many boys as girls identified as reading disabled (Rutter et al., 2007). Use of RTI in research may increase the incidence of inattentive or disruptive boys being identified as reading disabled there, too.

The Course of Reading Problems

Reading disabilities are a lifelong challenge. Over time, reading difficulties may shift from primarily decoding to comprehension, and performance will be further affected by learning environment and life demands, but the inherent impairment persists into adulthood.

With effective reading instruction and rich literacy experiences, children with reading disabilities can become accurate readers with adequate comprehension (Shaywitz et al., 2009). There are interventions that can improve reading accuracy and comprehension to within the average range (e.g., Foorman, Breier, & Fletcher, 2003; Shaywitz, Morris, & Shaywitz, 2008). However, adults with childhood diagnoses of reading disability continue to show immature word recognition strategies, lack of automaticity, and slow reading (Bruck, 1990, 1993; Lefly & Pennington, 1991). Slow readers will struggle with heavy reading loads and timed tests (Shaywitz et al., 2009). In addition, there are spelling and writing problems that exacerbate the academic difficulties of poor readers (Katusic, Colligan, Weaver, & Barbaresi, 2009).

Reading performance for poor readers can improve, but it can also get worse over time due to inadequate instruction, reading experiences, and recurrent lack of academic success (USDE, 2002). This escalating pattern of trouble has been called the Matthew effect, from the bible passage in the book of Matthew that says to those who have, more will be given, but from those who have nothing, even that will be taken away. The Matthew Effect was first applied by Walberg and Tsai (1983) to observations that the gap between good and poor students widens over time, with good students making progressively larger gains and poor students making progressively slower gains. Stanovich (1986) posited that the Matthew Effect might explain how a specific deficit in an underlying cognitive ability could lead to broad difficulties across reading performance. Stanovich originally posited phonemic awareness as the initial culprit, which affected acquisition of early decoding skills, leading to poor word recognition and slow, inaccurate reading. Poor readers subsequently suffered lack of practice, low expectations, and loss of motivation. They read less and learned less from their reading, thus missing out on an important source of advanced vocabulary, grammar, and concepts, leading to progressively worse academic performance over the school years.

It turns out that the initial cause of reading problems is not simply phonological awareness but rather a combination of weaknesses in phonological processing (Catts et al., 2012b). Language impairments persist and become more evident as academic demands increase, and reading comprehension scores may go lower as the measures rely less on word recognition (Catts, Adlof, & Weismer, 2006). Students can even emerge in later grades as reading disabled (Catts et al., 2012b). There is evidence that semantic deficits for children with reading comprehension disabilities worsen over time (e.g., Share & Silva, 1987; Stothard et al., 1998; Vellutino, Scanlon, & Spearing, 1995).

Despite the apparent worsening of reading performance over time, it is not clear that the gap between poor and good readers actually gets wider (Catts, Hogan, & Fey, 2003; Stothard et al., 1998). In a large-sample longitudinal study of readers from first to sixth grade, Shaywitz et al. (1995) found that the poor readers continued to be poor readers, but that their distance from good readers did not become wider in sixth grade. In a longitudinal study of children, Scarborough and Parker (2003) found that the gap between those identified as reading disabled and their typically developing peers maintained or even narrowed from sixth to eighth grade.

The mixed support for the Matthew Effect does not mean the problems go away. The evidence clearly shows that weak reading continues into adulthood. Those with marginal spoken language and cognitive abilities have more trouble as academic demands increase. Perhaps the moral to the story is not that children who start as poor readers get worse, but that they do not get better, especially if their environment does not support their reading and academic success. As Stanovich (1986) said, citing Morris, "to put it more simply—and more sadly—in the words of a tearful nine-year-old, already falling frustratingly behind his peers in reading progress, 'reading affects everything you do'"(p. 43).

Types of Reading Disability

Individuals with reading disability often show differential performance in word recognition and text comprehension. The former are slow and inaccurate at reading isolated words, nonwords, and sentences, but if they can recognize what is written, or have it read to them, have no difficulty comprehending the material. The latter show the inverse: troubles not with single-word and sentence reading but with understanding what they have read or what has been read to them.

A reading difficulty that is characterized by an inordinate difficulty learning how to read and a persistent problem with word recognition and fluent reading is called *dyslexia* (Catts et al., 2012a; Shaywitz et al., 2009). Because of the inconsistent use of the term dyslexia, a specific difficulty with word recognition without notable comprehension deficits may also be called *classic dyslexia*. With considerable effort and effective instruction, these children can become slow but accurate readers with adequate comprehension (Shaywitz et al., 2008; Torgesen et al., 2001).

There have been attempts to further subcategorize classic dyslexia. A distinction on regular or irregular word spelling has gone by a variety of labels: *phonological*, *dysphonetic*, or *audio-phonetic* versus *visuospatial*, *dyseidectic*, or *surface*. Those who have trouble with both types have been called *deep dyslexics*. It turns out that most dyslexic individuals make both kinds of errors (e.g., Murphy & Pollatsek, 1994; Stanovich, Siegel, & Gottardo, 1997). The few readers who have particular difficulties with sight words seem to have a milder dyslexia possibly accentuated by one of two seemingly opposite situations: lack of literacy experience or heavy phonics instruction (Catts et al., 2012a; Shaywitz et al., 2009).

Poor readers have also been distinguished based on accuracy versus speed of word recognition. Lovett (1987) found that children who were *accuracy disabled* were weaker across measures of decoding and comprehension and showed deficits in morphological and syntactic knowledge as well as rapid automatic naming. The *rate-disabled* readers were similar to normal readers in all the measures except rapid automatic naming, reflecting a weakness in phonological processing. Catts et al. (2012a) suggested that rate-disabled readers may be recently remediated and lack only further practice and automatization of reading. Thus, this distinction may be again one of severity and reading experience.

It turns out that slow reading may not a significant barrier to comprehension in untimed situations. Using a large longitudinal database of over 500 children tested in second, fourth, and eighth grades, Adlof, Catts, and Little (2006) found that all the children in the specific rate-deficit subgroup showed reading comprehension within the average range at every testing point. Only children who had concomitant spoken language deficits showed reading comprehension difficulties. Cutting, Materek, Cole, Levine, and Mahone (2009) found that children with specific reading comprehension deficits had no difficulty with reading single words and nonwords, but were slower in reading connected texts. This suggests that comprehension deficits slow rate, rather than the other way around (Catts et al., 2012a). Slowing down to read seems like an entirely reasonable response to difficulty understanding what you are reading. In sum, the efforts to subtype classic dyslexia have not been supported, and evidence indicates it is essentially a single entity operating around a core of underlying phonological processes that vary in severity (Morris et al., 1998; Stanovich & Siegel, 1994; Stanovich et al., 1997).

The distinction that has been upheld over time is word recognition versus comprehension. Students with a specific comprehension disability often progress adequately in reading in the early grades but are identified as reading disabled in late elementary grades when they struggle with more challenging reading material and academic knowledge. This condition has been called *poor comprehender* or *specific comprehension deficit* (Bishop & Snowling, 2004; Catts et al., 2003; Catts et al., 2006). *Hyperlexia* has been used (Catts et al., 2003; Gough & Tunmer, 1986), but this term, which refers to a splinter skill of exceptional decoding in the face of intellectual disability (Aram, 1997), is an inaccurate descriptor for poor comprehenders and has not been broadly adopted. Poor comprehenders show adequate or even fluent word recognition and reading of connected text but difficulty understanding what they have read and poor performance on spoken language tests (Nation et al., 2004; Catts et al., 2003).

The challenge in evaluating reading comprehension is bypassing decoding difficulties. Many researchers and educators have expected that a person who is an adequate decoder can read a passage and answer questions or complete Cloze sentences about the content to reveal comprehension ability. However, some comprehension tasks allow readers to compensate through their decoding skills. Catts et al. (2006) showed that, for good decoders with poor comprehension, reading comprehension worsened over the elementary grades as the instruments allowed less decoding compensation. In contrast, listening comprehension tasks did not show a change in performance over the grades. Thus, Catts et al. emphasized the need to evaluate listening rather than reading comprehension. This finding also validated an early model of reading called the Simple View of Reading, which predicted that reading performance could be predicted by knowing a person's decoding skills and listening comprehension skills (Gough & Tunmer, 1986; Hoover & Gough, 1990). Listening comprehension is mainly about language, so this strengthened the links between reading disability and spoken language impairment.

A third type of reading disability is deficits in both decoding and comprehension. This has been called *common*, *general*, or *mixed reading disability* (Catts et al., 2012a; Gough & Tunmer, 1986; Cutting et al., 2009). These readers show poor word recognition skills and poor listening comprehension. This is the most severely affected type of reading disability.

Catts et al. (2003) investigated the distribution of subtypes of reading disabilities at second grade. From the larger Epi-SLI corpus, 183 children were identified as poor readers who performed at least 1 standard deviation below the mean on a composite measure of reading comprehension. Catts et al. compared the poor readers on word recognition and listening comprehension (with spoken language measures). Catts et al. found that classic dyslexia comprised approximately 35% of the disabled readers. Approximately 15% showed a specific comprehension deficit and 36% showed a mixed reading disability. Finally, 13% were unspecified, with mild, balanced deficits in listening comprehension and word recognition.

Reading Disability and SLI: Different but the Same?

A fruitful avenue of investigation for subtyping reading disability is with underlying component cognitive abilities of phonological processing and linguistic skills. Using this perspective, the two fundamental manifestations of reading disability are dyslexia and SLI (Bishop & Snowling, 2004; Catts et al., 2006; Ramus, Marshall, Rosen, & van der Lely, 2013). Bishop and Snowling (2004) suggested that, rather than these being two distinct conditions, the "specific diagnosis the child receives is a function of the age of the child, the severity of the impairment, and the professional discipline of the person making the diagnosis" (p. 865).

Phonological processing is centrally involved in decoding or word recognition, whether by sounding out or by visual recognition of orthography. Reading words also involves semantics. The interplay of these skills is evident in reading tasks involving rapid and accurate word recognition, and has been called the *triangle model of reading*: a three-way reciprocal interplay of orthography, phonology, and semantics (Plaut, McClelland, Seidenberg, & Patterson, 1996). The earliest decoding efforts are focused

Box 5.4. *The Extended Triangle Model of Reading*

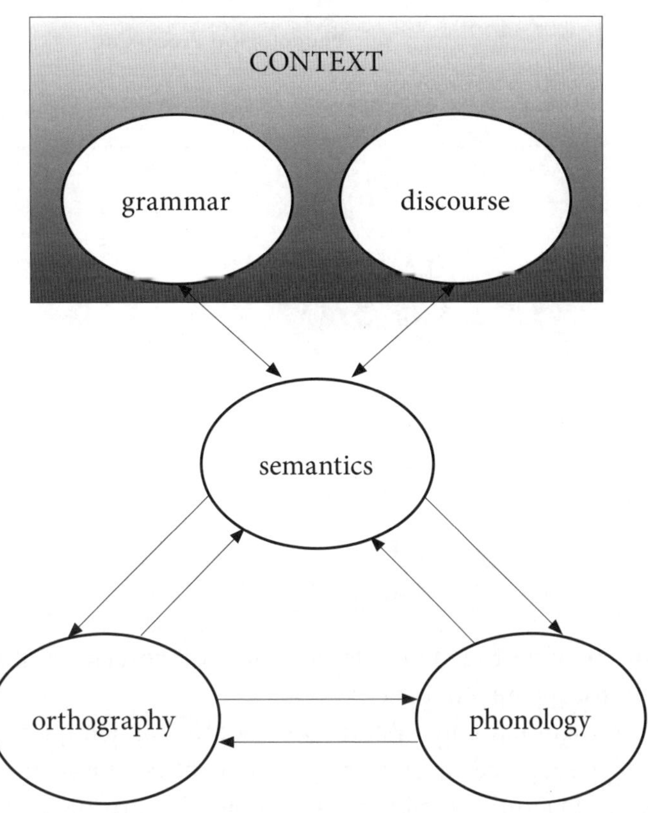

Note: From "Developmental Dyslexia and Specific Language Impairment: Same or Different?" by D. V. M. Bishop and M. J. Snowling, 2004, *Psychological Bulletin, 130*, p. 876. Copyright 2004 by American Psychological Association.

on linking orthography and phonology, and then, as the child (or computer model) learns more, this "learner" depends increasingly on semantic pathways for rapid recognition and for exception words. When reading goes beyond single-word recognition, connected text and comprehension of the discourse become involved in the reading process. Bishop and Snowling (2004) expanded Plaut et al.'s (1996) depiction to an "extended triangle model" of reading, which brings in the other language areas of syntax, discourse, and pragmatics (see Box 5.4).

This more comprehensive view of language brings SLI clearly into the picture of reading disability. Box 5.5 shows how dyslexia and SLI intersect when underlying abilities rather than simply reading performance is considered. Classic presentations of both dyslexia and SLI are characterized by deficits in aspects of phonological processing (Bishop & Snowling, 2004). The two conditions are differentiated by language skills, which, for classic dyslexia, are largely intact, while for classic SLI are notably low. There

Box 5.5. ***Relationship Between Reading Disability and SLI***

Semantics, Syntax, and Discourse	Phonological Processing: Poor	Phonological Processing: Adequate
Adequate	Classic Dyslexia	No Impairment
Poor	Classic SLI ⇩ Mixed Reading Disabled	SLI ⇩ Comprehension Reading Disabled

is a third dimension of time of manifestation, with SLI most apparent in preschool and classic dyslexia most apparent in the early grades.

Classic word-recognition-only dyslexia occupies the top-left quadrant of the figure with poor phonological processing but adequate semantics, syntax, and discourse skills. These children develop unremarkably as preschoolers but are identified as reading disabled in the early grades. These students will be flagged in kindergarten as showing insufficient progress in sound-letter knowledge, phonemic awareness, and simple nonword reading. If the student continues to struggle with reading in first grade, the RTI progress information and standard diagnostic measures will be used to identify reading disability.

SLI can be manifest with or without phonological processing deficits. What could be called "classic SLI" involves both phonological processing and language impairments. These children may be identified in preschool or kindergarten as SLI. If their deficits are severe enough to impact the early reading skills, they may be identified as reading disabled in the early grades. The emphasis in reading instruction and progress monitoring will be on word recognition. However, these students are likely to show deficits in reading comprehension, too. In the later elementary grades, the specialized reading instruction should expand its focus to include text comprehension as well as continued instruction in more advanced word recognition skills.

SLI with adequate phonological processing with noticeable spoken language delays in preschool or kindergarten will be identified as SLI and provided language support by SLPs. Given a home background that supports literacy development and adequate classroom instruction, these children are likely to progress adequately on decoding and spelling skills in the early grades. As these children progress through the primary grades and the language demands of their readings increase, their reading performance may drop so that they are then identified as reading disabled with a specific comprehension deficit. They are then served by reading specialists, possibly with secondary SLP language services. Alternately, neither the spoken nor written language deficits may be severe enough until later grades, at which point the child may be identified as reading disabled or language impaired.

Phonological processing and language can have interactive effects. For example, children with classic SLI might decode better than children with classic dyslexia because they have to work harder at it (Bishop & Snowling, 2004; Goulandris et al., 2000). Children with dyslexia can bootstrap their word recognition with better semantics and syntax (e.g., *This word is hard to sound out, but what words do I know that make sense in this sentence?*), which compensates for, but does not improve, their phonological decoding skills. This strategy is less available to children with classic SLI. As a result of not being able to depend on semantic or discourse skills, children with SLI must attend more carefully to the phonological and visual aspects of word decoding, leading to better word reading and spelling.

Interplay with other factors, such as general intellectual skills, world knowledge, or quality of instruction also affects outcomes (Bishop & Snowling, 2004). For example, a child with weak phonological processing but good executive function is likely to manage better than one who is less self-regulated. Furthermore, neither underlying skills nor observable behaviors directly translate into diagnostic labels or educational eligibility categories, which are subject to other factors, such as age of identification, eligibility criteria, testing measures, and primary versus secondary service decisions.

Two broad areas of ability that underlie reading competence are language and phonological processing. Children with SLI by definition are deficient in language and often are deficient in phonological processing. Children with reading disability are almost always deficient in phonological processing and are often deficient in language. The linguistic characteristics of reading disability and the phonological processing features of both disorders are presented next.

Language and Phonological Processing of SLI and Reading Disability

It is now generally agreed upon that deficits in awareness, storage, and retrieval of phonological representations lie at the core of reading disabilities (Bishop & Snowling, 2004; Catts et al., 2012b; Lyon et al., 2003; Shaywitz et al., 2009). Children with SLI, especially those whose difficulties persist to become reading problems, also have difficulties in this area. These cognitive skills are collectively called *phonological processing*. Awareness and working memory are most consistently included as components of phonological processing, but word finding is increasingly recognized as having phonological representation and access issues, too (e.g., Bishop & Snowling, 2004; Messer & Dockrell, 2006; Catts et al., 2012b). Current formulations of phonological processing recognize these three components and sometimes a fourth component of phonological production. SLPs are careful to distinguish among phonological processing, phonological processes (i.e., stopping, cluster reduction), and phonological production (i.e., speech sounds), but reading researchers are oblivious to these distinctions and use "phonological skills" to mean only phonological processing. Before further discussing the components of phonogical processing, the language features of reading disability will be presented.

Linguistic Characteristics of Reading Disability

As is apparent from the foregoing discussion of the relationship between SLI and reading disability, language is frequently deficient in individuals with reading disability, especially if the reading difficulties are manifest in comprehension. The reading research must be read carefully to determine what "language" difficulties are because "listening comprehension" may refer to passage comprehension or spoken language measures used by SLPs, and "language" may be considered to be phonological processing. In general academic achievement tests, language may mean spelling, punctuation, and formal grammar.

The word-recognition and fluency problems of dyslexia do not strongly involve language skills, but there is some effect even here from language deficits, especially in relation to semantics. Breadth (knowing a lot of words) matters more than depth (knowing a lot about words) for word recognition (Ouellette, 2006). Reading irregular and low-frequency words is particularly susceptible to weak vocabularies (Nation & Snowling, 1998b). Fluency, which involves reading rapidly, accurately, and with appropriate sentence prosody, is affected by syntax skills. Substantial deficits in receptive syntax have been found for children who show both decoding and comprehension problems, but not for comprehension problems alone (Cutting et al., 2009).

For reading comprehension, language matters a lot. Children with reading comprehension disability show low expressive and receptive vocabulary, grammar, and discourse (e.g., Catts et al., 2006; Cutting et al., 2009; Nation et al., 2004; Nation & Snowling, 1998a; Ramus et al., 2013; Scarborough, 1990). Nation et al. examined the spoken language skills of 8-year-olds who, despite reading fluently and accurately, had difficulty understanding what they read. Spoken language measures of semantics, morphosyntax, and metalinguistics showed low performance, with a substantial minority showing marked deficits. Nation and colleagues (2004) suggested that these children could have been considered undiagnosed SLI.

These deficits in spoken language precede the onset of reading instruction (e.g., Gallagher, Frith, & Snowling, 2000; Nation, Cocksey, Taylor, & Bishop, 2010). For example, Scarborough (1990) followed 52 children: 20 children who subsequently became disabled readers at second grade and 32 children who became normal readers. For the disabled readers, Scarborough found deficits at 30 months of age in utterance length, syntax complexity, and pronunciation accuracy. Expressive and receptive vocabulary deficits appeared at 3 years of age, and persisted into measurements at 5 and 8 years of age. From the Epi-SLI project, Catts, Fey, Zhang, and Tomblin (1999) found that, for second-grade poor readers, more than half had receptive (58%) and expressive (50%) spoken language deficits in kindergarten, compared to good readers (12% showed deficits). Among the poor readers, 39% showed vocabulary deficits, 56% showed grammar deficits, and 44% showed narrative deficits. Thus, problems in spoken language were 3 to 5 times greater among poor readers than among good readers.

Phonological Awareness

The component of phonological processing that has received the most attention, likely because it is very teachable, is phonological awareness: the ability to reflect on and manipulate the sounds of speech. Awareness of phonemes (e.g., "cat" has three sounds, /k/-/a/-/t/) is particularly important for alphabetic writing systems like English. There is a large body of evidence showing that preschool phonological awareness is predictive of later reading attainment, even when general cognitive ability is controlled (e.g., Bradley & Bryant, 1983; Lundberg, Olofsson, & Wall, 1980; Torgesen, Wagner, & Rashotte, 1994). Instruction in phonological awareness substantially improves reading outcomes (see Ehri et al., 2001), but the underlying deficits in phonemic awareness persist even when language and reading difficulties largely resolve (Bruck, 1993; Stothard et al., 1998).

Phonological awareness deficits have been found in children with SLI, particularly those who later develop reading problems (e.g., Catts, Adlof, Hogan, & Weismer, 2005; Fraser, Goswami, & Conti-Ramsden, 2010; Stothard et al., 1998). Consistent deficits in phonological awareness have been found in those with reading disability (e.g., Catts, 1993; Fraser et al., 2010; Gallagher et al., 2000; Torgesen et al., 1994). Performance has been found to be lower even than younger students matched on word reading level (Olson, Wise, Conners, Rack, & Fulker, 1989). For languages with more regular sound-letter correspondence patterns, weaknesses in phonological awareness have less of an impact on reading. For example, Landerl, Wimmer, and Frith (1997) found that German dyslexic readers with poor phonological awareness showed much better word reading performance than English dyslexic readers.

Phonological Memory

While phonological (or more specifically, phonemic) awareness is important in reading, deficits in other components of phonological processing, especially phonological memory, play a more critical role in severe, persistent reading problems. Phonological memory involves the short-term representation of speech sounds. Phonological memory is typically measured through memory-span tasks using digits, letters, or words, or repetition of polysyllabic sequences, such as *dopelate* or *blonterstapping*. Difficulty in these tasks occurs for children with SLI (e.g., Dollaghan & Campbell, 1998; Gathercole & Baddeley, 1990; Kamhi & Catts, 1986) and reading disability (e.g., Brady, Shankweiler, & Mann, 1983; Snowling, 1981; Torgesen, 1985).

Catts et al. (2012b) reported studies showing the memory issue is present even with visually presented verbal stimuli so long as they can be coded phonologically. In an unusual twist, Catts et al. reported that good readers, who rely more on phonological memory, have more difficulty with words that have close phonological representational ties, such as rhyming words, than poor readers. This rapidly decaying phonological memory likely affects not only sound-letter mapping but acquisition of vocabulary as children quickly forget the sounds of the new words they hear (e.g., Gathercole, Willis, Emslie, & Baddeley, 1992). Performance as preschoolers predicts later reading performance and, when early language and reading problems are resolved, nonword repetition deficits may continue (e.g., Catts, Fey, Zhang, & Tomblin, 2001; Gallagher et al., 2000; Nation et al., 2004; Stothard et al., 1998; Torgesen et al., 1994).

Phonological Code Retrieval

Phonological code retrieval is a third component of phonological processing. It is the process of locating and matching a string of speech sounds to word meaning. It may be observed as a word-finding problem in spoken language with substitutions, circumlocutions, or vague words. For reading, it appears as slower and less accurate performance on timed confrontation picture naming. Either of these can be present with intact receptive vocabulary (e.g., Catts, 1986; Denckla & Rudel, 1976). Evidence that these difficulties are phonologically based, not semantically based, was demonstrated by Hanly and Vandenberg (2010). In a picture-naming task, when participants said they knew the word, but could not recall it, they were asked to say what they knew semantically about the word. The children with reading disability experienced more tip-of-the-tongue episodes than typical readers but provided similar semantic information about the target word.

A measure of phonological retrieval independent of word familiarity is a task called *serial naming* or *rapid automatic naming*. This involves naming a sequence of colors, letters, numbers, or pictured objects as quickly as possible. Variation in rapid naming in preschoolers is predictive of later reading performance (e.g., Badian, 1994; Catts, 1993; Wolf, Bally, & Morris, 1986). Phonological retrieval problems, whether as word finding or rapid naming, are not always seen in SLI but are more likely to be present for those children who show reading problems (Messer & Dockrell, 2006). Children with reading disability have consistently been found to be slower on rapid naming tasks than typical readers (e.g., Denckla & Rudel, 1976; Vellutino et al., 1995). From the Epi-SLI project, Catts et al. (1999) found that 14% of their second-grade poor readers had phonological processing deficits alone, and 37% had it in combination with language deficits. This compared to the good readers, for whom 9% had deficits in phonological processing with or without language deficits. For phonological processing components, 17% had poor phonological awareness and 13% had poor rapid naming.

The combination of difficulties in phonological awareness and phonological code retrieval, as measured by rapid naming, has been thought to be a particular "double deficit" source of severe reading difficulties (Wolf & Bowers, 1999). This may be because, although rapid naming has a central phonological retrieval component, it also taps attentional, perceptual, memory, lexical, and articulatory elements (Wolf, Bowers, & Biddle, 2000).

Phonological Production

Speech sound problems are not a prominent feature of SLI or of reading disability. However there is evidence of subtle articulatory difficulties for phonologically complex words for both conditions (Elbro, Borstrom, & Petersen, 1998; Catts, 1986; Munson et al., 2005; Snowling, 1981). Many of the errors do not appear to be conditioned by the phonetic context but rather seem to be a function of inadequately specified phonological representations. Errors on rapid repetition of phrases containing common monosyllabic words (e.g., *brown and blue plaid pants*) suggest planning difficulties for speech sound sequences.

Other Possible Contributions to SLI and Reading Disability

There are other areas of perception and cognition that have been investigated as contributors to the language and reading difficulties of SLI and reading disability. Many children with poor language and reading skills show lower performance in these areas than their typically developing peers. However, the differences are usually slight and not consistently present. Furthermore, the relationship between these deficits and language or reading skills is unclear. Some deficits may cause language and reading problems, some may co-occur due to a third known or unknown common cause, and some deficits may combine to increase the severity of the communication and academic problems.

Auditory Processing

Below the level of speech-specific processing is auditory processing. Auditory perception has long been linked to developmental language and reading problems as reflected in the old label of "auditory dyslexia." Auditory processing has been investigated both as a contributing deficit in SLI and reading disability and as an independent, but often comorbid, disorder called *central auditory processing disorder*, or CAPD (the C may be left off) (Richard, 2012). Auditory processes that have been implicated include localization; lateralization; discrimination; pattern recognition; temporal integration, discrimination, ordering, and masking; competing signals; and degraded signals. CAPD is often evaluated by audiologists who may engage in auditory training exercises or offer classroom amplification. Management beyond that is likely to fall to SLPs, especially if there are deficits in language and academic performance. Despite the frequency with which CAPD is diagnosed, there is still a lack of professional consensus on its definition, components, identification, and treatment (Richard, 2012).

In relation to SLI and reading disabilities, researchers have investigated perception of speech signal components, such as formant transitions and voice onset time (e.g., Tallal & Piercy, 1974; Tallal, 1980) as well as perception of more general acoustic information, such as rapidly changing tones or speech in noise (Farmer & Klein, 1995). Difficulties have been more consistently present with speech than nonspeech sounds (e.g., Brier, Gray, Fletcher, Foorman, & Klaas, 2002). However, even then, differences are not consistently present: Hazan and colleagues (2009) examined discrimination of stop voicing contrast for adults with reading disability and found no significant group differences and inconsistent performance across related tasks within individuals. Although Tallal (2000) posited that temporal resolution of auditory information affected phonological representations, deficits have not been found to be consistently predictive of phonological processing or severity of reading deficit (e.g., Nittrouer, 1999; Share, Jorm, Maclean, & Matthews, 2002; but see Brier et al., 2002). In sum, auditory processing deficits have been found only in a minority of individuals with SLI or reading disability, and a causal role is not clear, with deficits possibly caused by other difficulties, such as inattention, working memory, or nonverbal intelligence (Bailey & Snowling, 2002; Catts et al., 2012b; Rosen, 2003).

Visuoperceptual Processing of Reading Disability

A popular belief is that reading disability is caused by visual-perceptual difficulties. A "word blindness" basis of reading disability would seem to make sense, given that reading involves looking at print and identifying the letters that form words. However, it turns out that this intuitive and long-held judgment is wrong.

Prominent features of dyslexia are often considered to be letter reversals and sequencing errors. Given the public's tenacious hold to this idea, there is surprisingly little systematic research examining this question (Catts et al., 2012b) and much of the work related to dyslexia dates from the 1970s. Children with poor reading do make reversal and sequencing errors, but they represent only a small proportion of the total reading errors (Fischer, Liberman, & Shankweiler, 1978; Liberman, Shankweiler, Orlando, Harris, & Berti, 1971). Liberman et al. found that reversible errors primarily involve letters that differ by rotational shifts, so remembering how the letters are spatially distinguished is critical (e.g., line down on the left of the circle versus up and on the right). In addition, the confused letters differ only by one phonetic feature (*b, d, p*). For sequencing errors (e.g., *saw/was, dog/god, girl/gril*), children with reading disability perceive letters as well as normal readers, as shown by letter copying, immediate letter recognition, and visual recall of unfamiliar letter shapes (e.g., Vellutino, Pruzek, Steger, & Meshoulam, 1973; Vellutino, Steger, DeSetto, & Phillips, 1975). Furthermore, in spelling, typical readers make the same kinds of spelling errors as dyslexic readers, just fewer of them (e.g., Holmes & Peper, 1977). This apparently notable problem turns out not to be not so notable (the first author, Ukrainetz, wrote in mirror writing in first grade and turned out to be an adequate reader).

One visuoperceptual explanation is that of erratic eye movements (Catts et al., 2012b). The sensation when we read is that our eyes move smoothly and continuously across and down the printed page. In fact, normal eye movement during reading involves a series of rapid left-to-right jerks, called *saccades*, with occasional reversed jerks, called *regressions*, followed by brief fixations. Poor readers have more and longer fixations, shorter saccades, and more regressions than typical readers. Eye movement differences have been observed for poor readers in nonreading, low-cognition visual tasks (e.g., Pavlidis, 1985; Rayner, 1978). However, these differences could be an effect, not a cause, of word recognition and comprehension difficulties with pauses and reversals increasing as the reader seeks to understand the material (Rayner, 1998).

Another visuoperceptual theory is *scotopic sensitivity syndrome* (Irlen as cited in Catts et al., 2012b). This condition involved oversensitivity to particular frequencies of light. Individuals with this condition were considered to be afflicted with perceptual distortions, reduced visual field, poor focus, eyestrain, and headaches. Irlen claimed that colored lenses or overlays reduced symptoms. Dyslexia was included in commercial promotions and the lens became a well-known alternative treatment (Silver, 1995). It is unclear whether children with reading disability have a higher incidence of scotopic sensitivity or, if present, that it explains the reading difficulties. In addition, not all studies have found the visual effect (e.g., Johannes, Kussmaul, Munte, & Mangun, 1996).

In sum, visuoperceptual explanations of reading disability have not been generally supported by research evidence. Furthermore, research findings in controlled studies of oculumotor exercises and colored lenses show a lack of effectiveness (e.g., Fletcher & Martinez, 1994; Blaskey et al., 1990; Keogh & Pelland, 1985; Metzer & Werner, 1984; Silver, 1995). A joint position statement by the American Academy of Pediatrics and American Academy of Ophthalmology (2009) strongly discouraged the use of colored lenses, eye exercises, and other behavioral vision therapies based on the lack of evidence of visuoperceptual causes or efficacy of treatment for reading disability.

Sensorimotor and Procedural Learning

There have been attempts to link auditory and visual performance based on features of the information being processed and common neurobiological pathways. One argument is that the phonological processing deficits of reading disability are caused by a general sensorimotor dysfunction that also affects aspects of visual function (Ramus, 2003, 2004). The scotopic sensitivity syndrome and erratic eye movements observed in some poor readers have been theorized to be due to lower level deficits in visual processing (Catts et al., 2012). There are two visual systems that are specialized in processing transient or sustained visual information. Individuals with reading disabilities have shown difficulty on visual tasks that involve the transient system (e.g., Lovegrove, Martin, & Slaghuis, 1986; Livingstone, Rosen, Drislane, & Galaburda, 1991). It has been proposed that a sluggish transient system disrupts parallel operations with the sustained system, leading to distortions and other visual problems. In what has been called the *general magnocellular theory of dyslexia*, this sluggish system leads to auditory, visual, and motor deficits (Ramus, 2003).

Another theory involves a somewhat higher level cross-modality difficulty in memory and learning for a specific type of information. Ullman (2004) has proposed a *procedural learning hypothesis* in which children with SLI have more difficulty learning procedural (sequences and rules) than declarative (conceptual and semantic) information. This difficulty is theorized to contribute to impairments observed in diverse linguistic and nonlinguistic abilities, including grammar, motor sequencing, temporal processing, lexical retrieval, dynamic visual imagery, and working memory (Ullman, 2004; Ullman & Pierpont, 2005). The areas of the brain identified for procedural memory involve the magnocellular pathways that process transient auditory and visual signals, thus research in these two areas may come converge in some way.

The evidence for either a general sensorimotor or a procedural memory deficit is very preliminary and neither of these is yet considered a primary cause of reading disability or SLI. A slight sensory or procedural learning deficit may occur in a subset of affected individuals, but even the causal link to language and reading difficulties is not clear. How sensorimotor and procedural memory interact and whether they are effects of more general limitations in attention or information-processing capacity is still under debate (Ramus, 2003; Stuart, McAnally, & Castles, 2001). For example, Gabriel, Stefaniak, Maillart, Schmitz, and Meulemans (2012) compared 6- to 12-year-old children with SLI to typically developing peers on nonverbal visual procedural tasks involving serial reaction time. The children with SLI were slower and made more errors with the responses, suggesting a procedural deficit that crossed into the visual modality. However, differences disappeared when the response was changed from a keyboard to a touch screen that simplified the motor and cognitive demands.

Attention and Information Processing

As Gabriel et al. (2012) showed, research investigation of perceptual factors in SLI and reading disability must control for effects of higher order differences in cognitive abilities, such as attention and executive function. Evidence is accumulating that there are differences in these areas that likely contribute to difficulties in language and reading.

Attention is a more complicated phenomenon than one would expect. Attention encompasses arousal and alertness; orienting and responding; searching and spotlighting; and selecting, sustaining, and dividing attention (Ashcraft & Radvansky, 2010). Attentional processes can be extremely rapid and reflexive or slow and deliberate. Some attentional acts take a lot of perceptual and cognitive resources and some take very little. Initial, reflexive, automatic attention occurs more to familiar events (i.e., we notice important stuff immediately) while subsequent intentional orienting and focusing occur more to novel events (i.e., we try to make sense of strange stuff) (Hogarth, Dickinson, & Duka, 2010). Hogarth et al. distinguished these two mechanisms as "looking for action" and "looking for learning," and add a third affective component: If we like what we notice, we will keep attending or "looking for liking."

The condition involving severe inattention, impulsivity, and overactivity, called attention-deficit/hyperactivity disorder (ADHD) has been tied to language and reading problems (Boada, Willcutt, & Pennington, 2012; Cantwell & Baker, 1987; McGrath et al., 2008). About one third of clinically referred children with SLI fit an ADHD profile. Studies using research-identified samples have shown a much lower, but still notable co-occurrence. Mueller and Tomblin (2012) found that children with SLI are 2 to 3 times more likely than typically developing children to have ADHD, but children with ADHD are much less likely to have SLI.

For reading disability and ADHD, estimates of comorbidity have varied widely, due both to how study participants were obtained and differences in identification criteria (Shaywitz, Fletcher, & Shaywitz, 1994). In research-identified samples, Shaywitz et al. reported that 36% of children with inattention as the primary condition had reading problems (either an ability-achievement discrepancy or scoring below the 25th %ile), while only 15% of children with reading problems had inattention (Shaywitz, Fletcher, & Shaywitz, 1994). The clinic-referred rates were 54% and 41%, respectively. Willcutt and Pennington (2000) found that the ADHD behaviors were consistent across contexts, so the co-occurrence was not likely due to the attention problems being caused by frustrations with reading. Willcutt and Pennington also reported that girls with reading disability had more inattention behaviors while boys with reading disability had more hyperactive and impulsive behaviors.

Although SLI and reading disability have a high co-occurrence of attentional difficulties, they seem to be different entities than ADHD. Children with a primary label of ADHD lack the phonological-processing deficit component (Boada et al., 2012; Willcutt et al., 2001). When significant attentional problems are present in reading disability, they are more often problems of inattention rather than hyperactivity or impulsivity, but even those can largely be accounted for by measures of general processing speed (Boada et al. 2012; Willcutt & Pennington, 2000).

Sustaining and allocating attention has been found to be weaker in children with SLI than in typically developing children. For visual attention alone, some studies have shown difficulty sustaining attention (e.g., Finneran, Francis, & Leonard, 2009) while others have not (e.g., Spaulding, Plante, & Vance, 2008). Archibald and Gathercole (2006) found that short-term and working memory for visuospatial stimuli were not significantly different for children with SLI in contrast to their performance on verbal memory tasks. Studies involving competing auditory-visual tasks and/or cross-modal processing suggest a domain-general resource limitation (Gillam, Cowan, & Marler, 1998; Leclercq, Majerus, Prigent, & Maillart, 2013; Leonard et al., 2007; Montgomery, 1993). For example, Hoffman and Gillam (2004) required school-age children with and without SLI to recall verbal and spatial stimuli in activities that varied in the number of task demands and the speed of item presentation. The children with SLI recalled less information and had more trouble coordinating within and across verbal and spatial modalities, suggesting lower capacity and weaker allocational resources. In addition, children with SLI show subtle difficulties in nonverbal tasks involving quantification, mental rotation, and dimensional thought (e.g., Cowan, Donlan, Newton, & Lloyd, 2005; Fazio, 1996; Johnston & Weismer, 1983; Johnston & Smith, 1989). Further evidence for a general processing limitation comes from studies indicating that some syntactic and narrative deficits can be explained by memory and attentional demands of the tasks (Colozzo, Gillam, Woods, Schnell, & Johnston, 2011; Leonard, Deevy, Fey, & Bredin-Oja, 2013; Robertson & Joanisse, 2010).

Executive function goes beyond attention and processing speed to include working memory, attention allocation, problem solving, rule learning, and reflective responding. It involves intentionally directing, reviewing, and modifying one's behavior to accomplish a goal. On detection and correction of erroneous or inserted story elements, Skarakis-Doyle and Dempsey (2008) found that preschool children with SLI had significantly more errors than both age- and language-matched controls. Parents and teachers of preschoolers with SLI have reported more difficulty with behaviors involving impulse and emotion control, transitioning between activities, managing task demands, and problem solving (Wittke, Spaulding, & Schechtman, 2013). Children with reading disability show difficulties on nonverbal puzzles (Cutting et al., 2009; Sesma, Mahone, Levine, Eason, & Cutting, 2009). Sesma et al. found that executive function performance explained variance in reading comprehension more than word recognition and did so in addition to effects of attention, fluency, and language skills.

Neurobiology and Genetics of SLI and Reading Disability

The Brains of Individuals With SLI or Reading Disability

The concept of SLI and reading disability as inherent learning problems necessitates a neurobiological basis. This belief has been present since the earliest descriptions of both developmental disorders (e.g., Orton, 1937), although investigators had to rely on presumed outward indicators, such as handedness or dichotic listening, to test theories such as lack of hemispheric lateralization. (In defense of left-handers like Ukrainetz, there is no association between handedness and reading disability; see Bishop, 1990.)

Answers to many questions about neurobiological mapping have hinged on development and access to appropriate imaging devices. The earliest research was conducted through autopsies of individuals who had histories of reading disabilities and delayed spoken language (e.g., Cohen, Campbell, & Yaghmai, 1989; Galaburda, Sherman, Rosen, Aboitiz, & Geschwind, 1985). One of the difficulties with interpreting brain differences in these studies was determining whether the differences were present during language and reading development or developed as result of a lifetime of impaired behaviors. Cortical and subcortical structure can now be examined in living individuals during language and reading tasks with computerized tomography (CT) scans and high-resolution magnetic resonance imaging (MRI). Metabolic activity and blood flow is visible with functional magnetic resonance imaging (fMRI), positron emission tomography (PET) scans, and evoked response potential (ERP) from scalp electroencephalography (Shafer & Maxfield, 2009). According to Shafer and Maxfield, ERP is the least expensive and easiest to use but is limited by what cortical signals can reach the scalp. Data from these tools can reveal differences and atypicalities during the developmental period. However, ascribing causes to differences must still be done cautiously.

There are considerable challenges to making sense of the research (Bishop & Snowling, 2004; Leonard & Eckert, 2008; Shaywitz et al., 2009). First, structural differences are often slight and diffuse. There is considerable inconsistency and conflicting findings concerning morphological asymmetry or abnormal gyral development. Functional imaging studies have obtained more consistent results, but there are caveats here too: A brain that lights up differently for a poor versus a good reader may only indicate that the poor reader is using different or more energy for this laborious task, not that the different brain activity is causing the reading problems. Second, while the brain measures may be done very carefully, the selection and ability profiling of the participants are often not. "Dyslexics" may simply be poor readers who appear normal otherwise. A major problem until recently has been lack of attention to word recognition and phonological processing versus comprehension and language in neurobiological study participants.

It turns out that SLI and reading disability overlap neurobiologically as well as phenotypically (Bishop & Snowling, 2004; Pennington & Bishop, 2009). Differences for both individuals with SLI and reading disability have been located to the temporo-parieto-occipital region of the left hemispheres (see Box 5.6). Differences have been located in the planum temporale (adjacent to Wernicke's area), responsible for receptive language processing, and the pars triangularis (within Broca's area), responsible for expressive language and speech production. For most people with normal language and reading, the left hemisphere is dominant and the left planum is larger than the right (leftward asymmetry).

A difference between SLI and dyslexia is in hemispheric lateralization. Although many articles link planar asymmetry with dyslexia (e.g., Catts et al., 2012b; Shaywitz et al., 2009), most studies that control for language abilities have not found this association but rather normal or exaggerated leftward asymmetry (Leonard & Eckert, 2008).

Box 5.6. ***Areas of Cortex Involved in Reading and Language***

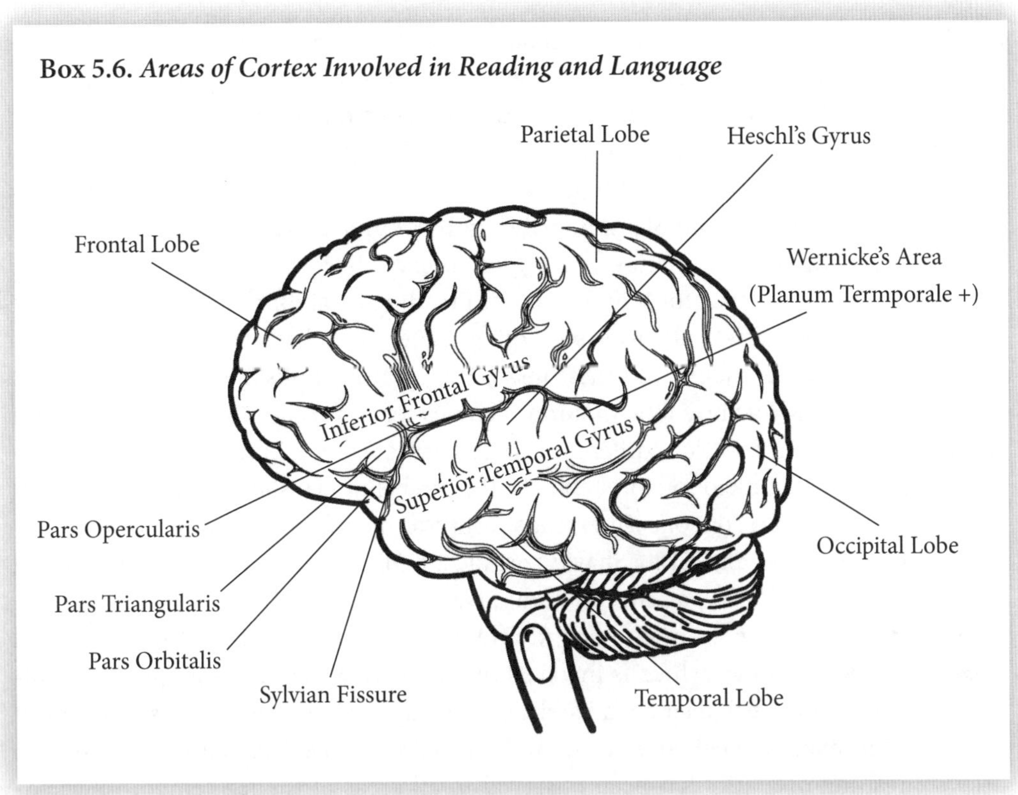

In a series of quantitative MRI analyses of children and adults with reading and language disorders, Leonard and colleagues (e.g., Gauger, Lombardino, & Leonard, 1997; Leonard & Eckert, 2008; Leonard et al., 2002) identified two clusters with contrasting anatomical and reading profiles. Normal children showed a linear relationship between reading skills and planar asymmetry, such that poorer readers had symmetry or rightward asymmetry of the planum temporale whereas better readers had leftward asymmetry. Individuals with language and reading disorders had two patterns of atypicality around this continuum. Children with deficits in multiple domains of written and oral language (whether SLI or reading disabled with comprehension problems) tended to have small or symmetrical cortical structures. They showed an enlarged right planum and lower volumes for the left pars triangularis, or planar symmetry and overall lower cortical volume. In contrast, children with phonologically based reading disabilities and college students with poor phonological decoding but good comprehension (classic dyslexia) had normal or exaggerated leftward planar asymmetry, sometimes with enlarged temporal lobes. In general, Leonard and Eckert found that more severely affected individuals had both more linear anomalies and more bilateral anomalies but that the anatomical risk factors deviated from the normal moderate brain size and asymmetry in opposing directions for language versus decoding problems.

Additional areas of abnormality have been identified subcortically, in the striatum of the basal ganglia, which projects to Broca's area and other inferior and premotor areas of the frontal lobe (Ullman, 2004; Ullman & Pierpont, 2005). The striatum consists of the caudate nucleus and the putamen. The caudate nucleus and its projection paths are associated with procedural memory, so anomalies in these structures could underlie a variety of the verbal and nonverbal deficits seen in SLI. According to Ullman and Pierpont, the projection paths control inhibition and excitation of frontal cortical pathways so that an imbalance between these two pathways has been thought to explain the hypo and hyper behaviors of both organic conditions like Parkinson's and Tourette's and developmental disorders like ADHD and SLI. Anomalies in these projection paths might be related to the overactivation of the inferior frontal area observed by Shaywitz et al. (1998) during phonological analysis tasks for individuals with reading disability. Alternately, maybe it shows the appropriate activation for struggling readers who have to try harder and involve more procedural memory in these tasks. The putamen links to motor control, thus possibly accounting for the subtle motor difficulties seen in some children with SLI and reading disability. In addition, differences have been observed in morphology and volume of another area linked to motor control, the cerebellum (Bishop & Snowling, 2004).

For reading, the area of concern extends from Wernicke's area into the posterior occipital region (Catts et al., 2012b; Shaywitz et al., 2009). Two areas can be distinguished for reading: (a) the dorsal parieto-temporal area, which is involved in phonemic word analysis, mapping sounds to letters, and attentional control; and (b) the left ventral occipito-temporal region, which is involved in automatic visual orthographic recognition. This latter area has also been implicated in rapid picture naming, suggesting it is involved in phonological code retrieval. Reduced or delayed activation in individuals with reading disability has been observed in all areas of the left temporo-parieto-occipital region (Shaywitz et al., 1998; Shaywitz et al., 2002). The magnocellular layers of the lateral geniculate nucleus, located at the junction of the occipital and temporal lobes, and their projection paths, have also been implicated in the processing of transient visual signals (Eden et al., 1996; Livingstone, Rosen, Drislane, & Galaburda, 1991), and possibly of even more general sensorimotor information (Ramus, 2003, 2004).

In a study of young adults identified as reading disabled in first grade, Shaywitz et al. (2009) reported that different neurobiological patterns were found for those who had improved to be slow but accurate readers from those who remained inaccurate and slow readers. The persistently poor readers had lower IQs and lower socioeconomic backgrounds (language skills were not reported). The improved readers showed similar activation to typical readers except during regular and nonword recognition tasks, when they continued to show the disruptions of posterior systems typical of reading disability. The persistently poor readers lacked the posterior differences but showed atypical connectivity patterns involving the right frontal region, associated with memory and executive systems.

Finally, brain activation is malleable from effective instruction, normalizing toward left temporo-parietal activation (Catts et al., 2012b). For example, Shaywitz et al. (2004) found that second- and third-grade readers with dyslexia who received a reading intervention that improved their reading accuracy, fluency, and comprehension demonstrated increased activation in both the left anterior and left posterior regions. Even anatomic features can be changed: Keller and Just (2009) showed increased myelination and improved organization of the white matter connections among reading-related brain regions for poor readers.

Heritability of SLI and Reading Disability

Both reading disability and SLI tend to run in families. Research on heritability compares the occurrence of SLI and reading disabilities in families versus the general population and in identical versus fraternal twins. Molecular genetics now allow researchers to investigate the genetic regions of chromosomes involved in these disorders.

Studies have shown a higher occurrence of language problems in the relatives of children with speech and language impairments (e.g., Lewis & Thompson, 1992; Tallal, Ross, & Curtiss, 1989; Tomblin, 1989). Lewis and Thompson administered interviews and questionnaires to parents of 165 children with and without speech sound and language impairment (called probands), matched on socioeconomic status. When compared to a matched control group, relatives of probands had higher rates of speech sound disorders and language impairment (13.6% versus 2.2%), reading problems (3.3% versus 1.0%), and histories of special education (5.3% versus 2.0%), but not stuttering or hearing impairment. The pattern was similar even for probands with only a speech sound impairment, suggesting a broad verbal heritable trait that can result in a speech, language, or reading disorder. Lewis noted that a higher incidence of all problems within the proband's nuclear family than in the extended family might have been due in part to heightened awareness and increased identification.

Across studies, having a first-degree relative with SLI increases chances of a family member being affected from about 7% to about 30% (Tomblin, 2009). For reading disability, Catts et al. (2012b) estimate that a sibling of a child with a reading disability has an approximately 40% chance of also having a reading disability and a parent has a 30% to 40% likelihood of experiencing reading difficulties. It should be noted that many retrospective identifications of SLI, reading disability, and other learning problems are loose. For example, Lewis and Thompson (1992) identified individuals as having a reading disability if they were: "(a) labeled as dyslexic in school or (b) had received tutoring for reading" (p. 589).

The family tree studies cannot untangle genetic relations from the influence of the caregiving and the literacy environment of the home; as Catts et al. (2012b) remind us, bad table manners and bad cake recipes also run in families. Studies of identical and fraternal twins circumvent this difficulty because they contrast on genetics not upbringing. In addition, prospective twin studies can use objective measures rather than depend on family report. Twin studies have shown coheritability for SLI and reading disability (Bishop, 2001; Stevenson, Graham, Fredman, & McLoughlin, 1987). The co-occurrence of reading disability in identical twins has been found to be 68% whereas co-occurrence in fraternal twins was only 40% (Light & DeFries, 1995). A number of twin studies have found that heritability increases if the impairment includes deficits in phonological processing (Bishop & Snowling, 2004). In a study involving preschoolers from the United States, Australia, and Scandinavia, researchers found a stronger genetic influence on phonological awareness, rapid naming, and verbal memory and a stronger environmental influence on vocabulary and print knowledge (Samuelsson et al., 2007). Finally, visual and auditory processing deficits do not show the heritability pattern seen for phonological processing (Bishop et al., 1999; Olson & Datta, 2002).

There is one extended family in the United Kingdom, called KE, that has been extensively studied for heritability of SLI. Fifteen family members across three generations have been reported to have severe speech and language impairments. Crago and Gopnik (Gopnik, 1990; Gopnik & Crago, 1991) proposed that this family's particular morphosyntactic difficulties revealed the existence of a genetic anomaly with a pattern suggesting a single dominant gene transmission. However, it became apparent that the family members had a high incidence of speech and orofacial apraxia, suggesting this was more than SLI (Tomblin, 2009). Regardless of the exact nature of the disorder, this family spurred studies identifying the genetic locations for language impairment.

Molecular genetics examines regions of the genome for polymorphic linkages or quantitative trait loci (Catts et al., 2012b; Tomblin, 2009). These loci involve multiple genes that work together (the genotype) to influence an observable behavior (the phonotype). For the KE family, a region on chromosome 7 designated as SPCH1 was found to be anomalous (Fisher, Vargha-Khadem, Watkins, Monaco, & Pembrey, 1998). The genetic anomaly was further specified to a FOXP2 gene for all affected members and for an unrelated case (Lai, Fisher, Hurst, Vargha-Khadem, & Monaco, 2001). However, subsequent studies of children with SLI have had mixed results in identifying FOXP2 abnormalities (e.g., O'Brien, Zhang, Nishimura, Tomblin, & Murray, 2003). Although the FOXP2 gene is involved in neural systems important for speech and language development, it does not appear to be a common cause of SLI (Tomblin, 2009).

Studies have shown evidence of linkages for dyslexia and SLI on a number of chromosomes, with some showing different locations for the two conditions (Bishop & Snowling, 2004; Catts et al., 2012b; Tomblin, 2009). It appears that a number of genes work together to influence reading ability and these genes affect different aspects of a learning disability (Plomin & Kovas, 2005). Differences in locations might indicate different etiologies, but Bishop and Snowling also suggested overlaps in areas of weaker association that were not picked up in these complex multivariate analyses. Catts et al. pointed out that reading is a relatively new human endeavor that involves many behaviors, so it is not surprising that it is not specifically coded in a single genetic location and that focusing on specific cognitive abilities, such as phonological memory, instead of broad diagnostic categories, is proving to be a more fruitful route.

Conclusion

This chapter reviewed two major types of learning disabilities appearing on a school SLP's caseload: SLI and reading disability. SLI is characterized by difficulties in spoken language. Reading disability is characterized by difficulties with written language. Reading disability can be subtyped as primarily word recognition problems (classic dyslexia), primarily comprehension problems, or both. The latter two conditions overlap with SLI and appear to differ mainly on severity and age of identification. Children with deficits in phonological processing, whether they have SLI or reading disability, are more likely to have serious reading problems. They also appear to have limitations in general cognitive processing and executive function. SLI and reading disability have distinctive neurobiological profiles and strong familial heritability. Both SLI and reading disability are lifespan issues: Although children can improve with effective intervention, they will continue to struggle in various ways with academic learning and reading.

References

Adlof, S. M., Catts, H. W., & Little, T. D. (2006). Should the simple view of reading include a fluency component? *Reading and Writing, 19*, 993–958.

American Academy of Pediatrics, Section on Ophthalmology; Council on Children with Disabilities; American Academy of Ophthalmology; American Association for Pediatric Ophthalmology and Strabismus; American Association of Certified Orthoptists (2009). Joint statement—Learning disabilities, dyslexia, and vision. *Pediatrics, 124*, 837–844.

Aram, D. M. (1997). Hyperlexia: Reading without meaning in young children. *Topics in Language Disorders, 17*, 1–13.

Aram, D. M., Ekelman, B. L., & Nation, J. A. (1984). Preschoolers with language disorders 10 years later. *Journal of Speech and Hearing Research, 27*, 232–244.

Archibald, L. M. D., & Gathercole, S. E. (2006). Visuospatial immediate memory in specific language impairment. *Journal of Speech, Language, and Hearing Research, 49*, 265–277.

Ashcraft, M. H., & Radvansky, G. A. (2010). *Cognition* (5th ed.). Boston, MA: Prentice-Hall.

Badian, N. A. (1994). Preschool prediction: Orthographic and phonological skills, and reading. *Annals of Dyslexia, 44*, 3–25.

Bailey, P. J., & Snowling, M. J. (2002). Auditory processing and the development of language and literacy. *British Medical Bulletin, 63*, 135–146.

Bedore, L. M., & Leonard, L. B. (1998). Specific language impairment and grammatical morphology: A discriminant function analysis. *Journal of Speech, Language, and Hearing Research, 41*, 1185–1192.

Beitchman, J. H., Nair, R., Clegg, M., & Patel, P. G. (1986). Prevalence of speech and language disorders in 5-year-old kindergarten children in the Ottawa-Carleton region. *Journal of Speech and Hearing Disorders, 51*, 98–110.

Berninger, V. (2008). Evidence-based written language instruction during early and middle childhood. In R. Morris & N. Mather (Eds.), *Evidence-based interventions for students with learning and behavioral challenges* (pp. 215–235). Mahwah, NJ: Erlbaum.

Bishop, D. V. M. (1990). *Handedness and developmental disorder*. Oxford, England: Blackwell Scientific.

Bishop, D. V. M. (2000). Pragmatic language impairment: A correlate of SLI, a distinct subgroup, or part of the autistic continuum? In D. V. M. Bishop & L. B. Leonard (Eds.), *Speech and language impairments in children: Causes, characteristics, intervention, and outcome* (pp. 99–112). New York, NY: Psychology Press.

Bishop, D. V. M. (2001). Genetic influences on language impairment and literacy problems in children: Same or different? *Journal of Child Psychology and Psychiatry, 2*, 189–198.

Bishop, D. V. M., & Adams, C. (1990). A prospective study of the relationship between specific language impairment, phonological disorders, and reading retardation. *Journal of Child Psychology and Psychiatry, 31*, 1027–1050.

Bishop, D. V. M., Bishop, S. J., Bright, P., James, C., Delaney, T., & Tallal, P. (1999). Different origin of auditory and phonological processing problems in children with specific language impairment: Evidence from a twin study. *Journal of Speech, Language, and Hearing Sciences, 62*, 155–168.

Bishop, D. V. M., Bright, P., James, C., Bishop, S. J., & van der Lely, H. K. J. (2000). Grammatical SLI: A distinct subtype of developmental language impairment? *Applied Psycholinguistics, 21*, 159–181.

Bishop, D. V. M., & Edmundson, A. (1987). Language-impaired 4-year-olds: Distinguishing transient from persistent impairment. *Journal of Speech and Hearing Disorders, 52*, 156–173.

Bishop, D. V. M., & Snowling, M. J. (2004). Developmental dyslexia and specific language impairment: Same or different? *Psychological Bulletin, 130*, 858–886.

Blaskey, P., Scheiman, M., Parisi, M., Ciner, E. B., Gallaway, M., & Selznick, R. (1990). The effectiveness of Irlen filters for improving reading performance: A pilot study. *Journal of Learning Disabilities, 23*, 604–610.

Boada, R., Willcutt, E. G., & Pennington, B. F. (2012). Understanding the comorbidity between dyslexia and attention-deficit/hyperactivity disorder. *Topics in Language Disorders, 32*, 264–284.

Botting, N., & Conti-Ramsden, G. (2003). Autism, primary pragmatic difficulties, and specific language impairment: Can we distinguish them using psycholinguistic markers? *Developmental Medicine and Child Neurology, 45*, 515–524.

Bradley, L., & Bryant, P. (1983). Categorizing sounds and learning to read: A causal connection. *Nature, 301*, 419–421.

Brady, S., Shankweiler, D., & Mann, V. (1983). Speech perception and memory coding in relation to reading ability. *Journal of Experimental Child Psychology, 35*, 345–367.

Breier, J. I., Gray, L. C., Fletcher, J. M., Foorman, B., & Klaas, P. (2002). Perception of speech and nonspeech stimuli by children with and without reading disabilitiy and attention deficit hyperactivity disorder. *Journal of Experimental Child Psychology, 82*, 226–250.

Bridges, M. S., & Catts, H. W. (2011). The use of a dynamic screening of phonological awareness to predict risk for reading disabilities in kindergarten children. *Journal of Learning Disabilities, 44*, 330–338.

Brinton, B., Fujiki, M., & Higbee, L. M. (1998). Participation in cooperative learning activities by children with specific language impairment. *Journal of Speech, Language, and Hearing Research, 41*, 1193–1206.

Bruck, M. (1990). Word recognition skills of adults with childhood diagnosis of dyslexia. *Developmental Psychology, 26*, 439–454.

Bruck, M. (1993). Word recognition and component phonological processing skills of adults with childhood diagnosis of dyslexia. *Developmental Review, 13*, 258–268.

Butler, K. G., & Wallach, G. P. (1982). *Language disorders and learning disabilities.* Rockville, MD: Aspen Systems.

Cantwell, D. P., & Baker, L. (1987). Prevalence and type of psychiatric disorder and developmental disorders in three speech and language groups. *Journal of Communication Disorders, 20*, 151–160.

Catts, H. W. (1986). Speech production/phonological deficits in reading-disordered children. *Journal of Learning Disabilities, 19*, 504–508.

Catts, H. W. (1993). The relationship between speech–language impairments and reading disabilities. *Journal of Speech and Hearing Research, 36*, 948–958.

Catts, H. W., Adlof, S. M., Hogan, T. P., & Weismer, S. E. (2005). Are SLI and dyslexia distinct disorders? *Journal of Speech, Language, and Hearing Research, 48*, 1378–1396.

Catts, H. W., Adlof, S. M., & Weismer, S. E. (2006). Language deficits in poor comprehenders: The case for the simple view of reading. *Journal of Speech, Language, and Hearing Research, 49*, 278–293.

Catts, H. W., Bridges, M. S., Little, T. D., & Tomblin, J. B. (1998). Reading achievement growth in children with language impairments. *Journal of Speech, Language, and Hearing Research, 51*, 1569–1579.

Catts, H. W., Compton, D., Tomblin, J. B., & Bridges, M. S. (2012). Prevalence and nature of late-emerging poor readers. *Journal of Educational Psychology, 104*, 166–181.

Catts, H. W., Fey, M. E., Zhang, X., & Tomblin, J. B. (1999). Language basis of reading and reading disabilities: Evidence from a longitudinal investigation. *Scientific Studies in Reading, 3*, 331–361.

Catts, H. W., Fey, M. E., Zhang, X., & Tomblin, J. B. (2001). Estimating risk for future reading difficulties in kindergarten children: A research-based model and its clinical implications. *Language, Speech, and Hearing Services in Schools, 32*, 38–50.

Catts, H. W., Hogan, T. P., & Fey, M. (2003). Subgrouping poor readers on the basis of reading-related abilities. *Journal of Learning Disabilities, 36*, 151–164.

Catts, H. W., Kamhi, A., & Adlof, S. M. (2012a). Defining and classifying reading disabilities. In A. Kamhi & H.W. Catts (Eds.), *Language and reading disabilities* (3rd ed., pp. 45–76). Boston, MA: Allyn & Bacon.

Catts, H. W., Kamhi, A., & Adlof, S. M. (2012b). Causes of reading disabilities. In A. Kamhi & H.W. Catts (Eds.), *Language and reading disabilities* (3rd ed., pp. 77–111). Boston, MA: Allyn & Bacon.

Chall, J. S. (1983). *Stages of reading development*. New York, NY: McGraw-Hill.

Cohen, M., Campbell, R., & Yaghmai, F. (1989). Neuropathological abnormalities in developmental dysphasia. *Annals of Neurology, 25*, 567–570.

Colozzo, P., Gillam, R. B., Woods, M., Schnell, R. D., & Johnston, J. R. (2011). Content and form in narratives of children with specific language impairment. *Journal of Speech, Language, and Hearing Research, 54*, 1609–1627.

Conti-Ramsden, G. (2003). Processing and linguistic markers in young children with specific language impairment. *Journal of Speech, Language, and Hearing Research, 46*, 1029–1037.

Conti-Ramsden, G. M., Botting, N. F., & Faragher, B. (2001). Psycholinguistic markers for specific language impairment (SLI). *Journal of Child Psychology and Psychiatry and Allied Disciplines, 42*, 741–748.

Conti-Ramsden, G. M., St Clair, M. C., Pickles, A., & Durkin, K. (2012). Developmental trajectories of verbal and nonverbal skills in individuals with a history of specific language impairment: From childhood to adolescence. *Journal of Speech, Language, and Hearing Research, 55,* 1716–1735.

Cowan, R., Donlan, C., Newton, E. J., & Lloyd, D. (2005). Number skills and knowledge in children with specific language impairment. *Journal of Educational Psychology, 97,* 732–744.

Craig, H. K., & Evans, J. L. (1993). Pragmatics and SLI: Within-group variations in discourse behaviors. *Journal of Speech and Hearing Research, 36,* 777–789.

Craig, H. K., & Washington, J. A. (1993). Access behaviors of children with specific language impairment. *Journal of Speech and Hearing Research, 36,* 322–337.

Cutting, L. E., Materek, A., Cole, C. A. S., Levine, T. M., & Mahone, E. M. (2009). Effects of fluency, oral language, and executive function on reading comprehension performance. *Annals of Dyslexia, 59,* 34–54.

Denckla, M. B., & Rudel, R. G. (1976). Rapid automatized naming (RAN): Dyslexia differentiated from other learning disabilities. *Neuropsychologia, 14,* 471–479.

Dockrell, J. E., Lindsay, G., & Connelly, V. (2009). The impact of specific language impairment on adolescents' written text. *Exceptional Children, 75,* 427–446.

Dollaghan, C., & Campbell, T. F. (1998). Nonword repetition and child language impairment. *Journal of Speech, Language, and Hearing Research, 41,* 1136–1146.

Eden, G. F., van Meter, J., Rumsey, J., Maisog, J., Woods, R., & Zeffiro, T. (1996). Abnormal processing of visual motion in dyslexia revealed by functional brain imaging. *Nature, 382,* 66–69.

Edwards, J., & Lahey, M. (1996). Auditory lexical decisions of children with specific language impairment. *Journal of Speech and Hearing Research, 39,* 1263–1273.

Edwards, J., & Munson, B. (2009). Speech perception and production in child language disorders. In R.G. Schwartz (Ed.), *Handbook of child language disorders* (pp. 216–231). New York, NY: Psychology Press.

Ehri, L. C., Nunes, S. R., Willows, D. M., Schuster, B. V., Yaghoub-Zadeh, Z., & Shanahan, T. (2001). Phonemic awareness instruction helps children learn to read: Evidence from the National Reading Panel's meta-analysis. *Reading Research Quarterly, 36,* 250–287.

Elbro, C., Borstrom, I., & Petersen, D. (1998). Predicting dyslexia from kindergarten: The importance of distinctness of phonological representations of lexical items. *Reading Research Quarterly, 33,* 36–60.

Farmer, M. E., & Klein, R. M. (1995). The evidence for a temporal processing deficit linked to dyslexia: A review. *Psychonomic Bulletin and Review, 2,* 460–493.

Fazio, B. B. (1996). Mathematical abilities of children with specific language impairment: A 2-year follow-up. *Journal of Speech and Hearing Research, 39,* 1–10.

Fazio, B. B., Naremore, R. C., & Connell, P. J. (1996). Tracking children from poverty at risk for specific language impairment: A 3-year longitudinal study. *Journal of Speech and Hearing Research, 39,* 611–624.

Federal Educational Eligibility Regulations, 34 C.F.R. § 300.8.b.10 (n.d.).

Fey, M. E., Catts, H. W., Proctor-Williams, K., Tomblin, J. B., & Zhang, X. (2004). Oral and written story composition skills of children with language impairment. *Journal of Speech, Language, and Hearing Research, 47*, 1301–1318.

Finneran, D. A., Francis, A. L., & Leonard, L. B. (2009). Sustained attention in children with specific language impairment (SLI). *Journal of Speech, Language, and Hearing Research, 52*, 915–929.

Fischer, F. W., Liberman, I. Y., & Shankweiler, D. (1978). Reading reversals and developmental dyslexia: A further study. *Cortex, 14*, 496–510.

Fisher, S., Vargha-Khadem, F., Watkins, K., Monaco, A., & Pembrey, M. (1998). Localisation of a gene implicated in a severe speech and language disorder. *Nature Genetics, 18*, 168–170.

Fletcher, J., & Martinez, G. (1994). An eye movement analysis of the effects of scotopic sensitivity correction on parsing and comprehension. *Journal of Learning Disabilities, 27*, 67–70.

Flower, L. S., & Hayes, J. R. (1980). The dynamics of composing: Making plans and juggling constraints. In L.W. Gregg & E.R. Steinberg (Eds.), *Cognitive processes in writing* (pp. 31–50). Hillsdale, NJ: Erlbaum.

Foorman, B. R., Breier, J. I., & Fletcher, J. M. (2003). Interventions aimed at improving reading success: An evidence-based approach. *Developmental Neuropsychology, 24*, 613–639.

Fraser, J., Goswami, U., & Conti-Ramsden, G. (2010). Dyslexia and specific language impairment: The role of phonology and auditory processing. *Scientific Studies of Reading, 14*, 8–29.

Friedmann, N., & Novodgrodsky, R. (2004). The acquisition of relative clause comprehension in Hebrew: A study of SLI and normal development. *Journal of Child Language, 31*, 661–681.

Fuchs, D., & Fuchs, L. S. (2006). Introduction to responsiveness-to-intervention: What, why, and how valid is it? *Reading Research Quarterly, 4*, 93–99.

Fujiki, M., Brinton, B., Isaacson, T., & Summers, C. (2001). Social behaviors of children with specific language impairment on the playground: A pilot study. *Language, Speech, and Hearing Services in Schools, 32*, 101–113.

Fujiki, M., Spackman, M. P., Brinton, B., & Hall, A. (2004). The relationship of language and emotion regulation to reticence in children with specific language impairment. *Journal of Speech, Language, and Hearing Research, 47*, 637–646.

Gabriel, A., Stefaniak, N., Maillart, C., Schmitz, X., & Meulemans, T. (2012). Procedural visual learning in children with specific language impairment. *American Journal of Speech–Language Pathology, 21*, 329–341.

Galaburda, A. M., Sherman, G. F., Rosen, G. D., Aboitiz, F., & Geschwind, N. (1985). Developmental dyslexia: Four consecutive patients with cortical anomalies. *Annals of Neurology, 18*, 222–233.

Gallagher, A., Frith, U., & Snowling, M. (2000). Precursors of literacy-delay among children at genetic risk of dyslexia. *Journal of Child Psychology and Psychiatry, 41*, 203–213.

Gallon, N., Harris, J., & van der Lely, H. (2007). Non-word repetition: An investigation of phonological complexity in children with grammatical SLI. *Clinical Linguistics and Phonetics, 21*, 435–455.

Gathercole, S. E., & Baddeley, A. D. (1990). Phonological memory deficits in language disordered children: Is there a causal connection? *Journal of Memory and Language, 29*, 336–360.

Gathercole, S. E., Willis, C. S., Emslie, H., & Baddeley, A. D. (1992). Phonological memory and vocabulary development during the early school years: A longitudinal study. *Developmental Psychology, 28,* 887–898.

Gauger, L. M., Lombardino, L. J., & Leonard, C. M. (1997). Brain morphology in children with specific language impairment. *Journal of Speech and Hearing Research, 40,* 1272–1284.

German, D. J. & Newman, R. S. (2004). The impact of lexical factors on children's word-finding errors. *Journal of Speech, Language, and Hearing Research, 47,* 624–636.

German, D. J., & Simon, E. (1991). Analysis of children's word-finding skills in discourse. *Journal of Speech and Hearing Research, 34,* 309–316.

Gillam, R. B., Cowan, N., & Marler, J. A. (1998). Information processing by school-age children with specific language impairment: Evidence from a modality effect paradigm. *Journal of Speech, Language, and Hearing Research, 41,* 913–926.

Gillam, R. B., & Johnston, J. R. (1992). Spoken and written language relationships in language/learning-impaired and normally achieving school age children. *Journal of Speech and Hearing Research, 35,* 1303–1315.

Goffman, L. (2004). Kinematic differentiation of prosodic categories in normal and disordered language development. *Journal of Speech, Language, and Hearing Research, 47,* 1088–1102.

Gopnik, M. (1990). Feature-blind grammar and dysphasia. *Nature, 344,* 715.

Gopnik, M., & Crago, M. B. (1991). Familial aggregation of a developmental language disorder. *Cognition, 39,* 1–50.

Gough, P. B., & Tunmer, W. E. (1986). Decoding, reading, and reading disability. *Remedial and Special Education, 7,* 6–10.

Goulandris, N. K., Snowling, M. J., & Walker, I. (2000). Is dyslexia a form of specific language impairment? A comparison of dyslexic and language impaired children as adolescents. *Annals of Dyslexia, 50,* 103–120.

Grigorenko, E. L. (2009). Dynamic assessment and response to intervention: Two sides of one coin. *Journal of Learning Disabilities, 42,* 111–132.

Hanly, S., & Vandenberg, B. (2010). Tip-of-the-tongue and word retrieval deficits in dyslexia. *Journal of Learning Disabilities, 43,* 15–23.

Hart, K. I., Fujiki, M., Brinton, B., & Hart, C. H. (2004). The relationship between social behavior and severity of language impairment. *Journal of Speech, Language, and Hearing Research, 47,* 647–662.

Hazan, V., Messaoud-Galusi, S., Rosen, S., Nouwens, S., & Shakespeare, B. (2009). Speech perception abilities of adults with dyslexia: Is there any evidence for a true deficit? *Journal of Speech, Language, and Hearing Research, 52,* 1510–1529.

Hinshelwood, J. (1905). Four cases of congenital word-blindness occurring in the same family. *The British Medical Journal, 2,* 1229–1232.

Hinshelwood, J. (1912). The treatment of word-blindness, acquired and congenital. *British Medical Journal, 2,* 1033–1035.

Hoffman, L. M., & Gillam, R. B. (2004). Verbal and spatial information processing constraints in children with specific language impairment. *Journal of Speech, Language, and Hearing Research, 47,* 114–125.

Hogarth, L., Dickinson, A., & Duka, T. (2010). Selective attention to conditioned stimuli in human discrimination learning: Untangling the effects of outcome prediction, valence, arousal, and uncertainty. In C. J. Mitchell & M. E. Le Pelley (Eds.), *Attention and associative learning from brain to behaviour* (pp. 71–98). Oxford, UK: Oxford University.

Holmes, D. L., & Peper, R. J. (1977). An evaluation of the use of spelling error analysis in the diagnosis of reading disabilities. *Child Development, 4*, 1708–1711.

Hooper S. R., & Montgomery, J. W. (1993). Prevalence of writing problems across three middle school samples. *School Psychological Review, 22*, 610–622.

Hoover, W. A., & Gough, P. B. (1990). The simple view of reading. *Reading and Writing, 2*, 127–160.

Johannes, S., Kussmaul, C. L., Munte, T. F., & Mangun, G. R. (1996). Developmental dyslexia: Passive visual stimulation provides no evidence for a magnocellular processing defect. *Neuropsychologia, 34*, 1123–1127.

Johnson, D., & Myklebust, H. (1967). *Learning disabilities: Educational principles and practice.* New York, NY: Grune & Stratton.

Johnston, J. R., Miller, J., & Tallal, P. (2001). Use of cognitive state predicates by language-impaired children. *International Journal of Language and Communication Disorders, 36*, 349–370.

Johnston, J. R., & Smith, L. D. (1989). Dimensional thinking in language impaired children. *Journal of Speech and Hearing Research, 32*, 33–38.

Johnston, J. R., & Weismer, S. E. (1983). Mental rotation abilities in language-disordered children. *Journal of Speech and Hearing Research, 26*, 397–403.

Kamhi, A., & Catts, H. W. (1986). Toward an understanding of developmental language and reading disorders. *Journal of Speech and Hearing Disorders, 51*, 337–347.

Katusic, S. K., Colligan, R. C., Weaver, A. L., & Barbaresi, W. J. (2009). The forgotten learning disability: Epidemiology of written-language disorder in a population-based birth cohort (1976–1982), Rochester, Minnesota. *Pediatrics, 123*, 1306–1313.

Keller, T. A., & Just, M. A. (2009). Altering cortical activity: Remediation-induced changes in the white matter of poor readers. *Neuron, 64*, 624–631.

Keogh, B. K., & Pelland, M. (1985). Vision training revisited. *Journal of Learning Disabilities, 18*, 228–236.

Kohnert, K., Windsor, J., & Ebert, K. (2009). Primary or "specific" language impairment and children learning a second language. *Brain and Language, 109*, 101–111.

Koutsoftas, A. D., & Gray, S. (2012). Comparison of narrative and expository writing in students with and without language-learning disabilities. *Language, Speech, and Hearing Services in Schools, 43*, 395–409.

Lai, C. S. L., Fisher, S. E., Hurst, J. A., Vargha-Khadem, F., & Monaco, A. P. (2001). A forkhead-domain gene is mutated in severe speech and language disorder. *Nature, 413*, 519–523.

Landerl, K., Wimmer, H., & Frith, U. (1997). The impact of orthographic consistency on dyslexia: A German-English comparison. *Cognition, 63*, 315–334.

Leclercq, A.-L., Majerus, S., Prigent, G., & Maillart, C. (2013). The impact of dual tasking on sentence comprehension in children with specific language impairment. *Journal of Speech, Language, and Hearing Research, 56*, 265–280.

Lefly, D. L., & Pennington, B. F. (1991). Spelling errors and reading fluency in compensated adult dyslexics. *Annals of Dyslexia, 41*, 143–162.

Leonard, C. M., & Eckert, M. A. (2008). Asymmetry and dyslexia. *Developmental Neuropsychology, 33*, 663–681.

Leonard, C. M., Lombardino, L. J., Walsh, K., Eckert, M. A., Mockler, J. L., Rowe, . . . DeBose, C. B. (2002). Anatomical risk factors that distinguish dyslexia from SLI predict reading skill in normal children. *Journal of Communication Disorders, 35*, 501–531.

Leonard, L. B. (1991). Specific language impairment as a clinical category. *Language, Speech, and Hearing Services in Schools, 22*, 66–68.

Leonard, L. B. (1998). *Children with specific language impairment.* Cambridge, MA: MIT Press.

Leonard, L. B., Davis, J., & Deevy, P. (2007). Phonotactic probability and past-tense use by children with specific language impairment and their typically developing peers. *Clinical Linguistics and Phonetics, 21*, 747–758.

Leonard, L. B., Deevy, P., Fey, M. E., & Bredin-Oja, S. L. (2013). Sentence comprehension in specific language impairment: A task designed to distinguish between cognitive capacity and syntactic complexity. *Journal of Speech, Language, and Hearing Research, 56*, 577–589.

Leonard, L. B., Miller, C., & Gerber, E. (1999). Grammatical morphology and the lexicon in children with specific language impairment. *Journal of Speech, Language, and Hearing Research, 42*, 678–689.

Lewis, B. A., & Thompson, L. A. (1992). A study of developmental speech and language disorders in twins. *Journal of Speech and Hearing Research, 35*, 1086–1094.

Liberman, I. Y., Shankweiler, D., Orlando, C., Harris, K., & Berti, F. (1971). Letter confusion and reversal of sequence in the beginning reader: Implications for Orton's theory of developmental dyslexia. *Cortex, 7*, 127–142.

Light, J. G., & DeFries, J. C. (1995). Comorbidity of reading and mathematics disabilities: Genetic and environmental etiologies. *Journal of Learning Disabilities, 28*, 96–106.

Liles, B. Z. (1985). Cohesion in the narratives of normal and language-disordered children. *Journal of Speech and Hearing Research, 28*, 123–133.

Liles, B. Z. (1987). Episode organization and cohesive conjunctives in narratives of children with and without language disorder. *Journal of Speech and Hearing Research, 30*, 185–196.

Lipka, O., Lesaux, N., & Siegel, L. (2006). Retrospective analyses of the reading development of Grade 4 students with reading disabilities: Risk status and profiles over 5 years. *Journal of Learning Disabilities, 39*, 364–378.

Livingstone, M., Rosen, G., Drislane, F., & Galaburda, A. (1991). Physiological and anatomical evidence for a magnocellular defect in developmental dyslexia. *Proceedings of the National Academy of Science, 88*, 7943–7947.

Lovegrove, W., Martin, F., & Slaghuis, W. (1986). The theoretical and experimental case for a visual deficit in specific reading disability. *Cognitive Neuropsychology, 3*, 225–267.

Lovett, M. W. (1987). A developmental approach to reading disability: Accuracy and speed criteria of normal and deficient reading skill. *Child Development, 58*, 234–260.

Lundberg, I., Olofsson, A., & Wall, S. (1980). Reading and spelling skills in the first school years predicted from phonemic awareness skills in kindergarten. *Scandinavian Journal of Psychology, 21*, 159–173.

Lyon, G. R., Shaywitz, S. E., & Shaywitz, B. A. (2003). A definition of dyslexia. *Annals of Dyslexia, 53*, 1–14.

MacLachlan, B., & Chapman, R. (1988). Communication breakdowns in normal and language-learning disabled children's conversation and narration. *Journal of Speech and Hearing Research, 34*, 549–558.

Marshall, C. R., & van der Lely, H. (2007). The impact of phonological complexity on past-tense inflection in children with grammatical-SLI. *Advances in Speech–Language Pathology, 9*, 191–203.

McFadden, T. U., & Gillam, R. (1996). An examination of the quality of narratives produced by children with language disorders. *Language, Speech, and Hearing Services in Schools, 27*, 48–57.

McGrath, L. M., Hutaff-Lee, C., Scott, A., Boada, R., Shriberg, L. D., & Pennington, B. F. (2008). Children with comorbid speech sound disorder and specific language impairment are at increased risk for attention-deficit/hyperactivity disorder. *Journal of Abnormal Child Psychology, 36*, 151–163.

McGregor, K. K., Newman, R. M., & Reilly, R. M., & Capone, N. C. (2002). Semantic representation and naming in children with specific language impairment. *Journal of Speech, Language, and Hearing Research, 45*, 998–1014.

McGregor, K. K., & Waxman, S. R. (1998). Object naming at multiple hierarchical levels: A comparison of preschoolers with and without word-finding deficits. *Journal of Child Language, 25*, 419–430.

Menn, L., & Stoel-Gammon, C. (2009). Phonological development: Learning sounds and sound patterns. In J.B. Gleason & N.B. Ratner (Eds.), *The development of language* (7th ed., pp. 58–103). Boston, MA: Pearson.

Messer, D., & Dockrell, J. E. (2006). Children's naming and word-finding difficulties: Descriptions and explanations. *Journal of Speech, Language, and Hearing Research, 49*, 309–324.

Metzer, R. I., & Werner, D. B. (1984). Use of visual training for reading disabilities: A review. *Pediatrics, 73*, 824–829.

Montgomery, J. W. (1993). Haptic recognition of children with specific language impairment: Effects of response modality. *Journal of Speech and Hearing Research, 36*, 98–104.

Morgan, W. (1896). A case of congenital word-blindness. *British Medical Journal, 2*, 1378.

Morris, R. D., Stuebing, K. K., Fletcher, J. M., Shaywitz, S. E., Lyon, G. R., Shankweiler, D. P., . . . Shaywitz, B. A. (1998). Subtypes of reading disability: Variability around a phonological core. *Journal of Educational Psychology, 90*, 347–373.

Mueller, K. L. & Tomblin, J. B. (2012). Examining the comorbidity of language impairment and attention-deficit/hyperactivity disorder. *Topics in Language Disorders, 32*, 228–246.

Munson, B., Kurtz, B. A., & Windsor, J. (2005). The influence of vocabulary size, phonotactic probability, and wordlikeness on nonword repetitions of children with and without specific language impairment. *Journal of Speech, Language, and Hearing Research, 48*, 1033–1047.

Murphy, L., & Pollatsek, A. (1994). Developmental dyslexia: Heterogeneity without discrete subgroups. *Annals of Dyslexia, 44*, 120–146.

Naidoo, S. (1972). *Specific dyslexia*. London, England: Pitman.

Nation, K., Clarke, P., Marshall, C. M., & Durand, M. (2004). Hidden language impairments in children: Parallels between poor reading comprehension and specific language impairment. *Journal of Speech, Language, and Hearing Research, 47*, 199–211.

Nation, K., Cocksey, J., Taylor, J. S., & Bishop, D. V. (2010). A longitudinal investigation of early reading and language skills in children with poor reading comprehension. *Journal of Child Psychology and Psychiatry, 51*, 1031–1039.

Nation, K., & Snowling, M. J. (1998a). Individual differences in contextual facilitation: Evidence from dyslexia and poor reading comprehension and specific language impairments. *Child Development, 69*, 996–1011.

Nation, K., & Snowling, M. J. (1998b). Semantic processing and the development of word-recognition skills: Evidence from children with reading comprehension difficulties. *Journal of Memory and Language, 39*, 85–101.

Newman, R. M., & McGregor, K. K. (2006). Teachers and laypersons discern quality differences between narratives produced by children with or without SLI. *Journal of Speech, Language, and Hearing Research, 49*, 1022–1036.

Nittrouer, S. (1999). Do temporal processing deficits cause phonological processing problems? *Journal of Speech, Language, and Hearing Research, 42*, 925–942.

O'Brien, E. K., Zhang, Z., Nishimura, C., Tomblin, J. B., & Murray, J. C. (2003). Association of specific language impairment (SLI) to the region of 7q31. *American Journal of Human Genetics, 72*, 1536.

Oetting, J. B., & McDonald, J. L. (2001). Nonmainstream dialect use and specific language impairment (SLI). *Journal of Speech, Language, and Hearing Research, 44*, 207–223.

Olson, R. & Datta, H. (2002). Visual-temporal processing in reading-disabled and normal twins. *Reading and Writing: An Interdisciplinary Journal, 15*, 127–149.

Olson, R. K., Wise, B., Conners, F., Rack, J., & Fulker, D. (1989). Specific deficits in component reading and language skills: Genetic and environmental influences. *Journal of Learning Disabilities, 22*, 339–348.

Orton, S. (1937). *Reading, writing, and speech problems in children*. London, UK: Chapman Hall.

Ouellette, G. P. (2006). What's meaning got to do with it: The role of vocabulary in reading and reading comprehension. *Journal of Educational Psychology, 98*, 554–566.

Owen, A. J., & Leonard, L. B. (2002). Lexical diversity in the spontaneous speech of children with specific language impairment: Application of D. *Journal of Speech, Language, and Hearing Research, 45*, 927–937.

Pavlidis, G. T. (1985). Eye movement differences between dyslexics, normal and slow readers while sequentially fixating digits. *American Journal of Optometry and Physiological Optics, 62*, 820–822.

Pennington, B. F., & Bishop, D. V. M. (2009). Relations among speech, language, and reading disorders. *Annual Review of Psychology, 60*, 283–306.

Plaut, D. C., McClelland, J. L., Seidenberg, M. S., & Patterson, K. (1996). Understanding normal and impaired word reading: Computational principles in quasi-regular domains. *Psychological Review, 103*, 56–115.

Plomin, R., & Kovas, Y. (2005). Generalist genes and learning disabilities. *Psychological Bulletin, 131*, 592–617.

Poll, G. H. (2011). Increasing the odds: Applying emergentist theory in language intervention. *Language, Speech, and Hearing Services in Schools, 42*, 580–591.

Prior, M., Sanson, A., Smart, D., & Oberklaid, F. (1995). Reading disability in an Australian community sample. *Australian Journal of Psychology, 47*, 32–37.

Ramus, F. (2003). Developmental dyslexia: Specific phonological deficit or general sensorimotor dysfunction? *Current Opinion in Neurobiology, 13*, 212–218.

Ramus, F. (2004). Neurobiology of dyslexia: A reinterpretation of the data. *Trends in Neurosciences, 27*, 720–726.

Ramus, F., Marshall, C. R., Rosen, S., & van der Lely, H. K. J. (2013). Phonological deficits in specific language impairment and developmental dyslexia: Towards a multidimensional model. *Brain, 136*, 630–645.

Rayner, K. (1978). Eye movements in reading and information processing. *Psychological Bulletin, 85*, 618–660.

Rayner, K. (1998). Eye movements in reading and information processing: 20 years of research. *Psychological Bulletin, 124*, 372–422.

Rescorla, L. (2005). Age 13 language and reading outcomes in late-talking toddlers. *Journal of Speech, Language, and Hearing Research, 48*, 459–472.

Rice, M. L., Oetting, J. B., Marquis J., & Bode, J. (1994). Frequency of input effects on word comprehension of children with specific language impairment. *Journal of Speech and Hearing Research, 37*, 106–121.

Rice, M. L., & Wexler, K. (1996). Toward tense as a clinical marker of specific language impairment in English-speaking children. *Journal of Speech and Hearing Research, 39*, 1239–1257.

Richard, G. J. (2012). Primary issues for the speech–language pathologist to consider in regard to diagnosis of auditory processing disorder. *Perspectives on Language Learning and Education, 19*, 78–86.

Robertson, E., & Joanisse, M. (2010). Spoken sentence comprehension in children with dyslexia and language impairment: The roles of syntax and working memory. *Applied Psycholinguistics, 31*, 141–165.

Robinson, N. M., & Robinson, H. B. (1976). *The mentally retarded child* (2nd ed.). New York, NY: McGraw-Hill.

Rosen, S. R. (2003). Auditory processing in dyslexia and specific language impairment: Is there a deficit? What is its nature? Does it explain anything? *Journal of Phonetics, 31*, 509–527.

Rutter, M., Caspi, A., Fergusson, D., Horwood, L. J., Goodman, R., Maughan, B., Moffitt, T. E., . . . Carroll, J. (2007). Sex differences in developmental reading disability: New findings from 4 epidemiological studies. *Journal of American Medical Association, 29*, 2007–2012.

Samuelsson, S., Byrne, B., Quain, P., Wadsworth, S., Corley, R., DeFries, J. C., . . . Olson, R. (2007). Genetic and environmental influences on prereading skills and early reading and spelling development in the United States, Australia, and Scandinavia. *Reading and Writing, 20*, 51–75.

Scarborough, H. S. (1990). Very early language deficits in dyslexic children. *Child Development, 61*, 1728–1743.

Scarborough, H. S., & Dobrich, W. (1990). Development of children with early language delay. *Journal of Speech and Hearing Research, 33*, 70–83.

Scarborough, H. S., & Parker, J. D. (2003). Matthew effects in children with learning disabilities: Development of reading, IQ, and psychosocial problems from grade 2 to grade 8. *Annals of Dyslexia, 53*, 47–71.

Schuele, C. M., & Tolbert, L. (2001). Omissions of obligatory relative markers in children with specific language impairment. *Clinical Linguistics and Phonetics, 15*, 257–274.

Schwartz, R. G. (2009). Specific language impairment. In R. G. Schwartz (Ed.), *Handbook of child language disorders* (pp. 3–43). New York, NY: Psychology Press.

Schwartz, R. G., Leonard, L. B., Messick, C., & Chapman, K. (1987). The acquisition of object names in children with specific language impairment: Action context and word extension. *Applied Psycholinguistics, 8*, 233–244.

Scott, C. M., & Windsor, J. (2000). General language performance measures in spoken and written narrative and expository discourse of school-age children with language learning disabilities. *Journal of Speech, Language, and Hearing Research, 43*, 324–339.

Sesma, H., Mahone, M., Levine, T., Eason, S., & Cutting, L. (2009). The contribution of executive skills to reading comprehension. *Child Neuropsychology, 15*, 232–246.

Shafer, V. L., & Maxfield, N. D. (2009). Neuroscience approaches to child language disorders. In R. G. Schwartz (Ed.), *Handbook of child language disorders* (pp. 532–548). New York, NY: Psychology Press.

Share, D. L., Jorm, A. F., Maclean, R., & Matthews, R. (2002). Temporal processing and reading disability. *Reading and Writing, 15*, 151–178.

Share, D. L., & Silva, P. A. (1987). Language deficits and specific reading retardation: Cause or effect? *British Journal of Disorders of Communication, 22*, 219–226.

Shaywitz, B. A. , Holford, T. R., Holahan, J. M., Fletcher, J. M., Stuebing, K. K., Francis, D. J., & Shaywitz, S. E. (1995). A Matthew effect for IQ but not for reading: Results from a longitudinal study. *Reading Research Quarterly, 30*, 894–906.

Shaywitz, B. A., Shaywitz, S. E., Blachman, B. A., Pugh, K. R., Fulbright, R. K., Skudlarski, P., . . . Gore, J. C. (2004). Development of left occipitotemporal systems for skilled reading in children after a phonologically based intervention. *Biological Psychiatry, 55*, 926–933.

Shaywitz, B. A., Shaywitz S. E., Pugh, K. R., Mencl, W. E., Fulbright, R. K., Skudlarski, P., . . . Gore, J. C. (2002). Disruption of posterior brain systems for reading in children with developmental dyslexia. *Biological Psychiatry, 52*, 101–110.

Shaywitz, S. E., Escobar, M. D., Shaywitz, B. A., Fletcher, J. M., & Makuch, R. (1992). Evidence that dyslexia may represent the lower tail of a normal distribution of reading ability. *The New England Journal of Medicine, 326*, 145–193.

Shaywitz, S. E., Fletcher, J. M., & Shaywitz, B. A. (1994). Issues in the definition and classification of attention deficit disorder. *Topics in Language Disorders, 14*, 1–25.

Shaywitz, S. E., Gruen, J. R., Mody, M., & Shaywitz, B. A. (2009). Dyslexia. In R. G. Schwartz (Ed.), *Handbook of child language disorders* (pp. 115–140). New York, NY: Psychology Press.

Shaywitz, S. E., Morris, R., & Shaywitz, B. (2008). The education of dyslexic children from childhood to young adulthood. *Annual Review of Psychology, 59*, 451–475.

Shaywitz, S. E., Shaywitz, B. A., Fletcher, J. M., & Escobar, M. D. (1990). Prevalence of reading disability in boys and girls. *Journal of the American Medical Association, 264*, 998–1002.

Shaywitz, S. E., Shaywitz, B. A., Pugh, K., Fulbright, R., Constable, R., Mencl, W., . . . Gore, J. C. (1998). Functional disruption in the organization of the brain for reading in dyslexia. *Proceedings of the National Academy of Sciences, 95*, 2636–2641.

Shriberg, L. D., & Kwiatkowski, J. (1994). Developmental phonological disorders I: A clinical profile. *Journal of Speech and Hearing Research, 37*, 1100–1126.

Shriberg, L. D., Tomblin, J. B., & McSweeny, J. L. (1999). Prevalence of speech delay in 6-year-old children and comorbidity with language impairment. *Journal of Speech, Language, and Hearing Research, 42*, 1461–1481.

Silver, L. B. (1995). Controversial therapies. *Journal of Child Neurology, 10*, S96–S100.

Skarakis-Doyle, E., & Dempsey, L. (2008). The detection and monitoring of comprehension errors by preschool children with and without language impairment. *Journal of Speech, Language, and Hearing Research, 51*, 1227–1243.

Snowling, M. (1981). Phonemic deficits in developmental dyslexia. *Psychological Research, 43*, 219–234.

Spaulding, T., Plante, E., & Vance, R. (2008). Sustained selective attention skills of preschool children with specific language impairment: Evidence for separate attentional capacities. *Journal of Speech, Language, and Hearing Research, 51*, 16–34.

Spector, J. E. (1992). Predicting progress in beginning reading: Dynamic assessment of phonemic awareness. *Journal of Educational Psychology, 84*, 353–363.

Stanovich, K. E. (1986). Matthew effects in reading: Some consequences of individual differences in the acquisition of literacy. *Reading Research Quarterly, 21*, 360–407.

Stanovich, K. E., & Siegel, L. S. (1994). Phenotypic performance profile of reading-disabled children: A regression-based test of the phonological-core variable-difference model. *Journal of Educational Psychology, 86*, 24–53.

Stanovich, K. E., Siegel, L. S., & Gottardo, A. (1997). Converging evidence for phonological and surface subtypes of reading disability. *Journal of Educational Psychology, 89*, 114–127.

Stevenson, J., Graham, P., Fredman, G., & McLoughlin, V. (1987). A twin study of genetic influences on reading and spelling ability and disability. *Journal of Child Psychology and Psychiatry, 28*, 229–247.

Stuart, G. W., McAnally, K. I., & Castles, A. (2001). Can contrast sensitivity functions in dyslexia be explained by inattention rather than a magnocellular deficit? *Vision Research, 41*, 3205–3211.

Stothard, S. E., Snowling, M. J., Bishop, D. V. M., Chipcase, B., & Kaplan, C. A. (1998). Language-impaired preschoolers: A follow-up into adolescence. *Journal of Speech, Language, and Hearing Research, 41*, 407–418.

Tallal, P. (1980). Auditory temporal perception, phonics, and reading disabilities in children. *Brain and Language, 9,* 182–198.

Tallal, P. (2000). Experimental studies of language learning impairments: From research to remediation. In D. V. M. Bishop & L. B. Leonard (Eds.), *Speech and language impairments in children: Causes, characteristics, intervention, and outcome* (pp. 131–155). Hove, England: Psychology Press.

Tallal, P., & Piercy, M. (1974). Developmental aphasia: Rate of auditory processing and selective impairment of consonant perception. *Neuropsychologia, 12,* 83–93.

Tallal, P., Ross, R., & Curtiss, S. (1989). Familial aggregation in specific language impairment. *Journal of Speech and Hearing Disorders, 54,* 167–173.

Thordardottir, E. (2008). Language-specific effects of task demands on the manifestation of specific language impairment: A comparison of English and Icelandic. *Journal of Speech, Language, and Hearing Research, 51,* 922–937.

Tomblin, J. B. (1989). Familial concentration of developmental language impairment. *Journal of Speech and Hearing Disorders, 54,* 287–295.

Tomblin, J. B., (1991). Examining the cause of specific language impairment. *Language, Speech, and Hearing Services in Schools, 22,* 69–74.

Tomblin, J. B. (2009). Genetics of child language disorders. In R.G. Schwartz (Ed.), *Handbook of child language disorders* (pp. 232–256). New York, NY: Psychology Press.

Tomblin, J. B., Records, N. L., Buckwalter, P., Zhang, X., Smith, E., & O'Brien, M. (1997). The prevalence of specific language impairment in kindergarten children. *Journal of Speech, Language, and Hearing Research, 40,* 1245–1260.

Tomblin, J. B., Records, N. L., & Zhang, X. (1996). A system for the diagnosis of specific language impairment in kindergarten children. *Journal of Speech and Hearing Research, 39,* 1284–1294.

Tomblin, J. B., & Zhang, X. (2006). The dimensionality of language ability in school-age children. *Journal of Speech, Language, and Hearing Research, 49,* 1193–1208.

Tomblin, J. B., Zhang, X., Buckwalter, P., & O'Brien, M. (2003). The stability of primary language disorder: Four years after kindergarten diagnosis. *Journal of Speech, Language, and Hearing Research, 46,* 1283–1296.

Torgesen, J. K. (1985). Memory processes in reading-disabled children. *Journal of Learning Disabilities, 18,* 350–357.

Torgesen, J., Alexander, A., Wagner, R., Rashotte, C., Voeller, K., & Conway, T. (2001). Intensive remedial instruction for children with severe reading disabilities: Immediate and long-term outcomes from two instructional approaches. *Journal of Learning Disabilities, 31,* 33–58.

Torgesen, J., Wagner, R., & Rashotte, C. (1994). Longitudinal studies of phonological processing and reading. *Journal of Learning Disabilities,* 27, 276–286.

Ukrainetz, T. A., & Gillam, R. B. (2009). The expressive elaboration of imaginative narratives by children with specific language impairment. *Journal of Speech, Language, and Hearing Research, 52,* 883–898.

Ullman, M. T. (2004). Contributions of memory circuits to language: The declarative/procedural model. *Cognition, 92,* 231–270.

Ullman, M. T., & Pierpont, E. I. (2005). Specific language impairment is not specific to language: The procedural deficit hypothesis. *Cortex, 41*, 399–433.

U.S. Department of Education Office of Special Education and Rehabilitative Services. (2002). *A new era: Revitalizing special education for children and their families.* Washington, DC: Author. Retrieved from http://www.ed.gov/pubs/edpubs.html.

van der Lely, H. (1996). Specifically language impaired and normally developing children: Verbal passive vs. adjectival passive sentence interpretation. *Lingua, 98*, 243–272.

van der Lely, H. K. J. (1997). Language and cognitive development in a grammatical SLI boy: Modularity and innateness. *Journal of Neurolinguistics, 10*, 75–107.

van der Lely, H. & Stollwerck, L. (1997). Binding theory and grammatical specific language impairment in children. *Cognition, 62*, 245–290.

Vellutino, F. R., Pruzek, R., Steger, J. A., & Meshoulam, U. (1973). Immediate visual recall in poor and normal readers as a function of orthographic-linguistic familiarity. *Cortex, 9*, 368–384.

Vellutino, F. R., Scanlon, D. M., & Spearing, D. (1995). Semantic and phonological coding in poor and normal readers. *Journal of Experimental Child Psychology, 59*, 76–123.

Vellutino, F. R., Steger, J. A., DeSetto, L., & Phillips, F. (1975). Immediate and delayed recognition of visual stimuli in poor and normal readers. *Journal of Experimental Child Psychology, 19*, 223–232.

Wagner, R. K. & Compton, D. L. (2011). Dynamic assessment and its implications for RTI models. *Journal of Learning Disabilities, 44*, 311–312.

Walberg, H. J., & Tsai, S. (1983). Matthew effects in education. *American Educational Research Journal, 20*, 359.

Wetherell, D., Botting, N., & Conti-Ramsden, G. (2007). Narrative skills in adolescents with a history of SLI in relation to nonverbal IQ scores. *Child Language Teaching and Therapy, 23*, 95–113.

Willcutt, E. G., & Pennington, B. F. (2000). Comorbidity of reading disability and attention-deficit/hyperactivity disorder. *Journal of Learning Disabilities, 33*, 179–191.

Willcutt, E. G., Pennington, B. F., Boada, R., Ogline, J. S., Tunick, R. A., Chabildas, N. A., & Olson, R. K. (2001). A comparison of the cognitive deficits in reading disability and attention-deficit/hyperactivity disorder. *Journal of Abnormal Psychology, 170*, 157–172.

Wittke, K., Spaulding, T. J., & Schechtman, C. J. (2013). Specific language impairment and executive functioning: Parent and teacher ratings of behavior. *American Journal of Speech-Language Pathology, 22*, 161–172.

Wolf, M., Bally, H., & Morris, R. (1986). Automaticity, retrieval processes, and reading: A longitudinal study in average and impaired readers. *Child Development, 57*, 988–1000.

Wolf, M., & Bowers, P.G. (1999). The double-deficit hypothesis for the developmental dyslexias. *Educational Psychology, 91*, 415–438.

Wolf, M., Bowers, P.G., & Biddle, K. (2000). Naming-speed processes, timing, and reading: A conceptual review. *Journal of Learning Disabilities, 33*, 387–407.

Zelaznik, H. N., & Goffman, L. (2010). Generalized motor abilities and timing behavior in children with specific language impairment. *Journal of Speech, Language, and Hearing Research, 53*, 383–393.

Chapter 6

Another Dimension to the Caseload: Bilingual Learners

Teresa A. Ukrainetz

A type of learner that intersects with all categories of disorder is a child who speaks more than one language. This chapter describes the process and educational implications of learning a second language. Dual language learners, both those fairly advanced in English and those newer to English, challenge speech–language pathologists (SLPs) and other educators, who must determine whether English language learners who are struggling in school have inherent language-learning impairments in addition to their linguistic and cultural differences (the difference versus disorder question) and how best to serve these children.

Who Are Bilingual Learners?

Developing bilinguals, bilingual learners, or dual language learners are children who receive regular input in two or more languages for some period from birth to adolescence. Children who enter school with English below that of their native-speaking peers are referred to as English language learners (ELL), children with English as a second language (ESL), with a further designation of fluent English proficient or limited English proficient. For young children, the standard is social use of language, but older students must meet academic standards of use. The reference for determining proficiency may be spoken and written tests normed on monolingual speakers or criterion measures of functional use designed specifically for English language learners. An English proficiency scale of functional use is presented in Box 6.1.

In the U.S., it is often assumed that English language learners are: (a) native Spanish speakers, (b) learning English in the early school years, (c) on an unusual developmental path, and (d) at risk for educational failure because of this path. While most American citizens and new arrivals fit the former two characteristics, the latter two are not true. Bilingualism is normal, not special: "globally, developing bilinguals are the rule rather than the exception" (Kohnert, 2010, p. 457). Bilingual speakers stand out in the U.S. because of its largely monolingual culture and schooling. Around the world, the vast majority of children learning two languages during childhood will become bilingually proficient for daily communication and academically successful in at least one language.

In the U.S., approximately 20% of students speak a primary language other than English (McCardle, Mele-McCarthy, Cutting, Leos, & D'Emilio, 2005). Statistics suggest that this proportion is higher than it is has ever been: The number of students designated as limited English proficient in grades K–12 in public schools increased by 72% from 1992 to 2002. In 1992, only 15% of U.S. teachers had one or more students with limited English proficiency, but by 2002, that had risen to 43% (McCardle et al., 2005). However, these numbers mask the longer term picture of immigration and linguistic diversity in the U.S. For example, census data showed that, in 1930, 25% of the U.S. school-age population was bilingual (Pintner & Arsenian, 1937), which is about what the figure is today. Bilingualism in the U.S. at that time involved largely "white" speakers of European languages (e.g., German, Yiddish, Russian, Italian, or Greek). The current association of bilingualism and cultural diversity with "persons of color," combined with more systematic documentation of linguistic status and more support for both learning

Box 6.1. ***Holistic Rating of English Language Proficiency***

Level	Rubric (Responses can be spoken or written to heard or read texts)
1	Responds using gestures, simple words, and phrases to demonstrate understanding in familiar situations and with familiar texts
2	Responds with some independence using acquired vocabulary in phrases and simple sentences to demonstrate understanding of story details (sequence, main idea, characters, setting) and basic situations
3	Responds with some complexity and moderate independence but some inconsistencies using expanded vocabulary and descriptive words for social and academic purposes
4	Responds with moderate independence using complex vocabulary with accuracy and demonstrates detailed understanding of social and academic language and concepts
5	Responds with high independence using extended vocabulary in social and academic discourse to negotiate meaning and apply knowledge across content areas; fluency sufficient to function in a classroom with native-English speakers; above the 35th percentile in reading and language on a standardized achievement test

Note: Rubrics paraphrased from the English Language Development scale described in Artiles et al. (2005) and used in California to classify ELL students; Limited English Proficient = Levels 1 to 4; Fluent English Proficient = Level 5.

English and maintaining native languages, leads to the impression that bilingualism is higher than ever before. Periods and patterns of immigration fluctuate over time, but cultural and linguistic diversity have always been part of the fabric of this country (Portes & Hao, 2002).

In U.S. public schools, 80% of second language students speak Spanish (McCardle et al., 2005). The 20% of non-Spanish bilingual speakers comprise 440 other languages, with Vietnamese running a distant second at 4%. Artiles, Rueda, Salazar, and Higareda (2005) reported that, for the 1998–99 school year, Hispanics comprised over 90% of ESL public school students in California. The next highest were Asian (3.3%) and White (2.5%), and then Filipino (0.7%), Black (0.3%), American Indian (0.1%), and Pacific Islander (0.1%). While many immigrants seek out communities where their language is spoken, some families may be linguistically isolated. Some may live among White, English-speaking families, while others, especially in urban areas, form a kaleidoscope of languages and cultures. Some immigrant children begin their U.S. schooling in the later grades, arriving with varying levels of native language literacy and life experiences.

In addition to immigrants and resident minorities, there is one more type of developing bilingual: Children whose English-speaking families choose to have them schooled in a second language. In the U.S. this is fairly rare, but in our neighbor to the north, it is almost commonplace for English-speaking Canadian children to be schooled in French (eight of the 13 nieces and nephews of this Canadian-American author attend French immersion). The performance of this group reveals important differences in how two languages may be acquired.

Living in Two Languages

Simultaneous Language Learning

Children who are exposed to both languages from infancy, in a manner sufficient to develop both languages, are simultaneous bilinguals. Simultaneous bilingual learners move through early language milestones in the same time and manner as monolingual children, using first words and word combinations at the same ages and for similar communicative purposes (e.g., Pearson & Fernandez, 1994; Petitto et al., 2001; Jackson-Maldonado, 2004). Although these children are fluent users of both languages by school entry, and may pass early English proficiency tests, just as for monolingual children, these children's two languages have considerable room for growth across the years of schooling and life experiences.

Simultaneous bilingualism typically arises because the two parents each speak a different native language. Another possibility is that one or both languages are spoken in the larger community and flow in varying combinations into the home. For example, Crago and Genesee (1996) found that, for an Inuit community in northeastern Canada where Inuktitut, English, and French were all spoken, there was wide variation in the proportion and patterns of use of the three languages in the homes of these multilingual families.

When each parent uses one language in a one-parent, one-language pattern, children show consistent differentiation, lack of confusion, and matching of language to interlocutor early on (Paradis, Genesee, & Crago, 2011). A more mixed presentation takes a little longer for children to sort out. However, so long as models and interactions continue for both languages, even in a mixed manner, simultaneous bilingual children will become proficient speakers of both languages. For learning three or more languages, proficiency also depends on input (Montanari, 2009). The more languages being learned, the more difficult it is to experience thorough input for each one, so it is less likely that a multilingual person will be proficient in all the languages he or she knows.

Infants and toddlers develop two languages as quickly as monolinguals develop one, with similar ages of attainment of first words, word combinations, and the vocabulary spurt, all used for similar communicative purposes (e.g., Pearson & Fernandez, 1994; Petitto et al., 2001). Early grammatical morphology also develops similarly (e.g., Jackson-Maldonado, 2004). Beyond early words, semantic and grammatical development of each varies with the nature of the languages involved and with the amount of exposure (Hammer et al., 2012; Paradis & Genesee, 1997; Patterson, 2000; Pearson, Fernandez, Lewedeg, & Oller, 1997). For example, Pearson and colleagues followed 25 simultaneous Spanish-English children from 8 to 30 months in a Spanish-speaking community of Miami. Using parent reports of the children's vocabulary and parental use, vocabulary size was found to be directly proportional to input. Early bilingual development is not dependent on cognitive level: Given consistent, rich bilingual exposure, even children with severe disabilities, such as Down syndrome, can become bilingual (Kay-Raining Bird et al., 2005; Feltman & Kay-Raining Bird, 2008).

Beyond toddlerhood, the dual language learner is not usually equally proficient or balanced in the two languages. The language of greater proficiency is the dominant or stronger language, and the other is the nondominant or weaker language. Dominance and language growth (or loss) are centrally affected by the amount and nature of the input, and as children have more outside-home experiences, dominance relations change. A language that is not spoken, but is understood to some degree, is called a passive language (Paradis et al., 2011). A language may disappear entirely if input is not maintained. However, vestigial memories can reappear. For example, several years ago, I was tutoring myself in Ukrainian for an upcoming trip to Ukraine. While I laboriously constructed utterances, my father, who had not spoken Ukrainian since early childhood, to our mutual surprise and delight, spontaneously emitted several fluent and appropriate utterances.

Which language is dominant fluctuates across age, context, and language areas. Children usually use their two languages with different conversants (e.g., family and friends versus teachers and other students), in different settings (e.g., playground versus classroom), for different topics (e.g., food versus zoo animals), or for different purposes (e.g., social storytelling versus narrative composition), resulting in different first language (L1) and second language (L2) performance across tasks (e.g., Kohnert, Kan, & Conboy, 2010; Ordonez, Carlo, Snow, & McLaughlin, 2002; Pena, Bedore, & Zlatic-Giunta, 2002). Vocabulary is notably sensitive to the language environment, and the size of the lexicon varies in proportion to the amount of exposure (Marchman, Martinez-Sussmann, & Dale, 2004; Patterson, 2000; Pearson et al., 1997). Although their total vocabulary expresses everything they want to say, young bilingual children show smaller vocabularies and lower vocabulary test scores for each language than monolinguals.

Unlike vocabulary, morphosyntax cannot be "added together" across languages. It is also challenging to measure because grammatical marking of concepts varies considerably across languages (e.g., noun gender markings in French). Mean length of utterance in morphemes may not be sensitive to grammatical complexity in languages that have few grammatical morphemes, like in the Hmong language (Kohnert et al., 2010), or that are highly agglutinative, like in the Tamil language (Raghavendra & Leonard, 1989). However, given similar rates of exposure, morphosyntax in young simultaneous bilinguals develops at a similar rate (Marchman et al., 2004).

Code-Mixing and Code-Switching

Children who begin developing two languages simultaneously generally keep the two languages separate. However, one language does sometimes intrude on the other language. This use of elements from two languages within an utterance or a unit of discourse is called code-mixing (Paradis et al., 2011) or code-switching (Poplack, 1980). This mixing can involve phonemes, inflectional morphemes, words, phrases, or clauses. Almost all simultaneous language learners code-mix to some degree. Paradis et al. report from children learning French and English at home in Montreal that code-mixing occurred less than 10% of the time and that it generally occurred between rather than within utterances.

Code-mixing is not just a developmental phenomenon; proficient bilingual adults do it too. Within-utterance mixes may result in odd or incorrect-sounding utterances, but each section of the utterance is well-formed (Paradis et al., 2011; Poplack, 1980). Balanced bilinguals juxtapose L1 and L2 where the elements do not violate the syntactic rules of either language. Adult code-mixing may occur to fill a lexical gap but is most often used for sociopragmatic reasons, such as a group identity marker to express intimacy and ethnic solidarity. They may code-mix as part of a narrative recount. They may code-mix to accommodate their less-proficient interlocutors or to show they are bilingual. Poplack's (1980, 1987) ethnographic studies found that Puerto Rican Spanish-speakers in New York fluently, rapidly, and frequently switched, suggesting they were expressing their dual identity as Puerto Rican and American. In contrast, code-switching by French Canadians in Ottawa occurred infrequently and involved expressions that were particularly apt for that context (*le mot juste*), with the original pronunciation preserved, suggesting a clear separation of languages and identity from English Canadians.

Sometimes nonbilingual parents or educators are concerned that code-mixing indicates lack of language skills or confusion about language use (Paradis et al., 2011). However, 2-year-old bilingual (and trilingual) children can adjust their language based on their interlocutor's language (Genesee, Boivin, & Nicoladis, 1996; Montanari, 2009). For young children, filling lexical gaps is the most common reason for mixing (Nicoladis & Secco, 2000). In addition to stretching their expressive abilities, children code-mix for similar sociopragmatic reasons as adults. How often, how fluently, and how grammatically children code-mix is affected by their language dominance, what language they are required to speak, and their perceptions of social support of their home language (Gutierrez-Clellen, Simon-Cereijido, & Leone, 2009). Code-mixing does not appear to reflect an impaired acquisition process: Children with SLI do not code-mix more often or differently from typically developing children (Gutierrez-Clellen et al., 2009).

Second Language Learning

For many children, there are consistent exposure and interactions in only one language from birth (L1), with exposure to L2 beginning later in childhood. The division between simultaneous and sequential bilingualism is placed at about 3 years of age (Paradis et al., 2011). The majority of ESL learners begin English acquisition in preschool or kindergarten.

Majority Versus Minority Languages

When considering bilingualism, especially in relation to sequential development, languages need to be distinguished as minority versus majority. Large parts of the population of almost every nation in the world are minority L1 and majority L2 (Kohnert,

2010; Paradis et al, 2011). These terms reflect the relative frequency of opportunities to use the language and the social value accorded native-speaker proficiency in the language. In the U.S., English is the majority language and all others are minority languages (or heritage languages, reflecting their role in ethnic identity). In Canada, French is an official language with extensive educational support throughout the country. However, French is still a minority language compared to the overwhelming dominance of English outside the province of Quebec.

Minority language speakers may be recent immigrants or may have descended from groups that precede the founding of the country. Even though their language may be the prevalent daily mode of communication in their local communities, English is still the language of the larger culture, education, and economy. There is no choice when it comes to their children learning English. The situation is very different for families who speak a majority language. They may choose to have their children be educated in a minority language. These latter children are surrounded by their L1 outside of school and do not have to deal with a new society and culture. This language status distinction has significant effects on the use and ultimate proficiency of L2 and maintenance of L1.

Children become sensitive to these differences in status early on. For example, in the English majority city of Edmonton, Paradis and Nicoladis (2007) found that French Canadian 4-year-olds adjusted their expectations about language comprehension based on which language was involved. Those whose French was dominant used their more limited English with English-speaking interlocutors. Those whose English had become dominant used English with both English-speaking and French-speaking conversational partners. Pearson et al. (1997) found that, in a Spanish-speaking community in Miami, toddlers learning Spanish and English required more exposures to Spanish to learn the same number of words as in English.

Spoken Second Language Development

The early period of second language acquisition moves from observation and imitation to productive use. An extended period of language development then follows before native-like proficiency, much like the years it takes for a monolingual child to achieve advanced competence in his or her sole language.

The early period of second language acquisition can be characterized into four phases: (a) home language use, (b) a nonverbal period, (c) formulaic language use, and (d) productive language use (Saville-Troike, 1987; Tabors, 2008). Tabors observed this pattern occur across diverse L1 learners in a Massachusetts preschool. The first phase was brief, often lasting only a few days. Some children skipped the second phase while others stayed in it for months. These children were largely silent, observing and listening, but also subvocally rehearsing what they heard, and engaging in private soundplay. They communicated nonverbally and varied in their interactiveness. In the third phase, formulaic language appeared: short, imitated social phrases (e.g., *excuse me, I don't know, be careful*) and play words (e.g., *zoom, hey, lookit*). The fourth state was the beginning of generative language. Utterances were initially telegraphic, combining all-purpose phrases with other words (e.g. *lookit X, I want X, how do you X?*). Proficiency quickly increased, so that although the children missed grammatical morphemes and had mispronunciations and errors, they communicated easily in diverse interactions.

Children can gain productive, functional use of L2 in less than a year (Saville-Troike, 1987; Tabors, 2008). However, there may still be a heavy reliance on context (Paradis et al., 2011). In adult-directed conversations, questions often require only short answers (e.g., *How do you like school? What is your favorite subject?*). Conversational competence is assisted by familiar topics, social routines, inference skills, and body language. Those who become involved in social interactions and use verbal and nonverbal cues will be more successful communicators. Fillmore (1979) determined a set of social and cognitive strategies that second language learners were observed to use to aid their acquisition of the second language (Box 6.2).

The longest period of second language development is between productive use and native-like competence. Called *interlanguage* by Selinker (1972), this L2 knowledge is systematic and rule governed but incomplete and changing. Most of the errors are common across L2 learners, regardless of L1. These are primarily developmental errors made by younger children acquiring English as their first language (Paradis et al., 2011). For grammatical morphology, the sequence of acquisition generally parallels that of English L1 learners, such as acquiring plural *-s* before past tense *-ed* and omitting morphemes (Dulay & Burt, 1974; Jia & Fuse, 2007; Paradis, 2005). One notable difference found by Dulay and Burt was the early acquisition of copula and auxiliary *be*, which emerged prior to articles *a/the*. The common sequence is present for L1 languages as different as Spanish and Cantonese.

Some L2 errors reflect strategies involved in communicating the ideas of an older child with the tools of a younger one. A common one is using general, all-purpose words to express specific meanings (Golberg, Paradis, & Crago, 2008; Harley, 1992; Tabors, 2008). For example, the verb *do* is used in this way by diverse L1 learners, in utterances

Box 6.2. ***Social and Cognitive Strategies for Second Language Learning***

1. Join a group and act as if you understand what is going on, even if you don't.
2. Assume that what people are saying is directly relevant to the situation. Guess!
3. Give the impression with a few well-chosen words that you can speak the language.
4. Get some expressions, even if telegraphic or formulaic, and start talking.
5. Look for recurring parts in the utterances you know.
6. Make the most of what you've got and don't worry much about being wrong.
7. Work on the big things; save the details for later.
8. Find friends who speak the language and count on your friends for help.

Note: Based on Fillmore (1979).

such as: *he do ribbit, ribbit* [says]; *I do the bigger one* [want]; *he do a baseball* [throws]; and *I can do any night* [play]; and *we do our name* [write] (Golberg et al., 2008, p. 53). Golberg et al. found that *do* was used in place of common as well as rare verbs, possibly due to word-finding difficulties in addition to lack of vocabulary.

Cummins (1979) proposed that a common underlying linguistic and cognitive proficiency causes a common sequence and rate of development of both languages so that development of one is likely to aid development of the other. Children learn new words equally quickly in their two languages: Kan and Kohnert (2008) administered structured novel-word learning tasks to 3- to 5-year-old Hmong children learning English and found that the children learned new words in the same number of trials in L2 as in L1, despite having less experience with L2. Furthermore, knowing a word in L1 makes it easier to be acquired in L2 (e.g., Perozzi & Sanchez, 1992; Pham, Kohnert, & Mann, 2011) and knowing more words in L1 is associated with knowing more words in L2 (e.g., Conboy & Thal, 2006; Kan & Kohnert, 2008, 2012; Kohnert et al., 2010). For example, Castilla, Perez-Leroux, and Restrepo (2009) found that, for Spanish-speaking 4-year-olds in an English preschool, Spanish performance at the beginning of the school year predicted success with English at the end of the year. This interdependence, where better L1 skills are associated with better L2 skills, is more pronounced for later L2 academic language and literacy (e.g., Proctor, August, Carlo, & Snow, 2006).

With continued L2 opportunities, learners will move from interlanguage to native-like competence. Children typically become proficient in daily language situations across a range of topics involving active participation in 2 to 3 years but take 4 to 5 years to reach native-like fluency (Saunders & O'Brien, 2006). Saunders and O'Brien reviewed longitudinal and cross-sectional studies of English language learners in a mix of English-only and bilingual education programs. Saunders and O'Brien found that the rate of change was fastest up to third grade and then progressed more slowly until the gap filled in fifth grade. The amount of English spoken within school was not predictive of differences in progress in general proficiency.

There is a critical period of language acquisition, but it is longer and less critical than many would think. Second language acquisition that begins prior to adolescence is most likely to result in native-like knowledge and skills across language areas (Collier, 1989). However, older children are more efficient L2 learners than younger children. For example, Ervin-Tripp (1974) tested English children's acquisition of French in Switzerland during their first 9 months of exposure. The 7- to 9-year-olds were superior to the 4- to 6-year-olds in spoken syntax, morphology, and pronunciation in natural conversation and structured tasks. This older-age advantage may be due to more developed metalinguistic and executive skills, along with greater proficiency in L1. In the long term, differences in second language competency due to age of initial exposure in childhood largely disappear (Collier, 1989).

Learning a Second Language as an Adult

So what about adult learners? Are adults too old to learn a second language without special aptitude and extreme dedication? Certainly, trying to learn Spanish in conventional L2 instruction in a high school foreign language class is unlikely to result in much beyond a rudimentary interlanguage. Many older adult immigrants achieve only the proficiency needed to manage in their workplaces. However, adults are very capable of becoming proficient in a second language and in about the same length of time with the same order of acquisition as children (Bailey, Madden, & Krashen, 1974; Gardner, 1991).

Adults do show great variation in ultimate L2 proficiency. Attitude, aptitude, and motivation all matter more for adults than children (Gardner, 1991). Adult language learning involves issues of cultural identity, social interaction with native speakers, and communicative incompetence. L2 acquisition may show hybridization in which the non-native speaker uses different structures from that of the target language (my friends and I called our version of French Franglaise and found it easier to understand than actual French!). Incomplete acquisition may result in permanent erroneous structures or fossilization (Selinker, 1972). Fossilization of phonology results in the foreign accent so common for adult bilingual speakers.

Although adults may always show their linguistic roots, those who seek out L2 input and use in actual communicative situations—requesting, protesting, and commenting across diverse topics and situations—become proficient in that language (Gardner, 1991). Adults who live in a foreign country and interact with native speakers of that country become competent social users of a second language. College students find that even just one semester abroad can lead to immense gains in L2 competence, especially if they form friendships in that language.

Second Language Progress Across Areas of Language

The rate and ease of second language acquisition varies across areas of language. For children of diverse L1s, phonology shows the fastest rate of acquisition, with only 1 to 2 years required for native-like proficiency of L2 (Paradis et al., 2011). When a child appears to have an accent, it often turns out that this is rather a dialectical variation of the community, such as a Spanish-influenced variety of English.

Paradis et al. (2011) report from their research with English language learners in Edmonton that, for 25 children followed longitudinally, some children's English grammar, vocabulary, and narrative skills were within the native-speaker range after just 1 year. After 3 years, others still lagged in vocabulary or grammar. High levels of grammatical competency were acquired in less than 2 years by Arabic preschoolers learning Swedish (Salameh, 2003). However, full proficiency in grammatical morphology in English may take 3 to 5 years (Paradis, Crago, Genesee, & Rice, 2003). Narrative macrostructure skills develop faster than microstructure skills, possibly because story grammar is more a conceptual than a linguistic skill (Paradis et al., 2011).

Vocabulary has the most variable course of acquisition. There are a relatively small set of phonological, morphosyntactic, and narrative structures to learn in any language. In contrast, the number of words a person can know is almost uncountable. The lexicon needed in daily communicative interactions will be acquired quickly, but the lexicon required in school is a moving target, with the native speakers rapidly acquiring new words each year. Oller, Pearson, and Cobo-Lewis (2007) found that it took Spanish L1 children until fifth grade (6 years) to achieve the same scores on receptive English vocabulary tests as same-age monolingual English-speaking peers in Miami. In contrast,

Golberg et al. (2008) found, for diverse L1 learners followed longitudinally from 5 to 7 years of age, using language samples and a standardized receptive vocabulary test, that English receptive vocabulary was at a native monolingual level in an average acquisition time of 34 months. On the final language sample, more different word types were used than by English L1 children with the same amount of exposure to English. The ratings of amount of home English exposure were similar for the two studies, but Golberg et al. speculated that, in contrast to the Miami students, the students in Edmonton may have used English more as the common language of communication.

Language performance differs by elicitation task, both due to task demands and measurement limitations. For example, Kohnert et al. (2010) elicited story retells and pictured object names from typically developing 3- to 5-year-olds in a bilingual preschool learning Hmong (L1) and English (L2). Hmong retells showed longer utterances and a greater diversity of words than English retells. However, for naming, English and Hmong performance were not significantly different. These children were rapidly acquiring the object lexicon of English while their story retellings reflected the greater diversity and grammatical control of their home language. Kohnert et al. found that the relationship between mean length of utterance (MLU) and vocabulary diversity was stronger for English than for Hmong and speculated that this might be due to L1 being at an earlier stage of development when the two measures are more closely associated. Kohnert also noted that MLU is not a sensitive indicator of complexity for Hmong, which lacks bound grammatical morphology.

Vocabulary may be distributed across topics rather than duplicated (Kohnert, 2010; Paradis et al., 2011). For example, I once evaluated an Urdu-speaking kindergartner. For a color-naming task, the interpreter switched to English to say that "we don't do that kind of thing in our language, parents would do that in English." In word-generation tasks (e.g., *Tell me all the clothes you can wear*), Pena et al. (2002) found that 68% of the lexical items produced by 4- to 7-year-old bilingual children were unique to either Spanish or English. For fourth- and fifth-grade Spanish L1 students, a cross-language influence was stronger for the more academic feature of superordinate terms than for more communicative description items (Ordonez et al., 2002).

This uneven performance across language areas and tasks means that a single language score for each language does not capture a dual language learner's competence in each language. Even for the language considered dominant at the time of the evaluation, performance in that language alone will not be comparable to those of monolingual L1 speakers.

First Language Influence on Second Language Learning

The two languages of developing bilinguals are functionally independent, but specific cross-language transfer occurs for phonology, semantics, and morphosyntax. These can involve facilitation or interference between the two languages. Interference appears as errors that reflect L1. These errors are much more noticeable than faster acquisition of correct forms (Kohnert, 2010).

Zdorenko and Paradis (2012) demonstrated both facilitation and interference with contrastive articles for children learning English. The presence of definite and indefinite articles in Spanish and Arabic facilitated those children's acquisition in English, while their absence in Mandarin and Cantonese impeded English acquisition. Paradis (2005) had hypothesized that languages that do not allow final consonant clusters (e.g., [ts] in "hats" or [kt] in "baked") or have sparse inflectional morphology, such as Cantonese, might result in more errors in English. Paradis found a trend in this direction, but, overall, patterns were more similar than different. One example of an odd but not incorrect transfer for Spanish and French learners of English is for possession: "the house of the dog" rather than "the dog's house" (Paradis et al., 2011, p. 118).

Cross-linguistic cognates share form and meaning in the two languages (e.g., *triangulo/triangle*) (Kohnert, 2010). Translation equivalents share the meaning but not the form (e.g., *cuadrado/square*). Spanish-speaking elementary graders have demonstrated a word-learning advantage for English vocabulary that is a cognate of Spanish words compared to learning of translation equivalents (Cunningham & Graham, 2000; Kelley & Kohnert, 2012).

Cross-language effects have been obtained for sentence comprehension and production. For example, English relies heavily on word order while Vietnamese has a more flexible word order and relies more on context for sentence interpretation. Pham and Kohnert (2010) found that, to determine the agent of a series of simple sentences (e.g., *The chair kicked the boy*), English monolingual children relied on word order and ignored animacy, even if the result did not make sense. In contrast, Vietnamese children relied on a mixture of animacy and word order. For relative clause acquisition, Yip and Matthews (2000) recorded instances of a Cantonese L1 child using the Cantonese pattern of preposing the relative clause in English utterances, such as, when a child was searching for his gift toy gun, "Where's the Santa Claus give me the gun?" (p. 204). Compound reversals occur for both French speakers learning English and English speakers learning French, such as brush-teeth for toothbrush (Nicoladis, 1999, 2002). Spanish-English and Hebrew-English children have been found to use the English requirement of overt subject mention (e.g., *I am drawing Mommy*) in Spanish and Hebrew when it is not pragmatically expected (Hacohen & Schaeffer, 2007; Paradis & Navarro, 2003).

Individual Variation in Dual Language Learning

There is considerable individual variation in the rate and pattern of acquisition of L1 and L2 (Gardner, 1991; Kohnert, 2010; Paradis et al., 2011). Developing bilinguals show diverse patterns of performance across language areas and learning strategies, even when age, context of acquisition, and socioeconomic status (SES) are taken into consideration. For example, Pham and Kohnert (2010) found that developing bilingual Vietnamese children varied in their use of word order versus animacy in sentence interpretation, with some children relying heavily on animacy to process English, some using word order to process Vietnamese, some using separate cues for each language, and others using a blending of cues for both languages.

Internal factors that can affect language acquisition include motivation, personality, and cognitive-linguistic ability. Persistent lack of motivation is rarely seen for minority L1 children (Portes & Hao, 2002; Paradis et al., 2011). There may be initial reluctance to move away from the comfort of L1, and a deliberate decision not speak the second language for a period of time (Tabors, 2008). Furthermore, the social need may not be as strong if there are peers who speak the L1. However, the social forces of the larger L2 community prevail and children enter the L2 learning process. Older students beginning English schooling may resist special instructional support, but that is an adolescent reaction to being singled out, not a lack of desire for English proficiency (Roessingh, Kover, & Watt, 2005). A child's personality and willingness to interact with others can affect progress. Social and outgoing children tend to progress more quickly in L2, especially early on (Fillmore, 1979; Strong, 1983; Tabors, 2008).

An internal factor that predicts language learning success is what could be called *language aptitude*. This aptitude is related to, but is not the same as, the general intelligence measured by IQ tests (Paradis et al., 2011). For adolescents and adult L2 learners, verbal analytic abilities have been found to be correlated with language learning success, while working memory was a better predictor of L2 proficiency for younger L2 learners (Harley & Hart, 1997). For English L1 first graders attending a French immersion program, Genesee and Hamayan (1980) found willingness to interact and explore the target language, along with verbal and nonverbal IQ, correlated with L2 performance in early writing, reading, and listening. Other studies have shown faster acquisition of English L2 with more outside-school use of English (e.g., Jia & Fuse, 2007).

Young children's progress in L2 is affected by the quantity and quality of verbal interactions in the home. Spanish-speaking children from higher SES homes show better English acquisition than those from a lower SES (Paradis et al., 2011). Golberg et al. (2008), found that, for diverse L1 children in Edmonton, children with mothers who had postsecondary education showed larger English vocabularies, even though those mothers were more likely to speak their L1 than English at home. Golberg also noted that the conventional SES measure may be problematic because parental education may not align with occupational level or family income.

First Language Development of Second Language Learners

For a minority L1, whether for simultaneous or sequential bilinguals, the level of support and use of L1 critically affects its continued presence and development. Until the introduction of L2, L1 will develop typically. After L2 exposure begins, differences can emerge that are all normal but not familiar to SLPs accustomed to the monolingual norms and criteria they use to judge language development.

Among early sequential bilingual children there is considerable individual variation, and uneven L1 and L2 acquisition is typical (Kohnert, 2010). In situations where L2 is the societally preferred language, language dominance typically shifts from L1 to L2 after several years of L2 experience, often with loss of L1 (Kohnert et al., 2010; Paradis et al., 2011). Spanish attrition can be seen in overuse of vague terms for objects, mixing English into Spanish, errors in verb morphology, noun gender, and adjective placement (Anderson, 2004). Anderson explains the negative effects on L1 of experiential factors, such as use of English at home, lack of L1 peers, lack of monolingual L1s in the community, and use of L1 in restricted domains (e.g., only talking to Grandma).

A shift in dominance from L1 to L2 can be expected within about 7 years of schooling for minority L1 children. Kohnert and colleagues (Jia, Kohnert, Collado, & Aquino-Garcia, 2006; Kohnert & Bates, 2002; Kohnert, Bates, & Hernandez, 1999) found, for Spanish L1 children and adolescents in California, on picture name verification, action naming, and timed naming speed tasks, that the two languages were balanced for the 6- to 8-year-olds with 2 to 4 years of exposure. Language dominance shifted to English for the 11- to 13-year-olds, with comprehension shifting before production. Although L2 performance exceeded that of L1, L1 performance on these basic processing tasks improved across the 5- to 20-year age range studied.

Some young L2 learners go through a time in which their L1 ability has declined considerably, but their L2 ability is still in the interlanguage period. This transitional period, sometimes called *semilingualism* or even non-non, has been viewed as a sort of linguistic vacuum analogous to language impairment (MacSwan, Rolstad, & Glass, 2002; Paradis et al., 2011). For young children, this may be manifested as a sudden shift in dominance with concomitant rapid loss of L1 occurs. However, at that age, it is not clear how deficient either language is nor that it reflects a permanent situation (Paradis et al., 2011). The L1 deficit may be experiential due to parents presenting impoverished models of L2 and demonstrating no L1. Often the judgment is made based on test scores that are referenced to monolingual speakers or that have other validity problems (e.g., MacSwan et al., 2002). If one examines how the child deals with daily communicative situations, one language or another is being used functionally. Although L2 is not yet fully developed, it is still systematic, generative, and functional and getting stronger every year.

It used to be thought that families should speak only the majority language, with the idea this will promote L2 competence, better cultural assimilation, and greater economic success. However, presence of L1 has important life functions. Parents are more likely to provide rich language models and interactions that lead to greater proficiency in L1, which is associated with better outcomes in L2 speaking, reading, and general academic success (Paradis et al., 2011). Adolescent immigrants to the U.S. who speak both languages at home with a strong bicultural atmosphere are more likely to graduate high school than their immigrant peers in English-dominant or English-limited households (Feliciano, 2001). Immigrants who maintain L1 more often have the close family and cultural connections associated with social and emotional health (e.g., Fillmore, 1991; Portes & Hao, 2002).

Given the benefits of maintaining L1, families are now encouraged to use their home language. The recommendation is to communicate in the language in which the family members can provide the best models, richest interactions, and strongest family connections. The school and larger community will provide the input needed for L2 proficiency and academic success. However, many immigrant families complain that their children refuse to speak their native language (Paradis et al., 2011). The parents speak it and the children answer back in English. This is most likely to occur if the L1 exists primarily in the family, without a surrounding L1 community or educational program. Such low ethnolinguistic vitality, along with an early focus on L2 attainment, leads to a loss of L1 over time and the negative outcomes associated with a lack of cultural identity (Anderson, 2004; Fillmore, 1991; Portes & Hao, 2002).

Portes and Hao (2002) described how, for immigrant groups across U.S. history, there is a "three-generation sequence" in which (a) first-generation immigrants learn as much English as needed to get by in their workplaces, (b) their children learn fluent English but maintain L1 in the home, and (c) their grandchildren take on English as the home language with loss of their heritage tongue. If the first generation arrives as teenagers or younger, then despite a family and community presence of the heritage language, their high fluency in English and rapid acculturation may result in an even more rapid loss. My family history reflects a two-generation loss of Ukrainian. My nephews—whose father emigrated to Canada from Sweden as a teenager—have learned only enough Swedish to cope in paternal family gatherings. Immigrant numbers may fluctuate and predominant groups vary, but the pattern even now is much more of assimilation and L1 loss than increasing bilingualism:

> Despite rapidly growing immigration, the U.S. Census reports that close to 90% of the American population speaks exclusively in English and that the rest is formed mainly by recently arrived immigrants. Recent research on the children of these immigrants documents an equally swift process of linguistic transition which leads to near universal English fluency and concomitant loss of parental languages in a few years.... To the extent that this process continues, the present will mirror the past as descendants of today's immigrants become rapidly integrated into the English monolingual mainstream. (Portes & Hao, 2002, p. 890)

Academic Achievement in a Second Language for Minority L1 Learners

Schooling in a second language in the U.S. concerns mostly L1 Spanish speakers, but there are many other L1 possibilities. In some urban schools, many different languages are spoken. While some of those may form strong ethnolinguistic communities, for others, there may be few speakers. All these children acquire spoken social English quite easily, but the advanced language knowledge and skills needed in school are another matter. Literacy and subject-area achievement are affected not only by language status, family characteristics, and instructional quality but also by the presence of academic instruction in the native language.

Social and Academic Uses of Language

A critical distinction in making sense of bilingualism is social versus academic uses of language. In the second language literature, these are called basic interpersonal communicative skills (BICS) and cognitive academic language proficiency (CALP) (Cummins, 1984). BICS is for daily social communication. It is thought of as spoken language only but includes informal written uses, such as grocery lists and texting. CALP is the decontextualized written and spoken language involved in transmitting, creating, and reflecting on school topics, abstract ideas, and new concepts. It occurs in classroom lessons, written compositions, formal presentations, and achievement tests. BICS and CALP are not fully distinct: Both occur in classroom interactions; many individual speech acts would be difficult to classify; and measures of English-language proficiency judge both social and academic uses. Despite the overlaps, the concepts of BICS and CALP are useful in explaining language acquisition (whether bilingual or monolingual).

Given regular exposure, L2 BICS takes only 2 to 3 years to acquire. Children (and adults) can become conversationally competent across a range of situations relatively quickly. In contrast, L2 CALP, with its involvement of more diverse vocabulary, complex grammar, informational discourse, and metalinguistic awareness, takes 5 to 7 years to achieve proficiency on par with native-speaking students across most areas of schooling (Collier, 1989; Cummins, 1984; Paradis et al., 2011). Furthermore, the two language functions can develop somewhat separately. Saville-Troike (1987) studied 7- to 12-year-old children of foreign graduate students. After 1 year of American schooling, little association occurred between spoken-English proficiency and academic performance. Only vocabulary diversity in a language sample correlated moderately and significantly with reading scores. Saville-Troike noted that determined students could succeed in classroom tasks with nonverbal interactions and access to peers who spoke their L1 to check on assignment comprehension.

Bilingualism and Cognition

CALP achievement is closely related to cognitive skills. Early studies suggested that bilingualism was damaging for cognitive performance, but Peal and Lambert (1962) and subsequent research that corrected methodological errors, such as controlling for SES, linguistic proficiency, and type of learning environment, have found either no difference or some cognitive advantages (Bialystok, 2007; Paradis et al., 2011). An early study by Pintner and Arsenian (1937) found no relation between presence of a second language and verbal intelligence or academic achievement among Jewish Yiddish-speaking children.

Cummins (1979) proposed that children who have low levels of bilingual proficiency are more likely to experience cognitive interference effects, while those who are highly proficient in the two languages will experience facilitative effects. This has been generally supported by subsequent research. Proficient bilingual adults and children consistently show better control than monolinguals of attention allocation, problem solving, and metalinguistics (Bialystok, 2007). According to Bialystok, research has shown no difference in general intelligence or working memory but does sometimes show slower rapid word retrieval. Bilingual adults and children seem better able to control attention and ignore misleading information in challenging tasks. For example, Bialystok (1988) found that first graders who were simultaneously bilingual French-English were superior to monolingual English children and children who were English L1 and partially French L2 proficient on metalinguistic tasks involving dealing with changing word meanings (e.g., *If we called a cat "dog," what sound would it make?*), explaining word concepts, and correcting grammatical errors. Interestingly, bilingualism may even help in older years, with a delay in onset of the symptoms of dementia (Bialystok, Craik, & Freedman, 2007).

Acquisition of CALP

CALP takes a long time to acquire, but given an adequate learning environment bilingual students will eventually equal their monolingual peers in achievement. Unfortunately, there is a disturbingly high proportion of English language learners who never develop adequate CALP skills. For example, Artiles et al. (2005) reported from California education data that about half the students classified as limited English proficient in elementary school continued into middle school in that classification. None of these students had arrived in the U.S. within the prior 3 years. In high school, almost half the ELL students had still not moved into the proficient classification. Only 14% of the high school ELL students were recent arrivals to the country. Over 90% of these students were Hispanic. In addition to gaps in advanced English competence, there is a consistent, large achievement gap between students who enter school with limited English proficiency and native-English speakers (Artiles et al., 2005; McCardle, Mele-McCarthy, & Leos, 2005). McCardle et al. reported that English language learners show the highest dropout rate, lowest achievement scores, largest mobility rate, and highest poverty of any student group.

This chronic low achievement is certainly cause for concern. However, one must be careful to separate out the effects of a second language from the effects of associated economic, cultural, and social challenges. While English language learners face educational challenges, so do monolingual English groups, such as African Americans and Native Americans (Institute of Education Sciences, 2011). Even poor White children have difficulties succeeding academically. Many of these monolingual English children would fail to meet standards of English proficiency "using extended vocabulary in social and academic discourse to negotiate meaning and apply knowledge across content areas" and would not score above the 35 percentile in reading and language (Artiles et al., 2005, p. 287).

Other reviews of research that compare ELLs to national norms rather than criterion standards find results comparable to those of monolingual American children. Collier (1989) reviewed research on L2 academic performance for children beginning English schooling at different ages. Across ages, Collier found students met national norms in fewer than 2 years in mathematics and basic writing skills (spelling, punctuation, and simple grammar points). For immigrants arriving at ages 8 to 12 years, with at least 2 years of L1 schooling in their home country, native-level proficiency on reading, social studies, and math in L2 took 5 to 7 years. Younger children arriving with no schooling in their first language took longer and were at risk of remaining below native levels of academic achievement. Collier found that adolescent arrivals were at the greatest risk of failing to acquire L2 academic competency, even if they arrived with a good L1 academic background (Collier, 1989). More recent work also finds the greatest academic risk for the youngest and oldest arrivals (e.g., Roessingh et al., 2005).

Transfer Effects on Learning to Read

For reading, word recognition skills are acquired quickly, with considerable positive transfer from L1 (e.g., Chen, Xu, Nguyen, Hong, & Wang, 2010; Dickinson, McCabe, Clark-Chiarelli, & Wolf, 2004; Uchikoshi & Marinova-Todd, 2012). For example, Oller et al. (2007) found that bilingual Spanish-English children across SES, language in the home, and educational setting, showed performance comparable to monolingual English children in basic reading (phonics) skills. Uchikoshi and Marinova-Todd found that Cantonese-speaking kindergartners performed below monolingual norms on receptive vocabulary for both languages but at or above average monolinguals on English letter-word identification and phonological awareness. This effect occurred whether the children were English dominant or Cantonese dominant. For the children attending Chinese after-school programs, cross-language facilitation from phonological awareness occurred on Chinese character recognition, despite the latter being iconic rather than sound based. This facilitation may be due to general perceptual-cognitive underpinnings of decoding skills, such as phonological memory.

Reading comprehension, which involves topic knowledge, vocabulary, and CALP, takes much longer to become on par with monolingual speakers (e.g., Oller et al., 2007; Roessingh et al., 2005). Students' achievement in this area is affected by educational programming, especially the provision of instruction in L1. L1 skills can transfer to and scaffold CALP proficiency (e.g., Carlisle & Beeman, 2000; Miller et al., 2006; Proctor et al., 2006). For example, Miller et al. (2006) examined the relations between lexical, syntactic, fluency, and discourse measures of oral narrative language and reading comprehension for more than 1,500 Spanish-English bilinguals in kindergarten to third grade. Results showed that oral language measures in either language predicted reading performance in both languages beyond the variance accounted for by grade.

Models of Schooling in a Second Language for Minority L1 Learners

There are a number of different approaches to educating minority second language learners. They vary on how L2 learning is supported and whether and how L1 learning is also supported in school. Each has different effects on the maintenance of L1 BICS, and the achievement of L2 CALP and academic success.

English-Only Schooling

For most children globally, L1 minority children are educated through the majority L2 without any particular attention to L1. This has been referred to as *sink-or-swim* or *submersion education* or by the more neutral label of *L2-only education* (Paradis et al., 2011). In many L2-only schools, ESL programs assist children in transitioning to English and American schooling.

Partial ESL programs provide: (a) several periods a week of English language instruction; (b) a teacher knowledgeable of the learners' sometimes diverse backgrounds, needs, and progress; and (c) a supportive microcommunity of L2 learners. The ESL teacher is a resource for other educators, an advocate for the ESL students, and a home-school link for the families of these children (e.g., Roessingh et al., 2005). ESL instruction may be even more extensive, with English learners grouped together for modified content area instruction and sometimes a paraeducator who provides translation of key concepts and instructions (Artiles et al., 2005; Rossell & Baker, 1996). This is sometimes called *structured ESL immersion*. In districts with many late L1 arrivals, ESL programs may be present in secondary schools.

It is difficult to determine the effectiveness of L2-only education because of the wide range of teaching quality, educational supports, L1 and L2 proficiency entering school, and language and life backgrounds (Paradis et al., 2011). However, second language learners can and do succeed in these settings. The presence of ESL support and the quality of the support appears to help educational outcomes (Roessingh et al., 2005). My mother was an ESL teacher in elementary and secondary grades, and she seemed to provide important educational and emotional support for her "mini United Nations" classroom. Children from some ethnolinguistic groups, particularly from Asian backgrounds, typically receive some kind of L2-only schooling but consistently meet or exceed the academic performance of White, monolingual English American children (Institute of Education Sciences, 2011).

Some minority L1 groups manage to succeed academically in L2-only schooling even with large cultural differences, poverty, low parental education, and traumatic life histories. For example, Hmong arrived in the last wave of Southeast Asian refugees in the 1980s. Hmong were mainly preliterate farmers or guerilla fighters from the rural highlands of northern Laos (Rumbaut, 1989). Rumbaut reported that Hmong arrived in the U.S. with the least education (a mean of 1.6 years) and after the longest time in refugee camps (a mean of 2.9 years) of any Southeast Asian group (Rumbaut, 1989). Their culture and life experiences, including the predominant religion of ancestor worship, were very different from that of White Americans. It turns out that Hmong children, born abroad and educated in the U.S., showed surprisingly strong levels of educational attainment. Ima and Rumbaut (Ima & Rumbaut, 1989; Rumbaut, 1989) found that Hmong students in California public schools in the 1980s had very low drop-out rates, grade point averages above White students, and standardized achievement test scores at or above the national average on mathematics and language. Even reading performance was within one standard deviation of the mean for Hmong students judged as English proficient.

Transitional Bilingual Education

Despite the pockets of success for L2-only education, overall immigrant and other minority students show persistent low achievement (Artiles et al., 2005; McCardle et al., 2005). Other models of education that involve L1 in some way have been developed. Bilingual education provides some schooling in L1 along with L2.

Transitional bilingual programs are the most common type of bilingual education in the U.S. (Paradis et al., 2011). The aim of these programs is to develop English proficiency in minority L1 children, with L1 used as a temporary crutch to achieve that aim (Paradis et al., 2011). They provide some literacy and academic instruction in L1 alongside instruction in L2 over a period of 1 to 3 years. As L2 proficiency is gained, use of English for academics increases and instruction in L2 decreases until the student is taught fully in English. In the U.S., these programs are offered mainly for Spanish L1 children.

In examining the effects of bilingual education, comparisons must be made to similar minority L1 learners in L2-only programs. That means not only the L1 and SES of individual children but the features of the families and communities in which the students live. Bilingual education is more likely to be offered where there are a large number of speakers of a particular language. Those communities are often poor, with low education and social disruption. Performance of children in these neighborhoods may differ from children from the same L1 and family income, but whose parents are well-educated (but underemployed) immigrants situated in better-off, primarily monolingual English neighborhoods. In addition, L2 performance must be examined over the long term, rather than early on, when instruction is largely in L1.

The research on bilingual education is additionally difficult to sort out because educational quality, the nature of L1 versus L2 instruction, and the degree of detail reported about instruction vary considerably (Lindholm-Leary & Borsato, 2006; Rossell & Baker, 1996). Rossell and Baker and others have argued that bilingual education is based more on cultural advocacy than educational benefit and that the time spent in L1 instruction hurts progress in English, what is called a *time-on-task* argument. Rossell and Baker's review of research found only a minority of studies showed transitional bilingual programs to be superior to L2-only education. However, significant problems in their exclusion and inclusion decisions affected the validity of their findings. Better analyses of the research and more recent studies have indicated that transitional bilingualism does not hurt L2 progress and is generally beneficial (Lindholm-Leary & Borsato, 2006; Paradis et al., 2011). Clearer and more consistently positive outcomes have been found for educational models that involve sustained uses of L1.

Additive Bilingual Education

So far, the models of education for developing bilinguals have been subtractive, aiming only at English proficiency (Box 6.3). Another approach to bilingual education is intended to develop proficiency and advanced academic achievement in both L1 and L2. Additive bilingual education occurs as developmental or late-exit bilingual and two-way bilingual programs (Paradis et al., 2011). Developmental bilingual programs are composed of only minority L1 children. The most common language split in these programs is 90% L1 and 10% L2 or 50% of each. Two-way programs aim for having half Spanish L1 speakers and half English L1 speakers, with instruction split between the two languages to promote mutual bilingualism. Instructional L1 is present in these programs for 4 or more years.

Additive L2 bilingual programs fare quite well compared to other forms of education for minority L1 learners. Systematic reviews of studies that consider SES, language status, and long-term effects have most often found that additive bilingual programs come out ahead compared to L1-only or even transitional bilingual programs (Lindholm-Leary & Borsato, 2006; Rolstad, Mahoney, & Glass, 2005; Thomas & Collier, 2002). Students in English-only instruction often show an initial advantage in English, but by the later elementary or middle school grades there is no difference or more often, a difference in favor of the bilingual program students (e.g., Shneyderman & Abella, 2009). At-risk students who have gone through some kind of bilingual education have been found

Box 6.3. ***Models of Education for Developing Bilingual Children***

Type	Duration	Target Students	BICS/CALP Proficiency	Aim
		L2-Only		
No supports	PreK–Gr12	Diverse minority L1s taught together	English	Subtractive
Partial ESL	3–4 years			
Immersion ESL	1–2 years			
		Bilingual		
Transitional	3–4 years	One minority L1	L1 basic and English full	Subtractive
Developmental	3+ years		English and L1	Additive
Two way	3+ years	Minority L1 and English L1	L1 and L2	Additive
		L2 Immersion for Majority L1s		
Early	K–Gr12	English L1	English and L2	Additive
Middle	Gr3–12			
Late	Gr7–12			

Note: English is the majority language in the U.S. and Canada; Spanish is most common for the bilingual programs in the U.S., and French is most common for the L2 immersion programs in Canada.

to be less likely to end up in special education in high school than those who had L2-only schooling (Artiles et al., 2005). The instructional time taken away from the majority language does not appear to inhibit its acquisition.

This lack of support for the time-on-task hypothesis for English is also evident in comparisons of the 90/10 and 50/50 program versions (Lindholm-Leary & Borsato, 2006; Paradis et al., 2011). Minority L1 students who receive greater exposure to English in the 50/50 programs show an initial advantage in English compared to those in 90/10 programs, but the advantage is small and temporary. By the end of third grade, the 50/50 and 90/10 programs show equal English proficiency. This is likely due to both the cognitive-linguistic scaffolding support coming from maintaining L2 proficiency and the ubiquity of English in the community, media, and country. In contrast, the minority L1, which has much less community exposure, benefits from greater time-on-task (Paradis et al., 2011). For example, Shneyderman and Abella (2009) found that, with 4 years of two-way bilingual instruction, students in the version that offered Spanish instruction in both language arts and a content area performed better in Spanish reading comprehension than those who received only Spanish language arts instruction.

Students in developmental bilingual programs show immediate transfer of decoding skills to English reading, but slower transfer of comprehension skills (Carlisle & Beeman, 2000; Proctor et al., 2006). Proctor and colleagues investigated the effects of Spanish literacy instruction on English reading in fourth-grade Hispanic students in a Spanish-English bilingual program. Stronger Spanish vocabulary was associated with stronger English reading fluency, particularly for the better readers. The students who had their initial reading instruction in Spanish exceeded those whose initial instruction was in English for Spanish alphabetic knowledge and fluency. For English alphabetic knowledge and fluency, the two groups performed the same. For oral language and reading comprehension, better performance aligned with the language of instruction.

Educating students in L1 and expecting L2 academic achievement works partly because of the larger presence of the majority L2, but also because the foundational skills and concepts for reading and writing involve basic cognitive processes that easily transfer between languages. For beginning readers, print concepts, letter names, letter-sound correspondence, phonological awareness, and work attack skills all move easily from one language to another. The transferability between languages is aided by structural similarity and the use of the same writing system. Even for languages with very different writing systems, such as Chinese, developing first language proficiency does not hinder the development of second language proficiency and academic performance in English (e.g., Uchikoshi & Marinova-Todd, 2012).

Second Language Schooling for Majority L1 Learners

Most of the educational attention is directed to low-SES minority L1 learners succeeding in majority L2 education. However, this is not the only L2 schooling possibility. Another option is majority language children being educated through a minority L2 language. In this approach, children are taught almost wholly in L2 for several years and then transition into bilingual L1 and L2 academic instruction that continues through to high school. French is the most common L2, but immersion programs in other languages also occur, such as the Mandarin immersion school attended by the son of a White SLP friend in Vancouver. L2 immersion education is an infrequent offering in the U.S. but is popular throughout Canada, including in western regions where French is not commonly spoken in the larger community.

Paradis et al. (2011) describe three timings for initiating academic and language immersion in L2: early (grades K/1), middle or delayed (4/5), and late (7–10). Early immersion commences with 100% of instruction in L2, initiates L1 reading and writing instruction in third grade, and shifts to 50% of each language across subject areas from fifth grade beyond. The idea of not teaching a child to read in English might seem disturbing, but as explained earlier, reading skills transfer easily between languages. I observed for my own nieces and nephews in French immersion that as soon as they could read in French, they could pick up a book in English and read it, too.

Middle and late programs provide some L2 language instruction in the grades preceding the initiation of L2 academic instruction and then begin subject area instruction in L2 in the grades specified. In delayed immersion, students commence and stay in 50% L2 instruction. Late immersion typically starts with 80% L2 then shifts to 50%. There are varying schedules of 50% delivery across the curriculum, such as assigning one subject to a language of instruction for a year or changing the language of instruction weekly. Students need to encounter all subjects in both languages over time so they know language-specific vocabulary, grammar, discourse, and writing conventions. All three varieties of L2 immersion aim for native-like proficiency in L2 and advanced functional achievement in all areas of academic performance.

Majority L1 students in immersion programs acquire a much higher level of functional proficiency in L2 across reading, writing, speaking, and listening than comparable students in conventional L2 classes (Paradis et al., 2011). Despite this high proficiency, full native-like L2 competence is elusive. Even in high school, Paradis et al. noted that students show some difficulties with French pronouns, verb tenses, prepositions, idiomatic expressions, and intrusions from English. Because the L2 is a minority language, time-on-task matters. Genesee and Hamayan (1980) found that children who used French more in class, at recess, and in halls, had higher French proficiency at end of kindergarten. But even those who freely converse in the L2 in school may not use it outside of school (Paradis et al., 2011). I have seen this dispreference for the non-native language for social interaction: Four nieces and nephews in one family who can easily converse in French at home, do not do so. Even my niece and nephew who have lived all their lives in Montreal and France converse almost solely in English with each other, their French-fluent parents, and their bilingual friends.

For academic achievement, evaluations of immersion programs indicate that L1 majority students generally attain the same levels as their peers in L1-only schooling (Paradis et al., 2011). English L1 students score as well on tests of math, science, and social studies administered in French as comparable students educated and tested in English and as well as French-speaking students educated and tested in French. Paradis et al. noted that French immersion students may have a lack of terminology and word-finding hesitations if tested in the noninstructional language, but these differences quickly disappear with a brief period of instruction in English.

While the immersion approach is widely recognized as successful for typical learners, there have been questions about suitability for at-risk students. Low-SES students fare as well in L1 achievement as comparable students in regular instruction and have the added benefit of L2 proficiency (Genesee & Jared, 2008; Paradis et al., 2011). For example, Holobow, Genesee, and Lambert (1991), in a two-way comparison of SES and ethnicity, found that low-SES and Black first-grade students in French immersion in Cincinnati attained the same levels of English and math as students in L1-only programs. For spoken French, the low-SES and Black students did not differ from the middle class or White students, although all were lower than Canadian children in the same kind of immersion program. For a French immersion program in Louisiana, state-standardized achievement performance in English language arts and math were higher for the immersion students, regardless of race or income, than for no-immersion students (Caldas & Boudreaux, 1999). Contrary to expectations, benefits were stronger for schools with many low income students.

There has been little investigation of the effect of L2 immersion education on majority L1 students with identified disabilities (Genesee & Jared, 2008; Paradis et al., 2011). Some early studies indicated that students with lower intellect or language impairment do no worse than in monolingual education (Bruck, 1978, 1982; Genesee 1976, 1978). Literacy and academic performance was similar to that of comparable students in English programs, with the added benefit of better French proficiency. Bruck (1985a, 1985b) compared children who were struggling in school and switched out of immersion to those who remained despite low academics. The switchers were distinguished by their negative attitudes toward school and showed more behavior problems, which continued after switching to monolingual education.

Early and late immersion seem to have different effects on spoken versus academic skills for students with lower IQs (Genesee, 1987). For early immersion, Genesee found that IQ predicted L2 academic performance but lower IQ students did better than expected on speaking and listening proficiency. For late immersion, with its greater use of CALP in spoken language interactions, IQ predicted both academics and spoken language proficiency. This suggests that, for at-risk students, early rather than later immersion is preferable. This may seem at odds with the idea of developing the native language before taking on a second language, but this illustrates the importance of considering language status: An English-speaking child with risk indicators in an English-speaking country succeeds better if the L2 subject area instruction begins earlier and when instruction is a social event, while a Spanish-speaking child with risk indicators in that same country is better off being educated in Spanish while also receiving instruction in English.

In sum, majority L1 children succeed in minority L2 immersion programs and gain the benefit of advanced proficiency in a second language. At-risk learners can also succeed, especially in early immersion. However, a major concern for students with low achievement is the lack of evidence-based intervention methodologies, such as RTI, for immersion education (Genesee & Jared, 2008). An additional challenge for students with low achievement in French immersion is the context of comparison. French immersion students most often come from higher SES families who view this model as an enrichment option. A struggling student, whether due to poverty, ability, or inclination, will look worse if peers are generally high achieving.

Language and Reading Intervention for Bilingual Students

Language and Reading Impairment in Bilingual Children

There are no epidemiological studies of the prevalence of SLI in children learning two languages (Kohnert, 2010). Rates of identification in special education do not inform on this question because of both over- and under-representation in these services (Artiles et al., 2005; McCardle et al., 2005). If SLI affects monolingual and bilingual children similarly, then approximately 7% of bilingual learners have SLI (Tomblin et al., 1997).

Like for monolingual children with SLI, bilingual children with SLI learn language at a slower pace and show lower levels of achievement than their typically developing bilingual peers. Bilingualism itself does not appear to result in additional or different language deficits for children with SLI compared to monolingual children with SLI of the same age and language background (e.g., Hakansson, Salameh, & Nettelbladt, 2003; Paradis et al., 2003; Salameh, 2003; Windsor, Kohnert, Lobitz, & Pham, 2010). Morgan, Restrepo, and Auza (2013) compared monolingual Spanish and bilingual Spanish-English children with typical and impaired language development on a variety of grammatical morphology tasks. The tasks differentiated the typically developing children from the children with language impairment, but none showed significant differences between the bilingual typically developing children and the monolingual children with language impairment. Like for typically developing children, first language skills predict growth in English for preschoolers with SLI (Gutierrez-Clellen, Simon-Cereijido, & Sweet, 2012). However, bilingual children with SLI may be particularly prone to losing their minority L1 despite use in the family (Restrepo & Kruth, 2000; Salameh, 2003).

Like for their monolingual counterparts, fundamental difficulties with marking of verb tense are present (Jackson-Maldonado, 2004; Paradis et al., 2003). For example, Paradis et al. compared the morphosyntax of eight French-English simultaneous bilingual 7-year-old children with SLI to age-matched monolingual English-speaking and French-speaking children with SLI. For French and English conversational language samples, the bilingual and monolingual SLI groups both showed greater accuracy with nontense (for English: *-ing*, *in/on*, plural *-s*) than tense (singular *-s*, past tense *-ed*, and irregular past tense) morphemes. Simon-Cereijido and Gutierrez-Clellen (2007) found that, from conversational language samples for preschoolers with and without SLI, a combination of MLU and a grammatical-error index discriminated language impairment equally well across bilingual, Spanish-dominant, and Spanish-only children.

Reading disability in bilingual children appears to involve the same factors as for monolingual children (Paradis et al., 2011). Specific problems with word recognition and additional problems with reading comprehension are both present, with similar contributions from phonological processing, alphabet knowledge, and oral language (Erdos, Genesee, Savage, & Haigh, 2010). Bilingual children with SLI show similar deficits in basic cognitive processes, such as phonological memory and word-learning ability (Kohnert, Windsor, & Ebert, 2009). Like for typically achieving bilingual children, the nature of L1 may accelerate or impede acquisition of word recognition skills: Poor phonemic awareness is less likely to impact acquisition of Chinese logographic characters or the more regular spelling system of Spanish. For alphabetic writing systems, the word attack skills will be similar, although specific orthographic patterns differ.

Reading comprehension has a larger scope of knowledge and skills than decoding. Many of these, such as executive functions, metalinguistic skills, and world knowledge, will transfer between L1 and L2 (e.g., Bialystok, 2007). Students who lack advanced proficiency in both languages, whether from impairment or lack of experience, can be expected to show reading comprehension problems. The world knowledge, areas of expertise, and literacy practices of minority immigrant children or children from isolated urban or rural communities may differ considerably from those of middle class suburban children.

Identification of Language Impairment in Bilingual Children

The tenet of SLI is that it involves inherent language-learning ability and will thus be manifest across languages. It would seem to be a simple matter, at least for second languages that are commonly present in a country, to determine that language learning is slower or atypical compared to peers. However, beyond the early milestones, dual language learning is a fluid process that appears to be more susceptible to internal and external factors than monolingual development (Kohnert, 2010; Paradis et al., 2011).

Not only does relative competence change over time, but, as Kohnert (2010) outlined, abilities may be uneven or distributed within and across linguistic domains and the two languages variably influence each other. In addition, considerable individual variation occurs despite similar language-learning circumstances. A tenet of determining a disorder is low performance in both languages. However, experientially caused L1 attrition can look a lot like language impairment (Anderson, 2004). As a result of all this variation, referencing an individual child's performance to group data or developmental norms, even those constructed on bilingual children, is problematic (Kohnert, 2010). In addition, bilingual learners have cultural differences and often deal with low SES and communities with social disruption. These cultural and contextual factors can affect student achievement, and must somehow be understood and taken into consideration when identifying and intervening with struggling students (Klingner, Artiles, & Barletta, 2006).

There are few validated procedures or measures for identifying language impairment in bilingual children. Moreover, SLPs generally lack expertise in using the ones that do exist (Caesar & Kohler, 2007; Roseberry-McKibbon, Brice, & O'Hanlon, 2005). Caesar and Kohler's survey of Michigan SLPs found a wide variability in procedures and measures used and a high reliance on English norm-referenced tests. In their survey, SLPs were asked to list five measures they used to assess bilingual students' language abilities in order of decreasing frequency. Of the 40 procedures and measures listed, two thirds were used by less than 10% of the respondents. Fewer than 2% of the respondents reported using measures published in languages other than English. Less than half the respondents used interpreters. Only one third of the respondents used language sampling and 10% used observation. Dynamic assessment was not reported by any of the respondents.

For Spanish, there are valid measures emerging, such as the *Bilingual English Spanish Oral Screener*, which examines morphosyntax and semantics in both languages for 4- and 5-year-olds (Pena, Gillam, Bedore, & Bohman, 2011). It seems to work well across dominance variations: Pena et al. reported that Spanish-dominant, balanced Spanish-English, and English-dominant bilingual children all scored lower than their monolingual Spanish or English peers, and none of the three bilingual groups fell disproportionately into the at-risk range. English tense morphology and story grammar measures, as well as parent questionnaires on early L1 development, have shown potential for discriminating diverse L1 children learning English (e.g., Cleave, Girolametto, Chen, & Johnson, 2010; Paradis, Schneider, & Duncan, 2013).

Measures of phonological processing appear to have good potential. Guiberson and Rodriguez (2013) found identification potential of Spanish nonword repetition task for Spanish-speaking preschoolers with and without language impairment. Even better, for older children, English nonword repetition has shown good results: Windsor, Kohnert, Lobitz, and Pham (2010) found that, for 6- to 11-year-old monolingual and sequential bilingual Spanish-English children, English four-syllable nonwords was a better predictor than Spanish nonwords at distinguishing children with and without SLI. These items likely stress the phonological memory system more and invoke linguistic experience less than the Spanish nonwords. Good predictive value of first-grade reading has been obtained from English measures of letter identification, phonological awareness, rapid automatized naming, and sentence repetition in Spanish-speaking kindergartners (e.g., Petersen & Gillam, in press). For these measures, care must be taken to minimize meaning demands. For example, for phonemic awareness, identifying the beginning phoneme in *dog* has less influence from knowledge of English than asking which of *cat*, *doll*, or *bed* begin with the same sound as *dog*.

The RTI programs for early reading that are now prevalent in elementary schools are promising in terms of determining which English learners have additional inherent learning impairments (Paradis et al., 2011; Xu & Drame, 2008). With the discrepancy method of identifying reading disability, young ELL students were often under-represented in special education in the early grades, but then as the IQ-achievement gap widened or language issues impacted reading comprehension more, late identification and even over-representation occurred in later grades (Artiles et al., 2005; McCardle et al., 2005). Diagnoses of language impairment may be avoided for the first several years of schooling because of the inability to determine the cause of low English scores. While it is appropriate to accommodate the second language acquisition process, this wait means that students are further behind before getting help. RTI helps both by providing early supplementary reading support without a label and collecting progress data that contributes toward more valid identification of inherent learning disability. However, RTI is a teaching-learning interaction that is impacted by cultural and linguistic differences, so behavior and outcome expectations based on English-speaking American children may not be equally applicable to learning problems in minority L1 groups (Xu & Drame, 2008).

An alternative that reflects the principles of RTI but avoids some of its weaknesses is dynamic assessment. Dynamic assessment is less susceptible to extraneous factors that enter the lengthier and broader focus of RTI instruction, such as child attendance, teaching quality, and multiple learning targets. Just as for monolingual children with reading disabilities (e.g., Bridges & Catts, 2011), dynamic assessment shows considerable promise for bilingual children. For example, Petersen and Gillam (in press) investigated the predictive validity of dynamic assessment for 63 bilingual Latino children at risk for language impairment or typically developing. A test-teach-test task involving nonsense-word decoding was administered in kindergarten. At the end of first grade, participants completed measures of word identification, decoding, and reading fluency. The dynamic assessment yielded high classification accuracy, with sensitivity and specificity above 80% for all three reading measures.

Determining a language impairment in bilingual learners is a much tougher challenge than decoding and spelling. While early language acquisition is a robust process that unfolds similarly across diverse and challenging life situations, determining difference from disorder for later language development is exceedingly difficult. Language comprehension and expression are complicated domains and more affected by the nature of the specific languages involved as well as the individual's life experiences. Valid RTI methodologies are not yet present for Spanish and even less so for other minority languages. Dynamic assessment is looking hopeful, with several studies showing excellent classification accuracy for bilingual learners and advances in ways of reducing administration times (e.g., Chanthongthip, 2013; Peña, Iglesias, & Lidz, 2001; Pena et al., 2006). The evidence is sufficiently impressive that versions that can be used clinically are urgently needed for identifying reading disability and language impairment.

In addition to considering the characteristics and developmental history of each child, best assessment practices involve the use of conventional and alternate measures with multiple measures in both languages, across language areas, and at different points in time (Kohnert, 2010; Paradis et al., 2011). It is important to remember that typically developing bilingual students can be low in both languages for various experiential home and school reasons, and so low performance in both languages is necessary but not sufficient for a language impairment. Procedures that minimize the effect of experience, such as nonword repetition and dynamic assessment, have considerable potential for differential diagnosis of bilingual learners.

Intervention With Bilingual Children

Identification of language impairment in bilingual children is a daunting endeavor. Fortunately, intervention is far less complicated. Just as for a monolingual child with a disorder, intervention is fundamentally an individualized endeavor in which the SLP matches the targets, procedures, and activities to the presenting characteristics of the child, and dynamically responds within the teaching-learning process. General principles of quality treatment, such as repeated opportunities for intense, systematically supported, explicit intervention (RISE+; see Chapter 2) in meaningful contexts, apply to bilingual children just as much as to monolingual children.

An important feature of intervention is recognizing and valuing the distinctive cultural and linguistic knowledge these children bring to the language-learning situation. Procedures include teaching through activities that draw on home experiences, using observational and cooperative learning, and making explicit the differences between home and school communication.

Another consideration is the language of intervention. Kohnert (2010) and others suggested that SLPs should move from the question of "Which language should we support in intervention with bilingual children?" to "How can we best support both languages needed by bilingual children with PLI [SLI]?" (p. 466). Clinical articles are emerging that describe bilingual methodologies, even in cases where the SLP does not speak both the child's languages (e.g., Kohnert & Derr, 2004; Kohnert, Yim, Nett, Kan, & Duran, 2005). However, research on this question is still minimal: Kohnert and Medina's (2009) systematic review located only four treatment studies that included bilingual children. All showed that English development was facilitated with use of L1 in treatment.

An example of bilingual intervention is Thordardottir, Ellis Weismer, and Smith (1997). In a single-subject alternating treatment research design, Thordardottir et al. examined the effects of monolingual versus bilingual vocabulary treatment for an Icelandic child of 4;11 in the U.S. The child's Icelandic was at the 2-year level receptively and 18 months expressively. Exposure to English had been minimal. The treatments involved individual semistructured play and following the child's lead. In the English condition, the bilingual SLP provided only English input and facilitations and did not respond to child initiations in Icelandic other than to say to "speak in English" (a third person matching the language of delivery was present in the room). In the bilingual condition, the SLP presented the novel vocabulary in both languages and responded with the language matching the child's initiations. Results showed comparable learning of English in the monolingual and bilingual conditions, with a slight advantage in the latter.

Pham et al. (2011) compared monolingual and bilingual treatment of a 3;11 Vietnamese preschooler with less than a year's exposure of English in a series of single-subject experiments comparing English-only and bilingual instruction. The receptive single-word vocabulary treatment involved listening to prerecorded audio files in Vietnamese and English and identifying pictures with corrective feedback from a clinician sitting beside him (not developmentally appropriate but good for experimental control). With the same total number of learning trials in the two conditions, results showed that the child was more attentive and learned as many English words with dual language instruction as with English-only instruction.

A randomized group experimental study of Spanish L1 preschoolers with SLI compared English-only and bilingual programs on growth in English (Gutierrez-Clellen et al., 2012). The two programs had parallel curricula involving academic enrichment in hands-on activities to develop vocabulary and numeracy skills for the same total time. In the bilingual condition, lessons were delivered in Spanish one day and in English the next. The program was additional to any SLP-delivered services, which were not specified. Guitierrez-Clellen et al. found greater growth in English MLU in the bilingual condition, and for the English-only condition, an interaction between Spanish skills and language of intervention, such that children with low Spanish MLUs did not do as well in English growth as those with higher Spanish MLUs.

For reading difficulties, the same intensive reading interventions targeting phonological processing and letter-sound knowledge that have been successful for monolingual children with reading deficits are similarly effective for bilingual children, whether delivered in L2 or L1 (e.g., Cirino et al., 2009; Lovett et al., 2008; Vaughn et al., 2006). For students in L2-only education, Lovett et al. found that with RTI delivered in English, diverse L1 learners made similar growth and achieved similar outcomes to English L1 children. Oral language abilities in English were highly predictive of final outcomes and growth for both groups of children. For bilingual Spanish-English education, Cirino et al. found that first-grade reading intervention that matched the language of classroom instruction showed benefits compared to students not receiving the intervention. Greater improvement was obtained for Spanish than for English reading performance. The Spanish intervention showed transfer to English letter-word recognition, but not to English reading fluency or oral language.

Despite clinical guidance and research evidence, Kohnert (2010) reported that SLPs largely provide treatment in only one language, usually English. Kohnert suggest several reasons for this, including: a shortage of bilingual SLPs, a belief that the SLP must speak the language to support its growth, and a belief that English-only intervention is best for educational outcomes. On the hopeful side, in the primarily White, monolingual state of Wyoming, our university program is educating more and more graduate students who have proficiency in Spanish and want to develop bilingual SLP expertise. A 2001 survey of SLP services to ELL students reported that most of the respondents had at least part of a course on bilingualism (73%) in their university preparation compared to only 24% in a 1990 survey (Roseberry-McKibbin et al., 2005). In both surveys, about 10% of respondents said they spoke another language fluently enough to provide services in that language. The two top concerns in both surveys was "lack of availability of other professionals who speak the students' languages" and "lack of knowledge of developmental norms in students' primary languages" (p. 55). Hopefully, better knowledge and skills in assessment and intervention methodologies for bilingual learners will show in the next survey.

Conclusion

There are many ways of becoming bilingual. Some children develop two languages simultaneously at home. Most acquire their second language in school. With adequate exposure, second language acquisition follows a similar course and time line as first language acquisition. An important factor in bilingual students' achievement of dual language proficiency and academic success is the majority versus minority status of L1 and L2. Many minority L1 children face the same challenges of poverty and cultural differences encountered by minority monolingual children, and encounter the same lack of proficiency in cognitive-academic uses of language.

Bilingual and immersion education provides students with the opportunity to be schooled in both their native language and a second language. Students of diverse languages, a range of abilities, and varying family backgrounds succeed in a variety of models of schooling, particularly those that support the linguistic and cultural characteristics of these students. Despite advances in research and practice, there remain significant challenges to identifying and intervening with bilingual learners who have language impairments and academic difficulties.

References

Anderson, R. T. (2004). First language loss in Spanish-speaking children: Patterns of loss and implications for clinical practice. In B. Goldstein (Ed.), *Bilingual language development and disorders in Spanish-English speakers* (pp. 187–211). Baltimore, MD: Brookes.

Artiles, A. J., Rueda, R., Salazar, J., & Higareda, I. (2005). Within-group diversity in minority disproportionate representation: English language learners in urban school districts. *Exceptional Children*, 71, 283–300.

Bailey, N., Madden, C., & Krashen, S. (1974). Is there a "natural sequence" in adult second language learning? *Language Learning, 24*, 235–243.

Bialystok, E. (1988). Levels of bilingualism and levels of linguistic awareness. *Developmental Psychology, 24*, 560–567.

Bialystok, E. (2007). Cognitive effects of bilingualism: How linguistic experience leads to cognitive change. *International Journal of Bilingual Education and Bilingualism, 10*, 210–223.

Bialystok, E., Craik, F. I. M, & Freedman, M. (2007). Bilingualism as protection against the onset of symptoms of dementia. *Neuropsychologia, 45*, 459–464.

Bridges, M. S., & Catts, H. W. (2011). The use of a dynamic screening of phonological awareness to predict risk for reading disabilities in kindergarten children. *Journal of Learning Disabilities, 44*, 330–338.

Bruck, M. (1978). The suitability of early French immersion programs for the language-delayed child. *Canadian Journal of Education, 3*, 51–72.

Bruck, M. (1982). Language-impaired children's performance in an additive bilingual education program. *Applied Psycholinguistics, 3*, 45–60.

Bruck, M. (1985a). Predictors of transfer out of early French immersion programs. *Applied Psycholinguistics, 6*, 39–61.

Bruck, M. (1985b). Consequences of transfer out of early French immersion programs. *Applied Psycholinguistics, 6*, 101–120.

Caesar, L. G., & Kohler, P. D. (2007). The state of school-based bilingual assessment: Actual practice versus recommended guidelines. *Language, Speech, and Hearing Services in Schools, 30*, 190–200.

Caldas, S., & Boudreaux, N. (1999). Poverty, race, and foreign language immersion: Predictors of math and English language arts performance. Learning Languages, 5, 4–15.

Carlisle, J. F., & Beeman, M. M. (2000). The effects of language of instruction on the reading and writing achievement of first-grade Hispanic children. *Scientific Studies of Reading, 4*, 331–353.

Castilla, A. P., Perez-Leroux, A. T., & Restrepo, M. A. (2009). Individual differences and the developmental interdependence hypothesis. *International Journal of Bilingual Education and Bilingualism, 12*, 1–16.

Chanthongthip, H. (2013). *Dynamic assessment of narratives: Efficient and accurate classification of bilingual students with language impairment* (Unpublished master's thesis). University of Wyoming, Laramie.

Chen, X., Xu, F., Nguyen, T., Hong, G., & Wang, Y. (2010). Effects of cross-language transfer on first-language phonological awareness and literacy skills in Chinese children receiving English instruction. *Journal of Educational Psychology, 102*, 712–728.

Cirino, P. T., Vaughn, S., Linan-Thompson, S., Cardenas-Hagan, E., Fletcher, J. M., & Francis, D. J. (2009). One-year follow-up outcomes of Spanish and English interventions for English language learners at risk for reading problems. *American Educational Research Journal, 46*, 744–781.

Cleave, P. L., Girolametto, L. E., Chen, X., & Johnson, C. J. (2010). Narrative abilities in monolingual and dual language learning children with specific language impairment. *Journal of Communication Disorders, 43*, 511–522.

Collier, V. P. (1989). How long? A synthesis of research on academic achievement in a second language. *TESOL Quarterly, 23*, 509–531.

Conboy, B. T., & Thal, D. J. (2006). Ties between the lexicon and grammar: Cross-sectional and longitudinal studies of bilingual toddlers. *Child Development, 77*, 712–735.

Crago, M., & Genesee, F. (1996, March). *Who speaks what language and why? Language use of families in an Inuit community*. Paper presented at the Annual Meeting of the American Association for Applied Linguistics, Chicago, IL.

Cummins, J. (1979). Linguistic interdependence and the educational development of bilingual children. *Review of Educational Research, 49*, 222–251.

Cummins, J. (1984). *Bilingualism and special education: Issues in assessment and pedagogy*. Clevedon, UK: Multilingual Matters.

Cunningham, T. H., & Graham, C. R. (2000). Increasing native English vocabulary recognition through Spanish immersion: Cognate transfer from foreign to first language. *Journal of Educational Psychology, 92*, 37–49.

Dickinson, D. K., McCabe, A., Clark-Chiarelli, N., & Wolf, A. (2004). Cross-language transfer of phonological awareness in low-income Spanish and English bilingual preschool children. *Applied Psycholinguistics, 25*, 323–347.

Dulay, H. C., & Burt, M. K. (1974). Natural sequences in child second language acquisition. *Language Learning, 24*, 37–53.

Erdos, C., Genesee, F., Savage, R., & Haigh, C. A. (2010). Individual differences in second language reading outcomes. *International Journal of Bilingualism, 15*, 3–25.

Ervin-Tripp, S. M. (1974). Is second language learning like the first? *TESOL Quarterly, 8*, 111–127.

Feliciano, C. (2001). The benefits of biculturalism: Exposure to immigrant culture and dropping out of school among Asian and Latino youths. *Social Science Quarterly, 82*, 865–879.

Feltman, K., & Kay-Raining Bird, E. (2008). Language learning in four bilingual children with Down syndrome: A detailed analysis of vocabulary and morphosyntax. *Canadian Journal of Speech–Language Pathology and Audiology, 32*, 6–20.

Fillmore, L. W. (1979). Individual differences in second language acquisition. In C. Fillmore, D. Kempler, & W. S.-Y. Wang (Eds.), *Individual differences in language ability and language behavior* (pp. 203–227). San Diego, CA: Academic Press.

Fillmore, L.W. (1991). When learning a second language means losing the first. *Early Childhood Research Quarterly, 6*, 323–346.

Gardner, R. (1991). Second-language learning in adults: Correlates of proficiency. *Applied Language Learning, 2*, 1–28.

Genesee, F. (1976). The role of intelligence in second language learning. *Language Learning, 26*, 267–280.

Genesee, F. (1978). A longitudinal evaluation of an early immersion school program. *Canadian Journal of Education, 3*, 31–50.

Genesee, F. (1987). *Learning through two languages: Studies of immersion and bilingual education*. Rowley, MA: Newbury House.

Genesee, F., Boivin, I., & Nicoladis, E. (1996). Talking with strangers: A study of bilingual children's communicative competence. *Applied Psycholinguistics, 17*, 427–442.

Genesee, F., & Hamayan, E. (1980). Individual differences in second language learning. *Applied Psycholinguistics, 1*, 95–110.

Genesee, F., & Jared, D. (2008). Literacy development in early French immersion programs. *Canadian Psychology, 49*, 140–147.

Golberg, H., Paradis, J., & Crago, M. (2008). Lexical acquisition over time in minority first language children learning English as a second language. *Applied Psycholinguistics, 29*, 41–65.

Guiberson, M., & Rodriguez, B. L. (2013). Classification accuracy of nonword repetition when used with preschool-age Spanish-speaking children. *Language, Speech, and Hearing Services in Schools, 44*, 121–132.

Gutierrez-Clellen, V. F., Simon-Cereijido, G., & Leone, A. E. (2009). Code-switching in bilingual children with specific language impairment. *International Journal of Bilingualism, 13*, 91–109.

Gutierrez-Clellen, V., Simon-Cereijido, G., & Sweet, M. (2012). Predictors of second language acquisition in Latino children with specific language impairment. *American Journal of Speech-Language Pathology, 21*, 64–77.

Hacohen, A., & Schaeffer, J. (2007). Subject realization in early Hebrew/English bilingual acquisition: The role of crosslinguistic influence. *Bilingualism: Language and Cognition, 10*, 333–344.

Hakansson, G., Salameh, E.-K., & Nettelbladt, U. (2003). Measuring language development in bilingual children: Swedish-Arabic children with and without language impairment. *Linguistics, 41*, 255–288.

Hammer, C. S., Komaroff, E., Rodriguez, B. L., Lopez, L. M., Scarpino, S. E., & Goldstein, B. (2012). Predicting Spanish-English bilingual children's language abilities. *Journal of Speech, Language, and Hearing Research, 55*, 1251–1264.

Harley, B. (1992). Patterns of second language development in French immersion. *French Language Studies, 2*, 159–183.

Harley, B., & Hart, D. (1997). Language aptitude and second language proficiency in classroom learners of different starting ages. *Studies in Second Language Acquisition, 19*, 379–400.

Holobow, N. E., Genesee, F., & Lambert, W. E. (1991). The effectiveness of a foreign language immersion program for children from different ethnic and social class backgrounds: Report 2. *Applied Psycholinguistics, 12*, 179–198.

Ima, K., & Rumbaut, R. G. (1989). Southeast Asian refugees in American schools: A comparison of fluent-English-proficient and limited-English-proficient students. *Topics in Language Disorders, 9*(3), 55–75.

Institute of Education Sciences (2011). *The Nation's Report Card: Reading 2011* (NCES 2012–457). Washington, DC: U.S. Department of Education, Institute of Education Sciences. Retrieved from http://nces.ed.gov/nationsreportcard/reading/

Jackson-Maldonado, D. (2004). Verbal morphology and vocabulary in monolinguals and emergent bilinguals. In B. Goldstein (Ed.), *Bilingual language development and disorders in Spanish-English speakers* (pp. 131–162). Baltimore, MD: Brookes.

Jia, G., & Fuse, A. (2007). Acquisition of English grammatical morphology by native Mandarin speaking children and adolescents: Age-related differences. *Journal of Speech, Language, and Hearing Research, 50*, 1280–1299.

Jia, G., Kohnert, K., Collado, J., & Aquino-Garcia, F. (2006). Action naming in Spanish and English by sequential bilingual children and adolescents. *Journal of Speech, Language, and Hearing Research, 49*, 588–602.

Kan, P. F., & Kohnert, K. (2008). Fast mapping by bilingual preschool children. *Journal of Child Language, 35*, 495–514.

Kan, P. F., & Kohnert, K. (2012). A growth curve analysis of novel word learning by sequential bilingual preschool children. *Bilingualism: Language and Cognition, 15*, 452–469.

Kay-Raining Bird, E., Cleave, P., Trudeau, N., Thordardottir, E., Sutton, A., & Thorpe, A. (2005). The language abilities of bilingual children with Down syndrome. *American Journal of Speech–Language Pathology, 14*, 187–199.

Kelley, A., & Kohnert, K. (2012). Is there a cognate advantage for typically developing Spanish speaking English-language learners? *Language, Speech, and Hearing Services in Schools, 43*, 191–204.

Klingner, J. K., Artiles, A. J., & Barletta, L. M. (2006). English language learners who struggle with reading: Language acquisition or learning disabilities? *Journal of Learning Disabilities, 39*, 108–128.

Kohnert, K. (2010). Bilingual children with primary language impairment: Issues, evidence, and implications for clinical actions. *Journal of Communication Disorders, 43*, 465–473.

Kohnert, K. J., & Bates, E. (2002). Balancing bilinguals II: Lexical comprehension and cognitive processing in children learning Spanish and English. *Journal of Speech, Language, and Hearing Research, 45*, 347–359.

Kohnert, K. J., Bates, E., & Hernandez, A. E. (1999). Balancing bilinguals: Lexical-semantic production and cognitive processing in children learning Spanish and English. *Journal of Speech, Language, and Hearing Research, 42*, 1400–1413.

Kohnert, K., & Derr, A. (2004). Language intervention with bilingual children. In B. Goldstein (Ed.), *Bilingual language development and disorders in Spanish-English speakers* (pp. 311–328). Baltimore, MD: Brookes.

Kohnert, K., Kan, P. F., & Conboy, B. T. (2010). Lexical and grammatical associations in sequential bilingual preschoolers. *Journal of Speech, Language, and Hearing Research, 53,* 684–698.

Kohnert, K., & Medina, A. (2009). Bilingual children and communication disorders: A 30-year research retrospective. *Seminars in Speech and Language, 30,* 219–233.

Kohnert, K., Windsor, J., & Ebert, K. (2009). Primary or "specific" language impairment and children learning a second language. *Brain and Language, 109,* 101–111.

Kohnert, K., Yim, D. S., Nett, K., Kan, P. F., & Duran, L. (2005). Intervention with linguistically diverse preschool children: A focus on developing home language(s). *Language, Speech, and Hearing Services in Schools, 36,* 251–263.

Lindholm-Leary, K. & Borsato, G. (2006). Academic achievement. In F. Genesee, K. Lindholm-Leary, W. M. Saunders, & D. Christian (Eds), *Educating English language learners: A synthesis of research evidence* (pp. 176–222). New York, NY: Cambridge University Press.

Lovett, M. W., De Palma, M., Frijters, J., Steinbach, K., Temple, M., Benson, N., & Lacerenza, L. (2008). Interventions for reading difficulties: A comparison of response to intervention by ELL and EFL struggling readers. *Journal of Learning Disabilities, 41,* 333–352.

MacSwan, J., Rolstad, K., & Glass, G. V. (2002). Do some school-age children have no language? Some problems of construct validity in the pre-LAS espanol. *Bilingual Research Journal, 26,* 395–420.

Marchman, V. A., Martinez-Sussmann, C., & Dale, P. S. (2004). The language-specific nature of grammatical development: Evidence from bilingual language learners. *Developmental Science, 7,* 212–224.

McCardle, P., Mele-McCarthy, J., Cutting, L., Leos, K., & D'Emilio, T. (2005). Learning disabilities in English language learners: Identifying the issues. *Learning Disabilities Research and Practice, 20,* 1–5.

McCardle, P., Mele-McCarthy, J., & Leos, K. (2005). English language learners and learning disabilities: Research agenda and implications for practice. *Learning Disabilities Research and Practice, 20,* 68–78.

Miller, J. F., Heilmann, J., Nockerts, A., Iglesias, A., Fabiano, L., & Francis, D. J. (2006). Oral language and reading in bilingual children. *Learning Disabilities Research and Practice, 21,* 30–43.

Montanari, S. (2009). Pragmatic differentiation in early trilingual development. *Journal of Child Language, 36,* 597–627.

Morgan, G. P., Restrepo, M. A., & Auza, A. (2013). Comparison of Spanish morphology in monolingual and Spanish-English bilingual children with and without language impairment. *Bilingualism: Language and Cognition, 16,* 578–596.

Nicoladis, E. (1999). "Where is my brush-teeth?" Acquisition of compound nouns in a French-English bilingual child. *Bilingualism: Language and Cognition, 2,* 245–256.

Nicoladis, E. (2002). What's the difference between 'toilet paper' and 'paper toilet'? French-English bilingual children's crosslinguistic transfer in compound nouns. *Journal of Child Language, 29,* 843–863.

Nicoladis, E., & Secco, G. (2000). Productive vocabulary and language choice. *First Language, 20*(58), 3–28.

Oller, D. K., Pearson, B. Z., & Cobo-Lewis, A. B. (2007). Profile effects in early bilingual language and literacy. *Applied Psycholinguistics, 28*, 191–230.

Ordonez, C. L., Carlo, M. S., Snow, C. E., & McLaughlin, B. (2002). Depth and breadth of vocabulary in two languages: Which vocabulary skills transfer? *Journal of Educational Psychology, 94*, 719–728.

Paradis, J. (2005). Grammatical morphology in children learning English as a second language: Implications of similarities with specific language impairment. *Language, Speech, and Hearing Services in the Schools, 36*, 172–187.

Paradis, J., Crago, M., Genesee, F., & Rice, M. (2003). French-English bilingual children with SLI: How do they compare with their monolingual peers? *Journal of Speech, Language, and Hearing Research, 46*, 113–127.

Paradis, J., & Genesee, F. (1997). On continuity and the emergence of functional categories in bilingual first-language acquisition. *Language Acquisition, 6*(2), 91–124.

Paradis, J., Genesee, F., & Crago, M. B. (Eds.) (2011). *Dual language development and disorders.* Baltimore, MD: Brookes.

Paradis, J., & Navarro, S. (2003). Subject realization and crosslinguistic interference in the bilingual acquisition of Spanish and English: What is the role of the input? *Journal of Child Language, 30*, 371–393.

Paradis, J., & Nicoladis, E. (2007). The influence of dominance and sociolinguistic context on bilingual preschoolers' language choice. *International Journal of Bilingual Education and Bilingualism, 10*, 277–297.

Paradis, J., Schneider, P., & Duncan, T. S. (2013). Discriminating children with language impairment among English language learners from diverse first language backgrounds. *Journal of Speech, Language, and Hearing Research, 56*, 971–981.

Patterson, J. L. (2000). Observed and reported expressive vocabulary and word combinations in bilingual toddlers. *Journal of Speech, Language, and Hearing Research, 43*, 121–128.

Peal, E., & Lambert, W. E. (1962). The relation of bilingualism to intelligence. *Psychological Monographs, 76*, 1–23.

Pearson, B. Z., & Fernandez, S. C. (1994). Patterns of interaction in the lexical growth in two languages of bilingual infants and toddlers. *Language Learning, 44*, 617–653.

Pearson, B. Z., Fernandez, S. C., Lewedeg, V., & Oller, D. K. (1997). The relation of input factors to lexical learning by bilingual infants. *Applied Psycholinguistics, 18*, 41–58.

Pena, E. D., Bedore, L. M., & Zlatic-Giunta, R. (2002). Category-generation performance of bilingual children: The influence of condition, category, and language. *Journal of Speech, Language, and Hearing Research, 45*, 938–947.

Pena, E. D., Gillam, R. B., Bedore, L. M., & Bohman, T. M. (2011). Risk for poor performance on a language screening measure for bilingual preschoolers and kindergarteners. *American Journal of Speech-Language Pathology, 20*, 302–314.

Pena, E. D., Gillam, R. B., Malek, M., Ruiz-Felter, R., Resendiz, M., Fiestas, C., & Sabel, T. (2006). Dynamic assessment of school-age children's narrative ability: An experimental investigation of classification accuracy. *Journal of Speech, Language, and Hearing Research, 49,* 1037–1057.

Peña, E., Iglesias, A., & Lidz, C. S. (2001). Reducing test bias through dynamic assessment of children's word learning ability. *American Journal of Speech–Language Pathology, 10,* 138–154.

Perozzi, J. A., & Sanchez, M. L. (1992). The effect of instruction in L1 on receptive acquisition of L2 for bilingual children with language delay. *Language, Speech, and Hearing Services in Schools, 23,* 348–352.

Petersen, D. B., & Gillam, R. B. (in press). Predicting reading ability for bilingual Latino children using dynamic assessment. *Journal of Learning Disabilities.*

Petitto, L., Katerelos, M., Levy, B. G., Gauna, K., Tetreault, K., & Ferraro, V. (2001). Bilingual signed and spoken language acquisition from birth: Implications for the mechanisms underlying early bilingual language acquisition. *Journal of Child Language, 28,* 453–496.

Pham, G., & Kohnert, K. (2010). Sentence interpretation by typically developing Vietnamese-English bilingual children. *Applied Psycholinguistics, 31,* 507–529.

Pham, G., Kohnert, K., & Mann, D. (2011). Addressing clinician-client mismatch: A preliminary intervention study with a bilingual Vietnamese-English preschooler. *Language, Speech, and Hearing Services in Schools, 42,* 408–422.

Pintner, R., & Arsenian, S. (1937). The relation of bilingualism to verbal intelligence and school adjustment. *Journal of Educational Research, 31,* 255–263.

Poplack, S. (1980). Sometimes I'll start a sentence in Spanish y termino en espanol: Toward a typology of code-switching. *Linguistics, 18,* 581–618.

Poplack, S. (1987). Contrasting patterns of code-switching in two communities. In E. Wande, J. Anward, B. Nordberg, L. Steensland, & M. Thelander (Eds.), *Aspects of multilingualism: Proceedings from Fourth Nordic Symposium on Bilingualism, 1984* (pp. 51–77). Uppsala, Sweden: Ubsaliensis S. Academiae.

Portes, A., & Hao, L. (2002). The price of uniformity: Language, family, and personality adjustment in the immigrant second generation. *Ethnic and Racial Studies, 25,* 889–912.

Proctor, C. P, August, D., Carlo, M. S., & Snow, C. (2006). The intriguing role of Spanish language vocabulary knowledge in predicting English reading comprehension. *Journal of Educational Psychology, 98,* 159–169.

Raghavendra, P., & Leonard, L. B. (1989). The acquisition of agglutinating languages: Converging evidence from Tamil. *Journal of Child Language, 16,* 313–322.

Restrepo, M. A., & Kruth, K. (2000). Grammatical characteristics of a bilingual student with specific language impairment. *Journal of Children's Communication Development, 21,* 66–76.

Roessingh, H., Kover, P., & Watt, D. (2005). Developing cognitive academic language proficiency: The journey. *TESL Canada Journal, 23,* 1–27.

Rolstad, K., Mahoney, K., & Glass, G. V. (2005). The big picture: A meta-analysis of program effectiveness research on English language learners. *Educational Policy, 19,* 572–594.

Roseberry-McKibbin, C., Brice, A., & O'Hanlon, L. (2005). Serving English language learners in public school settings: A national survey. *Language, Speech, and Hearing Services in Schools, 36,* 48–61.

Rossell, C. H., & Baker, K. (1996). The educational effectiveness of bilingual education. *Research in the Teaching of English, 30*, 7–74.

Rumbaut, R. G. (1989). Portraits, patterns, and predictors of the refugee adaptation process: Results and reflections from the IHARP panel study. In D.W. Haines (Ed.), *Refugees as immigrants* (pp. 138–186). Totowa, NJ: Rowman & Littlefield.

Salameh, E.-K. (2003). *Language impairment in Swedish bilingual children—epidemiological and linguistic studies* (Studies in Logopedics and Phoniatrics No. 4). Lund, Sweden: Lund University.

Saunders, W., & O'Brien, G. (2006). Oral language. In F. Genesee, K. Lindholm-Leary, W. Saunders, & D. Christian (Eds.), *Educating English language learners: A synthesis of empirical evidence* (pp. 24–97). New York, NY: Cambridge.

Saville-Troike, M. (1987). Bilingual discourse: The negotiation of meaning without a common code. *Linguistics, 25*, 81–106.

Selinker, L. (1972). *Interlanguage. International Review of Applied Linguistics, 10*, 219–231.

Shneyderman, A., & Abella, R. (2009). The effects of the extended foreign language programs on Spanish-language proficiency and academic achievement in English. *Bilingual Research Journal, 32*, 241–259.

Simon-Cereijido, G., & Gutierrez-Clellen, V. (2007) Spontaneous language markers of Spanish language impairment. *Applied Psycholinguistics, 28*, 317–339.

Strong, M. (1983). Social styles and the second language acquisition of Spanish-speaking kindergartners. *TESOL Quarterly, 17*, 241–258.

Tabors, P. O. (2008). *One child, two languages: A guide for preschool educators of children learning English as a second language* (2nd ed.). Baltimore, MD: Brookes.

Thomas, W. P., & Collier, V. P. (2002). *A national study of school effectiveness for language minority students' long-term academic achievement.* Santa Cruz, CA: Center for Research on Education, Diversity, and Excellence.

Thordardottir, E. T., Ellis Weismer, S., & Smith, M. E. (1997). Vocabulary learning in bilingual and monolingual clinical intervention. *Child Language Teaching and Therapy, 13*, 215–227.

Tomblin, J. B., Records, N. L., Buckwalter, P., Zhang, X., Smith, E., & O'Brien, M. (1997). The prevalence of specific language impairment in kindergarten children. *Journal of Speech, Language, and Hearing Research, 40*, 1245–1260.

Uchikoshi, Y., & Marinova-Todd, S. H. (2012). Language proficiency and early literacy skills of Cantonese-speaking English language learners in the U.S. and Canada. *Reading and Writing, 25*, 2107–2129.

Vaughn, S., Cirino, P. T., Linan-Thompson, S., Mathes, P. G., Carlson, C. D., Cardenas-Hagan, E., . . . Francis, D. J. (2006). Effectiveness of a Spanish intervention and an English intervention for English language learners at risk for reading problems. *American Educational Research Journal, 43*, 449–488.

Windsor, J., Kohnert, K., Lobitz, K., & Pham, G. (2010). Cross-language nonword repetition by bilingual and monolingual children. *American Journal of Speech–Language Pathology, 19*, 298–310.

Xu, Y., & Drame, E. (2008). Culturally appropriate context: Unlocking the potential of response to intervention for English language learners. *Early Childhood Education Journal, 35*, 305–311.

Yip, V., & Matthews, S. (2000). Syntactic transfer in a Cantonese-English bilingual child. *Bilingualism: Language and Cognition, 3*, 193–208.

Zdorenko, T., & Paradis, J. (2012). Articles in child L2 English: When L1 and L2 acquisition meet at the interface. *First Language, 32*(1–2), 38–62.

Chapter 7

Promoting Diverse and Deep Vocabulary Development

Karla McGregor & Dawna Duff

Building a diverse and deep vocabulary is a process that begins in infancy and continues into old age. The school years are a period of especially rapid vocabulary building. Rough estimates are that the average student learns about 1,000 new root words per year (Anglin, 1993; Biemiller, 2005). However, there is great variation around this mean. For example, at the end of second grade, children in the highest quartile will know roughly 8,000 root word meanings while those in the lowest quartile will know only 4,000 (Biemiller & Slonim, 2001). Many children on caseloads of speech–language pathologists (SLPs) fall into this lowest quartile. This chapter provides a rationale for vocabulary intervention for these children, presents information on vocabulary development and assessment, explains how to conduct effective vocabulary intervention, and reviews the research support for these practices.

A Rationale for Vocabulary Intervention

The activities that constitute schooling—classroom discussions, hands-on exploration, reading, test taking, and social interactions—are opportunities for vocabulary building. But, at the same time, success in these activities is related to the developmental status of the vocabulary itself. Take social success for example. In preschool classrooms, receptive vocabulary scores are a strong predictor of popularity. Children prefer other children who have larger vocabularies (Gertner, Rice, & Hadley, 1994). As for academic success, consider that among college students, vocabulary scores bear a positive correlation to exam scores (Dollinger, Matyja, & Huber, 2008) as well as standardized measures of academic achievement (Rohde & Thompson, 2007). These relationships may well feed each other in a reciprocal fashion. If the student with a large vocabulary has many friends, she will find herself in many communicative interactions that can further stimulate her vocabulary growth. Likewise, if the student with a large vocabulary earns excellent standardized test scores, he will likely be given opportunities for advanced studies that will further stimulate his vocabulary growth.

Much attention has been paid to the relationship between vocabulary and reading. Among schoolchildren, correlation between vocabulary size and reading comprehension typically falls between .6 and .8 and some researchers have found correlations as high as .93 (as summarized in Clarke, Snowling, Truelove, & Hulme, 2010; Pearson, Hiebert, & Kamil, 2007). Moreover, a child's vocabulary at one age is an important predictor of reading comprehension years later (Catts, Fey, Zhang, & Tomblin, 1999) and this is true even over long periods of time. Cunningham and Stanovich (1997) found that vocabulary in Grade 1 predicted how well students comprehended what they were reading in high school.

To comprehend what we read, we must be able to attach meanings to the words written on the page. In that sense, the relationship between vocabulary knowledge and reading comprehension is a given. However, the exact nature of the vocabulary–reading relationship is a matter of great debate. According to the instrumentalist hypothesis (Anderson & Freebody, 1981), the relationship is directly causal: Knowing more words enables better reading comprehension. Therefore, if we teach children the meanings of new words, their reading comprehension will improve. The bulk of supporting evidence involves teaching children new word meanings and measuring improved comprehension of texts that include the newly taught words (Baumann, Edwards, Boland, Olejnik, & Kame'enui, 2003; National Reading Panel, 2000). There are also effects of vocabulary intervention on comprehension of texts that do not contain taught words. These effects are much smaller in size but still significant (Stahl & Fairbanks, 1986). One possibility is that these interventions boost the children's metalinguistic skills in ways that increase word learning. For example, a child who has the metalinguistic capacity to recognize the similarity between a highly familiar word like *disagree* and an unfamiliar word like *disallow* will be in a good position to infer the meaning of the unfamiliar word and add it to his or her lexicon. Another possibility is that these interventions serve to reorganize the semantic system in ways that aid comprehension of other words (Landauer, Kireyev, & Panaccione, 2011). For example, imagine how teaching the words *extreme* and *drastic* could enable comprehension of a related but unfamiliar word like *radical*.

There may also be indirect causation such that vocabulary knowledge affects phonological awareness, which affects word reading skill, which in turn, affects reading comprehension. It is well established that phonological awareness is important to early reading development (Adams, 1990; Whitehurst & Lonigan, 1998). According to the lexical restructuring model, children first learn word forms as wholes but as they learn more words, especially words that sound similar to one another, their mental phonological representations become more fine-grained (Metsala & Walley, 1998). For example, if the word *cat* were represented as an underspecified whole then adding the words *cap* and *can* to the lexicon would force precision, otherwise comprehension would be compromised. With better represented information at the phonemic level, children can begin to isolate and manipulate phonemes in words. There is some research to support this view. Lonigan (2007) reported that children who received intervention for phonological awareness improved in phonological awareness (just as one would expect), but children who received an intervention for vocabulary improved in both vocabulary and phonological awareness.

In summary, success in academic contexts is related to vocabulary knowledge. Students with large vocabularies are more popular with their classmates and they perform better in school. Reading comprehension and vocabulary knowledge are strongly related and there is some evidence that this relationship is causal: Greater vocabulary knowledge aids reading comprehension and also aids the development of phonological awareness, a key component of learning to read. With the rationale for vocabulary intervention established, we turn to background that will inform intervention; specifically, we define *vocabulary development* and present an approach to the assessment of developmental status.

What Does It Mean to Build a Vocabulary?

A *vocabulary* is a store of word forms, their meanings, and their uses that accumulates over time. Vocabulary building is a formidable and never-completed feat of memory.

Webster's Third New International Dictionary of the English Language, Unabridged (Gove et al., 1981) contains 450,000 entries, and the editors lament that they could have easily added more were there space (p. 5a). Young native English-speaking adults are estimated to know 17,000 root words (Goulden, Nation, & Read, 1990). If words built by compounding as well as derivation of root words are included, then the estimate rises to 60,000 total words (Nagy & Herman, 1987). Moreover, knowledge of advanced vocabulary continues to increase across the adult years (Bowles, Grimm, & McArdle, 2005).

Vocabulary building is not only a large problem space, it is a complex one. For any given word in the vocabulary, the learner comes to represent the syntactic, morphological, phonological, and orthographic aspects of the word form, the potentially numerous literal and figurative meanings that are associated with that form, and the pragmatic rules that govern its use. Also, the learner establishes multiple relationships between that word and others, relationships that may involve co-ordination (words that are members of the same category such as *happy* and *sad*), collocations (words that are likely found together such as *happy* and *days*), superordination (words that relate hierarchically such as *happy* and *emotions*), and synonymy (words that have similar meanings such as *happy* and *content*) (Aitchison, 1994).

Because there are many words to learn and because it takes multiple exposures to a given word to learn all there is to know about it, at any point in developmental time, some words will be incompletely represented while others will be further along. In her seminal paper on children's incidental word learning, Carey (1978) puts it this way: "Suppose that, on the average, six months is required for the full acquisition of a new word. . . . If the child is learning nine new words a day, then he is working out the meanings of over 1,600 words at a time" (pp. 274–75). Put another way, word knowledge is not all-or-none but gradient. Take for example the word *truth*. A kindergartner knows what his parent means when asking, "Are you telling the truth?" but the parent has a more complete understanding that includes concepts such as *partial truth* and *relative truth*. Other adults may have an even richer understanding still, especially if they have professions in fields such as math, philosophy, or religion where the meaning of truth is specifically defined and debated.

Adding new words to the vocabulary store and enriching knowledge of familiar words require repeated exposures to those words and the ability to learn from those exposures. Exposure varies greatly from context to context and child to child. For example, parents of lower socioeconomic status (SES) address fewer and more directive words to their children than parents of greater means (e.g., *Sit down and eat* versus *Please come to the table so we can all have lunch*). These differences are reflected in dramatically different mean vocabulary sizes for these two groups of children (Hart & Risley, 1995).

An environment rich with opportunities for word learning is clearly necessary for optimal vocabulary development but likely not sufficient for many children with language impairment. These children require more exposures than unaffected children whether that exposure is oral (Gray, 2003; Nash & Donaldson, 2005) or written (McKeown, 1985; Shefelbine, 1990). They may also require these exposures to be simpler and more scaffolded. For example, some children with autism spectrum disorders will successfully link a new word to the object it names if their communication partner points to or touches the object, but they will fail if the partner's cue is a more subtle one like eye gaze (Parish-Morris, Hennon, Hirsh-Pasek, Golinkoff, & Tager-Flusberg, 2007). To add to the problem, many children with vocabulary difficulties are poor readers (Catts, Fey, Tomblin, & Zhang, 2002). As such, they limit their own exposure to new words and opportunities to enrich familiar words by reading more slowly, reading less, and understanding less of what they do read (Stanovich, 1986).

Given the diversity of word learning experiences and abilities, it might be surprising to know that order of acquisition is somewhat predictable. *The Living Word Vocabulary: A National Vocabulary Inventory* (Dale & O'Rourke, 1981) is a list of nearly 30,000 word roots (44,000 when multiple meanings are considered) and the percentage of students at Grades 4, 6, 8, 10, 12, 13, and 16 who understood each word as determined by a three-alternative forced choice assessment. Biemiller and Slonim (2001) assessed knowledge of a subset of words from this list in three different groups of children; two were drawn from communities representing a wide range of SES and a third from a community of upper-middle SES. Although the economically advantaged children knew more words, the strong tendency for all the children to know the majority of words from a given grade and from lower grades, together with the high correlation between the wide-ranging and advantaged SES groups, is evidence that root words are learned by schoolchildren in roughly the same order no matter the child's socioeconomic standing or vocabulary size. This developmental information can be valuable when selecting words as targets of intervention.

Of course not all words to be learned are root words. In fact, words built by derivation and compounding outnumber single root words in the English language (Goulden et al., 1990), and the increased rate of vocabulary growth in the elementary school years is largely driven by gains in knowledge of these multimorphemic forms (Anglin, 1993). Here too, order of acquisition is predictable because productivity of the specific word-building paradigm in question affects order and rate of attainment similarly across children (Bertram, Laine, & Virkkala, 2000; Clark & Cohen, 1984; Windsor, 1994).

Productivity is a function of type frequency (i.e., the number of different roots that can combine with a particular affix; Aronoff, 1976; Baayen, 1993) and transparency (i.e., how clearly the derived form relates phonologically, semantically, or orthographically to the root word; Clark, 1993). To get a sense of differences between productive and unproductive paradigms, think of a compound English word. More than likely, you thought of a noun + noun compound (e.g., *cupcake, parkbench*) rather than a preposition + noun compound (e.g., *in-group*). The latter is a highly productive paradigm in English; the former is not (Carstairs-McCarthy, 2002). Not surprisingly, noun + noun compounds are acquired in the early preschool years (Clark, 1993).

In English, compounding is more productive than derivation, and compounds tend to be learned earlier. For example, in the case of agentive nouns, English-speaking children first use compounds such as *farm-man* (Clark & Hecht, 1982) and later use derivatives such as *farmer* (Clark, 1993). There are productivity differences between derivational affixes as well, and these too predict order of acquisition. For example, the affixes *-less* (e.g., *hopeless*) and *-let* (e.g., *piglet*) are both productive, but *-let* is by far the less productive of the two and it is acquired later (Windsor, 1994). The ability to break down derivations (identify their roots) and build words via derivation (add derivational prefixes and suffixes) is largely acquired between Grades 1 and 6 (Carlisle, 1988, 2000; Lewis & Windsor, 1996); however, some derivatives remain below mastery even among adolescents (Nagy, Diakidoy, & Anderson, 1993; Windsor, 1994).

How Should Vocabulary Be Assessed?

Having established key aspects of vocabulary building, we now turn to assessment. The four points made above should serve to guide assessment. First, knowing a word involves knowing its form, meaning, and use. If a comprehensive assessment is desired, word knowledge in each of these domains should be measured. Second, learning a word is a gradual process, and thus many words in the vocabulary at any point in time will be partially known whereas others will be more deeply known. If an assessment of depth of word knowledge is desired, the assessment tools selected must be sensitive to this gradient of knowledge. The third important guide to assessment is that there are three types of words in the vocabulary: (a) roots, (b) roots that are combined to make compounds, and (c) roots that are inflected with derivational prefixes or suffixes. For an assessment to provide a valid measure of vocabulary development in the school years, all three types of words should be included. Finally, a large vocabulary requires many and rich exposures to words *and* a learner who readily benefits from those exposures. Therefore, static assessments of word knowledge should be complemented by dynamic measures of the child's word learning ability.

Static Assessment of Vocabulary Knowledge

Static assessment is often, but not always, accomplished via standardized, norm-referenced tests. There are some omnibus (all-in-one) standardized, norm-referenced tests that measure word knowledge in a comprehensive way. To provide but three of many examples, the *Clinical Evaluation of Language Fundamentals-Fourth Edition* (Semel, Wiig, & Secord, 2003), a test of oral language for children 5 to 21 years, includes subtests that tap word structure, word-to-word relationships, naming, defining, and word associations, as well as related skills such as rapid naming of words and pragmatic usage in the classroom. *The Comprehensive Assessment of Spoken Language* (Carrow-Woolfolk, 1999), a test of oral language for children ages 3 to 21 years, includes subtests that tap knowledge of antonyms, synonyms, and idioms, as well as the ability to infer meaning from context, interpret ambiguous words, and make pragmatic judgments about the use of words. Finally, the *Test of Adolescent and Adult Language-Fourth Edition* (Hammill, Brown, Larsen, & Wiederholt, 2007), a test of oral and written language for people ages 12 to 24 years, includes subtests that measure knowledge of antonyms, synonyms, analogies, word derivation, and spelling.

If omnibus measures such as these reveal concerns in a particular aspect of word knowledge, the SLP may wish to select additional, more focused assessments that will inform instructional decision making. These need not be norm referenced. If, for example, pragmatic aspects of word usage were a concern, additional assessments could be conducted in naturalistic contexts. Between-task comparisons may reveal the child's ability to modify word selection for a given context. For example, the child should use more literate or formal words in the written assignments contained in his or her portfolio than in a conversational language sample collected during a peer interaction.

When depth of vocabulary knowledge is of concern, probes that are sensitive to the knowledge gradient are required. One model is provided by Stallman, Pearson, Nagy, Anderson, and Garcia (1995). Stallman et al. developed a descriptive paper-and-pencil probe during which children select the best meaning for a given word at increasing levels of precision. At level I, for example, they are asked whether the word *flee* best goes with *picture/photo*, *gentle/silky*, or *go/leave*. To be correct, the child needs only know that *flee* involves movement. At level II, they match *flee* with *walk beside*, *run from*, *carry gently*, or *tiptoe quietly*. Here the correct response requires knowledge of the manner of movement associated with *flee*. Finally at the most precise level of knowledge, level III, they match *flee* to *sign out*, *hide under*, *escape quickly*, or *leave quietly*, thereby revealing their appreciation of the motives associated with *flee* (word examples from Stallman et al., 1995, p. 4).

Using a similar approach, Scott, Hoover, Flinspach, and Vevea (2008) developed a pencil-and-paper probe in which students answered questions tapping increasingly precise word knowledge (Box 7.1). Scott and colleagues selected the words for their probe from fourth-grade fiction and nonfiction texts. They were careful to include all word classes and many words were derived forms. The SLP can adapt such procedures according to the appropriate grade level for the student being assessed.

Box 7.1. ***Questions That Tap Depth of Word Knowledge***

1. Have you ever seen or heard of this word before?
2. How well do you know this word?
3. Can you think of another word that has something to do with this word?
4. What do you think this word means?
5. Do you think this word is a noun, verb, adjective, or adverb?

Note: Based on Scott et al. (2008, p. 329).

Dynamic Assessment of Word Learning

Any child who scores low on a static test of vocabulary knowledge should be tested for word learning ability. Because vocabulary knowledge is particularly dependent on experience and people from different communities have widely varying experiences, poor performance on a static test of vocabulary does not necessarily indicate a poor word learner. Rather, the test items might not validly reflect the vocabulary knowledge of the test taker. One commercially available option is *The Diagnostic Evaluation of Language Variance (DELV)-Criterion Referenced* (Seymour, Roeper, & deVilliers, 2003), a standardized measure of oral language for children of 4 to 9 years. Designed to avoid biases against nonstandard dialect speakers, it includes a process-based measure of word learning wherein the child's ability to map real verbs and novel verbs is determined.

Of course, commercially available standardized measures are not always necessary. One could also gauge word learning ability by observing the child's responses to vocabulary instruction in the classroom. For example, the SLP might observe a group lesson in which the child has multiple opportunities to participate. The SLP could compare the child to the other children in that group in terms of amount of responding, the adequacy of the responses, and the ability to revise responses given cues.

Whether vocabulary concerns are identified via static knowledge-based assessments or dynamic process-based assessments, the SLP must make a number of decisions about the intervention to be provided. We shall organize these decisions under the questions, *when*, *where*, *what*, and *how*.

When Should We Intervene?

Given that vocabulary development in the preschool years provides a foundation for academic participation and success in learning to read, vocabulary stimulation for those in impoverished environments and vocabulary intervention for those with identified language learning impairments should be provided as early as possible. Biemiller (2003) has argued that it is especially important to provide instruction in primary grades to promote reading comprehension in Grade 4 and beyond.

Despite the importance of early experiences, there is no sensitive period for word learning. Children become more efficient word learners as they mature, and adults readily add new words and refine their knowledge of familiar words throughout the lifespan. Moreover, the relationship between vocabulary and reading is hypothesized to be developmentally unlimited (Stanovich, 1986). That is, vocabulary knowledge predicts reading comprehension at any point in developmental time, albeit to different extents and for different reasons in beginning and more advanced readers. This is unlike the relationship between phonological awareness and reading, a relationship that weakens over time. To the extent that the instrumentalist hypothesis is correct, promoting a diverse and deep vocabulary will aid reading in both younger and older children.

Where Should We Intervene?

Vocabulary interventions can be equally beneficial when conducted one-on-one, in small groups, or in larger classroom settings (Marulis & Neuman, 2010). Under a response to intervention (RTI) approach, with its heirarchical levels of support, the instructional setting might be dictated by tier of support. Vocabulary stimulation may be provided in the general classroom setting where children learn new words incidentally from reading, hands-on activities, and classroom conversations as well as from didactic lessons embedded in each of these tasks.

For children in need of Tier II support, vocabulary intervention may occur in small-group settings. For children who receive the more intensive Tier III services, these settings may be supplemented by individualized intervention in pull-out settings (Justice, 2006). RTI is intended to focus on skills that are causally related to reading, and vocabulary is one of those skills (Justice, 2006). Although RTI is more often implemented to support the development of code-based skills such as phonemic awareness, phonics, and fluency, the SLP can advocate for including a vocabulary emphasis.

So what might vocabulary intervention look like in an RTI framework? Here are two examples from research conducted in real classrooms. Pullen, Tuckwiller, Konold, Maynard, and Coyne (2010) provided a vocabulary intervention where all children in first grade were taught new words in the classroom setting through storybook reading, child-friendly definitions, multiple exposures to the word within and outside of the story, and many chances to actively practice target words (Tier I). Children at risk for reading failure because of poor vocabulary were given more intensive instruction in small groups that involved more chances to do the same kinds of activities with the same words (Tier II); that is, they received a higher dosage. This kind of Tier II instruction did make a difference. At-risk children who received the Tier II intervention learned more vocabulary than at-risk children who received Tier I intervention only.

In the second example, Loftus, Coyne, McCoach, Zipoli, and Pullen (2010) provided a Tier I intervention in kindergarten classrooms that involved reading storybooks, giving a definition of the target word when it came up in the story and after the story was over, giving other examples of contexts for using the target word, and oral vocabulary activities like showing children a picture and asking if it was an example of the target word ("thumbs up") or not ("thumbs down"). Small groups of at-risk students received a repeat of the previous activities, plus new activities such as making a sentence including the word to describe a picture. They found that at-risk students who received the Tier II intervention learned nearly as many words as their more able peers in Tier I. If this approach were continued, then one might predict that children with poor vocabularies might be able to "keep up" if not "catch up" with their peers with better vocabularies.

Of course, the hallmark of any good intervention is generalization of gains. As in all school-based interventions, clinicians will want to facilitate generalization to home environments. McKeown, Beck, Omanson, and Pople (1985) reported that several vocabulary outcomes were improved when children were given points for bringing in examples of using, seeing, or hearing one of the target words outside the classroom. Beck, McKeown, and Kucan (2002) described in more detail the tools they used to motivate the children: leaflets describing different levels of achievement, tallies posted in the classroom, and certificates given every few weeks. They suggest that students can be asked to look for certain words in specific contexts (like *reasonable* in newspaper articles or TV advertisements). Students can also be given chances to suggest words that they have heard outside of the therapy room or classroom for others to learn.

What Should We Target During Intervention?

With hundreds of thousands of words in the English language, selecting words to target is a daunting task. There are two ways to make the task more tractable. The first is to consider the frequency and functionality of potential words. Beck, McKeown, and Kucan (2008) classify words into three tiers (a different use of tier than in the RTI frame-

Box 7.2. ***Selecting Target Vocabulary Words Using the "Tier Two" Approach***

1. Take a classroom text and ask the following questions about words you think might be candidates for direct instruction:
   a) Would you be more likely to find this word in written language than in spoken language? This should eliminate Tier One words, which will be familiar to students already. Tier Two words may also be used orally by mature language users.
   b) Would this word appear infrequently in written language in many contexts/topic areas? This should eliminate Tier Three words, which will not be as useful across many texts.
   c) Would you be able to explain this word using words the student already knows? This suggests that the word is a more mature way to refer to something the student is already somewhat familiar with. If the student has some conceptual understanding, then he or she may be more ready to learn the word.
   d) Can the word be worked with in a variety of ways? It will be easier to build a rich representation of words that have good instructional potential.
2. If you have underlined more words than you can reasonably teach, ask:
   a) Which words will help the child understand this text better?
   b) Which words will be most important across many texts?
3. Reduce the word list to a teachable number of Tier Two words.

Note: Based on Beck, McKeown, and Kucan (2002).

work). Tier One words (e.g., *baby, happy*) are high frequency and commonly used in oral language. Tier Two words (e.g., *coincidence, absurd, industrious*) are characteristic of literate language, more specific than the Tier One words, and more likely to be used across domains or subject areas than Tier Three words. Tier Three words (e.g., *peninsula, isotope*) are low frequency and apply to very specific domains. Because Tier One words are learned by most children without intervention and Tier Three words can be explained as they are needed to understand specialized content areas, Beck and colleagues recommend targeting Tier Two words for in-depth intervention.

Steps in identifying Tier Two words are summarized in Box 7.2. Potential words should be selected from read-aloud books (for prereaders) or textbooks found in the child's classroom. From these potential words, those that represent new labels for already familiar concepts are prioritized. For example, *absurd* would be a good choice for a child who already knows the meaning of words like *crazy* or *ridiculous*. This approach ensures functionality, as it is embedded in classroom language, and learnability, as teaching new words for old concepts ensures that the teaching is at a level that is challenging without being frustrating. There are likely to be a lot of Tier Two words identified. It is tempting to try to teach them all, but the SLP should be strict with him- or herself: For direct instruction (as opposed to simply enrichment through exposure), only a small number of words can be repeatedly presented and systematically taught in a meaningful way. Reduce the word list to a number that can really be learned by students in the available instructional time.

A complementary approach to target word selection is to consider order of acquisition. In *Words Worth Teaching: Closing the Vocabulary Gap* and the accompanying searchable CD-ROM, Biemiller (2010) has categorized word meanings by grade level (see examples in Box 7.3). He recommends using an adapted version of the tiers

Box 7.3. ***Example High and Low Priority Word Targets for Grades 3 to 6***

High Priority Words	Low Priority Words
appropriate: to be suitable for	**abhor:** to be disgusted with
accommodate: to help out	**lance:** to cut open
fatigue: loss of strength caused by hard mental or physical work	**obligation:** a personal duty
imply: to indicate without actually saying	**capacity:** a position served in
party: a political group	**hydraulic:** operated by water or another fluid

Note: Target low priority words only if needed for text comprehension or if required in the curriculum. Based on Beck, McKeown, and Kucan (2002).

approach to identify word meanings that are high or low priority for a given grade level. Once potential Tier Two words are selected from classroom texts, grade-level acquisition norms on the CD-ROM can be consulted to further cull the list. Culling is necessary to ensure that the learner is not overwhelmed by too many new words at any one time. For example, Johnson, Gersten, and Carnine (1987) found training 50 new words in many sets of two or three to be more efficient than training them in two sets of 25.

SLPs are highly familiar with order-of-acquisition approaches to goal selection in the domains of phonology, grammatical morphology, and syntax. Only recently have useful, large-scale databases of order-of-acquisition norms for words become available. In addition to Biemiller's (2010) norms for schoolchildren, SLPs may wish to consult the MacArthur-Bates Communicative Development Inventory Lex2005 database (http://www.sci.sdsu.edu/lexical/; Dale & Fenson, 1996) when providing intervention for children who are younger or who are very low functioning.

Another consideration is whether a potential target word belongs to a small or large morphological family. Large morphological families are preferred in that once you know the meaning of the root (e.g., *produce*) you have a chance to infer the meaning of many related words (e.g., *producer, producible, unproduced, reproduced*; Tyler & Nagy, 1990). Moreover, students read words from large families faster and more accurately, especially if the relationship between family members is transparent (Carlisle & Katz, 2006). A valuable guide to selecting word families by size, as well as regularity and productivity, is the work of Bauer and Nation (1993).

In addition to the question "What words?" the clinician must consider the question "What modality?" Beginning readers can understand and use more words orally than they can read. Therefore, their own reading will not provide a rich source of vocabulary learning. Ebbers and Denton (2008) put it this way: "As long as vocabulary remains trapped within the narrow boundaries of the printed page, word learning is restricted for students with limited decoding skills." (p. 92). For beginning readers, clinicians can target literate vocabulary via read-aloud books (books that adults read to children). This is an excellent idea because written language usually contains richer vocabulary than oral language. In fact, children's books contain a higher percentage of low frequency words than conversation between adults, even when those adults are college graduates (Hayes & Ahrens, 1988). Moreover, read-aloud books have been used in many successful intervention programs (e.g., Loftus et al., 2010; Pullen et al., 2010; Zipoli, Coyne, & McCoach, 2011). Many sorts of books can be used for reading aloud, including fictional chapter books, plays, and history and science texts. The language of more advanced books that will appeal to students can be simplified and supported by spoken interactions.

Biemiller (2005) found that from Grade 3 on, 95% of children could read more words aloud than they could define. Therefore, once children attain a Grade 3 reading level, they will meet many unfamiliar words representing many opportunities for learning as they read. Caution should be taken, however, when considering children who are many years behind their classmates in reading level. These children may well be learning new words from reading but these words will not be at grade level, so extra opportunities to meet and learn new words from spoken interactions should be provided. For all children, whether reading at or below grade level, it is useful to exploit all modalities: They should read, talk, and write about words.

How Should We Intervene?

There are three general and complementary approaches to promoting a diverse and deep vocabulary: We can enhance opportunities for incidental learning; we can take a more direct, didactic approach; and we can give children the skills they need to take responsibility for their own learning. Each will be considered in turn.

Increase Incidental Exposure

Because word learning is a gradual, incremental process, multiple exposures to a given word in a variety of meaningful contexts is essential for all word learners. For prereaders, parent-child book reading is one context that provides such exposure. The frequency with which parents read with their preschoolers accounts for 8% of the variance in their oral and written language outcomes (Bus, van IJzendoorn, & Pellegrini, 1995). For fifth graders, the amount of time spent reading silently at school predicts gains in reading comprehension (Taylor, Frye, & Maruyama, 1990).

Oral language in the classroom can also provide multiple exposures to new words. However, adults speaking to children sometimes fail to model varied and rich vocabulary or to provide the supports that allow children to understand such models. One strategy that addresses both of these failures is the "Teacher's Word Wall." On a wall of the classroom, the teacher posts a list of sophisticated words organized by the more common words they can replace. For example, under the common word *happy* appear the words *delighted*, *elated*, *pleased*, *tickled pink*, and *impressed* (Cavanaugh, 2010). The lists remind teachers to use a variety of words when praising the children's work and the organization of the list reminds children of the meanings of the new words. SLPs can work with teachers to create word walls for primary classrooms, and these can be developed not only as supports for classroom discourse but also for highlighting themes in current curricular materials and activities.

Faced with the findings that children need lots of exposures to words, it might be tempting to simply repeat a given activity over and over again. That would certainly save preparation time, but Stahl and Fairbanks (1986) found that vocabulary intervention where there were multiple exposures to a word in different contexts produced a bigger effect than multiple exposures in the same context. This makes sense, because to understand what a word means, we need to understand both when the word is appropriate and when it is not. A single context, even repeated many times, does not give children access to that important information.

When it comes to learners with vocabulary deficits, we must think carefully about whether maximizing the number of incidental learning opportunities is enough for them to make much-needed gains. The work of Nash and Donaldson (2005) is telling. They compared the word learning of schoolchildren with specific language impairment to that of their age mates and younger vocabulary-level mates. The children learned one set of new words incidentally by listening to tape-recorded stories and the other by receiving direct teaching. The children with SLI learned the spoken word *forms* in the incidental and direct teaching conditions equally well, and they learned better when given 12 exposures to each word than when given only six. However, those with SLI learned fewer word forms after 12 exposures than their age mates with normal language abilities had learned after only six (see also Gray, 2003). Clearly more exposure is not always enough for weaker learners. Moreover, all of the children, not only those with SLI, required direct instruction for optimal learning of word *meanings*. This finding is consistent with meta-analyses on the effect of vocabulary intervention on word learning and reading comprehension: Interventions that involve direct instruction are associated with larger effect sizes than those that depend on implicit opportunities for learning (Marulis & Neuman, 2010; National Reading Panel, 2000).

Teach Directly

In direct teaching, clinicians should aim to provide multiple and varied cues to support word learning as well as opportunities that encourage the child to process words deeply. Documented effects of direct word teaching include improved word knowledge, improved word retrieval, and improved reading comprehension.

To illustrate the effect of direct teaching on word learning, consider Biemiller and Boote (2006) who reported that children in kindergarten or first grade learned more

Box 7.4. ***A Direct Teaching Approach for Prereaders***

Day	Activity
One	Read the story aloud.
Two	Read the story aloud, targeting 7–10 words for explanation during reading. Reread the sentence with the target word. Provide an explanation of the target word.
Three	Same as for day two, but target 7–10 different words.
Four	Same as for day two, but target 7–10 different words.
Five	Review all the words discussed. Present new context sentences for target words that are not based on the story.

Note: Based on Biemiller and Boote (2006).

words if a book was read to them four times, rather than two times, even when no direct teaching was provided. However, teaching in the form of added explanation during the reading and review that included new examples of usage increased the amount of word learning beyond that resulting from repeated reading alone. This very simple protocol, illustrated in Box 7.4, took about 30 minutes per day and resulted in substantial vocabulary learning. The children learned about 40% of the presented words. The authors estimate that if 25 words a week were taught this way in the classroom, children would learn about 1,000 to 1,500 new words in the primary grades, an important gain.

McKeown and colleagues (1985) compared the benefits of three types of direct teaching on word learning and word retrieval. One fourth-grade classroom received traditional instruction in which the children associated each target word and its definition or synonym during in-class activities. A second classroom received rich instruction in which children identified the relationship between words, applied words in various contexts, and identified affective and cognitive aspects of the word meanings. A third classroom received extended/rich instruction that was the same as that used in the second classroom except that an activity designed to encourage use of the word outside of the classroom environment was added. Within each classroom, the number of exposures was also manipulated such that half of the words were assigned to a low frequency condition (4 exposures) and half to a high frequency condition (12 exposures). All three interventions, whether administered at low or high frequency, were enough to enhance knowledge of the new words as measured by a four-alternative multiple choice task that required selecting the best definition of a given word. However, the frequency and quality of instruction mattered for other outcomes as measured by recall of a story that contained the trained words, interpretation of sentences that contained the trained words, and a semantic decision task that measured speed of trained word retrieval. Extended/rich teaching that was high frequency resulted in optimal story recall. Sentence interpretation was maximized by frequent and rich or frequent and extended/rich teaching. Finally, word retrieval was best following extended/rich instruction.

When the goal is to facilitate reading comprehension, direct vocabulary instruction frequently takes place within the context of classroom reading materials. Adams (2010) recommended that a given topic be introduced with simple, short texts and supported by direct teaching of words and concepts related to that topic. Next, students can be introduced to increasingly complex texts on the same topic so that "each text bootstraps the language and knowledge that will be needed for the next" (Adams, 2010, p. 10). This proposal would have many implications for curriculum development, but SLPs could also use this strategy on a smaller scale by selecting simpler texts about an upcoming unit, directly teaching the vocabulary in the context of that text, and gradually adding more complex texts on the same topic. This would support the child's comprehension of grade-level materials used later in the classroom. Regardless of the language skills that the SLP is targeting with the child, linking to topics in the classroom ensures multiple and varied exposures to relevant vocabulary and concepts.

Is there an optimal time to discuss word meaning during classroom reading activities? Beck and her colleagues (Beck et al., 2002, 2008) recommended that words that are important to comprehension be clarified during reading (or during rereading, see Biemiller, 2010), by giving a brief explanation, then continuing with the text. If clarification *during* reading is not possible (for example, because the students are reading independently) then Beck et al. (2008) recommended clarification *near*, and preferably *after*, the point of use, by assigning shorter amounts of text and discussing each section. More in-depth discussion of new words should typically take place after the reading as well. The motivation for avoiding preteaching and relying instead on teaching during and after the reading activity rests in the teaching advantages that the reading context provides. The reading passage itself links the new vocabulary words together in a meaningful way thereby allowing incidental learning and a semantically coherent basis for didactic instruction.

Of course written texts are not the only context for direct vocabulary teaching, even when the ultimate goal is improved reading. Robust Vocabulary Instruction (Beck et al., 2002) is an approach to vocabulary development that emphasizes multiple and rich encounters in oral contexts to promote depth of semantic knowledge of words originally identified in the child's reading materials. Clarke and colleagues (2010) conducted a randomized, controlled trial comparing three interventions meant to ameliorate reading comprehension deficits. The long-term gains in reading comprehension were largest for the children who received an oral language intervention that included vocabulary instruction based on the principals of Robust Vocabulary Instruction, and these gains were largely mediated by improvements in oral-vocabulary knowledge. In Box 7.5, there are some examples of activities that are consistent with Robust Vocabulary Instruction. Notice how many ways there are to process the meaning of a word and how the activities promote much deeper processing than activities that simply present definitions.

Visual or graphic organizers are another way to promote deep processing about word learning. Visual organizers provide a structure and visual support for discussions about word meaning. They are not intended to be an independent activity but can easily be integrated into other kinds of discussions about word meaning (Steele & Mills, 2011).

Visual organizers take many forms. Semantic maps are one example (see Box 7.6). One way to use semantic maps is described by Stahl and Nagy (2006). First, children brainstorm familiar words about a topic, and they (or the SLP) write or draw them. Second, the SLP leads the children to group the words into categories by arranging them visually on the page. Finally, the SLP reads aloud a text containing the words and helps the children to revise the map to include new things they have learned from the book. Allen (1999) described a similar activity called "wordstorming" in which students brainstorm words individually then work in groups to combine the lists, categorize, and label each category.

There are a wide variety of other visual organizers that can be used. Stahl and Nagy (2006) recommend "word maps." These have a target word in the middle and four questions around it: What is it? What is it like? What are some examples? What are some

Box 7.5. ***Example Activities for Robust Vocabulary Instruction***

Presenting New Words After Reading a Text	Example
Contextualize the word for its role in the story	The woman moved *cautiously* across the wet floor. She was very careful as she walked on the wet floor.
Repeat the word to create a phonological representation	Say the word with me: *cautious*.
Explain the meaning of the word	*Cautious* people act very carefully because they want to avoid danger.
Give examples in contexts other than the ones used in the story	I would walk *cautiously* if I had bare feet and there were rocks on the ground. I would be *cautious* about inviting a stranger into my house.
Ask students to provide examples	What would make you *cautious*?
Repeat the word again	Let's say the word again: *cautious*.
Ask students for semantic judgments about examples	I'll tell you about some situations. You tell me if the person is being *cautious*. The bully was calling people names, so the boy went to the other side of the playground. The girl knew she could get a home run, and she swung her bat as hard as she could. The boy had never gone fishing before, and he didn't know if he wanted to touch the fish.
Ask students for True-False judgments	Are these true ("thumbs up") or false ("thumbs down")? I would feel *cautious* about phoning my best friend. People should be *cautious* about catching baseballs without a mitt.
Ask students to "show me how. . ."	To touch something *cautiously* To walk cautiously
Relate to other target words	"If someone *hurls* a ball, is he being *cautious*?"

Note: Based on Beck et al. (2002).

Box 7.6. ***Semantic Map Example***

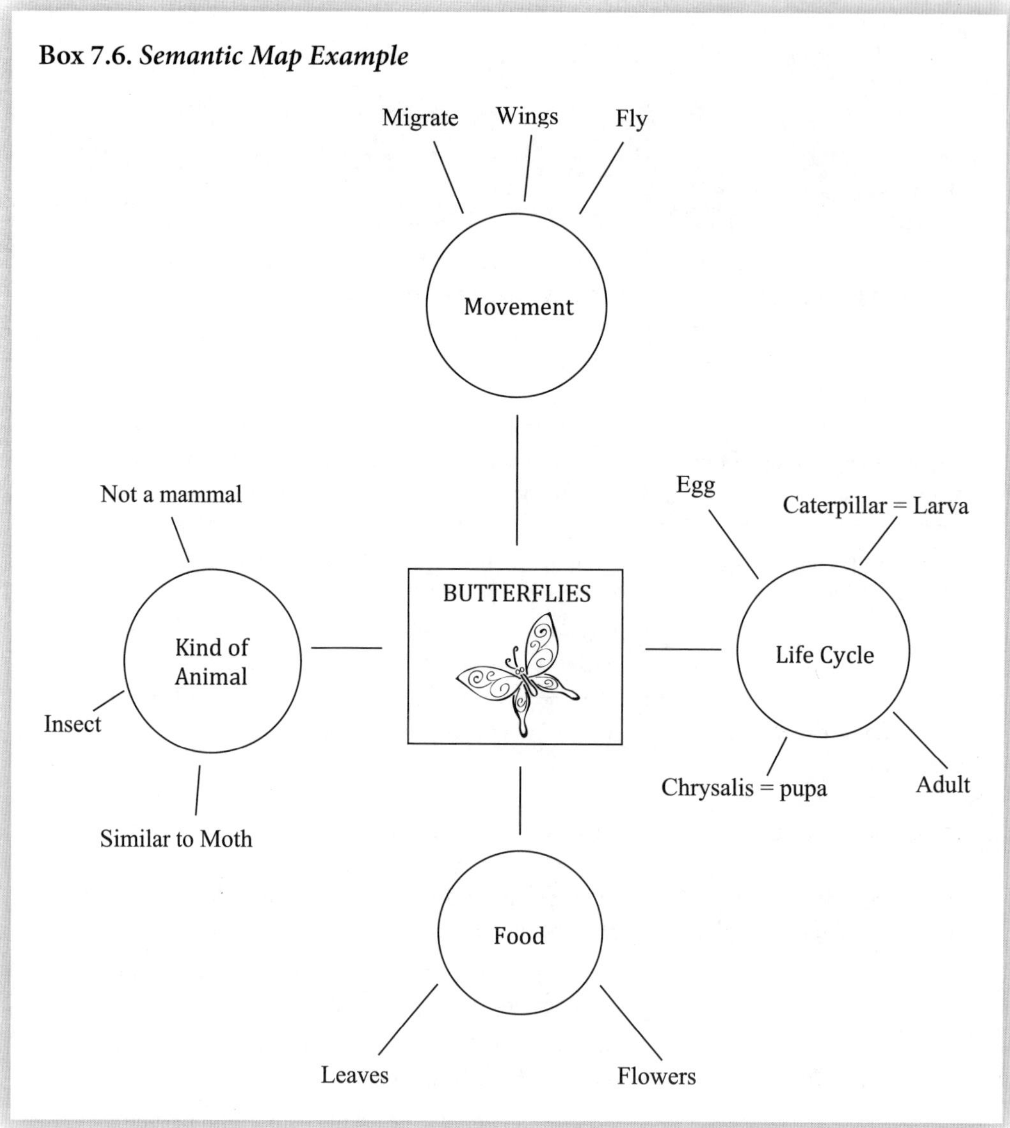

nonexamples? In a related activity, the same authors describe "four square" activities using a page folded into four parts, with sections devoted to the word, examples of the word, nonexamples of the word, and a word definition generated by students. Visual organizers might have different boxes for general information about a word and specific examples of a word (Allen, 1999) or spaces to put information about the context where a word is found, what the word is, what it is not, and an example that will help the student remember the word (Allen, 1999). Venn diagrams can be used to show how two words are similar and different.

A Note on Definitions

Teaching new words via definitions alone is not particularly effective. Definitions are limited in that they tend not to convey contextual nuances of meaning and usage. Chil-

Box 7.7. ***A Comparison of Typical and Child-Friendly Definitions***

Word	Typical Dictionary Definition	Child-Friendly Explanation
devious	straying from the course; not straightforward	If someone is *devious*, he is using tricky and secretive ways to do something dishonest.
suggestion	the act of suggesting	When someone *suggests* something, they tell you what they think you should do in a nice way.
exotic	foreign; strange; not native	Something that is *exotic* is unusual and interesting because it comes from another country far away.

Note: Based on Beck, McKeown, and Kucan (2008) and Steele and Mills (2011).

dren need to see how words are used and use them repeatedly across multiple contexts to gain robust knowledge.

Moreover, children often misunderstand definitions. For example, Miller and Gildea (1987) reported that after reading definitions, 63% of students' sentences using the words were odd. Children produced sentences such as, "Me and my parents *correlate*, because without them I wouldn't be here" and "I was *meticulous* about falling off the cliff" (p. 98). Word usage is a complex and subtle act. Clearly, these definitions did not tell children what they needed to know to use these words accurately. However, some dictionaries such as the *Collins Cobuild* (Sinclair, Hanks, Fox, Moon, & Stock, 1987) include more useful and child-friendly information (Beck et al., 2002, 2008). Some examples of traditional dictionary definitions versus child-friendly definitions are given in Box 7.7. Notice how the child-friendly definitions begin to explain how the words are used.

Although definitions alone are not effective teaching tools, they should not be avoided altogether. Teaching via context alone is not as effective as teaching via context plus definitions (Stahl & Fairbanks, 1986). Also, the ability to formulate definitions is an important academic skill as exam questions sometimes require definitional responses. Children can be taught both the form of definitions (i.e., category name plus characteristics) and the level of precision that definitions require. For example, the definition "an apple is a fruit that is red" is good in form but it is not precise enough to distinguish *apple* from *strawberry*, *raspberry*, or *cherry*.

Finally, as children gain greater awareness and become more responsible for managing their vocabulary limitations, they will need to be able to find and learn from definitions in the glossaries that accompany their texts as well as dictionaries and online resources. This point brings us to the third basic approach to promoting a diverse and deep vocabulary: to increase the child's own awareness of word knowledge and his or her ownership of strategies for learning and remembering words.

Increase Awareness and Ownership

Children's reflection on their own word knowledge is a useful starting point for metalinguistic interventions. Using self-assessment, children are encouraged to rate their own knowledge about words using descriptors such as: *I can define it, I know what it means, I know a little bit about it,* and *I don't know the word* (Dale & O'Rourke, 1986). One way to use this self-assessment would be to identify words in a text or lecture that may be challenging, and have students complete the chart individually. In small groups, students can then compare charts and share answers to move their knowledge "up" a level. The text or lecture notes can be reviewed and discussed to add further knowledge.

Older children may also benefit from understanding the rationale for their vocabulary learning efforts. Advance organizers that include an overview of new learning goals and new target words are a common tool for adolescents who face vocabulary challenges (Mastropieri & Scruggs, 2002; Swanson & Hoskyn, 2001). Over time, these students can become increasingly active in setting new goals and selecting new targets by previewing upcoming chapters and units of study. If children are able to reflect on their own word knowledge, they are likely able to benefit from metalinguistic approaches to learning new words.

One metalinguistic approach to vocabulary instruction is to directly teach children how to derive word meaning from context. Nagy (2010) argues that deliberately learning words from context differs from incidental word learning. Incidental word learning may involve more associative learning whereas explicitly trying to derive word meaning involves inference making and hypothesis testing about what a given word might mean. Knowing how to monitor your own word comprehension, stop at new words or new uses of words, and then figure out word meaning is an important life skill for students who must be increasingly independent at understanding and learning from challenging academic texts. Moreover, students who see themselves as clever *word detectives* will be empowered in their own learning.

The process of inferring meaning from context is complex. Readers need to find information in the text that might constrain the word meaning, weed out irrelevant information, bring in prior knowledge, and integrate information from multiple contexts (McKeown, 1985). After the child makes that first inference, he or she must be flexible enough to make a new inference after evaluating the sense of the first (Fukkink, 2005). Figuring out a way to teach students how to figure out meaning may sound daunting. The good news for clinicians is that it is not necessary to teach all of these steps or even a prescribed order and, in fact, trying to do so may not even be beneficial. When typical learners are asked to think aloud as they try to figure out word meaning, they may do all of these steps, or only some of them, and they may do them in a flexible order (Fukkink, 2005). In addition, elaborate strategies are not as helpful as simple ones, like reminding children to look for cue words in the story to help them to understand the hard words (Fukkink, 2005; Fukkink & de Glopper, 1998). The simplest possible strategy, just repeatedly asking children to guess the meaning of new words they read, can be useful as well (Carnine, Kame'enui, & Coyle, 1984). SLPs should demonstrate these strategies, talking through their own reading and how they would approach difficult words in a text.

Children with weak vocabularies or poor reading comprehension have more to learn about new words they encounter in text but actually learn less than their more skilled peers (Cain, Oakhill, & Elbro, 2003; Shefelbine, 1990). However, both children with average vocabularies and those with deficits can improve their skill in deliberately inferring word meanings from context through direct instruction (Cain, 2007; Fukkink & de Glopper, 1998; Goerss, Beck, & McKeown, 1999; Nash & Donaldson, 2005). Further, their skill grows at a reasonable pace. A meta-analysis of the effect of direct instruction on word inferencing showed an effect size of 0.43 standard deviations which could be ". . . cautiously interpreted as the difference that would be found after a period of two years of natural development" (Fukkink & de Glopper, 1998, p. 462). Because most of the interventions reviewed in the meta-analysis involved fewer than 6 hours of instructional time, these results are very encouraging. This kind of metalinguistic approach yields the sort of result SLPs and teachers look for—a moderately high impact—with a fairly limited time investment.

Below we describe two specific methods demonstrated to be effective in helping children learn to use context in service of word learning. Both were helpful for children who were aged 7 to 8 years and had either low vocabulary levels (Nash & Snowling, 2006) or diverse vocabulary levels (Cain, 2007). The first method was delivered in groups, the second with individuals. Resourceful clinicians will be able to adapt either.

In Nash and Snowling (2006), children were shown how to look for familiar words that might provide clues to the meaning of unfamiliar words. Semantic maps were generated, and then children were asked to generate definitions and think of ways to apply the word to their own experiences. The specific procedures are described in Box 7.8. Children who were given this kind of intervention learned these target words, just as children who were taught using definitions. But three months later, children who learned in this way were more able than those who learned using definitions alone to infer meanings for new words from context. They also had better comprehension of texts that contained the target words.

In Cain (2007), a different approach was used (see Box 7.9). Children did not look for clues in the text, but rather were simply asked what they thought the word meant. Some children were given feedback on their answer and other groups were asked to explain the answers (their own or the adult answer). Children did improve following feedback alone. However, when children were asked to explain an answer, they made greater gains in the quality of their definitions. Children made just as much improvement when asked to explain their own answer (which was sometimes right and sometimes wrong) than when asked to explain adults' answers.

One question that arises in this type of intervention is what kind of texts to provide. The examples above used texts where the meaning could be accurately derived from the

Box 7.8. ***Learning to Derive Meanings From Context: Looking for Context Cues***

Introduction:

Sometimes when we read, we read a word we've never seen before. I am going to show you a way to figure out what a new word means all by yourself. Any time you find a word you don't know, you can use this way to figure out what the word means.

Present the word:

Give each child a piece of paper with a short story at the top and a semantic map below it. The semantic map should have the same number of spokes as the number of "clue words" you will find. You can reproduce this at the large display for the whole group so that children are copying onto their own worksheets. Put the topic of the word in the center of the semantic map, and read it aloud as a group. Then have children read it individually.

Read an excerpt from the story aloud:

The tractor was blocking the road. Mom could not get the car around it. She had to shout to tell the driver the tractor was obstructing the car.

Look for clue words:

Remind the children that they are looking for "clue words" to help work out the meaning of the word. Ask children to identify and underline the clue words and then put them on the semantic map. In the example above, clue words would be "tractor," "blocking," "road," "car." Read all of the clue words aloud.

Generate a definition:

Ask the children to try to figure out what the word means. Continue to ask children until the correct meaning is generated. Ask the children to think of a time when they could use that word.

Note: Based on Nash and Snowling (2006).

context, at least by mature language users. Other texts are more ambiguous, so it is helpful to remind children that they will not necessarily be able to infer the correct meaning of an unfamiliar word from all texts (Goerrs et al., 1999). Clinicians should also attend to how many words might be unfamiliar to a given child: Fewer unfamiliar words mean the child has access to more context to figure out new word meanings, and this results in better word learning (Shefelbine, 1990). For example, if 1 in 10 words in a text is unknown, the chance of learning any given word is about 7%, but if only 1 in 150 words is unknown, the chance of learning that word goes up to about 30% (Swanborn & de Glopper, 1999). When training the skills of inferring from context, it is useful to scaffold the child's success by selecting texts in which structure is clarified by use of subtitles and clear anaphoric references (Herman, Anderson, Pearson, & Nagy, 1987). Keep in mind that when information about the target word occurs close to the word itself, word learning improves. This reduces short-term auditory memory demands, which helps

Box 7.9. ***Learning to Derive Word Meanings From Context: Practice Plus Explanation***

Introduction:

I have some stories that I am going to read out loud to you. I want you to follow the stories in the booklet in front of you. The person who wrote them got a bit stuck at times and didn't always know the right words to use, so they've put a made-up word in instead. At the end of the story I will ask you to explain the meaning of the word. For example, if I asked you what a "bed" was, you might tell me that it was a long piece of furniture that we sleep in.

Read the story aloud:

Ted was being chased by a bull. As he was running away, he looked over to the other side of the field and spotted a plicket. If he could get to the other side before the bull, he would be able to slip through to the next field. The bull could not follow him there.

After the story:

What do you think "plicket" means?

Feedback:

1. Explanation of the child's answer: *How did you figure out what plicket means?* (In this study, the child was asked the same question, regardless of whether the child's answer was right or wrong. In either case, the answer could be informative to the SLP.)

OR

2. Explanation of the adult's answer: *Yes, that's right. A "plicket" is a gap in the fence. I figured that out as well. How do you think I figured out that a "plicket" means a gap in the fence?* or *No, actually a "plicket" is a gap in the fence. How do you think I figured out that this made-up word "plicket" means a gap in the fence?*

Note: Based on Cain (2007).

all learners, but especially readers with poor comprehension (Cain et al., 2003). Finally, some texts will hold more helpful clues to the meanings of unfamiliar words than others. Those that include synonyms, antonyms, and other bases for inference are useful (Carnine et al., 1984). To illustrate, consider these lines from *The Call of the Wild*: Buck never came near Spitz without snarling and bristling *menacingly*. In fact, his conduct approached that of a bully. . . (London, 1965, p. 61). If the word *menacingly* were a target, the related words *snarling* and *bristling* before it and *bully* following it are useful cues.

In addition to teaching children to pay attention to the context surrounding a word for clues to meaning, we can teach them to pay attention to the components of the word itself. Ebbers and Denton (2008) dub the use of both as the "Outside-In Strategy": First look outside the word for clues, and then look inside the word for parts (p. 98; see also

Baumann et al., 2003). Because most words are composed of multiple morphemes, whether two roots or roots plus prefixes or suffixes, awareness of word structure can facilitate inferences about word meaning (Nagy & Anderson, 1984).

To benefit from paying attention to the word parts, the child must know what at least some of those parts mean. Knowledge of the root word is obviously helpful, but knowledge of the prefixes and suffixes that are attached to that root will help the student to make a more refined inference about the meaning of the whole. In general, it is better to teach prefixes before suffixes because prefixes tend to be more transparent and because suffixes often occur several at a time (e.g., paint-*er-ly*; will-*ful-ness*).

One way to teach prefixes and suffixes is to have students group words that begin or end the same way (e.g., *restart, retry, regroup, revisit*; Kieffer & Lesaux, 2007). Then the students can hypothesize what the given affix means by noticing what all of the words have in common. Students' recognition of the newly taught affix can be enhanced by asking them to find examples of new words that share the affix from their reading at home or at school.

Bowers and Kirby (2010) used sets of morphologically related words to teach fourth and fifth graders to use "morphological problem solving" in a highly metalinguistic way. The children were presented with morphological word families and were taught how to find meaning cues (morphemes) by noticing consistent spelling patterns. They practiced finding morphemes in words that were phonologically and orthographically transparent as well as in words that undergo shifts when affixed, making them less transparent. They were taught the value of morphemes by likening them to Lego pieces that can be rearranged into numerous structures. The students' gains generalized to new words within the morphological families they had studied; such gains were not demonstrated by students who had been randomly assigned to a control condition. Graves and Hammond (1980) reported the same pattern of generalized effects after they taught seventh graders the meanings of selected prefixes.

Bowers, Kirby, and Deacon (2010) conducted a meta-analysis of 22 studies in which children from preschool through eighth grade received interventions aimed at improving reading by instruction on morphology. All interventions targeted affixes (and some targeted roots as well) and all required students to identify morphemes in complex words. Activities included exercises in which children identified morphemes that word pairs shared in common, generated derivations when given a root and an affix, and applied new knowledge in novel contexts to make inferences about meaning. Compared to "business as usual" control groups, children receiving morphological intervention made greater gains in reading, spelling, and vocabulary knowledge. Effect sizes were larger for children with reading impairments than for those without and younger students (preschool to Grade 2) gained as much as older students (Grades 3–8). In general, interventions that incorporated morphological instruction into a more comprehensive program were more effective than those that involved morphological instruction only.

Notice how the term "comprehensive" echoes through this section on intervention. None of the interventions we reviewed are mutually exclusive. Rather, the best approach is a comprehensive approach that provides children with multiple, rich opportunities to learn words, to learn how to learn words, and to learn the power of words.

Conclusion

Diverse and deep vocabulary knowledge can make a real difference in a child's ability to communicate and learn successfully. We hope that having read this chapter you will know how to assess students' word knowledge and word learning abilities; how to select words to target; and how to meld increased exposure to words in context, direct teaching of word meanings, and coaching of metalinguistic strategies for optimal intervention effects. There is mounting high-level evidence that interventions aimed at promoting children's vocabulary development are efficacious. This evidence is not only instructive but also encouraging for the SLP and other professionals who serve children with limited vocabularies. Systematic instruction with explicit attention and repeated opportunities to understand and use words in rich, motivating contexts will help your students succeed across the curriculum.

References

Adams, M. J. (1990). *Learning to read: Thinking and learning about print.* Cambridge, MA: MIT Press.

Adams, M. J. (2010). Advancing our students' language and literacy: The challenge of complex texts. *American Educator, 34*(4), 3–11, 53.

Aitchison, J. (1994). *Words in the mind: An introduction to the mental lexicon.* Oxford, UK: Blackwell.

Allen, J. (1999). *Words, words, words: Teaching vocabulary in grades 4–12.* York, ME: Stenhouse.

Anderson, R. C., & Freebody, P. (1981). Vocabulary knowledge. In J. T. Guthrie (Ed.), *Comprehension and teaching: Research reviews* (pp. 77–117). Newark, DE: International Reading Association.

Anglin, J. M. (1993). Vocabulary development: A morphological analysis. *Monographs of the Society for Research in Child Development, 58*(10).

Aronoff, M. (1976). *Word formation in generative grammar.* Cambridge, MA: MIT Press.

Baayen, H. (1993). On frequency, transparency and productivity. In G. Booji & J. van Marle (Eds.), *Yearbook of morphology* (pp. 181–208). Netherlands: Kluwer.

Bauer, L., & Nation, I. S. P. (1993). Word families. *International Journal of Lexicography, 6*(4), 253–279.

Baumann, J. F., Edwards, E. C., Boland, E. M., Olejnik, S., & Kame'enui, E. J. (2003). Vocabulary tricks: Effects of instruction on morphology and context on fifth-grade students' ability to derive and infer word meanings. *American Educational Research Journal, 40*, 447–494.

Beck, I. L., McKeown, M. G., & Kucan, L. (2002). *Bringing words to life: Robust vocabulary instruction.* New York, NY: Guilford.

Beck, I. L., McKeown, M. G., & Kucan, L. (2008). *Creating robust vocabulary: Frequently asked questions and extended examples.* New York, NY: Guilford.

Bertram, R., Laine, M., & Virkkala, M. M. (2000). The role of derivational morphology in vocabulary acquisition: Get by with a little help from my morpheme friends. *Scandinavian Journal of Psychology, 41*, 287–296.

Biemiller, A. (2003). Vocabulary: Needed if more children are to read well. *Reading Psychology, 24*, 323–336.

Biemiller, A. (2005). Size and sequence in vocabulary development: Implications for choosing words for primary-grade vocabulary instruction. In A. Hiebert & M. Kamil (Eds.), *Teaching and learning vocabulary: Bringing research to practice* (pp. 223–242). Mahwah, NJ: Erlbaum.

Biemiller, A. (2010). *Words worth teaching: Closing the vocabulary gap.* Columbus, OH: McGraw-Hill SRA.

Biemiller, A., & Boote, C. (2006). An effective method for building meaning vocabulary in primary grades. *Journal of Educational Psychology, 98*(1), 44–62.

Biemiller, A., & Slonim, N. (2001). Estimating root word vocabulary growth in normative and advantaged populations: Evidence for a common sequence of vocabulary acquisition. *Journal of Educational Psychology, 93*(3), 498–520.

Bowers, P. N., & Kirby, J. R. (2010). Effects of morphological instruction on vocabulary acquisition. *Reading and Writing: An Interdisciplinary Journal, 23*, 515–537.

Bowers, P. N., Kirby, J. R., & Deacon, S. H. (2010). The effects of morphological instruction on literacy skills: A systematic review of the literature. *Review of Educational Research, 80*(2), 144–179.

Bowles, R. P., Grimm, K. J., & McArdle, J. J. (2005). A structural factor analysis of vocabulary knowledge and relations to age. *Journals of Gerontology Series B: Psychological Sciences and Social Sciences, 60*, P234–P241.

Bus, A. G., van IJzendoorn, M. H., & Pellegrini, A. D. (1995). Joint book reading makes for success in learning to read: A meta-analysis on intergenerational transmission of literacy. *Review of Educational Research, 65*, 1–21.

Cain, K. (2007). Deriving word meanings from context: Does explanation facilitate contextual analysis? *Journal of Research in Reading, 30*, 347–359.

Cain, K., Oakhill, J., & Elbro, C. (2003). The ability to learn new word meanings from context by school-age children with and without language comprehension difficulties. *Journal of Child Language, 30*, 681–694.

Carey, S. (1978). The child as a word learner. In M. Halle, J. Bresnan, & B. A. Miller (Eds.), *Linguistic theory and psychological reality* (pp. 264–297). Cambridge, MA: MIT Press.

Carlisle, J. F. (1988). Knowledge of derivational morphology and spelling ability in fourth, sixth, and eighth grades. *Applied Psycholinguistics, 9*, 247–266.

Carlisle, J. F. (2000). Awareness of the structure and meaning or morphologically complex words: Impact on reading. *Reading and Writing: An Interdisciplinary Journal, 12*, 169–190.

Carlisle, J. F., & Katz, L. A. (2006). Effects of word and morpheme familiarity on reading of derived words. *Reading and Writing, 19*, 669–693.

Carnine, D., Kame'enui, E. J., & Coyle, G. (1984). Utilization of contextual information in determining the meaning of unfamiliar words. *Reading Research Quarterly, 19*, 188–204.

Carrow-Woolfolk, E. (1999). *Comprehensive assessment of spoken language* (CASL). Circle Pines, MN: American Guidance Service.

Carstairs-McCarthy, A. (2002). *An introduction to English morphology: Words and their structure*. Edinburgh, UK: Edinburgh University Press.

Catts, H. W., Fey, M. E., Tomblin, J. B., & Zhang, X. (2002). A longitudinal investigation of reading outcomes in children with language impairments. *Journal of Speech, Language, and Hearing Research, 45*, 1142–1157.

Catts, H. W., Fey, M. E., Zhang, X., & Tomblin, J. B. (1999). Language basis of reading and reading disabilities: Evidence from a longitudinal investigation. *Scientific Studies of Reading, 34*, 331–361.

Cavanaugh, C. (2010, June 20). Preschool language intervention part 2. [Web log post]. Retrieved from http://vocablog-plc.blogspot.com/2010/06/preschool-language-intervention-part-2.html.

Clark, E. V. (1993). *The lexicon in acquisition*. Cambridge, MA: University Press.

Clark, E. V., & Cohen, S. (1984). Productivity and memory for newly formed words. *Child Language, 11*, 611–625.

Clark, E. V., & Hecht, B. F. (1982). Learning to coin agent and instrument nouns. *Cognition, 12*, 1–24.

Clarke, P. J., Snowling, M. J., Truelove, E., & Hulme, C. (2010). Ameliorating children's reading-comprehension difficulties: A randomized controlled trial. *Psychological Science, 21*, 1106–1116.

Cunningham, A. E., & Stanovich, K. E. (1997). Early reading acquisition and its relation to reading experience and ability 10 years later. *Developmental Psychology, 33*, 934–945.

Dale, E., & O'Rourke, J. (1981). *The living word vocabulary*. Chicago, IL: World Book/Childcraft International.

Dale, E., & O'Rourke, J. (1986). *Vocabulary builiding*. Columbus, OH: Zaner-Bloser.

Dale, P. S., & Fenson, L. (1996). Lexical development norms for young children. *Behavior Research Methods, Instruments, and Computers, 28*, 125–127.

Dollinger, S. J., Matyja, A. M., & Huber, J. L. (2008). Which factors best account for academic success: Those which college students can control or those they cannot? *Journal of Research in Personality, 42*, 872–885.

Ebbers, S. M., & Denton, C. A. (2008). A root awakening: Vocabulary instruction for older students with reading difficulties. *Learning Disabilities Research and Practice, 23*, 90–102.

Fukkink, R. G. (2005). Deriving word meaning from written context: A process analysis. *Learning and Instruction, 15*, 23–43.

Fukkink, R. G., & de Glopper, K. (1998). Effects of instruction in deriving word meaning from context: A meta-analysis. *Review of Educational Research, 68*, 450–469.

Gertner, B. L., Rice, M. L., & Hadley, P. A. (1994). Influence of communicative competence on peer preferences in a preschool classroom. *Journal of Speech and Hearing Research, 37*, 913–923.

Goerss, B. L., Beck, I. L., & McKeown, M. G. (1999). Increasing remedial students' ability to derive word meaning from context. *Journal of Reading Psychology, 20*, 151–175.

Goulden, R., Nation, P., & Read, J. (1990). How large can a receptive vocabulary be? *Applied Linguistics, 11*, 341–363.

Gove, P. B., & the Merriam-Webster Editorial Staff. (1981). *Webster's third new international dictionary*. Springfield, MA: Merriam-Webster.

Graves, M. F., & Hammond, H. K. (1980). A validated procedure for teaching prefixes and its effect on students' ability to assign meaning to novel words. In M. L. Kamil & A. J. Moe (Eds.), *Perspectives on reading research and instruction. Twenty-ninth yearbook of the National Reading Conference* (pp. 184–188). Washington, DC: National Reading Conference.

Gray, S. (2003). Word-learning by preschoolers with specific language impairment: What predicts success. *Journal of Speech, Language, and Hearing Research, 46*, 56–67.

Hammill, D. D., Brown, V. L., Larsen, S. C., & Wiederholt, J. L. (2007). *Test of adolescent and adult language* (4th ed.). Austin, TX: PRO-ED.

Hart, B., & Risley, T. R. (1995). *Meaningful differences in the everyday experience of young American children*. Baltimore, MD: Brookes.

Hayes, D. P., & Ahrens, M. G. (1988). Vocabulary simplification for children: A special case of 'motherese'? *Journal of Child Language, 15*, 395–410.

Herman, P. A., Anderson, R. C., Pearson, P. D., & Nagy, W. E. (1987). Incidental acquisition of word meaning from expositions with varied text structures. *Reading Research Quarterly, 22*, 263–284.

Johnson, G., Gersten, R., & Carnine, D. (1987). Effects of instructional design variables on vocabulary acquisition of LD students: A study of computer-assisted instruction. *Journal of Learning Disabilities, 20*, 206–213.

Justice, L. M. (2006). Evidence-based practice, response to intervention, and the prevention of reading difficulties. *Language, Speech, and Hearing Services in Schools, 37*, 284–297.

Kieffer, M. J., & Lesaux, N. K. (2007). Breaking down words to build meaning: Morphology, vocabulary, and reading comprehension in the urban classroom. *The Reading Teacher, 61*, 134–144.

Landauer, T. K., Kireyev, K., & Panaccione, C. (2011). Word maturity: A new metric for word knowledge. *Scientific Studies of Reading, 15*, 92–108.

Lewis, D. J., & Windsor, J. (1996). Children's analysis of derivational suffix meanings. *Journal of Speech and Hearing Research, 39*, 209–216.

Loftus, S. M., Coyne, M. D., McCoach, D. B., Zipoli, R., & Pullen, P. C. (2010). Effects of a supplemental vocabulary intervention on the word knowledge of kindergarten students at risk for language and literacy difficulties. *Learning Disabilities Research and Practice, 25*(3), 124–136.

London, J. (1965). *The call of the wild and other stories.* New York, NY: Grosset and Dunlap.

Lonigan, C. J. (2007). Vocabulary development and the development of phonological awareness skills in preschool children. In R. Wagner, A. Muse, & K. Tannenbaum (Eds.), *Vocabulary acquisition: Implications for reading comprehension* (pp. 15–31). New York, NY: Guilford.

Marulis, L. M., & Neuman, S. B. (2010). The effects of vocabulary intervention on young children's word learning. *Review of Educational Research, 80,* 300–335.

Mastropieri, M. A., & Scruggs, T. E. (2002). *Effective instruction for special education* (3rd ed.). Austin, TX: PRO-ED.

McKeown, M. G. (1985). The acquisition of word meaning from context by children of high and low ability. *Reading Research Quarterly, 20,* 482–496.

McKeown, M. G., Beck, I. L., Omanson, R. C., & Pople, M. T. (1985). Some effects of the nature and frequency of vocabulary instruction on the knowledge and use of words. *Reading Research Quarterly, 20,* 522–535.

Metsala, J. L., & Walley, A. C. (1998). Spoken vocabulary growth and the segmental restructuring of lexical representations: Precursors to phonemic awareness and early reading ability. In J. L. Metsala & L. C. Ehri (Eds.), *Word recognition in beginning literacy* (pp. 89–120). Mahwah, NJ: Erlbaum.

Miller, G. A., & Gildea, P. M. (1987). How children learn words. *Scientific American, 257,* 94–99.

Nagy, W. E. (2010). The word games. In M. G. McKeown & L. Kucan (Eds.), *Bringing reading research to life* (pp. 72–91). New York, NY: Guilford.

Nagy, W., & Anderson, R. C. (1984). How many words are there in printed school English? *Reading Research Quarterly, 19,* 304–330.

Nagy, W. E., Diakidoy, I. M., & Anderson, R. C. (1993). The acquisition of morphology: Learning the contribution of suffixes to the meanings of derivatives. *Journal of Reading Behavior, 25,* 155–170.

Nagy, W. E., & Herman, P. A. (1987). Breadth and depth of vocabulary knowledge: Implicationsfor acquisition and instruction. In M. G. McKeown & M. E. Curtis (Eds.), *The nature of vocabulary acquisition* (pp. 19–35). Hillsdale, NJ: Erlbaum.

Nash, H., & Snowling, M. J. (2006). Teaching new words to children with poor existing vocabulary knowledge: A controlled evaluation of the definition and context methods. *International Journal of Language and Communication Disorders, 41,* 335–354.

Nash, M., & Donaldson, M. L. (2005). Word learning in children with vocabulary deficits. *Journal of Speech, Language, and Hearing Research, 48,* 439–458.

National Reading Panel. (2000). *Teaching children to read: An evidence-based assessment of the scientific research literature on reading and its implications for reading instruction* (NIH Publication No. 00-4754). Washington, DC: U.S. Department of Health and Human Services, National Institute of Child Health and Human Development. Available at http://www.nationalreadingpanel.org/

Parish-Morris, J., Hennon, E., Hirsh-Pasek, K., Golinkoff, R., & Tager-Flusberg, H. (2007). Children with autism illuminate the role of social intention in word learning. *Child Development, 78,* 1265–1287.

Pearson, D. P., Hiebert, E. H., & Kamil, M. L. (2007). Vocabulary assessment: What we know and what we need to learn. *Reading Research Quarterly, 42,* 282–296.

Pullen, P. C., Tuckwiller, E. D., Konold, T. R., Maynard, K. L., & Coyne, M. D. (2010). A tiered intervention model for early vocabulary instruction: The effects of tiered instruction for young students at risk for reading disability. *Learning Disabilities Research and Practice, 25*(3), 110–123.

Rohde, T. E., & Thompson, L. A. (2007). Predicting academic achievement with cognitive ability. *Intelligence, 35,* 83–92.

Scott, J. A., Hoover, M., Flinspach, S. L., & Vevea, J. L. (2008). A multiple-level vocabulary assessment tool: Measuring word knowledge based on grade-level materials. In Y. Kim, V. J. Risko, D. L. Compton, D.K. Dickinson, M. K. Hundley, R. T. Jimenez, K. M. Leandor, & D. W. Rowe (Eds.), *57th yearbook of the National Reading Conference* (pp. 325–340). Oak Creek, WI: National Reading Conference.

Semel, E., Wiig, E. H., & Secord, W. A. (2003). *Clinical evaluation of language fundamentals–Fourth edition* (CELF-4). San Antonio, TX: The Psychological Corporation.

Seymour, H. N., Roeper, T. W., & deVilliers, J. (2003). *Diagnostic evaluation of language variation.* San Antonio, TX: The Psychological Corporation.

Shefelbine, J. L. (1990). Student factors related to variability in learning word meanings from context. *Journal of Reading Behavior, 12,* 71–97.

Sinclair, J., Hanks, P., Fox, G., Moon, R., & Stock, P. (1987). *Collins cobuild English language dictionary.* Glasgow, UK: Harper Collins.

Stahl, S. A., & Fairbanks, M. M. (1986). The effects of vocabulary instruction: A model-based meta-analysis. *Review of Educational Research, 56,* 72–110.

Stahl, S. A., & Nagy, W. E. (2006). *Teaching word meanings.* Mahwah, NJ: Erlbaum.

Stallman, A. C., Pearson, P. D., Nagy, W. E., Anderson, R. C., & Garcia, G. E. (1995). *Alternative approaches to vocabulary assessment* (Tech. Rep. No. 607). Urbana-Champaign: Center for the Study of Reading, University of Illinois.

Stanovich, K. E. (1986). Matthew effects in reading: Some consequences of individual differences in the acquisition of literacy. *Reading Research Quarterly, 21*(4), 360–407.

Steele, S. C., & Mills, M. T. (2011). Vocabulary intervention for school-age children with language impairment: A review of evidence and good practice. *Child Language Teaching and Therapy, 27,* 354–370.

Swanborn, M. S. L., & De Glopper, K. (1999). Incidental word learning while reading: A meta-analysis. *Review of Educational Research, 69,* 261–286.

Swanson, H. L., & Hoskyn, M. (2001). Instructing adolescents with learning disabilities: A component and composite analysis. *Learning Disabilities Research and Practice, 16,* 109–119.

Taylor, B. M., Frye, B. J., & Maruyama, G. M. (1990). Time spent reading and reading growth. *American Educational Research Journal, 27,* 351–362.

Tyler, A., & Nagy, W. (1990). Use of derivational morphology during reading, *Cognition, 36*, 17–34.

Whitehurst, G. J., & Lonigan, C. J. (1998). Child development and emergent literacy. *Child Development*, *69*, 848–872.

Windsor, J. (1994). Children's comprehension and production of derivational suffixes. *Journal of Speech and Hearing Research*, *37*, 408–417.

Zipoli, R. P., Coyne, M. D., & McCoach, D. B. (2011). Enhancing vocabulary intervention for kindergarten students: Strategic integration of semantically related and embedded word review. *Remedial and Special Education*, *32*(2), 131–143.

Chapter 8

The Place of Syntax in School-Age Language Assessment and Intervention

Catherine H. Balthazar & Cheryl M. Scott

Author Note: Preparation of this chapter was supported in part by Award Number R15DC011165 from the National Institute on Deafness and Other Communication Disorders (NIDCD). The content is solely the responsibility of the authors and does not necessarily represent the official views of the NIDCD or the National Institutes of Health.

School-age language intervention entails finding appropriate ways to support student performance in an increasingly academic, literate, and specialized language environment, with students whose skills and needs are diverse. Particularly as students progress into middle school and beyond, learning about different academic subjects means learning the language, including the syntax (grammar) of those subjects. Syntax can be viewed as the workhorse of meaning and a vehicle for acquiring knowledge (Scott, 2009) that sits squarely at the intersection of the content and function of the language of school. Children with language disorders fare poorly relative to their peers when it comes to meeting the language demands of school and adult society, and their difficulties are often evident in measures of syntactic performance. Although SLPs commonly assess and treat syntax in working with younger children, as children get older, interventions for this important language component may not keep up with the syntactic challenges that come with academic advancement.

What is the place of syntax assessment and intervention for school-age children? Sorting out the syntactic strengths and needs of the individual student and integrating them with the demands of the school environment is a challenging task that requires a solid understanding of both syntactic structure and syntactic development, but just as importantly, the functional implications of syntactic choices. Even the seasoned SLP, when comparing complex sentences found in academic contexts with the simple and perhaps agrammatic sentences of children with language disorders, may question how this problem can be addressed.

As a starting point for understanding the many roles and nuances of syntax in school-age language intervention, we begin by outlining a set of syntactic features that characterize academic language. We include a discussion of syntactic variation as a function of modality, genre, and discipline (or subject area). A description of what is known about the development of academic syntactic skills of students with typical and atypical language follows. Subsequently, we turn to clinical processes related to syntax. We describe an assessment process that involves extending uses of familiar procedures to closely examine syntactic features related to sentence complexity. We provide an overview of how to teach academic syntax in ways that are likely to result in meaningful gains in academic performance.

Syntax Fundamentals for Academic Language: Beyond Brown's Stages

Speech-language pathologists (SLPs) take pride in being "the language experts" among their colleagues who work with school-age children and adolescents. We can talk at length about "the components" of language, be it phonology, semantics, syntax, or pragmatics. When it comes to syntax and children, we are confident explaining early syntactic development—how the sentences of young children begin and grow to the point that a conversation with a 5-year-old reveals perfectly grammatical and sometimes quite lengthy sentences.

But switch the focus to an 11-year-old about ready for middle school who is struggling academically. What syntactic skills should be expected of this 11-year-old? Does syntax have anything to do with this student's problems reading textbooks, completing writing assignments, or understanding teacher directions and lectures in the classroom? These are difficult questions. Answers require taking a step back to examine syntax and its place in the broader scheme of school language. In this section, we identify the syntactic features that should be of most interest to SLPs who work with students, from early elementary through secondary grades, and explain how these forms "do the work" of school language, spoken and written.

Syntactic Features of Academic Language

We will concentrate on sentences that are characteristic of academic contexts. By this we mean sentences that a student is likely to encounter in the academic activities associated with school (e.g., listening to the teacher, presenting a report or participating in a group discussion, reading books, completing assignments that require writing). But academic language contexts can also occur outside of school in situations that call for communication of complex thoughts (e.g., a conversation with a peer about the suspected motivations behind another friend's actions, an argument to a parent about why an activity should be permitted, listening to a sermon, reading the newspaper, describing a nuanced movie plot). SLPs, when thinking about syntax, may imagine examining a child's language sample—in other words, the grammar associated with language production. In this chapter, however, we are equally concerned with sentences a student hears or reads and the challenges these present for comprehension. This multimodality perspective is consistent with the classroom experience. Although a written report about a Civil War battle provides evidence of how well a student can generate written sentences, embedded in that product is how well the student understood sentences that he or she read or heard about the battle in her preparations to write the paper. Thus, it is important for SLPs to be able to analyze grammatical features of sentences in textbooks and in the discourse context of classrooms as well as in written or spoken language output.

The sentence features of greatest interest for our purposes are listed in Box 8.1. The 16 syntactic forms and features listed are those that have appeared repeatedly in the literature as characteristic of academic language. Research questions and designs vary widely but include: (a) the purely descriptive, examining structures characteristic of two types of texts to see if there are differences (e.g., Biber, 1988, 2001); (b) examinations of language processing, such as comparisons of more- and less-complex sentences in terms of working memory (e.g., Magimairaj & Montgomery, 2012); and (c) comparisons of younger and older students, with and without language disorders, on sentence complexity features in spoken or written language samples (e.g., Scott & Windsor, 2000). All the examples in the chart are from a book of graded reading passages (Applegate, Quinn, & Applegate, 2008). The span from 2nd to 12th grade illustrates how these features play out in increasingly complex sentences (and texts) over the school years.

In the left-most column of Box 8.1, the syntactic features are organized according to the level of governing grammatical rule, whether phrasal (within noun phrases or verb phrases, #1–6), clausal/sentential (within a clause/simple sentence, #7–9), or multiclausal

Box 8.1. ***Syntactic Features Prominent in Academic Language***

FEATURE	EXAMPLES
1. NP: Premodification	• Many people have read about *that first great* explosion. (4th/info) [also #4] • Madison began to realize that *Hamilton's passionate political* style stood in sharp contrast to *his own subtle* style. (11th/info) [also #12] *Note:* Contributes to long nominal groups
2. NP: Postmodification	• Almost everyone in American had family members *who were immigrants themselves.* (3rd/info) [also #10] • He believed that these revolutions could be brought about only through an undermining *of the values of the controlling majority.* (11th/info) [also #3, 5, 12] *Note:* Contributes to long nominal groups
3. NP: Nominalization (verbs and adjectives changed to nouns)	• Over many years it had grown bigger from dozens of small *eruptions* and lava flows. (4th/info) [also #8] • Many people think that the *explosion* was the biggest that ever happened on earth. (4th/info) [also #10, 12, 13]
4. VP: Perfect aspect (HAVE + en, ed, irreg)	• He *had* always *wanted* to be a farmer and now he would have his chance. (3rd/nar) • Juan and Maria *had started* every day for the last two weeks talking about their Florida vacation. (4th/nar) [also #11]
5. VP: Passive (BE + en, ed, irreg)	• Most people just came looking for a better life. They *were called* immigrants. (3rd/info) • But he *was* soon *disillusioned* by the terror and tyranny that characterized both Lenin and Stalin. (11th/info) [also #8, 10]
6. VP: Combinations of mood, aspect, voice	• "*I've been missing* one of the best chances I've ever had," said Juan. (perfect + progressive) (4th/nar) [also #10] • Many of the tribal, civilian inhabitants of this region of Sudan *have been massacred.* (perfect + passive) (12th/info) • Ron suspected that he was most grateful for the full scholarship it would bring, a scholarship to a private university that the family *could* never *have afforded.* (mood + perfect) (11th/nar) [also #10, 12, 13, 14]
7. Clausal expansion via adverbial elements	• They use their wings to glide *from branch to branch in the tree without ever touching the ground.* (4th/info) • She was on the verge of *completely* losing control when she spied Jeff *nonchalantly* walking out of the theater's game room. (11th/nar) [also #10, 11, 13, 14]

(continues)

Box 8.1. (*continued*)

8. Phrasal coordination and series constructions	• *Her great pain and her great strength* made their way into her paintings. (4th/info) • Many countries in Africa struggle with *poverty, rebellions, famine, and disease* while other countries have *strong governments and economies with many resources.* (12th/info) [also #11] • The spores of the algae have *thick walls and fatty deposits* that enable them to withstand both *the extreme cold temperature of winter and the high summer temperatures* that would kill regular vegetative cells. (10th/info) [also #10, 14]
9. Non-canonical order	• It will take two weeks to train the sugar glider to accept you as its new home. (cleft construction) (4th/info) [also #12] • It was not until 1963 that Dr. Martin Schmidt explained the phenomenon by examining the strange light spectrum emitted by one of the "stars." (cleft construction) (12th/info) [also #1, 10] *Note:* Passive voice clauses/sentences are also examples of non-canonical order.
10. Relative clauses	• One animal *that helps others* is the wrasse. (2nd/info) [also #2] • The money *that the bank pays* is called interest. (3rd/info) [also # 2, 5] • The next player up hit the ball to left field and scored the two runs *that the team needed.* (3rd/nar) • But the buzz in the crowd was all about the recruiters from big-name colleges *who had come to scout Ron, their local football and baseball hero.* (11th/nar) [also #2, 4]
11. Adverbial clauses	• *If you leave your pet in another room*, it will glide back to you as soon as it sees you. (4th/info) [also #13] • She was trying desperately to control her anger *as she relived the events of the past few days*, events that dragged her memories back to the days of her youth when she felt so much like an outsider. (11th/nar) [also #10, 13]
12. Object complement clauses	• Jessie prayed *that the ride would end.* (2nd/nar) • They had to find out *if they were healthy enough to stay.* (3rd/info) • Mother knew *that they were going to use the overtime money to play for the hotel rooms and the plane tickets to Florida.* (3rd/nar) [also #8, 11, 14]
13. Combinations of subordinate and coordinate clauses	• Mr. Ruiz struggled *as he told the children that they would have to cancel their vacation.* (AC, OC) (4th/nar) • Ron knew *that his father had taken on the extra part-time job to earn the money to cover the expenses for Ron's participation in sports.* (OC, AC) (11th/nar) [also #3, 4, 14]

(continues)

Box 8.1. *(continued)*

14. Subordination depth	• Jill thought [that *if her team was going to win*, she would have to be the one to get the job done]. (Italicized AC is subordinate to OC in brackets) (4th/nar) [also #13] • And, if that were correct, the objects would be more than 3 billion light years away, [making them the most distant and, arguably, the most fascinating objects *ever discovered in our universe*]. (Italicized nonfinite RC is subordinate to AC in brackets) (12th/info) [also #1, 8]
15. Adverbial conjuncts	• Before she can start sipping your blood, she injects a little saliva to make it thinner. *Otherwise* it is like trying to drink a thick milk shake through a straw. (5th/info) • He believed that these revolutions could be brought about only through an undermining of the values of the controlling majority. Alexis de Tocqueville, *on the other hand*, was born in 1805 in Paris to an aristocratic family who had barely escaped the guillotine during the French Revolution of 1780. (11th/info)
16. Substitution and ellipsis	• People who save money in a bank earn interest. People who borrow from the bank must pay. Maybe Benjamin Franklin was thinking about *that* when he said, "A penny saved is a penny earned." (3rd/info) • Black holes suck in passing stars and clouds of gas and, in *doing so*, heat huge quantities of matter to such an extent that they emit stupendous amounts of light. (12th/info) [also #8]

All examples from graded reading passages; grade level and genre (narrative or informational) in parentheses; for examples that illustrate additional features, feature numbers are shown in brackets; NP = noun phrase; VP = verb phrase; RC = relative clause; OC = object complement; AC = adverbial clause.

Note: From the *Critical Reading Inventory: Assessing Students' Reading and Thinking* (2nd ed., pp. 128–372), by M. D. Applegate, K. B. Quinn, and A. J. Applegate, 2008, Upper Saddle River, NJ: Pearson Education, Inc. Copyright 2008 by the Pearson Education, Inc. Reprinted with permission.

(subordination/embedding operations, #10–14). The final two features (#15 and #16) can be governed by either grammatical rules (within sentences) or cohesion rules (between sentences).

To illustrate how level governs form more than does grammatical role, consider the noun phrase (NP). Although a NP may serve as the subject, direct object, or object of a preposition within a clause, the form stays the same (e.g., quantitative modifiers come before size modifiers), as shown below:

- *Increasing numbers of large Burmese pythons* are a worry to environmentalists. (NP functions as grammatical subject.)

- Park rangers are capturing *increasing numbers of large Burmese pythons* in the Everglades. (NP functions as grammatical object.)
- In *increasing numbers of large Burmese pythons*, biologists find large amounts of eggs. (NP functions as object of the preposition *in*.)

Likewise, at the level of the clause, a clause may be the main or subordinate clause within a multiclause sentence, but the clausal rules it follows are the same (e.g., subject-verb-object order). The three types of subordinate clauses listed (relative, adverbial, and object complement clauses) account for the large majority of subordinate clauses found in texts and in the spoken and written output of school-age children (Loban, 1976; Scott & Lane, 2008).

Box 8.2 shows four types of relative clauses that vary as a function of: (a) whether the relative clause modifies a noun that serves as the subject of the main clause or, alternatively, modifies a noun that complements the verb of the main clause (usually the direct object); and (b) whether the relative pronoun relates to the subject or object of the relative clause (see treatment of relative clauses in Perera, 1984; Romaine, 1984). Relative clauses that follow the main clause subject are frequently called *center embedded*

Box 8.2. ***Types of Relative Clauses***

Subject/Subject (SS): The relative clause modifies (and follows) the subject of the main clause; the relative pronoun replaces the subject of the relative clause.

The candidate *that won the primary* advances to the main election.

Based on: The candidate advances to the main election. (main clause)

~~The candidate~~ (that) won the primary (relative clause)

Subject/Object (SO): The relative clause modifies (and follows) the subject of the main clause; the relative pronoun replaces the object of the relative clause.

The candidate *that the party nominated* went on to win the election.

Based on: The candidate went on to win the election. (main clause)

(that) the party nominated ~~the candidate~~ (relative clause)

Object/Subject (OS): The relative clause modifies (and follows) the object of the main clause; the relative pronoun replaces the subject of the relative clause.

The swimmer beat his teammate *who had a world record in the 100m freestyle.*

Based on: The swimmer beat his teammate. (main clause)

~~The teammate~~ (who) had a world record in the 100m freestyle (relative clause)

Object/Object (OO): The relative clause modifies (and follows) the object of the main clause; the relative pronoun replaces the object of the relative clause.

The swimmer beat the teammate *that the referee disqualified.*

Based on: The swimmer beat the teammate (main clause)

(that) the referee disqualified ~~the teammate~~ (relative clause) because they are positioned in the center of the complex sentence, between the main clause subject and verb. Sentences with relative clauses of the subject/object (SO) variety are more difficult to comprehend (Gibson, 1998; Gibson & Warren, 2004).

Box 8.3 shows examples of relative, adverbial, and object complement clauses where the verb is nonfinite (i.e., not marked for tense or number). Forms of nonfinite verbs include infinitives, bare infinitives, and verbs with participial endings (*-ing* or *-ed*). By definition, nonfinite verbs can only occur in subordinate clauses. Examples of nonfinite subordinate clauses have been included because the lack of a fully marked verb can be confusing for identifying clause type.

In our assessment and intervention recommendations, we concentrate on multiclausal (complex) sentences because these types of sentences have been the focus of our research in the Building Complex Language Project (Balthazar, Koonce, & Scott, 2011; Scott & Balthazar, 2009, 2010). Specifically, we have looked for ways to assess school-age children's knowledge of sentences with adverbial clauses, relative clauses, and object complement clauses in both comprehension and production tasks. We then designed an intervention protocol to help students with language disorders develop greater fluency and conscious awareness of these sentences. Of course, SLPs can apply our suggestions in assessing and targeting other syntactic features comprising academic language. Noun

Box 8.3. ***Nonfinite Forms of Three Major Subordinate Clauses***

SUBORD. CLAUSE	NONFINITE EXAMPLES
Relative clauses	In an attempt <u>*to gain*</u> *greater insight into communist theory,* Gramsci moved to Moscow in 1921. (11th/info) After a childhood <u>*haunted*</u> *by fears of imprisonment*, he was sent to college at the age of sixteen. (11th/info)
Adverbial clauses	Most people just came <u>*looking*</u> *for a better life.* (RB) (3rd/info) So everyone in the family works <u>*to try*</u> *to pay the debt.* (3rd/info) In Botswana, another South African nation, agricultural and mining industries produce income <u>*to provide*</u> *education and health care for their populace.* (12th/info)
Object complements	Mom wants us <u>*to rake*</u> the leaves up. (4th/nar) Ben saw everyone <u>*looking*</u> at him but he knew deep down that he had lots of help last year. (4th/nar) A report of his finding, published in the *London Times*, caused some readers <u>*to conclude*</u> that the red color was rust from a meteoric iron deposit. (10th/info)

Note: All examples are from graded reading passages. The grade level and genre (narrative or informational) are shown in parentheses following each example.

Note: From the *Critical Reading Inventory: Assessing Students' Reading and Thinking* (2nd ed., pp. 128–372), by M. D. Applegate, K. B. Quinn, and A. J. Applegate, 2008, Upper Saddle River, NJ: Pearson Education, Inc.

phrase expansion via pre- and postmodification would be an especially important target because, as we show, long NPs appear as both subjects and objects in sentences and play a very prominent role in academic language.

Use of Academic Syntactic Features: The Wheres and Whys

One way to discover what is syntactically distinctive about sentences in academic language is to compare them with other types of language, for example, writing with speaking, and expository language with narrative language. Comparisons of written and spoken language modalities have shown that written sentences are lexically dense (a higher proportion of open-class, content words) and nominally embedded (a larger number of structures that pre- and postmodify head nouns of NPs such as adjectives, relative clauses, and prepositional phrases). Halliday (1985, 1987) referred to these types of sentences as hierarchical in nature. Spoken sentences, on the other hand, consist of clauses that are connected with coordinating and subordinating conjunctions, one after the other (a linear system). Biber (2001) concluded that one of the major differences in spoken and written sentences is that writers draw from a greater variety of syntactic features than speakers. Both Halliday and Biber cited processing differences inherent in the acts of speaking and writing for explanation of syntactic differences. The "here and now" pressures imposed by speaking bring about syntactic conjunction operations; that is, speakers like to "string together" clauses with coordinate and subordinate conjunctions. Writers are not under as much immediate time constraints and, as a result, hierarchical sentence features (e.g., object complement clauses, relative clauses, combinations of clause types within sentences, and greater depth of embedding) can take hold.

A genre comparison often made by applied linguists is that of narrative and expository (informational) texts. Although SLPs can consult a fairly extensive assessment and intervention literature on narratives, interest in expository text is recent (Nippold & Scott, 2010). Compared to narrative texts, sentences in expository texts favor: (a) NPs with extensive pre- and postmodification, (b) passives, (c) nonfinite forms of verbs, (d) phrasal coordination, and (e) nominalizations (Berman & Nir, 2010; Biber, 1988). Informational texts use nominalization processes to "recast" qualities (adjectives), happenings and experiences (verbs), and even logical relations (subordinate conjunctions) into abstract nouns (e.g., intense > intensity; to divide > division; because > reason; Fang, 2012). Nominalization allows a writer to "distill" previous information into one word and then proceed to expand on that information (e.g., *There was an intense reaction to the candidate's statement, but the intensity vanished almost overnight*). Halliday (2004) used the term *grammatical metaphor* (replacing one grammatical class with another) to describe this process. Sentences in expository texts (newspaper editorials, official documents, textbooks) are also longer on average than those in narrative texts (personal narratives, novels; Frances & Kucera, 1982).

In addition to modality and genre, sentence structure is influenced by subject matter, whether history, science, literature, or mathematics, as indicated in recent discussions of disciplinary literacy (Schleppegrell, 2001, 2004; Scott & Balthazar, 2010; Shanahan & Shanahan, 2008). The claim is that individual disciplines have their own ways of presenting information, and, because form follows function, distinctive sentences form. Fang

(2012) contrasts NP forms across disciplines. Science and history NPs are typically longer than those in literature, but what is truly interesting is the way the grammar "serves" the function of the discipline. In Fang's words, "scientific discourse privileges nouns, as they are a key grammatical resource for compacting information, creating technical objects, developing logical reasoning, facilitating discursive flow, and achieving precision" (p. 25). To illustrate, he provided the following example where NPs are underlined: "This uncontrolled dividing of cells can result from the failure to produce certain enzymes, the over production of enzymes, or the production of other enzymes" (p. 25). In this one sentence, several biological processes (*dividing, failure to produce, over production*) are nominalized from verbs (*divide, fail, produce*) and are logically related in a way that results in technical density achieved through language. History texts also use long NPs, but these serve different purposes than in science. They communicate how one thing leads to another, and therefore causality is carefully encoded in the choice of nouns, and even prepositions. Fang's (2012) analysis shows, with examples from school texts, the ways that grammar and lexical choices *combine* to serve unique discipline functions. Already there are calls for instruction that helps students explicitly recognize such discipline-specific uses of language (Shanahan & Shanahan, 2008). In the same vein, the Common Core State Standards (National Governors Association Center for Best Practices and the Council of Chief State School Officers, 2010) have discipline-specific standards in science, social studies, history, and technical subjects for Grades 6 through 12.

There is ample evidence that these grammatical features of academic language make sentences more difficult to process, for adults and children, by ear or by eye (Perera, 1984). A subject NP with extensive postmodification after the head noun puts distance (in words) between the subject and verb of the clause (e.g., in *The territory to the west of the Appalachian mountain range was divided into two parts*, eight words intervene between the head subject noun *territory* and the verb *was divided*). Coordinated phrases can do the same thing. Passive voice sentences disturb the more canonical subject-verb-object order of English and place the agent (subject) after the verb. Left-branching adverbial clauses (complex sentences where the adverbial clause comes first) postpone getting to the main clause information. The effect of the distance between a word and the word it relates to has been shown in experiments where adults take longer to verify information in sentences with greater distances (Gibson, 1998; Gibson & Warren, 2004). For 7- to 11-year old children, comprehension of object relatives (*the teacher that the girl liked taught math*) but not subject relatives (*the teacher that taught math was her favorite*) was related to working memory (Finney & Montgomery, 2011), perhaps due to the greater distance between the relative pronoun and the "trace" of the noun it replaces in object relatives.

A final perspective on characteristics of academic sentence structure is the question of the contribution to perceived text quality. Several recent investigations have compared ratings of writing quality with frequencies of particular syntactic features and measures such as sentence length and clause density. Using Coh-Metrix, an automated text analysis tool, McNamara, Crossley, and McCarthy (2010) compared frequencies of sentence-level complexity features with holistic ratings of quality in essays written by undergraduates. Of eight complexity measures examined, two were good differentiators of higher versus lower ratings: (a) the mean number of academic constituents per word, and (b) the number of words before the main clause. The first measure conveys an overall rate of production of academic syntax in the Coh-Metrix system (involving more features than the 16 listed back in Box 8.1). This finding would seem to indicate that readers respond positively to essays that adopt an academic tone via higher concentrations of academic structures. The second measure related to ratings focuses attention on the types of features that delay the main verb. The authors provided the following example where seven words precede the main verb *are*: "Thus, in syntactically simple English sentences there are few words before the main verb" (p. 69). An adverbial conjunct (*thus*) begins the sentence, followed by a prepositional phrase that functions as a (pre-posed) adverbial element, and contains a head noun (*sentences*) premodified by three words. Apparently raters appreciated the use of (a) adverbial elements that allow for elaboration within a clause (#7 back in Box 8.1), (b) information-packing mechanisms like NP premodification (#1), and (c) adverbial conjuncts (*thus* in this example) that provide for logical connections between sentences (#15).

In a study of narrative and persuasive essays written by seventh- and eighth-grade students, Beers and Nagy (2009) reported relationships between common measures of sentence complexity (clause length, sentence length, clause density) and quality ratings. Clause length was related to ratings of persuasive essays. Features that would lengthen clauses include NP pre- and postmodification (#1 and #2 back in Box 8.1), clausal expansion with adverbial elements (#7) and phrasal coordination (#8). All of these were mechanisms for "packing" information into a single clause. Quality ratings of narrative writing, however, were related to clause density (the average number of clauses per sentence), which the authors attributed to the use of adverbial clauses (the linear code mentioned earlier that is characteristic of narrative texts). The interesting point here is that genre has an influence on which syntactic features contribute to quality ratings.

When working with school-age students with language disorders, an SLP needs to have a clear picture of the sentence structures and their variations in different types of academic language. These structurally dense sentences allow complex information and thoughts to be communicated with precise meaning, but they are challenging to comprehend and produce. Next, we describe timelines for learning the grammar of academic language and review research on the performance of children with language disorders.

Learning and Using School Sentence Forms

School-Age Development

SLPs have been well served by developmental schedules for the acquisition of syntactic structures. Investigators have provided descriptions and explanations for systems that include basic morphosyntax (Brown, 1973), basic clause structure (Crystal, Fletcher, & Garman, 1976), and multiclause sentences (Diessel, 2004) that help clinicians decide (a) whether a child's language system is typical or not, and (b) if not, what the child needs to learn. Unfortunately, these descriptions take us only through the preschool years. For information about development of syntactic structures that contribute to higher-level language beyond preschool, Box 8.4 provides several sources and the types of information that can be found.

Box 8.4. ***Sources of Information on Development of Academic Syntax***

AUTHOR	AGES	CONTENT
Berman & Nir (2010)	9–10, 12–13, 16–17, 20–30 years	Describes sentence form in expository writing (discussing interpersonal conflict) in terms of temporal expression (tense, aspect, mood), clause types, and clause-linking connectivity. References include previous papers drawn from the same data set in a large, cross-linguistic investigation that includes comparisons of speaking and writing and narrative and expository text.
Nippold (2007)	School-age children, adolescents, and young adults	Reviews developmental literature on sentence length; subordinating, coordinating, and correlative conjunctions in terms of *both* comprehension and production; and adverbial conjuncts (intersentential connectives). Provides a bulleted account of syntactic milestones at ages 10, 15, and 25.
Nippold, Hesketh, Duthie, & Mansfield (2005)	8, 11, 13, 17, 25, 44 years	Empirical research provides measures of sentence length; clause density; as well as relative, adverbial, and nominal clause use in comparisons of conversational and expository genres (explaining a favorite game or sport).
Perera (1984)	School-age children, adolescents	Reviews developmental literature on clause patterns, NP and VP structure, coordination (compound sentences), and subordination (complex sentences—nominal, adverbial, relative, adjective + clause types) (separate treatments of both speaking and writing).
Romaine (1984)	School-age children, adolescents	Reviews developmental literature on two later-developing syntactic systems: relative clauses and passives.
Scott (1988)	School-age children, adolescents	Reviews developmental literature on sentence length, clause length, clause density (subordination index), NP and VP structure, subordination (nominal, adverbial, and relative clauses), adverbial conjuncts, and word order variations for theme and focus in written language. Reviews findings from early large-scale developmental studies of sentence structure in school-age children, including Hunt (1965, 1970), Loban (1976), O'Donnell, Griffin, & Norris (1967).
Scott (2012)	School-age children, adolescents	Reviews developmental literature on sentence form in writing, contrasts written form with spoken form, and compares narrative and expository form.

Even when SLPs are knowledgeable about later language development, it can still be difficult to pinpoint the grammatical knowledge of any one child and, accordingly, make decisions about the child's status relative to age peers. The reasons are many but include that the variety of contexts of use have expanded, and these contexts affect grammar (e.g., the child is writing as well as speaking but grammatical skills for speaking do not all predict writing). Another issue is that academic language is about grammatical choices rather than obligations. Even a kindly grandmother can tell if a child omits an obligatory past-tense marker or violates subject-verb agreement (although not in those terms perhaps), but it is much harder to judge whether a child speaks or writes with the appropriate amount and variety of multiclausal sentences for a particular discourse genre. And, while the child's productions can be accessed directly, syntactic comprehension within discourse is much harder to judge.

Nevertheless, some general principles emerge. On the production side, research has shown that quantitative measures of sentence complexity (e.g., sentence length and clause density) increase slowly throughout the school years into early adult years in both speaking and writing. To illustrate, Loban's (1976) data for spoken language showed an increase in words per sentence from 7.6 in the third grade to 11.7 in the 12th grade. The comparable figures for writing were 7.6 to 13.3. Nippold, Hesketh, Duthie, and Mansfield (2005) documented increases from 6.7 in 8-year-olds to 9.9 in 25-year-olds for spoken conversation, but when explaining a favorite game the range was larger, at 8.6 to 11.1 in the same speakers. The same principle of slow (but steady) growth has been shown for the measure of clause density. A typical figure for mid-elementary students is between 1.20 and 1.40 clauses per sentence. By the 12th grade, clause density is between 1.50 and 1.75, depending on task, modality, and genre (Nippold et al., 2005; Scott, 1988). Thus, for any one student, SLPs should not expect noticeable differences over time unless the measures are 2 or 3 years apart (Nippold, 2007; Scott, 1988).

Age-related changes in the production of subordinate clauses have received considerable attention. Studies document increased usage of all three major subordinate clause types. Although relative clauses occur less frequently than object complements and adverbial clauses overall, they show the most consistent age effects in cross-sectional studies and therefore provide a reliable marker of growth (Nippold et al., 2005; Nippold, Mansfield, & Billow, 2007; Scott & Lane, 2008). There are also age-related changes in the specifics of each type of subordination. For example, younger school-age children rarely use center-embedded relative clauses (SS and SO types, explained in Box 8.2) but are more likely to use relative clauses that modify object nouns that follow the verb (OS and OO types). Likewise, young elementary children often use conjunctions like *because*, *so*, *when*, and *(in order) to*, but it takes additional years before multiclause sentences with *even though*, *whereas*, *although*, *provided that* are seen with any frequency (Nippold, 2007; Perera, 1984; Scott, 1988).

As discussed previously, there is substantial evidence that genre, modality, topic, and task have significant effects on the occurrence of academic structures (Scott, 1994). Thus, another way to approach the topic of developmental change is to view it as the ability to produce texts that are matched to context. For example, when an 11-year-old writes a story and an informational report, the report is likely to contain more advanced sentence features. A persuasive piece (e.g., why school uniforms should not be required) at the same age should have the most advanced features of all (see Scott, 2012). Furthermore, the effects of modality and genre increase as students get older. For example, children's written sentences in early elementary years are much like those they would say; however, by mid-elementary years, written sentences begin to take on distinctly "written" features (Kroll, 1981; Perera, 1984, 1986). This divergence between speaking and writing increases further throughout the school years (Scott, 1988, 2012).

Children With Language Disorders

When thinking about how a school-age child with a language disorder might present during a language evaluation, the word *fluency* comes to mind. That is, not speech fluency, but sentence fluency, which is the ability to produce and comprehend complex sentence patterns with relative ease in academic contexts. It is not that the child never utters an adverbial clause or even a relative clause. Rather, the problem is that clauses are infrequent and might be restricted to earlier developing varieties (e.g., as noted previously, the child is unlikely to use a center-embedded relative clause). Generating written sentences in appropriate academic form is especially difficult, even for simpler sentences, such as pre-posing adverbials (e.g., *Quickly, the boy ran*). Instead, written sentences "sound" like they could be spoken (Scott, 2012). If we examine expository writing, we would find the gap between this child and an age peer with typical language especially pronounced (Scott & Windsor, 2000). Also, when writing, the child is likely to make grammatical errors that no longer occur when speaking, particularly in the realm of tense marking (Windsor, Scott, & Street, 2000).

One of the most robust research findings in research comparing children with and without language disorders is in the area of productivity: Children with language disorders produce too little language, regardless of task. Sentences that are produced are shorter, have reduced clause density, and show lower rates of usage of academic structures (Nippold, 2010a). Several studies have shown that these children have difficulty producing sentences that combine *different* types of subordinate clauses (Gillam & Johnston, 1992; Marinelle, 2004; Scott & Lane, 2008). And, sadly, as these children continue on through middle and high school, it is unlikely that gaps with age peers will narrow. As shown by Nippold and colleagues in large-scale longitudinal studies, spoken and written sentence complexity measures continue to distinguish adolescents with and without a history of SLI in 8th and 10th grades (Nippold, Mansfield, Billow, & Tomblin, 2008, 2009). Even if a child appears to catch up, problems with sentence complexity may return several years down the road, as shown by longitudinal data on narrative production of children who had been diagnosed with SLI as kindergartners (Fey, Catts, Proctor-Williams, Tomblin, & Zhang, 2004).

Comprehension of complex sentences is also a problem for children with language disorders. These sentences can be harder to parse (i.e., solve grammatically and derive meaning), whether one is listening or reading (Perera, 1984). Studies have shown that complex sentences containing passives, wh-questions, and relative clauses are poorly understood by children with SLI (Marinis & van der Lely, 2007; van der Lely & Battell,

2003). Montgomery and Evans (2009) reported that comprehension of complex sentences involving reversible passives and reflexive pronouns were harder for children with SLI (ages 6 to 12 years) compared to age peers, but the groups did not differ in comprehension of simple sentences. The common denominator in these reports is that children with SLI have a hard time understanding sentences that require them to resolve dependencies among grammatical elements that are distant (i.e., separated by intervening words/elements). Importantly, if listening comprehension is taxed by complex sentences, chances are that reading comprehension will also suffer (Adlof, Catts, & Lee, 2010; Kamhi & Catts, 2012). In fact, tenth graders who had been diagnosed with SLI as kindergartners continue to lag, reading only at a 6th grade level (Catts, Bridges, Little, & Tomblin, 2008). Scott and Koonce (in press) reviewed evidence of a robust relationship between syntactic ability and reading comprehension across the grades.

Combining information on the development of academic sentence structure in schoolchildren with typical development with information about weaknesses in children with spoken and written language disorders, we present a "top 10" list of principles in Box 8.5 to guide SLPs who offer services to this population. In the areas of both assessment and intervention, this list should help clinicians "fit" assessment tasks and observations with particular children as well as design meaningful interventions for those children.

What Explains Development of Academic Language Ability?

For children with both typical and atypical language, it is important to ask how academic sentence form is learned. Like language acquisition in preschool years, there is no explicit, organized instruction in production and comprehension of academic form. Although grammar is usually taught as part of a language arts curriculum, the lessons are not commonly organized around the types of features listed back in Box 8.1, nor is the usage potential of these forms taught or practiced, particularly in any direct way as applied to subject matter (history, math, or biology; Weaver, 1996; Weaver, McNally, & Moerman, 2001). The default explanation, then, is that the extant language provides the input, and academic form is learned implicitly through exposure and the ability to extract their distinctive properties. Recent findings of a positive relationship between statistical learning (indexed by the ability to learn an artificial grammar) and reading comprehension in college students would seem to lend support for this line of thinking (Misyak & Christiansen, 2011). Following this reasoning, it seems likely that children with the most input, those growing up in homes where they hear a lot of "book" language in parent/child reading routines and those who are good readers themselves, would be the same ones who are fluent producing and comprehending academic language.

Beyond exposure is need. Nippold (2010a) wrote that advanced syntactic development beyond the preschool years is driven by an expanding knowledge base and cognitive advances in the ability to reason, infer, and generalize. It would be difficult for any of us, child or adult, to adequately communicate in our complex world with simple sentences. Nippold's (2009) analyses of the language of adolescent chess players bore this out. In samples recorded when explaining how to play the game of chess to naïve lis-

Box 8.5. ***Top 10 Grammar Intervention Principles***

1. Sentence comprehension, while harder to observe than production, should be addressed.
2. Developmental norms are helpful to determine whether a child is "in the ballpark," despite slow growth and contextual variation.
3. Average sentence length roughly corresponds to chronological age to age 10.
4. By age 12, written sentences should be *at least* as long as spoken sentences.
5. Relative clauses, although less frequent than adverbial or object complement clauses, are good markers of developmental (or intervention) growth.
6. For all subordinate clause types, look for late-developing varieties to indicate developmental (or intervention) growth. This means: for adverbial clauses, adverbial conjuncts such as *unless, although, whereas* (not just *because* or *when*); for relative clauses, center-embedding (embedded after the subject of the main clause) and relative pronouns that stand for (deleted) objects; and for object complements, main clause verbs like *predict, suggest, claim* (not just *want* or *know*).
7. By age 10, a child's writing should contain sentences with distinctly written syntactic structures (that sound odd if spoken).
8. A good sign of grammatical fluency is combining several features within one sentence, for example an adverbial clause and a relative clause.
9. A child with a listening comprehension problem is likely to have a reading comprehension problem, regardless of decoding skills.
10. It is unlikely that students who struggle with academic language will improve on their own.

teners, quantitative measures of language complexity were substantially higher than in conversational interactions, even when the conversations centered on chess.

Exposure to academic language at home and school as well as need for academic language will vary widely. In combination with the effect of differences in inherent learning capacity, experiential differences result in considerable variation in grammatical performance. In reference to writing, Moffett (1968) reported that same-age children vary as much as children of very different ages. Although our suggestions for intervention will highlight explicit teaching of academic structures (as opposed to general language stimulation), SLPs can "up the ante" in collaborations with classroom teachers and parents. For example, to push their children's need for more sophisticated grammar and provide models for it, parents could discuss topics that lend themselves to arguing a point or delving deeply into a topic. The SLP should be the "go to" person for suggestions when it comes to implementing the complex language emphasis found in the Common Core State Standards.

Making the Case for Attending to School-Age Syntax

To this point, we have been building a case for why clinicians should pay attention to the grammatical structure and associated meanings of complex sentences characteristic of academic language. Fluency with these types of sentences allows students to be full participants in the language of learning. It takes many years to develop these types of sentence-level skills. Children with language disorders also progress, but evidence suggests they do not catch up to their age peers (Catts et al., 2008; Nippold et al., 2008, 2009). Written language, both composition and comprehension, is a real problem for these students, with obvious consequences for academic achievement. If sentences are the basic unit of analysis in language processing (Poirier & Shapiro, 2012) and the workhorse for encoding information in the academic world, we advocate a more central role for academic grammar in teacher and SLP education and in research agendas in school-age language disorders and learning disabilities. As a partial remedy, the remainder of this chapter presents information that will assist SLPs in uncovering specific problems with higher level sentence structure and suggest ways to intervene that build fluency with these forms, based on evidence available to date.

Assessment and Intervention for Academic Syntax

All students develop syntactic skills throughout the course of their education. As described previously, students must extend language skills into the written modality, learn lower frequency and topic-specific forms and meanings, develop awareness of language structure to make purposeful choices about what they say and write, and both understand and produce increasingly lengthy, detailed, and sophisticated pieces of discourse.

For a student with a language disorder, these demands are layered on top of developmental challenges with the structures of language. Basic morphological and syntactic features of oral language that were not mastered in early elementary school may require continued intervention, and even after acquisition in the oral modality, errors may re-emerge when language is produced in writing. Students with a language disorder often demonstrate limited productivity, especially in written expression. Furthermore, their discourse may be characterized by limited sentence fluency: that is, less varied and complex sentence structures.

Accordingly, school-age syntactic intervention extends beyond achieving mastery of particular structures (although that remains important). Students need help applying their language knowledge with more variety, flexibility, and productivity. Teaching particular complex language features at the general level may not be enough to "fix" the problems that landed students in the situation of having poor performance to begin with. Although we may be able to reduce the limitations that are affecting how a student performs, some higher-level language forms may never come easily or naturally. It could well be that a good part of what we teach is more like compensatory strategies than linguistic abilities, allowing students to purposefully work through what they need to read or write.

The treatment outcomes for these kinds of goals are not simply measured by percent correct use in obligatory contexts, as with acquisition of grammatical morphology. Rather, outcomes are measured through a combination of quantitative and qualitative observations that describe *how* a student performs comprehension and production tasks.

Beyond initially identifying particular syntactic problems, it is important to put in place some continuous assessment activities as an integrated part of intervention in order to keep in touch with how a student is performing both within intervention and with classroom materials and activities. Student performance with academic language is often inconsistent, spotty, and probably influenced by numerous linguistic and nonlinguistic factors (vocabulary, interest, experience, etc.) that make it hard to predict how syntactic problems will affect comprehension and production in any particular instance. Ongoing focused assessment during treatment, sometimes referred to as *dynamic* assessment, may help the clinician identify specific difficulties as they arise and then tailor intervention activities to strengthen knowledge and skills that are relevant to the student's education.

This kind of practice fits well within an integrated, collaborative service delivery model. Collaboration has long been advocated by language specialists concerned with school-age children (e.g., Nelson, 1989), and the model is currently gaining more traction given the advent of the Common Core standards and response to intervention (RTI) initiatives, which place special education service providers squarely in the middle of classroom practices and curriculum (Nelson & Van Meter, 2002; Whitmire, 2002). In the education literature, collaboration has been advocated as an essential means of improving literacy instruction, binding the teaching of literate language to the fundamentals of language competence (Moats, 2009; Sawyer, 2010). Practically speaking, it will be much easier to develop educationally relevant treatment activities and track student progress if there is an ongoing relationship between the clinician, who provides specialized support, and the teacher, who provides content and tests curricular performance.

Assessment and intervention procedures focused on school-age syntax build on two fundamental premises. The first is that the functional context of school should drive methods of assessment and intervention in order to achieve relevant outcomes. This means that our intervention will be successful to the extent that students are better able to meet academic standards, learn the contents of the curriculum, and perform specific classroom tasks. These, rather than more abstract general developmental milestones of syntax, serve as our benchmarks.

The second premise is that assessment and intervention should engage both oral and written modalities. The addition of reading and writing to the language picture may be more challenging (for both student and clinician), but the written modality has some important advantages. Print is a much more stable medium for teaching than is speech, and because much of the language with which a student will need support is encountered in written text, reading and writing activities are both practical sources for intervention content and functional environments for teaching. This is particularly true when it comes to expository language.

To illustrate our assessment and intervention guidelines, we will present Galen, a fictional case based on a composite of several students we have worked with in the course

Box 8.6. ***Introduction to Galen's Case***

Galen was a 13-year-old sixth-grader when he was evaluated for participation in our study. He had been diagnosed with a speech-language impairment in kindergarten and had been receiving services since first grade that were aimed at improving listening comprehension and grammatical accuracy. Later, after a difficult time in fourth grade, he was diagnosed with a learning disability. In fifth grade, Galen continued language intervention services, and resource room support was added for reading and mathematics. As he began sixth grade, the main goals on his IEP were to improve summarizing of oral information, following oral directions, written expression, reading fluency, reading comprehension, and mathematics skills. According to initial information, Galen's hearing and cognitive skills were within normal limits. His fifth-grade reading scores fell at the third-grade level for comprehension and word recognition. Galen's SLP at school suspected that some of his difficulties were related to weak syntactic knowledge or skill.

of our treatment study, the Building Complex Language Project (Balthazar et al., 2011; Scott & Balthazar, 2009, 2010). As you read the introduction to Galen's case in Box 8.6, notice any information that might relate to the state of his syntactic knowledge and skills.

Galen's file contained several preliminary indications that syntactic problems are contributing to poor performance, including: (a) a history of delayed language development and treatment for grammatical morphology and syntax; (b) poor scores on grammatical morphological and syntax subtests; (c) complaints of listening comprehension problems or difficulty following directions; (d) complaints of writing problems, such as low productivity, grammatical errors, simple and choppy sentences; and (e) indications of poor reading fluency or comprehension. Further evaluation was needed to go beyond this general information toward a grammatical intervention that would noticeably impact Galen's academic success.

Assessment as a Systematic Investigation

Assessing and Prioritizing

What could be done to further understand the role of Galen's syntactic skills in his language and learning performance? What could be done to help him do better? These are the kinds of questions that drive our next steps. Assessment information is collected to facilitate important clinical decisions, such as determining diagnosis, planning a treatment program, and measuring change (McCauley, 2001). The purpose of a detailed syntactic assessment with a student like Galen generally has less to do with diagnosis and more to do with treatment. The goal is to learn what a student knows about syntax and how that knowledge is demonstrated in the face of varying challenges in an academic environment.

Assessment with a case like Galen's should follow the guidelines provided in Box 8.7. These guidelines suggest a mixture of select norm-referenced tests as well as criterion-

Box 8.7. ***Syntactic Assessment Guidelines***

1. Consider detailed assessment of a student's syntactic knowledge and performance when there are any signs that a student may have syntactic weaknesses.
2. Use scores on norm-referenced tests of syntax as a starting point.
3. Analyze test performance for known patterns associated with syntactic difficulties.
4. Examine syntactic performance in written language as well as oral language.
5. Review samples of student assignments and classroom assessments for functional problems related to syntax.
6. Select appropriate criterion-referenced measures to thoroughly examine any problematic patterns and establish baseline performance.

referenced procedures, such as nonstandard uses of norm-referenced measures, dynamic assessment, clinician-created tasks, and language sample analysis. Oral language tests such as the *Clinical Evaluation of Language Fundamentals–Fourth Edition* (CELF-4; Semel, Wiig, & Secord, 2003), the *Test of Language Development: Primary–Fourth Edition* (TOLD-P:4; Newcomer & Hammill, 2008) and the *Comprehensive Assessment of Spoken Language* (CASL; Carrow-Woolfolk, 1999), from which we will draw examples, all include subtests designed to measure syntactic ability. There are also a few tests of written language used by SLPs, such as the *Test of Written Language–Fourth Edition* (TOWL-4; Hammill & Larsen, 2009) or the *Oral and Written Language Scales* (OWLS-II; Carrow-Woolfolk, 2011), which include subtests related to syntax.

Norm-referenced testing, while useful as a starting point, has important limitations, some of which may be moderated by extension or supplementation with criterion-referenced measures. One reason for going beyond the norm-referenced syntax subtests is that they may not contain examples of structures of interest (Balthazar & Scott, 2007). Also, the stimulus items tend to be drawn from basic, familiar, conversational, or narrative types of discourse and do not adequately sample the more challenging expository language. Another problem is that the sentences used in test items are rarely identified in terms of grammatical form, so a clinician may not be sure what specific forms are systematically represented. Because these measures do not provide a full inventory of the syntactic skills important in academic language, and because the skills are sampled in an artificially controlled way, they have limited functional applicability for setting goals and measuring progress (Scott & Balthazar, 2010).

Nevertheless, norm-referenced testing is often the entry point in assessment and is one source of information toward determining whether further syntactic testing is in order. Because the aim is to better identify problematic patterns and select goals accordingly, those tests can be supplemented in one of two ways. First, extension testing through additional stimulus items or follow-up questions can be used to explore errors on the standardized test items. Second, supplementation through language samples and

Box 8.8. ***Summary of Galen's Initial Assessment***

Galen's core language quotient on the *CELF-4* was 70, ranking in the 2nd percentile. His scores on most individual subtests fell at 6 or below (where scores of 7–10 are within one standard deviation of the mean), with scores of 6 on formulated sentences, 5 on recalling sentences, 4 on word definitions, and 8 on word classes. On the *CASL* sentence comprehension subtest, Galen scored 79, more than one standard deviation below the mean. For the *GORT-4*, his oral reading quotient (a combination of reading rate, accuracy, and comprehension) was 61, more than two standard deviations below the mean. Galen's conversational language during an initial interview did not contain any noticeable morphological or syntactic errors; however, samples of his written school work revealed numerous grammatical errors including verb tense, pronoun use, sentence fragments, and missing punctuation.

clinician-created measures can help connect error patterns in testing with functional problems in classroom communicative tasks.

In Galen's case, we first administered the CELF-4 and the *Gray Oral Reading Tests, Fourth Edition* (Wiederholt & Bryant, 2001), which were part of the standard evaluation procedures required for entry into our study. We also reviewed some work samples provided by his school SLP and engaged him in conversation. Box 8.8 summarizes the initial information that led us to explore his syntactic performance further. We needed to determine whether some of his language and reading problems might be rooted in weak syntactic knowledge, particularly multiclausal sentences.

Box 8.9 lists errors and error patterns we examined for Galen. Some of these problems with noun and verb phrases and multiclausal sentences can be observed through inspection of performance on items from a sentence production task like the CELF-4 Formulated Sentences subtest. For example, some older students with language disorders show nonfluent oral sentence formulation: Even though they eventually arrive at an acceptable sentence, there may be several false starts, mazes, and repetitions along the way. Students may have a difficult time regrouping after a false start, or may seem inflexible when attempting different ways to say the same thing, and therefore seem to get stuck on whatever option comes to mind first. On Formulated Sentences in the CELF-4, where the student must generate a sentence given a specific stimulus word, this predisposition can be fueled by the stimulus word provided, which students often attempt to use as the first word of the sentence. For example, for *until*, Galen produced, "*Until when the the the um orange shirted lady wouldn't buy a new bike until she saw a closed sign.*"

Students may demonstrate more grammatical errors on longer, more complex sentences than they do with shorter, simpler ones. Certain syntactic forms have been consistently identified as problematic for children with SLI, such as present- and past-tense markers on lexical verbs, auxiliary or copula forms of *be*, auxiliary *have*, and forms of *do* (e.g., Rice, Wexler, & Hershberger, 1998), as well as question forms, passives, and pronouns (e.g., van der Lely, 2005). There is some evidence that the language of children with language disorders may be subject to trade-offs between grammatical accuracy, particularly in the area of morphology, and increased sentence length and complexity

Box 8.9. ***Common Syntactic Problems for Students With Language Disorders***

AREA	PROBLEMS
Sentence fluency and diversity	1. False starts, mazes, repetitions in oral sentence formulation 2. Reduced amount of phrasal elaboration; choppy, simple-sounding writing; repetitive sentence structures 3. Difficulty constructing embedded clauses, particularly relative clauses 4. Atypical or awkward sounding object complement clauses 5. Inflexibility with attempting different ways to say the same thing
Grammatical accuracy in longer sentences or written language	1. Verb tense errors 2. Errors related to syntactic movement, embedding, and subordination, such as formulating or understanding questions, passives, relatives, and pronominal reference as well as relative clauses (especially center embedded and object relatives) and left-branching adverbial clauses
Lexical depth and diversity supporting complex sentences	1. Difficulty with the meaning and variety of adverbial conjunctions, such as infrequent use, overuse of one or a few conjunctions whether viable or not, and logical relationships are not expressed or interpreted accurately 2. Limited knowledge of metacognitive/cognitive state verbs 3. Atypical or awkward productions related to choice of adverbial conjunction or verb

(Owen, 2010). In other words, as students attempt longer and more complicated sentences, they tend to make more errors with morphological choices including verb tense. Subordinate clauses, pronominal reference, and subject-verb agreement are particularly difficult because syntactic features like embedded clauses or postmodified noun phrases place distance between a subject and its verb.

Additional patterns of performance can be observed if written language is sampled. There are often more grammatical errors in the written modality compared to spoken (Windsor et al., 2000). Another problem arises when students produce sentences that are grammatical, but slightly awkward, in that they do not choose the most common or adult-preferred forms. In some cases, this may also indicate semantic co-occurrence issues, such as with certain cognitive state verbs (e.g., *Danny did not mind* to wait [waiting] *in line at the cafeteria*). This may indicate that a student has not sufficiently fleshed out verb frame knowledge with when and how often certain grammatical and lexical options should be applied. Syntactic complexity is also associated with use of abstract nouns and metacognitive verbs in the written narratives of middle- and high-school-age students (Sun & Nippold, 2012). Limitations in lexical knowledge or variety, which obviously affect word use, also reduce the complexity of syntactic output. To illustrate, a child's knowledge of adverbial conjunctions may be restricted to *because*, *when*, and *so*. As a result, a variety of connections between ideas using other logical relationships, such as condition (e.g., *even if*) or concession (e.g., *although*) would not be expressed, and these missed opportunities would result in fewer subordinate clauses as well as less variety in sentence structures.

Strategic observation and analysis can help the clinician identify signals of specific syntactic problems like those back in Box 8.9. To determine what syntactic goals would be appropriate for Galen, we sifted through assessment information by: (a) analyzing his performance on individual items from the standardized tests, (b) analyzing narrative and expository writing samples, and (c) analyzing a written-sentence-combining task and a paraphrasing task. In particular, we explored his knowledge and use of three types of subordinate clauses that are found in complex sentences: adverbial clauses, object complement clauses, and relative clauses. Each analysis will be described and demonstrated with reference to those structures, but the steps in the assessment process would be similar for examining other forms, such as noun phrase expansion and verb phrase errors. The idea is to use available information to select aspects of syntactic functioning to treat or explore further.

Analyzing Performance on Complex Sentences

Analyzing test items and sentence productions for complex sentences begins with identifying when a sentence contains multiple clauses. A straightforward indicator of the number of clauses in a sentence is the number of verbs or verb phrases, whether the verbs are in finite (tense and number inflected) or nonfinite (participial or infinitival) form. When clauses are combined with a coordinating conjunction (e.g., *and*, *but*, *so*), this is known as a *compound* sentence. When clauses are combined so that there is a main clause and a subordinate (dependent) clause, either through use of a subordinating conjunction (*because*, *until*, *in order to*, etc.) or through embedding (relativization and complementation), we call it a *complex* sentence. Oftentimes, sentences are constructed with three or more clauses using any combination of coordination, subordination, and embedding. Definitions, examples, and developmental notes on verbs, clauses, and complex sentences are available in multiple resources (e.g., Justice & Ezell, 2008).

Analysis of Test Items for Sentence Complexity

Once multiclause sentences or opportunities for them have been identified, it is important to describe: (a) the type(s) of clause combining present, (b) specific conjunctions and verbs used in the process of combining clauses, and (c) any errors with choice of conjunction, use of verb, word order, or morphology (particularly verb inflection and pronoun reference). These quantitative and qualitative observations can be summarized in a checklist (see Appendix A).

Galen's oral responses on the CELF-4 Formulated Sentences subtest are presented in Box 8.10. For demonstration purposes, all items on the subtest, rather than just those between floor and ceiling, are listed. The responses contain several attempts at making complex sentences. Most of the opportunities for complex sentences on this subtest are created by the stimulus words provided, of which nine are adverbial conjunctions and require formation of complex sentences that contain an adverbial subordinate clause. Those sentences should definitely be analyzed, but there

Box 8.10. ***Galen's Responses to the CELF-4 Formulated Sentences Subtest***

Item	**Response**
children	The children are playing video games.
forgot	The girl forgot *to wear* [infinitival object complement] mittens.
always	Always brush your teeth.
car	The children are getting in the car.
gave	The parent gave the boy food.
never	Never let a dog *jump* [bare infinitive object complement] *on you . . . wearing* [nonfinite adverbial clause] *your new school clothes.*
finally	Finally the boy finish his test or assignments.
running	The boys and girls are running.
longest	The orange dog has the longest tail.
best	The boy looks best looking.
third	The girl *sweating* [reduced relative clause] is third in line.
quickly	The boy's quickly eating his breakfast or food.
if	If you are the . . . *if I forgot* [left-branching adverbial clause] *to get* [infinitival object complement] *on the bus,* walk to school.
and	And never let your dog out *when your cat's* [right-branching adverbial clause] *out.*
before	*Before buying* [left-branching adverbial clause] *my food,* you have *to put* [infinitival object complement clause] *it on the table or whatever that's called.*
because	*Because there's* [left-branching adverbial clause] *a blind man,* the dog is help him.
instead	*Instead of getting* [left-branching adverbial clause] *the green book* you will get the brown book.
unless	*Unless you are doing* [left-branching adverbial clause] *your homework* then don't play.
although	*Although your friend's riding* [left-branching adverbial clause] *a bike.*

(continues)

Box 8.10. *(continued)*

or	I like tomato or . . . I can't think.
until	Until when the the the um orange shirted lady wouldn't buy a new bike *until she saw* [right-branching adverbial clause] *a closed sign.*
otherwise	Otherwise, *if you don't have* [left-branching adverbial clause] *money enough money* your friends might pay for you.
neither	Neither I like the hamburger or the French fries.
however	*However you are doing* [left-branching adverbial clause] you should always work it.
as soon as	*As soon as I get done* [left-branching adverbial clause] *with breakfast* I will come outside and play.
in order to	*to . . . go* [left-branching adverbial clause] *outside* I have *to finish* [infinitival object complement] *my homework.*
even though	*Even though I like* [left-branching adverbial clause] *to play* [infinitival object complement] *basketball* I'd rather to play football.
as a consequence	You have a consequence *if you lie* [right-branching adverbial clause].

Note: Verbs underlined; subordinate clauses italicized; clause type in brackets following the subordinate clause verb.

were also a few other complex sentences that he produced, including spontaneous adverbial clauses and object complement clauses. Galen produced a total of 17 complex sentences, with 14 adverbial clauses, five object complements, and one reduced relative clause. He used adverbial conjunctions to indicate a variety of semantic relationships, including time, place, condition, concession, contrast, reason, and purpose. Two thirds of his adverbial clauses were left branching, or placed before the main clause, which is a lower frequency construction. However, three of the sentences he made with adverbial clauses contained subtle errors, in two cases because he probably needed to select a different conjunction (items 18 and 24), and in the other because he did not construct the subordinate clause verb phrase correctly (item 27, *I'd rather to play*). All six of the object complement clauses he used were infinitive or bare infinitive forms, and only four relatively common and generic verbs were in the main clauses: *let*, *have*, *like*, and *forget*.

These observations tell us some of Galen's strengths when it comes to complex sentences. In this type of task, Galen can produce both left- and right-branching adverbial clauses, he can express a variety of semantic relationships with adverbial conjunctions, and he can construct infinitive object complements using some basic verbs. There are also clues as to areas that might require more support, such as selecting and using certain adverbial conjunctions more accurately as well as expanding his range and use of cognitive state verbs that take object complements. There were no significant opportunities to observe his use of relative clauses on this subtest, so we cannot examine those abilities without further information.

Language Sample Analysis for Sentence Complexity

Language sampling is a basic component of the assessment process. Commonly, analysis involves transcribing, segmenting, and identifying clauses, so that descriptive statistics for complexity and productivity can then be derived, including mean length of C-Unit or T-unit (T-units are discussed here), number of total words, and clause density (also referred to as subordination index). Detailed discussions of procedures for language sampling and analysis a can be found in Nippold (2010b), Retherford (2000), and Hughes, McGillivray, and Schmidek (1997). There are some standard and even norm-referenced procedures for collecting an oral language sample, such as those described on the SALT website (SALT Software, 2010), or in formal tests like the *Test of Narrative Language* (Gillam & Pearson, 2004). But oral samples may not capture language needs in the written modality, and narrative samples may not predict performance on expository tasks (Scott, 2010). Given the importance of writing and exposition in academic performance evaluations, language should be sampled in those contexts as well. Samples can also be obtained from existing material that may have been collected for other purposes, such as norm-referenced language tests. Subtests on language measures such as the TOWL-4's Story Generation, for example, can be analyzed for specific features of complex syntax in addition to the features required by test scoring procedures that highlight writing conventions and narrative quality. Another source of written samples is class assignments (Kratcoski, 1998). Often teachers maintain work samples and evaluations in a portfolio to support their assessments of student progress, and accessing any such portfolios can be very helpful in planning and prioritizing treatment to maximize classroom impact (Nelson, 1989), particularly if language performance appears to suffer more in one subject area than another. These samples also offer the option to analyze a student's use of syntax in expository language.

For quantitative analysis, we start with a summary of overall length and complexity of sentences using the mean length of T-unit (MLT) and a clause density metric. MLT is calculated by dividing the total number of words in a sample by the total number of T-units (defined as a main clause and any subordinate clauses that are attached to it) (Hunt, 1970). For example, Galen's written summary in Box 8.11 has 15 T-units, numbered consecutively (this sample is intended as an illustration only; it's too short and restricted in context for a reliable and valid picture of student performance). The total number of words in the sample is 143, and thus the MLT is 143/15 or 9.53. MLT is sensitive to variables such as amount of subordination and noun phrase expansion; however, MLT does not indicate the relative proportions of features contributing to length (Scott, 2009). Thus, MLT may indicate when a student is using longer sentences, but not whether those sentences are being created mainly through phrasal expansion, clausal coordination, or complexity.

Box 8.11. ***Expository Writing: Galen's Summary of a Science Video***

1. people **have been trying** *to figure out* *why humans and clesure (creatures) sleep.* [3; infinitive object complement, wh object complement]
2. *the scincesties (scientists) **belive** (believe) *that creasurer (creatures) and human sleep* ***becuse*** *(because) they* ***are review*** *what he (they) did* [5; that object complement, right-branching adverbial clause, wh object complement]
3. *and they **say** *that you do something new and did* [3; coordinated that object complement]
4. and ***when*** *you get a good night sleep* you will do it 100x better [2; left-branching adverbial clause]
5. ****when*** *you sleep* you **think** *what you did.* [3; left-branching adverbial clause, infinitive object complement, infinitive object complement, wh- object complement]
6. *you will get picture in your heand (head) of *that (what) you did on that day* [2; wh object complement]
7. like fruit fles (flies) they Don't get a lot of sleep [1]
8. so they will sleep [1; left-branching adverbial clause]
9. *and sometime they look ***like*** *they are dead* **becus** *(because) they don't stand on their legs like houres (ours)* [3; right-branching adverbial clause, right-branching adverbial clause]
10. so they get like humans. [1]
11. mice do the same. [1]
12. *Scinecesties (scientists) have look into mices dream [1]
13. and they dream about it [1]
14. *and like that mouce (mouse) in the viedo (video) did [1]
15. and that night he dremed (dreamed) about it. [1]

T-units	Clauses	Total Number Words	Correct T-units	Correct Complex T-units
15	28	143	3	2

Note: Galen's spelling preserved; T-units numbered; number and types of dependent clauses in brackets; verb phrases for segmenting T-clauses underlined; adverbial conjunctions and object complement verbs bolded; subordinate and embedded clauses italicized; sentences with errors starred.

Clause density, on the other hand, reflects the amount of subordination present in a sample. It is calculated by summing the main and subordinate clauses and dividing that by the number of T-units (Hunt, 1970). In Galen's written summary, there are 28 total clauses and 15 T-units, so clause density is 28/15 or 1.87. Together, MLT and clause density offer a means of quantifying the amount of sentence complexity present in a sample. Both measures distinguish children with language disorders from typically developing peers (Fey et al., 2004; Nelson & Van Meter, 2002; Scott & Windsor, 2000), although differences have not been found consistently across all studies (see review in Scott, 2009).

Quantitative measures of language growth like MLT and clause density need to be followed up with some qualitative descriptions in order to capture important functional needs, or connect with curricular demands. For example, a student with a language disorder may be able to write longer sentences, resulting in a reasonable MLT, but in the face of a very challenging writing task may fall back on a limited number of familiar strategies for doing so, resulting in lower diversity or sentence fluency. SLPs who hope to advance academic aims should look to both quantitative and qualitative information.

Descriptive analysis can be done with the language samples as was done with the norm- and criterion-referenced test items. This will help the clinician to better understand how varied and sophisticated the syntax is in oral and written discourse of interest. In Galen's case, we see by the average clause density of almost 2 clauses per T-unit that this written expository sample has some complex sentences. But the subjective quality of the written summary was poor: It was very short, and sounded more like he was talking than writing. At age 13, we would expect to see written language taking on a more formal style using more of lower frequency, hierarchical sentence forms. Although there was a reasonable topic sentence and several details from the video he watched, the relationships between the details and the topic deteriorated as the passage progressed, and the coherence suffered. A reader would be hard-pressed to understand his summary of the video in anything more than a general sense.

Importantly, when we examined closely what kinds of sentences Galen used, and the meaning and variety of conjunctions and verbs associated with sentence complexity, specific needs were observable. Both adverbial and object complement clauses were produced, but no relative clauses. In the adverbial clauses, Galen used only the subordinating conjunctions *because*, *like* and *when*. In using *because* in #2, he would have been better served with a different logical connection—people don't sleep because they are reviewing what they did. The more accurate summary would have been "When people sleep, they are reviewing what they did," or possibly, "In order for the brain to review what they did, people must sleep." Here we may be seeing Galen falling back on the familiar *because* in his attempts to formulate a more complex relationship in writing, or we may be seeing his best understanding of what he heard, which in this case was a misunderstanding. The verbs used in object complement constructions included *try*, *figure out*, *believe*, *review*, *dream*, *look*, and *get*.

The functional impact of syntactic problems here is evident. Galen showed some strengths in that he appeared to understand and be able to discuss the overall theme of the video, and he used some varied and precise verbs in his initial description of the main idea (*figure out*, *review*, *believe*). But when he attempted to provide greater detail, he had a much more difficult time formulating grammatical, coherent text. The structure and sequence fell apart as he provided information out of sequence using general verbs like *say*, *try*, and *get* and did not explain the purpose of talking about mice. There were a few problems with pronoun choice and the use of the pronoun *it* where more specificity, and possibly even an object complement clause, would have served the purpose better. In this sample, using complex sentences goes hand in hand with a lot of morphosyntactic errors (see #2 where he omits plural, progressive *-ing*, and has trouble with pronominal reference). It is not likely that Galen does not know plurals or *-ing*, but rather that the challenge of the task overloaded his system, resulting in errors in forms he could manage conversationally. Galen's use of complex sentences is limited to object complements with a few early developing adverbials (*because, when*). Missing are greater variety of adverbials and relatives. These observations tell us that there are tangible ways that we could help this student improve his written summaries by using a greater variety of complex sentences, verbs, and conjunctions to meet particular communicative purposes, such as being specific and organized.

A useful follow-up is to have a student read and explain his or her written work. Galen's written summary, for example, could be revisited, with the SLP asking for more information or different ways to explain. He could be asked to expand on what he wrote by writing in the details in place of the pronoun *it*, in order to determine whether he understood and recalled those details and could formulate phrases or clauses to fit in the sentence. His understanding of the connection between sleep and memory could be questioned further, in order to assess whether he misunderstood the relationship when listening to the video, or whether he just needed a different adverbial conjunction to better express it. Student responses in these dynamic procedures can provide insight into both syntax-relevant vocabulary and sentence-structure-related comprehension gaps that might not be otherwise apparent.

Comprehension Assessment

So far, the discussion of assessing syntax has focused on tasks where there is some spoken or written production. However, the expression of syntactic knowledge is not confined to production. It should also be evaluated in language comprehension tasks. Problems with comprehension that are related to syntactic knowledge can be evident whether a student is listening or reading. In the Kamhi and Catts (2012) model of reading disabilities, listening comprehension difficulties complicate reading comprehension, either singly, or in combination with word recognition difficulties. Weaknesses in the syntactic domain will certainly impact reading comprehension (Scott, 2009).

As with production, norm-referenced tests of sentence comprehension can give a general indication of potential problem areas, and follow-up criterion-referenced testing may lead to more insights into specific functional problems. One example of a test follow-up might be to examine the difference in performance on a following-directions task when the clinician alters the directions to include more of the desired constructions. For instance, the CELF-4 Concepts and Following Directions subtest includes some coordination and subordination (e.g., *Point to the two cars that are to the right of a house, then point to the last house*) and postmodified noun phrases (*Point to the houses separated by a fish*), as well as adverbial clauses that violate order of mention (*Before you point to the shoe, point to the house*). This subtest also contains adverbial conjunctions such as *before, after, when*, and *unless*, in which the directions alternate between left-branching and right-branching adverbial clauses. So, during testing, if a student missed the left-branching items, a clinician could reverse the order of the clauses and check for comprehension when the adverbial clause was right-branching. If comprehension of additional spatial or sequencing or conditional conjunctions was of interest, some of the test items could be modified by replacing words like *before* and *unless* with *once* and *provided that.*

For other sentence comprehension tasks, SLPs can construct additional sentences, which include more examples of sentence types that were missed or which offer opportunities to investigate understanding of syntactic features that were not directly included. The CASL Sentence Comprehension task, for example, consists of comparisons between sentences that may contain several types of syntactic complexity. If a student were to miss the CASL comparison presented in Box 8.12, it would be difficult to determine whether left-branching adverbial clauses (*Because the team members were*

Box 8.12. ***Probe Procedure for Test Comprehension Errors***

CASL **Same/Different Sentence Comparison Subtest**

1. In spite of the hot weather, the baseball team's coach, who was eager for a win, made each team member practice daily.
2. Because the team members were eager for a win, they practiced every day even though the coach thought the weather was too hot.

(Answer: different)

1. Comprehension of left branching

a. In spite of the hot weather, the coach made each team member practice daily.

b. The coach made each team member practice daily in spite of the hot weather.

(Answer: same)

2. Comprehension of adverbial conjunctions

a. In spite of the hot weather, the coach made each team member practice daily.

b. Even though it was too hot, the coach made each team member practice daily.

(Answer: same)

a. Even though it was too hot, the coach made each team member practice daily.

b. Because it was so hot, the coach made each team member practice daily.

(Answer: different)

3. Comprehension of center-embedded relative clauses

a. The baseball team's coach, who was eager for a win, made each team member practice daily.

b. The baseball team's coach made each team member practice daily because he was eager for a win.

(Answer: same)

eager . . .), lexical challenges such as conditional adverbial conjunctions (*in spite of, even though*), object complement clauses (*the weather was too hot, each team member practice daily*), center-embedded relative clauses (*who was eager for a win*), or the combination of them is responsible. A series of follow-up comparisons could be developed like those shown. The number and type of follow-up items should be tailored to explore particular errors based on the student's prior comprehension and production performance.

There are also subtests that contain some complex sentences within larger pieces of text or discourse (such as CELF-4 Listening to Paragraphs, portions of the OWLS-II Listening Comprehension Scale, or Listening Comprehension on the *Woodcock Reading Mastery Tests, Third Edition*; Woodcock, 2011). Examinees listen to or read a passage and then respond to comprehension questions or paraphrase information. Discourse-level tasks may be regarded as more authentic than sentence-level tasks, to the extent that they are more contextualized or are similar to school tasks; however, it is more difficult to associate the responses to comprehension questions directly with knowledge of particular syntactic features. Even with careful content analysis, this type of procedure tells little about sentence-level syntax and comprehension.

Most passage comprehension measures are concerned with assessing whether a student understands and recalls the main idea and relevant details, not whether particular sentence structures are understood. Nonetheless, when using these stimuli, clinicians can add their own comprehension questions to focus on particular structures, such as center-embedded relative clause information and subject-verb links within an interrupted main clause. For example, the passage in Box 8.13 contains two relative clauses (in italics) that modify the main clause subject (underlined), and separate it from its verb (in bold). Follow-up comprehension questions can be phrased to specifically determine whether the verb has been assigned to the correct subject and whether the student understands the role and importance of the information in the embedded clause. This extension process can be applied throughout the school year for continuous assessment purposes by reviewing a student's reading material and developing syntax-focused comprehension questions.

Box 8.13. ***Probe Procedure for Passage Comprehension Errors***

Passage:

All insects *that go through incomplete metamorphosis* **must shed** their outer skeletons as they grow. A new larger skeleton then forms around its body. This process, *which is called molting,* **gives** the insect room to grow for a while.

Questions and Answers:

1. What must shed their outer skeletons? (insects)
2. Do all insects shed their outer skeletons as they grow? (no, only if they go through incomplete metamorphosis)
3. What process gives the insect room to grow? (molting)

Another approach is to have a student paraphrase what he or she is reading or listening to. This is similar to a think-aloud strategy for assessing comprehension, which may provide insight into underlying processes (Gillam, Fargo, & Robertson, 2009). After each sentence is presented, the clinician asks the student to explain what he or she learned using his or her own words. If a response does not show retention of critical information in the subordinate clause, a follow-up question is used to probe whether the student comprehended that information. We read a passage entitled "Passenger Cars," a historical piece about trains, aloud with Galen for this purpose, asking him after each sentence, "What do you know about passenger cars now?" If his paraphrase did not contain information from the subordinate clauses, a specific follow-up question was asked. The first few sentences in Box 8.14 illustrate. We did have to orient him first to the general topic since he thought the term *passenger cars* referred to automobiles rather than trains.

Notice that Galen doesn't quite get all of the details right from the first sentence, missing the referent (underlined) of the reduced relative clause (in italics). He most likely also did not understand the more infrequent comparative *little more than* as connecting *passenger cars* to *stagecoaches.* One can easily imagine how missing these cues while reading could compound over time and put a student at a real disadvantage when it comes to answering comprehension questions about the purpose and meaning of a reading passage.

Follow-Up Procedures for Investigating Sentence Complexity

Because many syntactic features of interest will not be fully sampled in just one subtest of a norm-referenced test, we are left with only partial insight into complex sentence knowledge. But we can supplement such subtests as needed for descriptive purposes, by either adding items (like additional stimulus words) or looking to other measures. With Galen, it would have been possible to follow up the initial observations about object

Box 8.14. ***Paraphrase Procedure to Probe Subordinate Clause Comprehension***

Examiner:	Early railroad passenger cars were little more than stagecoaches *fitted with special wheels* to help them stay on the tracks. What do you know about passenger cars now?
Student paraphrase:	That they have little wheels that help them stay on the tracks.
Examiner:	What were early passenger cars like? (stagecoaches)
Student:	They were like trains.
Examiner:	They didn't hold many passengers, and because they were made out of wood, they were fire hazards. What do you know about passenger cars now?
Student paraphrase:	They didn't hold a lot of people.
Examiner:	Why were they fire hazards?
Student:	Because it was made out of wood.

complements by asking him to make a few sentences using key stimulus words, such as cognitive state verbs like *decide*, *claim*, or *assume*. The words might be selected from those a clinician knows will be encountered, for example, in an upcoming classroom social studies unit. Additional subtests can also be modified for follow-up purposes. For example, the TOWL-4 Vocabulary subtest is a written version of a sentence elicitation task like the CELF-4 Formulated Sentences. The subtest has a few verb items that might elicit object complement clauses, such as *deny*, *specify*, and *alter*. One follow-up task could be a supplemental list of cognitive state verbs and subordinating conjunctions to obtain a larger sample of object complement and adverbial clauses. It is particularly helpful to instruct a student to combine or generate sentences without using the words *and*, *but*, *then*, and *or* in order to encourage the use of subordination rather than coordination. It is also helpful to give specific instructions. For example, the instruction "Finish this sentence by telling why: The woman went into the store–" obligates a causal construction using an adverbial conjunction (e.g., . . . *because she wanted a book*, or . . . *in order to find a book*, or . . . *so she could buy a book*).

To explore embedding of relative clauses, though, it is easier to develop a sentence combining task such as the one we gave Galen (Box 8.15). Our sentence completion task for eliciting complex sentences has been moderately correlated with the Recalling Sentences subtest of the CELF-4 ($r = .62$; Balthazar et al., 2011), and has been useful in helping us identify more subtle problems with sentence complexity for 10- to 14-year-old students, as well as to identify sample sentence types that are infrequent on standard-

Box 8.15. ***Galen's Written Sentence Combining Responses for Relative Clauses***

The pony express delivered mail across the western United States. The pony express consisted of horseback riders

The pony express *cosisted of horse back rider*.

The lineman tackled the quarterback. The quarterback fell to the ground.

The lineman *tackled the quarter back*.

Sam ate all the food. We made the food for the party.

Sam *ate all the food*.

The scientific method is a systematic approach to problem solving. Scientists use the scientific method.

The scientific method *is a systematic approach to problem solving*.

The Illini finally got a win. The press had been predicting the win all week.

The Illini *got a win*.

The doctor explained the complications to the patient's family. The doctor performed the surgery.

The doctor *performed the surgex*.

The human body requires vitamins. Vitamins regulate growth and normal functioning.

The human body *Requires vitamins*.

ized tests. Galen's responses to the items intended to elicit relative clauses are provided. Each pair of sentences contained information about the same noun, in order to elicit a longer sentence in which one stimulus sentence would be used as the main clause and the other would be converted to a relative clause. We then provided the subject noun of a sentence, in order to bias examinees to select one of the sentences as the main clause. The combining process was demonstrated twice with brief but detailed examples.

Galen did not make any attempts on this task to produce a relative clause despite the examples given. In fact, he did not produce any type of complexity, producing simple declarative sentences each time. Even after being redirected to try to get all of the information from both sentences into one longer sentence, he continued to produce the same types of responses. This dynamic procedure did not prove that Galen could not produce relative clauses but rather showed that he was unlikely to write them without even more practice and support. It also called into question whether he would be able to comprehend this type of construction. Galen's responses in comprehension tasks reflected similar patterns of performance to those observed previously, except that he produced two relative clauses when paraphrasing sentences that contained relative clauses, further supporting the idea that he can compose relative clauses but finds it difficult.

With any of these suggestions for eliciting particular types of sentences, it is good to remember that little is known about how well these tasks predict performance in actual use in the classroom. These assessment tasks call for a degree of explicit, conscious sentence formulation ability that differs from spontaneous use. On the other hand, these could be predictors of academic writing where there is more time to "be mindful." These assessment methods are useful for identifying and addressing curriculum-relevant and subject-specific syntax needs for both initial and ongoing assessment. By focusing analysis on problematic tasks and following up with targeted, dynamic assessments, a rich store of information can be collected to guide target selection and to suggest treatment activities that are likely to produce functional results.

Intervention for Academic Syntax

Developing Priorities and Goals

In the context of school, functional intervention means addressing goals in the Individualized Education Program (IEP) and advancing performance on educational standards and the local curriculum. Communication goals should reference school content by describing "the communication expectations underlying the standard" (Power-deFur, 2012, p. 11). As the Common Core standards are adopted across the country, more resources are becoming available to help SLPs adapt IEPs to clearly align with those standards (e.g., Rudebusch, 2012). Here, we highlight the special contributions of syntax within the context of the functional tasks the student must accomplish.

Syntactic competence supports many aspects of student functioning vis-à-vis curriculum standards. Curriculum standards that involve dense or discipline-specific language, discourse, logic, and organization provide a context within which to frame a syntactic goal. Student performance on syntactic structures occurring in that context can be assessed in order to establish the level of function and to estimate the amount of time and support necessary to reach the standard. In our view, the aims of syntactic intervention are to promote awareness and use of syntactic features in order to help students:

- deconstruct dense spoken and written language in academic contexts;
- understand the pragmatic motivations for particular syntactic forms, including specific uses in disciplinary language;
- use language structures fluently in oral and written discourse, particularly in expository contexts;
- understand and use syntactic features of the language of logic and organization; and
- use syntactic cues to support learning and comprehension strategies.

Returning to the example of Galen, we can see that there are several IEP goals related to language performance: summarizing oral information, following oral directions, written expression, and reading comprehension. We want to design his treatment to advance those goals. Notice that the goals refer to both production and comprehension in both oral and written modalities. Summarizing information and following directions are specifically mentioned as communicative functions that needed improvement. In oral and written modalities, across production and comprehension, expository activities such as these can be simulated and rehearsed, enabling syntactic treatment within functional contexts that is likely to impact these IEP goals.

Principles and Practices

Evidence from the fields of education and speech–language pathology regarding syntactic development and instruction has led to three principles that guide our clinical intervention framework. These principles reflect our best understanding of existing research, which is fairly sparse (see review in Balthazar & Scott, 2007), along with our clinical observations concerning effective practices. These three principles are: (a) to contextualize treatment within the student's own curriculum; (b) to practice in all modalities (reading, writing, speaking, and listening); and (c) to provide explicit metalinguisitc instruction about syntactic structure.

Returning to Galen's essay, as we think about these principles, recall that his performance with complex sentences was limited. He relied on basic (and early developing) adverbial conjunctions to connect ideas and tended to use relatively frequent and nonspecific verbs in infinitive object complement constructions. He did not produce any relative clauses in his written samples. On comprehension tasks, his standard score for Sentence Comprehension on the CASL was more than one standard deviation below the mean, and item analysis showed that he had difficulty when sentences contained three or more clauses. Importantly, his performance was not characterized by any complete absence of knowledge of particular syntactic structures. Rather, it was more an issue of fluent understanding and use of a variety of complex sentences. He made more mistakes when sentences became too long (more than two clauses) and following a direction depended on appreciation of every word and syntactic structure. He struggled to consciously construct complex sentences for purposes of writing a summary, and as a result became agrammatic beyond that observed when speaking.

It is easy to imagine some of the difficulties Galen could experience in trying to complete his school work, and it is hard to see how traditional "grammar" lessons could improve things. Galen's case illustrates a key point: Syntactic interventions should not simply be isolated grammar lessons delivered by the SLP (Silliman & Scott, 2009). To achieve use of targeted structures in the classroom and the achievement of academic standards, syntactic skills should be taught as a part of academic tasks such as understanding class readings, presenting a project, and writing a summary.

English and language arts instruction occurs across all grade levels, a large part of which focuses on English grammar in a decontextualized, metalinguistic manner. Students learn grammatical terms like *noun* and *punctuation* and are taught written English conventions. They learn to identify parts of speech and to use conventional rules in their writing. Unfortunately, this type of instruction, even for typical achievers, does not improve written expression or reading comprehension (Graham & Perin, 2007; Moats, 2009). Presumably this would be at least as true for students with language and learning problems who struggle both to learn in decontextualized, abstract grammar lessons and to carry this learning into functional applications.

For these reasons, it may seem counterintuitive to recommend metalinguistic grammar instruction. Yet we do see metalinguistic teaching as an important component of syntactic intervention, though not in the form of traditional grammar lessons. There are two primary reasons for this recommendation. First, in general education practices, there is a well-documented advantage to using particular metalinguistic procedures, notably sentence deconstruction and sentence combining, for improving written performance (Biancarosa & Snow, 2006; Graham & Perin, 2007). Although this comes from studies with typically developing students, such teaching methods hold promise for students with language disorders as well. Second, there are indications that for some students with language disorders, deliberate, repeated, explicit practice with syntactic structures can improve student writing. Hirschman (2000) provided third- and fourth-grade students with SLI 55 half-hour sessions of metalinguistic training over a 12-month period. These students improved both oral and written sentence complexity more than a control group. Hirschman noted that students with the poorest complex sentence usage at the beginning of the study appeared to benefit the most from the metalinguistic component of syntactic instruction. Perhaps children with weaker language abilities must rely more heavily on metacognitive strategies.

The use of metalinguistic means of teaching will be influenced by a student's age and cognitive skills. The complexity of explanations and amount of terminology need to fit a student's level of understanding. However, students do not need to be proficient in labeling parts of speech before they can be taught about complex sentence structure. In our experience, students learn any component concepts and labels over the course of the instruction through repeated examples and judicious explanation. So, for instance, one of the landmark features of a relative clause is that it tells about a noun. In the course of treatment, the nouns are always identified and discussed with respect to how they are modified by the relative clause, and as a result, the student becomes better acquainted with what nouns are and how to identify them. It is not necessary to wait to discuss relative clauses until a student is proficient in identifying nouns.

Metalinguistic instruction should be part of a larger treatment package that addresses form, content, and use. Students need to understand as both reader/listener and speaker/writer how syntactic forms are relevant for particular purposes. Pragmatic considerations, such as communicative purpose (e.g., informing, persuading, summarizing, recounting), motivate syntactic behaviors such as selecting a particular clause structure. Syntactic (e.g., phrase structure, clause structure) and semantic limitations (e.g., unfamiliar topics, underdeveloped vocabulary) can restrict ability to use language to meet those pragmatic requirements. Students need the depth and breadth of conceptual and linguistic experience to access the vocabulary and syntax needed for the pragmatic demands of academic tasks.

Metalinguistic Activities and Procedures

Metalinguistic methods for teaching syntax involve the explicit identification and manipulation of target structures. Instruction includes reasons for choosing such structures, and rules for doing so. The primary methods involve highlighting the properties of a desired structure in an organized and salient way, practicing segmentation of sentences into the relevant parts, and constructing sentences of the designated type.

Another feature of metalinguistic methods is verbal and visual cues. Most syntax intervention studies use these. For example, Ebbels (2007) used a system of shapes, colors, and arrows to teach past-tense morphology, comprehension of dative structures, and comparative questions. Levy and Friedmann (2009) spent 16 sessions over a period of six months teaching complex visual analysis codes and then used the codes to teach syntactic movement as found in relative clauses, wh-questions, and passive voice sentences.

There are many systems of features, definitions, tips, and cues. Often, local educators will follow a specific grammar curriculum with standard terminology. Clinicians would be well served to learn local systems, so that they can blend and build on anything with which students are familiar. Verbal and visual cues can be used flexibly at multiple levels, from segmenting words to writing essays. They can aid both comprehension and production, across oral and written modalities. Scaffolding may be provided by manipulating the length of the stimuli (number of clauses per sentence; number of sentences per sample); the familiarity of the content (grade level, curriculum, vocabulary); and the difficulty of the stimuli (concept load, information density, abstractness). Performance can also be scaffolded with the provision of visual supports (visual codes, written modality, key words and cues) and linguistic facilitations (modeling, expansion, extension).

Sentence Deconstruction

One metalinguistic method for helping students understand concepts such as "clause" or "phrase" is to break sentences down into their component parts. For this purpose, students can be shown how to identify the target linguistic unit and to take a sentence apart. Explicit grammatical instruction utilizing sentence deconstruction methods has

Box 8.16. *Sentence Deconstruction Procedure for Teaching Relative Clauses*

1. Introduction

We are going to start learning about a kind of complex sentence that is made with relative clauses. In this first activity, I will explain to you about relative clauses and then give you some examples of sentences that have relative clauses. Relative clauses start with a relative pronoun. Relative pronouns are THAT or a question word WHAT, WHICH, WHO, WHOSE, WHOM, WHEN, WHERE, HOW, and WHY. Relative clauses tell MORE about a NOUN. Relative clauses add information to make nouns more specific, colorful, or interesting, just like adjectives do. For example, in the sentence, "John ran the race" we might want to tell something more about the race. We could do this with an adjective, like "difficult"... "John ran the difficult race"; we could also use a relative clause, like "that was difficult"... "John ran the race that was difficult." We could also tell more about John with a relative clause, like "John, who didn't train at all, ran the race."

Examples:

The dog **that** bit my brother didn't have rabies. *(This one tells about the subject noun, "dog.")*

Mary wanted the new dress **that** was featured in the magazine. *(Tells about the object noun, "dress.")*

The hospital **where** I was born has been shut down. *(Tells about the subject noun, "hospital.")*

Lidia shared her lunch with the girl **who** didn't have one. *(Tells about the object noun, "girl.")*

2. Identifying Parts of a Sentence

Now I will show you some sentences with relative clauses in them. Listen as I read each one, then repeat it after me. Then we will find the verbs in this sentence. When there is more than one verb in a sentence, we know it is complex. Then you will help me find the relative pronouns and highlight the whole relative clause. We'll be sure to think about what each sentence means, too.

Examples (nouns underlined, verbs in boxes, and relative clauses in gray):

Kelly watched the movie **that** I recommended for her.

Nearly all of the proposals **that** the company has put forward have been accepted.

Scott's car, **which** broke down last night, is in the garage.

The veterinarian examined the dog **that** hurt its paw.

Any student **who** is vaccinated is unlikely to contract meningitis.

3. Deconstruction

Next, you are going to take some complex sentences and break them down into their separate parts: the main clause and relative clause. I have already circled the verbs to give you a clue about how to divide the sentence up. Another clue is to look for one of the relative pronouns you have been learning about. It will always be at the beginning of the relative clause.

Example:

Justin finally bought the new CD that was on the top 40 list for weeks.

Main clause: Justin finally bought the new CD.

Relative clause: The new CD was on the top 40 list for weeks.

been shown to be effective (Fang, 2006; Graham & Perin, 2007). Sentence deconstruction can be taught when structures are introduced at the sentence level, but once taught, can also be used at the discourse level as well, to help analyze and understand dense text material or to think of varied ways to construct a sentence or paragraph (see Box 8.16).

This lesson is designed to be supported with premade written materials that are placed in front of the student to show, as well as say, all of the instructions and examples. Notice in this lesson how the clinician provides definitions and examples and has simplified the task by using sentences with just two or three clauses. Notice also that the reasons for using the structure are described. Finally, the visual cues, such as highlighting, circling, and underlining, help to make the important features of the sentence more salient. Deconstruction tasks are helpful in parsing difficult sentences, like those containing relative or adverbial clauses. This strategy is one that can be especially helpful during reading tasks when a student has difficulty understanding a long and complex sentence.

Sentence Construction

Another way to focus attention on sentence structure is through sentence construction, through sentence combining or sentence completion. Students are given two separate but related sentences to combine into one longer sentence. An example of this type of task is the sentence completion probe discussed in the assessment section. This task can be used to teach as well as to test, as illustrated in Box 8.17.

Studies with typically developing adolescents have repeatedly shown that sentence combining is an effective way to increase both quality and accuracy of writing (Graham & Perin, 2007; Saddler & Graham, 2005). Less skilled writers tend to benefit more from this strategy than do more skilled writers. A systematic review of the effects of sentence-combining instruction compared with more traditional grammar-teaching methods reported results that favored sentence combining (Andrews et al., 2006), which supports the admonition against SLPs providing isolated grammar lessons. Some studies also have shown positive effects of sentence-combining practice on reading comprehension (Neville & Searles, 1991; Wilkinson & Patty, 1993). These studies suggest that sentence combining holds promise as a syntactic treatment procedure.

Sentence combining can be used for practicing most kinds of syntactic features of complex sentences and is especially relevant in the written composition process, where students can be taught to deliberately employ it in the process of revising their written work. It is a particularly useful way of teaching students to expand phrases using pre- and postmodification, and to produce sentences that combine two or more clauses with multiple levels of embedding.

Exposure and Practice in Context

In addition to metalinguistic instruction, students with language disorders need contextualized instruction. This means direct instruction in both the content and the strategies particular to disciplines such as history, language arts, and science (Deshler et al., 2001; Fagella-Luby, Graner, Deshler, & Drew, 2012). Treatment studies that combine metalinguistic instruction with context-based strategies are emerging in the language

Box 8.17. ***Sentence Construction Procedure for Teaching Relative Clauses***

Clinician: Now we are going to make some sentences using relative clauses. I will show you two smaller sentences, and you will pick the relative pronoun or question word to put them together with. You may type or write your answers on the computer or your worksheet, or you may ask me to write down what you say. The sentence in capital letters is the main clause, and this is the one we will use to tell the main idea that is happening in the sentence. The other sentence or phrase is the relative clause, and we will use it to tell more about one of the nouns in the sentence. To form a sentence with a relative clause, replace the X with relative pronoun or question word that makes sense. Put that with the whole clause in the blank. Sometimes the blank is after the main clause subject noun, and sometimes it comes after the main clause object noun. I'll help you read both sentences aloud together first, and then after you type or write your new sentence we will read the whole sentence out loud.

Examples:

THE CHURCH ______________ IS VERY OLD AND GRAND.

(X) My sister was married in the church.

Answer: The church where my sister was married is very old and grand.

RANCHERS IN THE WEST CLOSELY WATCH THE CATTLE ______________.

(X) The FDA inspectors have quarantined the cattle.

Answer: Ranchers in the West closely watch the cattle that FDA inspectors have quarantined.

intervention literature (Ebbels, van der Lely, & Dockrell, 2007; Hirschman, 2000; Katz & Carlisle, 2009; Levy & Friedmann, 2009; Scott & Balthazar, 2009). From these and other studies, we have found a number of good ways to keep the metalinguistic instruction grounded in functionality. Incorporation of these more contextualized procedures can help students produce target structures more frequently or apply their explicitly learned rules in meaningful ways.

Priming

The frequency with which students are exposed to target syntactic patterns is an important factor in their subsequent production performance. While explicit teaching methods are easily geared to provide language models at a much higher frequency than would be found ordinarily, there are some contextualized procedures for this as well. Gummersall and Strong (1999) demonstrated that typically developing children produced more subordinate clauses when retelling a story if, immediately before retelling, they heard the story a second time and repeated sentences with subordinate clauses. In another study, school-age children with language impairment doubled their rate of production of relative clauses after taking part in conversations where clinicians produced the same structures at an increased rate (Johnson, Marinellie, Cetin, Marassa, & Correll, 1999). A clinician's repeated use of target structures in a meaningful context, whether reading or conversation, may prime students for subsequent successful productions.

Paraphrasing

Another contextualized method of modeling and shaping sentence production is paraphrasing. The paraphrasing activity described previously for assessment can also be used for intervention. Paraphrasing offers opportunities not only for examining comprehension of specific complex sentences occurring in expository text, but also for teaching and expanding a student's syntactic knowledge and his or her ability to apply it in discourse.

Meaning Contrasts

Many of our students struggle with being specific in their speaking and writing and fail to appreciate the nuances of meaning communicated by word and structure choices. One way to develop understanding of the utility and necessity of particular structures is to highlight their meanings in contrast tasks. Sentence contrasting can be done with isolated pairs of clinician-generated sentences. To name a few more functional activities, sentence contrasting can easily be layered into discussions of academic readings, reviewing errors on comprehension questions from examinations, and developing a written report. The key is to identify what structural components to contrast. For example, Box 8.18 shows different ways to interpret sentences depending on the meaning of the adverbial conjunction *while*. Alternatively, the subtleties of meaning conveyed by the position of an adverbial clause could be emphasized. The discussions surrounding these kinds of contrasts can be both informative and interesting as SLP and student describe and refine their interpretations.

Embedding Syntax Instruction in the Writing Process

Student assignments can be the basis for other types of extended intervention activities. For example, "mini lessons" on sentence structure can be incorporated into the creation of a written product (Eisenberg, 2006; Nelson, 2010). Mini lessons are brief lessons that highlight particular syntactic forms that will occur in the language of a larger classroom project. They are given prior to or during the process of composing the project. They may involve expanding sentences, combining sentences, and contrasting structures. Nelson noted that students responded well to such mini lessons at all phases of the writing process, from drafting to revising and editing. A study by Hirschman (2000) taught 44 children with SLI who were 9 and 10 years of age to decompose and reconstitute multiclause sentences in the context of reading fables. When comparing pretest and posttest spoken and written language samples, the experimental group made significant gains compared with those in a control group. In Gillam, Gillam, and Reece (2012), children aged 6 to 9 years who participated in narrative literature-based activities with mini lessons demonstrated significant gains compared to a control condition in both story grammar and sentence measures, including indicators of syntactic complexity such as mental verbs and subordinating conjunctions.

Our case study can illustrate embedding syntax instruction within a writing activity. Galen's social studies class required an essay on why he liked his favorite music. His

Box 8.18. ***Meaning Contrast Procedure for Teaching Adverbial Construction***

Clinician: We've learned that the adverbial conjunction *while* can tell about time. But *while* also tells about how things are different, how they contrast with each other. Listen to these sentences and then think about what *while* means.

> Contestants for Miss America must each perform in a talent competition. Miss California sang an opera piece *while* Miss Louisiana played the harp.

Did Miss California and Miss Louisiana perform at the same time? Probably not. Here, *while* is used to show that they did something different.

Clinician: We've been talking about adverbial clauses and how they can be either before or after the main clause. People often say the most important things in their sentences last, so sometimes the adverbial clause gets moved to an earlier spot. Listen to these sentences and then think about which one you would use if you thought Lance Armstrong had been treated unfairly.

> Lance Armstrong finally admitted to using performance-enhancing drugs although he never tested positive during his Tour de France races.
>
> Although he never tested positive during his Tour de France races, Lance Armstrong finally admitted to using performance-enhancing drugs.

clinician used this assignment to form the basis of a unit on adverbial clauses and relative clauses. The essay assignment was presented a month before its due date. The clinician obtained the assignment instructions, the grading rubric, and a sample of a good student response from the prior year. The first step was to discuss with Galen what he understood about the required content and organization of the essay. This revealed that, although he had read and heard the directions in class, he had not clearly understood what he needed to do.

After reviewing the directions, the clinician then asked Galen to explain the requirements, the audience, and the expectations for good quality work. She used the sample paper to illustrate what the end product should look like, paying particular attention to the syntactic cues that provided organization and detail. In subsequent sessions, she diagrammed the content of the model essay and built an outline of the macrostructure. Galen was then assigned to research his topic and bring that information to the sessions. The clinician provided a blank web and helped him generate the content needed. He had to organize the content web into the typical five-paragraph essay structure outline as homework (Box 8.19). The clinician discussed this outline with him and they decided together that he needed more than five paragraphs, and a little grouping and organizing advice was given to revise the outline.

Galen then wrote a first draft, using his outline. It was evident from this first draft, shown in Box 8.20, that Galen needed support at multiple levels, including translating the outline into corresponding paragraphs of information, connecting ideas, filling in details, using language to organize, and using more formal and more diverse sentences, in addition to fixing style and grammar errors in the writing. It was also clear that there were many opportunities in working on this draft to give him specific practice learning

Box 8.19. ***Galen's Outline of an Essay***

Topic: Black Veil Brides (BVB)

Purpose: Explain why I like my favorite music

1. Music genre and style and CDs
    a. What's the difference between the new CD Set the World on Fire (STWOF) and the old CD We Stitch These Wounds (WSTW)
    b. What do your songs represent
2. BVB Army (fans)
    a. How does it feel to have fans that look up to the band
    b. How does it feel to have your own style of music and fans
3. What BVB represents
    a. The bands that inspired BVB to become a band
    b. The reason that Andy Six chose the name Black Veil Brides
4. History
    a. How many members have they had so far in the band over the years
    b. How did the band start
    c. What are the changes that the band has made so far
5. Opinions/explanations
    a. Do you still hang out with the old members of the band
6. Comparisons
    a. Do people mistake the genre for being Screamo or Heavy Metal

about and using more varied adverbial conjunctions to connect his ideas and using relative clauses to enhance details of nouns and provide more sentence variety.

Over the course of many subsequent sessions, the SLP reviewed issues and ways to improve content and organization, thinking of more details and rearranging them into a second draft. Although there were many ways she helped Galen draft this essay, the clinician kept her treatment focus on syntax, and in particular, relative and adverbial clauses. The clinician guided Galen to notice how sequencing words and adverbial conjunctions signaled logical connections, like *first*, *second*, *third* and *in order to*. One mini lesson involved grouping adverbial conjunctions into semantic categories. Another was combining choppy or run-on sentences using adverbial clauses.

In order to help him achieve the desired meanings, Galen needed more explanation and examples, so the SLP provided a series of mini lessons to illustrate the meanings and uses of different adverbial conjunctions. She explained that the placement of the

Box 8.20. ***Galen's First Draft of an Essay***

So far the history of the band members is really hard to explain. A lot of members and changes happened. Andy Six has kept in touch with former members and invited them to perform with them.

The BVB Army no only expands every day but it also expands on the internet with everyone. Kids get made fun of they see is a follower of the band BVB, so those people now see that they're not the only people out there. and there are other people out there to talk to.

the band the BVB came from Kiss and Motley Crue. The name BVB is the name when a nun marries herself to the church and they named the band this so they think this is a big accomplishment to take everything and spend it on marrying the church is really incredible.

People do mistake the band for Screamo it is actually Heavy Metal with Screamo.

The songs have feelings that have happened to the members of the band in their life and how the members reacted to them so they would take those members thoughts and turn them into a song.

Andy Six would tell the story of the song.

The changes the band has made so far is the makeup, a new drummer, and a new style of creative but yet entertaining music.

adverbial clause in the beginning of a sentence helped emphasize the main clause. In order to make his descriptions more specific, detailed, and interesting, in one mini lesson they listed more details about several of the nouns as short sentences. The clinician showed sentence combinations using relative clauses, and then had Galen turn the short sentences into two-clause sentences using relative clauses. Galen placed his new sentences back into the rest of the text on the following draft. Once this had been accomplished, the clinician reviewed the essay with him again, this time smoothing out the morphological and grammatical issues like tense, voice, and pronouns. Any remaining errors related to spelling and writing mechanics were worked on by Galen in his resource room. The end product in Appendix B shows Galen's achievements with adverbial clauses and relative clauses.

Conclusion

Whether assignments involve speaking or listening, reading or writing, there are abundant opportunities for systematically building syntactic skills within meaningful school contexts. Selectively and carefully assessing and teaching syntactic features is both a realistic and necessary part of the SLP's evolving role in the school. In the professional literature for SLPs, we increasingly encounter encouragement to "step up" to the challenge of helping students become more fluent with academic language. Because language is a huge domain that concerns many other educators who work with our students, we search for contributions that are distinctive and value added. The syntax assessment and intervention described in this chapter are just such contributions. It is our hope that further research and more "syntax-aware" clinicians will firmly establish the place of syntax in school-age interventions for oral and written language performance.

References

Adlof, S. M., Catts, H. W., & Lee, J. (2010). Kindergarten predictors of second versus eighth grade reading comprehension impairments. *Journal of Learning Disabilities, 43*, 332–345.

Andrews, R., Torgerson, C., Beverton, S., Freeman, A., Locke, T., Graham L., et al. (2006). The effect of grammar teaching on writing development. *British Educational Research Journal, 32*, 39–55.

Applegate, M., Quinn, K., & Applegate, A. (2008). *The critical reading inventory: Assessing students' reading and thinking* (2nd ed). Upper Saddle River, NJ: Pearson.

Balthazar, C. H., & Scott, C. M. (2007). Syntax-morphology. In A. J. Kamhi, J. J. Masterson, & K. Apel (Eds.), *Clinical decision making in developmental language disorders* (pp. 143–164). Baltimore, MD: Brookes.

Balthazar, C. H., Koonce, N., & Scott, C. M. (2011, June). *An exploration of the relationship of three experimental measures of complex sentence knowledge to CELF4 scores.* Symposium for Research on Child Language Disorders, Madison, WI.

Beers, S. F., & Nagy, W. E. (2009). Syntactic complexity as a predictor of adolescent writing quality: Which measures: Which genre? *Reading and Writing, 22*, 185–200.

Berman, R. A., & Nir, B. (2010). The language of expository discourse across adolescence. In M. A. Nippold & C. M. Scott (Eds.), *Expository discourse in children, adolescents, and adults* (pp. 99–122). New York, NY: Psychology Press.

Biancarosa, C., & Snow, C. E. (2006). *Reading next—A vision for action and research in middle and high school literacy: A report to Carnegie Corporation of New York* (2nd ed.) Washington, DC: Alliance for Excellent Education.

Biber, D. (1988). *Variation across speech and writing.* Cambridge, UK: Cambridge University Press.

Biber, D. (2001). On the complexity of discourse complexity: A multi-dimensional analysis. In S. Conrad & D. Biber (Eds.), *Variation in English: Multi-dimensional studies* (pp. 215–240). London: Longman.

Brown, R. (1973). *A first language: The early years.* Cambridge, MA: Harvard University Press.

Carrow-Woolfolk, E. (1999). *Comprehensive assessment of spoken language.* Torrance, CA: Western Psychological Services.

Carrow-Woolfolk, E. (2011). *Oral and written language scales* (2nd ed.). Torrance, CA: Western Psychological Services.

Catts, H., Bridges, M., Little, J., & Tomblin, J. B. (2008). Reading achievement growth in children with language impairment. *Journal of Speech, Language, and Hearing Research, 51*, 1569–1579.

Crystal, D., Fletcher, P., & Garman, M. (1976). *The grammatical analysis of language disability: A procedure for assessment and remediation.* London, England: Arnold.

Deshler, D. D., Schumaker, J. B., Lenz, B. K., Bulgren, J. A., Hock, M. F., Knight, J., & Ehren, B. J. (2001). Ensuring content area learning by secondary students with learning disabilities. *Learning Disabilities Research and Practice, 16*, 96–108.

Diessel, H. (2004). *The acquisition of complex sentences.* New York, NY: Cambridge University Press.

Ebbels, S. (2007). Teaching grammar to school-aged children with specific language impairment using shape coding. *Child Language Teaching and Therapy, 23*, 67–93.

Ebbels, S., van der Lely, H., & Dockrell, J. (2007). Intervention for verb argument structure in children with persistent SLI: A randomized control trial. *Journal of Speech, Language, and Hearing Research, 50*, 1330–1349.

Eisenberg, S. (2006). Grammar: How can I say that better? In T. A. Ukrainetz (Ed.), *Contextualized language intervention: Scaffolding preK–12 literacy achievement* (pp. 145–194). Austin, TX: PRO-ED.

Fagella-Luby, M. N., Graner, P. S., Deshler, D. D., & Drew, S. V. (2012). Building a house on sand: Why disciplinary literacy is not sufficient to replace general strategies for adolescent learners who struggle. *Topics in Language Disorders, 32*, 69–84.

Fang, Z. (2006). The language demands of science reading in middle school. *International Journal of Science Education, 28*(5), 491–520.

Fang, Z. (2012). Language correlates of disciplinary literacy. *Topics in Language Disorders, 32*, 19–34.

Fey, M., Catts, H., Proctor-Williams, K., Tomblin, J. B., & Zhang, X. (2004). Oral and written story composition skills of children with language impairment. *Journal of Speech, Language, and Hearing Research, 47*, 1301–1318.

Finney, M., & Montgomery, J. (2011, November). *Working memory's role in children's processing/comprehension of object relative sentences.* Paper presented at the annual meeting of the American Speech-Language-Hearing Association, San Diego, CA.

Frances, W. N., & Kucera, H. (1982). *Frequency analysis of English usage: Lexicon and grammar.* Boston: Houghton Mifflin.

Gibson, E. (1998). Linguistic complexity: Locality of syntactic dependencies. *Cognition, 68*, 1–76.

Gibson, E., & Warren, T. (2004). Reading time evidence for intermediate linguistic structure in long-distance dependencies. *Syntax, 7*, 55–78.

Gillam, R. B., & Johnston, J. R. (1992). Spoken and written language relationships in language/learning-impaired and normally achieving school-age children. *Journal of Speech and Hearing Research, 35*, 1303–1315.

Gillam, R., & Pearson, N. (2004). *Test of narrative language.* Austin, TX: PRO-ED.

Gillam, S. L., Gillam, R. B., & Reece, K. (2012). Language outcomes of contextualized and decontextualized language intervention: Results of an early efficacy study. *Language, Speech, and Hearing Services in Schools, 43*, 276–291.

Gillam, S. L., Fargo, J. D., & Robertson, K. S. C. (2009). Comprehension of expository text: Insights gained from think-aloud data. *American Journal of Speech–Language Pathology, 18*, 82–94.

Graham, S., & Perin, D. (2007). *Writing next—Effective strategies to improve writing of adolescents in middle and high schools: A report to Carnegie Corporation of New York.* Washington, DC: Alliance for Excellent Education.

Gummersall, D., & Strong, C. (1999). Assessment of complex sentence production in a narrative context. *Language, Speech, and Hearing Services in Schools, 30,* 152–164.

Halliday, M. A. K. (1985). *Spoken and written language.* Oxford, UK: Oxford University Press.

Halliday, M. A. K. (1987). Spoken and written modes of meaning. In R. Horowitz & S. J. Samuels (Eds.), *Comprehending oral and written language* (pp. 55–82). San Diego, CA: Academic Press.

Halliday, M. A. K. (2004). The language of science. In J. Webster (Ed.), *The collected works of M. A. K. Halliday* (Vol. 5). London, UK: Continuum.

Hammill, D. D., & Larsen, S. C. (2009). *Test of written language* (4th ed.). Austin, TX: PRO-ED.

Hirschman, M. (2000). Language repair via metalinguistic means. *International Journal of Language and Communication Disorders, 35,* 251–268.

Hughes, D., McGillivray, L., & Schmidek, M. (1997). *Guide to narrative language: Procedures for assessment.* Eau Claire, WI: Thinking Publications.

Hunt, K. (1965). *Grammatical structures written at three grade levels.* Champaign, IL: National Council of Teachers of English.

Hunt, K. (1970). Syntactic maturity in school children and adults. *Monographs of the Society for Research in Child Development, 35* (Serial No. 134, No. 1).

Johnson, C., Marinellie, S., Cetin, P., Marassa, L., & Correll, K. (1999, November). *Facilitating a child's syntactic style during conversational language intervention.* Paper presented at the annual meeting of the American Speech-Language-Hearing Association. San Francisco, CA.

Justice, L., & Ezell, H. (2008). *The syntax handbook: Everything you learned about syntax . . . but forgot!* Austin, TX: PRO-ED.

Kamhi, A., & Catts, H. (2012). *Language and reading disabilities* (3rd ed.). Upper Saddle River, NJ: Pearson.

Katz, L. A., & Carlisle, J. F. (2009). Teaching students with reading difficulties to be close readers: A feasibility study. *Language, Speech, and Hearing Services in Schools, 40,* 325–340.

Kratcoski, A. M. (1998). Guidlines for using portfolios in assessment and evaluation. *Language, Speech, and Hearing Services in Schools, 29,* 3–10.

Kroll, B. (1981). Developmental relationships between speaking and writing. In B. Kroll & R. Vann (Eds.), *Exploring speaking–writing relationships: Connections and contrasts* (pp. 32–54). Urbana, IL: National Council of Teachers of English.

Levy, H., & Friedmann, N. (2009). Treatment of syntactic movement in syntactic SLI: A case study. *First Language, 29,* 15–49.

Loban, W. (1976). *Language development: Kindergarten through grade twelve* (Research Report No. 18). Champaign, IL: National Council of Teachers of English.

Magimairaj, B. M., & Montgomery, J. W. (2012). Children's verbal working memory: Role of processing complexity in predicting spoken sentence comprehension. *Journal of Speech, Language, and Hearing Research, 55,* 669–682.

Marinellie, S. (2004). Complex syntax used by school-age children with specific language impairment (SLI) in child-adult conversation. *Journal of Communication Disorders, 37,* 517–533.

Marinis, T., & van der Lely, H. (2007). On-line processing of wh-questions in children with G-GLI and typically developing children. *International Journal of Language and Communication Disorders, 42,* 557–582.

McCauley, R. J. (2001). *Assessment of language disorders in children.* Mahwah, NJ: Erlbaum.

McNamara, D. S., Crossley, S. A., & McCarthy, P. M. (2010). Linguistic features of writing quality. *Written Communication, 27,* 57–86.

Misyak, J., & Christiansen, M. (2011). Statistical learning and language: An individual differences study. *Language Learning, 61*(1), 1–30.

Moats, L. (2009). Knowledge foundations for teaching reading and spelling. *Reading and Writing, 22,* 370–399.

Moffett, J. (1968). *A student-centered language arts curriculum, grades K–13: A handbook for teachers.* Boston, MA: Houghton Mifflin.

Montgomery, J. W., & Evans, J. L. (2009). Complex sentence comprehension and working memory in children with specific language impairment. *Journal of Speech, Language, and Hearing Research, 53,* 269–299.

National Governors Association Center for Best Practices and Council of Chief State School Officers. (2010). *Common core state standards for English language arts and literacy in history/social studies, science, and technical subjects.* Washington, DC: Author. Retrieved from http://www.corestandards.org/

Nelson, N. W. (1989). Curriculum-based language assessment and intervention. *Language, Speech, and Hearing Services in Schools, 20,* 170–184.

Nelson, N. (2010). *Language and literacy disorders: Infancy through adolescence.* Boston, MA: Allyn & Bacon.

Nelson, N. W., & Van Meter, A. M. (2002). Asssessing curriculum based reading and writing samples. *Topics in Language Disorders, 22,* 35–59.

Neville, D., & Searls, E. (1991). A meta-analytic review of the effect of sentence combining on reading comprehension. *Reading Research and Instruction, 31,* 63–76.

Newcomer, P. L., & Hammill, D. D. (2008). *Test of language development: Primary* (4th ed.). Austin, TX: PRO-ED.

Nippold, M. A. (2007). *Later language development: School-age children, adolescents, and young adults* (3rd ed.). Austin, TX; PRO-ED.

Nippold, M. A. (2009). School-age children talk about chess: Does knowledge drive syntactic complexity? *Journal of Speech, Language, and Hearing Research, 52,* 856–871.

Nippold, M. A. (2010a). Explaining complex matters: How knowledge of a domain drives language. In M. A. Nippold & C. M. Scott (Eds.), *Expository discourse in children, adolescents, and adults* (pp. 41–61). New York, NY: Psychology Press.

Nippold, M. A. (2010b). *Language sampling with adolescents.* San Diego, CA: Plural.

Nippold, M. A., Hesketh, L. J., Duthie, J. K., & Mansfield, T. C. (2005). Conversational versus expository discourse: A study of syntactic development in children, adolescents, and adults. *Journal of Speech, Language, and Hearing Research, 48,* 1048–1064.

Nippold, M. A., Mansfield, T. C., & Billow, J. L., (2007). Peer conflict explanations in children, adolescents, and adults: Examining the development of complex syntax. *American Journal of Speech–Language Pathology, 16,* 179–188.

Nippold, M. A., Mansfield, T. C., Billow, J. L., & Tomblin, J. B. (2008). Expository discourse in adolescents with language impairments: Examining syntactic development. *American Journal of Speech–Language Pathology, 17,* 356–366.

Nippold, M. A., Mansfield, T. C., Billow, J. L., & Tomblin, J. B. (2009). Syntactic development in adolescents with language impairments: A follow-up investigation. *American Journal of Speech–Language Pathology, 18,* 241–251.

Nippold, M., & Scott, C. (2010). *Expository discourse in children, adolescents, and adults.* New York, NY: Psychology Press.

O'Donnell, R., Griffin, W., & Norris, R. (1967). *Syntax of kindergarten and elementary school children: A transformational analysis* (Research Rep. No. 8). Champaign, IL: National Council of Teachers of English.

Owen, A. J. (2010). Factors affecting accuracy of past tense production in children with specific language impairment and their typically developing peers: The influence of verb transitivity, clause location, and sentence type. *Journal of Speech, Language, and Hearing Research, 53,* 993–1014.

Perera, K. (1984). *Children's writing and reading: Analyzing classroom reading.* London, UK: Blackwell.

Perera, K. (1986). Grammatical differentiation between speech and writing in children aged 8 to 12. In A. Wilkinson (Ed.), *The writing of writing* (pp. 90–108). London, UK: Falmer Press.

Poirier, J., & Shapiro, L. P. (2012). Linguistic and psycholinguistic foundations. In R. Peach & L. Shapiro (Eds.), *Cognition and acquired language disorders: An information processing approach* (pp. 121–146). St. Louis, MO: Elsevier Mosby.

Power-deFur, L. (2012). Unpacking the standards for intervention. *Perspectives on School-Based Issues, 13,* 11–16.

Retherford, K. (2000). *Guide to analysis of language transcripts* (3rd ed). Austin, TX: PRO-ED.

Rice, M. L., Wexler, K., & Hershberger, S. (1998). Tense over time: The longitudinal course of tense acquisition in children with specific language impairment. *Journal of Speech, Language, and Hearing Research, 41,* 1412–1431.

Romaine, S. (1984). *The language of children and adolescents.* New York, NY: Basil Blackwell.

Rudebusch, J. (2012). From Common Core state standards to standards-based IEPs: A brief tutorial. *Perspectives on School-Based Issues, 13,* 17–24.

Saddler, B., & Graham, S. (2005). The effects of peer-assisted sentence-combining instruction on the writing performance of more and less skilled young writers. *Journal of Educational Psychology, 97,* 43–54.

SALT Software. (2010). *SALT Software Resources.* Retrieved from http://www.saltsoftware.com/resources/

Sawyer, D. (2010). Improving reading instruction: A call for interdisciplinary collaboration. *Topics in Language Disorders, 30*(1), 28–38.

Schleppegrell, M. (2001). Linguistic features of the language of schooling. *Linguistics and Education, 12,* 431–459.

Schleppegrell, M. (2004). *The language of schooling: A functional linguistics perspective.* Mahwah, NJ: Erlbaum.

Scott, C. (1988). Spoken and written syntax. In M. Nippold (Ed.), *Later language development: Ages 9 through 19* (pp. 45–95). San Diego, CA: College Hill.

Scott, C. (1994). A discourse continuum for school-age students: Impact of modality and genre. In G. Wallach & K. Butler (Eds.), *Language learning disabilities in school-age children and adolescents: Some underlying principles and applications* (2nd ed., pp. 219–252). Columbus, OH: Macmillan/Merrill.

Scott, C. M. (2009). A case for the sentence in reading comprehension. *Language, Speech, and Hearing Services in Schools, 40,* 184–191.

Scott, C. M. (2010). Assessing expository texts produced by school-age children and adolescents. In M. A. Nippold, & C. M. Scott (Eds.), *Expository discourse in children, adolescents, and adults* (pp. 191–214). New York, NY: Psychology Press.

Scott, C. (2012). Learning to write. In A. Kamhi, & H. Catts (Eds.), *Language and reading disabilities* (3rd ed., pp. 244–268). Boston, MA: Pearson.

Scott, C., & Balthazar, C. (2009). *Building complex sentences: An intervention feasibility study for school-age children with oral and written language disorders.* Poster presented at the Symposium for Research in Child Language Disorders, Madison, WI.

Scott, C., & Balthazar, C. (2010). The grammar of information: Challenges for older students with language impairments. *Topics in Language Disorders, 30,* 288–307.

Scott, C., & Koonce, N. (in press). Syntactic contributions to literacy learning, In E. Silliman, A. Stone, & G. Wallach (Eds), *Handbook of language and literacy: Development and disorders* (2nd ed.), New York, NY: Guilford.

Scott, C., & Lane, S. (2008, June). *Capturing sentence complexity in school-age children with/without language impairment.* Paper presented at the Symposium for Research in Child Language Disorders, Madison, WI.

Scott, C., & Windsor, J. (2000). General language performance measures in spoken and written narrative and expository discourse in school-age children with language learning disabilities. *Journal of Speech, Language, and Hearing Research, 43,* 324–339.

Semel, E., Wiig, E., & Secord, W. (2003). *Clinical evaluation of language fundamentals* (4th ed.). San Antonio, TX: Harcourt.

Shanahan, T., & Shanahan, C. (2008). Teaching disciplinary literacy to adolescents: Rethinking content area literacy. *Harvard Educational Review, 78,* 40–59.

Silliman, E., & Scott, C. (2009). Research-based oral language intervention routes to the academic language of literacy. In S. Rosenfield, & V. Berninger, *Implementing evidence-based academic interventions in school settings* (pp. 107–145). New York, NY: Oxford University Press.

Sun, L., & Nippold, M. A. (2012). Narrative writing in children and adolescents: Examining the literate lexicon. *Language, Speech, and Hearing Services in Schools, 43,* 2–13.

van der Lely, H. (2005). Domain-specific cognitive systems: Insight from grammatical-SLI. *Trends in Cognitive Sciences, 9,* 53–59.

van der Lely, H, & Batell, J. (2003). Wh- movement in children with grammatical SLI: A test of the RDDR hypothesis. *Language, 79*, 153–181.

Weaver, C. (1996). *Teaching grammar in context*. Portsmouth, NH: Boynton/Cook.

Weaver, C., McNally, C., & Moerman, S. (2001). To grammar or not to grammar: That is not the question! *Voices from the Middle, 8*(3), 17–33.

Whitmire, K. (2002). The evolution of school-based speech–language services: A half century of change and a new century of practice. *Communication Disorders Quarterly, 23*, 68–76.

Wiederholt, J. L. & Bryant, B. R. (2001). *Gray oral reading test* (4th ed.). Austin, TX: PRO-ED.

Wilkinson, P., & Patty, D. (1993). The effects of sentence combining on the reading comprehension of fourth-grade students. *Research in the Teaching of English, 27*, 104–125.

Windsor, J., Scott, C., & Street, C. (2000). Verb and noun morphology in the spoken and written language of children with language learning disabilities. *Journal of Speech, Language, and Hearing Research, 43*, 1322–1336.

Woodcock, R. (2011). *Woodcock reading mastery tests* (3rd ed.). San Antonio, TX: Pearson.

Appendix A: Complex Sentence Observation Checklist

Student: ____________ **Date:** ________ **Sample Type/Source:** ________		
Feature	**Description**	**Attempts & Errors**
Adverbial Conjunctions Used	**Time** when, after, before, since, until, while, as, once **Place** where, wherever **Condition** even if, if, unless, in case, provided that **Concession** although, while, whereas **Contrast** while, whereas **Reason** because, since, as **Purpose** (in order) to *, in order that, so (that) **Result** so (that) * *in order to* is the exception, but if you can insert *in order* and it makes sense, it is usually an adverbial clause	
Adverbial Clause Position	**Left Branching** The adverbial conjunction and dependent clause are before the main clause. **Right Branching** The adverbial conjunction and dependent clause are after the main clause	

<table>
<tr><td>Object Complements Used</td><td>that John forgot <u>that</u> his mother was coming to pick him up early.
wh John wondered <u>whether</u> his mother would be on time.
infinitive John's mother remembered <u>to pick</u> him up on time.
gerund John's mother tried <u>picking</u> him up early, but it was too hard.
John's mother saw him <u>waiting</u> in the parking lot.
bare infinitive John let his mother <u>pick</u> him up early.</td><td></td></tr>
<tr><td>Verbs Used That Can Take Object Complements</td><td>Agree, Ask, Assert, Assume, Attempt, Be, Begin, Believe, Catch, Claim, Decide, Do, Expect, Explain
Feel, Find, Forget, Have, Hear, Help, Hypothesize, Indicate, Identify, Imply, Know, Learn, Leave, Let
Make, Observe, Predict, Promise, Realize, Remember, Report, Request, Require, Rule, Say, See, Show, Smell
Speculate, Start, Suggest, Taste, Tell, Try, Understand, Want, Wish, Wonder, Worry, Other:</td><td></td></tr>
<tr><td>Relative Clauses Used</td><td>Center Embedded The relative clause comes after the subject of the sentence, separating it from its verb.
End Embedded The relative clause comes after the object of the sentence.
Subject Relative The relative clause subject pronoun refers to the noun it modifies; usually the clause is in active voice.
Object Relative The relative clause subject pronoun refers to a direct or indirect object; usually the clause is in passive voice.
Reduced Relative The relative pronoun and verb are omitted from the sentence.</td><td></td></tr>
<tr><td>Relative Pronouns Used</td><td>That, Which, Where, When
Who, Whom, Whose</td><td></td></tr>
</table>

Appendix B: Galen's Final Essay

Healing, Vengeance, and Tears

The Black Veil Brides is a unique band. This band, *which mixes Screamo and Heavy Metal*, has a sound *that is very popular.* Black Veil Brides, *which started as a high school group*, has music based on emotional reactions to real life experiences *since all members contribute to writing the music.*

The band started in high school with Andy Sixx and four friends in about 2004. Andy Sixx is the center of the band *because he started it and he composes the songs and is also the lead singer.* Andy Sixx shaped the band by changing the members *in order to get better recognition.* Another reason *that he changed the members* was because of the way they acted. In 2006, the first band broke up and Andy Sixx invited six more people with the original drummer to the band. In 2008, the band broke up again and then Jay Holiday and Sandra joined, followed by Ashley Purdy and Jake Pitts in 2009. Two months later, Jay Holiday left and Jinx took his place. In 2010, Sandra left and in 2011, CC Coma joined.

The bands *that inspired the Black Veil Brides* were Kiss and Motley Crue. Kiss inspired the make-up *while Motley Crue inspired the music and the way the band dressed.* On an interview on You-Tube Andy Sixx explained that the name Black Veil Brides comes from clothing *that a nun wears when she marries herself to the church.* They named the band this *because they think it is an incredible accomplishment* to take everything that you've earned and spend it on marrying the church.

The songs *that the band plays* represent feelings *that have happened to the members of the band in their lives*, and how the members reacted to them. One example of how they would turn thoughts into songs is the song "Rebel Love Song" *which tells about one of Andy Sixx's relationships.* Andy Sixx was dating a girl named Scout, and Scout's parents didn't agree with Andy Sixx, and they wanted them to stop seeing each other. So it is basically a modern Romeo and Juliet story.

People do mistake the band for Screamo *when really the band mixes Heavy Metal with Screamo.* Screamo and Heavy Metal are the same *in that they use the same instruments, which are electric guitars, two-piece drumsets, and bass guitars.* Vocalists sing loudly and sometimes growl the words. *Whereas Screamo and Heavy Metal are similar,* they also are different. Screamo is about letting anger out by screaming or growling into the microphone. They usually sing about how life isn't fair and they don't like the way God made their lives. Heavy Metal is singing about something *that happened in your life that was hidden away. Instead of saying it* you decide to express it by singing it. The styles and topics are different. The clothing and costumes are different. And Heavy Metal is older.

Even though Black Veil Brides have 5 CDs each one is different. Their CDs We Stitch These Wounds and Set The World On Fire are good examples. The first CD represents Andy Sixx's way of dealing with people making fun of him. *Instead of taking his anger out on himself or others* he would stitch the wounds by writing them in a journal. Whereas We Stitch These Wounds is about healing, Set The World On Fire, *which came from his reaction to 9-11*, represents getting revenge on people.

Because Andy Sixx was constantly getting made fun of, he thought that when he made the band they would have a web page *where people who were just like him* could talk to each other. The Black Veil Brides Army is basically the fans *that like the band*. It expands by 100 people per day *while it also expands on the internet and on facebook.*

In conclusion, the band Black Veil Brides has had a long but yet interesting history in the way they are, the way they feel about their fans, and how many members they have in the band. They also have expressed in most songs the power of healing, vengeance, and tears.

Chapter 9

Telling a Good Story: Teaching the Structure of Narrative

Teresa A. Ukrainetz

Narratives can occur in intervention in so many ways it is impossible to cover them all in a single chapter. Stories can be used to enliven and contextualize lessons on almost anything: vocabulary, grammar, pragmatics, spelling, science concepts, and even arithmetic. Alternatively, narrative structure and quality can be the direct instructional target. Literary analysis and creative writing classes teach sophisticated knowledge and skills to advanced learners. For younger students and students with language impairments, instruction and intervention are directed at fundamental competence with organizing the actions and events of a story, linking sentences into a cohesive whole, and using elaborated language to add detail and interest. This chapter addresses these three ways of teaching narrative as a target of intervention: story grammar, cohesion, and story art. Intervention recommendations follow a contextualized skill approach. Whole and part activities include sharing children's literature as model and inspiration, practicing individual language skills within simple activities, and integrating targeted skills in the creation and sharing of stories. Children's literature, customized narratives, and pictography are the structural scaffolds that support construction of this complex discourse.

Why Narrative Matters

Distinctive Features of Narrative Discourse

Narratives are central to our lives. Narratives are used to report on, evaluate, and regulate activities. They provide an implicit common organization of experience and feelings of emotional solidarity (McCabe, 1991). Community is established, history maintained, and children are socialized through the daily flow of narratives (Bauman, 1986). We not only talk in stories but think in them: The narrative mode of thought seems to organize much of our understandings and experiences (Bruner, 1986).

A narrative is a verbal recapitulation of a past experience or, more simply, a telling of what happened (Labov, 1972; Moffett, 1968). The "what happened" is often characterized by genre: fictional or imaginary stories versus experiential or biographical personal narratives. However, that distinction does not really hold: Both imagination and experience are woven into any tale. In this chapter, narrative, story, and even tale are used interchangeably.

Narratives have other distinctive discourse features. Narratives involve both events, the "landscape of action," and what the participants in those events think or feel about the events, the "landscape of consciousness" (Bruner, 1986, p. 99). Consciousness also comes from the narrator whose perspective affects how a story is told: The same event will be narrated very differently if the point of the story is to show how brave versus how foolish the protagonist was. In contrast to conversational discourse, narrative discourse is generally *monologic* or told by a single speaker (Ninio & Snow, 1996). When a narrative occurs within a conversation, it has opening and closing markers (e.g., *One time, I . . . and that was what happened to me*) that indicate to other conversants that the narrator intends to hold the floor for an extended turn (Labov, 1972). If a narrative is coconstructed, as sometimes happens among familiar conversants, one person will usually indicate ownership of the tale (e.g., *Hey, let me tell the story!*).

Narrative is a particularizing form of discourse. This means a narrative is about a specific event that occurred at a specific (real or imaginary) point in time (e.g., *Once last winter, I got stuck . . .*). This contrasts with expository discourse, which deals with, in addition to abstract and hypothetical ideas, timeless or repeated events (e.g., *I am going to explain how not to get stuck*). Unlike dramatic discourse, which involve present-tense commentaries about ongoing events (e.g., *He is driving into that snowdrift! Oh no, it is above his wheels. He is spinning. He is really stuck!*), narratives are set in the past (Longacre, 1983; Moffett, 1968; Schriffrin, 1981). They move from the past toward the present with temporally ordered statements that match the chronology of the event. Diversions from this are marked with time words and verb adjustments (e.g., *Before that happened* or *Ten years earlier*).

Narratives involve many cognitive and linguistic skills. The construction of a narrative requires at least four different kinds of knowledge (Hudson & Shapiro, 1991; Johnston, 1982): (a) knowledge of the world, including scripts of how events typically proceed and specific understandings of people, objects, and actions; (b) knowledge of words and grammar needed to construct effective sentences; (c) knowledge of how to link those sentences into a coherent, cohesive discourse whole; and (d) knowledge of how communication operates in context (i.e., why this story is being told and what an audience needs to know to achieve the narrator's purpose). If that was not enough to daunt any narrator, Johnston (2008) reminded us that a narrator must also have sufficient cognitive processing capacity to manage all these demands simultaneously.

Narratives are deeply social events, so it is not surprising that narrative structure can vary with culture and context. There is the topic-associated, poetic, and contextualized style associated with African American storytelling (Gee, 1989; Labov, 1972; Michaels, 1991), the four-part, pause-signifier structure of Athapaskan Indian storytelling (Scollon & Scollon, 1988), and the short, minimalist, and implicit style reported for Japanese American and Korean storytelling (Lai, Lee, & Lee, 2010; Minami, 2002). Some cultural communities emphasize orderly and factual recounts, while others encourage embellishments and tall tales (Heath, 1983). Even in mainstream American culture, informal stories about familiar events shared among family and friends may jump from topic to topic, with implicit references, and communication carried in tone and gesture. *Tell Me a Story Mama* (Johnson, 1989) is a wonderful example of this nonchronological, implicit storytelling as a little girl and her mother reminisce about the mother's childhood and the bonds that hold a family together. In advanced storytelling, narrators may explore alternate time ordering, event structure, and character perspectives, such as stream-of-consciousness writing.

Narratives and School

Narrative competence matters for success in school. Despite the many creative ways stories can be structured, children must be able to produce the topic-centered, chronologically ordered, decontextualized narratives valued in school. The kinds of knowledge and language skills needed to produce and understand stories like these begin with early life experiences and continue through school through both direct instruction and incidental learning.

Box 9.1. ***Common Core Expectations for K–4 Narrative Structure***

Kindergarten	Use a combination of drawing, dictating, and writing to narrate a single event or several loosely linked events in the order in which the events occurred, and provide a reaction to what happened.
Grade 1	Write narratives that recount two or more sequenced events, with some details regarding what happened, temporal words to signal event order, and some sense of closure.
Grade 2	Write narratives that recount a well-elaborated event or short sequence of events, with details of actions, thoughts, and feelings as well as temporal words and closure.
Grade 3	Write narratives to develop real or imagined events using effective technique, descriptive details, and clear event sequences. Introduce a situation and a character. Use dialogue, actions, thoughts, and feelings to show character response, along with temporal words and closure.
Grade 4	Write narratives like above with added aspects of a variety of transitional words and phrases, concrete and sensory details to convey experiences precisely, and a coherent conclusion.

Note: Based on National Governors Association Center for Best Practices and the Council of Chief State School officers (2010).

Young children who engage in focused, elaborated talk with their parents about experiences have larger vocabularies and longer, more complex, and informative narratives than children whose parents do not engage in such talk (Peterson, Jesso, & McCabe, 1999; McCabe & Peterson, 1991). Frequency of storybook reading and quality of adult interactions around storybooks have been correlated with language development (De-Temple & Snow, 2003; van Kleeck & Vander Woude, 2003).

In school, narratives are used to teach and display academic knowledge and language skills. Well-formed narratives with elaborated language are specified in the academic standards of many states (Petersen, Gillam, Spencer, & Gillam, 2010). In the Common Core State Standards (National Governors Association Center for Best Practices and the Council of Chief State School Officers [NGA-CSSO], 2010), from kindergarten to twelfth grade, students must comprehend and analyze the structure of literary texts and recount experiences using effective techniques, well-chosen details, and well-structured event sequences. Common Core expects kindergartners to tell a story in time order, second graders to give details of actions, thoughts, and feelings in their narratives, and fourth graders to effectively transmit subtleties of narrative events (Box 9.1).

Language Impairment and Narrative

Narratives are complex discourse events that challenge weak language learners. Expressive narrative structure and quality differentiates elementary grade children with language impairment or learning difficulties from those with typical achievement

(Boudreau & Hedberg, 1999; Catts, Fey, Zhang, & Tomblin, 1999; Fey, Catts, Proctor-Williams, Tomblin, & Zhang, 2004; Gillam & Carlile, 1997; Gillam & Johnston, 1992; Hayward, Gillam, & Lien, 2007; McFadden & Gillam, 1996; Newman & McGregor, 2006). Differences have been found in episodic structure (e.g., Roth & Spekman, 1986; Siegmuller, Ringmann, Strutzmann, Beier, & Marschik, 2012), cohesion (e.g., Liles, 1985, 1987), story art (e.g., Celinska, 2004; Ukrainetz & Gillam, 2009), and comprehension of themes (Williams, 1993). Vocabulary and grammar tested in narrative tasks is a better predictor of persistent language impairment and future academic difficulties than when they are tested in word and sentence tasks (Bishop & Edmundson, 1987; Fazio, Naremore, & Connell, 1996; Wetherell, Botting, & Conti-Ramsden, 2007). This may be due to the greater processing demands of narratives: A marker for children with language impairment is an uneven profile within narratives, with stories that show poor content but grammatical adequacy or elaborated content but grammatical errors (Colozzo, Gillam, Wood, Schnell, & Johnston, 2011).

Fortunately, students with language impairments can improve their narrative performance. Petersen's (2011) systematic review of group and single-subject controlled studies found moderate to large treatment effects for embedding vocabulary, grammar, and narrative structure into activities involving generating and retelling imaginative and personal narratives using children's literature, picture supports, and interactive scaffolding such as prompting, modeling, and recasting. Despite these overall positive findings, Petersen notes that narrative intervention studies have had small sample sizes, limited experimental control, and considerable variation in procedures and materials. I have noticed that some studies provide explicit therapeutic instruction that can be clearly linked to outcomes, while others engage children in unfocused story activities not clearly related to outcomes. Thus, in addition to research evidence, SLPs should continue to use their clinical expertise in designing and delivering quality narrative intervention.

Story Grammar Analysis

Story grammar structure deals with how statements are organized into problem-solution units called *episodes*. Episodes describe an animate being's motivations and goals, the efforts to achieve the goals, and the outcomes of such efforts. Statements composing an episode are causally linked, meaning each physical or mental event occurs as a result of a prior event and leads to another event. Story grammar originated as a mental schema for the way people typically organize their recalls of events (Mandler & Johnson, 1977; Mandler, Scribner, Cole, & DeForest, 1980; Stein & Glenn, 1979). Story grammar is commonly used by teachers and SLPs to guide students in understanding and composing narratives ("grammar" here refers to the macrolevel of discourse organization, not the microlevel of syntactic organization).

Pre-episodic Organization

For young children, narratives may not have a goal-directed unity of action. The narratives of toddlers and preschoolers are most often collections of utterances loosely linked by a theme, temporal order, or prosodic line (Applebee, 1978; Botvin & Sutton-Smith, 1977; Peterson & McCabe, 1983; Sutton-Smith, 1986). Applebee describes five types of early narratives: heaps, sequences, primitive narratives, unfocused chains, and focused chains. A simpler three-way typology, based on Peterson and McCabe, is used here.

The earliest pre-episodic structure is a *descriptive sequence*. These thematic or verse collections of statements do not really have the features of a narrative, but they are called narratives because they occur in contexts where we would expect a narrative (i.e., the child is trying to tell what happened or the adult asks for a story). Box 9.2 presents five frog stories that exemplify different story grammar organizations. The narratives were obtained by McFadden (1998) in a comparison of writing, drawing, and pictographic narrative planning aids for second graders, based on the title and cover picture of a set of frog stories (e.g., Mayer, 1969). The first story is a descriptive sequence: The boy, the dog, and the frog could have caught the fish in any order, with no statement affecting another.

Box 9.2. ***Five Frog Stories***

1) **A Boy, a Dog, a Frog, and a Friend**

One day a boy and a dog and a frog and a friend were fishing. The boy caught one fish. The dog caught two. And the frog caught none.

2) **One Frog Too Many**

Once there was a boy. He loved to play in the pond right across from his house. One day he was playing in the pond. And he found a frog. And he took it home and put it in his room and went to eat dinner. He went back to his room. And there were frogs jumping everywhere. And he kept all the frogs.

3) **Frog, Where Are You? (Version A)**

Once there was a boy, a dog, and a frog. Once the frog left. And he went into the forest. And the boy kept looking for him. And then finally the frog came out. And they all went home.

4) **Frog, Where Are You? (Version B)**

A boy had a frog. The frog jumped off. He went into some trees. In a minute he was no longer in sight The boy called and called for him. And then he saw that his frog had took a scary path. So he decided to take the scary path. So he took the scary path. And it was very, very creepy. Then he saw something jumping. He grabbed it. And it was his frog.

5) **Frog and a Friend**

There was a boy. And he had a frog. Then he lost his frog. He looked downstairs. But he was not there. So he looked in his room. The window was opened. So he went outside. He did not find him. So he looked by a pond. Then he heard a sound. So he went to a hollow log. He found two frogs.

Note: Narratives from second graders, based on the title and cover picture of Mercer Mayer (1969) frog books, using writing, drawing, or pictography as planning notations. Based on McFadden (1998).

The next levels of organization are the *action sequence* and the *reactive sequence.* In an action sequence, the series of actions show temporal relations between the propositions. Action sequences are more like actual narratives: this happened, then this, next this, and last this. These productions can have a sense of a beginning, middle, and end. In the second frog story of Box 9.2, the statements could not be re-ordered without changing the meaning of the story. In *reactive sequences,* causal relations are present, but the complication is resolved automatically, without any goal-directed actions on the part of an agent (Peterson & McCabe, 1983). For example, *The rock crushed the frog* and *So the frog died,* are causally linked, but there were no motivating feelings or attempts to resolve the complication.

Episodic Organization

The first decision in a story grammar analysis is whether or not the story is episodic. If there is a disequilibrium or complication that a character is seeking to resolve, then the story is episodic. If not, then the story is one of the pre-episodic organizations just described. Sometimes, the distinction can be subtle: In the second story back in Box 9.2, the boy's frog turns into *frogs jumping everywhere.* While the story title suggests this ought to have been a concern, the narrator did not present it as such. Thus, that narrative is only a pre-episodic action sequence.

If a narrative is judged to be episodic, the variety of elements present and the type of episode are then determined. There are six elements that comprise an episode (Box 9.3). The elements combine to form episodes. A *basic episode* consists of only three parts: (a) a complication, (b) some evidence of goal directedness, and (c) a consequence. Indications that the character is trying to resolve the complication can vary from obvious statements, such as, *I have a plan to fix that problem,* to more subtle indicators, such as going outside after noticing a pet frog is missing. Other types of episodes have fewer or additional elements (Box 9.4). Young children often produce the first two types: *incomplete* and *abbreviated* episodes that leave the audience wondering "So what happened?" or "How did that happen?" Published literature often involves complicated episodic structure such as *embedded* and *interactive* episodes. In addition to episodic elements, narratives include setting information and additional details of actions, thoughts, or feelings that are not part of the causal problem-solution structure of the episodes.

Episode types can be confusing because different authors define them differently, especially in terms of what is considered a complete episode: Peterson and McCabe (1983) say a complete episode has only the three required elements described previously, while Westby (2012) lists five elements for a complete episode. Few stories, even well-formed, adult ones, include every element in every episode. However, when teaching children to produce episodic stories, SLPs often require all episodic elements plus setting information and sometimes an initial action and a final story resolution. As a result of this variation, I called the minimally complete three-part unit a "basic episode" and leave it to each SLP to decide what constitutes a complete episode for her students' situations.

The two *Frog, Where Are You?* stories from Box 9.2 illustrate two levels of episodic structure. One story is a basic episode consisting of a complication, attempt, and consequence. The other story is an elaborated episode consisting of a complication, three attempts, a plan, a consequence, and a reaction. Not all statements in a story have epi-

Box 9.3. ***Story Grammar Elements***

Elements of an Episode		
Complication	Event that causes an agent's internal state or action; also known as an initiating event, a disequilibrium, or a problem	*The boy's pet frog was gone.*
Motivation	Feeling or cognition resulting from the complication and leading to an attempt, also called internal response or motivating state	*The boy was sad and puzzled.*
Plan	Intentions resulting from motivation, leading to an attempt; also called internal response	*He decided to look in the long grass.*
Attempt	Actions resulting from motivating state and leading to a consequence	*He searched through the grass.*
Consequence	Successful or unsuccessful outcomes of attempts; also called resolutions or outcomes	*He found his frog.*
Reaction	Feeling or cognition resulting from the consequence but not motivating further attempts; end of the episode	*He was glad.*
Nonepisodic Elements		
Setting	Characters, surroundings, and habitual states and actions	*A little boy had a pet frog that he took outside on nice days.*
Actions and States	Isolated emotional or cognitive states and physical actions	*The boy was annoyed at his sister. He went downstairs for breakfast.*

Note: Based on Peterson and McCabe (1983).

sodic roles. Statements that are not causally related to the preceding or following statement are called states and actions. For example, in the fourth frog story, *In a minute, he was no longer in sight* is an action that adds detail, but is not a story grammar element.

Story grammar is a functional analysis, meaning it is concerned, not with specific word choices, but how the words operate in a story. For example, feeling words like *He was sad* can play multiple roles in a story. In the third frog story, the emotional statement of *very, very creepy* is a reaction because it results from the prior statements but does not lead to any subsequent statements. In another story, the same words could be a setting statement. It could even be an emotional motivation if it resulted in the boy altering his search. Multiple episode stories can be complicated because a single statement

Box 9.4. ***Types of Story Grammar Episodes***

Episode Type	Episodic Elements
Incomplete Episode	Complication + Motivating State or Attempt
Abbreviated Episode	Complication + Consequence
Basic Episode	Three parts: Complication + Motivation, Plan, or Attempt + Consequence
Complex Episode	Complication + Multiple Attempts + Consequences
Elaborated Episode	More episodic elements than Basic
Embedded Episode	An episode occurring within a larger episode
Interactive Episode	Two or more characters with interrelated complications

Notes: Based on Peterson and McCabe (1983).

may play two roles, such as a resolution being the next complication or even someone else's complication (e.g., a child finding his lost frog becoming a problem for the mother who doesn't want the frog in the house).

Story grammar analysis can be difficult when narratives lack explicitness. Box 9.5 shows how a story is broken down to determine story grammar elements. For this complex episode story from Box 9.2, some statements were labeled consequences but the role had to be inferred. An explicit statement that one of the two frogs the boy had found was his pet frog or that he preferred these two frogs to his lost frog would more clearly have shown that this consequence resolved the complication.

Development of Episodic Structure

The episodic structure of children's narratives develops from preschool through the elementary grades. The stories of preschoolers are often descriptive, action, and reactive sequences. Goal-directed problem-solution units emerge around kindergarten, with basic episodes clearly established by 8 years of age (Botvin & Sutton-Smith, 1977; Peterson & McCabe, 1983). Internal responses, attempts, and consequences increase in frequency and variety from 8 to 11 years of age (Peterson & McCabe, 1983). The frequency of basic and embedded episodes continues to increase through the age of 14 years (Roth & Spekman, 1986). Written narratives lag in comparison to spoken narratives, especially for beginning writers. The descriptive and action sequence frog stories back in Box 9.2 were written by second graders. Even for older students, writing can affect story performance: Freedman (1987) reported that only half of the fifth-grade students in his study achieved the level of plot development that all of the 7-year-olds in Botvin and Sutton-Smith (1977) had achieved orally.

Box 9.5. ***Story Grammar Analysis of "Frog and a Friend"***

Utterance	Story Grammar Element
There was a boy / and he had a frog.	Setting: Who
Then he lost his frog.	Complication
He looked downstairs.	Attempt 1
But he was not there.	Consequence 1
So he looked in his room.	Attempt 2
The window was opened.	Consequence 2
So he went outside.	Attempt 3
He did not find him.	Consequence 3
So he looked by a pond.	Attempt 4
Then he heard a sound / so he went to a hollow log.	Attempt 5
He found two frogs.	Consequence 4

It is difficult to specify more precisely the developmental order for episodic structure because even simple variations in the elicitation task affect narrative performance (Fiestas & Pena, 2004; Merritt & Liles, 1989; Mills, Watkins, & Washington, 2013; Schneider, 1996; Schneider & Dube, 2005; Ukrainetz & Gillam, 2009). For example, picture sequences and story retelling will dictate story structure more than a single picture or a story starter (e.g., *One dark and gloomy night*...). Elaborated episodes can be obtained from kindergartners with retelling tasks, while scenic pictures tend to result in descriptions even from older students. Thus, it is important for clinicians to notice how tasks affect child narrators in order to elicit more than one narrative in an assessment and to use the same elicitation task to make comparisons between children or over time.

Cohesion Analysis

Cohesion is the glue of discourse. It employs vocabulary and grammar choices to link sentences and sentence parts into larger, understandable units of discourse (Halliday & Hasan, 1976). Cohesion is not specific to narrative, but rather operates in all discourse, from children's earliest conversations to sophisticated expository texts.

Cohesive Conjunction

Conjunctive cohesion involves conjunctions and adverbials to indicate relations between sentences. They can express additive (*in addition to*, *also*), adversative (*however*, *instead*), temporal (*first, next*), causative (*because, as a result*) or continuative (*anyway*) meanings (Halliday & Hasan, 1976). For example, consider: *She had guests coming to dinner. She needed to go to the store. She did not have time. She changed the menu plans at the last minute. It was a success.* While each sentence is semantically and syntactically correct, the relations between these sentences become clearer with the addition of *so, however, as a result, nevertheless.*

Narratives tend to unfold in chronological manner, so unlike exposition, sequential adverbials are not critical. However, it is helpful to model and elicit from young students *then* and *next* for each event to obtain an orderly action progression. Any step out of chronological order requires time words (e.g., *Before that happened, years earlier*). A key feature of narratives is causal relations among episodic elements. Words like *because, so,* and *as a result* help create the links from complication through the efforts to resolve it to the final reaction.

Conjunctive cohesion enables both clear communication and sophisticated composition. Basic connectives help organize narrative and exposition (e.g., reducing use of *and* and increasing appropriate use of *or, but, because, first, next, last*). Older students will benefit from increasing their awareness and appropriate use of more nuanced connectives (e.g., *instead, despite, in order to, nevertheless*) in their compositions.

Pronominal Reference

Pronominal reference involves ties between pronouns and their referents. *Anaphoric ties* occur when the referent precedes the pronoun, such as in *Lily reached for her coat. Cataphoric ties,* which sound more literary, reverse the order of referent and pronoun: *Her name was Lily.* Both these are *endophoric*, meaning that the referents are located in the words alone, which is the aim for school discourse. In informal conversations, where physical cues or background information are available, cohesion may be *exophoric*, meaning the referent is outside the text (e.g., *Put that here*).

Pronominal reference is a critical device for keeping track of characters within narratives. Clear pronominal reference is challenging when there are several possible referents or there are several sentences between the referent and the pronoun. Even fine literature can stumble on this: There are many confusing passages about the multiple female characters in Jane Austen's (1811/1996) *Sense and Sensibility.*

Cohesive use of pronouns differs from syntactic usage. At the syntactic level, correctness is the issue (e.g., the referent is a boy and the pronoun is in object position, so *him* is used). In contrast, for cohesive usage, appropriateness and clarity must be judged (e.g., Is it clear to whom *him* refers?). While syntactic use of pronouns is mastered early in childhood, clear cohesive use can be challenging in informal discourse even for adults, leading many a listener to wonder who did what to whom. Conventions in writing dictate that a pronoun is used only 2 to 3 times before the referent is restated, even if there is only one referent involved, and that the referent is restated at the beginning of each paragraph (notice that none of these paragraphs start with "it").

Other Cohesive Devices

There are other cohesive devices that are less commonly addressed in language intervention. In addition to pronominal reference, there are other reference ties (e.g., *this/that, a/the, here/there*). The articles *a/the* are among the earliest grammatical morphemes to be produced, but it takes longer to know to use "a boy" for the first mention and "the boy" thereafter. In the very simple descriptive sequence frog story back in Box 9.2, *a/the* are contrasted correctly, possibly because this was by a second grader rather than a preschooler.

Lexical cohesion involves simply repeating a word from a prior sentence, such as the word *frog* in the frog stories. Lexical repetition is the most basic way to cohere sentences. Lexical substitution involves the provision of different words that have the same referent (e.g., *pet* and *amphibian* both refer to the *frog* initially mentioned). Children do not typically provide substitutions spontaneously (Crowhurst, 1987) and need explicit guidance and an adequate vocabulary to do so.

Parallel structures involve repeating a syntactic structure. The same words can be used or the similarity can derive from the syntactic structure. The first frog story in Box 9.2 has parallelism in the "caught" sentences. The third frog story creates parallelism by linking the sentences with *and* and similar length sentences. Sentences with predicate lists that lack parallel structure do not flow well (e.g., *I see an otter, bears sunning, lizards are there, and a raccoon runs away*).

Finally, ellipsis, or zero substitution, involves the omission of an item retrievable from elsewhere in the text (e.g., *May I go to the store? You may*). Ellipsis is frequent in conversation but also occurs in formal writing (for example, here, I omitted saying *ellipsis* again after *but*). Elliptical sentences would be odd or incomplete in isolation, but make sense in position between other sentences. Ellipsis of "fish" can be seen in the first frog story in which "the boy caught one fish and the dog caught two." Ellipsis instruction would focus what can be left out when.

Development of Cohesion

Children move from exophoric to endophoric cohesion from preschool into the school years as they learn to represent their meanings more fully in their words (Crowhurst, 1987; Pelligrini, Galda, & Rubin, 1984). Connective cohesion develops from additive to temporal to causal relations. By 8 years of age, children can generally provide clear and cohesive spoken narratives (Pelligrini et al., 1984). However, sophistication in cohesion, especially in written contexts, continues to develop through adolescence and beyond (Bennett-Kastor, 1984; Crowhurst, 1991; Klecan-Aker & Hedrick, 1985; Neuner, 1987). Over the grades, students learn to use a greater variety and frequency of cohesive forms. For pronominal reference, the distance between cohesive ties increases, while ambiguous usage decreases.

Story Art Analysis

Story grammar and cohesion deal mainly with the transmission of information or what is called the *referential function of narrative* (Labov, 1972). Skillful narrators also strive to achieve the expressive function of narrative: obtaining emotional involvement and rhetorical appreciation from their audience (Kernan, 1977; McFadden & Gillam, 1996). Story art analysis attempts to quantify the language elements that take a story from a

Box 9.6. ***Holistic Rating of Story Quality***

Rating	Rubric
Weak	Description or poorly organized, uncaptivating story
Adequate	Event recount without a central climax, a bare-bones narrative with no elaboration, a narrative without an ending, or a confusing narrative with strong descriptive elements
Good	Captivating story that contained problems and resolutions, even with some organizational problems
Strong	Easily understood narrative with clear, integrated story line, elaboration, interesting word choices, and captivating features like climax, ending twist, or personal voice

Note: Based on McFadden and Gillam (1996, p. 203).

basic event recount to something more. It involves the effective techniques and descriptive details specified in the Common Core.

There is no single accepted method of evaluating the artfulness of a story. Not only are there many ways of providing "the magic of story," but what one audience may appreciate may not be valued by another. Overall quality can be rated with a single holistic score or with several trait scores. For example, Box 9.6 shows a holistic scoring rubric developed by McFadden and Gillam (1996), based on what a team of scorers found they valued from spoken and written imaginative narratives from elementary grade students. Holistic scoring is often used for standardized exam essays. Such rubrics, especially if they are developed based on actual student stories, can provide useful estimates of overall quality. However, global scores provide little guidance for instruction and are not sensitive to learning progress.

Expressive Elaboration

Expressive elaboration analysis provides a quick, reliable way to track individual elements that contribute to narrative quality. Expressive elaboration was derived from a more impressionistic linguistic analysis called *high point*, which examines how narrator perspective is transmitted to an audience and how the emotional *high point* or climax of a personal narrative is expressed (Kernan, 1977; Labov, 1972; Labov & Waletsky, 1967; Peterson & McCabe, 1983). Ukrainetz et al. (2005) developed this more quantified version using a large corpus of imaginative narratives elicited during norming of the *Test of Narrative Language* (TNL; Gillam & Pearson, 2004). Story art, as measured with expressive elaboration, is more likely to be displayed in tasks for which students have a sense of performance or storytelling (Mills et al., 2013; Ukrainetz & Gillam, 2009). For example, Mills et al. found that higher expressive elaboration scores were obtained from a wordless picture book narration than a fictional story when elicited in a formal testing context.

Box 9.7. *Elements of Elaborated Expression*

Element	Example
Appendages (story signals)	
Introducer	*One day, Once there was a boy.*
Abstract	*Frog, Where Are You? This is about how a boy lost his pet frog.*
Theme	*The frog was still lost. The boy kept looking for his lost frog.*
Coda	*The boy learned a lesson that day about looking after his frog.*
Ender	*The end*
Orientations (beyond a simple setting)	
Name	*Joe, Mrs. Pendley*
Relation	*teacher, sister, pet*
External	*It rained all day, playing in the pond*
Personality	*The boy was lonely, the frog was brave*
Evaluations (emphasis and detail)	
Modifiers	*quickly, so, almost, really, weird, three**
Expression	*woke up on the wrong side of the bed, as fast as he could, all the way*
Repetition	*very very fast, looked and looked*
Internal	*decided, thought, wanted, angry, tired*
Dialogue	*He called, "Where are you?!"*

*Interesting modifiers, not common words like *some, other, another, little, outside, after*

Note: Elements from Ukrainetz et al. (2005) and Ukrainetz and Gillam (2009).

In expressive elaboration analysis, presence of 14 artful elements is scored across three categories: appendages, orientations, and evaluations (see Box 9.7). Appendages involve statements that introduce, comment on, and conclude the story. These are elements that clearly distinguish an intentional story from more casual event recounts. A story title or foreshadowing statement like, "This story will be about . . ." is an *abstract.* "Once there was . . ." is an *introducer,* while "The End" is an *ender.* A *theme* is a restatement of the main idea during the story. Stories can conclude with the sophisticated element of *coda*, which wraps up the story with a lesson learned or brings the listener back to the present. Orientations provide background information on the habitual actions and nature of the characters or the surrounding *external conditions*. They general occur at the beginning of the narrative. Rather than simply stating "a boy and a frog," specific character *names*, *relations*, and *personality* features receive credit.

The largest category is evaluations. Evaluations are elements that contribute detail or emphasis. Word *repetition* and character *dialogue* are easy to use. *Expressions* such as "quick as a wink" tend to stand out, but interesting *modifiers* are more difficult to judge reliably. In our research, we excluded very common descriptors that did not add noticeable quality to the narratives, such as "more, good, another." If we had heard or read the students' stories rather than reading transcripts, we might have added an element to score paralinguistics, such as intonation, gestures, and or exclamatory punctuation.

In addition to story art elements, a story's plot shape can be noted (Box 9.8). Evaluations are generally concentrated around the complication where an emotional high point or climax is desired (Labov, 1972; Peterson & McCabe, 1983). Not all stories have a climax and a resolution. Some stories are confusing descriptions or flat recounts. Some children build their stories toward a climax, but end there, leaving the audience hanging about the outcome.

Looking back at Box 9.2, we see that none of the frog stories provide appendages or orientations. The narrators do not foreshadow the point of the story or end with a moral. They also give little orientation information. The first two stories have no high points: They simply describe and list events. However, there are some artful elements.

Box 9.8. *The Shape of a Story Plot*

Disorganized		Are you just confused?
Flat		Is the story ho-hum?
End at high point		Are you left hanging on the cliff?
Classic		Does the story build to a climax then resolve in a satisfying way?

Note: Based on Labov (1972) and McCabe and Peterson (1983).

The first story has the appendage, *One day*, cueing that the narrator intended this to be a story. The second story has an orientation about the boy's love of playing in the pond. The fourth story shows clear story art mainly through evaluation elements. There are details about where the frog went and how fast he disappeared. The climax of the story is the lengthy search, with words like *kept looking* and *finally* and the parallel structures about taking a scary path. Descriptive words (*creepy, scary, grab*) and word repetitions (*called and called*; *very, very*) are used. In contrast, the final frog story, which has similar episodic complexity and control of cohesion, has little story art. This story reads like an event report, rather than a desperate search for a beloved pet.

Development of Story Art

Story art shows some developmental progression. Using Labov's (1972) high-point scheme with structured elicitations, Peterson and McCabe (1983) found that preschoolers tend toward confused or chronological plot patterns in their personal narratives while 5-year-olds often end at the high point. By 7 years of age, half of the children in Peterson and McCabe's study could tell personal narratives with the components of a classic plot, although end-at-high-point was a noticeable occurrence until 9 years of age. For narratives in natural preschool conversational settings from 3- to 6-year-olds, Kuntay (2002) found that variations in provision of a coherent problem-resolution structure were more dependent on characteristics of the recounted event and the interactional situation than on developmental features.

A high-point study by Celinska (2004) of personal narratives elicited in naturalistic conversations from 10-year-olds with and without learning disabilities showed globally coherent personal narratives with classic structure for the typically developing children. Celinska found that boys with learning disabilities had narratives of similar length, organization, and coherence to those of their typically developing peers, but the narratives of the girls with learning disabilities were significantly lower. The investigators linked this lower performance to a body of research that has shown lower verbal and cognitive skills and more severe academic deficits for girls than for boys diagnosed with learning disability.

In terms of types of story art elements, appendages are infrequent in children's personal and imaginative narratives but increase in presence and variety from 5 to 12 years of age (Peterson & McCabe, 1983; Ukrainetz et al., 2005; Umiker-Sebeok, 1979). Orientations are more common and increase further with age in the detail, variety, and tailoring to audience needs. Evaluations are most frequent and showed the greatest age changes, particularly between 5 and 9 years of age. Interesting word choices and character dialogue are the most frequent evaluation elements. Sophistication in artful storytelling continues to develop through adolescence (Kernan, 1977; Labov, 1972).

For story art, audience matters. Haden, Haine, and Fivush (1997) found that girls from 3 to 6 years of age provided longer stories than did boys, with more orientations and evaluative elements, in their past-event reminiscing with parents (despite a lack of overall difference in language ability). Although mothers and fathers did not differ in how they structured their reminiscing, the children provided more orientations and evaluations with their fathers than with their mothers. Lai et al. (2010) compared South Korean and Taiwanese preschoolers on the narrative structure of stories about visiting the doctor.

Box 9.9. ***The Art of Present Tense and Short Sentences to Build Tension***

8-year-old: One afternoon, Ashley and Alex and their family went camping. And then Ashley and Alex got lost in the woods. They found this park. And then they saw (thr*) five aliens in the park. Ashley wanted to introduce herself. *Alex says no. And then she grabs him and walks. And they say hi. And then he runs away. And then she tries to go find him.* But she never found him. So she played with the aliens and asked them to come again.

11-year-old: One beautiful foggy Tuesday morning, Michael and Sonia, they were brother and sister. So they woke up. And they decided to go for a walk. Since it was summer they loved the nice breeze and the weather. So they decided to go out to a forest just to watch and sit down and talk and enjoy the weather. *And then they hear some noises. They hear people talking. They hear things moving. So they go out. And they go behind a bush. And they look. And they can't believe their eyes...*

Note: Stories based on the *Test of Narrative Language* (Gillam & Pearson, 2004) alien picture.

Taiwanese children at 3 and 4 years of age used more internal state terms while the Korean children transmitted those meanings through intonation, gesture, and eye contact. However, the Korean children showed a developmental leap to more sequentially organized and elaborated narratives at 5 years. These differences were consistent with differences in the emphases of the preschool curriculum and caregiving interactions in the two countries.

The expressive elaboration analysis captures story art sufficiently for treatment goals and tracking progress. However, SLPs should be open to creative alternatives not included in the scoring scheme. For example, stories are usually told in past tense. Present tense or tense mixing by children is typically an indicator of linguistic immaturity or lack of discourse control. Also, students are encouraged to use long, complex sentences. However, strategic use of short, present tense sentences can add emphasis and build tension. Box 9.9 shows effective use of these typically undesirable features. These stories could serve as models to show students that grammar is not just a tedious requirement but has communicative power.

The Tools of Narrative Intervention

For any job, the right tools make all the difference. Before turning from analyzing narratives to teaching them, Box 9.10 presents an assessment tool: a list of guiding questions to help an SLP work through the three prior analyses. In this section, three tools (or structural scaffolds) for teaching narrative structure will be presented: children's literature, customized stories, and a visual representational system.

Children's Literature

Good literature serves as a model, a context, and a source of inspiration for the lessons to follow. Children's literature consists of picture books and chapter books enjoyed by

Box 9.10. ***A Pocket Reference for Narrative Structure Evaluation***

What to Look for in Story Grammar Analysis

1. Is there a complication that bothers someone in the story?
2. If no, then is this pre-episodic story organized descriptively, chronologically, or causally?
3. If yes, then what is the best episode—is there a basic, complex, or elaborated episode?
4. Which episodic elements (e.g., motivation, plan, attempt, reaction) are present?
5. Are the elements expressed explicitly or are you inferring a lot?

What to Look for in Cohesion Analysis

1. Does the story hang together clearly?
2. Are there helpful connecting words like *first, next, however*?
3. Is it clear to which characters the pronouns are referring?
4. Can reference be made clearer by changing more pronouns to nouns?
5. Do the incomplete sentences have appropriate ellipses?

What to Look for in Story Art Analysis

1. Overall, does this sound like a story and is it enjoyable?
2. Are there appendages, orientations, and evaluations?
3. Which elements are present and which are missing?
4. Which are used well and which need strengthening?
5. Which of the weaker elements would be simple to teach?

both children and adults. Even general interest science books can qualify as children's literature. Merriam-Webster (1993) defines *literature* as writings in prose or verse having excellence of form or expression concerning ideas of permanent or universal interest. Thus, children's literature is any quality written composition that has value beyond its instructional applications.

Children's literature is an immensely useful intervention tool. Storybook sharing introduces children to the language, ideas, and types of information important in narrative (Justice, Skibbe, & Ezell, 2006; van Kleeck & Vander Woude, 2003). Parents and teachers prompt children to predict events (e.g., *What do you think will happen next?*), analyze motivations (e.g., *Why did the wolf huff and puff and blow the house down?*), or identify print (e.g., *What does N-O say?*). Story structure and many other language skills are readily and enjoyably taught through children's literature (Owens & Robinson, 1997; Ukrainetz, 2005; Ukrainetz & Trujillo, 1999). Reading and guided discussion of storybooks with follow-up activities lead to better story retelling, book concepts, and story comprehension (Martinez & Roser, 1985; Morrow, 1985; Morrow, O'Connor, & Smith 1990). Morrow and colleagues found that simply repeatedly reading the same story promotes more child talk, more spontaneous commenting, and increased quality of thought. Young children can become familiar enough with favorite storybooks that they can recite entire stories (Sulzby & Zecker, 1991; Trousdale, 1990).

Books should be selected based on the narrative structure and the appeal of the story. Look for stories that either present a clear central problem with multiple attempts to solve or ones that contain several problems that are resolved more quickly. Interactive episodes in which one character's solution becomes another's problem are more challenging but can be handled with story grammar charts that identify the dual functions of particular actions or feelings. For younger students, a clear pattern is important. Older students gain important text analysis skills through the process of breaking a more complicated story into its episodic elements.

Patterns can be made clearer by simplifying the story text. Covering the printed text with clear packing tape allows written changes to be taped on the page without damaging the book. The reading level of books is of little concern because the students are not reading independently. Students often enjoy books above and below their grade level. Authors often write in the same style across books, allowing repeated, similar opportunities for episodic structure and other language goals.

In Ukrainetz (2006), I describe favorite books that employ examples of particular episodic structures, cohesion, and narrative art. Beck and McKeown's *Text Talk* (2005) provides storybooks and lessons that include attention to story structure. Storybooks that demonstrate multiple basic or complex episodes are listed in the Appendix. Acquiring children's literature is an inexpensive and enjoyable habit, but there is no need for a large collection. Just one good book can start an SLP on the path to literature-based intervention.

Customized Narratives

Customized narratives are created specifically for teaching particular skills. They lack the artistry and nuance of good literature, but this simplicity is their strength, clearly and repeatedly presenting particular structure and content in a whole discourse context. Sets of customized narratives can be constructed that are controlled for complexity, length, interest, and other factors. Story structure and other language skills have been successfully assessed and taught through customized narratives (Hoffman, Norris, & Monjure, 1990; Petersen et al., 2010; Petersen et al., 2014; Spencer & Slocum, 2010; Swanson, Fey, Mills, & Hood, 2005).

One way to customize is to abbreviate a storybook. After a book is shared, for follow-up activities, the story is shortened and simplified so children can retell the whole story and include target language structures. A few key illustrations of the basic storyline or of a single episode can be copied and made into sequenced picture cards. Clinicians can create short stories that parallel a storybook's theme and plot (Gillam, Gillam, & Reece, 2012; Gillam, McFadden, & van Kleeck, 1995; Gillam & Ukrainetz, 2006). These are often followed by student-created parallel stories that contain the target language skills. These parallel stories are first steps toward students creating their own stories with the target structures. I used to have students cooperatively create stories after sharing *Promise Is a Promise* (Munsch & Kusugak, 1988). While I wanted the theme to reflect broken promises, my students' parallel creations invariably fell along a boogeyman theme. This was fine because the intervention goal of students generating stories with complex episodes was still achieved.

Both imagination and life events can be the source of customized narratives. For the cohesion lesson in this chapter, I composed a fanciful story to demonstrate vague pronoun use. For demonstrating complex episodes and pictographic sketching, I made up a story about my brother and I paddling a canoe that tipped over and our attempts to rescue ourselves. Some interventions are organized fully around customized narratives (Petersen et al., 2010; Petersen et al., 2014; Spencer & Slocum, 2010; Swanson et al., 2005).

Pictography

The notation system of pictography allows quick and easy representation of events and story elements for recall, revision, and retelling. The spoken word is a transitory acoustic event. Children can enjoy listening to whole stories, but for the conscious, sustained attention needed to improve language and learning skills, the SLP needs a way to represent stories visually. This visual aid should be quick, easy, and flexible. It can be a tool used only by the SLP, but is more powerful if it can be used by the students themselves in the speech room, and even better, in the classroom.

For fluent readers and writers, the answer is obviously writing. However, for our students, writing is too slow and laborious, and the act of text production so fully occupies mental resources that story content and organization are forgotten. The dynamic and pleasurable interchange involved in narrative creation grinds to a halt under the demand of student writing. In the early grades, drawing may be used as a prewriting strategy to stimulate story ideas and record some story details. However, drawings are of limited aid. The static, detailed images do not lend to depicting story progression and the aesthetic involvement distracts from the task of narrative composition.

An alternative notation that employs aspects of both drawing and writing is picture-writing or *pictography*. Pictography represents concepts rather than specific words, like Chinese logography. Pictography is composed of simple sketches, organized in a left-to-right, chronological order, with scenes linked by arrows (see Box 9.11). The beginning, middle, and end of a story can be represented with just three sketches or branching sketches can represent complex episodic structure (see Box 9.12).

Pictography is a type of graphic organizer, along with semantic webs, which uses networks of words, phrases, or pictures to depict relationships among concepts. Content-based pictography, in which the icons represent specific story events, is presented here. An alternative system is structure-based icons, such as story grammar markers, which can be used to guide any story construction. For example, Box 9.13 shows story grammar icons from the Petersen and Spencer *Story Champs* program (see http://www.languagedynamicsgroup.com).

In introducing pictography, the SLP demonstrates pictographic creation. The SLP thinks aloud during the process, demonstrating how to select key ideas, make simple sketches, and organize the content (e.g., *This story is about a boy named Tim . . . here,*

Box 9.11. ***Clinician's Pictography for Scary Visitor Story***

This is for a story about a scary visitor who turned out to be the children's mother with a new hairstyle and hands full of groceries.

Note: From "Stickwriting Stories: A Quick and Easy Narrative Representation Strategy," by T. A. Ukrainetz, 1998, *Language, Speech, and Hearing Services in Schools*, 29, p. 199. Copyright 1998 by American Speech-Language-Hearing Association. Adapted with permission.

Box 9.12. ***Clinician's Pictography for Multiple Attempts to Solve a Problem***

This is for a story about multiple attempts to right a tipped-over truck.

Note: From "Stickwriting Stories: A Quick and Easy Narrative Representation Strategy," by T. A. Ukrainetz, 1998, *Language, Speech, and Hearing Services in Schools, 29*, p. 205. Copyright 1998 by American Speech-Language-Hearing Association. Reprinted with permission.

Box 9.13. ***Story Grammar Icons***

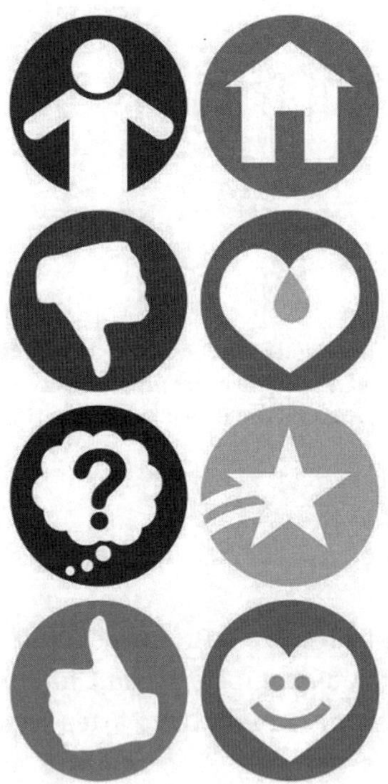

Note: From *Story Champs* intervention program (see http://www.languagedynamicsgroup.com). The icons are also color-coded (e.g., thumb-down problem icon is red and the thumb-up successful consequence is green).

a quick stickman for Tim . . . one day, Tim was out walking in the park . . . a tree will remind me this is a park . . . on a snowy winter day . . . one snowflake, that is just enough to remember . . .). To avoid the *I can't draw* syndrome, the SLP comments on how poor her first stick figure is, but says that it is *good enough to remember.* As the students plan their own stories, the SLP talks them through their sketching, commenting on their selection of key notations and organization from left-to-right with arrows. To keep the focus on the story rather than on the drawing, emphasis is always on *quick and easy* and *just enough to remember.* The only writing used is key words or punctuation symbols, such as *No!* or a question mark in a thought bubble above a character's head.

Pictography provides memory and organizational support, allowing planning, recall, discussion, and revision of any event-based discourse, including narratives, historical annals, and procedural exposition. As students compose or revise, they can add, subtract, reorder, or revise events and details. Pictography serves as both an SLP's tool to support language development and as a student's compensatory strategy for story composition. Pictography works well in cooperative groups where one student can devote attention to story generation while another student scribes. Pictography can also assist listening comprehension: The SLP periodically stops reading a story and has students

Box 9.14. ***Frog in a Restaurant Pictography by a Second Grader***

Note: From "Stickwriting Stories: A Quick and Easy Narrative Representation Strategy," by T. A. Ukrainetz, 1998, *Language, Speech, and Hearing Services in Schools, 29*, p. 200. Copyright 1998 by American Speech-Language-Hearing Association. Reprinted with permission.

sketch that part of the story. Students are likely to attend better and recall more than if they simply listen.

I first started using pictography to plan customized narratives before treatment sessions, and realized that, if a literate, competent adult found this tool useful, my students might find it likewise. Students from kindergarten to seventh grade learned easily what they called "stickwriting" (see Box 9.14). Students used it willingly within the speech room and, with teacher permission, in the classroom. One teacher commented that she was able to skip the first written draft on story compositions. Many SLPs with whom I have shared pictography have found it to be easy to use and very helpful. My research has shown this quick, flexible tool increases the length, temporal organization, and quality of students' narratives compared to story planning with pictures or writing (McFadden, 1998; Ukrainetz, 1998).

A benefit for older students might be improving their note taking. Students tend to write full sentences with correct spelling even when explicitly directed to use only key words (Bereiter & Scardamalia, 1982). I found that my sixth and seventh graders started spontaneously "sneaking" in written words (see Box 9.15). They had to be fast enough to keep within the *quick and easy* rule. Because they tended to select only words that they could have pictorially represented, they used mainly nouns and verbs, which proved to be an effective key word strategy. I have not tried intentionally teaching this strategy to older students, but it certainly has potential.

Teaching Narrative Structure

Early Narrative Intervention

The first step in narrative intervention for very young or expressively limited students is having them independently recount a simple event. As Westby (1985) long ago explained, narratives are particularly good for bridging between the conversational style of the home and the literate style of decontextualized, monologic discourse expected in

Box 9.15. ***Key Word Planning Arising From Pictography***

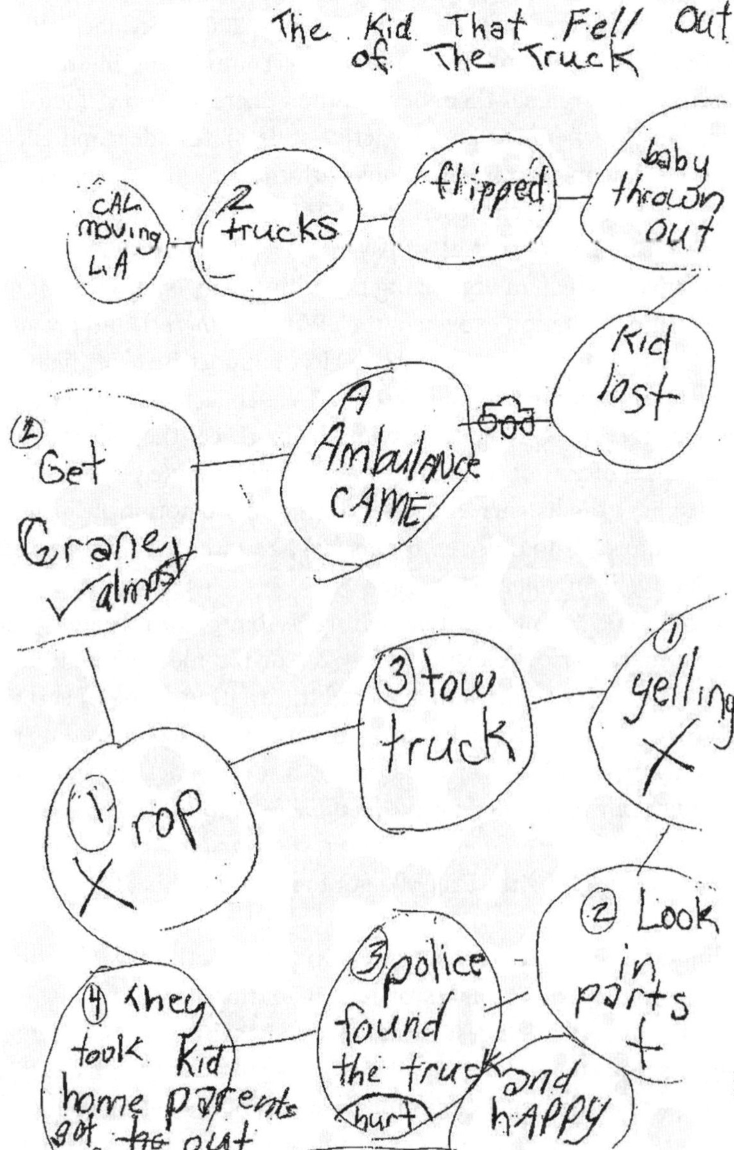

Note: This is for a two-episode story of righting a tipped-over truck and finding a lost child by older elementary students with learning disabilities.

school. Preschoolers and kindergartners with language impairment are likely to have small vocabulary, short utterances, grammatical immaturities, and passive communicative styles. Despite these language limitations, these young students have the potential to tell whole stories by themselves. The aim of this level of narrative intervention is to help students become more active, independent communicators.

Young children do not typically tell stories at home as single-speaker monologues. Rather, they are surrounded by familiar peers and adults who support their tellings as coconstructed events in dramatic play, conversation, and storybook sharing (e.g., Galda & Pelligrini, 1988; Haden et al., 1997; Kuntay & Senay, 2003; McCabe & Peterson, 1991; Odegaard, 2007; Sachs, Goldman, & Chaillé, 1985). Young children are supported into verbal reminiscing that stretches them beyond their "here and now" focus.

Some parents and teachers use an interactive style that models and elicits a variety of story structure elements in story creations with their children, while others provide much less support (Harris & Schroeder, 2012). The narrative support that children receive can be conversational, historical, or psychological (Ninio & Snow, 1996). Conversational support involves help in organizing the telling (e.g., *First, we went where?*), presenting the types of information expected (e.g., *Who was there?*), and providing needed details (e.g., *Tell what you said to him*). Historical support involves helping the child sort out what happened in the original event and which aspects of the event should be recounted for the story. Psychological support helps reveal the teller's emotional perspective. A narrator is often not trying to report information (e.g., about scary dogs) so much as trying to have the listener understand his or her emotions (e.g., fear and courage). Adults help put words to those emotions (e.g., *You were really scared of that dog! I was too. I was shaking in my shoes!*).

A basic way to support young children's tellings is to provide repeated, guided opportunities to tell a simple story. For example, my 2-year-old niece had an important personal narrative to tell. She and her father shared the exciting event several times on the way home and then she told it to each family member she encountered. With each telling, Amy could say more of it on her own: *getting a sliver in her eye, going to the doctor to get it out, lying calmly on the table while he pulled it out, the doctor saying how brave she was, how most little kids would have cried but she didn't, and daddy buying her a toy as a reward for her courage.* By the time she got to her aunt, this little girl could tell her heroic tale independently.

Story retelling and dramatic reenactments in group settings with adult guidance allow children to manage long pieces of text (Culatta, 1994; Morrow, 1985, 1986). Owens and Robinson (1997) suggest using group chanting to retell segments of stories to allow peer support and not call notice to any single child. Physical movements that accompany parts of the story can improve recall of the action elements of narratives (Biazak, Marley, & Levin, 2010). The group setting results in more thematically relevant and coherent storytelling through children emulating or elaborating on the topics and content presented by other children in their narratives (Kuntay & Senay, 2003).

While the rich language of children's literature is beneficial for developing vocabulary and grammar comprehension, for the purpose of children's retelling, a predictable retelling routine and a salient, repeatable version of the story are helpful. Kirchner's (1991) reciprocal reading involves a structured sequence of prompting involving a reading a book aloud several times and pausing at moments for a Cloze response (finishing the adult's sentence). With repetitions, the Cloze response involves progressively longer segments of text. Finally, the child can retell the story in its entirety. From these retell-

Box 9.16. *Preschoolers' Cooperative Mushroom Story Pictography*

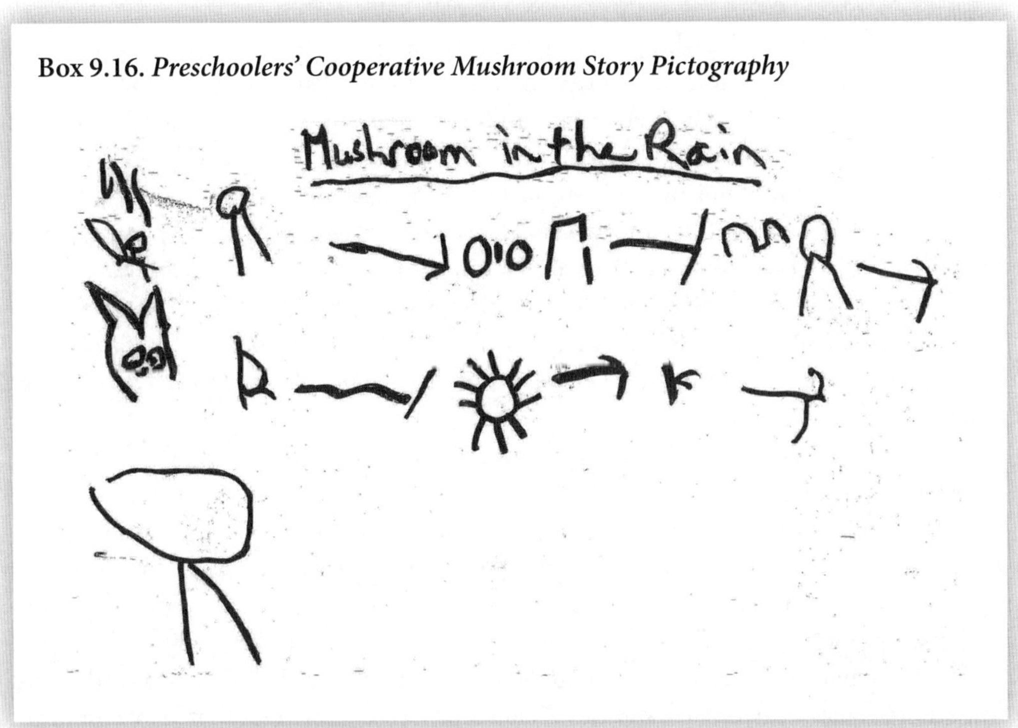

ings, children can move to creating parallel stories. Visual props available in preschool classrooms, such as felt boards and toys, can support the tellings. For retelling *Mushroom in the Rain* (Ginsburg, 1974), I emphasize the repetitive requests to get under the mushroom and skip the fox encounter and mushroom growth lesson. One group of preschoolers invented the refrain "Skootch over!" each time a critter responded that there was not space for anyone else. Even the least able child could call out that refrain.

For the retellings, on a whiteboard (or an iPad), the SLP pictographically sketches the desired story events, with the children assisting the retelling. The children then chorally retell the story from the pictography. After that, the SLP goes back to the beginning, and asks each child to take a turn telling one episode, with prompting as needed. Then, each child has a turn drawing a scene while another child narrates the episode (see Box 9.16). This pictography may not be recognizable for long, but it serves as a temporary mnemonic for an immediate retelling. The activity culminates with each child telling the entire story from the student or SLP pictography.

With these guided repeated tellings, children learn to tell the main events of the story in order on their own. While additional language skills, such as character feelings and causal relations may be modeled, the aim is for each student to produce a short independent recount of the basic "beginning/middle/end" sequence of the story. The students are then ready to tackle the internal structure of their stories, which is where this chapter goes next.

Teaching Story Grammar

Story grammar structure is commonly taught in the elementary grades. While terminology varies, students often have a basic understanding of setting, character, problem, feelings, and solutions. Teaching students how these elements combine into elaborated episodic structure and how to identify them in literature leads to better metalinguistic awareness, discourse comprehension, and narrative production. Controlled studies have shown that students taught to stop during listening or reading to answer questions or map story structure improve in their narrative comprehension (Babyak, Koorland, & Mathes, 2000; Crabtree, Alber-Morgan, & Konrad, 2010; Taylor, Alber, & Walker, 2002). Students taught story structure improve their own narrative structure and content compared to prior performance or control groups (Goddard & Sendi, 2008; Hayward & Schneider, 2000; Justice, Swanson, & Buehler, 2008; Nathanson, Crank, Saywitz, & Ruegg, 2007; Petersen et al., 2010; Petersen et al., 2014; Spencer & Slocum, 2010; Swanson et al., 2005).

Graves and Montague (1991) compared using story grammar cue cards to planning time alone or planning time and a simple review of story grammar elements. Upper elementary and junior high students used story grammar cue cards during planning time to remind them of basic episodic elements to include in their narrative compositions: setting, character, problem, plan, and ending. The students checked off story parts as they incorporated them. This procedural facilitation helped students self-monitor and resulted in longer and qualitatively better stories compared to the other two conditions. The students with learning disabilities dictated or wrote narratives that were similar in quality to those of typically achieving students.

In a multiple baseline across subjects design, Crabtree, Alber-Morgan, and Konrad (2010) taught three high school students with learning disabilities to identify story grammar elements in short fiction stories to improve their reading comprehension. In the baseline phase, students read and listed facts from the story and then were tested on story comprehension. In the treatment phase, for each story, students stopped at three points to identify story grammar elements. Then they were tested on story fact recall and comprehension questions. The results showed a noticeable improvement in reading comprehension during and following treatment.

Several treatment studies address the episodic structure of children's own narrative productions. Hayward and Schneider (2000) taught 13 4- to 6-year-olds with language impairment in a lagged baseline mixed group and single-subject design. Treatment involved narrating picture cards, story retelling, reformulating scrambled stories, using iconic story grammar cue cards, and identifying missing story components. Children learned to include more story information and moved from pre-episodic sequences into episodic structure. In contrast, Westerveld and Gillon (2008) were less successful with their story grammar intervention. Ten 7- to 9-year-old children with reading disabilities, in a treatment versus waitlist control design, received 12 hours of treatment over 6 weeks involving analyzing children's literature for story grammar elements using interactive scaffolding and story mapping. Mercer Mayer frog stories were retold and comprehension questions asked about them. Results showed improved story comprehension but no change in story retelling.

In a more systematic manner, Swanson et al. (2005) provided a 6-week narrative-based language intervention to 10 7- to 8-year-old children with language impairments. Posttest performance was compared to normative data obtained in the same way in another study. The treatment involved a cyclical goal attack strategy for three syntactic and three narrative goals with repeated retellings of customized stories and generations of stories from pictures. Results showed that, while syntactic complexity did not improve, eight of the children made significant improvements on a narrative quality rating that assessed complexity of episodic structure and character, setting, and ending. Other recent controlled studies have successfully taught multiple language skills, including story grammar structure, in a similar, but even more structured, manner (Petersen et al., 2010; Petersen et al., 2014; Spencer & Slocum, 2010).

As the foregoing research demonstrates, explicit attention to story grammar, cohesion, and story art improves children's narrative production and comprehension across a range of ages and ability levels. Students can learn to analyze and produce simple stories that incorporate complex, elaborated episodic structure. The general instructional approach involves introducing the elements of story grammar, teaching students to identify these elements in children's literature or customized narratives, and then using this organization to develop or improve their own narratives. It is important to provide repeated opportunities to hear, analyze, and create narratives; interactive scaffolds that systematically support learning; and the structural scaffolds of stories with obvious story grammar structure and visual cues such as pictography.

Before sharing the story, to determine initial knowledge of story grammar terminology, the SLP asks children to generate story parts: what comes at the beginning of a story, what comes in the middle, and how stories end. As the children offer words, the SLP introduces terminology for each element and enters the term in a story grammar chart (see Box 9.17). The storybook is introduced by showing the cover and reading the title of the book. The children guess the who, where, and when of the story, a problem that the story is about, and how the character might attempt to resolve the problem. The SLP fills in the prediction column of the chart with key words for each of the story grammar elements.

After predicting the story, the SLP begins reading. The whole story is read once with only brief attention to analysis of each episode. The complication, internal responses, attempts to solve, and consequence are charted. Predictions are compared to actual happenings. After reading the storybook, the episodes are reviewed with greater attention to each episode and story grammar element. Not all the story grammar chart boxes may be filled (e.g., *There was only one episode with one problem that was solved in this story. And the author did not say how the girl felt about losing her dog. What words give you an idea how she feels?*). Using pictography, each student charts an episode from the story. The students then cooperatively retell the entire story by narrating individual pictographically represented episodes.

Next, students create their own parallel stories using pictography. The planning starts with the setting components of who, when, and where in the first scene. Then the actions leading to a complication are sketched. Multiple attempts to resolve each complication are sketched like back in Box 9.13. Students take turns narrating their stories from their pictography. They can revise or add an attempt and then tell the story again. To provide another opportunity to internalize this structure, students can take turns playing reporter. They interview and audio-record each other about each adventure, with attention to the attempts made and their consequences. The recordings are played and the students identify and discuss the attempts and alternatives.

Box 9.17. ***Story Grammar Chart***

Element	Prediction	Episode #1	Episode #2	Episode #3
Setting: • Characters • Place • Time				
Complication (problem)				
Motivation (feeling)				
Plan (idea to solve)				
1st Attempt and Conse-quence (outcome)				
2nd Attempt and Consequence				
Last Attempt and Final Consequence (resolution of complication)				
Reaction (end feeling)				

In addition to the multiple attempts to resolve the problem, the SLP can teach other story grammar elements. Students often fail to employ the thought and feeling words involved in character descriptions, motivations, plans, and reactions (Peterson & McCabe, 1983). Montague and Graves (1992) included three lessons on character development in their study. They started with a discussion of the role of characters in stories: their identities, attributes, and motivations as well as the problems they encounter. The instructor and students identified action, idea, and emotion words that described the characters in the shared storybook. The next lesson involved writing a cooperative story with a focus on the affective qualities of the characters. The instructor recorded ideas on chart paper. The students then dictated the story using story grammar cue cards. The story was written on chart paper and audio-recorded. The instructor created a customized story with all words reflecting character cognition and emotion deleted, which the students then evaluated and compared to their cooperative story.

Montague and Graves (1992) went beyond "inserting feeling words" to considering the feelings and cognitions that were appropriate to a character and related well to the story. A further refinement would be to focus more on the functional role of the targeted story grammar element (e.g., the many ways *sad* can be used, as an enduring character attribute, an emotional motivation, or a final reaction that ends a story episode).

Teaching Pronominal Reference

Cohesion involves the appropriate selection of words and phrases to unify text. It overlaps with syntax (conjunction, predicate structure, pronouns) and vocabulary (lexical variety). However, a cohesion skill that can be taught without calling on a lot of language resources is pronominal reference.

Stories with multiple characters provide opportunities for confusing and clear pronoun reference. After listening to the story for enjoyment, a second reading with discussion is used to become aware of character reference (see Box 9.18). The basic strategy is to go backward (anaphoric reference) to the closest noun mentioned to determine to whom the pronoun is referring. However, students may need to go further back until the reference makes sense (e.g., *The fox ate the bird, the mouse, and the bug. Then he felt full*) or even determine whether it is cataphoric instead (e.g., *He was so satisfied, that old fox*). After making students aware of how pronominal reference operates, a customized confusing parallel story can analyzed (see Box 9.19). The students then cooperatively fix the story and discuss their decisions. Students can delete nouns to make their own confusing story versions and have a peer figure out what is happening in the story and make plausible improvements. Cohesion is best taught through written work. Students do not need to be competent readers or writers, but print allows everyone to look at the words used.

Making Stories Artful

The best way to start instruction in story art is to enjoy a good story together. Awareness of story art comes through the ways storybooks are commonly shared, such as noting an intriguing title, the way the story grabs your interest, how certain phrases are used as refrains, and which words are particularly evocative. Word choices, word repetitions,

Box 9.18. ***Pronominal Reference Discussion***

One day an ant was caught in the rain. "Where can I hide?" he wondered. He saw a tiny mushroom peeking out of the ground in a clearing, and he hid under it. He sat there, waiting for the rain to stop. We just read about an ant. Here the author says "ant" to let us know who the first character is. Then the author uses the pronoun "he." How many times does the author use "he"? Is four times okay? Does this confuse the reader? Why is this okay?

On the next page, a butterfly joins him. *The butterfly says, "I am so wet I cannot fly,"* and the ant says, *"How can I let you in? There is barely room enough for one."* Who is "I"? Is "I" the butterfly or the ant? Does that depend on who is talking?

Here it says: *They moved over, and there was room enough for the sparrow.* Now the animals are described as "they." Who are "they"? How do we know?

Now the fox says, *"Have you seen the rabbit? Which way did he go?"* Who is "he"? "He" refers back to rabbit. How do we know? We go back to the the first place that identifies an animal. *The fox turned up his nose, flicked his tail, and ran off.* "His nose" is whose nose? That is the fox. How do you know that? What did we do for the rabbit? Yes, we go backward to find out to which character the pronoun refers.

Note: Based on Ukrainetz (2006).

Box 9.19. ***A Confusing Story Involving an Owl, a Woodpecker, a Termite, and Two Boys.***

There once was an owl who tried to make a home in a hole in a tree. It couldn't fit. It was too big. So it asked it to make the hole bigger. It tried, but it couldn't. So it asked it to help. It tried to help, but it was in a hurry. It needed a hole to lay its eggs. Then they came along. It asked them to help. He stood on his shoulders. He reached up high with his pocket knife. He dug out more space in the hole. He peered in and thought that was a comfy, safe spot for his new friend. They found there was enough space for all of them, so they decided to try to live together. They thanked them and moved into their new home, just in time for it to lay its eggs. The end.

Note: Based on Ukrainetz (2006).

parallel structures, sentence structure, dialogue, and even punctuation choices can be noted. After raising awareness of what makes a story appealing, a few artful techniques are then taught.

Artful story instruction starts with explicit identification of the elements that will be treatment goals from the three categories of appendages, orientations, and evaluations. Both the SLP and students should know exactly what is being taught and learned among the myriad ways of telling a good story. Students learn those elements through rich models, simple models, and their own creations. A familiar storybook is revisited, with the targeted story art elements identified and discussed. A written list of targets helps keep everyone focused and allows tracking of the times the students have identified or produced the artful element (see Box 9.20). Moving from listening to speaking

Box 9.20. ***Tracking Opportunities for Learning Story Art Treatment Targets***

Student Name:				
Activity Date:				
Activity ➔ **Objectives ⬇**	**Storybook**	**SLP Story**	**Student Story**	**Story Sharing**
Appendage Title Theme Coda				
Orientation Personality				
Evaluation Repetition Expression				

Note: Check each time a student identifies, discusses, or uses a targeted story art element. Amount of support can be noted: 1 = independent; 2 = a response prompt; 3 = multiple prompts.

begins by having children narrate a familiar storybook in which the story art elements have been introduced. If the focus is on evaluations within the climax, then just the exciting middle event may be reshared.

Stories with classic plot shapes work well for story art instruction. The classic plot shape involves a buildup to the climax, then a resolution and a windup that ends in a satisfying manner (Labov, 1972). Suspenseful stories usually have a classic shape and a lot of evaluations, such as interesting modifiers, expressions, repetitions, and dialogue. The frog books involve both these as the boy strives to resolve whatever muddle he and his frog find themselves in.

Students can create their own versions of the frog books. An artful but abbreviated story can be built from a small number of pictographic scenes or a selection of the illustrations. Narratives created in earlier story grammar or cohesion lessons can be used. With the visual support and the familiarity of the plotline, referential information and organization is already present, so the focus can be kept on artful elements. Key words and phrases can be written into each pictographic scene or picture by the SLP as the artful revisions and additions are made.

For *Frog, Where Are You?*, the SLP might model beginning a story with appendage and orientation elements. The rather bland story title could be improved (e.g., *Curiosity Almost Killed the Frog*). Teachers sometimes call this, or other audience-catching beginnings, the "story hook." Then an orientation about the characters' personalities could be modeled (e.g., *Once there was a boy who truly loved his little frog. His frog was always curious*). Known vocabulary is used, because the aim is to teach how to use words artfully, not to teach new words. The SLP can show how a theme is used by restating the title after beginning the story (e.g., *This was the day the frog's curiosity would get it in trouble*). This thematic repetition does not add linguistic load to the telling and helps the student keep his story on track.

Next, a few evaluative elements are introduced around the climax of the story. For the lost frog story, the climax is the search, when tension is built by making the boy progressively more concerned and frustrated. A simple element is repetition: No additional vocabulary is needed. Existing descriptive words can be expanded into expressive phrases with simple additions like changing *worried* or *anxious* to *even more worried* or *even more anxious*. Similes are fun and manageable for students: Instead of being knocked over a cliff by a deer, he is *tossed in the air like a rag*. Saying "even more" or "like an X" several times can be repetitious, but practice using one structure is needed to learn the words well enough for independent use.

Finally, story endings can be addressed. Instead of just resolving the complication and expressing a reaction to fulfill story grammar expectations, one more step achieves a satisfying ending. A coda about what the main character learned can be taught. After the boy finds his frog and expresses relief, a coda can be added, such as *Both the boy and his frog learned that curiosity is okay—but tell your friends where you are going*. Voila! An artful story that holds an audience from beginning to end has been created.

After discussing and revising the story for the treatment goals, the story is told and retold, as a pleasurable telling as well as for skill practice. Students should be encouraged to use intonation and gesture in their story sharing. Story art is meant to be enjoyed by both narrator and audience, so this part should be fun. Giving students periodic opportunities to share their creations with an audience, whether through presentations or publications, will increase their motivation to engage in the work of crafting quality stories (Hubbard, 1985).

The possibilities of story art are almost endless, but only a few can be systematically addressed in language intervention. However, SLPs who use literature and storytelling during intervention will provide rich incidental exposure to artful storytelling. Story art is modeled every time a good story is shared and an element is noted. Even brief attention can reap later rewards as students remember and refer to favorite stories for ideas and inspiration.

Conclusion

Stories occupy much of the daily discourse of home and school. This chapter addressed teaching children to tell whole stories on their own, with improved story grammar, cohesion, and story art. Increasing awareness and use of these types of story structure improves narrative production and comprehension for students from preschool and into the secondary grades. Research evidence and clinical experience have shown that intervention that has an explicit skill focus over repeated opportunities, with systematic scaffolding from clinician interactions around children's literature, customized narratives, and pictography, leads to noticeable improvements in students' narrative competence.

References

Alborough, J. (1993). *Cuddly dudley*. Cambridge, MA: Candlewick Press.

Applebee, A. N. (1978). *The child's concept of story: Ages two to seventeen*. Chicago, IL: University of Chicago Press.

Austen, J. (1811/1996). *Sense and sensibility*. New York, NY: Dover.

Babyak, A. E., Koorland, M., & Mathes, P. G. (2000). The effects of story mapping instruction on the reading comprehension of students with behavioral disorders. *Behavioral Disorders, 25*, 239–258.

Bauman, R. (1986). *Story, performance, and event: Contextual studies of oral narrative*. Cambridge, MA: Cambridge University Press.

Beck, I. L., & McKeown, M. G. (2005). *Text talk*. New York, NY: Scholastic.

Bennett-Kastor, T. L. (1984). Cohesion and predication in child narrative. *Journal of Child Language, 13*, 353–370.

Bereiter, C., & Scardamalia, M. (1982). From conversation to composition: The role of instruction in a developmental process. In R. Glaser (Ed.), *Advances in instructional psychology* (Vol. 2, pp. 1–64). Hillsdale, NJ: Erlbaum.

Biazak, J. E., Marley, S. C., & Levin, J. R. (2010). Does an activity-based learning strategy improve preschool children's memory for narrative passages? *Early Childhood Research Quarterly, 25*, 515–526.

Bishop, D. V. M., & Edmundson, A. (1987). Language-impaired 4-year-olds: Distinguishing transient from persistent impairment. *Journal of Speech and Hearing Disorders, 52*, 156–173.

Botvin, G. J., & Sutton-Smith, B. (1977). The development of structural complexity in children's fantasy narratives. *Developmental Psychology, 13*, 377–388.

Boudreau, D. M., & Hedberg, N. L. (1999). A comparison of early literacy skills in children with specific language impairment and their typically developing peers. *American Journal of Speech–Language Pathology, 8*, 249–260.

Brett, J. (1989). *The mitten*. New York, NY: Putnam.

Brett, J. (1992). *Trouble with trolls*. New York, NY: Penguin.

Brown, M. (1985). *Arthur's tooth*. New York, NY: Little, Brown.

Bruner, J. (1986). *Actual minds, possible worlds*. Cambridge, MA: Harvard University Press.

Catts, H. W., Fey, M. E., Zhang, X., & Tomblin, J. B. (1999). Language basis of reading and reading disabilities: Evidence from a longitudinal investigation. *Scientific Studies in Reading, 3*, 331–361.

Celinska, D. K. (2004). Personal narratives of students with and without learning disabilities. *Learning Disabilities Research and Practice, 19*, 83–98.

Colozzo, P., Gillam, R. B., Wood, M., Schnell, R. D., & Johnston, J. R. (2011). Content and form in the narratives of children with specific language impairment. *Journal of Speech, Language, and Hearing Research, 54*, 1609–1627.

Crabtree, T., Alber-Morgan, S. R., & Konrad, M. (2010). The effects of self-monitoring of story elements on the reading comprehension of high school seniors with learning disabilities. *Education and Treatment of Children, 22*, 187–203.

Cronin, D., & Lewin, B. (2000). *Click, clack, moo*. New York, NY: Scholastic.

Crowhurst, M. (1987). Cohesion in argument and narration at three grade levels. *Research in the Teaching of English, 21*, 185–201.

Crowhurst, M. (1991). Interrelationships between reading and writing persuasive discourse. *Research in the Teaching of English, 25*, 314–338.

Culatta, B. (1994). Representational play and story enactments: Formats for language intervention. In J. F. Duchan, L. E. Hewitt, & R. M. Sonnenmeier (Eds.), *Pragmatics: From theory to practice* (pp. 105–119). Englewood Cliffs, NJ: Prentice-Hall.

DeTemple, J. M., & Snow, C. E. (2003). Learning words from books. In A. van Kleeck, S. A. Stahl, & E. B. Bauer (Eds.), *On reading books to children* (pp. 16–36), Mahwah, NJ: Erlbaum.

Fazio, B. B., Naremore, R. C., & Connell, P. J. (1996). Tracking children from poverty at risk for specific language impairment: A 3-year longitudinal study. *Journal of Speech and Hearing Research, 39*, 611–624.

Fey, M. E., Catts, H. W., Proctor-Williams, K., Tomblin, J. B., & Zhang, X. (2004). Oral and written story composition skills of children with language impairment. *Journal of Speech, Language, and Hearing Research, 47*, 1301–1318.

Fiestas, C. E., & Pena, E. D. (2004). Narrative discourse in bilingual children: Language and task effects. *Language, Speech, and Hearing Services in Schools, 35*, 155–268.

Freedman, A. (1987). Development in story writing. *Applied Psycholinguistics, 8*, 153–170.

Galda, L., & Pelligrini, A. D. (1988). Children's use of narrative language in peer interaction. In B. A. Rafoth & D. L. Rubin (Eds.), *The social construction of written communication* (pp. 175–194). Norwood, NJ: Ablex.

Gee, J. P. (1989). Two styles of narrative construction and their linguistic and educational implications. *Discourse Processes, 12*, 287–307.

Gillam, R. B., & Carlile, R. M. (1997). Oral reading and story retelling of students with specific language impairment. *Language, Speech, and Hearing Services in Schools, 28*, 30–42.

Gillam, R. B., & Johnston, J. R. (1992). Spoken and written language relationships in language/learning-impaired and normally achieving school-age children. *Journal of Speech and Hearing Research, 35*, 1303–1315.

Gillam, R., McFadden, T. U., & van Kleeck, A. (1995). Improving narrative abilities: Whole language and language skills approaches. In M. E. Fey, J. Windsor, & S. F. Warren (Eds.),

Language intervention: Preschool through the elementary years (pp. 145–181). Baltimore, MD: Brookes.

Gillam, R. B., & Pearson, N. (2004). *Test of narrative language.* Austin, TX: PRO-ED.

Gillam, R. B., & Ukrainetz, T. A. (2006). Language intervention through literature-based units. In T. A. Ukrainetz (Ed.), *Contextualized language intervention: Scaffolding preK–12 literacy achievement* (pp. 59–94). Austin, TX: PRO-ED.

Gillam, S. L., Gillam, R. B., & Reece, K. (2012). Language outcomes of contextualized and decontextualized language intervention. *Language, Speech, and Hearing Services in Schools, 43,* 276–291.

Ginsburg, M. (1974). *Mushroom in the rain.* New York, NY: Aladdin.

Goddard, Y. L., & Sendi, C. (2008). Effects of self-monitoring on the narrative and expository writing of four fourth-grade students with learning disabilities. *Reading and Writing Quarterly: Overcoming Learning Difficulties, 24,* 408–433.

Graves, A., & Montague, M. (1991). Using story grammar cueing to improve the writing of students with learning disabilities. *Learning Disabilities Research and Practice, 6,* 246–250.

Haden, C. A., Haine, R. A., & Fivush, R. (1997). Developing narrative structure in parent-child reminiscing across the preschool years. *Developmental Psychology, 33,* 295–307.

Halliday, M. A. K., & Hasan, R. (1976). *Cohesion in English.* London, UK: Longman.

Harris, Y. R., & Schroeder, V. M. (2012). What the Berenstain Bears can tell us about school readiness: Maternal story grammar style and preschool narrative recall. *Journal of Early Childhood Research, 10,* 176–195.

Hayward, D. V., Gillam, R. B., & Lien, P. (2007). Retelling a script-based story: Do children with and without language impairments focus on script and story elements? *Journal of Speech-Language Pathology, 16,* 235–245.

Hayward, D., & Schneider, P. (2000). Effectiveness of teaching story grammar knowledge to preschool children with language impairment. *Child Language Teaching and Therapy, 16,* 255–284.

Heath, S. B. (1983). *Ways with words: Language, life, and work in communities and classrooms.* Cambridge, UK: Cambridge University Press.

Hoffman, P. R., Norris, J. A., & Monjure, J. (1990). Comparison of process targeting and whole language treatments for phonologically delayed preschool children. *Language, Speech, and Hearing Services in Schools, 21,* 102–109.

Hubbard, R. (1985). Second graders answer the question "Why publish?" *Reading Teacher, 38,* 658–662.

Hudson, J. A., & Shapiro, L. R. (1991). From knowing to telling: The development of children's scripts, stories, and personal narratives. In A. McCabe & C. Peterson (Eds.), *Developing narrative structure* (pp. 89–136). Hillsdale, NJ: Erlbaum.

Johnson, A. (1989). *Tell me a story mama.* New York, NY: Orchard Books.

Johnston, J. R. (1982). Narratives: A new look at communication problems in older language-disordered children. *Language, Speech, and Hearing Services in Schools, 13,* 145–155.

Johnston, J. R. (2008). Narratives: Twenty-five years later. *Topics in Language Disorders, 28,* 93–98.

Justice, E. C., Swanson, L. A., & Buehler, V., (2008). Use of narrative-based language intervention with children who have cochlear implants. *Topics in Language Disorders, 28*, 149–161.

Justice, L. M., Skibbe, L., & Ezell, H. (2006). Using print referencing to promote written language awareness. In T. A. Ukrainetz (Ed.), *Contextualized language intervention* (pp. 389–428). Austin, TX: PRO-ED.

Kernan, K. (1977). Semantic and expressive elaborations in children's narratives. In S. Ervin-Tripp & C. Mitchell-Kernan (Eds.), *Child discourse* (pp. 91–102). New York, NY: Academic Press.

Kirchner, D. M. (1991). Reciprocal book reading: A discourse-based intervention strategy for the child with atypical language development. In T. M. Gallagher (Ed.), *Pragmatics of language: Clinical practice issues* (pp. 307–332). San Diego, CA: Singular.

Klecan-Aker, J. S., & Hedrick, D. L. (1985). A study of the syntactic language skills of normal middle school children. *Language, Speech, and Hearing Services in the Schools, 16*, 2–7.

Kuntay, A. C. (2002). Occasions for providing resolutions (or not) in Turkish preschool conversational narratives. *Narrative Inquiry, 11*, 411–450.

Kuntay, A. C., & Senay, I. (2003). Narratives beget narratives: Rounds of stories in Turkish preschool conversations. *Journal of Pragmatics, 35*, 559–587.

Labov, W. (1972). *Language in the inner city*. Philadelphia: University of Pennsylvania Press.

Labov, W., & Waletzky, J. (1967). Narrative analysis: Oral versions of personal experience. In J. Helm (Ed.), *Essays on the verbal and visual arts* (pp. 12–44). Seattle: University of Washington Press.

Lai, W. -F., Lee, Y. -J., & Lee, J. (2010). Visiting doctors' offices: A comparison of Korean and Taiwanese preschool children's narrative development. *Early Education and Development, 21*, 445–467.

Liles, B. Z. (1985). Cohesion in the narratives of normal and language disordered children. *Journal of Speech and Hearing Research, 28*, 123–133.

Liles, B. Z. (1987). Episode organization and cohesive conjunctives in narratives of children with and without language disorder. *Journal of Speech and Hearing Research, 30*, 185–196.

Longacre, R. (1983). *The grammar of discourse*. New York, NY: Plenum.

Lunge-Larsen, L., Preus, M., & Arroyo, A. (1999). *The legend of the lady slipper*. Boston, MA: Houghton Mifflin.

Mandler, J. M., & Johnson, N. S. (1977). Remembrance of things parsed: Story structure and recall. *Cognitive Psychology, 9*, 111–151.

Mandler, J. M., Scribner, S., Cole, M., & DeForest, M. (1980). Cross-cultural invariance in story recall. *Child Development, 51*, 19–26.

Martinez, M., & Roser, N. (1985). Read it again: The value of repeated readings during story time. *Reading Teacher, 38*, 782–786.

Mayer, M. (1969). *Frog, where are you?* New York, NY: Dial.

McCabe, A. (1991). Preface: Structure as a way of understanding. In A. McCabe & C. Peterson (Eds.), *Developing narrative structure* (pp. ix–xvii). Hillsdale, NJ: Erlbaum.

McCabe, A., & Peterson, C. (1991). Getting the story: A longitudinal study of parental styles in eliciting narratives and developing narrative skill. In A. McCabe & C. Peterson (Eds.), *Developing narrative structure* (pp. 217–254). Hillsdale, NJ: Erlbaum.

McFadden, T. U. (1998). The immediate effects of pictographic representation on children's narratives. *Child Language Learning and Teaching, 14*, 51–67.

McFadden, T. U., & Gillam, R. (1996). An examination of the quality of narratives produced by children with language disorders. *Language, Speech, and Hearing Services in the Schools, 27*, 48–57.

Merriam-Webster. (1993). *Merriam-Webster's collegiate dictionary* (10th ed.). Springfield, MA: Author.

Merritt, D. D. & Liles, B. Z. (1989). Story grammar ability in children with and without language disorder: Story generation, story retelling, and story comprehension. *Journal of Speech and Hearing Research, 30*, 539–552.

Michaels, S. (1991). The dismantling of narrative. In A. McCabe & C. Peterson (Eds.), *Developing narrative structure* (pp. 303–352). Hillsdale, NJ: Erlbaum.

Miller, J. P. (1954/1982). *The little red hen*. New York, NY: Golden Books.

Mills, M. T., Watkins, R. V., & Washington, J. A. (2013). Structural and dialectal characteristics of fictional and personal narratives of school-age African American children. *Language, Speech, and Hearing Services in Schools, 44*, 211–223.

Minami, M. (2002). *Culture-specific language styles: The development of oral narrative and literacy*. Tonawanda, NY: Multilingual Matters.

Moffett, J. (1968). *Teaching the universe of discourse*. New York, NY: Houghton Mifflin.

Montague, M., & Graves, A. (1992). Teaching narrative composition to students with learning disabilities. In M. Pressley, K. R. Harris, & J. T. Guthrie (Eds.), *Promoting academic competence and literacy in schools* (pp. 261–277). San Diego, CA: Academic Press.

Morrow, L. M. (1985). Reading and retelling stories: Strategies for emergent readers. *The Reading Teacher, 38*, 871–875.

Morrow, L. M. (1986). Effects of structural guidance in story retelling on children's dictation of original stories. *Journal of Reading Behavior, 18*, 135–152.

Morrow, L. M., O'Connor, E. M., & Smith, J. K. (1990). Effects of a story reading program on the literacy development of at-risk kindergarten children. *Journal of Reading Behavior, 22*, 255–272.

Munsch, R., & Kusugak, M. (1988). *A promise is a promise*. Toronto, Canada: Annick.

Munsch, R., & Martchenko, M. (1996). *Stephanie's ponytail*. Toronto, Canada: Annick.

Nathanson, R., Crank, J. N., Saywitz, K. J., & Ruegg, E. (2007). Enhancing the oral narratives of children with learning disabilities. *Reading and Writing Quarterly, 23*, 315–331.

National Governors Association Center for Best Practices and Council of Chief State School Officers (2010). *Common Core State Standards for English Language Arts and Literacy in History/Social Studies, Science, and Technical Subjects*. Washington, DC: Author. Retrieved from http://www.corestandards.org/

Neuner, J. L. (1987). Cohesive ties and chains in good and poor freshman essays. *Research in the Teaching of English, 21*, 92–105.

Newman, R. M., & McGregor, K. K. (2006). Teachers and laypersons discern quality differences between narratives produced by children with or without SLI. *Journal of Speech, Language, and Hearing Research, 49*, 1022–1036.

Ninio, A., & Snow, C. E. (1996). *Pragmatic development.* Boulder, CO: Westview.

Odegaard, E. E. (2007). What's worth talking about? Meaning-making in toddler-initiated co-narratives in preschool. *Early Years: An International Research Journal, 26*, 79–92.

Owens, R. E., & Robinson, L. A. (1997). Once upon a time: Use of children's literature in the preschool classroom. *Topics in Language Disorders, 17*(2), 19–48.

Pelligrini, A., Galda, L., & Rubin, D. (1984). Context in text: The development of oral and written language in two genres. *Child Development, 55*, 1549–1555.

Petersen, D. (2011). A systematic review of narrative-based language intervention with children who have language impairment. *Communication Disorders Quarterly, 32*, 207–220.

Petersen, D., Gillam, S. L., Spencer, T., & Gillam, R. B. (2010). Effects of literate narrative intervention on children with neurologically based language impairments: An early stage study. *Journal of Speech, Language, and Hearing Research, 53*, 961–981.

Petersen, D. B., Brown, C. L., Ukrainetz, T. A., DeGeorge, C., Spencer, T. D., & Zebre, J. (2014). Systematic individualized language intervention on the personal narratives of children with autism. *Language, Speech, and Hearing Services in Schools, 45*, 67–86.

Peterson, C., Jesso, B., & McCabe, A. (1999). Encouraging narratives in preschoolers: An intervention study. *Journal of Child Language, 26*, 49–67.

Peterson, C., & McCabe, A. (1983). *Developmental psycholinguistics: Three ways of looking at a child's narrative*. New York, NY: Plenum.

Roth, F. P., & Spekman, N. J. (1986). Narrative discourse: Spontaneously generated stories of learning-disabled and normally achieving students. *Journal of Speech and Hearing Disorders, 51*, 8–23.

Sachs, J., Goldman, J., & Chaillé, C. (1985). Narratives in preschoolers' sociodramatic play: The role of knowledge and communicative competence. In L. Galda & A. D. Pelligrini (Eds.), *Play, language, and stories: The development of children's literate behavior* (pp. 45–61). Norwood, NJ: Ablex.

Schneider, P. (1996). Effects of pictures versus orally presented stories on story retellings by children with language impairments. *American Journal of Speech–Language Pathology, 5*, 86–95.

Schneider, P., & Dube, R. V. (2005). Story presentation effects on children's retell content. *American Journal of Speech–Language Pathology, 14*, 52–60.

Scieszka, J. & Smith, L. (1989). *The true story of the three little pigs*. New York, NY: Viking.

Scollon, R., & Scollon, S. B. K. (1988). *Narrative, literacy, and face in interethnic communication.* Norwood, NJ: Ablex.

Shaw, N. (1986). *Sheep in a jeep.* Boston, MA: Houghton Mifflin.

Siegmuller, J. Ringmann, S., Strutzmann, E., Beier, J., & Marschik, P. B. (2012). A crucial marker for specific language impairment at the preschool age: Narrative competence. *Sprache - Stimme - Gehor, 36*, 65–75.

Spencer, T. D., & Slocum, T. A. (2010). The effect of narrative intervention on story retelling and personal story generation of preschoolers with risk factors and narrative language delays. *Journal of Early Intervention, 32*, 178–199.

Stein, N. L., & Glenn, C. G. (1979). An analysis of story comprehension in elementary school children. In R. Freedle (Ed.), *New directions in discourse processing* (Vol. 2, pp. 53–120). Norwood, NJ: Ablex.

Stevens, J. (1987) *The three billy goats gruff*. New York, NY: Harcourt.

Stevens, J. (1995). *Tops and bottoms*. New York, NY: Harcourt.

Sulzby, E., & Zecker, L. B. (1991). The oral monologue as a form of emergent reading. In A. McCabe & C. Peterson (Eds.), *Developing narrative structure* (pp. 175–214). Hillsdale, NJ: Erlbaum.

Sutton-Smith, B. (1986). The development of fictional narrative performances. *Topics in Language Disorders, 7*(1), 1–10.

Swanson, L. A., Fey, M. E., Mills, C. E., & Hood, L. S. (2005). Use of narrative-based language intervention with children who have specific language impairment. *American Journal of Speech–Language Pathology, 14*, 131–143.

Taylor, L., Alber, S., & Walker, D. (2002). The comparative effects of a modified self-questioning strategy and story mapping on the reading comprehension of elementary students with learning disabilities. *Journal of Behavioral Education, 11*, 69–87.

Trousdale, A. M. (1990). Interactive storytelling: Scaffolding children's early narratives. *Language Arts, 67*, 164–173.

Ukrainetz, T. A. (1998). Stickwriting stories: A quick and easy narrative representation strategy. *Language, Speech, and Hearing Services in Schools, 29*, 197–206.

Ukrainetz, T. A. (2005). What to work on how: An examination of the practice of school-age language intervention. *Contemporary Issues in Communication Sciences and Disorders, 32*, 108–119.

Ukrainetz, T. A. (2006). Teaching narrative structure: Coherence, cohesion, and captivation. In T. A. Ukrainetz (Ed.), *Contextualized language intervention: Scaffolding preK–12 literacy achievement* (pp. 195–246). Austin, TX: PRO-ED.

Ukrainetz, T. A., & Gillam, R. B. (2009). The expressive elaboration of imaginative narratives by children with specific language impairment. *Journal of Speech, Language, and Hearing Research, 52*, 883–898.

Ukrainetz, T. A., Justice, L. M., Kaderavek, J. N., Eisenberg, S. L. Gillam, R. B., & Harm, H. M. (2005). The development of expressive elaboration in fictional narratives. *Journal of Speech, Language, and Hearing Research, 48*, 1363–1377.

Ukrainetz, T. A., & Trujillo, A. (1999). "You know, I just don't know what else you'd do?" Five SLPs' perspectives on children's literature in speech–language intervention. *Contemporary Issues in Communication Sciences and Disorders, 26*, 35–48.

Umiker-Seboek, D. J. (1979). Preschool children's intraconversational narratives. *Journal of Child Language, 6*, 91–109.

van Kleeck, A., & Vander Woude, J. (2003). Booksharing with preschoolers with language delays. In A. van Kleeck, S. A. Stahl, & E. B. Bauer (Eds.), *On reading books to children: Parents and teachers* (pp. 58–94). Mahwah, NJ: Erlbaum.

Westby, C. E. (1985) Learning to talk—talking to learn: Oral-literate language differences. In C. S. Simon (Ed.), *Communication skills and classroom success: Therapy methodologies for language-learning disabled students* (pp. 181–213). San Diego, CA: College-Hill.

Westby, C. E. (2012). Assessing and remediating text problems. In H. W. Catts, & A. G. Kamhi (Eds.), *Language and reading disabilities* (3rd ed., pp. 163–225). Boston, MA: Allyn & Bacon.

Westerveld, M. F., & Gillon, G. T. (2008). Oral narrative intervention for children with mixed reading disability. *Child Language Teaching and Therapy*, *24*(1), 31–54.

Wetherell, D., Botting, N., & Conti-Ramsden, G. (2007). Narrative skills in adolescents with a history of SLI in relation to nonverbal IQ scores. *Child Language Teaching and Therapy*, *23*, 95–113.

Williams, J. P. (1993). Comprehension of students with and without learning disabilities: Identification of narrative themes and idiosyncratic text representations. *Journal of Educational Psychology*, *85*, 631–641.

Appendix: Children's Literature With Episodic Structure

Episode With Multiple Attempts to Solve	
Frog, Where are You? (Mayer, 1969)	One of six wordless picture books about the adventures of a boy and his frog. Language structures and complexity can be matched to the student. All six books recommended. Photocopies well for picture sequence cards.
The Little Red Hen (Miller, 1954/1982)	Hen asks all her friends to help her plant her garden; they all turn her down. She plants by herself and the others learn to regret their laziness.
Cuddly Dudley (Alborough, 1993)	Penguin seeks solitude from his numerous brethren, but decides he has too much aloneness. Main episode with multiple attempts to solve, leading to two brief complications with the last unresolved.
Arthur's Tooth (Brown, 1985)	Arthur's tooth is loose but it won't come out. He is last in his class to lose a tooth. He and his friends try all sorts of ways to get his tooth to fall out.
Stephanie's Ponytail (Munsch & Martchenko, 1996)	Stephanie wants to be different. Her classmates laugh at her but keep copying her. Eventually, she gets the last laugh. The problem is implied rather than stated.
Click, Clack, Moo: Cows That Type (Cronin & Lewin, 2000)	Cows go on strike for better living conditions, then the hens join them. After their dispute is resolved, the ducks embark on their own labor action. Including the farmer's point of view makes it an interactive episode, but it is essentially a simple story.

Multiple Basic, Complex, Elaborated, or Interactive Episodes	
The Three Billy Goats Gruff (Stevens, 1987)	Three goats try to cross a bridge guarded by a troll. The first two succeed by offering a bigger brother. The biggest goat really solves the problem.
The Mitten (Brett, 1989)	A series of animals crawl into a stretchy mitten lost in the snow. The text involves unclear reasons for crawling in, but could be modified.
Sheep in a Jeep (Shaw, 1986)	A verse story of the misadventures of six sheep in a jeep. The language is sparse, so the episodic structure is easy to identify.
Mushroom in the Rain (Ginsburg, 1974)	A series of creatures seek to hide from the weather. Each asks to get under the crowded mushroom, is rebuffed, but asks again, and space is made. Also good for wet words, conditional verbs, and persistent requesting.
Trouble with Trolls (Brett, 1992)	A very modern little girl and her dog encounter troublesome trolls while ski mountaineering. Multiple episodes on the way up the mountain and the final deal-making squeezes in five quick episodes.
The True Story of the Three Little Pigs (Scieszka & Smith, 1989)	Wolf's version of the tale: all the pig trouble arose out of innocent attempts to borrow a cup of sugar. The alternate perspective is enjoyed by older students and leads into creating other parallel bent-fairytales.
Promise Is a Promise (Munsch & Kusugak, 1988)	A modern Inuit girl breaks a promise to her mother and then must fulfill her promise to the dreaded Quallupiluit. Complications along the way provide other short episodes. The solution is the Quallipiluit's problem.
Legend of the Lady Slipper (Lunge-Larsen, Preus, & Arroyo, 1999)	An Ojibwe tale of a young girl's harrowing winter trip to obtain medicines for her people. She encounters a series of brief complications on her journey. Language is rich with metaphor.
Tops and Bottoms (Stevens, 1995)	Hare, impoverished but industrious, tricks Bear, land-rich but lazy, into share-cropping deals. Hare's and Bear's problems and solutions interact, and Bear learns some life lessons.

Chapter 10

Informational Discourse: Teaching the Main Course of Schooling

Carol Westby, Barbara Culatta, & Kendra M. Hall-Kenyon

Cognitive psychologist John Black has described expository texts as the meat and potatoes of the world because they deliver new information and explain new topics. In contrast, stories and other narrative texts are the dessert of the world. They are interesting and enjoyable, but they are simply variations on well-learned themes (Black, 1985). Although most students may prefer dessert to the main course, speech–language pathologists (SLPs) can elevate students' interest in and increase their benefit from "meat-and-potatoes" expository texts. This chapter focuses on ways to scaffold students from acquiring earlier narrative skills to performing within higher level expository discourse skills. It first explores the nature and development of informational and expository discourse and text skills and then illustrates how SLPs, in collaboration with classroom teachers, can enhance students' acquisition of early developing informational discourse skills and also facilitate higher level comprehension and production of oral and written expository discourse.

Nature and Development of Informational and Expository Discourse

Informational or expository discourse, designed to convey factual information about the natural or social world, can be challenging for some students. The term *discourse*, which deals with units of language longer than the sentence, is similar to the term *text*, with discourse typically being associated with oral language and text typically being associated with written language.

Expository discourse and texts represent the primary way that students gain new information in school, particularly beyond third grade. Expository discourse and texts describe, inform, and explain, typically providing generalized information on a topic with logical or sequential links in formats suited to the specific purpose (e.g., listing, describing, or comparing). The term *informational discourse* or *informational text* has broader meaning that refers to presentation of factual information. It can include presentation of information about a specific person or event in a sequential narrative format. Informational expository and narrative discourse contrasts with fictional accounts of ideas and events. Although most of the informational discourse and texts in schools are in expository formats, some informational discourse and texts, particularly those in the early grades, are presented in conversational and narrative formats.

Early informational discourse and text formats lay the cognitive and linguistic foundations that students need for the more abstract expository discourse of the later grades. This section identifies the linguistic characteristics of informational texts, delineates the various forms of informational discourse from conversation to argumentation, and explores processes within adult-child conversations that facilitate the development of informational discourse skills.

Characteristics of Informational Discourse

There are a number of characteristics that impact the complexity of informational discourse. As discourse functions progress from causal conversations and fictional narratives to expository functions of persuasion and argumentation, content becomes more decontextualized, vocabulary less familiar, syntax more complex, and organization more varied. The characteristics of informational discourse that influence its complexity are considered in this section.

Decontextualized Demands

Informational discourse is typically decontextualized, requiring the ability to understand and speak about events that are removed in time and space or that are abstract or difficult to visualize (Dickinson & Sprague, 2001; Hedberg & Westby, 1993; Hicks, 1990; Zwiers, 2008). When physical context is not available, the discourse language must rely on more specific vocabulary and complex syntax to make the ideas and the relationships among those ideas more explicit. Students need to know how to process and produce demanding text-level language, with its complex vocabulary, grammar, and organizational structures—features that are typically present in what is referred to as academic language (Zwiers, 2008). Teaching students to deal with expository texts entails teaching them to deal with the higher order language skills that comprise the tasks they encounter both in and out of school (Duke & Pearson, 2002).

To comprehend and produce informational texts, students must use these higher order language skills to analyze, evaluate, synthesize, persuade, predict, explain, compare, interpret, and infer. They must recognize the decontextualized nature of informational texts and realize that not all the content that is essential to understanding an informational text is directly stated. They must be able to retrieve relevant background knowledge and make logical inferences from the text content. For example, a text that states that pesticides can interfere with the life cycle of bees and birds requires the reader to know that pesticides are strong chemicals used to kill bugs, that bugs typically eat plants that people grow to eat, that such chemicals are poisonous, that such powerful unnatural agents could also be toxic enough to harm larger animals, and that these chemicals are likely to be transmitted to animals when they land on or eat the fruits and plants that have been sprayed.

Vocabulary

Informational discourse employs more abstract and technical vocabulary than do conversational and narrative discourse because the topics involved are less familiar, more decontextualized, more generalized, and more theoretical. Informational discourse also requires the use of key words that connect ideas in meaningful ways and signal the overall organization of the text.

Expository texts typically contain words used to describe abstract ideas and concepts (e.g., *democracy, freedom*) that relate to higher order thinking (Zwiers, 2008). In addition, the process of nominalization that tends to occur in expository texts contributes to the abstract and technical nature of the vocabulary. Nominalization turns a simple word into a complex derivative. Processes and sequences or time periods are turned into things (*pollute* becomes *pollution*, *destroy* become *destruction*, *migrate* becomes *migration*). In nominalization, verbs and adjectives are made into nouns that then become subjects or objects in clauses or sentences (e.g., *Pollution of streams and lakes* [the subject of the sentence] has caused *the destruction of habitats and disruption in the migration of waterfowl* [the object of the sentence]). Abstract and technical vocabulary words, such as nominalized terms, are difficult not only because they deal with less familiar concepts but also because of their length and complex syllabic structure. In addition, students don't encounter many opportunities to learn these words in daily life, since they occur primarily in academic settings.

Texts become lexically dense when a number of nominalized and abstract words are present. A high lexical density indicates a large amount of information-carrying words, and a low lexical density indicates relatively few information-carrying words. Since each of these words can refer to complex ideas, there is a lot of information in the sentences and paragraphs that contain them. Words such as *migration* and *revolution*, for example, condense lengthy explanations into individual words (Zwiers, 2008). Texts that explain and interpret tend to use more nominalized words to refer to complex phenomena or processes. Nominalization compacts information and creates a high level of abstraction that removes concrete referential information (Halliday & Martin, 1993). The frequent use of nominals and other abstract and unfamiliar vocabulary in informational discourse makes it difficult for the reader or listener to use context from the sentence or paragraph to infer the meanings of the words.

Certain words occur in discourse and texts to signal the relationships between ideas; they serve the important grammatical functions of tying ideas together. Many, but not all, signal words are conjunctions or connectives that relate ideas within and across sentences and support the coherence of ideas. These words signal how new ideas relate to previous ones and offer clues to the overall organization of the text (Meyer & Rice, 1984). Different expository text structures tend to have particular key words or phrases associated with them. For example, compare/contrast texts can use the words *different, same, alike, similar, although, but, however, contrasted with, compared to, yet, still,* and *instead* to signal their organization. Connecting words such as *but, yet, so, because,* and *as a result* can signal cause-effect structure. Similarly, words such as *first, second, then,* or *finally* indicate that the text is organized as a sequence.

Syntactic Patterns

Informational texts tend to use more complex syntactic structures than conversational and narrative discourse do because they are expressing unfamiliar and abstract relationships among people, objects, events, and ideas through the use of sentences with multiple dependent or subordinate clauses: adverbial, adjectival, and nominal. Adverbial clauses modify the verb, adjectival clauses modify the noun, and nominal clauses serve as nouns in subject and object positions. Students must be able to use complex syntactic patterns with dependent clauses if they are to understand or express relationships in informational texts, such as those in the examples from a text about peregrine falcons (see Box 10.1).

Discourse Structures

Informational texts have varied organizational discourse structures, in contrast with fictional narrative texts, which typically have a basic episodic plot structure. Five gen-

Box 10.1. *Types of Dependent Clauses Common to Informational Texts*

Adverbial	*Birds such as falcons, eagles, hawks, owls, and vultures are called birds or prey because they eat other birds and small animals.* (p. 6)
Adjectival	*DDT was sprayed on crops to kill the insects that ate them.* (p. 12)
Nominal	*They [the ornithologists] saw that when a mother peregrine sat on her eggs to keep them warm, they broke.* (p. 10)

Note: Based on Jenkins (1996).

eral text structures reflect how informational texts are typically organized: description, procedure-sequence, compare-contrast, cause-effect, problem-solution, and enumeration (Meyer & Freedle, 1984; Meyer & Poon, 2001). Box 10.2 explains the main organization features of each.

The organization of informational texts is loosely related to a text's function. Some of the most common functions are to describe, relate steps in a sequence or procedure, explain, analyze-evaluate, and argue-persuade (Box 10.2). An explanation, which may involve giving reasons for events, may draw upon a cause-effect structure. A persuasive or argumentative piece might also be organized with a cause-effect structure or with a compare-contrast structure to provide various pros and cons or to state different points of view. Although different informational texts can be organized in different ways (Coffin, 2006; Martin, 2002), the organization must fit with the author's purpose. For example, historical discourse, whose role is that of chronicling past events, is often organized as a sequence, but historical discourse that serves the functions of explaining and arguing can be framed in compare/contrast, cause/effect, or problem/solution organizations.

Continuum of Informational Discourse Skills

SLPs must understand the nature of discourse development in order to support children's acquisition of informational skills. From very early on, information is incorporated into conversations parents have with young children. Moffett (1968) delineated a number of discourse genres that first occur in home contexts and then become more academically based. Moffett proposed that children develop types of discourse that serve four different functions. These talk types are differentiated along two continuums: from casual conversation to focused argumentation and from the present and specific to the hypothetical and general.

The first type of discourse is conversation. In casual conversations, people engage in dialogue, discussing topics familiar to them and frequently asking about and commenting on immediate contexts and events. In somewhat more structured conversations, they "record" what is happening in a dramatic commentary on events. When engaged in recording, a speaker has long stretches of monologues that tend to require reports of events.

Box 10.2. ***Basic Organizational Structures of Informational Discourse***

Structure	Description
Description	A topic or concept is described by referring to its characteristics, features, or attributes. Examples are a book on animal camouflage (the kinds of animals that use camouflage, where they live, how they look, when they use camouflage) or a newspaper article describing a person (his or her appearance, where and when the person lived, and what memorable acts the person does or did).
Sequence	Items or events are listed in a chronological order. A text could give instructional procedures (e.g., how to make a kite) or relate a time-ordered series of events (e.g., from frogs laying eggs, to tadpoles emerging from the eggs, to tadpoles changing into frogs).
Causation	Ideas or events are presented as causes that lead to results or effects. For example, science books give causes of physical events (e.g., earthquakes, thunder and lightning, sinking of the *Titanic*) or history books refer to actions or beliefs that affect other actions and beliefs (e.g., religious persecution influenced the Pilgrims' decisions to come to America, or the Boston Tea Party ignited the Revolutionary War).
Problem/ Solution	The main ideas are organized into: (a) a *problem* and one or more proposed or known *solutions,* or (b) a *question* and its *answer*. For example, troubleshooting manuals present problems and possible solutions (e.g., the problem is the game box doesn't work, and proposed solutions are to check the power cord and connections), and scientific articles raise a question or problem and then seek to give an answer or solution (e.g., germs and illness are problems while washing hands and vaccinations are solutions).
Comparison	The ways that things, concepts, ideas, or events are similar or different are presented. For example, a compare/contrast text could consider similarities and differences among animals in preparation for deciding what pet to buy or it could compare cultural variations of *Cinderella.*
Argumentative/ Persuasive	Positions are presented with supports or reasons for the positions. Often reasons that both support and do not support the position are stated. A final conclusion is given based on whether the reasons support or do not support the position. For example, a text might give reasons for having a pet or argue for what a community should do with trash.

Box 10.2. (*continued*)

Enumeration	Things, ideas, or events are related by listing them together as a string of co-occurring items or with linking words like *first, second, and,* or *another*. Enumeration can occur within any of the other discourse structures. For example, a list of ingredients in recipes (a sequence text), a list of reasons for recycling trash (a problem-solution text), or a list of effects of the Civil War (a causation text).

Note: Informational texts have a primary discourse structure, but other types are also typically present. Based on Meyer, Young, and Bartlett (1989) amd Meyer and Poon (2001).

The second type of discourse is reports or accounts of past events. Reporting, which Moffett (1968) also refers to as narrating, is relating what happened. It typically involves talking about and giving accounts of past events, which may be less familiar to participants and more decontextualized than conversations within an immediate context. In terms of content and structure, the process of reporting has been viewed as a bridge between conversation and expository discourse because its linguistic characteristics and cognitive demands are midway between conversation and exposition and contain elements of both (Westby, 1994). Some reports or narratives can serve as a means of presenting new factual information.

The third type is informational discourse, which deals with conveying generalizations about objects, people, or events. It covers what typically happens rather than specific happenings (Moffett, 1968). For example, rather than a story or a personal experience involving a particular frog, an informational text describes what is known about frogs and their common experiences.

Finally, there is theoretical or argumentative discourse, in which what may, will, or could happen is related. The theoretical focus uses information from expository texts to generate and support hypotheses, while discourse with an argumentative slant uses information to persuade. The theoretical/argumentative genre requires knowledge of a subject and may be used to make a point, delineate a position, view a topic from more than one perspective, or encourage adoption of a particular point of view. For example, students might be asked to argue why it is important for scientists to investigate what is causing frogs to disappear.

Interactional Processes That Facilitate Informational Discourse Skills

Much of children's early exposure to informational discourse occurs in conversations (Bova, 2011; Orsolini, 1993; Snow & Beals, 2006). Within conversational contexts parents often engage in processes that support the development of early informational discourse. Certain types of adult-child interactions are strongly associated with improvements in children's language scores and better academic performance in school. For example, the number of conversational turns is more highly correlated with children's performance on a language test than with the number of adult words they hear (Zimmerman et al., 2009). In addition to the number of conversational turns, other aspects of parental interactional processes facilitate higher-level language skills in children. In this section the topic of how facilitative processes operate while parents engage children in interactions for different purposes is explored. The processes, presented below along a quasi-developmental continuum, begin with explaining immediate events and end with arguing and persuading. These processes are also helpful in guiding decisions about early-intervention practices with very young children.

Explain and Problem-Solve in Immediate Situations

Children begin to acquire informational discourse skills when engaged in explanations about what's immediately happening (Bova, 2011; Frazier, Gelman, & Wellman, 2009). As children interact with parents in everyday situations, opportunities arise for explanations and problem solving. Parents explain why they behave in certain ways and how to accomplish desired tasks, and why certain situations or phenomena occur, starting with events that are immediately occurring.

Donaldson (1986) documented the development of different types of explanations in children, beginning in the preschool years. Children and adults explain the purpose for objects, machines, or actions (e.g., why we need to go to the store, why we look both ways before crossing the street); procedures while making and doing things (e.g., how to make cookies, how to build a snowman, how to put a toy together when we've lost the directions); and causes and effects of actions (e.g., why you can't just take something you want in a store, why school was canceled because of the storm). Even 3- and 4-year-old children engage in causal explanations required for tasks involving physical, psychological, or logical relations, and they generally use the connectives *because* and *so* correctly. These early explanations, as they relate to events that are very familiar or immediately happening, lay the cognitive and linguistic foundations for cause-effect and problem-solution informational texts.

Elaborate and Explain Information in Storybooks

Children acquire some informational discourse skills during book reading (Price, van Kleeck, & Huberty, 2009). Within shared book reading, children experience adults commenting on and explaining ideas and relating story ideas to real-life information. Explanations occur as parents tell what would happen in real life or why certain typical cause-effect relationships operate. In addition, comparisons are often associated with book reading, as the adult compares the events in the story with the experiences of the child. Thus rather than just labeling and describing objects and events in books, adults explain, elaborate, and evaluate (Reese, Cox, Harte, & McAnally, 2003; Sigel, Stinson, & Flaugher, 1991).

Co-construct and Reflect on Past Events

Opportunities to relate information removed from time and space, including personal experiences that happened in the past, support higher-level language (Fivush, 2011; Reese et al., 2003). Children who participate in interactions that use decontextualized references to non-immediate content in the preschool years do better academically in later years (Sigel et al., 1991).

In addition to supporting decontextualized language skills, mothers who scaffold and elaborate children's contributions to the reporting of past events help them develop strategies for remembering and evaluating experiences (Fivush & Fromhoff, 1988; Hudson 1990; Peterson & McCabe, 1994). If a child does not recall a detail or a piece of information, a mother can provide the next piece of the event or explanation, integrating details already recalled, combining both of their contributions into a coherent account of what occurred. Such parents also ask many open-ended questions that both provide the child with some information and encourage the child to recall additional information (e.g., "What did we do in the zoo today?"). They integrate their children's responses into the ongoing narrative to weave together a story that includes multiple components such as the who, what, when, and where of the event (e.g., "That's right, we watched the trainers feeding the seals. Was there anyone else with us?"). In reminiscing interactions, children tend to be exposed to abstract concepts and rare words that correlate to later vocabulary scores (Snow & Beals, 2006), complex syntactic patterns that code temporal and causal relationships, and communicative functions that relate to critical thinking (Orsolini, 1993; Sigel et al., 1991). In the process, children learn to produce explicit monologue discourse, which is essential in school contexts. Mothers who do a lot of elaborative reminiscing when engaged in conversations about past events set the stage for their children's development of explicit decontextualized language.

In addition to learning how to give accounts of past experiences and develop decontextualized language in the process, recounting and reminiscing about personal experiences serve to support evaluating and generalizing—critical processes for learning in school. Mothers who do a lot of elaborative reminiscing when engaged in conversations about past events model strategies for evaluating experiences (Fivush, 2011; Fivush & Fromhoff, 1988; Hudson, 1990; Peterson & McCabe, 1994). When reminiscing, these parents talk about the nonimmediate and, as a consequence, their language begins to take on the characteristics of academic talk. They explain and evaluate (e.g., "I think the monkeys screamed because they were frightened when the lions roared. I was frightened too. Were you?"). Also in the process of elaborating past experiences, parents relate specific events to general knowledge or information. They make generalizations (e.g., "Frogs eat insects. Some brightly colored frogs are poisonous").

Negotiate, Persuade, and Argue

Although argumentative or persuasive informational discourse is frequently considered the most complex type of verbal communication, its elements develop out of the social negotiations that children engage in to make a point, assert a right, or negotiate for possessions. Children learn to persuade and argue when told "no" or when they seek something adults do not permit (Weiss & Sachs, 1991). By age 3, children understand and generate the principle components of an argument, either in face-to-face interaction or individual interviews. The ability to construct detailed, coherent rationales in defense of a favored position improves with age, but even young children show some competence in producing arguments in support of a claim (why I should get to stay up longer, why I should get a puppy for my birthday; Clark & Delia, 1976; Eisenberg & Garvey, 1981; Orsolini, 1993; Stein & Miller, 1993; Weiss & Sachs, 1991) and in understanding the structure of an argument (Chambliss & Murphy, 2002).

In sum, the scaffolding that occurs as parents interact with their children to achieve certain functions serves as the basis for the development of informational discourse skills in young children. The same processes can be applied in teaching informational discourse skills to children with language deficits in school. In turn, these early-developing informational skills can lay the foundation for teaching the more complex expository-text skills involved in comprehending and producing written expository texts.

Intervention: Facilitating Skills Within Early Informational Discourse

Many students arrive at school without the developmental underpinnings for comprehending and producing informational texts. In an effort to facilitate acquisition of foundational skills, SLPs can provide students with early supported experiences that begin with conversations and narratives about informational topics. In this way, students learn to talk about unfamiliar, decontextualized topics.

Although not responsible for teaching curricular content, SLPs should collaborate with teachers to align information-based intervention with curricular topics and goals. This section addresses ways SLPs, with teacher involvement, can improve children's informational discourse skills. To illustrate the intervention process, examples using content related to the topic of *caring for animals and the places they live* and drawn from collaborative projects the authors have conducted in preschool and elementary-grade classrooms are presented.

Much of the research on teaching students to comprehend and produce oral and written expository texts has focused on teaching metacognitive strategies to reflect on the features and organize the language components involved in the comprehension and production processes. This assumes that students have declarative knowledge essential for the expository discourse (content information, vocabulary, and syntax) that they employ in functional activities. Students cannot be metacognitive in regard to comprehending and producing expository texts if they do not have foundational language skills and if they don't have some degree of competence with academic language and some basic informational discourse skills. This section identifies various early informational discourse skills that can be addressed in school contexts along with the interactional processes that serve to facilitate them.

Informational Talk: Explaining and Problem Solving in Immediate Situations

Conversational interactions within immediate clinic- or classroom-based activities can be used to support the development of informational discourse skills. Exchanges that involve the sharing of information within immediate experiences can be used to model and support those skills. Children can be given the opportunity to recognize and practice using informational functions in exchanges that occur within school-based contexts. These exchanges can address concrete and immediate situations that can also reference events and information that are more remote, more abstract, or less familiar (Dore, 1986; Tough, 1977). Informational discourse often involves explaining and describing how aspects of immediate events relate to information that is removed in time and space (Coffin, 2006; Martin, 2002).

Informational functions and structures can be modeled within interactive hands-on experiences created to extend or establish background knowledge. Providing concrete experiences applied to the content in a curricular unit or text can support decontextualized language as well as build background knowledge. While the event is immediate, it provides opportunities to talk about how the situation or experience relates to things that are more abstract or remote (removed in time and space) and less familiar (Hicks, 1990).

As an example, the SLP working in the collaborative project focusing on caring for animals and their surroundings provided students with a hands-on activity that related to a pet hamster that kept trying to escape from its cage. As a relevant hands-on experience, the SLP arranged for students to build a better hamster cage, one that would fit the hamster's needs. In addressing the notion of how an animal's home must fit its needs, the SLP talked about hamsters' needs and natural desires (e.g., to get exercise, explore new places, and have places to hide and sleep during the day) and gave the students various materials to work with. She arranged for the students to plan for and build a cage that the hamster would like and that would meet its needs.

The contextualized conversation that occurred in the process of building a better hamster cage modeled a problem-solution structure: the students contributed ideas, and the SLP scaffolded the organization. The SLP reminded the students why they were creating a plan for a new cage (to solve the problem of the hamster not being "happy" and not being able to be freed because it wouldn't survive) and what problems or needs the hamster had (get exercise, not be bored, have access to food and water, etc.) and asked questions about what they decided to do in their design to solve these problems. The students explained why they chose what they did in making a better hamster cage. The organized conversation about the content within the immediate context was designed to support decontextualized language use and also to model a common informational structure, that of problem-solution.

Explanations of Stories or Story Events: Elaborating Content

Some of the earliest contexts for exposing students to informational content are those occurring within interactions around storybooks. The reading of a fictional book provides opportunities to comment on and discuss real-world information that relates to the story's ideas. SLPs can select books that address the targeted curricular content (e.g., the notion that animals' habitats must be compatible with their needs) and elaborate on information related to story events. The information comes not from the story but from side conversations and discussions about what happens in real life. In the project on caring for animals and their habitats, information about an animal's needs was introduced with the telling of *Mouse Mess* (Riley, 1997), a story about a mouse living under a family's stairway instead of outside in the woods. This served as a jumping-off point for comments and explanations about how real mice can take care of themselves in the woods. Within the interactions around the book, the SLP related content to background knowledge, introduced relevant information, and organized discussions in a way that served to model an expository text structure (e.g., compare-contrast of pets versus wild animals and problems-solutions related to having a mouse in the house).

A common way to address information within a storybook context is to activate background knowledge. For example, within the theme of caring for animals and their habitats, the SLP can ask the students what they know about mice and the places they live (e.g., "Have you ever seen a mouse? Where? When do mice usually sleep? How do mice get food?"). The SLP can also provide information about the best living environment for mice and illustrate that with props or pictures (e.g., show a replica or picture of a mouse's nest). In this way, the instructor draws parallels between content in the story and basic knowledge about the subject.

During book reading, SLPs diverge from the telling to orally elaborate relevant information and discuss how the story content relates to the students' lives. In doing so, they can contrast fantasy with fact (e.g., "What would really happen when . . . ? In real life would you ever be able to . . . ?"). For example, in reading the *Mouse Mess* book, the SLP can contrast events in the story (e.g., the mouse raking up cereal with a fork, building a "sand" castle with brown sugar, taking a bath in a teacup) to what real mice would do and how real mice take care of themselves when they live outdoors. In comments during reading or a discussion, the SLP can explain that certain animals usually live outside. Other animals, the kind we call *pets*, usually live in homes with people. Sometimes an animal that usually lives outside tries to get into someone's house, but there are reasons why they don't belong. And sometimes an animal that likes to be free but lives in a house as a pet gets outside the house. Explanations for why we want to help animals and what responsibility we have to treat animals kindly, even when they encroach on our space, can lead to discussions that serve higher functions.

Discussions of Content: Imposing a Structure

The SLP can organize a discussion related to story content that deepens conceptual understanding and models an informational text structure. Outlining problems and their potential solutions, reporting a sequence of events that typically occur in real life, and comparing and contrasting story events with real-life events all support exposing students to different ways of organizing information. A salient discussion that differentiated between what is real and what is imaginary, and was organized using the compare-contrast structure, was used in reference to the *Mouse Mess* story. The SLP contrasted how a mouse that lives outdoors satisfies its needs versus how the mouse in the story took care of itself. In discussing the story, the SLP contrasted what real mice do versus what the fictional mouse in the story did. The SLP talked about how the mouse in the story slept during the day and was awake at night, just like real mice ("But a real mouse wouldn't cover himself up with a blanket; he'd make a nest out of twigs or leaves or grasses. A real mice wouldn't use a fork to rake up its food; it would just hold the food with its paws and eat it. But both a real mouse and the story mouse search for food, and both need a warm, cozy place to sleep").

Decontextualized Discourse: Narrating Past Experiences

Reporting past experiences can serve as an oral form of informational discourse. The report can be about an event the SLP or an acquaintance experienced, a situation the teacher and students shared, or an event an individual child experienced. In addition to elaborating the content and scaffolding the telling, the personal account can model a particular informational text structure (e.g., sequence, compare-contrast, or problem-solution).

An example of one SLP's account concerned a squirrel that got into her house and created a terrible problem because it couldn't get its needs met in the house. Her account and discussion reflected a problem-solution structure. She introduced students to the problems she encountered and explained how the squirrel was frightened and possibly dangerous, how he could squeeze under doors and could not be shooed outside, and how he made such a horrible mess. She also related what she did and asked her students what they would have done to address or "fix" the problem. She commented on how she needed to solve the problem but still needed to respect the squirrel's right to live and remain unharmed while also making sure that it didn't destroy the house or harm her. In discussing the situation, the SLP explained how the squirrel could make itself flat enough to squeeze under doors and scamper all over the house. So, as a solution, she sealed off the space under the doors with rolled-up blankets in order to keep the squirrel in one room so that she could safely catch it. Once the squirrel was in one room, she then had the problem of catching it without her or the squirrel getting hurt. To solve this problem, she bought a trap and placed some nuts inside. She caught the squirrel when the trapdoor closed, carried the trap far away from the house, and let the squirrel loose in a wooded area.

Accounts of events the students have experienced can also be used to co-construct organized informational discussion. Children can be asked if they have had similar experiences (e.g., finding a spider in the classroom, finding an animal in a strange place) that relate to the underlying purpose or theme (e.g., helping or rescuing a lost or confused animal). To scaffold the discourse so that students convey their own experience, the SLP can ask students to tell stories that relate to a targeted topic and can scaffold the organization so that it reflects a particular text structure (e.g., "Let's talk about the problem we had with an animal being in the wrong place and what you did to solve the problem").

Expository Discourse: Scaffolding Generalized Accounts

Narrative discourse reports on what happened in a specific event to particular people, animals, or objects. In contrast, expository discourse provides generalized information about categories of people, animals, objects, or events. Because of its personal nature, a narrative account relates to a specific and familiar situation and is likely to be less complex than a text about generalized information or a script for how things usually happen in certain situations. The process of relating and discussing personal experiences, either those experienced by the SLP or the students, can be presented in a way that addresses knowledge of a subject rather than specific details of something that happened at one particular time.

The specific experience with the squirrel was reworked and turned into a general description of the nature of squirrels and the procedures to follow when a person encounters a wild animal in his or her space. After presenting her account of discovering the squirrel in her home, the SLP engaged students in a scaffolded conversation about why wild animals should not be kept in houses (e.g., they can be dangerous and can bite or scratch if they feel threatened, they will destroy the home, they can carry diseases, they will be frightened, and they won't be able to survive). The generalized information could be related to procedures for catching and removing a wild animal (e.g., call the forest service for information, buy a trap, put food in the trap, take the trapped animal far away from houses and let it loose in the woods) or to characteristics about that particular wild animal (e.g., how squirrels can scamper up almost anything, run fast, and squeeze through small spaces; how they can carry diseases; and how they are always searching for food to take to their nests). The discussions dealing with general information about squirrels can be organized as a description; if the focus is on getting the squirrel to be where it belongs, the discussion can be framed as a procedure, sequence structure, or problem-solution.

Role-playing relating to informational topics, in addition to conversations about how things operate generally, is another way of providing students with experience talking about topics in general ways and distanced from personal experience (Naremore, Densmore, & Harman, 1995). Role-play situations represent real events or replicate exchanges that people tend to have for particular reasons. Some examples could include: a newscaster who tells why it's important to keep animals away from pesticides, a park ranger who explains how feeding wild animals prevents them from searching for food on their own, a member of a community who explains why it is important to plant flowers that will attract bees, or a salesperson who compares a poisonous bug-control product with one that will not harm larger animals. Role-play can replicate information-based exchanges that can convey general information in a way that exemplifies a particular text structure (e.g., compare-contrast, problem-solution, cause-effect, sequence).

Argumentative Discourse: Providing Opportunities to Negotiate and Persuade

Although preschool children can argue with and even persuade their parents and peers, sophisticated, logical argumentation requires much further development in abstract reasoning, world knowledge, and expository-discourse skills. Successful persuasion also involves subtle social and rhetorical skills that engage emotional appeal and avoid putting others on the defensive (but those go beyond the scope of this chapter).

To provide a strong logical argument, students must identify a problem and then compare and evaluate information that could be used to solve that problem. They must be able to identify the cause-effect relationships that might exist for all of the possible solutions they consider. Informational exchanges that relate to negotiating, arguing, and persuading can occur as part of situations that arise in classroom contexts or that are arranged to provide a provocative or controversial topic to discuss or evaluate. Such events can illustrate particular informational functions and specific text structures. This rationale approach to arguing and persuading (or even just negotiating a middle ground) gives rise to the informational discourse that is needed in academic activities.

For well-structured argumentation, the SLP models how an arguer proposes an interpretation of events and defends it with a series of supportive facts or evidence. The arguer must also explain how immediate and familiar events relate to remote and abstract ones. The SLP models and involves the children in reflecting on and evaluating a concept or in grappling with a situation that is unfamiliar or removed from immediate and personal experience. Sustained, purposeful, supportive conversations about informational topics that involve negotiating meaning promote academic and decontextualized language (Zwiers, 2008).

The various reasons for negotiating, arguing, and persuading can be framed in an organized way and conveyed within common informational text structure. For example, the SLP might want to propose arguments that would serve to raise awareness of animal issues and to advocate for animal rights. The SLP can model well-formed arguments and scaffold the children as he or she compares and contrasts the views of scientists who test new medicines on animals with the views of animal rights advocates (e.g., both have important goals, both want the animals to be treated humanely but differ in that the animal rights group doesn't want animals to even be confined to cages or used for research). Persuasive discourse can also occur as individuals discuss problems and solutions related to saving endangered animals. Different texts and text types can be used to make an argument if information is presented in a purposeful, logical, and organized fashion.

Intervention: Supporting Expository Text Comprehension and Production

Once students are able to engage in conversation-based informational discourse skills, SLPs should begin to support students in comprehending and producing more-complex expository discourse and written texts. As in the earlier interventions, SLPs use interactional exchanges to scaffold performance but also target higher level skills and more decontextualized academic language. In this section, intervention processes are applied to comprehending and producing texts dealing with saving animals.

Discuss and Elaborate Written Expository Texts

SLPs must make decisions about how to support students' comprehension of informational texts. Curriculum-based texts provide content the student is familiar with while interactions around the texts provide supportive metacognitive processes and facilitative strategies. While the intervention will vary based on the needs of the students, it might include strategies such as relating known to unknown information, modifying the complexity of the text, identifying the text's organization, and connecting ideas. The text referred to in this section, *Falcons Nest on Skyscrapers* (Jenkins, 1996), concerns the near extinction of peregrine falcons because of the use of pesticides on crops.

Relate the Known to the Unknown

Because informational texts are dependent on world knowledge and include new information, conversations about what students know can influence their comprehension (Best, Floyd, & McNamara, 2008). In the *Falcons Nest on Skyscrapers* text, the SLP can contrast familiar events with information presented in the text. Prior to reading the text, the students could be asked to talk about what it feels like to lose something valuable and never get it back or why parents keep chemicals like cleaning supplies out of the reach of young children.

In addition to discussing ways in which texts are similar to students' own knowledge and experiences, SLPs help students connect with the content of the text by discussing ways in which situations in the texts are similar to their own experiences. Zarnowski (2006) recommended that teachers draw their attention to how aspects of life in the texts are different from as well as similar to those of the students. In the caring-for-animals theme, the SLP scaffolds students in filling out compare-contrast matrices and T-charts to document differences and similarities between familiar and new content.

For example, the Jenkins text begins with a description of falcons to help readers understand the causes of the birds' decline and why losing this species matters. Falcons can be contrasted with common birds (e.g., sparrows or robins) that the students are likely to have encountered. A T-chart can be used to visually represent the comparison of the two types of birds (Box 10.3): one column on the chart for the smaller common birds and the other for the larger hunting birds, and rows for the different dimensions being considered (e.g., what they look like, what they eat, how they have babies, and where they live). The chart helps demonstrate similarities and differences, such as that both small and big birds eat living things but that what they eat differs in size (e.g., worms and mosquitoes versus mice and pigeons). Then the SLP can help the students see that the bigger hunting birds serve an important purpose (e.g., by eating animals that hurt crops or by controlling the number of pigeons that carry disease). This comparison can lead to a more in-depth discussion about why people should make sure that falcons (or large hunting birds in general) don't become extinct.

Modify Complexity and Unpack the Content

Written texts can be made accessible to students by adjusting the content and structure through spoken presentation. Expository texts should not just be read as written; in-

Box 10.3. ***Matrix to Demonstrate Compare/Contrast Structure***

Attributes	**Small Common Birds** **(e.g., sparrows, robins, swallows, chickadees)**	**Large Hunting Birds** **(e.g., hawks, eagles, owls, falcons)**
Appearance		
Diet		
Reproduction		
Location		

stead the formal language should be paraphrased or simplified, and the ideas discussed (Price et al., 2009). Through these supportive conversations about expository texts, the SLP unpacks the content and simplifies the complexity of the sentences and vocabulary.

SLPs must help students deal with content that is essential for comprehending an expository text. This includes explaining the meaning of obscure and abstract words in simple, child-friendly language (Beck, McKeown, & Kucan, 2002). The SLP also explains the meanings of nominal words that refer to complex processes. The SLP uses strategies such as recasting (conveying the same thing in different ways) and build-ups and breakdowns (pairing complex with simple ways to express the same idea) to exemplify the meaning and function expressed in complex syntactic patterns. The SLP also draws students' attention to how the clauses serve to modify ideas.

Adjusting complexity also entails helping students understand information that is not directly stated, that is, invisible or implicit content (Blank, 2002; Culatta, Blank, & Black, 2010). The SLP fills in missing information or calls attention to clues needed to make inferences. While talking through the ideas in a text to make it less dense, the SLP expands on and connects what is stated to what is implied. For example, one dense paragraph in the book Falcons Nest on Skyscrapers refers to ways to solve the problem of falcons becoming extinct:

> Falcon researchers working at the special laboratory called The Hawk Barn were determined to save the peregrine falcon. They collected young peregrines from

> the wild and raised them in their lab. These birds mated and laid eggs. After the eggs hatched, the scientists taught the nestlings how to survive in the wild. (Jenkins, 1996, p. 14)

The SLP can make this information understandable by breaking it into problem-solution units. The SLP helps students understand that the problem was a threat to the population of falcons and the solution was to arrange for the few falcons to live in a lab that was closely matched to their natural environment so they could safely lay eggs and the newly hatched baby falcons could be protected. Then the scientists had another problem: the baby falcons that had been protected from birth could not survive in the wild. So, to solve this problem, the scientists themselves would have to teach the baby falcons how to survive in the wild.

Make Connections Between Ideas

Part of adjusting complexity entails helping students connect ideas within and between sentences to achieve local cohesion. The SLP can show students how clauses modify ideas and call attention to or add explicit conjunctions and key words or phrases (e.g., *problem, solution, so, to solve the problem*) that connect ideas within and across sentences and signal the structure of the text. The SLP adds or calls attention to conjunctions and adverbials that signal relationships and make a text cohesive.

Cohesive connections are often part of grammatically complex phrases and clauses. SLPs can help their students process connectives in an oral medium with stress, intonation, pauses, or gestures (Wallach, 2008). Zwiers (2008) suggested pairing gestures with conjunctions and cohesive devices as the SLP talks about the text. For example, for words that signal opposing thoughts (e.g., *nevertheless, on the other hand, despite, yet*), one would first move a hand in one direction and then lift it in a 180-degree arc in the other direction to express or signal a contradiction or opposing ideas; to communicate cause and effect (e.g., *therefore, as a result, thus, consequently, for this reason*), the SLP would move his or her hands forward in a rolling motion.

The text about the plight of falcons has examples of connections that could be added or emphasized, as illustrated by this short paragraph:

> Not long ago, peregrine falcons lived practically all over the world. But in the 1950s, they began to disappear very rapidly. No one knew why. Bird experts, or ornithologists, were alarmed. Something had to be done quickly, or the peregrines would become extinct. (Jenkins, 1996, p. 10)

Although one of the oppositional ideas is signaled with *but*, causal connections between the bird's plight and the people's reactions are not stated with conjunctions (e.g., words such as *because*, *so*, *therefore*, and *as a result* are missing in places where there is implied causality). With the connections added, one sentence could be changed to: "Because the peregrines were becoming extinct, ornithologists had to figure out what was wrong and come up with a solution."

Identify or Call Attention to Text Structure

Instruction in identifying a text's structure improves students' comprehension and recall of information in expository texts (Hall, Sabey, & McClellan, 2005; Meyer & Poon, 2001; Sweet & Snow, 2003; Weaver & Kintch, 1991; Westby, Culatta, Lawrence, & Hall-Kenyon, 2010; Williams, Hall, & Lauer, 2004; Williams, Stafford, Lauer, Hall, & Pollini, 2009). Highlighting text organization helps students make meaningful connections among key ideas (Ukrainetz, 2006). The SLP calls attention to the organization as she names or describes it, talks about how ideas are related, highlights or adds devices that signal the organization, and guides students in a discussion that reflects the text's organization. Not all texts, however, are clearly organized, and not all connections between ideas are explicitly stated in a text (Hall-Kenyon & Black, 2010). Signal words (e.g., *because, however, although, consequently*) can be added in oral comments or explanations even though the ideas or relationships are inferred. The SLP can fill in implied connections and words that signal the structure.

The book *Falcons Nest on Skyscrapers* has different parts with different structures. One part, a description, gives information about falcon birds; another part, cause-effect, addresses why the falcons were becoming extinct; and yet another part, problem-solution, provides ideas for how to stop poisoning the birds and bring back the falcon population. While the different structures in the book are discernable, being based on logical relationships among events or information, some were explicitly signaled while others were implied. In introducing, telling, or discussing the book about the plight of the falcons, the SLP can call attention to important ideas and their relationships and explicitly label the organization.

In giving an oral preview for the part of the text that deals with the cause-effect structure, the SLP might say, "We'll learn why falcons dwindled and what caused their numbers to decrease—what caused their baby birds not to live." During the telling, the SLP might draw attention to the cause-effect relationships that are explicitly stated in the book:

> DDT was sprayed on crops to kill the insects that ate them. The poison was supposed to be just strong enough to kill insects but not strong enough to harm other creatures. But birds ate the poisoned insects. Then peregrines ate the birds that had eaten the poisoned insects. The DDT did not kill the birds or the peregrines. But it did have another effect on them. The DDT made the peregrines' eggshells too thin. When the mother falcons sat on them, they broke. No baby falcons, or eyases, could hatch. (Jenkins, 1996, pp. 12–13)

In addition, during a discussion the SLP might add in connectors or key phrases to help students understand the cause-effect relationships among the ideas in the text. Consider the number of opportunities to add cause-effect signal words in the following chain of ideas: *because* farmers wanted to stop bugs from eating their crops, they sprayed the crops with pesticides (poisons to kill bugs), and, *as a result*, the poisoned plants *caused* the bugs that ate them to become poisonous; *so* when the birds ate the bugs, they also ate the poison. *Therefore* when the falcons ate those smaller birds, the poison got into the falcons' bodies and harmed their eggs. This *caused* the eggshells to be thin and weak, *so that* (*because of this*) when the mother sat on them, the eggs broke before the babies inside were big enough to survive.

Co-construct a Representation

The SLP can involve students in jointly constructing a representation of a text. Graphic representations (visual displays that convey the main ideas and organization of a text) can help students deal with expository texts. Text comprehension and production is supported as the SLP involves students in the mapping process, adds signaling devices, and teaches the content from the map (Duke & Pearson, 2002; Pearson & Duke, 2002; Williams, et al., 2005; National Reading Panel, 2000). Illustrations of these processes will be applied to Internet texts that deal with helping abused, injured, or endangered animals.

The level of complexity of the task will depend on the nature of the text and the amount of support. In involving students in representing texts, the SLP should begin by selecting well-organized texts. As children's proficiency grows, more-complex texts can be introduced. Selection of the representation must fit the function and structure of the text, either the author's or the SLP's purpose, and content and structure of the text (Hall-Kenyon & Black, 2010).

When teaching a text about how zoos or animal shelters need to replicate the habitat of the animals they keep, the SLP involved the students in mapping a simple problem-solution text. Some zoos receive animals that were orphaned when young, became disoriented, or were injured and couldn't be returned to the wild. Problems occur when these animals try to adapt to living in a confined space, in which case the zookeepers or rescue workers must adapt the available space to fit the needs of the animals. For example, after telling and reading a text about rescuing monkeys that were mistreated when they were kept as pets (Dokken & Ampika, 2010), the SLP and students represented the text as a problem-solution structure (e.g., problem: pet monkeys are often abandoned or killed when they get older and aggressive; solution(s): raise money to provide a shelter, make it illegal to have monkeys as pets, teach the monkeys to get along with other monkeys and to live in trees again, then release them into the wild). The SLP provided the framework and talked the students through the process of filling in the map.

In using a Cloze map, the SLP presents a graphic organizer with some cells filled in and supports the students as they select phrases and sentences or props to put in cells that represent a particular idea and afterward discuss the relationship among the ideas. Children can help fill in missing elements, but the SLP will signal the higher order relationships and structure. The SLP also reminds students how the information in the cells relates to the overall organization and main idea of the text (Culatta, Hall-Kenyon, & Black, 2010). Cells that label columns and rows in graphic representations can serve as headings that label the ideas and can imply the text's structure. Expansion of the information in the headings and overviews can be presented verbally.

Add and Highlight Signal Words

Instruction in attending to or identifying signal words can facilitate text comprehension (Seidenberg, 1989; Spyridakis & Standal, 1987). In the process of mapping a text, the SLP can draw attention to key terms or phrases that point to a text's structure and serve to connect ideas. When signals highlight the structure of a text, recalled versions closely resemble the structure of the original text (Lorch & Lorch, 1995; Lorch, Lorch, & Inman, 1993; Meyer, Brandt, & Bluth, 1980; Meyer & Poon, 2001; Millis & Just, 1994).

In many cases, even well-organized texts do not have many of the logical connections explicitly stated, and thus they need to be added in telling or representing a text. In guiding a child in representing a text, the SLP can add or highlight signal devices. In a matrix, the signal devices are added orally as the SLP scaffolds the representation and talks about the text during the process. In other forms of representation, such as a flowchart or tree diagram, the signal devices can be physically added to the arrows or lines linking cells populated with important ideas. The students help fill in the information in the cells, and the SLP highlights the organizational framework in the exchange. The SLP can also involve the students in retrieving words to connect ideas, drawing on sentence-combining techniques (Killgallon & Killgallon, 2000).

Talk Through the Content From the Graphic Organizer

The representation of a text can be combined with an oral presentation or telling of the text. The SLP models the retelling from the graphic representation and then provides the student with an opportunity to tell or teach the same text or content from the representation.

Support for comprehension can occur as the SLP talks through the graphic organizer with attention to structure (Culatta, Blank, & Black, 2010; Hall-Kenyon & Black, 2010). This produces an oral version that serves as a model for a well-structured text. The SLP may fill in the cells of the map as he or she talks through the text. In the telling, with the map as the representation, the SLP repeatedly models ways to specify the text structure by adding signaling devices, labeling and describing the overall structure, referring to hierarchical relationships signaled in the headings, or adding key words that connect ideas and suggest the overall structure.

Once the SLP has modeled telling or teaching a text from a representation, he or she can arrange for students to talk or rewrite the text from a graphic organizer. Telling or retelling or talking through a text with the aid of a graphic organizer enables children to generate an organized informational text and supports comprehension and content knowledge. In retelling the text from a graphic representation, the students can learn to differentiate between main ideas and supportive details (Meyer et al., 1980). The retelling provides children with the chance to connect the important elements and see the global structure along with the details and to make connections between higher and lower elements.

To be successful, students need sufficient supports, which can consist of questions, concrete props, and sentence-completion responses. The retelling can occur in a Cloze or co-constructed procedure. Rather than retelling the text themselves, the students use the maps generated by the SLP and the SLP's supportive response to the students' contributions. The SLP partially fills in the ideas (oral or written) presented in a targeted text, and students select options from choices or fill in the supportive details (Torgesen, Rashotte, & Greenstein, 1988). The SLP can ask connection questions such as, "What is being compared?" or "How do the zoo and the 'wild' differ in terms of where rescued owls sleep? How do the environments differ in terms of how vultures get their food?" In supporting the retelling, the SLP can label the structure, point out the elements of the structure, and model and scaffold the students' telling of the text from the organizer (Piccolo, 1987).

Model Text Production

SLPs can scaffold students' oral and written expository skills by exposing them to and modeling the construction of well-formed texts. In modeling and constructing, the students are given clear and explicit examples to follow and are alerted to the features they need to replicate. Examples of the intervention procedures will be illustrated with texts that deal with the role that bees play in people's lives and actions that can be taken to protect them.

Provide Model Texts as Exemplars

A model text is an ideal piece of writing that exemplifies the characteristics that the SLP wants students to produce when they generate their own text. With a model text, the SLP provides an example of a text worth imitating and points out a key feature or two (e.g., organization, signal devices, or cohesive connections). The model text provides students with a very clear example of what to follow as they generate a similar product (Gallagher, 2011).

A number of Internet sites contain texts for students that address issues related to the role that bees play in the environment and the threats to their existence. One text, *The Case of the Missing Bees* (http://www.timeforkids.com/news/case-missing-bees/11806), which contains a problem-solution structure, deals with solving the mystery of colony collapse disorder. Using this as a model text could help students identify the problem-solution structure and key signal devices (e.g., subheadings, signal words or phrases, and clear topic sentence or introductory statement). The text states that there are most likely two problems that cause the death of bees: a fungus and a virus. To keep the bees alive (the problem), beekeepers should treat the bees with medicine to get rid of the fungus, because the fungus is easier to treat than the virus (the solution). The beekeepers also need to find ways to stop the fungus and virus from spreading (the problem), and so they must keep observing and testing the bees to learn more about what is hurting them (the solution).

Children can be given a reason for producing structured text that would require them to use the feature(s) shown in the model text(s). To evoke a problem-solution text about bees, students can replicate the structure and copy the key features of a model text to create a similar well-formed text without producing an exact copy of the model text (e.g., include an overview that explicitly states the main idea and signal the organization with words that specify the relationships among the ideas). Through guided interactions following exposure to a model text, students are led to "see" and construct a complex web of ideas and information (Blank, 2002; Cazden, 1988; Mercer & Hodgkinson, 2008; Silliman & Wilkinson, 1994). The purposes of the text, to convince people to be concerned about bees and to find ways to keep them healthy and reproducing, fit with or are compatible with the organization.

One option for supporting writing with assistance from model texts, referred to as *dictogloss*, is to arrange for students to rewrite the exact same text but to do it paraphrasing the content, modeling the use of the same signaling devices and following the same structure (Smith, 2011; Wajnryb, 1990). The students model their text after the targeted characteristics and structure of a model text but signal the content and structure (e.g., introduction, signal devices, relationships among ideas) in their own words. The students are first exposed to the model text in ways that raise their familiarity with the content and structure (e.g., listening to the text being read several times, taking and sharing notes, discussing or representing the content) and then rewrite or co-construct the text with help from a peer or instructor. The students then share their rewrites with others and compare their rewritten version with the original text.

Model the Writing Process

Complementing modeling the *product* of writing is modeling the *process* of writing (Gallagher, 2011). It is important to show how to get from an assortment of ideas to a well-structured, effective text (Box 10.4). In modeling how to compose informational texts, the SLP talks through the thinking process as the students observe and then arranges for students to generate their own similar text. Prior to implementing parallel or modeled writing, the SLP decides what function or purpose the target text, along with its content and structure, should serve (Pearson & Myrick, 2012). As with writing from a model text, a clear purpose helps dictate the structure or make it logical. Knowing that you are trying to accomplish a specific communicative purpose such as explaining or persuading rather than just writing an assigned composition also helps motivate the text-generation process. Content based on information the students have already had some experience with should be selected.

In conducting a lesson, an SLP, Barb Smith, writes in the presence of the students, making the writing visible via chart paper, overhead or computer projector, or smart board. The SLP discusses her thinking as she plans to write. To model the composition process, the SLP specifies a purpose and an organization. The SLP activates or retrieves what she knows about a topic, provides a reason for writing about the topic, and then talks through and exemplifies her own writing. The SLP talks about her planning and organization of the content with a graphic representation, outline, or notes and then engages in the writing processes or models writing from that representation. The SLP can create an overview that may signal the purpose and organization and specify the main idea. Throughout the process, the SLP engages in parallel talk as she comments on what she is doing and verbalizes the words and sentences while writing them. The SLP

Box 10.4. *Cognitive Modeling of the Composition of Informational Text*

Planning to write:

1. What is my purpose for writing? What am I trying to tell my readers with this paper? Am I trying to describe something, tell the sequence of events, actions or steps, explain a process, solve a problem, or compare and contrast two or more things or ideas?
2. What are the main points I want to make? Let's look back at my purpose for writing. I'll write down the main ideas. Now, what information could support those ideas? How can I back up my main points with some details or examples?
3. How should I organize the information if I'm trying to describe something, relate a sequence, explain a process, solve a problem, or compare and contrast two or more things or ideas? I can use a graphic map or a chart to group the big ideas. I can use a matrix if I am comparing two or more items. I can use a timeline if I am describing a sequence. I can use a web for describing. I can use a flowchart for connecting problems to solutions.
4. I will write sentences about each part of the map or chart and sort the sentences into the best order, such as a time order for a procedure or each main idea with its supporting details for a description or an explanation.
5. I will put those sentences into paragraphs and use key words that will connect ideas. If my purpose is to compare two pieces of information, I will use key words such as *but*, *however*, *also*, and *alike* to indicate similarities and differences. If my purpose is to explain a sequence of events, I will use words like *next*, *then*, or *finally* to indicate the order of each item.

Reviewing and revising:

1. I will read my paper and see if it makes sense and if it fits my purpose. If I am describing something do my words help me see a mental picture? If I am giving a set of steps, can the reader follow the procedure? If I am addressing causes of happenings or problems, can the reader understand how the causes and outcomes are connected? When making comparisons, can the reader understand how the things I am comparing are the same or different?
2. I might have to add or drop ideas or change groupings.
3. I might have to change my words or sentences to say something better.
4. I will review the information in my paper to make sure that it is accurate. I might have to check other sources to make sure the information is correct.
5. I will review my use of signal words, like *next, as a result, one solution is,* and *in contrast* to be sure my reader will know how the ideas are connected.

restates the purpose, emphasizes, or state reasons and strategies she uses for signaling the organization and for selecting conjunctions to signal the connections between ideas.

In modeling the writing of a persuasive or argumentative piece about protecting bees, the SLP might first discuss her thinking about the importance of bees and why she wants to write about that topic (e.g., something she read that got her thinking about how bees are at risk or a conversation she had with a friend who keeps bees). The SLP then talks about her decision to use a particular organizational pattern (e.g., cause-effect, problem-solution, compare-contrast) and how that relates to the purpose of the text (e.g., "I am going to use the cause-effect structure because I want my audience to understand what things harm bees and how the loss of bees affects the environment"). She might then create a graphic organizer (a flowchart) that connects the reasons why bees are dying (cause) and the impact that has on the environment (effect). Once the graphic organizer is created, she might also talk about decisions related to what content from the graphic organizer she will include and which key words she will use to connect the ideas in her writing.

After modeling writing, the SLP then involves the students in the writing process. The text is jointly constructed and becomes a model for the students' own writing. SLPs support students' ability to signal organization by scaffolding their use of text structure to write about their content learning (Vukelich, Evans, & Albertson, 2003). The SLP evokes information from the students about what they are learning (perhaps as the SLP fills in a graphic representation), selects a text structure that would fit a logical purpose for sharing that information, and then models the writing of a text using that content. In a similar way, the SLP can support students' retrieval of information in a well-organized way, perhaps with the aid of a graphic reorientation, as she lets students write their own text following the same structure.

Educational Expectations for Informational Discourse

Informational texts can be difficult for students to comprehend. The Common Core State Standards (National Governors Association Center for Best Practices and the Council of Chief State School Officers [NGA-CSSO], 2010) delineates the competencies for the comprehension and production of informational texts expected of students from kindergarten through twelfth grade. The Common Core lists what students are expected to do but does not provide any guidelines for enabling students to meet these standards. Teachers are expected to adopt an approach to language that is significantly more in-depth than that required by previous standards.

As part of their roles and responsibilities, SLPs are to collaborate with school personnel to provide services that support instructional programs (American Speech-Language-Hearing Association, 2010). Currently, this collaboration involves supporting at-risk students and students with disabilities with respect to the Common Core. SLPs can provide unique contributions by addressing the linguistic and metalinguistic foundations of curriculum learning for students with disabilities as well as for other learners

Box 10.5. ***Informational Discourse Foundations for Common Core Competencies***

Fifth-Grade Competencies (NGA-CSSO, 2010)	**Informational Discourse Foundations**
Determine two or more main ideas of a text and explain how they are supported by key details; summarize the text	• Use a graphic organizer to retell an expository text
Explain the relationships or interactions between two or more individuals, events, or concepts in a historical, scientific, or technical text based on specific information in the text	• Signal words • Connective words • Dependent clauses
Determine the meaning of general academic and domain-specific words and phrases in a text relevant to a grade topic or subject area	• Talk about the nonimmediate • Disciplinary vocabulary • Nominalization
Compare and contrast the overall structure (e.g., chronology, comparison, cause/effect, problem/solution) of events, ideas, concepts, or information in two or more texts	• Engage in varied informational discourse functions in conversations in immediate and nonimmediate situations
Analyze multiple accounts of the same event or topic, noting similarities and differences in the point of view they represent	• Theory of mind: recognize that persons have thoughts, ideas, and beliefs that may differ • Recognize factors that influence ideas and beliefs
Explain how an author uses reasons and evidence to support particular points in a text, identifying which reasons and evidence support which point(s)	• Negotiate, persuade, argue about personal experiences/desires • Take the perspectives of others
Integrate information from several texts on the same topic in order to write or speak about the subject knowledgeably	• Recognize similarities and differences between texts • Use language to compare and contrast information in texts • Organize information into a structured discourse

who are at risk for school failure or for those who struggle in school settings. The link between the Common Core and school curricula, along with demands for more educationally and functionally relevant IEP goals, make it necessary that SLPs understand the language underpinnings for the Common Core standards and develop assessments and interventions strategies to assist students with disabilities in meeting meet those standards (Roberts, 2012). Second- through fifth-grade students are to meet the following standard for informational text: "By the end of the academic year, students are to read and comprehend informational texts, including history/social studies, science, and technical texts, at the high end of the grade complexity band independently and proficiently." Box 10.5 shows the competencies that are the basis of this standard for fifth-grade students and the foundational skills and knowledge that these competencies require. The competencies are taken from the reading standards but are easily taught within spoken interactions. The role of the SLP is to work with students and collaborate with teachers to develop these foundational skills.

Conclusion

The activities described in this chapter demonstrate how to use instructional discourse to build the vocabulary, syntactic patterns, abstract and decontextualized language, and discourse structures students require to comprehend and to produce informational texts. SLPs can use instructional discourse as a context or medium for making text elements clear and for assisting students in navigating through the complex nature of expository texts (e.g., function, nominalization, syntactic complexity). This article has considered these challenges and suggested ways of handling them in classrooms, particularly in elementary grades. Through instructional discourse, students can be supported in transitioning from conversation and narrative texts to informational texts used in history, social studies, and science. Once students have these foundational skills, SLPs can more easily implement metacognitive strategies to facilitate advanced comprehension and production of expository texts.

References

American Speech-Language-Hearing Association. (2010). *Roles and responsibilities of speech-language pathologists in schools* [Professional issues statement]. Available from www.asha.org/policy

Beck, I. L., McKeown, M. G., & Kucan, L. (2002). *Bringing words to life.* New York, NY: Guilford.

Best, R. M., Floyd, R. G., & McNamara, D. S. (2008). Differential competencies contributing to children's comprehension of narrative and expository texts. *Reading Psychology*, 29, 137–164.

Black, J. B. (1985). An exposition on understanding expository text. In B. K. Britton & J. B. Black (Eds.), *Understanding expository text: A theoretical and practical handbook for analyzing explanatory text* (pp. 249–267). Hillsdale, NJ: Erlbaum.

Blank, M. (2002). Classroom d iscourse: A key to literacy. In K. G. Butler & E. R. Silliman (Eds.), *Speaking, reading, and writing in children with language learning disabilities: New paradigms in research and practice* (pp. 151–173). Mahwah, NJ: Erlbaum.

Bova, A. (2011). Functions of "why" questions asked by children in family conversations. *Procedia—Social and Behavioral Sciences, 30*, 776–782.

Cazden, C. B. (1988). *Classroom discourse: The language of teaching and learning.* Portsmouth, NH: Heinemann.

Chambliss, M. J., & Murphy, P. K. (2002). Fourth and fifth graders representing the argument structure in written texts. *Discourse Processes, 34,* 91–115.

Clark, R. A., & Delia, J. G. (1976). The development of functional persuasive skills in childhood and early adolescence. *Child Development, 47,* 1008–1014.

Coffin, C. (2006). *Historical discourse: The language of time, cause, and evaluation.* London, England: Continuum.

Culatta, B., Blank, M., & Black, S. (2010). Talking things through: Roles of instructional discourse in children's processing of expository texts. *Topics in Language Disorders, 30,* 308–322.

Culatta, B., Hall-Kenyon, K. M., & Black, S. (2010). Teaching expository comprehension skills in early childhood classrooms. *Topics in Language Disorders, 30,* 323–338.

Dickinson, D. K., & Sprague, K. E. (2001). The nature and impact of early childhood care environments on the language and early literacy development of children from low-income families. In S. B. Neuman & D. K. Dickinson (Eds.), *Handbook of Early Literacy Research* (pp. 263–280). New York, NY: Guilford Press.

Dokken, N., & Ampika, M. (2010). Free the monkeys. *Wild Life Rescue, 10,* 4, 6.

Donaldson, M. (1986). *Children's explanations: A psycholinguistic study.* New York, NY: Cambridge University Press.

Dore, J. (1986). The development of conversational competence. In R. Schiefelbusch (Ed.), *Language competence: Assessment and intervention* (pp. 3–60). San Diego, CA: College-Hill.

Duke, N. K., & Pearson, P. D. (2002). Effective practices for developing reading comprehension. In A. E. Farstrup & S. J. Samuels (Eds.), *What research has to say about reading instruction* (3rd ed., pp. 205–242). Newark, NJ: International Reading Association.

Eisenberg, A. R., & Garvey, C. (1981). Children's use of verbal strategies in resolving conflicts. *Discourse Processes, 4,* 149–170.

Fivush, R. (2011). The development of autobiographical memory. *Annual Review of Psychology, 2,* 559–582.

Fivush, R., & Fromhoff, F. (1988). Style and structure in mother-child conversations about the past. *Discourse Process, 11,* 337–355.

Frazier, B. N., Gelman, S. A., & Wellman, H. M. (2009). Preschoolers' search for explanatory information within adult-child conversation. *Child Development, 80,* 1592–1611.

Gallagher, K. (2011). *Write like this: Teaching real-world writing through modeling and mentor texts.* Portland, ME: Stenhouse.

Hall, K. M., Sabey, B. L., & McClellan, M. (2005). Expository text comprehension: Helping primary grade teachers use expository texts to their full advantage. *Reading Psychology, 26,* 211–234.

Hall-Kenyon, K. M., & Black, S. (2010). Learning from expository texts: Classroom-based strategies for promoting comprehension and content knowledge in the elementary grades. *Topics in Language Disorders, 30,* 339–349.

Halliday, M. A. K., & Martin, J. R. (1993). *Writing science: Literacy and discursive power.* Pittsburgh, PA: University of Pittsburgh Press.

Hedberg, N., & Westby, C. E. (1993). *Analyzing storytelling skills: From theory to practice.* Tucson, AZ: Communication Skill Builders.

Hicks, D. (1990). Narrative skills and genre knowledge: Ways of telling in the primary grades. *Applied Psycholinguistics, 11*, 83–104.

Hudson, J. A. (1990). The emergence of autobiographical memory in mother-child conversation. In R. Fivush & J. Hudson (Eds.), *Knowing and remembering in young children* (pp. 166–196). New York, NY: Cambridge University Press.

Jenkins, P. B. (1996). *Falcons nest on skyscrapers.* New York, NY: HarperCollins.

Killgallon, D., & Killgallon, J. (2000). *Sentence composing for elementary school.* Portsmouth, NH: Heinmann.

Lorch, R. F., Jr., & Lorch, E. P. (1995). Effects of organizational signals of text-processing strategies. *Journal of Educational Psychology, 87*, 537–544.

Lorch, R. F., Jr., Lorch, E. P., & Inman, W. E. (1993). Effects of signaling topic structure in text recall. *Journal of Educational Psychology, 85*, 281–290.

Martin, J. R. (2002). Writing history: Construing time and value in discourse of the past. In M. J. Schleppegrell & M. C. Colombi (Eds.), *Developing advanced literacy in first and second languages: Meaning with power* (pp. 87–118). Mahwah, NJ: Erlbaum.

Mercer, N., & Hodgkinson, S. (2008). *Exploring talk in school.* Los Angeles, CA: Sage.

Meyer, B. J. F., Brandt, D. M., & Bluth, G. J. (1980). Use of top-level structure in text: Key for reading comprehension of ninth-grade students. *Reading Research Quarterly, 16*, 72–103.

Meyer, B. J. F., & Freedle, R. O. (1984). Effects of discourse type on recall. *American Educational Research Journal, 21*(1), 121–143.

Meyer, B. J. F, & Poon, L. W. (2001). Effects of structure strategy and signaling on recall of text. *Journal of Educational Psychology, 93*, 141–160.

Meyer, B. J. F., & Rice, G. E. (1984). The structure of text. In R. Barr, M. L. Kamil, P. Mosenthal, & P. D. Pearson (Eds.), *Handbook of Reading Research* (Vol. I, pp. 319–352). New York: Longman.

Meyer, B. J. F., Young, C. J., & Bartlett, B. J. (1989). *Memory improved: Reading and memory enhancement across the life span through strategic text structures.* Hillsdale, NJ: Erlbaum.

Millis, K. K., & Just, M. A. (1994). The influence of connectives on sentence comprehension. *Journal of Memory and Language, 33*, 128–147.

Moffett, J. (1968). *Teaching the universe of discourse.* New York, NY: Houghton Mifflin.

Naremore, R. C., Densmore, A. E., & Harman, D. R. (1995). *Language intervention with school-aged children: Conversation, narrative, and text.* San Diego, CA: Singular.

National Governors Association Center for Best Practices and Council of Chief State School Officers. (2010). *Common Core State Standards.* Washington, DC: Author. Retrieved from http://www.corestandards.org

National Reading Panel. (2000). *Teaching children to read: An evidence-based assessment of the scientific research literature on reading and its implications for reading instruction* (NIH Publication No. 00-4754). Washington, DC: U.S. Department of Health and Human Services, National Institute of Child Health and Human Development. Available at http://www.nationalreadingpanel.org/

Orsolini, M. (1993). "Because" in children's discourse. *Applied Psycholinguistics, 14,* 89–120.

Pearson, P. D., & Duke, N. K. (2002). Comprehension instruction in the primary grades. In C. C. Block and M. Pressley (Eds.), *Comprehension instruction: Research-based best practices* (pp. 247–258). New York, NY: Guilford Press.

Pearson, S., & Myrick, P. (2012). *Arts of persuasion: Learn NC editions.* Available from http://www.learnnc.org/lp/editions/artspersuade/640

Peterson, C., & McCabe, A. (1994). A social interactionist account of developing decontextualized narrative skill. *Developmental Psychology, 30,* 937–948.

Piccolo, J. A. (1987). Expository text structure: Teaching and learning strategies. *Reading Teacher, 40,* 38–47.

Price, L. H., van Kleek, A., & Huberty, C. J. (2009). Talk during book sharing between parents and preschool children: A comparison between storybook and expository conditions. *Reading Research Quarterly, 44,* 171–194.

Reese, E., Cox, A., Harte, S., & McAnally, H. (2003). Diversity in adults' styles of reading books to children. In A. van Kleeck, S. A., Stahl, E. B. Bauer (Eds.), *On reading books to children: Parents and teachers* (pp. 37–57). Mahwah, NJ: Erlbaum.

Riley, L. A. (1997). *Mouse mess.* New York, NY: Blue Sky.

Roberts, K. L. (2012). The Common Core state standards on reading and writing informational text in the primary grades: What are they, and what are the linguistic demands? *Seminars in Speech and Language Pathology, 33,* 146–159.

Seidenberg, P. L. (1989). Relating text-processing research to reading and writing instruction for learning disabled students. *Learning Disabilities Focus, 5,* 4–12.

Sigel, I. E., Stinson, E. T., & Flaugher, J. (1991). Socialization of representational competence in the family: The distancing paradigm. In L. Okagaki & R. Sternberg (Eds.), *Directors of development: Influences on the development of children's thinking* (pp. 121–144). Hillsdale, NJ: Erlbaum.

Silliman, E. R., & Wilkinson, L. C. (1994). Discourse scaffolds for classroom intervention. In G. P. Wallach & K. G. Butler (Eds.), *Language learning disabilities in school-age children and adolescents* (pp. 27–52). New York, NY: Merrill.

Smith, K. (2011). Dictogloss: A multi-skill task for accuracy in writing through cooperative learning. *Teachers helping teachers—Proceedings of 2011 conferences, seminars, and workshops.* Retrieved from http://tht-japan.org/proceedings/2011/069-080_smith.pdf

Snow, C., & Beals, D. E. (2006). Mealtime talk that supports literacy development. *New Directions for Child and Adolescent Development, 111,* 52–66.

Sweet, A. P., & Snow, C. E. (2003). *Rethinking reading comprehension.* New York, NY: Guilford.

Spyridakis, J. H., & Standal, T. C. (1987). Signals in expository prose: Effects on reading comprehension. *Reading Research Quarterly, 22,* 285–298.

Stein, N. L., & Miller, C. A. (1993). The development of memory and reasoning skill in argumentative contexts: Evaluating, explaining, and generating evidence. In R. Glaser (Ed.), *Advances in instructional psychology* (Vol. 4, pp. 285–335). Hillsdale, NJ: Erlbaum.

Torgesen, J. K., Rashotte, C. A., & Greenstein, J. (1988). Language comprehension in learning disabled children who perform poorly on memory span tests. *Journal of Educational Psychology, 80*, 480–487.

Tough, J. (1977). *The development of meaning.* New York, NY: Wiley.

Ukrainetz, T. A. (2006). The many ways of exposition: A focus on text structure. In T. A. Ukrainetz (Ed.), *Contextualized language intervention: Scaffolding preK–12 literacy achievement* (pp. 246–288). Austin, TX: PRO-ED.

Vukelich, C, Evans, C, & Albertson, B. (2003). Organizing expository texts: A look at possibilities. In D. M. Barone & L. M. Morrow (Eds.), *Literacy and young children: Research-based practices* (pp. 261–288). New York, NY: Guilford.

Wajnryb, R. (1990). *Grammar dictation.* Oxford, England: Oxford University Press.

Wallach, G. (2008). *Language intervention for school-aged children.* St. Louis, MO: Mosby.

Weaver, C. A., & Kintsch, W. (1991). Expository text. In R. Barr, M. L. Kamil, P. Mosenthal, & P. D. Pearson (Eds.), *Handbook of reading research* (Vol. 2, pp. 230–244). White Plains, NY: Longman.

Weiss, D. M., & Sachs, J. (1991). Persuasive strategies used by preschool children. *Discourse Processes, 14*, 55–72.

Westby, C. E. (1994). The effects of culture on genre, structure, and style of oral and written texts. In G. Wallach & K. Butler (Eds.), *Language learning disabilities in school-age children and adolescents* (pp. 180–218). Columbus, OH: Merrill.

Westby, C. E., Culatta, B., Lawrence, B., & Hall-Kenyon, K. (2010). Summarizing expository texts. *Topics in Language Disorders, 30*, 275–287.

Williams, J. P. Hall, K. M., & Lauer, K. D. (2004). Teaching expository text structure to young at-risk learners: Building the basics of comprehension instruction. *Exceptionality, 12*, 129–144.

Williams, J. P., Hall, K. M., Lauer, K. D., Stafford, K. B., DeSisto, L. A., & deCani, J. S. (2005). Expository text comprehension in the primary grade classroom. *Journal of Educational Psychology, 97*, 538–550.

Williams, J. P., Stafford, K. B., Lauer, K. D., Hall, K. M., & Pollini, S. (2009). Embedding reading comprehension training in content-area instruction. *Journal of Educational Psychology, 101*, 1–20.

Zarnowski, M. (2006). *Making sense of history.* New York, NY: Scholastic.

Zimmerman, F. J., Gilkerson, J., Richards, J. A., Christakis, D. A., Xu, D., Gray, S., & Yapanel, U. (2009). Teaching by listening: The importance of adult-child conversations to language development. *Pediatrics, 124*, 342–349.

Zwiers, J. (2008). *Building academic language: Essential practices for content classrooms.* San Francisco, CA: Jossey-Bass.

Chapter 11

Playing the Classroom Game: Supporting Students Who Are Environmentally at Risk

Celeste Roseberry-McKibbin

"It's all about making the implicit explicit" (Brinton & Fujiki, 2011). In the 21st century, the sociocultural face of the U.S. is changing rapidly. Our schools reflect this change, with increasing numbers of students coming to school as English language learners (ELLs) and many coming from impoverished backgrounds. Schools are striving to successfully support and serve the needs of these ELL and low socioeconomic status (SES) students. Schools provide remedial and special education services to assist struggling students to succeed academically. However, there is little to help at-risk students to understand and implement the social "rules of the game," that are also involved in school success. These implicit rules of success are what Nelson (1989) called the "hidden" curriculum of the classroom. These at-risk students form a significant proportion of the caseloads of many speech–langauge pathologists (SLPs). SLPs have a distinctive role in addressing the social-communicative competencies of their students in the classroom (American Speech-Language-Hearing Association [ASHA], 2010). This chapter explains practical assessment and intervention strategies for SLPs that help at-risk ELL and low-SES students play the school interactional game successfully.

Our Shifting Society: Demographic and Socioeconomic Trends

The U.S. Census Bureau (2010) indicated that the number of foreign-born residents is projected to rise from 31 million in the year 2000 to 48 million in 2025. It is projected that in 2030, 43% of U.S. citizens will be from a culturally diverse background, meaning one with non–Anglo-Western ancestry. By mid-century, through both immigration and births, the Hispanic population is expected to triple (Box 11.1). From the 1997–1998 to the 2008–2009 school year, the general population of students in the U.S. grew by 7.2% to 49.5 million (Education Week, 2012). During the same period, the number of ELLs enrolled in America's public schools increased from 3.5 million to 5.3 million, or by 51% (National Clearinghouse for English Language Acquisition, 2011).

Box 11.1. *U.S. Demographics by Race and Ethnicity*

	1970	2000	2050
White	83.7%	70.0%	50.0%
Black	10.6%	12.0%	13.0%
Hispanic	4.5%	13.0%	24.0%
Asian	1.0%	4.0%	9.0%
Native American	0.4%	0.9%	1.0%

Note: Data from U.S. Census Bureau (2010).

Children from linguistically and culturally diverse backgrounds who are ELLs sometimes perform quite well in school, especially if their families are not dealing with other challenges such as poverty or unemployment. Being a proficient bilingual has many cognitive, linguistic, and social advantages (Grech & McLeod, 2012). Children who become proficient-bilingual educated adults enrich society in a wide variety of ways and are very sought after as potential employees in the U.S. and abroad.

However, many ELLs experience difficulty in school (Hernandez, 2011; Kayser, 2012; Paradis, Genesee, & Crago, 2011; Roseberry-McKibbin, 2014). Nationwide, only 12% of students with limited English scored "at or above proficient" in mathematics in fourth grade, compared to 42% of students not classified as ELLs. The gap was much wider in eighth-grade math, where 5% of ELLs were proficient or above proficient, compared to 35% of non-ELLs. On a national reading test, in eighth grade, only 3% of ELLs scored at or above proficiency compared to 34% of non-ELLs (Education Week, 2012). There are a number of reasons why ELLs struggle in mainstream American schools.

One major reason is that ELLs come to kindergarten (or later grades) speaking little or no English and must learn academics in this new language. Often, schools do not support or accommodate these students successfully. There are few bilingual classrooms, which are classrooms that teach in both English and the native language, gradually transitioning students to English-only instruction. Instead, most classes in American public schools are taught in English only, with few if any special provisions for ELLs. In addition, many ELLs come from cultural and environmental backgrounds that do not match those of U.S. schools, which are based on Western middle-class culture. The lack of familiarity with English coupled with environmental mismatch issues leaves these students very susceptible to school failure, even if they have normal underlying language-learning ability (Nixon, McCardle, & Leos, 2007). According to Rosa-Lugo, Mihai, and Nutta (2012):

> In the absence of careful planning and implementation of effective instructional practices, English learners are at risk of becoming academic underachievers with limited vocational and economic opportunities. The level of academic achievement among English learners, measured as a subgroup, is lower than that of proficient English-speaking learners. (p. 5)

Another change in the U.S. in the past few decades is an increase in the numbers of children from low-SES homes. The Great Recession, which began in 2007, has caused even more children to be impacted by poverty. According to the most recent federal data, in the 2008–2009 school year, there were 954,914 homeless children and youth enrolled in public schools. This represents a 20% increase from the 2007–2008 school year and a 41% increase from the 2006–2007 school year (National Association for the Education of Homeless Children and Youth, 2011).

Statistics show that nationally 27% of White children, 30% of Asian children, 61% of African American children, and 63% of Hispanic children come from backgrounds of poverty (National Center for Children in Poverty, 2005). The standard of living for those in the bottom 10% of the population is lower in the U.S. than in any other developed nation except the United Kingdom. Some states have been more impacted than others. In California, for example, in 2011 an estimated 2.2 million children were living in poverty. Children of color in California were four times more likely than White children to be born into economically fragile households. Sixty-nine percent of Hispanic and 71% of African American children in California were classified as "income poor" compared to 32% of White children. Eighty-two percent of poor children came from homes where at least one parent was working (Posnick-Goodwin, 2011).

According to Terry, Connor, Thomas-Tate, and Love (2010), findings across multiple studies show that there is widely varying achievement among children in U.S. schools, with children from some environments experiencing early difficulty. When these children enter kindergarten, achievement gaps are observable even before they start learning to read. According to Terry et al., the most salient child characteristics that predict academic success are race/ethnicity and SES. Belonging to a racial or ethnic minority group and living in poverty place children at greater risk for poor education, health, and social outcomes (Centre for Social Justice, 2011). Low SES puts children at particular risk for behavior, language, and academic problems, regardless of their race or ethnicity (Qi & Kaiser, 2004).

When at-risk students arrive at school, they find that school culture predominantly reflects the values of middle-class White Americans. For example, most SLPs are middle-class, White females whose intervention practices are grounded in their own cultural practices and beliefs (Hammer, 2011). The background experiences, views of schooling, and interactional behaviors of at-risk children make them vulnerable to mismatches with mainstream schools in a number of areas that will be described in this chapter.

It is imperative that SLPs, classroom teachers, and other educators who work with at-risk children in the schools be aware of these mismatches so that students are not mistakenly diagnosed with language impairments or other disabilities (Davis & Banks, 2012; Grech & McLeod, 2012; Justice, 2010). In addition, awareness enables educators to help these students learn and negotiate the cultural and pragmatic rules of the mainstream classroom and thereby successfully play the classroom game.

The Costs of Not Attending to the Implicit School Curriculum

School can be viewed as a social as well as an academic game whose rules successful students need to follow in order to win. Academic rules are usually explicit, that is, obvious and discussed openly. Teachers typically make expectations of the academic curriculum clear in content areas such as math, science, and social studies. While students may still not do what needs to be done, the reason is not usually that of not knowing what to do. But what about the more subtle social rules of the implicit curriculum? How are they learned? Where are they taught? Who teaches them? What happens to the student who enters school having had little experience with or knowledge of these implicit rules? Society—as well as most educators—assume that children will somehow automatically learn, automatize, and follow these rules. Those who do are the ones who will succeed.

Many children, especially ELL and low SES, do not absorb and follow the social rules of school without direct, explicit instruction. They struggle beginning in kindergarten and can eventually manifest problematic social patterns of behavior characterized by poor verbal and nonverbal communication skills (Ebert & Kohnert, 2011; Hill & Coufal, 2005; Liiva & Cleave, 2005; McCormack, Harrison, McLeod, & McAllister, 2011; Redmond, 2011). Left unattended, poor communication skills increase students' risk of later substance abuse and encounters with the juvenile justice and prison systems (Armstrong, 2011; ASHA, 2007; Fogle, 2013; Linares-Orama, 2005). A study by Blanton and Dagenais (2007) of adjudicated (involved in the court system) and nonadjudicated adolescents showed that adjudicated adolescents had vocabulary and overall language scores lower than those of nonadjudicated adolescents. According to Blanton and Dagenais, "SLPs need to look at methods for identifying and providing interventions for adjudicated adolescents and students with behavior problems before they are adjudicated or incarcerated" (p. 314).

Common Challenges in the Hidden Curriculum of the Classroom

Educators' Lack of Awareness

Becoming competent in following the rules of the hidden curriculum of the classroom involves developing skills in two areas: communicating in the discourse of the classroom and following classroom routines. Before discussing specific assessment and intervention strategies for helping at-risk students succeed in these areas, it is important to understand the nature of the difficulties that they are vulnerable to experiencing. As a foundation for helping students succeed, professionals must understand how at-risk students' backgrounds might not match the expectations of the typical mainstream school classroom.

First and foremost, at-risk low-SES and ELL students need to communicate successfully with their classroom teachers. They need to comprehend what teachers are saying and to express themselves appropriately. They also need to understand and to follow classroom rules. While these may seem like straightforward tasks to White, monolingual, English-speaking, middle-SES families, many at-risk students struggle to communicate appropriately with their teachers and to follow classroom rules.

It is my experience that some mainstream White middle-SES English-speaking professionals may feel frustration with at-risk students, especially if these students come to kindergarten with no preschool experience. Because teachers have many demands on their time and may teach large numbers of students, they often believe that they cannot take time to teach at-risk students the "culture of the classroom," that is, the social rules for successful interaction in the formal school setting. Teachers who are asked to tackle the social rules of classroom interaction in addition to academic content can feel overwhelmed.

SLPs can be supportive here, helping children inside the classroom in individual small group or large all-class formats (more about these later). In addition, SLPs can educate classroom teachers about the nature of the difficulties that some at-risk students experience. If teachers better understand the challenges experienced by at-risk students, they will be in a stronger position to help these students succeed in the classroom setting.

Thus, while it is important for students to learn and follow the social rules of the classroom, it is also critical for teachers and other educators to increase their awareness of and sensitivity to the challenges experienced by many at-risk students (Davis & Banks, 2012). With awareness of the cultural mismatches between home and school, educators are then much less likely to mislabel students as needing special education if it is not warranted and better able to provide effective, sensitive interventions to help students adjust to and succeed in classroom settings.

At-Risk Students' Lack of Experience With Instructional Discourse

A major challenge experienced by many at-risk students is their lack of familiarity and experience with classroom discourse, disadvantages that can lead to social interaction difficulties as well as academic failure.

Classroom discourse has also been called academic or instructional discourse. Merritt, Barton, and Culatta (1998) stated that instructional discourse "is the particular type of exchange used in classrooms during teacher-student interactions for the purpose of enhancing knowledge, guiding comprehension, or developing skills" (p. 145). The goal of instructional discourse is to teach new information and skills through connected utterances or through a sustained exchange that communicates meaning (Merritt et al., 1998). Children gain competence in this type of discourse through formal schooling.

Many ELL students come to school with at least basic knowledge of informal oral English communication. Referred to as basic interpersonal communication skills, or BICS, this communication is contextualized, supported by environmental cues, and assumes a shared reality among listeners (Cummins, 2000; Roseberry-McKibbin, 2007, 2014). For typically developing children, BICS takes 2 to 3 years to develop to a native-like level.

The other type of competence is cognitive academic language proficiency, or CALP. CALP is decontextualized, impersonal, and does not assume a shared reality. For typically developing ELL students, CALP takes 5 to 10 years to develop to a native-like level (Cummins, 1999; Paradis et al., 2011). CALP requires competence in instructional discourse. Instructional discourse has three major distinguishing characteristics: (a) it is decontextualized, (b) it involves connected utterances that are used in a sustained exchange, and (c) there is a power asymmetry between the teacher and the students, with the teacher mediating who can speak and when. Cazden (2001) stated:

> Classrooms are complex social systems. . . . In typical classrooms, the most important asymmetry in the rights and obligations of teacher and students is over the right to speak. . . . Teachers have the right to speak at any time and to any person; they can fill any silence or interrupt any speaker; they can speak to a student anywhere in the room and in any volume or tone of voice. And no one has any right to object. (p. 54)

Box 11.2. ***Examples of an Initiation-Response-Evaluation (IRE) Instructional Interaction***

Teacher: Why was the Civil War fought?

Student: (after raising hand and being called upon) To free slaves and end slavery.

Teacher: That's right. President Lincoln wanted to end slavery and have freedom for all Americans.

Teacher: Why is it important to recycle?

Student: I don't think it's important. At my house, we just throw everything in the trash.

Teacher: We can throw some things in the trash, but it is best to recycle when we can. It is important for us to recycle items like paper, glass, and plastic so that we reduce pollution and climate change.

Cazden (2001) outlined a typical model of instructional discourse as: initiate (teacher), respond (student), evaluate (teacher). The teacher asks a question, the student answers, and then the teacher evaluates the response (Box 11.2). In this IRE model, with her or his questions, the teacher determines the amount, form, and content of the target response. Teachers ask known-information questions, meaning they ask questions for which they already know the answer. Teachers use these questions to determine whether or not the material has been read, understood, and memorized, and, if needed, they add corrective information (Hulit, Howard, & Fahey, 2011). This directive teaching style emphasizes recall of details. Students must master the IRE routine in order to interact successfully in the classroom (Ritzman, Sanger, & Coufal, 2006).

For ELL students who are trying to become familiar with instructional discourse so they can achieve CALP, it is challenging to interpret information in a decontextualized context accompanied by nonshared assumptions. It is also challenging to participate in sustained exchanges with limited English skills. Many ELL students may not be accustomed to connected discourse and sustained exchanges in the home (Chan & Chen, 2011).

In Anglo-Western culture, children are viewed as important and legitimate conversational partners who actively engage in ongoing interactions with adults (Hanson, 2011; Hart & Risley, 1999; van Kleeck, 2006). Children are expected to verbally display their knowledge and to look an adult in the eye when doing so. Boys and girls are expected to learn together as equals. Children are expected to display their knowledge in front of others. Independence and autonomy are valued. American classrooms reflect all these values, but they clash with the values of cultures such as Hispanic and Middle Eastern, which include interdependence, collectivism, and familism (Kayser, 2012; Sharifzadeh, 2011).

In some cultures, children are to be seen and not heard. Averting eye gaze when speaking with an adult is a sign of respect. In these cultures, it is considered inappropriate for children to initiate conversation with adults or to actively and verbally assert themselves (Cheng, 2012; Jacob, 2011; Joe & Malach, 2011; Roseberry-McKibbin, 2013, 2014; van Kleeck, 2006). For them, adult control is a given. These children are not encouraged to think independently, negotiate, make choices, or plan ahead. Rather than engaging in conversation with adults, the children primarily learn by listening and watching. They demonstrate what they have learned discreetly, on their own or in groups. Many Hispanic and Middle Eastern girls from traditional homes may have been socialized to be silent, letting the males dominate. These girls may defer to boys, only displaying their knowledge in the company of other girls. Thus, in the mixed gender of the classroom, these girls may remain silent, missing opportunities for interaction and learning (Heckler, 2009; Kayser, 2012; Sharifzadeh, 2011).

White, middle-class parents generally value individualism, progress, and achievement. In contrast, many Hispanic parents may not push for achievement or developmental milestones. There is a more relaxed attitude toward development of early skills (Chan & Chen, 2011; Zuniga, 2011) and an emphasis on interdependence rather than independence. Parents emphasize the language of affiliation and connection. The emphasis upon interdependence among family members is reflected in language that tends to be contextualized and personal (Westby & Inglebret, 2012). For example, Hispanic children are expected to participate enthusiastically in family activities. They often have more interactions with siblings and peers than with adults (Zuniga, 2011). These children may struggle when they arrive in a classroom where the teacher controls interactions, expects students to interact with her directly, and discourages personal sharing and helping each other on assignments.

There are many similarities between the discourse of the classroom and that used in middle-SES Anglo-European homes (Hanson, 2011). These children are often involved in decision making with their parents from very early in life. They are given choices, even as toddlers, about what they want to eat and play with. Middle-SES children, early in life, are encouraged to develop negotiation skills. Thus, middle-SES children enter school with a discourse style from home that matches what the school expects. In addition, middle-SES caregivers' child-directed speech mirrors the teachers' question-and-answer discourse style.

In contrast, low-SES children may be more strictly controlled, given few choices and few opportunities to develop this language of negotiation (Hart & Risley, 1995; Neuman, 2009). Many low-SES parents, because of long work hours and time spent taking buses, along with limited child-care options, often have to leave their children alone. These parents try to establish clear boundaries to keep their children safe but often end up restricting the children's autonomy, using strict obedience and punitive measures: "The verbal give-and-take so common in middle-class homes is replaced by absolute authority" (Neuman, 2009, p. 17).

For low-SES students from some homes, an informal speaking register is not unusual. This informal register may include, among other things, arguing, interrupting, challenging authority, and even using pofanity (Payne, 2003; Roseberry-McKibbin, 2013). When children from these homes arrive at kindergarten, they may use this informal register with teachers and other authority figures if not explicitly cautioned. I will never forget Jeffrey, an angelic, blond, blue-eyed kindergartener from a low-SES home who looked at me during a therapy session and said, "No, b----." Shocked, I gave him a very stern lecture about bad language, school rules, and how I would take him to the principal if he ever said that to me again. Jeffrey began to cry and apologize, and said, "But

Box 11.3. ***Noncongruence of Other Cultures With Instructional Discourse***

Instructional Discourse	Noncongruent Home Discourse
1. Eye contact with teacher	1. Look away as a sign of respect
2. Initiate interaction with teacher; method depending on classroom rules	2. Do no initiate, especially verbally, with an adult
3. When teacher initiates, maintain the interaction by adding information	3. Give a brief answer and stop
4. Individual verbal display of knowledge	4. Do not display knowledge or point to yourself; do things in groups
5. Students expected to answer questions about their opinions, preferences	5. Do not express your opinions; adults say, "you'll do it this way because I said so"
6. Interact and learn in mixed-gender groups	6. Boys and girls learn separately
7. Teacher talks; students listen	7. Talk to other children freely
8. Teachers explain content and procedures	8. Observe and listen to learn content and procedures
9. Teachers ask known-information questions with specific answers expected	9. Not asked known-information questions; viewed as illogical
10. Teachers expect students to follow routines and rules	10. No school-like routines in background if children have not attended preschool
11. Activities occur for prescribed periods scheduled by teacher	11. Do activities for as long as you want, no adult-prescribed schedule

Note: Compiled from Armstrong (2011), Battle (2012), Chan and Chen (2011), Mokuau and Tauili'ili (2011), Roseberry-McKibbin (2007, 2013), Santos and Chan (2011), Stockman (2010), On-Line Teacher Resource (2011).

my dad always calls my mom that." In other situations, I have had to work very hard in language intervention to help low-SES students learn that they are not to interrupt an adult, or even another student, who is speaking but rather politely wait for their turn to talk. Box 11.3 compares and contrasts typical Anglo-Western cultural expectations to those that are typical in the home environments of many at-risk students.

In the classroom, teachers often use indirect requests (Hulit et al., 2011; O'Neill-Perrozi, 2009; Owens, 2010). For example, if students are talking, a teacher may say: "It's pretty hard to hear with all the noise in here." Mainstream students will interpret this to mean: "Stop talking." But some low-SES students who are used to very directive language at home (e.g., "Shut up right now!") will interpret the teacher's statement literally, as just a comment on the noise and keep on talking. Alternatively they may interpret an implied directive as indicating that the teacher is fearful and not deserving of respect (Delpit, 1995; Payne, 2003; Roseberry-McKibbin, 2013). Box 11.4 contains examples of contrasting home and classroom directives.

Box 11.4. ***Contrasting Explicitness of Adult Directives at Home and School***

Low-SES Homes	School
Shut up!	I can't hear Jose with all the talking in here.
Sit down right now.	We can't begin the lesson until everyone is seated.
Wait your turn!	We need to let Heather finish what she is saying.
Stop bugging me! Get lost!	You need to sit at your desk until I say you can get up.

For many students from low-SES homes, success in school is not important. On the other hand, early in life mid-SES students are given the "big picture": Do well in school and follow the rules to get into a good college, obtain a well-paying job, drive a nice car, and live in a nice home in a good neighborhood where you can raise children to have the same advantages. Their path is clear. Whenever these mid-SES children are bored at school and reluctant to comply with rules, they are reminded by their parents that delayed gratification, such as doing homework when they would rather be playing video games, or working quietly in class even though they would rather be talking or texting, will eventually pay off in a materially prosperous adulthood accompanied by an excellent quality of life.

For low-SES students, however, the "big picture" is not as clear. Some low-SES students come from homes where their caregivers are too busy surviving and providing for life's basic necessities to spend time engaging in interactions about the importance of school. Those students whose background is one of generational poverty, where several generations of families have depended on welfare and have experienced little formal schooling, do not see the relevance of school, or its rules, at all. An additional challenge for low-SES children, especially those who are highly mobile (e.g., homeless or of migrant status), is that their chaotic and unpredictable lifestyle does not teach skills such as prioritizing and planning ahead (Neuman, 2009; Roseberry-McKibbin, 2013). These students may need substantial guidance to learn, internalize, and follow classroom rules and routines successfully.

At-Risk Students' Unfamiliarity With Classroom Social Routines

When students enter kindergarten, and every year after that, they need to learn and follow classroom social routines or scripts (Brinton & Fujiki, 2011; Westby, 2006). This may present challenges for low-SES students, as they frequently come from backgrounds where routines are not common. Middle-class parents build routines (e.g., visiting the local library, going grocery shopping, eating out at restaurants, going to church, attending team sports practices) in their children's worlds that the children internalize over time. Along with these routines, parents develop a set of oral scripts, predictable language sequences that condition children to expect what is next and to know how to act appropriately. Low-SES children often are not exposed to these routines in their daily lives and may come to school without a basic oral script set. Many low-SES children have lived in circumstances with casual, informal, unpredictable, continuously shifting schedules, especially if they are homeless or of migrant status (Geiss, 2011). The order, regimentation, and time-sensitivity of school are a great shock to them (Neuman, 2009; Roseberry-McKibbin, 2013).

In terms of at-risk ELL students, some classroom social rules and routines may be especially hard for those from cultural backgrounds where they are taught to interact with peers and siblings and to work collaboratively (Davis & Banks, 2012). Mainstream U.S. school classrooms are extremely individualistic and emphasize routines involving independent work. This environment is difficult for children from collectivist backgrounds, which emphasize interdependence and cooperation. Some of these children are raised in homes where family members live in very close proximity to one another and where physical affection is the norm. Everyone shares everything. There may be few rules, especially if parents work long hours and children have had a great deal of unsupervised time (Zuniga, 2011). The regimented, structured routines of school may be completely unfamiliar, and students may unknowingly violate the rules involved in these routines and incur their teachers' displeasure. Box 11.5 has a list of classroom routines that are typical of most mainstream U.S. classrooms that SLPs can use in classroom observations to evaluate whether or not a student of concern is following specific routines behaviors successfully.

At-Risk Students' Deficits in Self-Regulated Learning

Making good choices in school and seeing the benefits of delayed gratification involve "self-regulation," which is also called "executive functioning." Students need to take charge of their own learning, organize their materials, attend to tasks, do independent seatwork, manage their time, prioritize, and plan ahead (Haynes & Pindzola, 2012; Ziolkowski & Goldstein, 2011). Such self-regulated "thinking language" grows out of social support and scaffolding from attentive, supportive people in the child's environment, especially in families where problem solving and delayed gratification are encouraged.

Deficits in self-regulation may be evident in physiological or neurological differences. For example, Blair and colleagues (2011) longitudinally studied a sample of 1,292 low-SES children. They found that high cortisol levels in infancy, caused by stress early in life, were uniquely associated with executive functioning skills at the age of 3 years.

Farah, Noble, and Hurt (2005) examined the neurocognitive performance of 60 African American children, 30 from low- and 30 from mid-SES homes, enrolled in Philadelphia public school kindergartens. The children were tested on a battery of tasks designed to assess the functioning of five key neurocognitive systems. Farah and colleagues found that the more advantaged children performed better on the test battery as a whole. There were large and significant differences between low- and mid-SES children on tasks designed to tap skills in both the left/perisylvian language system and the prefrontal executive control system. In addition, those from low-SES backgrounds had significantly greater difficulties in areas of the brain that control working memory,

Box 11.5. ***Classroom Routines Assessment Checklist***

Expectations	Violation of Expectations
When you arrive in the morning	
Come to class prepared with homework done	Arrive without supplies or homework done
Read the directions on the board	Ignore directions
Empty your backpack	Leave your backpack unemptied
Put your jacket on its hook	Leave your jacket on the floor
Keep your things organized	Be messy, leave things in disarray
Begin the morning assignment	Wander around, sit and do nothing, talk
In general	
Do not touch others' property or person without permission	Touch others' property or person without permission
Sit straight in your chair	Tilt in your chair or wander around
Stay in your seat unless permitted to leave	Wander around the room
Look the teacher in the eye	Look around you and not at the teacher
Think about what the teacher is saying	Think about something else
Don't talk unless asked to	Talk to your friends
Raise your hand if you have something to say	Call out when you have something to say
Work carefully; don't rush	Rush and finish as fast as possible
Be quiet in lines, hallways, restrooms	Talk and wander around outside classroom
Always do your best	Work only when you feel like it

which has a negative impact on executive functioning. According to the investigators, brain disparities in the areas of memory, language, and cognitive control can affect life paths. Lack of cognitive control may negatively impact self-regulation and problem-solving ability. Memory and language deficits have a negative impact on acquisition of academic skills and, eventually, the ability to pursue higher education and a well-paying job.

In sum, it is important for educators to be aware of the challenges faced by at-risk (low-SES and ELL) students in the classroom setting. These challenges include difficulty interacting competently via the medium of instructional discourse, following expected classroom routines, and being self-regulated learners. SLPs can support these students through assessment of the classroom environment and intervention to help students increase their competence in interacting successfully in classroom discourse and routines.

Assessment of At-Risk Students' Classroom Performance

In order to evaluate at-risk students' classroom performance and genuinely understand them and their ways of interacting with peers and teachers, the SLP needs to get into the classroom to make multiple observations over time (Haynes & Pindzola, 2012; Nelson, 2010; Roseberry-McKibbin, 2014). Interviews with students and their teachers are also needed. Norm-referenced test performance and even language sampling is not enough to understand the patterns of strengths and weaknesses with instructional discourse.

There are several ways in which SLPs can evaluate students. They can use the material in Boxes 11.3 and 11.5 as checklists for observing and recording classroom behaviors. They also can use the lists to guide student interviews. For example, the SLP can ask questions such as, "What is the rule if you want to say something while the teacher is talking?"

Videotaping classroom interactions and reviewing these tapes with students and teachers can be especially helpful. Students and teachers are then able to see their own performance and reflect on what happened and what they could do differently the next time. Most recently, SLPs have begun using iPad technology to this end (Archer & Bateson, 2011; DeCurtis & Ferrer, 2011; Roseberry-McKibbin, Bryla, Faherty, & Johnson-Garcia, 2012). As an anecdotal example, I offer the following experience: I recently used my iPad with a low-SES second-grade boy who was having continuous social difficulties in the classroom. When he was able to view his facial expressions and body language on my iPad, not only was he very taken with the technology, but he also improved his behavior at once. Because iPads are often considered very "cool," even among high school students, using them to video-record the students and then show them their behaviors can be highly effective.

When SLPs conduct multiple observations in the classroom over time and record students' behaviors, they are in an ideal position to collaborate with teachers. This collaboration can lead to a version of response to intervention (RTI) aimed at classroom interactions that is very promising with at-risk students who are having difficulty communicating in the classroom.

A Response to Intervention Model for Classroom Pragmatics

Response to intervention (RTI) has been discussed previously in terms of early identification and support for reading. RTI is particularly effective for addressing the needs of students who are at risk of being misclassified as needing special education (Brown & Sanford, 2011; Davis & Banks, 2012; Education Week, 2012; Wyatt, 2012). The goal of RTI is to help support at-risk students by providing them with the conceptual academic knowledge they need in content areas such as math and reading. Within a pragmatics-focused RTI, SLPs can collaborate with teachers to increase or modify the support that students receive in the classroom to help them better cope with instructional discourse, follow social routines, and regulate their own learning.

There are many models of collaboration for implementation of RTI (Brice & Brice, 2007). Sometimes SLPs work with students individually and sometimes in small groups. Other times, they provide direct, whole-class instruction. If appropriate services can be provided in the classroom, SLPs should work directly with students in that setting. At the Tier 1 level, SLPs can provide indirect services, such as giving teachers lists of suggestions to implement. In Tier 2 interventions, SLPs can guide instructors or work directly with students who are having difficulty (Rudebusch & Wiechmann, 2011). Tier 3 interventions involve referral for special education services. Even for these students, SLPs can work in the classroom. Nippold (2011) emphasized that classroom-based intervention does not have to occur at the cost of individualized therapeutic services. Rather, SLPs should aim for students receiving both through collaboration with teachers.

Although classroom-based service delivery is recommended, especially for pragmatic skills, Brandel and Loeb (2011) found that pullout remains the most prevalent service delivery option. Brandel and Loeb surveyed almost 2,000 SLPs nationwide about the factors they considered when making service delivery decisions. It was found that students with moderate-severe disabilities participated in intervention from two to three times a week for 20–30 minutes in groups outside the classroom. Students with the least severe disabilities received intervention once a week for 20–30 minutes in groups outside the classroom. While student characteristics were a factor cited in decision making about intensity and type of service delivery, caseload size and years of experience seemed to be more important factors.

It is very beneficial for SLPs to work closely with classroom teachers, serving at-risk students inside the classroom, because this increases the students' awareness of the demands of the curriculum and of the social rules and routines of the classroom. SLPs can help struggling students learn and follow the social rules of the classroom in relating appropriately to their teachers and peers (Davis & Banks, 2012). Some studies show that service delivery to at-risk students inside the classroom can be beneficial and effective (e.g., Nungesser & Watkins, 2005; Thiemann & Goldstein, 2004). However, there are very few direct comparisons of classroom-based and pullout services for speech–language intervention (Meline & Kaufman, 2010). For assessment, Haynes and Pindzola (2012) stated that:

> The diagnostician cannot fully understand the . . . child unless he or she is familiar with the child's learning environment. Sometimes, the most potent treatment recommendations include curricular, instructional, and learning strategy modifications. Without examining these areas in a thorough assessment, a clinician cannot hope to make effective suggestions for remediation. (p.149)

In sum, for assessment and intervention, SLPs should spend at least some time supporting at-risk students and collaborating with teachers inside the general education classroom. Through an RTI model, SLPs can help these students develop adequate comprehension and expression skills, and successfully participate in expected classroom social routines. As a foundation for addressing these areas, it is important to first create an emotional connection with the students.

Intervention to Increase At-Risk Students' Classroom Success

Creating an Emotional Connection

Before presenting any formal explanation of practical intervention strategies to increase at-risk students' classroom communication effectiveness, it is important to discuss a foundational concept: emotional buy-in on the part of students (Leroy & Symes, 2001). Research and my clinical experience show that teachers who try to teach rules and skills before making an emotional connection with their students often find their efforts fruitless.

For many students from low-SES homes, home life may involve chaos and emotional neglect, or it may involve strict obedience and punitive measures. For these students and their families, school may be perceived as a strange and fearful environment with few benefits for them. If at-risk ELL and low-SES students do not connect emotionally with the educators who are trying to help them, the students may compliantly follow instructions and appear to be learning but not not really internalize or generalize the content and skills being taught. As mentioned earlier, for those in generational poverty who do not see the relevance of school, emotional buy-in is absolutely critical, because in the absence of it, they will at best cooperate only on the surface and at worst openly rebel (Covington & Teel, 1996; Payne, 2003; Roseberry-McKibbin, 2013).

In terms of ELL students, as previously described, in many cultures students come from close-knit, emotionally warm, and physically demonstrative families in which they have become accustomed to the language of affiliation and connection. These students may have substantial difficulty with the impersonal, detached, and decontextualized instructional discourse of the classroom. For these ELL students, the adjustment is major indeed, and an emotional connection with the teacher is crucial.

In terms of establishing an emotional connection with students, many middle-SES mainstream professionals may not be aware that this is important or know how to obtain this connection. It is expected that students will listen, follow rules, and generalize what they are taught, "because I said so, and it's good for you." But with at-risk students—both ELL and low-SES—for whom this is insufficient, how can educators establish the necessary foundational emotional relationships that will motivate these students to want to learn? How can educators connect emotionally with these students in a time-efficient manner that still permits the required amount of work to get done?

There are a number of ways to connect with students. Some suggestions are presented in Box 11.6. For many mainstream educators, these suggestions may seem outside appropriate professional boundaries. Accustomed to depersonalized "professional" communication, these educators may believe that the suggestions in Box 11.6 are inappropriate.

Box 11.6. ***Establishing an Emotional Connection With At-Risk Students***

1. When first getting to know at-risk students, don't demand too much verbalization and give plenty of verbal space.
2. Give an appropriate touch or hug.
3. Ask the student to help with a small chore or errand such as erasing the board, taking a note to the principal's office, or collating and stapling papers.
4. Show pictures of your own pet or family members so that students see you as a human being with a personal life.
5. Within bounds of discretion, talk about your personal life, especially graduating from college and why college has helped you become a successful professional.
6. Be generous with praise, no matter how small the attempt or how inaccurate the answer. For example, instead of focusing on whether or not the answer is "right," say something like "Emily, I love how you raised your hand and used your words," or "Thank you for sharing that. I like that you shared your idea with me and your friends."
7. Talk with students informally about nonacademic topics they are interested in (e.g., TV, movies, family, pets) to encourage comfortable, personal interactions.
8. Talk with students about their own dreams and hopes for the future. Encourage them to remember that society has many resources, outside the family, for supporting individuals with talent and willingness to work hard.

Note: Based on Davis and Banks (2012), Roseberry-McKibbin (2007, 2013), Zuniga, (2011).

The reader is invited to cautiously try out the ideas and see if their implementation creates greater success in motivating at-risk students to learn and succeed in school.

In addition to providing emotional support and establishing emotional connections themselves, educators can recruit peer mentors (Davis & Banks, 2012; Paul & Norbury, 2012). For example, Olszewski-Kubilius, Lee, Ngoi, and Ngoi (2004) conducted an extensive research project in which they worked with at-risk ELL gifted elementary and middle school students from low-SES backgrounds. The collaborative effort of a university-based gifted center and local high school districts, the Project EXCITE program was designed to train and prepare gifted ELL low-SES students in elementary and middle schools for advanced tracks in science and math in high school. These researchers recruited successful high school and college students from culturally and linguistically diverse backgrounds to serve as role models, helping the younger students visualize the path that they were expected to prepare for and eventually take. The older students tutored younger ones, served as teaching assistants for after-school sessions, and spoke to parents and students about their experiences of achieving in high school. Peer relationships were carefully monitored by Project EXCITE staff, and families were included whenever possible.

Results of the Project EXCITE program showed that most of its students were retained in the program and earned high grades in science and math at school. An important finding was a 300% increase in at-risk low-SES ELL students qualifying for an advanced math class in sixth grade after two years of involvement in the program. The researchers stated that among the most potent variables contributing to the success of this project were the provision of older role models and clustering gifted students with their peers in order to provide support against the perception that they were "acting White" (p. 154). Thus, this study showed that using peer models to help provide at-risk students with emotional support can be effective.

In another study, Gandara (2004) described the Puente Project, which, among other strategies, engaged older Hispanic students from California colleges as role models to work with low-SES Hispanic high school students, encouraging them to prepare to enter four-year colleges. Students also were kept together in cohorts to encourage them to form friendships, an important variable in student engagement that reduces the likelihood that students will drop out of school. As a result, many Puente students indicated that they associated with other Puente students. In addition, Puente students were less likely than non-Puente students to drop out of high school. This program was very successful: 43% of Hispanic high school students who participated in the Puente Project attended four-year colleges, in contrast with 24% of high school Hispanic students who were not involved in the Puente Project.

In sum, professionals can work to establish personal emotional connections with at-risk students as a foundation for helping these students succeed in the classroom setting. Research demonstrates that in addition, provision of emotional support by peer role models from similar backgrounds is a major variable in helping these at-risk students succeed.

Increasing Communicative Flexibility

Increasing at-risk students' classroom communication skills is a complex and challenging task. As previously stated, many ELL and low-SES students come to school having had little experience with the instructional discourse of the classroom. For these students, learning is not automatized. Many academic tasks require controlled processing. While a child is constructing meaning, she has to simultaneously store components in short-term memory while actively accessing long-term memory. As classroom interaction and exchanges become more difficult, processing breakdowns are more likely to occur (Merritt et al., 1998). Students whose first language is not English as well as low-SES children must allocate attentional, cognitive, and linguistic resources to tasks that for other students are basic and automatic.

To support these students, educators can utilize the principle of constructivism, allowing students to use their own prior knowledge and experiences to make connections with and learn new information (Merritt et al., 1998). Children's prior experiences are incorporated into explanations of why what happens in the classroom happens. For example, teachers can ask what rules are followed at home and compare them to classroom expectations. For children from chaotic homes, the lack of predictability can be compared to the security of having classroom routines.

Teachers and other educators also need to increase students' functional flexibility, the ability to use language for a variety of communication purposes (Turnbull & Justice, 2012). Middle-SES students often have adequate functional flexibility, as they tend to be exposed to a variety of conversational partners and experiences. Some at-risk children, due to a lack of opportunity or cultural practices, may have had few conversational experiences with nonfamily members before they reach kindergarten. Thus, these children's functional flexibility is limited.

Educators can increase students' functional flexibility by giving them more opportunities to participate and interact in class. As discussed, the IRE model that is so typical of classrooms often does not permit much time for students to talk and interact; the teacher controls communication. It is critical to give students as many opportunities as possible to talk and interact with each other as well as with the teacher.

One aspect of an interactive discourse style of teaching is having students share with each other. This is actually comfortable for many ELL students, who are accustomed to interacting more with peers and siblings than with adults. Activities like group projects and discussions facilitate more interaction than passive listening while the teacher talks. Box 11.7 contains practical ideas for giving students more opportunities to converse and to interact in the classroom setting.

An interactive teaching style encourages students to participate, gives them feedback, and acknowledges their contributions (Merritt et al., 1998; Owens, 2010). Comments further the exchange. If student responses are irrelevant, the teacher can offer accepting yet constructive feedback. Teachers can also balance questions with comments (Box 11.8). Teachers and other educators tend to ask many questions and give few comments:

> Balancing questions with comments helps teachers and SLPs avoid the "domination trap," that is, the unfortunate habit of dispensing information as if the adult is the final authority for all that is correct and true in the classroom. Nothing obliterates a discussion faster than students' perception that the adult "knows it all." If teachers use more comments and open-ended and opinion-based questions, students see that there is more than one right answer. (Merritt et al., 1998, p. 166)

In order to increase student interaction and build students' communication skills, some educators use the technique of *revoicing* (Hulit et al., 2011). Students speak, and the teacher restates their contribution in a more formal academic manner, rephrasing rather than evaluating the response or giving simple feedback (Box 11.9). Revoicing models academic discourse, at the same time as accepting the student's idea (Westby, 2006). Educators can also ask higher order questions to help students gradually increase their functional flexibility and to promote higher order thinking, such as those of Bloom's taxonomy (Bloom, Benjamin, & Krathwohl, 1956; Box 11.10).

In sum, SLPs and teachers can help increase at-risk students' facility with classroom instructional discourse by increasing opportunities for students to interact. When students have more opportunities to interact, their functional flexibility increases, which in

Box 11.7. *Increasing Students' Conversational Experiences*

- ☑ Arrange the physical setting of the classroom to promote conversation. Individual desks and carrels help students focus for independent work, but they discourage interaction. Provide learning centers, interactive classroom displays, and large tables for group work.
- ☑ Allow students, especially young ELLs, to respond nonverbally if they do not want to speak. For example, create conversational turns (e.g., "If the sun is shining, clap your hands," "If it is recess time, stand up.").
- ☑ Use information talk instead of questions. At-risk students may become anxious under repeated questioning. We can "pour words" into students' actions so that they hear rich language without having to respond (e.g., "You are cleaning up your desk and putting things into your backpack. I like how you are organizing your homework folder.").
- ☑ Bring in volunteers to have conversations with students about their interests or about what they are doing in school.
- ☑ Increase student-to-student conversations. Students can be assigned to work on projects together and can engage in cooperative learning activities.
- ☑ Look for chances to talk one-on-one with students. For example, talk with students while distributing materials or carrying out routines (e.g., "We are going to get ready to go home. I am passing out your math homework for tomorrow. You can put it in your math folder.").
- ☑ Use transition times to comment on positive student action (e.g., "Thank you for lining up quietly before we go to lunch.").
- ☑ Talk to individual students as they complete their work (e.g., "You finished that crossword puzzle on the continents. Great job!").
- ☑ Instead of letting students work silently, talk them through lessons (e.g., "We are looking at pictures of things that begin with /b/. Oh, look! You found a *balloon*. Here is another thing that begins with /b/. It's a *basket*.").
- ☑ Respond in ways that promote continued talk. For example:

  Student: My grandma and I went to the mall.

  Educator: That sounds like fun. Tell us about what you did there.

  A way to discourage continued talk would be to respond, "That's nice. Hope you had fun."
- ☑ Provide opportunities for students to use language and interact during the learning process. For example, if the class is learning about the zoo, students who have been to the zoo can be encouraged to share these experiences with the class.
- ☑ Give all students opportunities to practice various language functions, including negotiating, problem solving, making requests, and explaining concepts.

Note: Adapted from Kaderavek (2011), Paul and Norbury (2012), Roseberry-McKibbin (2013), and Weiner (2001).

Box 11.8. ***Responding to Students With Questions Versus Comments***

Educator Question	Educator Comment
Student: I think Johnny Appleseed helped a lot of hungry people get food.	
Educator: How did he do this, Joey?	Educator: His apples fed many hungry pioneers.
Student: I don't understand why we need to recycle. It's more work than just throwing things in the garbage.	
Educator: Why do people tell us to recycle?	Educator: A lot of garbage is dumped into our oceans, especially plastic.
Student: I don't think watching TV is so bad. We do it at home a lot.	
Educator: What could you be doing instead of watching TV?	Educator: People who watch a lot of TV often don't have time for other important things.

turn increases their overall communication effectiveness and helps them better follow and respond to the classroom's social routines.

Training "The Guy in My Head"

In order for students to successfully participate in the expected social routines of the classroom, as previously discussed, they need adequate self-regulatory or executive functioning skills. Educators need to give students the confidence and the tools to eventually internalize the orders and directions they hear in their environments and to convert them into self-talk that they use to direct themselves (Nelson, 2010). For ELL and low-SES students who are at risk for difficulties with executive functioning, there are a number of strategies that can be implemented by SLPs and other professionals to help build self-regulation.

It is helpful to assist students in creating lists of tasks, prioritizing these tasks, and keeping planning calendars. Most mainstream students come from homes where these habits have been cultivated from early childhood. However, for many at-risk students, calendars and checklists of activities are novel and unfamiliar. When these students are specifically taught to use these organizational devices, their learning improves immensely.

Initially, teachers and SLPs can teach at-risk students to verbalize their activities. They can then help at-risk students transition from talking about their agendas to using private, internal speech. As one of my students said, "I listen to the guy in my head." Educators can talk with at-risk students about "the guy (or girl) in your head" who helps you

Box 11.9. ***Revoicing Student Responses to Model Instructional Discourse***

Student: Um, it's important to use things again so we can save the earth.
Teacher: Yes, Sammy, it is important to recycle, and to reuse things so that we reduce pollution and help our air be cleaner.

Student: We shouldn't eat too much junk food. We need to eat things that are good for us.
Teacher: Yes! Eating junk food, like candy and doughnuts, is not nutritious. We need to eat nutritious food like fruits, vegetables, and foods containing protein.

Teacher: Why did the pioneers decide to move west?
Student: Because they were not happy where they were.
Teacher: The pioneers wanted better lives for themselves as well as more opportunities to be independent and own land, and they believed that moving west would help them accomplish these goals.

Teacher: Why did Johnny Appleseed plant apple trees?
Student: Because he liked apples.
Teacher: He did like apples, and he knew a lot of other people did too. He knew that many people were hungry and that apples were healthy, so he wanted to plant trees to give people apples for all their lives.

Box 11.10. ***Examples of Questions and Response Forms Based on Bloom's Taxonomy***

1. Identify information (knowledge): *Point to the picture of the dog.*
2. Yes/no questions (comprehension): *Did Miguel feed the hungry dog?*
3. Closed choice set (comprehension): *Was the dog a big or little dog?*
4. One-word answer (knowledge): *What did Miguel feed the dog?*
5. Elicit information (comprehension): *What did the dog do after Miguel fed her?*
6. List (application): *Name some other things that Miguel could feed the dog.*
7. Explain (analysis): *Why is it so important to feed animals on a regular basis?*
8. Bring together (synthesis): *What other things should we do to take care of animals?*
9. Explain (evaluation): *How will we know when we have successfully taken care of an animal?*

think, organize your learning, and plan ahead. Work-plan contracts, such as that in Box 11.11, increase at-risk students' success in following classroom routines by having them plan ahead and assume responsibility for their work. Taking these steps gives students experience in thinking in advance about the steps needed to complete a task and taking responsibility to make sure each step is completed in a sequential and timely manner.

Box 11.11. ***Work-Plan Contract***

Student Name: ______________________________ Date: ___________

Teacher Name: ______________________________ Date: ___________

Assignment: ______________________________

This assignment will be turned in by __________________________(date)

If I complete this assignment according to the steps outlined in this contract, I will receive a grade of _____.

To complete this assignment, I will complete the following:

Day 1/Date ____ ______________________________

Day 2/Date ____ ______________________________

Day 3/Date ____ ______________________________

Day 4/Date ____ ______________________________

Day 5/Date ____ ______________________________

I understand that I am responsible for completing my work at the dates assigned above. If I do not complete this work according to the above timelines, I will either: 1) redo the assignment for a higher grade, or 2) accept a lower grade.

______________________________ ______________________________

Teacher Signature Student Signature

Note: Based on Covington and Teel (1996) and Roseberry-McKibbin (2013).

To help create internal structure, educators can also give students choices, such as: "You have 5 minutes. If you choose to finish your paper, you may go to the reading corner and select a book. If you choose not to finish your paper, you may not go to the reading corner." In this way, students see that they indeed have control over their own actions and that their choices have consequences. This realization creates the internal structure that students will eventually need if they want to be professionally successful adults. Box 11.12 can be used to help students concretely learn to make choices and experience consequences. When at-risk students internalize the fact that they create their own choices and consequences, they can become more successful at following classroom routines and teacher expectations.

Box 11.12. ***Making Explicit a Student's Choices and Consequences***

My Choices and Consequences Student name________________ Date________	
The choice I made: __________ __________ __________	The consequence of my choice: __________ __________ __________
Next time, I could choose to: __________ __________ __________	The consequence of that choice would be: __________ __________ __________
Next time, I could also choose to: __________ __________ __________	The consequence of that choice would be: __________ __________ __________
I know that each choice I make leads to a consequence. I will make good choices so that I can experience good consequences.	

Note: From *Increasing the Language Skills of Children in Poverty: Practical Strategies for Educators*, 2nd ed. (p. 330), by C. Roseberry-McKibbin, 2013, San Diego, CA: Plural. Copyright 2013 by Plural. Reprinted with permission.

Another practical way that professionals can help students increase their executive functioning and overall skills in following classroom social routines is by de-emphasizing innate ability (e.g., "You're so smart!") and emphasizing effort, diligence, and hard work. At-risk students from some cultures, such as many Asian cultures, will relate well to this strategy (Chan & Chen, 2011). Research has shown that low-SES students who tend to exhibit some behaviors of learned helplessness because of their backgrounds respond very well to an emphasis on hard work as the path to success (Bronson & Merryman, 2009; Covington & Teel, 1996). Accustomed to hardship and numerous "roadblocks," these students can profit immeasurably from being taught that they can acquire a great deal of control over their own learning. Students relate to the idea of "exercising their brains" through repetition to improve their "wobbly" skills (Nelson, 2010): Just as athletes lift weights, do push-ups, swim, or run laps to build their strength and endurance, students, too, can increase their brain power and sharpen their skills through exercise and repetition.

Dweck (2007) and her team at Columbia conducted a study of the effects of praise on students in 20 New York schools that involved a series of experiments with 400 low-SES fifth graders. Dweck and her colleagues found that students who were praised for being smart gave up easily when presented with challenging tasks. They also performed poorly on difficult tests. Praise that emphasized natural intelligence took the control of the task out of the students' hands and did not provide them with a good model for responding to a failure. In contrast, students who were praised for their effort and diligence did better on tests than children praised for being smart. Emphasizing effort gives a child a variable that he or she can control.

In another study, Blackwell, Trzesniewski, and Dweck (2007) engaged several hundred low-SES students at Life Sciences Secondary School in East Harlem, New York, in a semester-long intervention to improve math scores. Students were split into experimental and control groups. The control group received instruction in study skills. The experimental group received instruction in study skills as well, but they were also given a special module on how intelligence is not innate. This special module consisted of two extra lessons, a total of 50 minutes on how the brain acts like a muscle; giving it a harder workout makes you smarter. The students read aloud an essay about how the brain grows new neurons when challenged, saw pictures of the brain, and acted out skits about the effect of effort on the brain. Results showed that the students in the experimental group improved their study habits and grades to a significantly greater extent than did the controls. The only difference between the two groups was that students in the experimental group were taught that working the brain harder makes it smarter and that effort pays off.

Neuman (2009) discusses helping these children through repeated exposures to controllable challenges. This means giving students difficult learning tasks with adequate support so that they can succeed. The support needs to be given in a way so that students perceive that their success is due solely to their own efforts. As children master each challenge, their self-confidence and ability to rely on their own internal abilities grow.

Box 11.13. ***Teaching Students Classroom Rules***

1. Post the list of numbered rules on the bulletin board and explain the class rules.
2. Practice the rules and provide cues and reminders (e.g., nonverbally pointing to a rule).
3. Provide external rewards for following the rules (e.g., student choice of where to sit).
4. If a student violates a rule, call out the student's name and the rule number. Have the student mark the violation on the board.
5. Enforce a consequence on the student (e.g., loss of recess time).
6. Fade the cues over time.

Note: Based on Westby (2006).

In sum, SLPs and other educators can help at-risk students develop their executive functioning skills. They can do this through strategies such as (a) helping students create prioritized lists of tasks, (b) teaching students to talk through routines and organizational plans and to internalize this as self-talk, and (c) sharing with students the belief that hard work and exercise make you smarter and better at everything, including learning and following classroom routines.

Making the Implicit Explicit

When teaching students classroom social routines, SLPs can make implicit rules explicit. For example, classroom rules can be posted. The teacher can review them at the beginning of the year, discussing them daily for the first month (Box 11.13). During the second month of school, the teacher can discuss and review the rules weekly. As the school year progresses, the teacher can discuss and review the rules less and less frequently.

Teachers can change their scripts over the school year, progressively decreasing the number of reminders they give students (Box 11.14). Teachers and SLPs can use a simple format to help all students in the classroom learn classroom social routines and successfully carry them out. After the teacher instructs the entire class about social routines, SLPs can work with small groups of at-risk students to help them review what the teacher said, rehearse the routines and rules, and even act out compliance with the rules

Box 11.14. ***Changes in Teacher Scripts From Beginning to End of the Year***

Early in Year	Later in Year
1. Teacher models each activity for children.	1. Teacher models fewer activities.
2. All activities are determined and structured by the teacher.	2. Class votes on some activities.
3. Teacher repeats directions and rules.	3. Teacher states directions and rules once, then says, "If you don't know, ask a friend."
4. Teacher puts notes on board for students to finish work.	4. Teacher uses fewer notes about getting work done.
5. Teacher tells class when it is time to begin and end activities.	5. Teacher sets clock to cue students that they are to begin and end activities.
6. Teacher reminds students each Monday that homework packet is due Thursday.	6. Teacher stops reminding students of Thursday deadline.
7. Students work together as partners and class solves problems with teacher.	7. Class works together as a large group to solve problems.
8. Students must raise their hands to answer, but calling out is accepted and not penalized.	8. Calling out is not accepted and is penalized.

Note: Based on Roseberry-McKibbin (2013) and Westby (2006).

Box 11.15. ***Progression of Teaching Classroom Routines***

Whole class instruction by the teacher

Small group or individual instruction in mini-lessons by the SLP

Hands-on opportunity to apply the new skill in the classroom

(Box 11.15). Many at-risk ELL and low-SES students benefit from small group or individual reinforcement of what their teacher has told the whole class about classroom routines, such as raising one's hand before speaking. These students benefit from repetition and hands-on chances to practice in an individual or small group format.

Paul and Norbury (2012) and Westby (2006) recommend the strategy of having in-class "mini lessons" with groups of students. Each mini-lesson begins with a discussion of a classroom routine. After discussing the routine, students engage in an activity involving that routine. Some take the role of students, and others take the role of the teacher. For example, in a mini-lesson, the student playing the role of the teacher asks the "students" to discuss what they need to do to prepare for an upcoming field trip. The "teacher" reminds the "students" to raise their hands and not interrupt. If a "student" interrupts, the group discusses this and encourages that person to listen without interrupting and to wait for his or her turn to talk.

Another practical strategy for helping at-risk students learn to follow classroom routines is to have a "rule of the week." Teachers can reward students who are doing especially well with this rule. For example, if the rule of the week is "Sit up straight in your chair," the teacher, the SLP, or a classroom aide can look for students who are performing this task especially well. Each student will have a small bowl or container on his or her desk to hold a fun token (e.g., a shiny play-money coin) that the educator will deposit each time the student follows the rule successfully. At the end of the week, the students who have earned a predetermined total number of tokens receive a sticker or prize. I have found that many at-risk students respond better to "being caught being good" than to being punished for rule violations. While it is certainly appropriate to have students face the consequences for violating classroom social rules, it can be more effective to reward them when they are following the rules successfully.

In addition to being rewarded for following rules successfully, many students enjoy seeing adults demonstrate or role-play what not to do. This is an activity that can also involve students. For example, the teacher and SLP can have a "conversation" in front of the class. The SLP can violate many rules: she can interrupt without raising her hand, slouch in her chair, dump her backpack on the floor so that things spill out everywhere, and so forth. Students can be asked to list the rules that the SLP is breaking. If they can specifically list all the exact rules that are being broken, they get a sticker. In addition, an iPad can be used to video-record several students (who have been primed in advance) violating social classroom rules. These videos can be played for the class as a whole, and students can search for and list the rules that are being broken.

Conclusion

This chapter addressed common challenges experienced by students who are at risk for school failure. These at-risk students may be ELLs, or they may be from low-SES homes, or both. They are vulnerable to school failure because of mismatches between what they experience in their home environment and what schools that are based on mainstream mid-SES Anglo-European culture and values expect. At-risk students often have difficulty with the academic language of the classroom as well as with lack of knowledge of expected classroom social routines. SLPs can collaborate with teachers to assess and intervene in the classroom setting, helping students succeed in communicating in academic language. They can help at-risk students successfully follow classroom social routines by establishing emotional connections with their students, by increasing their belief that effort can make a difference and by improving their self-regulatory skills. SLPs can make implicit rules explicit in a fun, engaging format. In these ways, educators can help at-risk students succeed in school and become productive members of society.

References

American Speech-Language-Hearing Association. (2007). *Special populations: Prison populations—2004 edition.* Baltimore, MD: Author. Retrieved from http://www.asha.org/Research/reports/prison_populations/

American Speech-Language-Hearing Association (2010). *Roles and responsibilities of speech-language pathologists in schools* [Professional issues statement]. Baltimore, MD: Author.

Archer, J. C., & Bateson, S. (2011, November). *Using the iPad as a clinical and educational tool.* Paper presented at the annual convention of the American Speech-Language-Hearing Association, San Diego, CA.

Armstrong, J. (2011, August 30). Serving children with emotional-behavioral and language disorders: A collaborative approach. *The ASHA Leader*, 1–7.

Battle, D. E. (2012). Communication disorders in a multicultural and global society. In D. E. Battle (Ed.), *Communication disorders in multicultural and international populations* (4th ed., pp. 2–19). St. Louis, MO: Elsevier/Mosby.

Blackwell, L. S., Trzesniewski, K. H., & Dweck, C. (2007). Implicit theories of intelligence predict achievement across an adolescent transition: A longitudinal study and intervention. *Child Development, 78*, 246–263.

Blair, C., Granger, D. A., Willoughby, M., Mills-Koonce, R., Cox, M., Greenberg, M. T., . . . Fortunato, C. K. (2011). Salivary cortisol mediates effects of poverty and parenting on executive functions in early childhood. *Child Development, 82*, 1970–1984.

Blanton, D. J., & Dagenais, P. A. (2007). Comparison of language skills of adjudicated and nonadjudicated adolescent males and females. *Language, Speech, and Hearing Services in Schools, 38*, 309–314.

Bloom, B. S., & Krathwohl, D. R. (1956). *Taxonomy of educational objectives: The classification of educational goals, by a committee of college and university examiners. Handbook 1: Cognitive domain*. New York, NY: Longman.

Brandel, J., & Loeb, D. F. (2011). Program intensity and service delivery models in the schools: SLP survey results. *Language, Speech, and Hearing Services in Schools, 42*, 461–490.

Brice, A. E., & Brice, R. G. (2007). School language and classroom programs for children with language impairment: Collaborating with parents and school personnel. In C. Roseberry-McKibbin, *Language disorders in children: A multicultural and case perspective* (pp. 441–464). Boston, MA: Allyn & Bacon.

Brinton, B., & Fujiki, M. (2011, June). *Facilitating social communication in children with autism spectrum disorders and language impairment: Interventions to enhance social and emotional competence.* Paper presented at the annual University of the Pacific Summer Colloquium, Stockton, CA.

Bronson, P., & Merryman, A. (2009). *NurtureShock*. New York, NY: Twelve/Hachette Book Group.

Brown, J. E., & Sanford, A. (2011). *RTI for English language learners: Appropriately using screening and progress monitoring tools to improve instructional outcomes*. Washington, DC: Center on Response to Intervention at American Institutes for Research. Retrieved from http://www.rti4success.org/pdf/rtiforells.pdf

Cazden, C. (2001). *Classroom discourse: The language of teaching and learning* (2nd ed.). Portsmouth, NH: Heinemann.

Centre for Social Justice. (2011, February). *Mental health: Poverty, ethnicity, and family breakdown* [Interim policy briefing]. London, England: Centre for Social Justice.

Chan, S., & Chen, D. (2011). Families with Asian roots. In E. W. Lynch & M. J. Hanson, *Developing cross-cultural competence: A guide for working with children in their families* (4th ed., pp. 234–318). Baltimore, MD: Brookes.

Cheng, L-R. L. (2012). Asian and Pacific American languages and cultures. In D. E. Battle (Ed.), *Communication disorders in multicultural and international populations* (4th ed., pp. 37–60). St. Louis, MO: Elsevier/Mosby.

Covington, M. V., & Teel, K. M. (1996). *Overcoming student failure: Changing motives and incentives for learning*. Washington, DC: American Psychological Association.

Cummins, J. (1999). Beyond adversarial discourse: Searching for common ground in the education of bilingual students. In I. A. Heath & C. J. Serrano (Eds.), *Annual editions: Teaching English as a second language* (pp. 204–224). Guilford, CT: Dushkin/McGraw-Hill.

Cummins, J. (2000). *Language, power, and pedagogy: Bilingual children in the crossfire*. Bristol, UK: Multilingual Matters.

Davis, P., & Banks, T. (2012). Intervention for multicultural and international clients with communication disorders. In D. E. Battle (Ed.), *Communication disorders in multicultural and international populations* (4th ed., pp. 279–295). St. Louis, MO: Elsevier/Mosby.

DeCurtis, L., & Ferrer, D. (2011, November). *Embracing iPad technology with toddlers using traditional therapy techniques*. Paper presented at the annual national convention of the American Speech-Language-Hearing Association, San Diego, CA.

Delpit, L. (1995). *Other people's children: Cultural conflict in the classroom*. New York, NY: The New Press.

Dweck, C. S. (2007). The perils and promise of praise. *Educational Leadership, 65*(2), 34–39.

Ebert, K. D., & Kohnert, K. (2011). Sustained attention in children with primary language impairment: A meta-analyis. *Journal of Speech, Language, and Hearing Research, 54*, 1372–1384.

Education Week. (2012, January). *English-language learners*. Retrieved from http://www.edweek.org/ew/issues/english-language-learners

Farah, M. J., Noble, K. G., & Hurt, H. (2005). *Poverty, privilege, and brain development: Empirical findings and ethical implications.* Retrieved from http://www.psych.upenn.edu/~mfarah

Fogle, P. T. (2013). *Essentials of communication sciences and disorders*. Clifton Park, NY: Delmar.

Gandara, P. (2004). Building bridges to college. *Educational Leadership, 62*, 56–60.

Geiss, S. A. (2011, March). *Language and literacy issues in children who are homeless or living in poverty.* Paper presented at the annual convention of the California Speech and Hearing Association, Los Angeles, CA.

Grech, H., & McLeod, S. (2012). Multilingual speech and language development and disorders. In D. E. Battle (Ed.), *Communication disorders in multicultural and international populations* (4th ed., pp. 120–147). St. Louis, MO: Elsevier/Mosby.

Hammer, C. S. (2011). Broadening our knowledge about diverse populations. *American Journal of Speech–Language Pathology, 20*, 71–72.

Hanson, M. J. (2011). Families with Anglo-European roots. In E. W. Lynch & M. J. Hanson (Eds.), *Developing cross-cultural competence: A guide for working with children and their families* (4th ed., pp. 80–109). Baltimore, MD: Brookes.

Hart, B., & Risley, T. R. (1995). *Meaningful differences in the everyday experience of young American children*. Baltimore, MD: Brookes.

Hart, B., & Risley, T. R. (1999). *The social world of children learning to talk*. Baltimore, MD: Brookes.

Haynes, W. O., & Pindzola, R. H. (2012). *Diagnosis and evaluation in speech pathology* (8th ed.). Upper Saddle River, NJ: Pearson.

Heckler, E. E. (2009). Home and school language matches and mismatches. In A. E. Brice & R. G. Brice, *Language development: Monolingual and bilingual acquisition* (pp. 314–339). Boston, MA: Allyn & Bacon.

Hernandez, R. (2011). Literacy starts in the family. *California Educator, 15*(4), 10.

Hill, J. W., & Coufal, K. L. (2005). Emotional/behavioral disorders: A retrospective examination of social skills, linguistics, and student outcomes. *Communication Disorders Quarterly, 27*, 33–46.

Hulit, L. M., Howard, M. R., & Fahey, K. R. (2011). *Born to talk: An introduction to speech and language development* (5th ed.). Boston, MA: Allyn & Bacon.

Jacob, N. (2011). Families with South Asian roots. In E. W. Lynch & M. J. Hanson (Eds.), *Developing cross-cultural competence: A guide for working with children in their families* (4th ed., pp. 437–462). Baltimore, MD: Brookes.

Joe, J. R., & Malach, R. S. (2011). Families with American Indian roots. In E. W. Lynch & M. J. Hanson (Eds.), *Developing cross-cultural competence: A guide for working with children in their families* (4th ed, pp. 110–139). Baltimore, MD: Brookes.

Justice, L. M. (2010). *Communication sciences and disorders: A contemporary perspective* (2nd ed.). Boston, MA: Allyn & Bacon.

Kaderavek, J. N. (2011). *Language disorders in children: Fundamental concepts of assessment and intervention*. Boston, MA: Allyn & Bacon.

Kayser, H. (2012). Hispanic and Latino cultures in the United States and Latin America. In D. E. Battle (Ed.), *Communication disorders in multicultural and international populations* (4th ed., pp. 102–147). St. Louis, MO: Elsevier/Mosby.

Leroy, C., & Symes, B. (2001). Teachers' perspectives on the family backgrounds of children at risk. *McGill Journal of Education, 36* (1), 45–60.

Liiva, C. A., & Cleave, P. L. (2005). Roles of initiation and responsiveness in access and participation for children with specific language impairment. *Journal of Speech, Language, and Hearing Research, 48*, 868–883.

Linares-Orama, N. (2005). Language-learning disorders and youth incarceration. *Journal of Communication Disorders, 38*, 311–319.

McCormack, J., Harrison, L. J., McLeod, S., & McAllister, L. (2011). A nationally representative study of the association between communication impairment at 4–5 years and children's life activities at 7–9 years. *Journal of Speech, Language, and Hearing Research, 54*, 1328–1348.

Meline, T., & Kauffman, C. (2010). A speech–language pathologist's dilemma: What is the best choice for service delivery in the schools? *EBP Briefs, 5*(4), 1–14. Bloomington, MN: Pearson.

Merritt, D. D., Barton, J., & Culatta, B. (1998). Instructional discourse: A framework for learning. In D. D. Merritt & B. Culatta, *Language intervention in the classroom* (pp. 143–174). San Diego, CA: Singular.

Mokuau, N., & Tauili'ili, P. (2011). Families with Native Hawaiian and Samoan roots. In E. W. Lynch & M. J. Hanson (Eds.), *Developing cross-cultural competence: A guide for working with children in their families* (4th ed., pp. 365–391). Baltimore, MD: Brookes.

National Association for the Education of Homeless Children and Youth. (2011). *Facts about homeless education*. Retrieved from http://www.naehcy.org/facts.html

National Center for Children in Poverty. (2005). *Basic facts about low-income children: Birth to age 18*. Retrieved from http://nccp.org.pub_lic06html

National Clearinghouse for English Language Acquisition. (2011). *The growing numbers of English language learner students (1998/99–2008/09)*. Available at http://www.ncela.us/publications

Nelson, N.W. (1989). Curriculum-based language assessment and intervention. *Language, Speech, and Hearing Services in Schools, 20*, 170–184.

Nelson, N. W. (2010). *Language and literacy disorders: Infancy through adolescence*. Boston, MA: Allyn & Bacon.

Neuman, S. B. (2009). *Changing the odds for children at risk: Seven essential principles of educational programs that break the cycle of poverty*. Westport, CT: Praeger.

Nippold, M. A. (2011). Language intervention in the classroom: What it looks like. *Language, Speech, and Hearing Services in Schools, 42*, 393–394.

Nixon, S. M., McCardle, P., & Leos, K. (2007). Implications of research on English language learners for classroom and clinical practice. *Language, Speech, and Hearing Services in Schools, 38*, 272–277.

Nungesser, N. R., & Watkins, R. V. (2005). Preschool teachers' perceptions and reactions to challenging classroom behavior: Implications for speech–language pathologists. *Language, Speech, and Hearing Services in Schools, 36*, 139–151.

Olszewski-Kubilius, P., Lee, S. Y., Ngoi, M., & Ngoi, D. (2004). Addressing the achievement gap between minority and nonminority children by increasing access to gifted programs. *Journal for the Education of the Gifted, 28*, 127–158.

O'Neil-Perozzi, T. (2009). Feasibility and benefit of parent participation in a program emphasizing preschool language development while homeless. *American Journal of Speech–Language Pathology, 18*, 252–263.

The On-line Teacher Resource. (2011). *Classroom rules: Elementary level*. Retrieved from http://www.teach-nology.com

Owens, R. E. (2010). *Language disorders: A functional approach to assessment and intervention* (5th ed.). Boston, MA: Allyn & Bacon.

Paradis, J., Genesee, F., & Crago, M. B. (2011). *Dual language development and disorders: A handbook on bilingualism and second language learning* (2nd ed.). Baltimore, MD: Brookes.

Paul, R., & Norbury, C. F. (2012). *Language disorders from infancy through adolescence: Listening, speaking, reading, writing, and communicating* (4th ed.). St. Louis, MO: Mosby/Elsevier.

Payne, R. K. (2003). *A framework for understanding poverty* (4th ed.). Highlands, TX: aha! Process.

Posnick-Goodwin, S. (2011). Living and learning in poverty. *California Educator, 16*(3), 10–21.

Qi, C. H., & Kaiser, A. P. (2004). Problem behaviors of low-income children with language delays: An observation study. *Journal of Speech, Language, and Hearing Research, 47*, 595–609.

Redmond, S. M. (2011). Peer victimization among students with specific language impairment, attention-deficit/hyperactivity disorder, and typical development. *Language, Speech, and Hearing Services in Schools, 42*, 520–535.

Ritzman, M. J., Sanger, D., & Coufal, K. L. (2006). A case study of a collaborative speech–language pathologist. *Communication Disorders Quarterly, 27*, 221–231.

Rosa-Lugo, L. I., Mihai, F. M., & Nutta, J. W. (2012). *Language and literacy development: An interdisciplinary focus on English learners with communication disorders*. San Diego, CA: Plural.

Roseberry-McKibbin, C. (2007). *Language disorders in children: A multicultural and case perspective*. Boston, MA: Allyn & Bacon.

Roseberry-McKibbin, C. (2013). *Increasing the language skills of children in poverty: Practical strategies for educators* (2nd ed.). San Diego, CA: Plural.

Roseberry-McKibbin, C. (2014). *Multicultural students with special language needs: Practical strategies for assessment and intervention* (4th ed). Oceanside, CA: Academic Communication.

Roseberry-McKibbin, C., Bryla, J., Faherty, K., & Johnson-Garcia, D. (2012, March). *Snaps, apps, and raps: iPad use with speech and language impaired students.* Paper presented at the annual convention of the California Speech and Hearing Association, San Jose, CA.

Rudebusch, J., & Wiechmann, J. (2011, August 30). How to fit response to intervention into a heavy workload. *The ASHA Leader*, 1–7.

Santos, R. M., & Chan, S. (2011). Families with Filipino roots. In E. W. Lynch & M. J. Hanson, *Developing cross-cultural competence: A guide for working with children in their families* (4th ed., pp. 319–364). Baltimore, MD: Brookes.

Sharifzadeh, V.-S. (2011). Families with Middle Eastern roots. In E. W. Lynch & M. J. Hanson, *Developing cross-cultural competence: A guide for working with children in their families* (4th ed., pp. 392–437). Baltimore, MD: Brookes.

Stockman, I. (2010). A review of developmental and applied research on African American children: From a deficit to difference perspective on dialect differences. *Language, Speech, and Hearing Services in Schools, 41*, 23–38

Terry, N. P., Connor, C. M., Thomas-Tate, S., & Love, M. (2010). Examining relationships among dialect variation, literacy skills, and school context in first grade. *Journal of Speech, Language, and Hearing Research, 53*, 126–145.

Thiemann, K. S., & Goldstein, H. (2004). Effects of peer training and written text cueing on social communication of school-age children with pervasive developmental disorder. *Journal of Speech, Language, and Hearing Research, 47*, 126–144.

Turnbull, K. L., & Justice, L. M. (2012). *Language development from theory to practice* (2nd ed.). Upper Saddle River, NJ: Pearson.

U.S. Census Bureau (2010). *Census brief: Overview of race and Hispanic origin.* Retrieved from: http://www.census.gov/prod/cen2010/briefs/c2010br-o2.pdf

van Kleeck, A. (2006). Cultural issues in promoting interactive sharing in the families of preschoolers. In A. van Kleeck (Ed.), *Sharing books and stories to promote language and literacy* (pp. 179–230). San Diego, CA: Plural.

Weiner, C. (2001). *Preparing for success: Meeting the language and learning needs of young children from poverty homes.* Youngtown, AZ: ECL.

Westby, C. (2006). There's more to passing than knowing the answers: Learning to do school. In T. A. Ukrainetz (Ed.), *Contextualized language intervention: Scaffolding preK–12 literacy achievement* (pp. 319–388). Austin, TX: PRO-ED.

Westby, C., & Inglebret, E. (2012). Native American and worldwide indigenous cultures. In D. E. Battle (Ed.), *Communication disorders in multicultural and international populations* (4th ed., pp. 76–101). St. Louis, MO: Elsevier/Mosby.

Wyatt, T. (2012). Assessment of multicultural and international clients with communication disorders. In D. E. Battle (Ed.), *Communication disorders in multicultural and international populations* (4th ed., pp. 243–278). St. Louis, MO: Elsevier/Mosby.

Ziolkowski, R. A., & Goldstein, H. (2011). Kevin: A school-age child with behavioral disorders and language-learning disabilities: Applying contextualized written language and behavioral supports. In S. S. Chabon & E. R. Cohn, *The communication disorders casebook: Learning by example* (pp. 291–302). Upper Saddle River, NJ: Pearson.

Zuniga, M. (2011). Families with Latino roots. In E. W. Lynch & M. J. Hanson (Eds.), *Developing cross-cultural competence: A guide for working with children and their families* (4th ed., pp. 190–233). Baltimore, MD: Brookes.

Chapter 12

Awareness, Memory, and Retrieval: Intervention for the Phonological Foundations of Reading

Teresa A. Ukrainetz

The processes involved in the awareness, storage, and retrieval of phonological representations are central to the act of reading. Phonological awareness is the most familiar and most teachable of these cognitive processes. However, researchers have turned their attention increasingly to phonological memory, also called verbal working memory, and to phonological code retrieval, known as word-finding or rapid naming. These cognitive skills that are referred to collectively as *phonological processing.* Phonological production, which involves speech sounds, is also sometimes included in this collective. This chapter addresses the other three processes and what is known about working directly and indirectly with them. The guidance provided in Ukrainetz (2006a) for intervening in a contextualized skill manner at the phoneme level of awareness continues to inform this chapter. The main change in the past decade is that phonemic awareness has shifted from being a distinctive endeavor of the speech–language pathologist (SLP) to being taught within regular and supplementary reading instruction. SLPs still offer distinctive expertise in this critical oral language area, but coordination of services with teachers is more important than ever.

Phonological Awareness Fundamentals

Why Be Aware of Phonology

This book is about language: semantics, syntax, discourse, and pragmatics. However, when language is mapped into print, phonology starts to matter, not in terms of communication, but rather in terms of how the sounds of speech map to letters. Phonological awareness is the understanding that words are composed of discrete sounds that can be separated and manipulated (e.g., *chase* has three sounds, /tʃ/-/ei/-/s/; change /tʃ/ to /k/ and you get *case*). This oral language skill is critical to written language success. Phonological awareness enables children to understand the alphabetic principle, to notice the regular ways that letters represent sounds in written words, and to generate possibilities for words that are only partially sounded out (Al Otaiba, Kosanovich, & Torgesen, 2012). Phonological awareness is important because of the role it plays in reading and spelling. The phoneme level of phonological awareness is learned primarily through interactions with print, as children learn about mapping letters to sounds. Despite its tight relationship with reading and spelling, phonological awareness exists independent of print (so that the phonemes of a word can be segmented without knowing how to spell the word).

Phonological awareness is one of the strongest kindergarten indicators of later reading difficulties and is frequently deficient in children with specific language impairment (SLI) and reading disability (Catts, Adolf, Hogan, & Weismer, 2005; Catts, Fey, Zhang, & Tomblin, 2001; Fraser, Goswami, & Conti-Ramsden, 2010). Deficiencies often persist in older poor readers even if their language and reading difficulties largely resolve (Bruck, 1993; Stothard, Snowling, Bishop, Chipcase, & Kaplan, 1998). Despite its persistence, phonological awareness is a developmentally limited contributor to reading performance (Hogan, Catts, & Little, 2005; Stanovich, 1986). This means that its contributions are most apparent when children are learning to read and are much less so as children get older and many other contributing factors, such as vocabulary, reading practice, and motivation, come into play.

Types and Tasks of Phonological Awareness

Phonological awareness operates on the speech units of syllables, onset-rimes, and phonemes. Phonological awareness tasks have differing degrees of involvement of other language skills and cognitive operations: some are purely sound based while others are aided by knowing the meanings of the words being manipulated or having a strong auditory working memory. Tasks can be distinguished as requiring shallow or deep levels of awareness (Schuele & Boudreau, 2008). Shallow awareness tasks involve minimally active mental judgments, such as generating rhymes or matching initial phonemes of words. Deep awareness tasks involve more demanding phoneme manipulations (e.g., change /g/ in *glad* to /p/ and you get *plaid*). There are many tasks that fall between shallow and deep, so this metaphor is more of a sloping beach rather than a rock shelf.

For reading and spelling in alphabetic writing systems (i.e., phoneme-grapheme based systems), *phonemic awareness*, which involves knowing that words can be broken into discrete and manipulable *phonemes*, is the critical type of speech awareness. Phonemes are the smallest units of contrastive speech, which means using different phonemes changes the meaning of a word (e.g., *rap-lap* are two differnt words, so /r/ and /l/ are different phonemes). Phonemes are often called "speech sounds" although syllables and words are also speech sounds (but bigger than phonemes).

There is also a level of awareness that taps speech at a level beyond that of phonemes. Awareness of the articulatory and acoustic features of phonemes, such as voicing, aspiration, or place of articulation, is *phonetic awareness*. Phonetic awareness may even include noticing noncontrastive features, such as aspiration in English (e.g., [p^{h}ad] is a breathy version of *pad* that does not change its meaning). Noncontrastive pairs of *phones*, called *allophones*, may vary phonotactically (e.g., aspirated stops in word-final but not word-initial position) or by dialect (e.g., [awnt] vs. [aent] for *aunt*), but the variations do not affect word meaning in that language. When SLPs conduct close transcriptions of speech with diacritics, they are using their expert level of phonetic awareness that goes beyond the phonemic level needed for reading and spelling. One popular beginning reading program that will be explained later in this chapter includes explicit, extended attention to this level of phonetic awareness. Although this deep *phonetic* awareness may be helpful in articulation treatment or in adult second language instruction, there is no evidence that native speakers need this additional level of awareness to learn to read and spell.

Teachers do not use the term *phonetic* the same way SLPs do. When teachers say "phonetic spelling," they mean using reasonable but not correct phoneme-grapheme correspondences, such as *KAM* for *came* or *SERKIS* for *circus*. This kind of spelling is also called invented, emergent, or developmental spelling (Ukrainetz, 2006b). *Phonemic decoding* is a term used for reading printed words with regular enough spelling patterns so that speech sound units can be mentally invoked, in contrast to irregular words, which require primarily visual recognition. *Phonics* refers to reading curricula that focus on sound-letter correspondence in an explicit, structured manner.

Phonological awareness involves two other supraphonemic units of speech: rhyme and syllable. Rhyming words are created from an onset, an initial consonantal segment, and a rime, which is the rest of the word. Rhyming involves words and nonwords that differ only by their onsets (e.g., /s/-/aed/, /b/-/aed/, /gl/-/aed/). Generating a nonsense rhyming word pair reveals where the division is in a word (e.g., *dedicate-redicate*). Syllables are rhythmic consonant-vowel units (e.g., *ba-na-na*, *ex-pla-na-tion*) apparent as intensity pulses on a spectrogram (Gillon, 2004). Multisyllabic words usually have one stressed syllable. The position of that spoken stress can change meaning (e.g., *rational* versus *rationale*) or vary dialectically (e.g., *décal* in American versus equal stress in Canadian). There is more than one way to divide a word syllabically. Gillon recommends following Treiman's principles: (a) each syllable has a vowel; (b) as many consonants as possible begin a stressed syllable (e.g., *pa-tról* not *pat-ról*); and (c) each syllable contains allowable consonant clusters (e.g., *on-ly* not *onl-y* or *o-nly*). Allowable combinations of phonemes (e.g., no nasal velars word initially in English, [ŋo]) and syllables (e.g., Italian preference for open CV syllables) involve *phonotactics*.

Although part of phonological awareness and predictive of later reading performance (Wagner, Torgesen, & Rashotte, 1994), rhyme and syllable awareness contribute little to the development of phonemic awareness or reading (Engen & Hoien, 2002; Hoien, Lundberg, Stanovich, & Bjaalid, 1995; Nation & Hulme, 1997; Storch & Whitehurst, 2002; Wood & Terrell, 1998). For example, Hoien et al. found little relationship between syllable and phoneme awareness (correlations of .1 to .2) for kindergartners and first graders. Wood and Terrell showed that good and poor readers did not significantly differ on syllable segmentation. First-grade syllable awareness explains less than 1% of unique variance in word decoding (Engen & Hoien, 2002). Syllable and onset-rime awareness may be important in syllabic writing systems, such as Mycenean Greek and Cherokee, or in systems that combine logographs with syllable representation, such as Chinese and Japanese (see en.wikipedia.org/wiki/Syllabary). However, these two units play very minor roles in learning to read and spell in English.

Phonological awareness curricula and assessment measures may include two other kinds of awareness under the label of phonological awareness (e.g., Adams, Foorman, Lundberg, & Beeler, 1998; Notari-Syverson, O'Connor, & Vadasy, 1998). *Auditory awareness* involves judgments about environmental sounds (e.g., a dog barking versus a bell ringing). Auditory awareness may promote listening skills and attention to sound, but these skills can be achieved much more directly with phonological activities. There is no evidence that nonspeech listening activities are needed for learning to read and spell (Ukrainetz, 2008).

Tasks such as dividing compound words into root words and breaking up sentences into component words are often clumped within phonological awareness, but these are really types of *semantic awareness*. An indication of whether a task is primarily phonological or semantic is whether it can be done without understanding the spoken item. Two-syllable compound words can be divided into their component words without knowing what the words mean by using syllable division (e.g., *hot-dog*), so they could be considered phonological. In contrast, the root words of multisyllabic compounds (e.g., *extra-ordinary*) and words of sentences cannot be segmented purely phonologically. A good illustration of this occurs when you try to segment a sentence in a language you do not know (e.g., *jevoudraisavoirdulaitsilvousplait*): You can do it by phonemes or syllables, but not by words.

Development of Phonological Awareness

Phonological awareness is in a gray zone between the natural unfolding of language and the instructional dependency of literacy: it emerges "naturally" with literacy experiences but is also very teachable. The emergence of phonological awareness has much less developmental ordering than is often thought (Anthony et al., 2002; Anthony, Lonigan, Driscoll, Phillips, & Burgess, 2003). Rhyme and syllable tasks are accomplishable by children as young as 3 years, but so are phoneme tasks (e.g., Chaney, 1992; Maclean, Bryant, & Bradley, 1987). Fox and Routh (1975) reported that segmenting sentences into words, words into syllables, and syllables into phonemes all showed similar steep growth trajectories between 3 and 4 years of age. Bradley and Bryant (1985) noted, in trying to teach children to categorize words by rhyme and first phoneme, that it was easier to start with phonemes because there were fewer words that rhymed than words that started with the same sound, and because it was easier to explain first sounds than rhyming. With current preschool literacy practices, deeper levels of phoneme isolation and matching are now expected (Good, Simmons, Kame'enui, Kaminski, & Wallin, 2002; McGee, 2005).

The tasks used to demonstrate phonemic awareness do show some limited developmental ordering. Awareness develops from easy word-initial phoneme tasks to mid-level tasks involving word-final phonemes and blending and segmenting of phonemes in simple syllable structure words (Box 12.1). The most difficult level is segmenting words with harder kinds of consonant clusters and multiple syllables. Manipulations like phoneme deletion, substitution, and transposition are also in the "hardest" category.

Even this limited ordering of difficulty can be further affected by task features, such as the number and type of alternatives and the presence of pictures and manipulatives. For example, first phoneme matching tasks all fall within the "easier" level. However, judging whether two phonemes are the same in a four-word array is harder than in a three-word array. Within the same activity, it is more difficult to make difference judgments than similarity judgments. A four-word-array matching task (e.g., "Which one starts with a different sound, *dog*, *dream*, *cat*, or *doll*?") involves working memory and vocabulary. However, how memory and vocabulary interact with phonemic awareness may not be predictable: Is it easier to mentally review four items for their speech sounds if you know the meanings or if you do not? If you are looking at pictures while the words are spoken but other labels pop into your mind, will those pop-ups interfere with the intended labels? For classroom group-administered testing, test-taking ability can significantly impact performance (e.g., remembering to locate the test item on the page, position the pencil, wait for the question, scan the pictures, review the possibilities, and circle the correct answer). When tasks are kept equivalent in cognitive and memory demands, achievements among rhyme, syllable, and phoneme are almost parallel. The developmental order of phonological awareness is, in fact, not very ordered.

Box 12.1. ***Phonemic Awareness Tasks***

Easier
• Generating alliterative words: *What are words that start with /b/? What are names that start like Tom and Teresa?* • Matching or categorizing words by initial phonemes: *Do these words start with the same sound: dog, sun? Which start with the same sound: dog, log, doll?* • Isolating or identifying initial phonemes: *What is the first sound in dog? What is the first sound in dog, doll, and day?* • Blending onset-rime into words: *What word is this, /d/-/awg/, /spl/-/aet/?*
Harder
• Isolating final phonemes: *Tell me the last sound in dog.* • Matching final phonemes: *Which words have the same last sound: dog, log, doll?* • Blending phonemes into simple words: *What word is this: /d/-/aw/-g/, /m/-/ae/-/n/.* • Segmenting simple words into phonemes: *Say the sounds in up, dough, dog, cheese, stop.*
Hardest
• Segmenting words with triple clusters and final clusters: *Say the sounds in jump, strikes.* • Segmenting and blending multisyllabic words: *Say the sounds in jumping and higher.* • Deleting and substituting in simple words: *Take the /d/ off dog, add a /b/, what do you get?* • Transposing in simple words: *Switch the /d/ and /g/ in dog, what do you get?*

Reciprocal Relations With Reading and Spelling

Phonemic awareness develops *along with* and as *a consequence of* learning to read and write. Although children can be taught phonological awareness without reference to print, the primary route to an awareness of phonemes is through learning to read and spell, through self-directed exploration (Richgels, 1995; Richgels, Poremba, & McGee, 1996), and formal sound-letter instruction (Dahl, Scharer, Lawson, & Grogan, 1999; Ehri & Wilce, 1986). As preschoolers learn about letter names, letter sounds, and the forms and functions of print, they are simultaneously learning that *Dora*, *Delia*, and *Donophrio* all start with the /d/ sound and that *Donophrio* has the most sounds in his name. A child who writes *cat* with three letters is aware not only that letters represent sounds but also that this word has three of those distinct, individual small sounds. Even "semiphonetic" spelling, like *KT* for *cat*, shows awareness of first and last phonemes. After children begin learning to decode words, their performance on phonemic awareness tasks increases quickly, especially for languages with consistent sound-letter patterns (e.g., Cossu, Shankweiler, Liberman, Katz, & Tolar, 1988; Durgunoglu & Oney, 1999).

Phonemic awareness not only arises through reading and spelling but is also shaped by orthographic knowledge. Ehri and Wilce (1986) reported that children who were able to spell very few words judged the middle of *bump* and *tent* to be single nasalized vowels and the consonant cluster of *truck* to be a single affricate, while children who knew how to spell many words separated them into two phonemes. Experience with spelling can reveal to children word segments not previously noticed or pronounced (e.g., *bicycle* pronounced as /baisɪko/ or *didn't* pronounced as /dInt/).

The effect of print on awareness varies with writing system and language. Chen et al. (2004) found that children learning the Chinese logo-syllabic script show advanced onset-rime understanding. Chen et al. also found that Cantonese-speaking children showed more advanced awareness of tones than Mandarin-speaking children did, which they attributed to the more complicated tone system of Cantonese. Durgunoglu and Oney (1999) reported that Turkish-speaking kindergartners and first graders were more proficient in both syllable manipulation and final phoneme deletion than were English-speaking children. This was linked to the features of the respective spoken languages and how each is mapped into writing.

The effect of knowing how to read and write is evidenced in the performance of adults who cannot read alphabetic systems. Neither illiterate adults nor adults who are literate only in Chinese characters can add or delete phonemes of spoken words (Read, Yun-Fei, Hong-Yin, & Bao-Qing, 1986; Morais, Cary, Alegria, & Bertelson, 1979). Although phonemic awareness arises from reading, a lasting ability is easily obtained: both poor, rural, Portuguese adults who had only rudimentary reading skills and Chinese adults who had once learned alphabetic writing but could no longer use it were able to perform the phoneme tasks easily.

The Research Evidence for Phonological Awareness Instruction

Phonological Awareness for Typical Learners

There is a large body of research showing that direct instruction in phonological awareness leads to higher levels of phonological awareness and positively impacts acquisition of word reading and spelling performance for a range of ages and ability levels. In a meta-analysis, Ehri et al. (2001, summarized in National Reading Panel, 2000) examined the outcomes on phonemic awareness, reading, and spelling of more than 60 controlled group studies. In the studies reviewed, children from preschool to sixth grade were taught awareness of a variety of phonological skills using diverse procedures and activities for varying lengths of time.

Ehri et al. (2001) found that statistically significant outcomes were consistently obtained. Using effect size, which allows comparison of the magnitude of change in studies with different procedures, Ehri and colleagues found moderate to large effects on phonemic awareness, moderate effects on short-term reading and spelling, and small effects for long-term reading outcomes. Some specific features that affected outcomes were determined by comparing selected studies or by statistically controlling for particular variables. Instruction focused on one to two phonemic skills produced better results than instruction on three or more skills. Programs that included letter training were more effective than those teaching phonological awareness without print. Small group instruction was superior to classroom or individual instruction, and instruction for 5 to 18 hours was superior to shorter or longer periods of instruction. Students from a range of socioeconomic backgrounds, ages, and ability levels made significant and substantial progress on phonemic awareness and transfer to spelling and reading.

Making sense of the evidence across different studies can be difficult because studies vary not only in research design (e.g., a no-treatment or an alternate treatment control) but also in treatment features, such as what skills are taught, for how long, in what ways, to whom, in what size groups, and combined with what other language or literacy skills. Studies that systematically compare specific features of instruction are helpful but uncommon. Instead, answers are sought by comparing the outcomes of studies that have many similar features but differ with respect to a few key elements. For example, some evidence pertaining to phonemic versus phonological awareness instruction comes from comparing two early, well-respected studies.

Lundberg, Frost, and Peterson (1988) investigated a phonological awareness program that became the basis for the commercial program *Phonemic Awareness for Young Children* (Adams et al., 1998). In this study, 235 Danish children, with a mean age of 6;0 years, received 8 months of daily 15-minute whole class instruction on identifying nonverbal sounds, completing rhyming activities, segmenting sentences, segmenting syllables, isolating phonemes, and blending and segmenting phonemes. Children in the training group showed significant improvements in phonemic-level skills compared to 155 children in a no-treatment group. Results for phoneme segmenting compared to those for no-treatment showed a significant moderate effect size ($d = 0.69$).

Ball and Blachman's (1988) phonemic awareness instruction formed the basis of the commercial program *Road to the Code* (Blachman, Ball, Black, & Tangel, 2000). Ball and Blachman randomly assigned 89 kindergartners with a mean age of 5;8 years to one of three conditions: phoneme segmentation plus letter-sound intervention, semantic knowledge plus letter-sound intervention, and no-treatment control. In the first condition, groups of five children were taught phoneme segmentation in four 20-minute sessions per week for 7 weeks using a say-it-and-move-it method with letter tiles. The segmentation treatment condition showed significantly better phoneme segmenting and word reading skills with large effect sizes ($d = 1.85$, $d = 1.67$) compared to those shown by the no-treatment control and the language-letter treatment conditions.

Both of these studies obtained gains that were statistically significant compared to those of the control conditions, meaning the average change was greater than could be expected by chance. Lundberg et al. (1988) reported a moderate effect size compared to that of the no-treatment condition, whereas Ball and Blachman (1988) reported much larger effect sizes compared even to the language-letter treatment, which also received the benefits of print and small group instruction. This comparison provides evidence that, for kindergartners, focusing on advanced phonemic awareness skills produces larger gains in a much shorter time than does teaching an array of awareness skills.

Phonological Awareness Intervention for At-Risk Learners

Children who are at risk for reading difficulties are presented with a double challenge: they often have deficiencies in phonemic awareness, and they must keep up with their peers whose progress has been accelerated by direct instruction. Ehri et al. (2001) found that older children with reading disabilities made smaller gains than typically developing children, but children below second grade with risk indicators, such as low socioeconomic status, low early literacy, language impairment, or developmental delay, showed *larger* gains in phonological awareness and better transfer to reading and spelling than typically developing learners.

In addition to generally greater gains, young at-risk learners show more enduring benefits from instruction. Ehri et al. (2001) found that, in contrast to typical learners whose advantages over their non-instructed peers typically shrink over time, at-risk learners demonstrated substantially larger relative effects at follow-up evaluations than they did immediately following intervention. For example, Byrne and Fielding-Barnsley (1991, 1993) found immediate improvement from preschool phonological awareness instruction compared to the regular curriculum, but the instructional advantage was maintained into kindergarten only for children with low initial levels of phonemic awareness. Higher phonological awareness skills corresponded with higher reading achievement in kindergarten, but many of the higher achievers in the control condition gained phonemic awareness without explicit instruction, apparently figuring out phonemic awareness as they learned to read and spell.

Hatcher, Hulme, and Snowling (2004) conducted a large sample study of reading instruction with typical and at-risk preschoolers. Phonics-based reading instruction alone was compared to additional explicit phonemic awareness instruction. Results were similar to the Byrne and Fielding-Barnsley (1991, 1993) study with no significant differences for the typical learners in a kindergarten follow-up, but sustained benefits from the phonemic awareness instruction for the at-risk learners.

Most of the studies reviewed by Ehri et al. (2001) identified the lower learners simply through pretest performance or socioeconomic status. Children with low initial levels of literacy may be typical learners who have had insufficient exposure to literacy experiences, or they may be children with inherent learning impairments. The former can be expected to make leaps in understanding when given the opportunity, whereas the latter are likely to make much slower progress. However, even preschoolers and kindergartners with language impairment show large and lasting positive effects from phonemic awareness intervention (e.g., Gillon, 2000, 2002; Hund-Reid & Schneider, 2013; van Kleeck, Gillam, & McFadden, 1998; Warrick, Rubin, & Rowe-Walsh, 1993).

Intensity and Distribution of Intervention

Efforts to optimize phonological awareness instruction have addressed the issues of how much instruction should be given, what skills should be taught, and how instruction should be organized. These three factors are interrelated, so that optimal skill combinations and schedules require less instructional time. Phonological awareness is now regularly taught in kindergarten and even preschool, so estimations of how much treatment time is needed must consider what is being delivered in the regular classroom in what may be called *tiered instruction.*

Ehri et al. (2001) found that total treatment durations from 5 to 18 hours produced similar results. Evidence suggests that children with language impairment need the longer side of that estimate (Ukrainetz, 2009). For example, Gillon (2000, 2002, 2005) found that 20 hours of a phoneme-level treatment in biweekly 1-hour sessions that included attention to speech sound production produced significant and enduring gains for preschoolers and kindergartners with speech and language impairments. Denne, Langdown, Pring, and Roy (2005) failed to obtain significant gains in a 12-hour version of the same program. Carson, Gillon, and Boustead (2013) were successful with that 20-hour program distributed across 10 weeks of 30-minute whole class lessons for 5-year-olds with and without language impairment. The children with language impairment showed significant improvement on phoneme blending and segmenting, and five of the seven met age expectations for word reading accuracy and comprehension. However, they did not show the transfer to untaught phoneme deletion and nonword spelling skills exhibited by the typically developing children.

Ukrainetz, Ross, and Harm (2009) investigated whether intensity or distribution of treatment mattered for 41 kindergartners at risk for reading difficulties. Half the children were Spanish-speaking English language learners. Three groupings balanced for age, English learner status, and learner level were randomly assigned to one of three conditions: (a) phonemic awareness instruction concentrated into 3 times per week for 8 weeks in the fall of the school year, (b) phonemic awareness instruction dispersed across 1 time per week for 24 weeks, and (c) vocabulary instruction with the same incidental attention to self-regulatory behaviors as a control condition. Small groups were taught first and last phonemes, blending, and segmenting in 30-minute sessions with print and nonprint activities. Each child obtained at least 5 response opportunities for each skill each session.

Ukrainetz and colleagues (2009) found that neither intensity nor schedule of treatment had much of an effect. The treatment children with mild deficits showed no significant benefits compared to the control children, who had received classroom instruction and incidental attention to self-regulatory behaviors (Box 12.2). However, children with greater deficits had both stronger effects in December from greater treatment intensity and better performance in March from both concentrated and dispersed intensity.

By the end of the school year, almost all the children across the three conditions, regardless of their proficiency in English, had met grade-level benchmarks in phoneme segmentation, letter names, and nonsense word reading. The few children who had not were spread across the three conditions. For most of the children, the classroom phonemic awareness instruction plus additional attention to learning behaviors were enough. The few children who did not catch up to their peers still showed a lot of improvement, but their more persistent learning difficulties require longer term support. These children were flagged at the end of the study for special education assessments in the following fall. This differential growth pattern over the school year (and the great improvement in the performance of almost all the English language learners) matches

Box 12.2. ***Treatment Scheduling Effects for At-Risk Kindergartners***

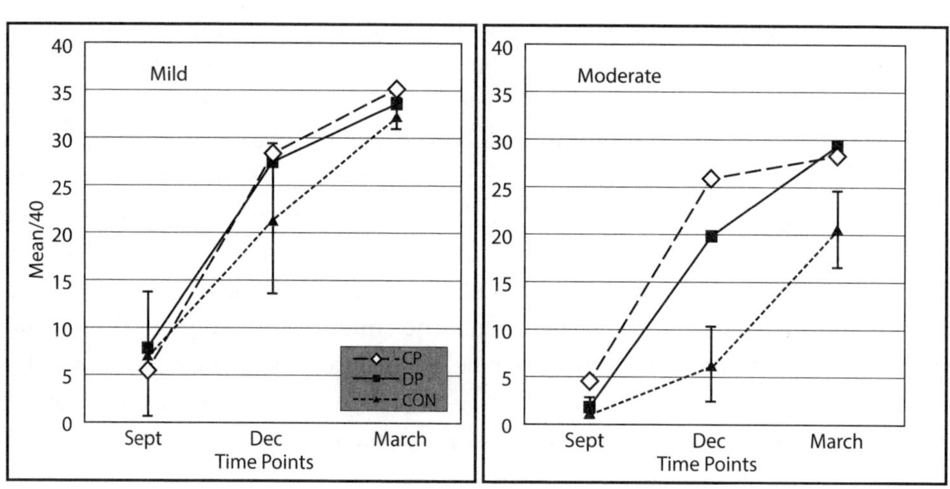

Phonemic awareness performance for children with mild and moderate DIBELS deficits in concentrated (CP), dispersed (DP), and vocabulary control (CON) conditions at across time with 95% confidence interval on CON.

Note: "An Investigation of Treatment Scheduling for Phonemic Awareness with Kindergartners at Risk for Reading Difficulties," by T. A. Ukrainetz, C. L. Ross, and H. M. Harm, 2009, *Language, Speech, and Hearing Services in Schools, 40*, p. 93. Copyright 2009 by American Speech-Language-Hearing Association. Reprinted with permission.

the expectations of dynamic assessment and response to intervention in revealing inherent learning strengths and impairments despite initial low performance on a static measure.

Skill Selection and Ordering

There are many phonological awareness skills that can be taught. Ehri et al. (2001) reported that teaching one to two skills produced better results than teaching three or more skills. However, Ehri did not examine what or how skills were taught. The developmental evidence suggests that awareness of units larger than a phoneme does not precede awareness of phonemes. A close look at the instructional evidence indicates that the most efficient route is to teach only a few key phoneme skills rather than a large array of sound awareness skills.

The earlier comparison of Lundberg et al. (1988) and Ball and Blachman (1988) showed larger gains in a shorter time for phoneme-level instruction for kindergartners. The Lundberg et al. treatment was used in a shorter 18-week version by Brady, Fowler, Stone, and Winbury (1994) and again obtained only a moderate effect size. A phoneme focus makes even more sense now that kindergarten is all about reading instruction. In an investigation of two-tiered kindergarten instruction, Schuele et al. (2008) did not find significant effects on word reading or spelling from a yearlong classroom application of the Adams et al. (1998) program of listening, sentence, word, syllable, rhyme, and phoneme skills. In the second tier of support, Schuele and colleagues provided lower achieving children additional intervention with a more restricted focus on syllable, rhyme, and phoneme skills as well as letter-sound instruction. These children did not improve in their word reading but showed improved developmental spelling at the end of the school year. In Ukrainetz et al. (2009), almost all the at-risk kindergartners reached grade-level expectations on phoneme segmentation and word reading with phoneme-only instruction.

Rhyme and syllable activities are often recommended as introductory steps toward phoneme skills for preschoolers but may not even be helpful at that young age. Ukrainetz (2008) conducted a systematic review of the literature published in the prior 10 years and located 10 studies of preschoolers with language impairment. Amost any type of phonological awareness instruction showed statistically significant outcomes in phonemic awareness, letter-sound knowledge, word reading, and spelling. However, larger effect sizes were obtained in less time with phoneme-level skills compared to combinations that included rhyme and syllable instruction. A packet of basic phoneme-level skills (first and last sound generation, isolation, and categorization) coupled with letter-sound instruction had the strongest results (Byrne & Fielding-Barnsley, 1991; Hindson et al. 2005). Phoneme segmenting and blending, combined with letters, were successfully introduced, but accomplishments varied (Gillon, 2005; Hesketh, Dima, & Nelson, 2007; Hindson et al., 2005, Yeh, 2003).

In terms of the order of introduction of skills, the developmental and instructional evidence suggest only that there are only general gradations of difficulty. Rhyme, syllable, and first phoneme tasks are all easier tasks. Phoneme segmentation and blending are harder and vary in difficulty within those skills by phonotactic and phoneme features. The evidence supports teaching one phoneme skill at a time in a vertical ordering of skill mastery (Carson et al., 2013; Hund-Reid & Schneider, 2013; Schuele et al., 2008). The evidence also supports a horizontal order of teaching multiple complementary phoneme skills in an integrated manner with scaffolding matched to task difficulty to young and at-risk learners (Gillon, 2000, 2002, 2005; Ukrainetz, Cooney, Dyer, Kysar, & Harris, 2000; Ukrainetz, Nuspl, Wilkerson, & Beddes, 2011; Ukrainetz, Ross, & Harm, 2009).

An example of a horizontal, integrated multiple skill format in a preschool storybook-based curriculum comes from Justice et al. (2010). The curriculum involved 60 large group lessons over 30 weeks with 15 commercial storybooks. Each lesson addressed two of four domains—vocabulary, narrative, print, and phonological awareness—before, during, and after the storybook sharing. There were six syllable, rhyme, and phoneme tasks addressed in each phonological awareness lesson. The Justice curriculum was effective for a range of abilities, but the effects were smaller for children with lower language skills. These scripted lessons mixed syllable and rhyme tasks with phoneme tasks, but the curriculum could be adapted to teach only a few phoneme skills in a more responsive and supportive manner that would further benefit all the children.

Horizontally organized contextualized intervention programs that address only a few phoneme skills have been successful with typically developing and at-risk preschoolers and kindergartners (Ukrainetz et al., 2000; Ukrainetz et al., 2009; Ukrainetz et al., 2011). Ukrainetz et al. (2011) demonstrated not only that preschoolers could learn phoneme segmenting and blending in a horizontal ordering but that prior syllable instruction was not a helpful addition. Thirty-nine preschoolers were randomly assigned to three conditions of twice-weekly small group instruction: (a) 2 weeks of syllable instruction followed by 4 weeks of phoneme isolating, blending, and segmenting instruction, (b) 4 weeks of multiple phoneme skill instruction, or (c) 4 weeks of first phoneme instruction. The children were taught using a mix of single skill and integrated skill activities, such as card games, and sound talk embedded in shared verse book reading and message writing. (These activities and procedures will be explained further later in this chapter.)

Ukrainetz et al. (2011) found that first phoneme isolation was easily mastered by all of the children, many of whom did so within the first few sessions. The children who were taught phoneme blending and segmenting showed moderate to large significant gains. However, for the children first taught syllables, there was no advantage and more initial confusion between syllables and phonemes. After 4 weeks of multiple-phoneme skill instruction, the children showed impressive gains in advanced phoneme skills: half the preschoolers could blend six or more words correctly; 9 children could segment VC, CV, and CVC words correctly; and many of the children could provide some partially correct segmenting responses, even to difficult words (e.g., *brag* as /br-ae-g/, *plop* as /pl-aw-p/, *plant* as /pl/-/ae/-/nt/, *liver* as /lɩ-v-er/, and *seashell* as /si/-/ʃ/-/el/).

Teaching phonemic awareness through rhyming books and writing can be just as effective as a vertically structured skill mastery approach. Torgesen, Wagner, Rashotte, Herron, and Lindamood (2010) compared the effects of two instructional programs adapted for computer-assisted instruction with animation and digitized speech for first graders with low reading performance, taught in small groups for a total of 80 hours distributed across the school year to a no-treatment condition that received a nonspecified mix of regular and supplemental instruction. One was the *Lindamood Phoneme Sequencing Program* (LiPS; Lindamood & Lindamood, 2011), which teaches phonemic awareness along with phonetic spelling and word decoding using say-it-and-move-it teaching procedures in a tightly structured, discrete skill, hierarchical structure. It also addresses phonetic awareness through making children aware of the articulatory features associated with each phoneme, accompanied by a special lexicon for phonemic categories (e.g., lip poppers, tongue tappers). The other program, called *Read, Write and Type* (Herron, 1995), employed an engaging story line to lead children in activities that provided explicit instruction and practice in phonemic awareness, phonetic spelling, and keyboarding. Phoneme manipulation was systematically introduced in the context of rhyming stories, practiced during spoken language activities, and then further practiced on the computer in phonemic awareness and spelling activities. Torgesen et al. reported that the discrete skill approach and the more contextualized skill approach resulted in similar significant moderate effects compared to the no-treatment control on phonemic awareness, phonemic decoding, reading accuracy, and reading comprehension. The phonemic awareness and decoding benefits continued to be demonstrated for both conditions in follow-up testing at the end of second grade.

The Role of the SLP in Phonemic Awareness Intervention

Previous generations learned to read and write despite the lack of direct instruction in phonemic awareness. Although typically developing children show large immediate responses to instruction, their advantages in both phonemic awareness and reading compared to noninstructed peers often disappears over time (Ehri et al., 2001). Despite the lack of enduring benefit, in the general determination to have children acquire reading earlier and faster, direct instruction in phonemic awareness is now a standard part of reading instruction (National Reading Panel, 2000; Schuele et al., 2008). Assessment measures used within tiered instructional models, such as *Dynamic Indicators of Basic Early Literacy Skills* (DIBELS; Good & Kaminski, 2002; see http://dibels.uoregon.edu/), include phonemic awareness tasks to identify children in need of supplemental "strategic" or heavier "intensive" reading intervention to move them into segmenting and reading simple words and nonwords by the end of kindergarten.

This emphasis on phonemic awareness in tiered reading instruction has affected the SLP's role. Formerly, this spoken language skill was considered a distinctive, if not unique, purview of the SLP (Ukrainetz, 2006c; Ukrainetz & Fresquez, 2003; Schuele & Boudreau, 2008). Children with language impairment and other risk indicators for reading difficulties need help even more now that typically developing children are receiving the boost in the regular classroom. They may be receiving this adequately through reading instruction—or they may not (Phillips, Clancy-Menchetti, & Lonigan, 2008; Schuele et al., 2008). However, if phonemic awareness is classified as a reading intervention goal rather than as a speech–language goal, this sometimes means SLPs are not permitted to directly address it.

Whether or not SLPs can directly treat phonemic awareness, they need to be flexible and creative in finding ways to support the development of phonemic awareness in children with language impairment. Phonemic awareness instruction can be embedded as mini-lessons within treatment of other speech and language goals. SLPs who are well integrated into their schools can consult and collaborate with teachers to guide them toward more effective tiered instruction. SLPs have a deeper understanding of phonological awareness (Spencer, Schuele, Guillot, & Lee, 2008) that enables them to evaluate curricular programs, suggest modifications, or demonstrate how to better scaffold learning (McGee & Ukrainetz, 2009; Schuele et al., 2008). The simple idea of talking about sounds in words outside a formal lesson can be novel for teachers. Gillon (2004) provides ideas for embedding phonemic awareness comments in classroom lessons and activities, such as having each child tell the sound beginning his or her name during roll call. When writing a word on a board, teachers can think aloud about speech sounds (e.g., "Hmm, I need to write *happy*. What *are* the sounds in *happy*? /h/-/ae/-/p/-/i/."). The SLP may be able to take treatment programs and modify them for large group, teacher-delivered instruction. For example, Carson et al. (2013) adopted Gillon's (2000, 2005) individualized, 1-hour treatment sessions on phonemic awareness with speech production goals for use by teachers without the speech component in daily, short, more-scripted, large group lessons.

The Structure of Intervention

The aim of phonemic awareness instruction is not to teach a phoneme-by-phoneme or word-shape-by-word-shape skill. Rather, it is to teach a robust awareness that phonemes are separable and manipulable as well as to nurture the ability to use that awareness so that children can better learn about how phonemes and graphemes map onto each other in reading and spelling.

Phoneme Isolation, Blending, and Segmenting Skills

Even at the phoneme level, there are many skills or skill variations that can be taught, but only a few are instructional priorities. For example, first-phoneme awareness can be shown in categorizing, matching, generating, and isolating tasks. These variants provide practice opportunities and help develop a robust awareness of first phonemes. However, children do not need to master or even experience every one. There are three skills that are priorities for intervention: phoneme blending, segmenting, and isolating. Phoneme blending involves having children guess a word from the component phonemes spoken by the instructor. Phoneme segmenting is the inverse, with the children saying the component phonemes of a target word. Word familiarity, phonotactic shape, and phoneme features affect the task difficulty of both these skills. First phoneme isolation is the first step and building block of phonemic segmenting and blending. If students can say the first sound of a given word, they are already partway into phoneme segmenting (e.g., "What is the first sound in the word *cat*? Now say all the sounds in *cat*."). Reflecting this, first phoneme isolation is sometimes called first-phoneme segmentation or even onset-rime segmentation (e.g., "Let's break this word into two parts: the first sound and the rest of the word: /k/-/aet/.").

Tasks involving isolating and making judgments about phonemes in other word positions are distinctly more difficult than first-phoneme tasks. For last-phoneme tasks, students need to hold the whole word in working memory and consider the last segment. In teaching final sounds, phoneme segmentation can scaffold the supposedly easier final-phoneme isolation (e.g., "What is the last sound in *cat*? /k/. Not the first but the last sound. /k/-/ae/-/t/, /t/ is the last sound."). Last-phoneme isolation is a reasonable part of the basic skill treatment package, but it is a step up from first-phoneme isolation. Medial-phoneme isolation is even harder. Medial phonemes will usually be vowels, which are less categorically produced or perceived, and vary with syllable stress, dialect, word context, and speed of articulation. Furthermore, they are notoriously irregular to spell in English, so pairing them with letters will increase teaching challenges and shift the focus from phonemic awareness to phonics. Medial-phoneme awareness is best accomplished incidentally through the process of teaching phoneme blending and segmenting.

Other Phoneme Skills

First-phoneme tasks other than isolating, such as judging, matching, and sorting, are fairly easy to master, even for at-risk preschoolers. They add variety without significantly increasing the learning challenge. They also usually involve an isolation act. For example, in a matching card game, the child names the two cards for every turn, isolates the first phonemes, and then judges if they are the same or different. That results in two response opportunities for phoneme isolating for every act of phoneme matching.

Phoneme tasks of matching, categorizing, or sorting usually involve visual supports such as picture cards. The SLP needs to be attentive to the memory, vocabulary, and motor demands of these tasks. If the word depicted is unfamiliar, the child will have trouble remembering it to focus on the phonemes. Holding, touching, and organizing their "wins" of objects and pictures in games can distract young children. Despite the possible complications, these activities help children become accustomed to a variety of task formats and response requirements that may be required in testing. Children should not fail items because they are distracted or confused by the task features. For example, in the beginning kindergarten level of the popular *Dynamic Indicators of Basic Early Literacy Skills* (DIBELS; Good & Kaminski, 2002, p. 3), the tester says, "This is *tomato, cub, plate, doughnut* [points to pictures]. Which picture starts with /d/?" This involves scanning four pictures, remembering the labels for each picture, and judging whether each word starts with the target sound.

Although the focus should be on phonemes, if children will be tested on syllables, some practice in that testing format is also recommended. Syllable segmentation is quite easy to learn and does not need to precede phoneme-level instruction. Rather, it can be presented as needed for test-taking preparation (e.g., "We have been learning to break words into little sounds, but today we need to practice breaking words into big sounds. You will have a test next week where you will have to do this, so let's practice a bit.").

Rhyming does not need to be taught prior to phoneme skills and does not even need to be a direct treatment goal. Rhyming is a useful tool and an enjoyable way to highlight the sound structure of words. Phonemes can be isolated and manipulated in the context of rhyme, without directly targeting rhyming as a skill to master. In addition, rhyming sets of words come into play in phonics programs that organize word spelling by rime units (e.g., *p-an, r-an, m-an*) called analogy phonics (National Reading Panel, 2000). An SLP may choose to spend a brief time teaching children to identify and produce rhyming words. Most children can learn rhyming fairly quickly, but for those children who have particular difficulty with rhyming, the SLP should move on rather than spend more time on rhyme at the expense of phoneme instruction. Testing for rhyme and syllable skills in kindergarten may be continued despite the research evidence against it if they are listed in state academic expections (Box 12.3).

Phoneme deletion, substitution, and transposition tasks are not skills that are needed for early reading. Children will be able to perform them much better after they learn to read. Phoneme deletion is often present in tests because it is appropriate for older children and can be administered and scored faster and more reliably than segmentation and blending (e.g., *Comprehensive Test of Phonological Processing–Second Edition*; Wagner, Torgesen, Rashotte, & Pearson, 2013). Bridges and Catts (2011) found a dynamic phoneme deletion to be an excellent predictor of end-of-year reading achievement for kindergartners, surpassing both the DIBELS Initial Sound Fluency task and a static version of the deletion task. This does not mean that deletion should be directly taught but that it is a valuable diagnostic task for future reading difficulties.

Box 12.3. ***Phonological Awareness Standards in the Common Core***

Kindergarten: Demonstrate understanding of spoken words, syllables, and sounds (phonemes).

a. Recognize and produce rhyming words.

b. Count, pronounce, blend, and segment syllables in spoken words.

c. Blend and segment onsets and rimes of single-syllable spoken words.

d. Isolate and pronounce the initial, medial vowel, and final sounds (phonemes) in three-phoneme (consonant-vowel-consonant, or CVC) words (not including final /l/, /r/, or /x/).

e. Add or substitute individual phonemes in simple, one-syllable words to make new words.

Grade 1: Demonstrate understanding of spoken words, syllables, and sounds (phonemes).

a. Distinguish long from short vowel sounds in spoken single-syllable words.

b. Orally produce single-syllable words by blending phonemes, including consonant blends.

c. Isolate and pronounce initial, medial vowel, and final phonemes in spoken single-syllable words.

d. Segment spoken single-syllable words into their complete sequence of individual phonemes.

Note: From National Governors Association Center for Best Practices and Council of Chief School Officers (2010, p. 15).

Thus, the first priority treatment goals are phoneme isolating, segmenting, and blending simple words. Final phoneme may be a fourth skill goal. If only one phonemic awareness goal can be listed because other language goals are needed, then it should be phoneme isolating for preschoolers and phoneme segmenting for kindergartners. Phoneme matching, categorization, generation, and even rhyming may be engaged in to support achievement of the primary isolating, blending, and segmenting skills.

Vertical and Horizontal Goal Order

Another intervention decision is how to order skill instruction. Many intervention programs use a vertical structure to teach target skills, which means one skill is taught at a time. Within each skill or task area, there may be additional steps involving the number of response alternatives, phonotactic features, or phoneme features. Mastery may be required at each stage, or a set time may be spent on each skill. However, even with vertical ordering, mastery of one step is not a prerequisite to the next step, not all speech units or tasks merit equal teaching time, and the critical skill of phoneme segmenting takes the

Box 12.4. ***Single-Skill Instruction in a Vertical Sequence***

Week	Skill	Activities
1	Rhyme	Bingo, odd-one-out
2	Initial phoneme	Bingo, matching, odd-one-out
3	Final phoneme	Bingo, matching, odd-one-out
4 & 5	Phoneme blending	Drawing, singing, bingo; mainly 2–3 phoneme words; 4-phoneme words and consonant clusters to extend students
6 & 7	Phoneme segmenting	Drawing, singing, bingo; mainly 2–3 phoneme words; 4-phoneme words and consonant clusters to extend students
8 & 9	Phoneme manipulation	Letter cards and white board for manipulating letters and sounds in words to create new words
10	Review	Reviewing prior nine weeks of activities with focus on phoneme segmenting and blending

Note: Based on Carson et al. (2013).

most time (e.g., Gillon, 2004; Phillips et al., 2008; Schuele & Boudreau, 2008). An example of a simple vertical ordering from Carson et al. (2013) that focuses on phonemes and employs a variety of tasks for learning and practice within one level is presented in Box 12.4.

Treatment can also be provided in a horizontal skill order that is explicit and systematic but more closely approximates how children develop phonemic awareness and other language and literacy skills (McFadden, 1998; Ukrainetz, 2006a, 2006b). Several complementary skills are addressed in several different activities or combined within one activity in each treatment session. Varying levels of challenge can provide children of different skill levels within a group with opportunities for success. Simpler skills provide children with consistent opportunities for success, supportively introduce them to challenging skills, and scaffold more difficult skills through the simpler skills. This integrated approach allows flexible application of skills as needed, which better reflects how phoneme skills are used in reading and spelling.

Even within the phoneme level, giving children a mix of tasks can provide opportunities that are not available in a vertical goal structure. Preschoolers are not typically exposed to phoneme segmentation in a vertical skill order because it takes too long to work through all the earlier steps. In a horizontal structure, this challenging but critical task is introduced early on, affording more time and learning opportunities. Sometimes, unexpected strengths may emerge. For example, Ukrainetz et al. (2011) reported that a preschooler in the study was able to score only 2 correct out of 10 on first-phoneme isolating

Box 12.5. ***Instructional Cycle for Horizontal Integrated Skill Instruction***

Session	Activities	Skills
1	a. Open Skill Question b. Naming c. Verse Book d. One Game e. Close Skill Question	a. What and why from one child b. Naming has one skill c. Book has three skills d. Game has one skill e. Specific what answer from each child
2	a. Open Skill Question b. Naming c. 2–3 Games d. Close Skill Question	See Session 1; Games each address one skill
3	a. Open Skill Question b. Naming c. Writing d. 1–2 Games e. Close Skill Question	See Session 1; Writing has four skills

Note: First- and last-phoneme isolation, segmenting, and blending skills are taught in each session. The three-session cycle is repeated with progressively less scaffolding. Based on Ukrainetz et al. (2009).

at the end of treatment. However, this child blended 8 out of 10 words and partially segmented many words. Engaging in phoneme isolating, blending, and segmenting simultaneously allowed this child to learn what made sense to him.

A horizontal ordering approach can use a whole-part contextualized skill framework to explicitly and systematically provide focused practice on particular skills in contrived or "part" activities and integrated use in naturalistic or "whole" activities (see Chapter 3). An example of this is in Box 12.5, where treatment occurred as repetitions of a three-session unit consisting of: (a) one session of sound talk embedded in a rhyming book, (b) one session of single-skill activities, and (c) one session of sound talk embedded in shared writing (Ukrainetz et al., 2009).

Intervention With RISE

Some kind of phonological awareness instruction is commonly present in kindergarten and even in preschool. However, children with learning difficulties need more supportive and systematic instruction than do typically developing children. The features associated with effective interventions are RISE: repeated practice opportunities, intense service delivery, systematic learning support, and an explicit focus on target skills (Box 12.6).

First is the "E" of an *explicit focus* on treatment skills. In an integrated horizontal skill ordering approach to intervention, explicit, systematic attention is distributed

Box 12.6. ***RISE Applied to Phonemic Awareness Intervention***

Critical Element	Description
Repeated opportunities	Total response opportunities per child per 20–30 min session Distributed across phoneme isolating, blending, and segmenting In name play, single skill contrived activities, and sound talk in verse books and writing
Intensity	20 hours of instruction on phoneme-level awareness, with most of it in individualized intervention
Systematic support	*Structural scaffolds*, such as small groups to optimize participation, simple activities for massed practice, and verse books to highlight form over content and tie to contexts of use *Amount and type of interactive scaffolding* matched to task difficulty and child need *Interactive linguistic scaffolds*, such as stressing the target sound and expanding a partial into full word segmentation *Interactive regulatory scaffolds*, such as obtaining the child's full attention and waiting expectantly for a response
Explicit skill objective	Maintain a clear focus with therapeutic attention only on phonemic awareness and other skills addressed only incidentally

across three to four skills in a mix of whole and part activities supported by some structural scaffolding and considerable interactive scaffolding, the latter of which is matched to task difficulty and child need. Vertical skill ordering requires similar intensity and repeated opportunities, but in this case explicit attention is given to one skill at a time, with more use of contrived activities and less interactive scaffolding. Many possibilities for enriching other language and literacy skills may arise, especially in whole activities or when print is present. While attention to other skills may occur in periodic "teachable moments," the focus of instruction should be on the treatment goals. To reinforce the goal focus, children should be told at the beginning of the session, reminded during the session, and asked at the end of the session what they are learning. The answer should be related to phonemic awareness, such as "saying sounds in words," "first sounds," or "counting sounds," with the reason for learning being help with reading, writing, or spelling. This opening and closing skill review also applies to vertical skill ordering, but is particularly important when multiple skills are addressed and when whole communicative activities with many nontarget skills are used.

The second consideration is how much treatment, which consists of the "R" of *repeated opportunities* within a session and the "I" of overall treatment *intensity*. Two treatments offered two times per week for eight weeks can represent very different amounts of treatment, depending on how intervention is structured. Warren, Fey, and Yoder (2007) proposed a dosage framework, with intensity measured in terms of a *dose*:

"the number of properly administered teaching episodes during a single intervention session" (p. 71). Doses are delivered in *dose forms*, which are the activities employed to deliver the teaching episodes, such as picture labeling or play conversation. One dose in structured drills may comprise 100 responses in a 20-minute session, whereas in a writing activity, a dose may be only 20 responses in the same length of time. The more dilute writing dose may require more doses for comparable results, or it may be successful with a similar number of doses due to its greater meaningfulness. For phonological awareness, it is not clear which dose intensity is optimal for which type of learner, but thinking about intensity in this format is helpful for treatment planning and progress measurement.

The basic unit of a teaching episode in phonemic awareness instruction is composed of an instructor initiation, a child response, and an evaluation—*response opportunities* that reflect how much active teaching and learning is occurring in treatment. Response opportunities are easy to control in a highly structured procedure in which a single elicitation leads to a single answer with a predesignated prompt. It is a little more complicated with more dynamic instructional procedures (Ukrainetz, 2009). For example, one teaching episode with an individual child might involve an extended series of prompts, repeated attempts, and evaluations. An SLP might use simple subskills to achieve a more complex skill. For example, the SLP might ask: "Now say the sounds in *blue*. What is the first sound in *blue*? Yes, /b/. Now try again and say all the sounds in *blue*." The two tasks embedded in this request could be counted as two isolating and one segmenting response opportunities or as a single extended segmenting opportunity. Other counting complications are: instructor models, choral responses, children listening to each other's responses, and children answering questions directed at others. However, even an approximate count of response opportunities, with notations of the nature of the elicitations, responses, and scaffolds, will show children's learning progress.

So how intense should phonemic awareness intervention be? For preschoolers and kindergartners with language impairment, a total of approximately 20 hours of individual or small group instruction seems to be needed. If some explicit instruction is occurring in the classroom, then less intervention time will be needed. If other language skills are also being addressed, then more total treatment time will be needed. Within a session, at least 20 response opportunities should be planned for each child. If multiple skills are being addressed, then children should have at least five opportunities for each skill in a session.

Possibly the most important part of RISE is the systematic learning support. In an integrated, horizontally ordered approach, the responsive support of scaffolding is particularly important. In a vertically ordered skill mastery approach, treatment activities are contrived to enable the child to perform with a minimum of interactive support. The SLP may provide occasional prompts, but the child is expected to perform largely independently. However, in more contextualized interventions, the SLP must support the learning of multiple skills with dynamic adjustments based on the child's verbal responses and nonverbal indicators. These structural and interactive scaffolds will be discussed further after presenting the activities within which intervention procedures operate.

Intervention Activities

Phonemic awareness intervention activities are presented as name play, contrived picture and object activities, and interactions involving printed text. The name play makes efficient use of transition times. The contrived activities provide massed practice opportunities for individual skills. The contextualized skill activities provide opportunities for integrated applications in meaningful print situations. These activities can be used with an isolated single or an integrated skill focus in vertical or horizontal skill ordering, with tightly or loosely controlled phonotactic and phoneme choices.

Name Play

Name play is a short, flexible activity that requires no special materials. Children enjoy playing with the sounds in their names and in the names of their friends and families. It works well as a warm-up or as a transition activity to occupy children while they are waiting for materials to be set up or distributed. The name play activity arose originally in Ukrainetz et al. (2000), when the children spontaneously took an interest in the instructor's name tag, requesting her to read it and to count the sounds in it during each session.

Names with the same first or last phonemes can be generated. The SLP models how to isolate the first sound in his or her name and then generates the names of two acquaintances (real or imaginary) with the same first sound. Then each child does the same. Categorizing can be used after isolating the first sound in the names (e.g., "Your name is Sam. Which of these names starts with the same sound as *Sam*: *Ezra*, *Cody*, or *Sarah*?"). Across activities, "same" questions are easier than "different" questions, so mixing them up will keep children alert and flexible. Names can be enhanced with appealing adjectives, such as *Terrific Teresa, Lovely Laura, Smart Sarita,* or *Rocking Ron.* Sometimes a child will insist that he is *Burrito Ted* and refuse to go along with the alliteration. Pointing out the */b/ and /t/* difference and showing how the two phonemes are articulated is an awareness lesson in itself. Names can be guessed when the SLP pronounces the component phonemes. Children enjoy comparing the length of their names. First, middle, and last names provide everyone with the opportunity to have the longest name, although phoneme segmenting and counting works best with short names.

Single-Skill Picture and Object Activities

Contrived activities are designed specifically to teach a skill without any larger communicative purpose. They are based on children's card games and object play, such as "I spy" or Bingo, but modified to practice phoneme awareness. Depending on whether the desire is for vertical or horizontal ordering, the games within a session can all target a single skill, or each can target a different skill.

A selection of single-skill activities for isolating, blending, and segmenting is presented in Box 12.7. The basic component of these contrived activities is a predictable, repetitive, but entertaining format that maintains a focus on phonemes and provides repeated opportunities for practice. Any of the activities can be modified to teach skills other than what is stated. Primary skill targets are listed, but often other phonemic awareness skills are involved in getting to the answer. Phoneme blending and segmenting can be combined in a single activity. For example, in the "Guess the Food" blending game, after the children have become familiar with the procedure, I have a child who has some segmenting competence "be the teacher" and announce the phonemes, and then I have the other children guess the word. (Children need to be able to provide at least one onset-rime segmentation with a small pause so that it is blendable by the others.)

For the picture cards, there are commercial phonemic kits and supplies, but rummaging through the typical SLP toolbox will reveal picture sets that work fine. Item complexity can be controlled by selecting cards with particular phonotactic shapes and phoneme contrasts. Articulation picture cards provide multiple exemplars of particular phonemes in initial, medial, and final positions. Phonological process cards work well for phoneme segmentation because they control phonotactic shape. For instance, a "cluster reduction" card pack provides 3-phoneme (e.g., *sick*, *lick*) versus 4-phoneme (e.g., *stick*, *slick*) words. Print can be present on the picture cards, but children may notice the letters and use them to match, categorize, isolate, and segment instead of the phonemes.

Commercial curricula (e.g., Adams et al., 1998; Blachman et al., 2000; Notari-Syverson et al., 1998) provide additional activity ideas without committing to the entire program. Most simple computer games can be adapted to provide play-drill for phonemes by embedding clinician-child sound talk within the activities. There are computer programs with speech output that are designed to be used without interactive SLP support, such as Earobics (Cognitive Concepts, 1997). There are undoubtedly iPad applications for this purpose.

In these contrived contexts, meaning is not essential, so nonwords words can be used, providing absolute control over word shape and phoneme composition. The Fill-in-the-Blank game can easily work with nonwords. This activity is similar to the Say-It-and-Move-It activity used in *Road to the Code* (Blachman et al., 2000). The structure may be increased further by color coding the chips or tiles to match particular phonemes or phoneme categories but doing so will add an extraneous memory load. These activities can move from blank to letter tiles. If there are only a few letters or if phonetic spelling is used, the focus may still stay on phonemic awareness. However, as soon as the letter-sound correspondence goes beyond the most basic level, instruction will focus on spelling, not phonemic awareness.

Sound Talk Through Verse Books

Phonemic awareness can be taught within interactions around print. These reading and writing activities can occur in two ways: sharing of verse books and message writing (McFadden, 1998; Ukrainetz, 2006a, 2006b). In these activities, it is difficult to keep the focus entirely on one skill, and there is no particular need to, because the skills build on each other naturally. Word and phoneme complexity can be loosely controlled by the SLP choosing to talk only about particular words or word shapes. The focus is always on the sounds in the spoken words, not the letters on the page (i.e., "We are talking about sounds [*point to ear*] not letters [*point to eye*].").

Box 12.7. *Some Single-Skill Contrived Activities*

Phoneme Isolation and Matching
Concentration. Picture cards with labels that elicit two to four different first or last phonemes are spread face down on the table. The children take turns choosing two cards, identifying the pictures, isolating the phonemes, and determining if the two phonemes are the same or different. This judgment is on sounds, not on the pictures or on any letters printed on the cards. If the cards match in first sound, the child keeps the pair, if not, the pair is returned to the table. The winner is the one with the most pairs.
Puzzles. A simple puzzle with woodcut figure pieces works for first or last phoneme isolation. For each puzzle piece, children identify the sound in the vehicle, or food, or animal name. For animals, children will need to be directed that this is about the sounds in the names, not the sounds that the animals make. An additional matching or categorization judgment could be made before the pieces are returned, again with identification of the target phoneme.
Go Fish! In this familiar card game, one child asks another for a card beginning with the same sound as one in his or her hand of four cards. Little hands have trouble holding several cards, so the "hand" may be laid on the table behind a barrier. This game has several components that have to be coordinated. The child must choose a card to ask about, isolate the phoneme, and then ask for a card starting with that sound. The other child must examine each of his or her cards to determine which starts with that sound and then give the card. The recipient must judge that the two sounds do match. If the child does not have a matching card, he or she says, "Go Fish!" and the other child selects a card from the face-down pile. If that card matches a card in the hand, it is kept, and if not, discarded. This game should not have more than six different phonemes so there are a lot of matching opportunities. Again, the winner is the one with the most pairs.
Phoneme Blending and Segmenting
Guess the Food! For sound blending, children guess the word from the parts from a known array of words. Six to eight plastic food items are displayed and labeled. My plastic food array includes: *apple*, *peach*, *orange*, *bread*, *hot dog*, and *pizza* (really a piece of pie, which is easier, but the children always called it pizza). The food items are dropped into an opaque bag and the tension mounts. The SLP grasps one item in the bag, provides the segmented word (e.g., /b/-/r/-/E/-/d/), and each child takes a turn guessing the word. Children like to hold, examine, and even pretend-nibble their objects, but to reduce distractions, the SLP can remove the items after identification.
Listen to the Whole Word. Another word blending game uses picture cards. Four pictures are spread face up on the table. Words with the same starting sounds and similar lengths (e.g., *bat*, *bun*, *back*, *ball*) are used to prevent guessing based only on the first sound or word length. The children are told to guess which word the SLP is saying.

(continues)

Box 12.7. (*continued*)

Phoneme Segmentation
Catching Fish. This game is a favorite with children. Paper fish with paperclips attached are spread on the floor. Reversed chairs can be set in a circle so children kneel and lean over the chair back to fish in the "water," although I have learned that children are equally entertained by catching fish sitting at the table, which is a whole lot faster and simpler to accomplish. With a magnetic "fishing rod," the child catches a fish. The clinician asks the child the picture label, then has the child "cut the fish" by segmenting the word into phonemes. Children track who caught the "biggest" fish. A magnetic "tool picker-upper" from the hardware store makes a fine fishing rod. It helpfully lacks the swinging potential of a magnet on a string, although the SLP still needs to retrieve the rod immediately from the successful fisher.
Fill-in-the-Blanks. The children are given a paper with four squares drawn. Each child is told to listen to a word and place a chip in each square for each sound. The child is told that not all the blank spaces may be needed. The SLP demonstrates several 1- to 4-phoneme words, having the children copy the segmentation and chip placement. Then the children place their chips while the clinician simply segments the word. Finally, the child says each phoneme as he or she places the chip in the square. In a more controlled version of this, the number of squares can be matched to the word length, gradually moving from 2 to 3 to 4 phonemes. Points can be earned for correct answers.

The materials for the shared reading activity are simply enjoyable verse books with a minimum of text. (See the Appendix for books that work well.) Any book can be used, but the salience of meaningful stories takes attention away from the structure of speech sounds and makes stopping to talk about sounds more artificial. Rhyming verses provide natural stopping points that allow sound talk. Rhyme is not a treatment goal in these activities, but rather a structural scaffold used to highlight the sounds of speech. The SLP helps the children identify the rhyming words but quickly segues to teaching the targeted phoneme skills on those rhyming pairs. Books can be read initially without discussion and then reread for sound talk. Alternately, sound talk may accompany the first reading, as long as the pleasure of reading is maintained. The whole book does not have to be shared each session, but rather it can be shared in installments over several sessions along with other phonemic awareness activities.

Easier and more difficult tasks co-occur within book sharing. The SLP provides more support for harder words or chooses to talk about the phonemes of easier words. For example, in a favorite verse book of mine, one of the rhyming stories contains *cat*, *rat*, and *aristocrat*. I touch my nose and look snobby for *aristocrat* as we examine the picture of a cat looking very elegant. The children savor this new "yummy word," but we do not do much phonemically with it beyond isolating the first sound. We segment and count the phonemes in *cat* and *rat*, and then observe that "*aristocrat* has a lot of sounds, but we won't try to count them."

Talk about sounds within verse book sharing is supported by the structural scaffold of a predictable sequence, called a sound talk episode (McFadden, 1998). The sound talk episode is comprised of an integrated set of phonemic awareness tasks carried out on words in the text at intervals during the book sharing. The basic sound talk episode consists of four parts: (a) identify the rhyming words; (b) isolate the first phoneme of each word; (c) segment the sounds in the words; and (c) judge which is the longer word (Box 12.8). For kindergartners, the episode can be extended by inserting the last phoneme isolation after the first phoneme isolation and by adding phoneme blending after segmenting. For blending, the SLP sounds out the phonemes of another rhyming word for the children to blend. As children become accustomed to the tasks, the questions can be asked out of order or selectively.

Other literacy knowledge and skills may be addressed through brief incidental comments about interesting vocabulary, personally relevant topics, arithmetic opportunities, and print concepts. For example, print concepts arise when the SLP and the children identify the book title, author, and illustrator, and find the page number for a particular verse. In Ukrainetz et al. (2000), during a reading of *Drummer Hoff*, one child suggested that she knew this was a "long part in the story" because there were so many words on that page. During another book reading, a child commented that he knew that a certain part of the story needed to be read loudly because there was an "explanation point" (i.e., exclamation point) in the writing. The children became excited over new storybooks and discussed vocabulary such as *private*, *corporal*, and *general* (*Drummer Hoff*), and demonstrated the concept of upside down (*Silly Sally*). Counting the sounds and comparing length provided mini-lessons in adding and subtracting. As is evident, this book reading activity is rich in language and literacy possibilities. However, the therapeutic focus is on phonemic awareness, with RISE provided only for that treatment goal.

Sound Talk Through Writing

Writing is a powerful context for becoming aware of the phonemic construction of words, especially when children are spelling phonetically rather than conventionally. Writing a verse from a story just heard, generating a pretend grocery list, writing a message to Dad, writing a story, or describing a picture are examples of communicative writing activities. The key element to this instruction is the SLP, who talks through the process (Box 12.9). As the clinician writes, he or she elicits from the children isolation and segmentation of the phonemes in each word. The number of letters required can be predicted. The SLP demonstrates how to think through phoneme isolation and segmentation for the purpose of writing. Every word and every phoneme do not have to be discussed. Instead the SLP chooses which words and word parts will be used for the sound talk.

The children can take turns writing parts of the message. The sound talk is the same, but one child spells the word while that same child or another uses best guesses on its spelling. Having an alphabet strip available to consult alleviates children's concerns about letter formation. After writing the message, the SLP and children reread the sentences, identify component sounds, and count the number of sounds in those words

Box 12.8. ***An Illustration of a Sound Talk Episode on a Verse***

SLP: {reading} The story of Fred. This is a boy named Fred. He hates to go to bed. He hides out in the shed, and stays awake instead. Do you hear words that rhyme? {reads again, stressing rhyming words}

Sara: Fred-bed. [IDENTIFY RHYMING WORDS]

Deepa: Shed.

SLP: {segmentation} Yes, all those words rhyme, *Fred-bed-shed*. What's the first sound in *Fred {points to upper teeth touching lower lip}*?

Sara: /f/ [FIRST-PHONEME ISOLATION]

SLP: And *bed*? /b/-/b/-/bEd/

Deepa: /b/

SLP: Good job. Let's count the sounds in *Fred*. Put your fingers out for each sound. /f/-/r/-/E/-/d/. [PHONEME SEGMENTATION]

Children: {raising a finger for each sound and saying along with the SLP} /f/-/r/-/E/-/d/.

SLP: How many sounds?

Children: {count fingers} 4 sounds!

SLP: How many in *bed*? /B-e-d/.

Children: {raising a finger for each sound and saying along with the SLP} /b/-/E/-/d/.

SLP: How many sounds? [COUNT THE PHONEMES]

Sara: 3 sounds.

SLP: Which one is longest?

Children: Fred.

SLP: Yes, *Fred* is the longest word. It has four sounds, /f/-/r/-/E/-/d/.

Note: From *Terrible Teresa and Other Very Short Stories* (pp. 8–9), by M. Cuetara, 1997, Boston, MA: Dutton/Penguin. Copyright 1997 by the Mittie Cuetara. Reprinted with permission. Based on Ukrainetz (2006a, p. 452).

again. The key is to maximize the amount of sound talk while still composing a brief, satisfying message.

During the writing and sound talk, children predict how many letters there are from the number of phonemes. The SLP can note when the one phoneme for one grapheme rule is violated: "Oh well, spelling is funny sometimes, but usually it matches the

Box 12.9. ***Sound Talk Through Shared Writing***

SLP: Tell me what you want to say and I'll write it down.

John: I went to the zoo today.

SLP: I /w-E-n-t/, what's the first sound I need?

John: /w/

SLP: Yes, /w/. /w-E-n-t/. What's the last sound?

John: /t/

SLP: Yes, /t/. Whew, four sounds in that word. That's lots to write. To, /t/-/u/. That's easy, /t-t-t/ and /uuu/, just two sounds {writes them as says them}. The zoo, /z/-/u/ {stretched out}. What's the first sound I need?

John: /u/

SLP: Listen again, /zzz-u/

John: /z/

SLP: Yes, /z/. I like /z/ words, *zoo, zebra, zoom*. Then the last sound?

John: /u/

SLP: You got it. /u/. Last word, *Today*, /t/ - /u/ - /d/ - /ay/. You count those sounds, fingers out.

John: /t/ - /u/ - /dai/. Three.

SLP: Hmm, let me check. /t/-/u/-/d/-/ai/. I count four. /d-ai/ are two sounds. Four sounds, four letters. Hmm, it's written with five letters. Oh well, sometimes spelling is strange. We wrote, "I went to the zoo today."

Note: From *Contextualized Language Intervention: Scaffolding PreK-12 Literacy Achievement* (p. 454), by T. A. Ukrainetz, 2006a, PRO-ED: Austin, TX. Copyright 2007 by the PRO-ED. Reprinted with permission.

sounds." Encouraging children to use their best guesses and to line up the number of letters with the number of sounds is appropriate for beginning writers and helps them figure out both phonemic awareness and spelling. Kindergartners will correct each other's attempts with *th*, *ll*, and silent *e* suggestions. This is fine, but the target child's guess should also be supported, and the writing should not get bogged down in the complexities of spelling. The objective is not to hinder correct spelling but to keep the focus on sound analysis, with spelling expectations matched to each child's level.

Scaffolding Learning

Scaffolding is the intentional, strategic support provided by more competent partners to enable children to complete a task they could not accomplish independently (Vygotsky, 1978; Wood, Bruner, & Ross, 1976). It enables the child to successfully respond and understand how to do better the next time. Over repeated opportunities for learning, children gradually internalize the assistance provided and become better able to perform the task on their own.

Structural Scaffolds

Scaffolding is most often considered to take the form of interactive facilitations, but it can also be closer to the literal idea of a temporary structure erected to support a building under construction. This structural scaffolding consists of the environmental simplifications that an instructor programs into activities to help children succeed in the target skills. Pictures and objects help children remember the words being analyzed, while tiles and letters help children remember the number and position of phonemes in words. Routinized activities provide predictability so that children do not have to think about what comes next. Rhyming words in verse books and invented spelling scaffold a focus on sound. Predictable sound talk episodes enable children to think about sounds in words instead of what comes next. Small groups are the components of the structural scaffold of peer models and enthusiasm, while individual intervention provides more practice opportunities and more responsive support. In large groups, choral responses increase the number of response opportunities for each child.

Highly structured tasks that are matched to a child's current performance require very little interactional scaffolding. When phonemic awareness is embedded in more complicated reading and writing activities, then more interactive scaffolds are needed. Activities need to be structured so they provide sufficient meaning and interest but still maintain a focus on the target skill. Some activities can be needlessly complicated, such as a group role play in which children are assigned phoneme identities and then move around the room to respond to the teacher's call for particular phonemes to form different words.

Interactive Scaffolding

Interactive scaffolding involves the facilitative moves made by the instructor to help a child answer better but also, and even more important, to learn the skill being addressed and to become more independent in its use. SLPs need to be able to match the nature and amount of help to give the child, and to note when a task is too easy or too complicated to advance the child's learning. The interactive scaffolding moves used to support children's responses and move them toward success and independence are the same in vertical and horizontal approaches, but they are used more in activities with less structural control.

Scaffolding may be regulatory or linguistic. Regulatory interactive scaffolds, such as naming a child before asking a question, pausing, and then repeating the question, encourage a hesitant or inattentive child to answer in some way. Linguistic scaffolds provide children with more information, enabling them to give a better answer. These aids include expanding a partial to a full segmentation, slowing word enunciation, stressing sounds, giving physical cues, and giving the answer. Interactive scaffolding possibilities are known in advance, but enactment is dynamic and responsive to each child's needs in the moment.

Scaffolding matches the expected difficulty of the task (first sound versus segmentation), word position (first versus middle), word shape (single versus multisyllabic), and phoneme (continuant versus vowel). Assistance may range from a high degree (e.g., needing to hear stress on the target word in the prompt and hear other children's responses) to a middle level (e.g., needing the word slowed down to count the segments) to a low level (e.g., needing only repetition of the sentence containing the target word). Box 12.10 shows the types and amounts of interactive scaffolding that are needed at each of these levels for isolating, blending, and segmenting.

Progress toward independence can be measured by tallying how many prompts are needed to enable a child to successfully respond and understand how to do better the next time. To track progress in treatment, children's responses can be scored as requiring no, low, mid, or high levels of scaffolding. If a child can perform at 90% or better at a particular scaffolding level, a lower level of support can be given in the next session. If the child shows little progress, scaffolding may stay high throughout the intervention, and the child may not achieve independence for that particular task. That may mean that a preschooler can identify first sounds fully independently and last sounds with medium support.

Scaffolding Blending and Segmentation

Phoneme segmentation is a particularly difficult task. In contrast to the rhythmic divisions of syllable or onset-rime segmentation, it is awkward and jarring to stop at each individual phoneme. This level of segmentation is actually impossible for stops (a schwa vowel is appended), extends the continuants, and exaggerates liquids, glides, and vowels. However, it is the level required for an alphabetic writing system.

In a blending task, the SLP presents each phoneme separately but in close succession, and the child identifies the word. For reading, children are taught to "sound out" printed words by stretching and linking the phonemes continuously with no micro-pauses between. However, to become aware of all the individual phonemes of the word, the separation is needed. Successful blending seems almost to be an all-or-none achievement: children cannot do it, and then they can. In the interval, they answer with random words or with words that start with the same phoneme. A structural scaffold restricts the word array (e.g., "Look at these pictures and guess what word I am saying."). It also controls the foil choices, starting with only two choices and having all the words start with different phonemes, or having different word lengths. For interactive scaffolding, the phonemes can be presented in faster succession or in onset-rime segmentation (e.g., SLP: "What fruit am I holding? /p/-/i/-/tʃ/?" Child: "Apple?" SLP: "Listen again: /p/-/itʃ/." Child: "Peach!").

Phoneme segmentation instruction can be broken into many steps. In the move-it-and-say-it procedure, children learn to represent a phoneme with a movable tile and then to move tiles for phonemes in progressively more complicated word shapes in one-phoneme increments (V, CV, CVC, CCVC, etc.). If they struggle, a cue is provided; if they struggle a lot, they are moved back a step. This progression works well. However, it requires special materials and is an activity unto itself: it cannot be used within shared reading or writing activities or even within picture and object games.

Box 12.10. ***Levels of Scaffolding for Isolating, Blending, and Segmenting Phonemes***

Level	Scaffolding	Isolation	Blending	Segmentation
None	Question asked with no support	What is the first sound in *ball*? [correct answer]	What word is this, /b/-/r/-/e/-/d/? [correct answer]	You count the sounds in *man*. I am listening. [correct answer]
Low	Question asked with target sound stressed or word repeated	What is the first sound in *ball* {first sound stressed}? [correct answer] or [letter answer] *B* is the letter. What is the sound? [correct sound]	I am thinking of a word. What word is this, /b/-/r/-/e/-/d/? [no answer] Listen to the sounds again, /b/-/r/-/e/-/d/. [correct answer]	You count the sounds in *man*. Get ready. Count the sounds in *man*. {silently mouths sounds as child says them} [correct answer]
Mid	Target sound stressed or word re-peated plus another prompt	What is the first sound in *ball*? [wrong answer, /k/] No, listen again, and watch my lips {points and repeats sound}, b-b-b-all? [correct sound]	/b/-/r/-/e/-/d/ is repeated. [wrong answer, *beans*] Close, that starts with /b/. Listen again {onset-rime}: /br/-/ed/. [correct answer]	You count the sounds in *man*. Fingers up and say it with me: /m/-/ae/-/n/. Fingers and si-lent mouthing while child says each aloud with fingers. [correct answer]
High	Answer pro-vided after unsuccessful prompting or without prompting	What is the first sound in *b-b-ball*? [wrong answer, *ball*] No, just the sound. Listen and watch my lips {points and repeats sound}, *b-b-b-all*. [no answer] It is /b/. You say /b/. [imitated answer]	/b/-/r/-/e/-/d/ [wrong answer after repetition and onset-rime prompt] What am I say-ing? /b/-/r/-/e/-/d/. /b/-/r/-/e/-/d/ is *bread*. Say it with me. [imi-tated answer]	Let's count the sounds in *man*. Fingers up and say it with me: /m/-/ae/-/n/. [imitated answer]

In contrast, there is a simple structural scaffold that can become the children's own tool. It can apply in any activity involving phonemic segmentation. It can be carried in a pocket and used in the classroom in impromptu practice activities. That tool is a set of fingers. By raising their fists in the air or placing them on the table or floor in front of them and then extending a finger for each phoneme, children have a highly effective representational and counting device. The table and fist provide an anchor for limited motor coordination. Box 12.11 shows a sequence of steps for teaching phoneme segmentation using fingers. Children quickly get the idea that fingers match sounds in words, but it takes repeated opportunities and strategic withdrawal of support for children to become independent segmenters. The SLP listens and watches for indicators of achievement and struggle, and provides just enough assistance to keep children "in the zone" of optimal learning challenge and moving toward independence.

For teaching segmenting, the adult should model the correct target, even for segmentation of hard words during book sharing or writing activities, which children may segment initially with onset-rime (e.g., *hunt* as /h/-/ʌnt/ or with missing phonemes (*hunt* as /h/-/ʌ/-/t/). Depending on whether the approach is vertical skill mastery or repeatedly cycling through the skill in the horizontal ordering, children may not be required to be totally correct. Instead, the SLP judges whether or not the child met the expectation at that point and commends the parts that were correct.

The Very Start of Phonemic Awareness

There are some young children who need an extra push to start noticing that speech sounds are separate from the meanings they carry. When asked for the first sound in *mad*, despite the SLP stretching and stressing the /m/ and pointing to her or his mouth, some children persist in saying the whole word, related words, or an unrelated sound. These are not the children who provide a letter name response, which shows they are aware of the difference between the two but have jumped past the phoneme to the letter. This letter focus is easily corrected by the SLP guiding the student to listen (point to the ear) for the sounds and accepting only phoneme not letter responses).

A brief period of phoneme production practice will accustom children to thinking about speech sounds. This involves stopping a word after the first sound and practicing saying the sound (e.g., "Listen to *boy*. The first sound is a /b/, /b/-/b/-/b/. Look at my lips. Everyone say the /b/ sound. Feel your lips move. Look at everyone's lips saying /b/-/b/. What is the first sound in *boy*? Let's say it, /b/."). To help children separate speech sounds from words, the articulatory movements are exaggerated, repeated, and extended. Children look at each other or at themselves in a mirror and notice their mouth and throat movements. Scaffolds during the lesson have the children look at the SLP's lips (with finger cues such as an index finger over the lips for /ʃ/ or at the neck for /g/) and imitate the sounds. This exercise is then contrasted with the /g/ from *ghost* or the /m/ from *man*, for which a brief practice period ensues. Simply having children focus their attention on sounds at the beginning of the session and, based on their errors, again periodically during the session, orients even 3-year-olds within one to two sessions.

Box 12.11. ***The Finger Method for Learning to Segment***

Demonstration and Imitation

1. The SLP says she is going to count all the sounds in a word and puts her hand by her face. The SLP says each phoneme of the word very clearly and extends a finger close to her face.
2. The SLP tells the children to, "Get ready, fists on the table." The children put their fists on the table, look at the SLP, and get ready to copy. The SLP says each phoneme of the word and extends a finger close to her face. The children extend fingers and say each phoneme along with the SLP.

Performing with Assistance

3. The SLP says the word with no fingers while the children say the word and extend fingers.
4. The SLP extends fingers but delays momentarily in saying the phonemes to let the children get slightly ahead.
5. The SLP extends fingers and silently mouths the phonemes while the children say the word and extend fingers.

Emerging Independence

6. The SLP says it is one of the children's turns to lead and only mouths the sounds while the child says the word and everyone else extends fingers.
7. A child independently segments by saying the sounds and extending fingers.

From Phonemic Awareness to Phonological Processing

Phonological processing refers to the cognitive skills involved in awareness, storage, and retrieval of phonological representations (Bishop & Snowling, 2004). Two other components of phonological processing are verbal working memory, also referred to as phonological memory, and word retrieval, also referred to as phonological code retrieval. Deficits in these two components are frequently present in children with specific language impairment and reading disabilities (Bishop & Snowling, 2004; Catts et al., 2005; Fraser et al., 2010). In addition, phonological production (i.e., speech sound pronunciation) is sometimes included as a fourth component of phonological processing. Children with specific language impairment or reading disability who do not have clinical levels of speech production problems often show subtle articulatory difficulties with phonologically complex words and word sequence repetitions (Edwards & Munson, 2009). Intervention for phonological production is not addressed here beyond the incidental benefits obtained from the multisyllabic word exercises involved in addressing the other areas of phonological processing.

Phonemic Awareness for Older Students

This chapter has focused on intervention in preschool and the early grades, teaching isolation, blending, and segmenting with phonotactically simple words or with expectations of partially correct performance for more difficult words. The goal of phonemic awareness intervention is not to teach how to manipulate all the phonemes of English in all possible combinations and word shapes. Rather, the goal is to enable children to achieve the idea that speech is composed of phonemes and be able to conduct basic operations on phonemes in simple words.

Beyond second grade, the benefits of phonemic awareness instruction for poor readers are less clear. Ehri et al. (2001) found that second- to sixth-grade students with average cognitive ability but below grade level reading showed smaller effect sizes than other student groups did. The gains these students made also showed smaller transfer effects to reading and no transfer to spelling. Ehri et al. suggested that this might have been because the students were already more advanced in phonological awareness skills and so had less room to gain or because they were being taught advanced forms of phonological awareness that are harder to acquire.

Despite the reduced benefits, it is still generally recommended that reading and spelling intervention for older students include some attention to phonemic awareness (Al Otaiba et al., 2012; see Chapter 16). Integrating attention to phonemes into phonics-based interventions has been found to be effective for older students with reading disabilities (e.g., Berninger et al., 2008; Torgesen et al., 2001; Torgesen et al., 2010). One way to do this is with LiPS (Lindamood & Lindamood, 2011), which has shown excellent results in teaching phoneme segmentation and word decoding for at-risk first graders and for older students with reading disabilities (Torgesen et al., 2001; Torgesen et al., 2010). However, it is not alone in its success; other programs with the RISE quality indicators and much less attention to phonemic awareness, such as the Torgesen-led studies, have had similarly strong results in improving phonemic awareness and reading.

Even students in the secondary grades with milder reading difficulties may benefit from individualized attention to phonemic awareness integrated into reading and spelling lessons (e.g., Apel & Masterson, 2001; Apel & Swank, 1999). For longer words (e.g., *su-per-sti-tious*), attention to the syllable in combination with morphological analysis is more helpful than phoneme-by-phoneme segmentation. Older students with reading disabilities usually have basic phonemic and syllable awareness and know basic phoneme-grapheme correspondence, as evidenced by their reasonable invented spellings. What they lack is more advanced spelling knowledge (e.g., rules for use of a silent *e* or a *tion*) and a large store of accurate mental graphemic images.

There is a risk to overtraining sensitivity to phonemic distinctions. Older children who are extensively drilled in identifying subtle phoneme contrasts may get frustrated when their close listening and phonetic spelling are penalized (e.g., spelling *butter* as *BUDDER* and *dogs* as *DOGZ*). Once children have achieved basic competence in phonemic awareness and know how to spell, it may be better to let their spelling influence their perception, segmenting *butter* with a medial /t/ and *dogs* with a final /s/. This perception may not be fully accurate, but it reflects how literate adults casually perceive words and how these perceptions result in correct spelling.

Phonological Memory Intervention

One potential benefit of working on advanced phonemic awareness skills is that it may be a way to approach less accessible components of phonological processing. There is some indication that even basic phonemic awareness instruction improves phonological memory (van Kleeck, Gillam, & Hoffman, 2006). It seems reasonable that "workouts" with advanced phonemic awareness tasks, such as the segmentation of longer words and the deletion, substitution, and transposition of phonemes in words, might improve phonological memory. Substitution and transposition tasks clearly draw on phonological memory and other cognitive skills. If these tasks are done without memory supports, such as color-coded tiles and letters, they certainly would tax phonological processing abilities. Even with memory supports, they require sustained attention, memory, retrieval, and problem solving. Learning to use Pig Latin may be an entertaining way to stretch phonological processing abilities (Box 12.12).

There is evidence that systematic practice with phonological items can improve memory. For example, Maridaki-Kassotaki (2002) randomly assigned 120 6- to 9-year-old Greek children to treatment and control conditions. The treatment condition group received nonword repetition exercises for 15-minute sessions 4 days a week for 7 months, and showed significantly better nonword repetition and reading than the no-treatment group. Garcia-Madruga et al. (2013) taught third graders in a set of experimenter-designed tasks addressing attentional focus, attention switching, connecting with prior knowledge, semantic updating in working memory, and inhibition. Compared to a no-

Box 12.12. ***How to Speak Pig Latin***

Pig Latin takes the first consonant or consonant cluster of an English word, moves it to the end of the word, and adds the suffix *ay* [eɪ] to every word.

pig → *igpay*

banana → *ananabay*

truck → *ucktray*

happy → *appyhay*

For words that begin with vowel sounds or a silent letter, "way" or "yay" or "ay" (depending on the version) is added at the end of the word. Examples are:

egg → *eggway*

inbox → *inboxway*

Mentions of Pig Latin date back to magazine articles in the late 1800s. A few Pig Latin words, such as *ixnay* for *nix*, *amscray* for *scram*, and *upidstay* for *stupid* have been incorporated into American English slang.

Note: From http://en.wikipedia.org/wiki/Pig_Latin

treatment control, the treatment group showed improved IQ scores, reading comprehension, and executive processes, including working memory.

Emerging research suggests that significant benefits can be obtained from computer-based training on demanding visuospatial and verbal tasks (Boudreau & Constanza-Smith, 2011; Gillam & Gillam, 2012). A particular task called *dual n-back* has been proposed to improve not only working memory but also other aspects of intelligence and executive functioning. As Gillam and Gillam explained, *n-back* involves listing to or looking at a stream of letters or numbers and deciding whether the item matches one that occurred a designated number of items earlier. In a 2-back task, participants listen to "1-4-5-7-5-2-7-2-7-3-6-8-6" and press a button for the underlined items because those appeared 2 places earlier. In the dual version, participants look at and listen to different sequences simultaneously (see http://www.soakyourhead.com). The training involves moving incrementally from 1-back to 2-back and so on. Positive effects have been obtained for children in two controlled studies (Jaeggi, Buschkuehl, Jonides, & Shah, 2011; Wener & Archibald, 2011). A commercial computer program for children, called CogMed (2012), has been developed based on this n-back paradigm. CogMed has been subjected to several controlled studies that indicated improved attention and working memory (Holmes, Gathercole, & Dunning, 2009; Klingberg et al., 2005) and improved reading (Dahlin, 2011).

Despite these promising results, Gillam and Gillam (2012) and Holmes et al. (2010) cautioned that it is still early to embrace CogMed and other memory drill treatments. With only comparisons to no-treatment conditions, it is not yet known which treatment features are responsible for the benefits. They could be the result of ancillary treatment features such as the effect of the additional monitoring and encouragement at school and at home. Also unknown is whether the outcome measures would respond equally well to other language interventions that demand mental rehearsal and manipulation. It is also not clear what is being changed in these interventions. Holmes et al. (2010) suggested changes in their study may have been due not to capacity improvement, but to improved control of voluntary attention and strategy use: a majority of the 8- to 11-year-old students in their study reported concentrating harder to improve performance. Strategies included closing their eyes, rehearsing items, and tracing visual patterns with their eyes. Holmes et al. did not determine whether or not students applied these concentration strategies to school activities. Finally, it remains to be seen whether benefits extend as far as problem solving, language learning, or academic learning. Gillam and Gillam noted that similar impressive benefits were initially obtained with Fast ForWord (Scientific Learning Corporation, 2012), but research has since demonstrated that benefits were not specific to Fast ForWord but rather could be obtained with a variety of quality treatments with RISE features.

For students with deficits in verbal working memory, there are other ways to improve daily life performance. Boudreau and Constanza-Smith (2011) described the many factors that impinge on verbal working memory, including the student's language skills, knowledge base, and learning skills. Improving a student's language and metalinguistic skills is likely to improve memory function by making academic tasks less overwhelming. Working with the student and his or her teachers to modify environmental demands and learning supports can also improve performance. In a randomized experimental study, Berninger et al. (2008) found that for fourth- to sixth-grade children with reading disability, explicit orthographic and morphological training improved pseudo word reading and real word spelling, but that phonological working memory benefitted from a more indirect route: hands-on, engaging, problem-solving science instruction.

Phonological Retrieval Intervention

Some children with language or reading problems have trouble accurately and quickly accessing the phonological code representing the meanings they know (Messer & Dockrell, 2006). This may be seen in conversational discourse in the form of hesitations, pauses, and fillers (e.g., *um, you know*). A person may travel around the word that is on "the tip of the tongue" with substitutions and circumlocutions. A reader with phonological retrieval problems may be slower to "recognize" the meaning of a printed word sounded out. While anyone involved in stressful speaking or reading tasks can exhibit these behaviors, the slowness in retrieving words in confrontation naming is characteristic of children with reading disability (e.g., Denckla & Rudel, 1976; Vellutino, Scanlon, & Spearing, 1995).

The combination of difficulties in phonological awareness and phonological code retrieval, as measured by rapid naming, has been thought to be a particular "double deficit" source of severe reading difficulties (Wolf & Bowers, 1999). Rapid naming has a central phonological retrieval component, but it also taps attentional, perceptual, memory, lexical, and articulatory elements and thus involves many aspects of cognitive processing (Wolf, Bowers, & Biddle, 2000). Rapid naming is a robust predictor of many aspects of reading, even across orthographies for different languages (Kirby et al., 2010). While reading fluency would be expected to be more affected than individual word recognition, Kirby et al. reported that it is the opposite: students with naming deficits are slow at learning to recognize new words, but their response to fluency training is similar to that of students without naming deficits in both accuracy and rate.

Language interventions addressing word retrieval have used combinations of: (a) improving word depth and elaboration in traditional semantics treatment, (b) using phonological and semantic cues to aid word retrieval, and (c) teaching children how to cue and organize themselves (McGregor & Leonard, 1995). In general, while deeper vocabulary knowledge and cueing intervention are effective in accuracy and latency of word retrieval in confrontation naming tasks, there is little generalization to untrained words and none to communicative and reading tasks (e.g., Bragard, Schelstraete, Snyers, & James, 2012). Word-finding is not generally addressed as a goal in language intervention but rather as an ancillary aspect of spoken language treatments addressing the improvement of narrative and expository discourse performance.

In the reading literature, training involves rapid letter-naming exercises or exercises with a broader array of items (Kirby et al., 2010). The rapid letter-naming interventions have obtained some immediate increase in letter-naming speed and reading fluency, but the improvements have been temporary or required additional orthographic training. Studies that address rapid naming of letters, colors, numbers, and objects in combination with phoneme awareness and word level reading skills have obtained significant effects on letter naming but not on object and color naming. Rapid naming performance can also improve somewhat as a function of reading intervention. For example, Torgesen et al. (2010) found that both LiPS and a phonics program with less explicit attention to phonemic awareness showed significant benefits compared to the no-treatment control on rapid naming of digits but not the naming of letters at posttesting. At the one-year follow-up, letters but not digits were significantly better.

The research indicates that rapid naming can be improved through a variety of structured programs, both those specifically aimed at rapid naming and those with a broader reading focus. However, it appears that phonological code retrieval is difficult to improve, that students can improve their reading without accompanying improvements in retrieval speed, and that gains in reading may not be due to any gains in speed of retrieval (Kirby et al., 2010). Based on these outcomes, rapid naming exercises do not appear to be a good use of valuable treatment time.

Conclusion

In this chapter, methods of teaching phonemic awareness to preschool and early primary-grade children at risk for reading difficulties were presented. Evidence indicates that the most efficient way to help children acquire the critical skills of phoneme isolation, blending, and segmentation is to teach them at the phoneme level with no prior syllable or rhyme awareness instruction, even for preschoolers. Phonemic awareness can be taught in a vertical progression of single-skill contrived activities with structural control over phonotactic shape and phoneme features. Alternately, it can be taught in a horizontal integrated ordering in which complementary phoneme skills are addressed together within structured single-skill activities and sound talk embedded in shared reading and writing activities, with interactive scaffolding systematically matched to task difficulty and child need.

Phonemic awareness is a highly teachable skill, but it is only one component of a larger collection of cognitive abilities, collectively called phonological processing, that are critical to fluent reading. Two other components are phonological memory, also called verbal working memory, and phonological code retrieval, also called rapid naming. There is some evidence that direct training can improve verbal working memory, but both memory and retrieval can be aided through broader language and literacy interventions.

References

Adams, M. J., Foorman, B. R., Lundberg, I., & Beeler, T. (1998). *Phonemic awareness in young children: A classroom curriculum*. Baltimore, MD: Brookes.

Al Otaiba, S., Kosanovich, M. L., & Torgesen, J. K. (2012). Assessment and instruction for phonemic awareness and word recognition skills. In A. Kamhi & H. W. Catts (Eds.), *Language and reading disabilities* (3rd ed., pp. 112–145). Boston, MA: Allyn & Bacon.

Anthony, J. L., Lonigan, C. J., Burgess, S. R., Driscoll, K., Phillips, B. M., & Cantor, B. G. (2002). Structure of preschool phonological sensitivity: Overlapping sensitivity to rhyme, words, syllables, and phonemes. *Journal of Experimental Child Psychology, 82,* 65–92.

Anthony, J. L., Lonigan, C. J., Driscoll, K., Phillips, B. M., & Burgess, S. R. (2003). Phonological sensitivity: A quasi-parallel progression of word structure units and cognitive operations. *Reading Research Quarterly, 38,* 470–487.

Apel, K., & Masterson, J. J. (2001). Theory-guided spelling assessment and intervention: A case study. *Language, Speech, and Hearing Services in Schools, 32,* 182–195.

Apel, K., & Swank, L. K. (1999). Second chances: Improving decoding skills in the older student. *Language, Speech, and Hearing Services in Schools, 30,* 231–242.

Ball, E. W., & Blachman, B. A. (1988). Phoneme segmentation training: Effect on reading readiness. *Annals of Dyslexia, 38,* 208–225.

Berninger, V. W., Winn, W. D., Stock, P., Abbott, R. D., Eschen, K., Lin, S.-J., & Nagy, W. (2008). Tier 3 specialized writing instruction for students with dyslexia. *Reading and Writing, 21,* 95–129.

Bishop, D. V. M., & Snowling, M. J. (2004). Developmental dyslexia and specific language impairment: Same or different? *Psychological Bulletin, 130,* 858–886.

Blachman, B. A., Ball, E. W., Black, R., & Tangel, D. M. (2000). *Road to the code: A phonological awareness program for young children.* Baltimore, MD: Brookes.

Boudreau, D., & Costanza-Smith, A. (2011). Assessment and treatment of working memory deficits in school-age children: The role of the speech–language pathologist. *Language, Speech, and Hearing Services in Schools, 42,* 152–166.

Bradley, L., & Bryant, P. (1985). *Rhyme and reason in reading and spelling.* Ann Arbor: University of Michigan Press.

Brady, S., Fowler, A., Stone, B., & Winbury, N. (1994). Training phonological awareness: A study with inner-city kindergarten children. *Annals of Dyslexia, 44,* 26–59.

Bragard, A., Schelstraete, M.-A., Snyers, P., & James, D. G. H. (2012). Word-finding intervention for children with specific language impairment: A multiple single-case study. *Language, Speech, and Hearing Services in Schools, 43,* 222–234.

Bridges, M. S. & Catts, H. W. (2011). The use of a dynamic screening of phonological awareness to predict risk for reading disabilities in kindergarten children. *Journal of Learning Disabilities, 44,* 330–338.

Bruck, M. (1993). Word recognition and component phonological processing skills of adults with childhood diagnosis of dyslexia. *Developmental Review, 13,* 258–268.

Byrne, B., & Fielding-Barnsley, R. (1991). Evaluation of a program to teach phonemic awareness to young children. *Journal of Educational Psychology, 83,* 451–455.

Byrne, B., & Fielding-Barnsley, R. (1993). Evaluation of a program to teach phonemic awareness to young children: A 1-year follow-up. *Journal of Educational Psychology, 85,* 104–111.

Carson, K. L., Gillon, G. T., & Boustead, T. M. (2013). Classroom phonological awareness instruction and literacy outcomes in the first year of school. *Language, Speech, and Hearing Services in Schools, 44,* 147–160.

Catts, H. W., Adolf, S. M., Hogan, T. P., & Weismer, S. E. (2005). Are SLI and dyslexia distinct disorders? *Journal of Speech, Language, and Hearing Research, 48,* 1378–1396.

Catts, H. W., Fey, M. E., Zhang, X., & Tomblin, J. B. (2001). Estimating the risk of future reading difficulties in kindergarten children: A research-based model and its clinical implications. *Language, Speech, and Hearing Services in Schools, 32*, 38–50.

Chaney, C. (1992). Language development, metalinguistic skills, and print awareness in 3-year-old children. *Applied Psycholinguistics, 13*, 485–514.

Chen, X., Anderson, R. C., Li, W., Hao, M., Wu, X., & Shu, H. (2004). Phonological awareness of bilingual and monolingual Chinese children. *Journal of Educational Psychology, 96*, 142–151.

CogMed. (2012). *CogMed working memory training.* Upper Saddle River, NJ: Pearson. Retrieved from http://www.cogmed.com

Cognitive Concepts. (1997). *Earobics: Auditory development and phonics program* [Computer software]. Cambridge, MA: Author.

Cossu, G., Shankweiler, D., Liberman, I. Y., Katz, L., & Tolar, G. (1988). Awareness of phonological segments and reading ability in Italian children. *Applied Psycholinguistics, 9*, 1–16.

Cuetara, M. (1997). *Terrible Teresa and other very short stories.* Boston, MA: Dutton/Penguin.

Dahl, K. L., Scharer, P. L., Lawson, L. L., & Grogan, P. R. (1999). Phonics instruction and student achievement in whole language first-grade classrooms. *Reading Research Quarterly, 34*, 312–341.

Dahlin, K. I. E. (2011). Effects of working memory training on reading in children with special needs. *Reading and Writing, 24*, 479–491.

Denckla, M. B., & Rudel, R. G. (1976). Rapid automatized naming (RAN): Dyslexia differentiated from other learning disabilities. *Neuropsychologia, 14*, 471–479.

Denne, M., Langdown, N., Pring, T., & Roy, P. (2005). Treating children with expressive phonological disorders: Does phonological awareness therapy work in the clinic? *International Journal of Language and Communication Disorders, 40*, 493–504.

Durgunoglu, A., & Oney, B. (1999). A cross-linguistic comparison of phonological awareness and word recognition. *Reading and Writing, 11*, 281–299.

Edwards, J., & Munson, B. (2009). Speech perception and production in child language disorders. In R. G. Schwartz (Ed.), *Handbook of child language disorders* (pp. 216–231). New York, NY: Psychology Press.

Ehri, L. C., Nunes, S. R., Willows, D. M., Schuster, B. V., Yaghoub-Zadeh, Z. & Shanahan, T. (2001). Phonemic awareness instruction helps children learn to read: Evidence from the National Reading Panel's meta-analysis. *Reading Research Quarterly, 36*, 250–287.

Ehri, L. C., & Wilce, L. S. (1986). The influence of spellings on speech. In D. B. Yaden & S. Templeton (Eds.), *Metalinguistic awareness and beginning literacy* (pp. 101–113). Portsmouth, NH: Heinemann.

Engen, L., & Hoien, T. (2002). Phonological skills and reading comprehension. *Reading and Writing: An Interdisciplinary Journal, 15*, 613–631.

Fox, B., & Routh, D. K. (1975). Analyzing spoken language into words, syllables, and phonemes: A developmental study. *Journal of Psycholinguistic Research, 4*, 331–342.

Fraser, J., Goswami, U., & Conti-Ramsden, G. (2010). Dyslexia and specific language impairment: The role of phonology and auditory processing. *Scientific Studies of Reading, 14*(1), 8-29.

Garcia-Madruga, J. A., Elosua, M. R., Gil, L., Gomez-Veiga, I., Vila, J. O., Orjales, I., & Duque, G. (2013). Reading comprehension and working memory's executive processes: An intervention study in primary school students. *Reading Research Quarterly, 48*, 155–174.

Gillam, R. B., & Gillam, S. L. (2012). N-back and CogMed working memory training: Proceed with caution. *Perspectives on Language Learning and Education, 19*(3), 108–116.

Gillon, G. T. (2000). The efficacy of phonological awareness intervention for children with spoken language impairment. *Language, Speech, and Hearing Services in Schools, 31*, 126–141.

Gillon, G. T. (2002). A follow-up study investigating benefits of phonological awareness intervention for children with spoken language impairment. *International Journal of Language and Communication Disorders, 37*, 381–400.

Gillon, G. T. (2004). *Phonological awareness: From research to practice.* New York, NY: Guilford.

Gillon, G. T. (2005). Facilitating phoneme awareness development in 3- and 4-year-old children with speech impairment. *Language, Speech, and Hearing Services in Schools, 36*, 308–324.

Good, R. H., & Kaminski, R. A. (2002). *Dynamic indicators of basic early literacy skills* (6th ed.). Eugene, OR: Institute for the Development of Educational Achievement.

Good, R. H., Simmons, D., Kame'enui, E., Kaminski, R. A., & Wallin, J. (2002). *Summary of decision rules for intensive, strategic, and benchmark instructional recommendations in kindergarten through third grade* (Technical Report 11). Eugene: University of Oregon.

Hatcher, P. J., Hulme, C., & Snowling, M. (2004). Explicit phoneme training combined with phonic reading instruction helps young children at risk of reading failure. *Journal of Child Psychology and Psychiatry, 45*, 338–358.

Herron, J. (1995). *Read, write, and type.* San Rafael, CA: Talking Fingers.

Hesketh, A., Dima, E., & Nelson, V. (2007). Teaching phoneme awareness to pre-literate children with speech disorder: A randomized controlled trial. *International Journal of Language and Communication Disorders, 42*, 251–271.

Hindson, B., Byrne, B., Fielding-Barnsley, R., Newman, C., Hine, D. W., & Shankweiler, D. (2005). Assessment and early instruction of preschool children at risk for reading disability. *Journal of Educational Psychology, 97*, 687–704.

Hogan, T. P., Catts, H. W., & Little, T. D. (2005). The relationship between phonological awareness and reading: Implications for the assessment of phonological awareness. *Language, Speech, and Hearing Services in Schools, 36*, 285–293.

Hoien, T., Lundberg, I., Stanovich, K. E., & Bjaalid, I. (1995). Components of phonological awareness. *Reading and Writing: An Interdisciplinary Journal, 7*, 171–188.

Holmes, J., Gathercole, S. E., & Dunning, D. L. (2009). Adaptive training leads to sustained enhancement of poor working memory in children. *Developmental Science, 12*(4), F9–F15.

Holmes, J., Gathercole, S. E., Place, M., Dunning, D. L., Hilton, K. A., & Elliott, J. G. (2010). Working memory deficits can be overcome: Impacts of training and medication on working memory in children with ADHD. *Applied Cognitive Psychology, 24*(6), 827–836.

Hund-Reid, C., & Schneider, P. (2013). Effectiveness of phonological awareness intervention for kindergarten children with language impairment. *Canadian Journal of Speech–Language Pathology and Audiology, 37*, 6–25.

Jaeggi, S. M., Buschkuehl, M., Jonides, J., & Shah, P. (2011). Short- and long-term benefits of cognitive training. *Proceedings of the National Academy of Sciences of the United States of America, 108*, 10081–10086.

Justice, L. M., McGinty, A. S., Cabell, S. Q., Kilday, C. R., Knighton, K., & Huffman, G. (2010). Language and literacy curriculum supplement for preschoolers who are academically at risk: A feasibility study. *Language, Speech, and Hearing Services in Schools, 41*, 161–178.

Kirby, J. R., Georgiou, G. K, Martinussen, R., Parrila, R., Bowers, P., & Landerl, K. (2010). Naming speed and reading: From prediction to instruction. *Reading Research Quarterly, 45*, 341–362.

Klingberg, T., Fernell, E., Olesen, P., Johnson, M., Gustafsson, P., Dahlstrom, K., Westerberg, H. (2005). Computerized training of working memory in children with ADHD: A randomized, controlled trial. *Journal of the American Academy of Child Adolescence and Psychiatry, 44*, 177–186.

Lindamood, P., & Lindamood, P. (2011). *The Lindamood phoneme sequencing program for reading, spelling, and speech* (4th ed.). Austin, TX: PRO-ED.

Lundberg, I., Frost, J., & Peterson, O.-P. (1988). Effects of an extensive program for stimulating phonological awareness in preschool children. *Reading Research Quarterly, 23*, 263–284.

Maclean, M., Bryant, B., & Bradley, L. (1987). Rhymes, nursery rhymes, and reading in early childhood. *Merrill-Palmer Quarterly, 33*, 255–281.

Maridaki-Kossotaki, K. (2002). The relation between phonological memory and reading ability in Greek-speaking children: Can training of phonological memory contribute to reading development? *European Journal of Psychology of Education, 17*, 63–73.

McFadden, T. U. (1998). Sounds and stories: Teaching phonemic awareness in print contexts. *American Journal of Speech–Language Pathology, 7*, 5–13.

McGee, L. M. (2005, December). *The role of wisdom in evidence-based preschool literacy curriculum*. Paper presented at the presidential address to the National Reading Conference, San Antonio, TX.

McGee, L. M., & Ukrainetz, T. A. (2009). Using scaffolding to teach phonemic awareness in preschool and kindergarten. *Reading Teacher, 62*, 599–603.

McGregor, K. K., & Leonard, L. (1995). Intervention for word-finding deficits in children. In M. E. Fey, J. Windsor, & S. F. Warren (Eds.), *Language intervention: Preschool through the elementary years* (pp. 85–106). Baltimore, MD: Brookes.

Messer, D., & Dockrell, J. E. (2006). Children's naming and word-finding difficulties: Descriptions and explanations. *Journal of Speech, Language, and Hearing Research, 49*, 309–324.

Morais, J., Cary, L., Alegria, J., & Bertelson, P. (1979). Does awareness of speech as a sequence of phonemes arise spontaneously? *Cognition, 7*, 323–331.

Nation, K., & Hulme, C. (1997). Phonemic segmentation, not onset-rime segmentation, predicts early reading and spelling skills. *Reading Research Quarterly, 32*, 154–167.

National Governors Association Center for Best Practices and Council of Chief State School Officers. (2010). *Common Core State Standards for English Language Arts & Literacy in History/Social Studies, Science, and Technical Subjects*. Washington, DC: Author. Retrieved from http://www.corestandards.org

National Reading Panel. (2000). *Teaching children to read: An evidence-based assessment of the scientific research literature on reading and its implications for reading instruction* (NIH Publication No. 00-4754). Washington, DC: U.S. Department of Health and Human Services, National Institute of Child Health and Human Development. Retrieved from http://www.nichd.nih.gov/publications/nrp

Notari-Syverson, A., O'Connor, R. E., & Vadasy, P. F. (1998). *Ladders to literacy.* Baltimore, MD: Brookes.

Phillips, B. M., Clancy-Menchetti, J., & Lonigan, C. J. (2008). Successful phonological awareness instruction with preschool children. *Topics in Early Childhood Special Education, 28*(1), 3–17.

Read, C., Yun-Fei, Z., Hong-Yin, N., Bao-Qing, D. (1986). The ability to manipulate speech sounds depends on knowing alphabetic writing. *Cognition, 24,* 31–44.

Richgels, D. J. (1995). Invented spelling ability and printed word learning in kindergarten. *Reading Research Quarterly, 30,* 96–109.

Richgels, D. J., Poremba, K. J., & McGee, L. M. (1996). Kindergarteners talk about print: Phonemic awareness in meaningful contexts. *The Reading Teacher, 49,* 632–642.

Schuele, C. M., & Boudreau, D. (2008). Phonological awareness intervention: Beyond the basics. *Language, Speech, and Hearing Services in Schools, 39,* 3–20.

Schuele, C. M., Justice, L. M., Cabell, S. Q., Knighton, K., Kingery, B., & Lee, M. W. (2008). Field-based evaluation of two-tiered instruction for enhancing kindergarten phonological awareness. *Early Education and Development, 19,* 726–752.

Scientific Learning Corporation. (2012). *Fast ForWord Language Program* [Computer program]. Retrieved from http://www.scilearn.com/products/fast-forword-language-series

Spencer, E. J., Schuele, C. M., Guillot, K. M., & Lee, M. W. (2008). Phonemic awareness skill of speech–language pathologists and other educators. *Language, Speech, and Hearing Services in Schools, 39,* 512–520.

Stanovich, K. E. (1986). Matthew effects in reading: Some consequences of individual differences in the acquisition of literacy. *Reading Research Quarterly, 21,* 360–407.

Storch, S. A., & Whitehurst, G. J. (2002). Oral language and code-related precursors to reading: Evidence from a longitudinal structural model. *Developmental Psychology, 38,* 934–947.

Stothard, S. E., Snowling, M. J., Bishop, D. V. M., Chipcase, B., & Kaplan, C. A. (1998). Language-impaired preschoolers: A follow-up into adolescence. *Journal of Speech, Language, and Hearing Research, 41,* 407–418.

Torgesen, J. K., Alexander, A. W., Wagner, R. K., Rashotte, C. A., Voeller, K. K., & Conway, T. (2001). Intensive remedial instruction for children with severe reading disabilities. *Journal of Learning Disabilities, 34,* 33–58.

Torgesen, J., Wagner, R., Rashotte, C., Herron, J., & Lindamood, P. (2010). Computer-assisted instruction to prevent early reading difficulties in students at risk for dyslexia: Outcomes from two instructional approaches. *Annals of Dyslexia, 60,* 40–56.

Ukrainetz, T. A. (2000). An investigation into teaching phonemic awareness through shared reading and writing. *Early Childhood Reasearch Quarterly, 15,* 347–348.

Ukrainetz, T. A. (2006a). Scaffolding young students into phonemic awareness. In T. A.

Ukrainetz (Ed.), *Contextualized language intervention: Scaffolding preK–12 literacy achievement* (pp. 429–467). Austin, TX: PRO-ED.

Ukrainetz, T. A. (2006b). Using emergent writing to develop phonemic awareness. In L. M. Justice (Ed.), *Clinical approaches to emergent literacy intervention* (pp. 225–259). San Diego, CA: Plural.

Ukrainetz, T. A. (2006c). EBP, RTI, and the implications for SLPs: Commentary on L. M. Justice. *Language, Speech, and Hearing Services in Schools, 37*, 298–303.

Ukrainetz, T. A. (2008). Phonemic awareness instruction for preschoolers: The evidence for prephonemic versus phonemic tasks. *EBP Briefs, 2*, 47–58.

Ukrainetz, T. A. (2009). Phonemic awareness: How much is enough within a changing picture of reading instruction? *Topics in Language Disorders, 29*, 344–359.

Ukrainetz, T. A., Cooney, M. H., Dyer, S. K., Kysar, A. J., & Harris, T. J. (2000). An investigation into teaching phonemic awareness through shared reading and writing. *Early Childhood Research Quarterly, 15*, 331–355.

Ukrainetz, T. A., & Fresquez, E. F. (2003). What *isn't* language?: A qualitative study of the role of the school speech–language pathologist. *Language, Speech, and Hearing Services in Schools, 34*, 284–298.

Ukrainetz, T. A., Nuspl, J. J., Wilkerson, K., & Beddes, S. R. (2011). The effect of syllable instruction on phonemic awareness in preschoolers. *Early Childhood Research Quarterly, 26*, 50–60.

Ukrainetz, T. A., Ross, C. L., & Harm, H. M. (2009). An investigation of treatment scheduling for phonemic awareness with kindergartners at risk for reading difficulties. *Language, Speech, and Hearing Services in Schools, 40*, 86–100.

van Kleeck, A., Gillam, R. B., & Hoffman, L. M. (2006).Training in phonological awareness generalizes to phonological working memory: A preliminary investigation. *Journal of Speech–Language Pathology and Applied Behavior, 1*, 228–243.

van Kleeck, A., Gillam, R. B., & McFadden, T. U. (1998). A study of classroom-based phonological awareness training for preschoolers with speech and/or language disorders. *American Journal of Speech–Language Pathology, 7*, 65–76.

Vellutino, F. R., Scanlon, D. M., & Spearing, D. (1995). Semantic and phonological coding in poor and normal readers. *Journal of Experimental Child Psychology, 59*, 76–123.

Vygotsky, L. (1978). *Mind in society: The development of higher psychological processes*. Cambridge, MA: Harvard University Press.

Wagner, R. K., Torgesen, J. K., & Rashotte, C. A. (1994). Development of reading related phonological processing abilities: New evidence of bidirectional causality from a latent variable longitudinal study. *Developmental Psychology, 30*, 73–87.

Wagner, R. K., Torgesen, J. K., Rashotte, C. A., & Pearson, N. A. (2013). *Comprehensive Test of Phonological Processing–Second Edition*. Austin, TX: PRO-ED.

Warren, S. F., Fey, M. E., & Yoder, P. J. (2007). Differential treatment intensity research: A missing link to creating optimally effective communication interventions. *Mental Retardation and Developmental Disabilities Research Reviews, 13*, 70–77.

Warrick, N., Rubin, H., & Rowe-Walsh, S. (1993). Phoneme awareness in language-delayed children: Comparative studies and intervention. *Annals of Dyslexia, 43*, 153–173.

Wener, S. E., & Archibald, L. M. D. (2011). Domain-specific treatment effects in children with language and/or working memory impairments: A pilot study. *Child Language Teaching and Therapy*, *27*, 313–330.

Wolf, M. & Bowers, P. G. (1999). The double-deficit hypothesis for the developmental dyslexias. *Educational Psychology*, *91*, 415–438.

Wolf, M., Bowers, P. G., & Biddle, K. (2000). Naming-speed processes, timing, and reading: A conceptual review. *Journal of Learning Disabilities*, *33*, 387–407.

Wood, C., & Terrell, C. (1998). Poor readers' ability to detect speech rhythm and perceive rapid speech. *British Journal of Developmental Psychology*, *16*, 397–413.

Wood, D., Bruner, J. S., & Ross, G. (1976). The role of tutoring in problem solving. *Journal of Child Psychology and Psychiatry*, *17*, 89–100.

Yeh, S. S. (2003). An evaluation of two approaches for teaching phonemic awareness to children in Head Start. *Early Childhood Research Quarterly*, *18*, 513–529.

Appendix: Verse Books for Talking About Phonemes

Brown, M. W. (1982). *Goodnight moon*. New York, NY: Harper Trophy.

Carlstrom, N. W. (1986). *Jesse Bear, what will you wear?* New York, NY: Aladdin.

Cuetara, M. (1997). *Terrible Teresa and other very short stories*. New York, NY: Dutton Children's Books.

Emberly, B. (1967). *Drummer Hoff*. New York, NY: Aladdin.

Guarino, D. (1989). *Is your mama a llama?* New York, NY: Scholastic.

Hutchins, P. (1988). *Where's the baby?* New York, NY: Greenwillow Books.

Numeroff, L. (1995). *Chimps don't wear glasses*. New York, NY: Scholastic.

Shaw, N. (1986). *Sheep in a jeep*. Boston, MA: Houghton Mifflin.

Teague, M. (1995). *How I spent my summer vacation*, New York, NY: Crown.

Wolff, A. (1990). *Baby beluga*. New York, NY: Crown.

Wood, A. (1992). *Silly Sally*. San Diego, CA: Harcourt.

Chapter 13

Teaching the Fundamentals of Reading: Word Identification and Fluency

Pamela E. Hook & Elizabeth C. Crawford-Brooke

Despite some improvement over the last few years, one third of fourth graders display basic deficits in reading (Institute of Education Sciences, 2011). Most children who have not succeeded in reading by Grade 4 never catch up with their typically achieving peers, particularly in the area of reading fluency (Torgesen, Alexander, et al., 2001). The costs of this early reading failure are great. Accompanied by low self-esteem and anxiety, both of which interfere with learning, such failure often results in behavioral issues and is associated with the large percentage of adolescents who drop out of school (Lesnick, George, Smithgall, & Gwynne, 2010). Literacy difficulties extend into adulthood, often contributing to continued low self-esteem and reduced employment opportunities. Despite these dire statistics, the large majority of children have the potential to be good readers. This potential can be realized with quality early-reading instruction. This chapter provides an overview of the stages of reading development and the deficits associated with word identification and fluency. It will review best practices in reading instruction and explain principles and methods of effective assessment and intervention.

The Role of the SLP in Reading Acquisition

Given the complex, reciprocal relationship between spoken and written language, it is not surprising that approximately two thirds of children with oral language deficits also have difficulties reading and writing (Catts, Fey, Zhang, & Tomblin, 1999; Stackhouse & Wells, 1997; Tallal, 1988). The American Speech-Language-Hearing Association (ASHA) has strongly endorsed the position that language impairments encompass receptive and expressive language in spoken and written forms (ASHA, 2001).

Many children will receive both speech–language and reading services in the schools. A recent study of over 150,000 kindergarteners and first graders in Virginia indicated that one quarter of the children receiving speech–language services also received reading services (Gosse, Hoffman, & Invernizzi, 2012). Children who received speech–language services received reading services at twice the rate of children who were not receiving speech–language services.

Identifying and intervening with young children at risk for reading failure is critical for the development of reading proficiency. While it is difficult to predict with a high degree of certainty which young children will develop reading difficulties, nearly 75% of poor readers in second grade have an early history of spoken-language deficits (Catts, Kamhi, & Adloff, 2012). Speech–language pathologists (SLPs) have the knowledge of the phonological system and the training in phonemic awareness that are fundamental to helping young children and struggling readers to develop word identification skills and thus are particularly well positioned to help teachers and parents identify the "red flags" of reading disabilities and to help establish appropriate intervention. Their knowledge and training also enable SLPs to outperform other educators, such as reading, special education, kindergarten, and first-grade teachers, at segmenting words that have a complex relationship between speech and print (Spencer, Schuele, Guillot, & Lee, 2008). In addition, throughout the grades, SLPs contribute to the academic language skills students need for general reading comprehension and for reading to learn across subject areas. Finally, ASHA (2001) considers the role of the school SLP to include direct instruction in word recognition and reading fluency.

Despite their training in phonemic awareness and academic language, and ASHA's statement of their role in reading instruction, SLPs often have limited knowledge of the specific relationships between spoken and written language and even less of how to teach reading. Even if SLPs do not provide direct intervention in basic reading skills, they need to know how reading works, how to teach it, and how it relates to oral language to be part of the educational team providing unified, coherent intervention for students with academic difficulties.

Processes Involved in Word Identification

The reading process can be divided into two basic components: identification of the printed word, which is more related to the written code, and reading comprehension, which is more related to the meaning or content (Hoover & Gough, 1990). Word identification, also referred to as word recognition, occurs through processes involved in sounding out (decoding) or recognizing the word as a whole. As readers become more proficient, they develop fast, automatic word recognition, which is essential for reading fluency and comprehension. Even mild difficulties in word identification focus a reader's attention on the code instead of meaning, which leads to fragmented sentence and text comprehension (Lyon, Shaywitz, & Shaywitz, 2003; Torgesen, Rashotte, & Alexander, 2001). On the other hand, lack of vocabulary, conceptual, or even grammatical skills will affect the accuracy and speed of word recognition (e.g., try to read aloud the ingredients of your shampoo). There are two major components to word recognition, one that involves the phonological system and one the visual orthographic system.

Phonological Processing

In developing accurate word identification skills, children initially rely heavily on the phonological system to develop their ability to map sounds onto print. Phonological processing involves perceiving, remembering, producing, and manipulating speech sound information.

The aspects of phonological processing that are important for reading are phonemic awareness, phonological working memory, and rapid automatic naming (Adams, 1990; Ehri et al., 2001; Gathercole, Willis, & Baddeley, 1991; Manis & Friedman, 2001; Snowling, 2000; Wolf, 1997; Wolf & Bowers, 1999). Phonemic awareness skills that are closely related to sounding out written words involve segmenting and blending phonemes. Although many children develop phonemic awareness naturally, about 25% of middle-class first graders and substantially more of those who come from less literacy-rich backgrounds need direct instructional support (Adams, 1990). Phonological memory is particularly important when students are trying to sound out unfamiliar words that contain many phonemes. Nonword repetition is often used to evaluate the ability to temporarily hold increasingly complex phonological representations in memory. Rapid automatic naming, which involves the speed at which phonological representations of words are retrieved from mental storage, is measured with tasks that involve timed serial labeling of common objects, colors, numbers, or letters. All these processes are most important early in reading acquisition, especially when children are sounding out words rather than using automatic visual recognition (Ehri et al., 2001; Gathercole et al., 1991; Wolf & Bowers, 1999).

Orthographic Processing

Although reading is generally viewed as being based on the spoken language system, it obviously involves visual processing as well. Specifically, word identification involves the ability to identify letters and specific letter patterns through the orthographic processing system (Badian, 1997, 2005; Share & Stanovich, 1995). As with phonological processing, orthographic processing involves the ability to visually perceive, remember, and produce letter symbols. Children develop awareness of the letter patterns found in English orthography as well as the ability to store and retrieve those patterns. Orthographic memories for specific letter patterns, or mental graphemic representations (MGRs), are critical for developing automatic word identification (Apel, 2009). These exact mental images of the letters in a word allow recognition of printed words by sight without sounding them out. Word identification, therefore, requires the interaction of two kinds of processing, phonological and orthographic, in order to access lexical information in long-term memory storage (Adams, Foorman, Lundberg, and Beeler, 1996).

Processing Involved in Fluency

Historically there has been some controversy as to how fluency should be defined. There is now general consensus that a fundamental component of fluency is speed of reading and that fluency involves automaticity, defined as fast, accurate, and effortless word identification at the single-word level. At the text level where students are required to read phrases, sentences, and paragraphs, reading speed and automatic word recognition are both important. There is less agreement on how other skills, such as syntax and discourse comprehension, are involved in fluent reading. See Torgesen, Rashotte, and Alexander (2001) for a discussion of this issue. There is, however, a growing consensus that fluency requires not only automatic word identification but also control of prosody, which includes correct intonation, phrasal reading, and rhythm (Bashir & Hook, 2009; Kuhn, Schwanenflugel, & Meisinger, 2010; Torgesen, Rashotte, & Alexander, 2001). Prosody has been found to predict unique variance in reading comprehension and in reading fluency after controlling for word reading (Miller & Schwanenflugel, 2008; Schwanenflugel, Hamilton, Kuhn, Wisenbaker, & Stahl, 2004). For an in-depth review of this literature, see Holliman, Wood, and Sheehy (2012).

Kuhn and Stahl (2003) stressed that proficient reading involves not only accurate and automatic word decoding but also prosodic interpretation of text. Thus, fluent reading incorporates elements from syntax, morphology, semantics, discourse, and pragmatics. For our purposes, this broad, more inclusive definition of fluency will be used because it reflects the importance of developing automatic application of appropriate phrasing and prosodic features needed for comprehension. Fluency also involves anticipation of what will come next in the text and facilitates reaction time, which is particularly important for comprehension (Wood, Flowers, & Grigorenko, 2001).

Reading fluency should be directly addressed, particularly in the case of children who do not develop this skill naturally. Many students who struggle to learn to read are able, with appropriate instruction, to compensate for initial reading problems by becoming accurate decoders but still fail to reach a level of sufficient fluency to become fast and efficient readers. Although the research clearly indicates that a systematic alphabetic approach to teaching beginning and struggling readers is more effective than a whole word approach (Adams, 1990; Chall, 1983, 1996; Snow, Burns, & Griffin, 1998), the most effective way to teach fluency is less well understood.

Stages of Reading Development

One could consider that reading development begins at birth since it builds on the spoken language system. Several stage theories of reading acquisition have been developed to explain the steps that children go through in acquiring written language skills, for example, Chall (1983), Ehri (1994), and Frith (1985). These stage theories are based on the assumption that the acquisition of reading skills progresses in a somewhat hierarchical order. In actuality, these stages often overlap, and even efficient readers use strategies developed in earlier stages when they come across words that are unfamiliar. The stage theories also do not address how children develop into smooth and efficient readers.

Share (1995) suggested that rather than going through stages, children use a "self-teaching" strategy. What this means is that through repeated experience with phonologically decoding (sounding out) individual words letter by letter, children discover and remember patterns of letter-sound correspondence. The more times they encounter and phonologically decode a word, the stronger the orthographic representation for the word becomes. Students can visually recognize words that they encounter frequently from some or all of their letters. Other less frequently read words must still be sounded out. Thus, through their own attempts to sound out words, beginning readers are in a mix of stages for different words (Kamhi & Catts, 2012).

Despite the limitations of stage theories, they are helpful for delineating which aspects of spoken and written language play the most significant roles at different points in the reading acquisition process. Following is a brief discussion of Chall's stage theory and Frith's phases of reading acquisition that gives a general sense of the challenges inherent in integrating the spoken and written language systems.

Chall (1983) divided reading acquisition into six basic stages, each with a qualitatively different goal to accomplish (Box 13.1). Although the basic goals remain the same, current standards are pushing the age of acquisition of reading skills earlier into kindergarten and even preschool. Thus, the timing of the stages has been altered from Chall's original description. In Chall's Stage 0, the goal is to acquire the rule systems that govern all aspects of the spoken language system (phonology, morphology, syntax, semantics, discourse, and pragmatics). To a startling degree, typically developing children usually

Box 13.1. ***Chall's Stages of Reading***

Stage	Label	Current Ages/ Grades	Description
0	Prereading	Birth to 5 Years	Spoken language and phonological awareness
1	Initial Reading or Decoding	Kindergarten and First Grade (was Grades 1–2)	Letter-sound correspondence, phonemic awareness, and basic word recognition
2	Confirmation, Fluency, and Ungluing from Print	End of First and Second Grade (was Grades 2–3)	Consolidating word decoding skills, becoming fluent, and focusing on comprehension
3	Reading for Learning the New	Third through Eighth Grade	Gaining new knowledge from reading of texts with clear content and structure; establishing foundational knowledge and skills
4	Multiple Viewpoints	High School	Dealing with multiple viewpoints, layers of facts and concepts, in lengthy, complex texts
5	Construction and Reconstruction	College	Purpose-driven and strategic reading; not everyone achieves this

Note: Based on Chall (1983).

accomplish this goal by the age of 3, well before they begin kindergarten. Although language continues to develop throughout the elementary years and well into adulthood (depending on an individual's life experiences, vocabulary can increase throughout the life span), the basic language skills needed for comprehending simple texts are developed in this first stage.

Reading requires not only the acquisition of these rule systems but also an awareness of the structure of language systems (metalinguistic awareness). In the preschool years, children begin to develop an awareness of the rules of the phonological system. They become aware that the phonological system has patterns that exist outside of the semantic system, as is evident in their enjoyment of rhymes (e.g., nursery rhymes) and games that involve hearing beginning sounds. At this time, they are also learning to recognize very high frequency words as wholes—sort of like pictures without an understanding of the letter-sound relationships. Frith (1985) refers to this as logographic reading.

During kindergarten, as children become more aware of individual sounds within words (phonemic awareness) and use their knowledge of letter-sound correspondences, they move into Chall's Stage 1 (cracking the code). They understand how the sound system maps onto the orthographic system of letters and letter patterns and how to apply phonic word attack strategies.

Frith (1985) developed a theory of reading and spelling development that also highlights the changing importance of phonological and orthographic processing skills as children move through the steps involved in the acquisition of word identification and spelling skills. Frith notes that children learn to spell alphabetically (through the analysis of the phonological system and the application of phonics) before they learn to read alphabetically and that alphabetic reading precedes orthographic reading (recognizing words automatically as wholes). Children move from reading logographically to alphabetically to orthographically. It is interesting to note that Frith emphasizes that children learn to read orthographically before they learn to spell orthographically because spelling requires retrieval of exact letter patterns whereas reading requires only partial recognition of those patterns and is often aided by context. An example of this ability to read with only partial recognition of words is clear from the following text:

> Aoccdrnig to a rscheearch at Cmabrigde Uinvervtisy, it dseno't mtaetr in waht oerdr the ltteres in a wrod are, the olny iproamtnt tihng is taht the frsit and lsat ltteer be in the rghit pclae. The rset can be a taotl mses and you can sitll raed it whotuit a pboerlm.

Here, all of the letters in a word are present, but only the first and last letters are in the proper position. Fluent readers are able to easily use the context to determine the actual word even though the MGR has been substantially altered—a seemingly amazing feat. This is a complex process involving the use of context as well as the use of partial orthographic cues by an advanced reader and has no bearing on how a student who is not fluent should be taught to read.

During first grade, children are expected to move into Chall's Stage 2 (developing fluency), where they improve their ability to recognize words quickly and accurately as wholes (automatically) and to use the syntactic, morphological, semantic, and pragmatic cues available in text to read smoothly and with expression (fluently). Paragraph reading is now expected in the middle of first grade, but expectations for speed of reading increase substantially in second grade. In oral reading, most students are fairly fluent readers by the end of second grade, moving from around 30 words per minute in first grade to around 100 words per minute by the end of Grade 2 or beginning of Grade 3 (Good & Kaminski, 2010). Older students and adults achieve an oral reading rate of around 180 to 200 words per minute.

In summary, through the first three stages of reading acquisition, the route to automatic word identification skills moves from the holistic recognition of a small number of words, much like pictures or logographs, through a phase of sounding out the letters in words, called alphabetic or phonological decoding. Repeated phonological decoding of words leads to the formation of MGRs and a shift into orthographic word recognition, which is essential for fluent reading. A large store of these detailed graphic representations, achieved through extensive reading, enables students to move from the stage of learning to read into reading to learn. However, sounding-out skills always remain important; we all revert back to alphabetic reading when we are confronted with an unfamiliar word.

Once children have achieved fluency, they are no longer *learning to read* but shift into Stage 3, where the emphasis changes to *reading to learn*, usually between third and fourth grade. The type of text shifts from primarily narrative to primarily expository, and the language complexity of the written material (including vocabulary level, sentence complexity, and text structure) begins to increase dramatically. The conceptual demands and importance of background knowledge also increases. Fluent reading at this point is essential. As children move up into high school and beyond (Stages 4 and 5), there is increasing emphasis on higher order thinking skills, such as comparing viewpoints and constructing knowledge, and strategic techniques that suit different purposes of reading, such as skimming for particular information.

Best Practices in Reading Instruction

Over the last 50 years or more, there has been strong disagreement about the best way to teach children how to read. This lack of consensus has resulted in what has been dubbed the "Reading Wars." The fundamental differences in philosophy among these educators stem from how they view the process of reading. One view is that instruction should focus primarily on teaching words as wholes, giving more attention to the meaning than they would with word attack strategies. This strategy, which was initially implemented in the 1950s as a "sight word" approach, had students look repeatedly at isolated printed words and memorize how to say them (Look/Say). In the "whole language" approach, reading acquisition is viewed as a top-down, natural, and implicit process like oral language acquisition. Students learn to read by reading or, in other words, by being exposed to orthographic patterns within the context of meaningful text and inferring the rules. Both narrow sight word instruction and the more comprehensive whole language instruction are considered meaning-based approaches. Another view, called a code-based approach, focuses directly on teaching systematic sound-based or phonic word attack strategies. This is considered a more bottom-up, artificial, and explicit process that, unlike spoken language, requires direct instruction.

Reviews of the research have consistently indicated that a balanced approach, that combines a systematic focus on the code with important aspects of language comprehension, yields the best overall results when considering both word identification and comprehension outcomes. As early as 1967, Jeanne Chall published what was at the time a highly controversial book, *Learning to Read: The Great Debate* (revised in 1996), in which she summarized the research in the area of reading acquisition. Chall concluded that a code-based approach had the best results for word recognition skills but that attention to meaning was still needed (Chall, 1996). Consistent with these conclusions, Marilyn Adams published another comprehensive review of the research in 1990 showing that a systematic focus on the code and on phonological awareness yielded better results than sight word and context-based approaches (Adams, 1990). As with Chall, however, Adams stressed the need for balance in the curriculum and noted that aspects of both code-based and meaning-based approaches were needed for readers to become skilled at both word recognition and text comprehension.

In 1998, the National Reading Council, a panel of experts chaired by Catherine Snow, published a report entitled "Preventing Reading Difficulties in Young Children" (Snow et al., 1998) that reviewed research related to challenges and instruction in the early stages of literacy acquisition. It concluded that instructional approaches that are more phonemically explicit have the strongest impact on the reading growth of children at risk for reading disabilities and that intensive preventive intervention can bring the word reading skills of the majority of children at risk solidly into the average range.

In 2000, the National Reading Panel (NRP), comprised of a diverse committee of reading experts, identified and summarized studies in Grades K–12 that met established criteria for being evidence based. They identified five areas fundamental to strong reading instruction: phonemic awareness, phonics, and fluency as well as vocabulary and text comprehension strategies. The first three related primarily to identifying words accurately and quickly, whereas the latter two pertained mostly to constructing meaning. Reviewers determined that the approaches to instruction varied along a continuum from incidental to systematic. Incidental instruction involves subtle models, prompts, and feedback during extensive exposure to meaningful print that requires the learner to infer orthographic rules and patterns. Systematic instruction is characterized by explicit, structured, and sequential teaching of orthographic knowledge with review and practice. The NRP found that across all areas of reading instruction, especially for children with reading disabilities, the most effective teaching approaches were systematic. Some of the systematic methods included multisensory presentation, which means, in addition to the natural visual and auditory modalities, providing tactile-kinesthetic input. It recommended that instruction be tailored to the ability level of each individual student rather than be delivered as scripted group instruction. This avoids boring those students who have already intuited the rules and are ready to move on.

Results of the NRP meta-analysis for systematic phonics instruction as it relates to word identification indicated overall moderate effect sizes in K–1 but only small effect sizes in Grades 2–6. However, for children with reading disabilities in Grades 2–6, the effect size was quite large (standardized mean difference of 0.74). The NRP also found a moderate effect of phonics instruction on reading comprehension in kindergarten and first grade. This effect also lasted into later grades for children with reading disabilities. These results make sense because older students who are poor readers will benefit longer from instruction focused on improving their basic reading skills.

In the area of fluency, the NRP found only 14 studies that were sufficiently rigorous and similar enough to allow a meta-analysis. These studies focused on guided repeated reading with corrective feedback typically compared with an approach that emphasized increasing the amount of reading through incentives for silent reading of more books. The meta-analyses indicated small to moderate effects of guided repeated reading on reading accuracy (0.55), speed (0.44) and comprehension (0.35) across student groups in Grades K–6. While average readers in Grades K–4 showed moderate effects on overall reading from guided repeated reading, children with reading disabilities showed moderate effects up to twelfth grade. Again, older struggling readers benefited from the same instruction given to younger readers but for longer.

Types of Reading Assessments

Reading assessments that determine deficits in word recognition and reading fluency inform decisions about the presence of a reading disability and eligibility for intervention services. In addition, it is important to assess the many skills involved in these two areas of reading to plan appropriate instruction for each student.

Under the reauthorization of the Individuals with Disabilities Education Act (IDEA) in 2004, local educational agencies were given the option to use a response to intervention (RTI) model when determining whether or not a student has a learning disability. In addition, the RTI model is designed to identify students who struggle, plan instruction, and monitor progress. (See National Association of State Directors of Special Education, 2005.) Regardless of whether or not a school or district has adopted an RTI model for assessment and intervention, personnel will need to develop an assessment plan to identify students who are at risk, monitor students' progress, diagnose students' strengths and weaknesses, and assess whether or not they learned the information expected in the given time frame (Torgesen, 2006). This section will explain the types of reading assessments used for each of these purposes.

Assessments of reading skills often involve SLPs. For example, SLPs typically evaluate phonological awareness, phonological memory, and rapid automatic naming using measures such as the *Comprehensive Test of Phonological Processing–Second Edition* (CTOPP-2; Wagner, Torgesen, Rashotte, & Pearson, 2013). If a student struggles with phonemic awareness, one expects that student to have difficulty learning to map sounds to letters and acquiring phonic word attack strategies. If a student has poor phonological memory, she or he will struggle with sounding out and recognizing long, multisyllabic words. If a student struggles with rapid naming, the student will most likely have difficulties with automatic word identification and fluency. In addition, an SLP's findings on spoken language skills need to be integrated with word recognition and reading fluency skills to understand the sources of a student's difficulties with reading comprehension.

Screening

A screening measure, often referred to as a universal screener because it can be given to all students, is primarily administered at the beginning of the year to determine which students are on track and which students are at some level of risk for reading failure. These screeners are quick and easy to administer and score with a minimum of training. Typically screeners do this by comparing the student's performance to a national norm or standard. Screenings that are designed to identify children at risk for reading failure in kindergarten cannot examine reading skills directly; instead they examine areas related to reading: phonemic awareness, speed of processing, and sound-letter knowledge. As students progress through the grades, screening shifts to the reading skills of word identification, fluency, and comprehension. Two examples of screeners that assess areas related to word identification and fluency are *Dynamic Indicators of Basic Early Literacy Skills Next* (DIBELS Next; Good & Kaminski, 2010) and *AIMSweb* (Pearson Publishing, 2001). If the screener identifies a student as being at some level of risk, more frequent progress monitoring of that student as well as a potentially diagnostic assessment to complete a profile of strengths and weaknesses to help drive an instructional plan may be necessary.

Progress Monitoring

Progress monitoring tools provide educators with a means to monitor a student's learning frequently. There are two types of progress monitoring tools. The first type assesses more general reading skills, such as phonological awareness, phonics, and fluency. These tests typically establish grade-level, criterion-based benchmarks and sometimes have norm-referenced scores to accompany the benchmarks. The second type of progress monitoring tool is more specific to a particular curriculum and is typically criterion referenced (Torgesen, 2006). Progress monitoring measures can be administered as often as weekly if a close check on growth is needed. If the students were only identified as having a mild level of risk, then progress monitoring might only occur on a monthly basis (Fletcher, 2006; Fuchs & Fuchs, 2006; Vellutino, Scanlon, Small, & Fanuele, 2006). If the students were found to be on target or low risk for reading failure on the screener, then typically three times a year is sufficient for progress monitoring. DIBELS Next and *AIMSweb* are used for progress monitoring of basic reading skills. Informal assessments, such as reading inventories, which ask students to read passages of various levels to assess their decoding skills and sometimes contain comprehension questions and letter name/sound fluency assessments, can also be used.

When progress-monitoring students, it is important to make sure that the measure being used is sensitive enough to capture small amounts of growth, both through being closely tied to what is taught and through having items that differentiate levels of performance. Also, the probes need to be equated for difficulty. For example, when assessing oral reading of paragraphs, each passage should be at the same general level. This will ensure that you are comparing apples to apples and not wondering if the limited growth is due to the second passage being harder than the first passage.

Diagnostic

The purpose of diagnostic assessments is to determine the nature of a problem and to make eligibility decisions. Diagnostic evaluations build a profile of the general strengths and weaknesses of a student. Unlike universal screeners, diagnostic measures are designed to be given only to a small subset of students. Diagnostic tests are longer than screeners or progress monitoring tools and are administered as part of a comprehensive battery. They often require someone with specialized training to administer, score, and interpret. They are generally administered as part of the identification process for special education. Some examples of diagnostic assessments that measure skills related to word identification and fluency are the CTOPP-2; the *Woodcock Reading Mastery Tests–Third Edition* (WRMT-III; Woodcock, 2011), which includes subtests on word identification and word attack using nonsense words as well as a subtest on passage comprehension; and the *Gray Oral Reading Tests–Fifth Edition*, which assesses oral reading fluency and passage comprehension scores (GORT-5; Wiederholt & Bryant, 2012).

Outcome

These first three types of assessments can be thought of as formative assessments and can help to inform instructional decisions along the way. The fourth and final assessment type, outcome measures, is a summative assessment. These tests determine whether or not a student has learned a given set of facts in a specific time frame. For example, a unit test can be thought of as a summative assessment of that particular unit. State assessments given at the end of each school year are the most common summative assessments. Rather than measuring learning over a particular unit or month, end-of-year assessments measure cumulative achievement across the year compared to grade-level norms or standards. Most often there is some measure of reading comprehension included in academic summative assessments, although they can include subtests related to word recognition. Some examples of outcome measures are *Stanford Achievement Test* (Pearson, 2012), *Gates-MacGinitie Reading Tests* (MacGinitie, MacGinitie, Maria, Dreyer, & Hughes, 2002), *Group Reading Assessment and Diagnostic Evaluation* (Williams, 2001), and state assessments (e.g., MCAS in Massachusetts, FCAT in Florida).

Areas of Assessment for Word Identification and Fluency

Methods of assessing each of the component skills of word recognition and reading fluency will be briefly reviewed in this section. Unlike most language assessments, assessments of these component skills often have a timed element. This is not done to stress the student but to test speed, which is a factor as important as accuracy.

Speed reflects automaticity and fluency. To become an efficient reader, it is essential that the student be able not only to read a word correctly in isolation but also to do it quickly in connected text without expending significant energy and attention. Many students can become accurate readers, but achieving that goal can be a slow and laborious process that is very frustrating. Thus, certain assessments need to have some timing element in order to determine how automatically the student can perform reading-related tasks. Without automaticity, a reader will not be able to focus cognitive energy on gaining the meaning of the text, which is the ultimate goal of reading.

Although automaticity and fluency are often used interchangeably, automaticity more directly applies to rate and accuracy at the letter-sound and word level, while fluency applies to connected text and includes, along with automaticity, prosody and syntactic chunking. Fluency assessments of connected text should contain not only rate and accuracy elements but also the means to assess a student's ability to read with correct intonation and phrasing, which aid in comprehension.

An interesting issue is how reading aloud, which is often required in assessment and intervention, relates to silent reading, which is the ultimate goal. When beginning readers read, they benefit from reading out loud, probably because of the auditory feedback that helps them to monitor what they are reading. Struggling readers often continue to read out loud or subvocalize even when asked to read silently. Even fluent readers sometimes revert to reading difficult text out loud in order to better focus their attention on meaning. On the other hand, there are students who have more difficulty reading aloud and who struggle with the memory and motor components of the task. Their attention is pulled away from the meaning. Retrieval and articulation issues can interfere further with comprehension. For these students, it is suggested that oral reading be avoided as much as possible (German & Newman, 2007). For this reason, it is important to consider the effects of reading aloud or silently on performance and to assess both when possible.

Word Identification

The most basic type of testing for prereading skills is knowledge of letter names. Research has shown that letter name knowledge is one of the strongest predictors of early reading success (Torgesen, 2002). The most common method of assessing letter name knowledge is simply to present a letter to a student and ask its name. Some assessments present the letter in a variety of fonts and sizes, and some assessments combine a letter-naming task with asking for the letter sound. Both accuracy and speed of letter naming are important components of assessment and are often a part of a screening battery, particularly at the kindergarten level.

In addition to knowledge of letter names for the youngest students, it is important to assess knowledge of letter-sound correspondence for students of all ages to serve as a baseline for developing systematic intervention. Assessment should include single consonants, long and short vowel sounds, consonant digraphs (*sh*, *th*, *ch*, and *wh*), and two- and three-letter consonant blends such as *st*, *spr*, as well as vowel combinations such as *oo*, *ow*, and *ou*. The Graphemes subtest on the *Phonological Awareness Test–Second Edition* (Robertson & Salter, 2007) can be used for systematically assessing letter-sound knowledge.

The next level of assessment is word level, which encompasses applying knowledge of letter-sound correspondence to decode single-syllable and multisyllable words as well as recognizing words as wholes. For purposes of assessment in reading, there are two types of words, regular and irregular. Regular or decodable words are those that follow common patterns and rules that allow each letter of a word to be phonemically decoded or sounded out. Irregular words do not completely follow the letter-sound correspondence rules. Irregular words are often referred to as *sight words* because they need to be learned as whole words (recognized by sight) instead of being sounded out. However, *sight words* also refers to irregular words that have been seen so often that they are recognized visually without having to work out how to phonologically decode them (e.g, *the*, student names), as well as to regular words that started out being recognized by phonological decoding but are now also automatically visually recognized as MGRs. For a complete assessment, performance on all three types of words (regular, irregular, and high frequency) needs to be evaluated.

When assessing the ability to sound out words, it is important to get an accurate measure of what students can decode compared to words that they have encountered frequently enough to have learned to recognize them as wholes. In order to truly assess a

Box 13.2. *The Six Syllable Types*

1. Closed—*nOt* (when closed in by a consonant, vowel makes a short sound)
2. Open—*nO* (when ends in a vowel, vowel makes a long sound)
3. Silent *E*—*nOtE* (when ends in vowel + consonant + *e*, vowel makes a long sound)
4. Vowel combination—*nAIl* (the two vowels together make a sound: e.g., *ai, ay, oa, ea, oi, oy*)
5. *R* controlled—*bIRd* (when contains a vowel + *r*, vowel sound is changed: e.g., *ar, or, ir, ur, er*)
6. Consonant-*L*-*E*—*noBLE* (when C + *le* is at the end of a word, "E" is silent)

student's ability to apply the rules of decoding, it is recommended that nonsense or pseudowords be included. This ensures that the students have not memorized the word from prior exposure but instead are applying the rules of decoding (e.g., knowing that the nonsense word *bepe* would be pronounced */bip/* because of the silent *e* at the end of the word). The decoding subtest on the *Phonological Awareness Test–Second Edition* (Robertson & Salter, 2007) can be used for assessing application of letter-sound correspondence to decoding pseudowords based on the six syllable types described in Box 13.2.

A frequently used test to measure accuracy of word identification and phonic word attack strategies for pseudowords is the WRMT-III (Woodcock, 2011). The Word Identification subtest presents words that are regular or irregular but arranged by difficulty level based on frequency by grade level. The Word Attack subtest contains a list of nonsense words to measure a student's accuracy in decoding single- and multisyllable words. In order to measure automaticity at the word level, the *Test of Word Reading Efficiency–Second Edition* (Torgesen, Wagner, & Rashotte, 2011), for example, presents both real and nonsense words. The difference in scores on these two kinds of tests can be used to determine if automaticity of word identification is an issue that would be expected to interfere with fluency and thus comprehension. To assess high frequency words, the most common list is the Dolch list, which divides these words by grade level beginning with preprimer and ending with third grade.

Fluency

Reading fluency assessment usually includes rate and accuracy (automatic word recognition in context). In order to be able to evaluate accuracy and speed directly, assessment of reading fluency is often done through oral reading fluency measures such as the DIBELS Next Oral Reading Fluency subtest. Here, the student is asked to read one or more passages aloud and is scored on the number of words read correctly in 1 minute. These measures tend to be fast and efficient to administer. Another commonly used test of oral reading fluency is the GORT-5, which is a diagnostic test that involves reading passages of increasing difficulty level and answering questions to determine comprehension of the content. This test, however, is fairly time consuming. In addition to assessing oral reading fluency, there is a need to determine speed of silent reading in order to estimate the effectiveness of a student in the more natural silent reading environment. As noted earlier, there are also some students who will read silently much more easily than orally. Many tests of silent reading comprehension are timed and can give a sense of this ability but should be combined with an oral reading test if scores in silent reading are low. Rate measures are necessary to determine the need for the accommodation of extended time on achievement tests.

Rate and accuracy assessment is a fairly straightforward quantifiable process. However, other aspects of fluency are more difficult to measure (Fuchs, Fuchs, Hosp, & Jenkins, 2001; Hudson, Lane, & Pullen, 2005). Prosody and syntactic chunking or phrasing are often more subjective and are usually assessed informally through checklists or rating scales that rate "word-by-word reading" versus reading with appropriate intonation. The GORT-5 has a rating scale that can accommodate evaluation in this area.

Characteristics of Good Instruction

Good instruction in reading shares characteristics with good instruction in all aspects of spoken and written language. The most commonly used types of instruction developed for struggling readers share the following characteristics: explicit teaching of concepts; structured, sequential, and systematic sequence of presentation; multisensory delivery involving auditory, visual, and tactile/kinesthetic modalities; and systematic and intensive opportunities for review and practice (Henry & Hook, 2006). Although these approaches are often referred to as "multisensory structured language" (MSL), the most important characteristics are that they are highly structured and are implemented with sufficient intensity. Many MSL programs also incorporate mnemonics to aide recall of the arbitrary, nonmeaningful letter symbols.

The focus of these programs is to increase metalinguistic skills by making the rules governing the structure of both oral and written language explicit. This is important because intuiting these rules is difficult for children who struggle with reading. Instruction is highly scaffolded in the beginning, but students are expected to take on more responsibility until they can ultimately perform independently. In order to deliver this type of specialized reading instruction, professionals need intensive, supervised training in one of the many MSL approaches. Some examples of these types of programs are *Orton Gillingham* (Gillingham & Stillman, 1997), *Specialized Program Individualizing Reading Excellence* (Clark-Edmands, 2008), *Lindamood Phoneme Sequencing Program* (Lindamood & Lindamood, 2011), *Wilson Reading Program* (Wilson Language Training Corporation, 2010), *Lively Letters* (Telian, 2001) and *Reading by the Rules* (Weiss-Kapp, 2005).

The intensity of the instruction depends on the severity of the deficits and how quickly the student responds to intervention. The RTI model discussed earlier in relation to assessment incorporates a three-tiered model for intervention (Berninger,

Stage, Smith, & Hildebrand, 2001). In this model, Tier 1 instruction for reading is designed for the regular education classroom and is delivered through a combination of large and small group instruction. It should include systematic instruction in phonemic awareness, phonics, fluency, vocabulary, and comprehension. Students who struggle are placed in Tier 2 small group instruction, where they receive increased intensity and scaffolding. This instruction is often focused more narrowly on the code aspects of reading: phonemic awareness, phonics, and fluency. Students' responses to this intervention are carefully measured through progress monitoring assessments. If the students do not improve sufficiently, they move to Tier 3, where specialized, intensive, individualized reading instruction is provided. Progress for Tier 3 students is monitored often, sometimes weekly, to determine if changes in instruction are needed.

Word Identification Intervention

Intervention in the area of word identification should involve systematic work, not only in phonic word attack strategies but also in the area of structural analysis (prefix, stem, and suffix), particularly when working with children in third grade and up. Both of these types of strategies are designed to expand the breadth and precision of the MGRs and by so doing lead to more automatic and fluent reading. Teaching of phonic word attack strategies involves training in awareness of the phonological system and linking that to the orthographic system, whereas structural analysis focuses more on the morphological structure of words. In a recent study of first- to third-grade children, morphological awareness was found to be a significant predictor of both accuracy and speed of word identification, nonword reading, text reading speed, and comprehension (Kirby et al., 2011). The relatively new *Common Core State Standards*, developed to serve as the scope and sequence for language arts and other subject area instruction in the public schools, supports a focus on phonics instruction, particularly in kindergarten and first grade, and begins introducing simple concepts related to structural analysis in second grade (National Governors Association Center for Best Practices and Council of Chief State School Officers, 2010).

English orthography presents a particularly challenging problem for acquiring strong word identification skills in that it is only semialphabetic in nature. In other words, there is not as direct a relationship between sounds and letters as there is in more alphabetic or transparent languages, such as Spanish or Serbo-Croatian. For example, in English, there are around 44 phonemes and only 26 letters. Many letters have more than one sound (e.g., long and short vowels or hard and soft *c* and *g*). To make matters even more complicated, many sounds can be spelled in different ways (e.g., there are at least seven fairly common ways to spell /ei/: b*a*by, r*ai*n, pl*ay*, b*a*k*e*, n*eigh*bor, th*ey*, v*ei*n).

Despite these complexities, phonological decoding works in reading much of English. Up to 84% of English is regular for reading if students know enough about the structure of the orthographic system, and knowing how to phonically attack words is a critical reading skill. As a result, the word identification procedures explained next are mainly types of phonic word attack strategies that teach students the rules and patterns of English orthography and how to map sounds onto print. However, irregular word instruction procedures will also be presented. These procedures to aid memorization also provide additional repeated opportunities for review and for practice of regular word reading. This is helpful because students who struggle with reading and spelling acquisition may have difficulty remembering all the rules that explain English spelling.

Incorporating Phonemic Awareness Into Phonics

Before explaining the teaching procedures, it should be noted that there is often confusion about the difference between phonemic awareness and phonics. Put simply, phonics is a teaching approach that involves associating sounds with letters to read printed words, while phonemic awareness is an underlying phonological processing skill that involves knowing that spoken words are composed of individual sounds and being able to manipulate those sounds. Phonemic awareness is necessary when applying phonics to reading but can be taught in activities that do not involve letters (e.g., hearing two spoken words and judging whether they begin with the same phoneme). However, training methods that combine phonemic awareness with direct instruction in how letters map onto sounds (phonics) are more effective at improving word identification than phonemic awareness or phonics instruction alone (Ball & Blachman, 1991; Bus & van IJzendoorn, 1999; Senechal, Ouellette, Pagan, & Lever, 2012). Phonics instruction that includes integration of direct instruction in phonemic awareness is important, particularly for struggling readers. Thus, instruction in phonic word attack strategies should incorporate attention to phonemic awareness skills along with instruction in letter-sound correspondence, syllable types, and rules for syllable division.

Letter-Sound Correspondence

Developing automatic recall of letter-sound correspondences is an important first step in learning how to decode words. Although a structured and systematic approach is important, there is no absolute order in which these correspondences need to be taught. When determining the exact sequence of letter-sound instruction to be used, several criteria should be considered, including frequency, simplicity, visual distinctiveness, and phonological properties. For example, the consonants *m* and *s* (compared to *b, d, p*) are good choices for initial instruction because they occur in many words, have only one sound, are visually distinct from one another, and are continuants so that the sounds can be extended to aid in blending activities. See Gillingham and Stillman (1997) for a specific scope and sequence based on these characteristics.

Some programs focus attention on the phonological properties of words as an aid to recall of the letter-sound correspondence (e.g., pairing the consonants *b* and *p* despite the visual similarity because of the similarity in articulation). See Lindamood Phoneme Sequencing Program (*LiPS*; Lindamood & Lindamood, 2011), *Lively Letters* (Telian, 2011), and *WKRP Reading by the Rules* (Weiss-Kapp, 2005) for examples of this approach. Again, when examining different sequences within programs, it is not necessarily the specific order that is important but rather the systematic and structured approach to teaching described above.

Articulatory Cues and Mnemonics

One reason that learning letter-sound correspondences is difficult for some children is that neither the sound nor the letter has meaning; thus, learning to associate them requires rote memorization, which may be particularly difficult for children with poor phonological or orthographic memory. In order to aid recall, a common technique employed by MSL programs is the use of tactile-kinesthetic cues. For example, Orton-Gillingham–based programs often use techniques such as tracing on a rough surface or sky writing to help solidify the associations among the auditory, visual, and tactile-kinesthetic modalities.

As noted earlier, other programs such as LiPS use tactile-kinesthetic cues from the articulators to help students identify what their mouth is doing when they are producing sounds. They organize sounds into "minimal pairs" based on similarities in articulation and varying only in voicing (e.g., /p/-/b/, /d/-/t/, or /k/-/g/) or other characteristics of the sounds, such as being "nose" sounds (/m/-/n/-/ŋ/). They pair consonants that differ only in voicing in order to emphasize the tactile-kinesthetic aspects of sounds to help anchor the phonological characteristics. LiPS also uses the concept of a vowel circle, which illustrates the position of the tongue and jaw when forming the vowels to help struggling readers discriminate between vowel sounds, many of which are articulated in a very similar fashion. This is particularly helpful for the short vowels, which are very close in production and often confused (e.g., short *i* and short *e*; short *e* and short *a*; short *u* and short *o*). All of these approaches are structured and systematic in their presentation, explicitly teach the rules governing the phonological and orthographic structure of the language, and include extensive opportunity for practice. This creates strong metalinguistic awareness of the phonological structure of spoken language.

Many programs also incorporate meaningful associations to help children learn letter-sound correspondences. Orton-Gillingham–based programs often use a key word that is always associated with the letter and serves to elicit the sound; often a picture is presented in the beginning and is later removed as these associations become automatic. For example, children learn to respond with the letter name, keyword, and sound in response to the letter and picture (e.g., they would say, "*o*, octopus, /a/" in response to the letter card for the short sound of *o*).

Other programs, such as *Lively Letters*, *WKRP Reading by the Rules*, and LiPS, use stories, pictures, mouth-shape cues, and voicing characteristics to help with storage and retrieval of letter-sound associations. For example, in the *Lively Letters* program, letters are not only grouped by articulatory characteristics but also described as individuals with personalities. For example, in an introduction to the consonant pairs *b* and *p*, red lips become a part of the letter, and the students are told that the first thing to do when they make these sounds is put their lips together (this can help with confusion between *b/d*) and then puff out air (known as a "lip puffer"); the *b* is described as having a circle down low, resembling a little baby who makes lots of *noise* (voiced sound) while the *p* is described as a tall mother with the circle up high, telling her baby to be *quiet* (unvoiced sound). Boxes 13.3 and 13.4 show examples of an Orton-Gillingham keyword picture card and a *Lively Letters* paired consonant card. Ultimately, these auditory and visual

Box 13.3. ***Memorization Aids of Key Word Pictures***

Orton-Gillingham

Note: From *The Gillingham Manual: Remedial Training for Children With Specific Disability in Reading, Writing, and Penmanship*, by A. Gillingham, and B. Stillman, 1997, Greenville, WI: School Specialty. Copyright 1997 by School Specialty. Reprinted with permission.

Box 13.4. ***Memorization Aids of Paired Consonant Cards***

Lively Letters

Note: From *Lively Letters*, by N. Telian, 2007, Weymouth, MA: Reading with TLC. Copyright 2007 by Reading with TLC. Reprinted with permission.

cues are removed so that the student recalls the letter-sound association automatically without scaffolding.

Segmenting and Blending With Letters

Once some letter-sound correspondences have been established, the following segmenting techniques are excellent for bridging between phonemic awareness and phonics instruction. For instruction in words that are regular for reading and spelling, it is often helpful to use activities that involve both decoding and encoding. Russian psychologist David Elkonin (1973) devised what has become a classic technique for developing both phonemic awareness and the application of exact letter-sound correspondence while specifically addressing segmentation and blending skills. It begins by utilizing tokens to represent sounds, and then incorporates the letters that represent those sounds. This Say-It-and-Move-It (SIMI) activity is highly structured and can be systematically adjusted to represent words of increasing phonological complexity (e.g., VC, CVC, CCVC, CCVCC and CCCVC), depending on an individual student's abilities. SIMI employs all the important aspects of multisensory structured language techniques: explicit training of segmentation and blending, systematic and sequenced application of phonic word attack strategies, and multisensory delivery (involving motor movement as well as visual and auditory processing).

For encoding or spelling practice using the SIMI technique, the student uses a series of tokens (e.g., colored blocks, pennies, paper clips) or letter tiles comprised of the letter-sound correspondences that have been presented. The teacher says a word, and the student repeats it. The student then segments the word or word part into individual phonemes while moving one token or letter down to a segmented line or series of boxes for each sound in the word (Box 13.5). Consonant digraphs, two consonants that make one sound (e.g., *THink, puSH*), are considered in these activities as one sound whereas consonant blends (e.g., *BLack, siLK*) are separated. The "silent *e*" (e.g., *maKE*) can be coded with a special marker. Words with more complicated orthographic patterns are avoided (e.g., *enough* has 3 phonemes but 6 letters). Once the word has been successfully segmented, the student blends the individual phonemes into a recognizable word while running his or her finger underneath the letters and then writes it on a piece of paper.

Box 13.5. ***Say-It-and-Move-It Activity to Teach Letter-Sound Correspondence***

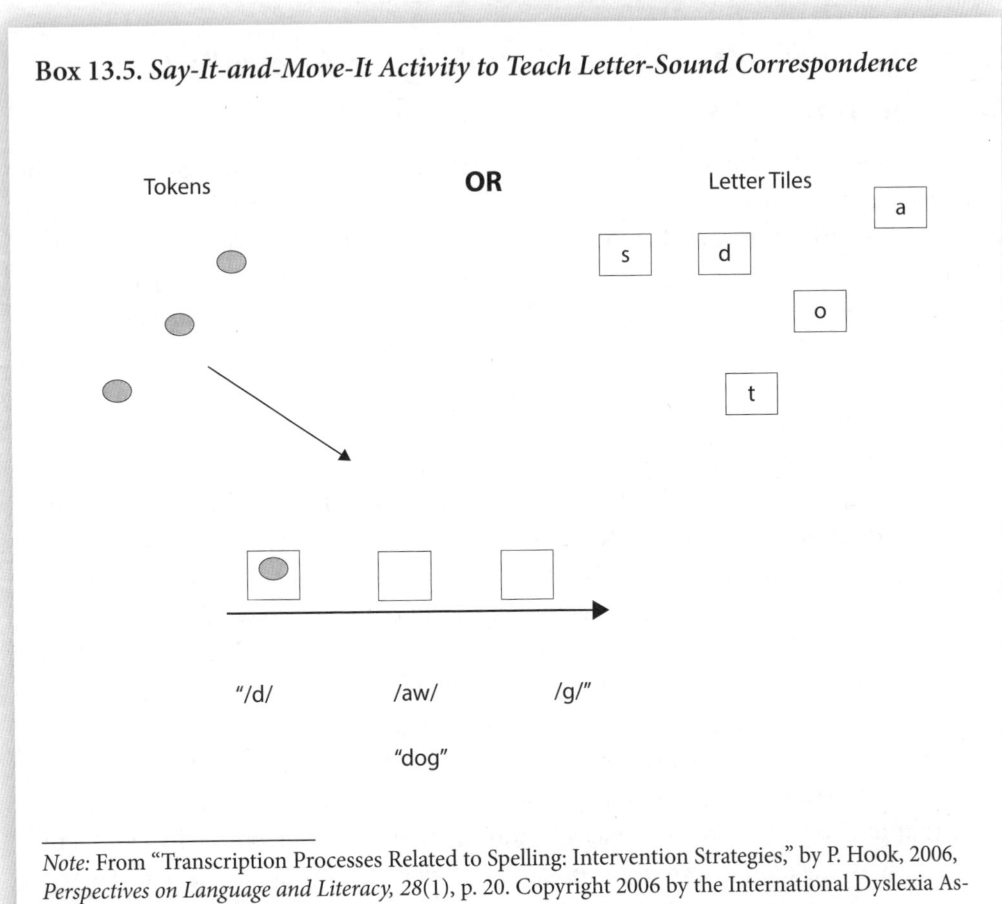

Note: From "Transcription Processes Related to Spelling: Intervention Strategies," by P. Hook, 2006, *Perspectives on Language and Literacy, 28*(1), p. 20. Copyright 2006 by the International Dyslexia Association. Reprinted with permission.

For decoding or reading practice, the teacher constructs a word or word part with letter tiles and has the student move letter tiles while pronouncing the phoneme that corresponds to each grapheme (or digraph). The student then blends the sounds together to decode the word or word part. This task allows the student to closely monitor the letter-sound correspondence. As students progress, it may be sufficient for the teacher to touch each letter as the students say the sound. This scaffolding is gradually decreased until they can independently read regular words.

Another technique to increase ability to manipulate letters and sounds as well as to monitor exact letter-sound correspondence involves creating chains of words or word parts that vary in only one phoneme (e.g., starting with *ip* and successively changing the spelling to represent *op, top, tap, pat, pet, pest, pets*). This technique is based on the kinds of errors that struggling readers often make: substitutions, additions, reversals, omissions, and transpositions. Students manipulate either tokens or letters to make changes in the visual pattern where they hear the changes in the auditory pattern. For example, for encoding, the teacher says, "If that says *ip*, make it say *op*"; while for decoding, the teacher would add *t* at the beginning and say, "If that says *op* what does this say?" Student responds, "*Top*." Some of the published programs that contain systematic use of this technique are LiPS, *Lively Letters*, and SPIRE.

Application of Letter-Sound Knowledge in Controlled Orthography Texts

In addition to SIMI activities, phonics instruction must include systematic application of letter-sound knowledge to reading words in context. Therefore, students who struggle with word identification need to be given text that is controlled for letter-sound correspondence and does not include unfamiliar irregular words or words that have concepts that have not been introduced. This kind of text, called *controlled orthography*, allows students to directly apply the skills that they are learning. If texts include irregular words, the students will learn a guessing strategy based perhaps on the pictures that will not work for them in the long run.

This application of phonics knowledge should begin as soon as students have learned a few letter-sound correspondences rather than after all of the letters have been presented. Students should be asked to read and spell words using those letters. For example, if the first letters taught in a carefully constructed sequence are *m, s, t, l, a*, then the following words could be constructed (maybe out of letter tiles) and read: *am, at, Al, Sam, sat, Sal, mat*. In addition, some nonsense words could be introduced (*lam, mal, sal, lat*) to further reinforce the application of phonic word attack strategies, particularly when working with older students. The ability to read nonsense words becomes very important when students move to the two-syllable level, where many of the syllables are not real words. Irregular high frequency words need to be systematically introduced in order that phrases and short sentences containing controlled orthography can be presented such as: *the mat, a mat, at the mat, sat on the mat, Sam sat on the mat* (Henry & Redding, 2012). As students learn the orthographic structure of English, the majority of words become decodable and can be included in a controlled orthography text.

Syllable Types

Because English has both a complex phonology and orthography, it is essential that struggling readers who have trouble with word identification understand the syllabic structure of the written code, which at times may differ from the rules that govern the spoken language. It is this written structure that signals how the vowel will be pronounced and is fundamental to reading one- and two-syllable words. To accomplish this, many MSL phonics programs teach six syllable types and their corresponding rules for pronunciation through the orthographic pattern of the letters within the syllable (refer back to Box 13.2.). For example, if asked to pronounce the nonword *nim*, the majority of people will produce /I/ for the *i*, whereas for *ri*, they will use /i/. It is the orthographic pattern of the syllable that signals the vowel sound: a consonant following a single vowel signals the short sound (closed syllable), whereas a syllable that ends in a vowel usually has the long sound (open syllable).

Good readers are not typically consciously aware of these aspects of English orthography (that the first syllable type is closed and the second is open), but they have intuited the "rules" often through analogy to known words (e.g., they might associate the syllable *nim* with the real word *him* or *nimble* or the syllable *ri* with *hi* or *rifle* to determine the pronunciation). Because they have adequate phonological awareness and orthographic memory, they are able to invoke these associations automatically, with little or no conscious effort. This is the first step in moving from the need to apply phonic word attack strategies to identify a word to becoming an orthographic or automatic reader. Struggling readers, on the other hand, have difficulty seeing and hearing these analogous patterns and benefit enormously from systematic instruction in the orthographic structure of English and how it maps onto English phonology. Highlighting, underlining, or enhancing the saliency of the visual pattern in some way is recommended to direct the student's attention to the critical components of the orthographic image.

Stories designed to differentiate the syllable types can also help in aiding memory by adding a meaningful component. For example, for a closed syllable, it is suggested that the consonant at the end is like a gate or door closing the vowel in and creating a short sound. *WKRP Reading by the Rules* (Weiss-Kapp, 2005) suggests that when explaining closed and open syllable pronunciation, the following mnemonic be used: every syllable has a vowel, and that vowel wants to go for a walk. If it runs into a consonant (i.e., in a closed syllable), it can only go for a short walk (creating a "short walk syllable," where the vowel makes its short sound). If it does not run into a consonant (i.e, in an open syllable), it can go for a long walk (creating a "long walk syllable," where the vowel makes its long sound). A systematic scope and sequence for teaching these syllable types can be found in most MSL programs.

Syllable Division

Once students have mastered one or more of the syllable types, they may be ready to move on to strategies for syllable division. Younger students may remain working on one-syllable words while older students may want to move on to two- or some three-syllable words once closed syllables are mastered. For example, they could easily read

Box 13.6. ***Ways of Dividing Multisyllabic Words Into Component Syllables***

1. VC/CV *heL/Met, coM/Pete*
2. V/CV *la/Bor, po/Ta/To*
3. VC/V *tiM/id, traV/el*

words like *funnel* or even *fantastic* once they know how to pronounce closed syllables and know the appropriate rule for syllable division. Visually recognizing the orthographic patterns that allow them to determine where to divide these words will help in deciphering them. There are three main syllable division patterns: between two consonants, before a consonant, or after a consonant (Box 13.6).

Students are taught to first find the vowel letters in a word that have a sound (every syllable has only one vowel sound). This avoids confusion with a syllable that contains a silent *e* as in the word *com/pete.* They then look at what comes between the letters that make the vowel sounds. The first pattern (VC/CV) indicates that when there are two consonant letters between the sounded vowels, you divide between them, creating a closed initial syllable with a short vowel. When syllable division is first introduced, the second syllable is also closed, as in *velvet*, but after other syllable types have been introduced, the same rule can be applied to words with any of the syllable types (e.g., *ban/jo, com/pete, sus/tain, con/form, sam/ple*). The second two-syllable division patterns, which involve VCV, can be divided either before the consonant, creating an open syllable with a long vowel as in *la/bor,* or after the consonant, indicating an open syllable with a short vowel as in *trav/el.*

WKRP Reading by the Rules (Weiss-Kapp, 2005) has a helpful way of teaching students to flex between the first two orthographic syllable division patterns. Rather than drawing a line between the consonant and vowel (e.g., *li/lac, trav/el*), the student moves a letter tile between the vowels, thus creating a strong visual or orthographic pattern of the resulting syllable type. Students learn to flex very quickly between the open syllable first (more frequent) and the closed syllable (e.g., saying, *li/lac* versus *lil/ac* or *le/mon* versus *lem/on*) to come up with the correct word. Most MSL programs have systematic instruction in these as well as more complex rules for syllable division.

Morphological Structure

Application of phonic word attack strategies is heavily dependent on awareness of the structure of language at the level of phonology and is essential for identifying one- and two-syllable words. However, these strategies may not work as well for multisyllabic words (more than two syllables) because so many of the syllables are unaccented and do not lend themselves to analysis by syllable type. This is where awareness of the morphological structure of language can be helpful (Carlisle, 2004). As with phonic word attack strategies, many students intuit the relationships, but for struggling readers, the rules governing the morphological structure of words must be explicitly taught (Carlisle, 2003).

Morphological awareness involves the understanding that words are made up of prefixes, stems, and suffixes (the minimal meaningful units of language or morphemes) in both their spoken and written form. In application to reading (and spelling), morphological instruction involves teaching the rules that govern the spelling of these morphemes and thus the pronunciation of the written words. One of the advantages of teaching word identification strategies through morphological structure is that there is a finite number of prefixes, stems and suffixes that recur in many words (e.g., ***export***, *de-**port***, *trans**port***; and ***ex**plore*, ***ex**plain*, ***ex**tract*). These word parts also have meaning (e.g., *trans* means "across" and *port* means "to carry"), which can be helpful for storing and retrieving the orthographic representations to aid word identification. A secondary benefit for language is that morphological analysis also increases vocabulary knowledge.

Based on their origin, English words can be divided morphologically into words stemming from Anglo-Saxon, Latin, or Greek. Anglo-Saxon–based words tend to be higher frequency and to deal with everyday life (*coat, food, rain*), wherea Latin-based words are often associated with government or law (*constitution, administration, structure*) and Greek with math, science, and the theater (*geometry, synthesis, proscenium*). Learning to read words with Latin and Greek origins can be an extreme challenge for a struggling reader. For example, many multisyllabic words, such as *contemptuous, continuance*, and *industrious* often appear as a jumble of letters to a struggling reader. There are, however, important orthographic rules that apply to most of these types of words that enable students to identify them. Think about the word *contemptuous*, for example. The ability to automatically identify *con* as the prefix, *tempt* as the stem, and *ous* as the suffix can greatly aid in deciphering the word. In addition, it is helpful to know that the *t* in *-tu-* is pronounced /ch/ and that the *u* after it is a connective that links the stem *tempt* to the suffix *ous*.

There are many words that contain one of more of these elements of structure (e.g., *nature, natural*—ligatured *tu*; *annual, continual*—connective *u*). Knowledge of these structural components opens up a multitude of words that would otherwise be unavailable to struggling readers. There are also many accent placement rules that are determined by morphological patterns. (Accent usually falls on the stem, but in some cases it falls in other places in the word, e.g., *separate*, where the accent falls on the prefix *se*.) When presented in a systematic way, these rules are not difficult for students to master. (See Henry, 2010, for a systematic sequence and scripted lesson plans for teaching morphological structure and Steere, Peck, & Kahn, 1988, for a thorough treatment of accent placement as well as rules related to morphological structure.)

Aids for Irregular Word Memorization

Phonic word attack strategies are particularly helpful for dealing with words that are regular for reading. However, dealing with irregular words (e.g., *busy*) places much more strain on the orthographic memory system. Students must memorize the specific spelling of each word. One irregular-word teaching procedure is having students repeatedly trace or write the letters of the word under discussion. Another is fading of letter cues while copying, simultaneously naming letters, and then ultimately writing from memory (e.g., *busy*: *b _ sy, b_ _ y, b _ _ _, _ _ _ _,* _____). In addition, air writing may be employed to create an "after image" to enhance memory for the orthographic representation; the students then close their eyes and attempt to answer orthographic-specific questions such as, "What is the third letter in *busy*?" This technique can also be used to enhance the development of MGRs for regularly spelled words (Bell, 1997).

Intervention for Automaticity and Fluency

In addition to learning to apply knowledge of syllable patterns, syllable division, and structural analysis to identify words, students must be able to see these patterns automatically and read individual words as wholes. Fast and accurate word identification is critical for fluency and comprehension, facilitating the ultimate goal of reading for learning and pleasure. Most students who learn to apply phonic and morphological word attack strategies can become quite accurate in their reading. However, because of an insufficient store of strong MGRs, some students have trouble moving up to the level of fluent reading. In addition to orthographic memory deficits, students may also have rapid automatic naming deficits that interfere with reading fluency.

Fluency is particularly important if students are to move from the stages of *learning to read* in kindergarten, first, and second grades to *reading to learn* in third grade and beyond. Students who struggle often remain slow and laborious in their word identification, a deficit that causes comprehension problems, particularly in timed situations. Many adults continue to struggle with reading and require extended time when taking tests because of lack of automaticity and fluency.

Linking Phonology and Orthography for Word Automaticity

There are several procedures that have been developed to strengthen orthographic representations and thus increase automaticity and fluency (Hook & Jones, 2002). Extensive practice in pattern recognition that focuses on the six syllable types, irregular words, and ultimately multisyllabic words is often the key. Fischer (1995) has developed a series of drills based on interaction between the orthographic and phonological processors. The first step, referred to as "training the orthographic processor," is designed to enhance students' attention to orthography at the single-syllable level by having them mark the vowels in a series of contrasting syllables (e.g., *tap*, *mop*, *mope*, *tape*; *rid*, *stride*) in which the vowel will be either long or short. The only way to determine vowel pronunciation is by processing the orthographic cues related to the syllable type (e.g., closed vs. silent *e*). Another technique that Fischer refers to as "linking the orthographic and phonological processors" involves having the student pronounce the vowel based solely on the letter patterns contained in the word without actually reading the word. Other ways of emphasizing orthographic patterns are card sorts where students sort different syllable types visually into appropriate categories as quickly as possible and then say the vowel sounds.

Once these orthographic patterns are automatically recognized, speed drills consisting of lists of six to eight isolated words with contrasting vowel sounds can be introduced (Clark-Edmands, 2008; Fischer, 1995). For example, to contrast closed syllables with silent-*e* syllables containing the vowel *I*, six to eight words can be repeated randomly on a page and read for 1 minute (*rid*, *ride*, *hid*, *hide*, *kit*, *kite*). Individual goals are established, and the number of words read correctly within a minute is recorded in successive sessions. The same word lists are repeated in sessions until the goal has been achieved for several (usually three) sessions in a row. When selecting words for these word lists, the use of high frequency words within a syllable category may increase the likelihood of generalization to text reading. See the SPIRE program (Clark-Edmands, 2008) for word lists based on frequency.

Speed drills can also be used for irregular words (e.g., *from*, *of*, *come*, *some*, *one*) as well as multisyllable words that incorporate higher level concepts of structural analysis (prefix, stem, and suffix). At the multisyllable level, automatically recognizing the visual patterns related to syllable division as well as prefixes, stems, and suffixes (morphological chunks) can be very helpful. The SPIRE program (Clark-Edmands, 2008) contains speed drills that at first mark these syllable breaks as well as prefixes and suffixes, and then fade the cues as the student progresses through the drill (*pro/tec/tive*, *neg/a/tive*, *ad/he/sive*, *sen/si/tive*, *ex/plo/sive*, *de/tec/tive*, *pro/duc/tive*).

Fluency Through Repeated Readings

One of the most commonly used methods for improving reading fluency at the text level is repeated readings. This involves simply having the students read the same passage several times until a satisfactory fluency rate (usually defined as correct words per minute) is achieved. This method was originally developed under the premise that reading passage-level text multiple times increases familiarity with the text, which leads to automatic word recognition, improved fluency, and freed-up cognitive resources for comprehension (Kuhn & Stahl, 2003; LaBerge & Samuels, 1974).

The research on repeated readings, however, shows inconsistent results. Repeated readings of the same text have been found to be effective in increasing reading rate for those paragraphs, with 3 or 4 readings of the text as the optimum number (Meyer & Felton, 1999; National Reading Panel, 2000). Research has indicated that repeated readings improve reading rate for practiced passages (Ardoin et al., 2007; Rasinski, 1990) as well as for similar, unpracticed passages or passages with overlapping features or vocabulary (Ardoin et al., 2007; Martin-Chang & Levy, 2005; Rashotte & Torgeson, 1985). Some prior research has also documented gains for novel, untrained passages (Martens et al., 2007). However, generalization may be limited somewhat to the specific words being practiced. Furthermore, a high number of single, rare multisyllabic words in a text negatively impact the effectiveness of repeated readings (Heibert, 2005). Years ago, Rashotte and Torgeson (1985) suggested that repeated readings may not be any more effective than equivalent amounts of nonrepetitive reading; they observed improvements in fluency only for passages similar to those practiced. A recent meta-analysis using very rigorous standards has indicated that repeated reading does not appear to be an evidence-based practice for students with or at risk for learning disabilities (Apichatabutra, Baker, Chard, Doabler, & Ketterlin-Geller, 2009).

Instead of repeated readings of a single text, students should read a lot of diverse, real texts, which increases language skills and content knowledge as well as fluency. In order to encourage the strongest generalization, it is recommended that texts contain high frequency words in order to provide as many exposures as possible to these words.

Whether or not teachers use decodable text, they should choose text for fluency practice that students are able to read independently with around 95% accuracy.

Fluency Through Phrasing and Chunking Text

Although speed and accuracy are considered the important factors at the single-word level, fluent reading at the text level involves the additional application of intonation and phrasal chunking. Speed is therefore not necessarily the appropriate goal in the beginning; one must often caution students to slow down and monitor their prosody to increase their comprehension. Although periodic timing of the reading of connected text is important for monitoring progress in developing fluency, more important is the focus on applying prosodic features and syntactic chunking. Reading with natural prosody has been found to be strongly facilitated by repeated readings of text printed with spaces between phrases and at the ends of lines at clause boundaries, thereby providing visible support for sentence structure (LeVasseur, Macaruso, & Shankweiler, 2008). The incorporation of a multisensory component of scooping or drawing an arc under predetermined syntactic chunks of text may benefit some students. One program that has sentences and paragraphs that are designed to include scooping is the *Wilson Reading Program* (Wilson Language Training Corporation, 2010).

The following is a suggested progression for repeated readings of paragraphs that incorporates systematic work at the phrase and sentence levels as well as the motor component of scooping or having students trace lines (with either their finger or a pencil) that indicate the syntactic chunks. It is important that the syntactic chunks be identified for students because they will not be able to do so themselves. Arcs can either be drawn under the phrases and the student can trace over them, or spaces can be inserted to show where the scoop should begin and end. Transparent overlays can be prepared ahead of time and a marker used for the scooping if the text cannot be marked.

The students can read the paragraph aloud, either after a brief discussion of the content to give them some anticipatory set or completely cold, with no introduction to the text ahead of time. This can be tape-recorded as a baseline for comparison with successive readings. Students can be asked to read the passage silently and to find any words they do not recognize. They then read the passage with a rhythm that matches the scooping actions until they are relatively fluent with appropriate prosody (see Box 13.7). After this reading, the students read the paragraph as a whole without scooping. If the oral reading was recorded, they can compare their performance on the two readings in terms of accuracy, rhythm, and speed. Timing at this level may be incorporated once rhythm has been clearly established.

Students with fluency problems often read in a monotone without applying appropriate intonation and prosody or attending to punctuation. A simple exercise that can help

Box 13.7. ***Phrasal Chunks Scooped for Reading Intonation Practice***

As the athletes ran quickly down the road, the cars stopped to honk their horns.

Box 13.8. ***Question-Answering for Intonation Practice***

- *Who* is running? The *boy* is running down the street.
- *What* is the boy *doing*? The boy is *running* down the street.
- *Where* is the boy running? The boy is running *down the street.*

raise the students' awareness of punctuation is to have them circle the period at the end of sentences in the passage while they are reading orally and practice dropping their voices. They can also read the same sentence in different ways, depending on the end punctuation: *The cat ran. The cat ran! The cat ran?* Having the student first point to the sentence that you are reading is a helpful way to increase awareness of intonation if he or she struggles with this task. To help with placing appropriate emphasis or stress on words, the same sentence can be read in different ways to answer specific questions. For example, the simple sentence, "The boy is running down the street" can be read in three different ways to answer the questions that follow it (Box 13.8).

Developing Anticipatory Set

Improving the use of syntactic chunking and prosody enables students to strengthen their ability to anticipate what will come next in a text. In addition, knowledge of the content also helps to develop an anticipatory set and enhances fluency and comprehension (Wood et al., 2001). Through the activation of prior knowledge and a preview of what will happen in the story, students can learn to predict text content. Summarizing the story, discussing the characters, or previewing the pictures to get ideas of what the story may be about can also improve anticipatory sets and thus enhance fluency. Other commonly used strategies, such as reviewing the vocabulary and comprehension questions before reading the passage, may also be helpful in this regard. In addition, the use of Cloze procedure activities, which involve determining a missing word by using the sentence context, can develop a conscious use of syntactic and semantic cues as well as heighten attention to meaning, thus improving the student's ability to anticipate what may come next. Plus, students need to read a lot. In addition to improving language skills, reading comprehension, and content knowledge, reading literature and informational texts will increase and improve breadth and solidity of orthographic patterns for automatic word recognition and fast, accurate reading fluency.

Conclusion

To provide integrated services for students at risk for reading failure, it is essential that professionals in the fields of reading and speech–language pathology pool their resources. Prevention of problems in reading through early identification and appropriate intervention requires careful assessment of the specific patterns of spoken and written language skills. Whether SLPs pursue specialized training in teaching word identification and reading fluency skills or choose to consult with those who do, it is important that SLPs know the processes involved in word recognition and reading fluency as well as the recommended instructional practices for poor readers.

References

Adams, M. (1990). *Beginning to read: Thinking and learning about print.* Cambridge, MA: MIT Press.

Adams, M., Foorman, B., Lundberg, I., & Beeler, T. (1996). *Phonemic awareness in young children.* Baltimore, MD: Brookes.

American Speech-Language-Hearing Association (2001). *Roles and responsibilities of SLPs with respect to reading and writing in children and adolescents* [Position statement]. Rockville, MD: Author.

Apel, K. (2009). The acquisition of mental orthographic representations for reading and spelling development. *Communication Disorders Quarterly, 31*(1), 42–52.

Apichatabutra, C., Baker, S., Chard, D., Doabler, C., & Ketterlin-Geller, L. (2009). Repeated reading interventions for students with learning disabilities: Status of the evidence. *Exceptional Children, 7,* 263.

Ardoin, S., McCall, M., & Klubnick, C. (2007). Promoting generalization of oral reading fluency: Providing drill versus practice opportunities. *Journal of Behavioral Education, 16,* 54–69.

Badian, N. (1997). Dyslexia and the double deficit hypothesis. *Annals of Dyslexia, 47,* 69–88.

Badian, N. (2005). Does a visual-orthographic deficit contribute to reading disability? *Annals of Dyslexia, 55,* 28–52.

Ball, E., & Blachman, B. (1991). Does phoneme awareness training in kindergarten make a difference in early word recognition and developmental spelling? *Reading Research Quarterly, 24,* 49–66.

Bashir, A., & Hook, P. (2009). Fluency: A key link between word identification and comprehension, *Language, Speech, and Hearing Services in Schools, 40,* 196–200.

Bell, N. (1997). *Seeing stars.* San Luis Obispo, CA: Gander Educational.

Berninger, V., Stage, S., Smith, D., & Hildebrand, D. (2001). Assessment for reading and writing intervention: A 3-tier model for prevention and intervention. In J. Andrews, D. Saklofske, & H. Janzen (Eds.), *Ability, achievement, and behavior assessment: A practical handbook* (pp. 195–223). New York, NY: Academic Press.

Bus, A. G., & van IJzendoorn, M. H. (1999). Phonological awareness and early reading: A meta-analysis of experimental training studies. *Journal of Educational Psychology, 91,* 403–414.

Carlisle, J. (2003). Morphology matters in learning to read: A commentary. *Reading Psychology, 24,* 291–322.

Carlisle, J. (2004). Morphological processes that influence learning to read. In A. Stone, E. Silliman, B. Ehren, & K. Apel (Eds.), *Handbook of language and literacy: Development and disorders* (pp. 318–339). New York, NY: Guilford Press.

Catts, H. W., Fey, M. E., Zhang, X., & Tomblin, J. B. (1999). Language basis of reading and reading disabilities: Evidence from a longitudinal investigation. *Scientific Studies in Reading, 3*, 331–361.

Catts, H. W., Kamhi, A.G., & Adlof, S. (2012). Defining and classifying reading disabilities. In H.W. Catts & A.G. Kamhi (Eds.), *Language and reading disabilities* (3rd ed., pp. 45–76). Boston, MA: Allyn & Bacon.

Chall, J. (1983). *Stages of reading development*. New York, NY: McGraw-Hill.

Chall, J. (1996). *Learning to read: The great debate*. New York, NY: McGraw-Hill.

Clark-Edmands, S. (2008). *Specialized program individualizing reading excellence*. Cambridge, MA: Educator Publishing Service.

Ehri, L. (1994). Development of the ability to read words: Update. In R. Ruddell, M. Ruddell, & H. Singer (Eds.), *Theoretical models and processes of reading* (pp. 323–358). Newark, DE: International Reading Association.

Ehri, L., Nunes, S., Willows, D., Schuster, B., Yaghoub-Zadeh, Z., & Shanahan, T. (2001). Phonemic awareness instruction helps children learn to read: Evidence from the National Reading Panel's meta-analysis. *Reading Research Quarterly, 36*, 250–287.

Elkonin, D. B. (1973). U.S.S.R. In I. Downing (Ed.), *Comparative reading* (pp. 551–580). New York, NY: Macmillan.

Fischer, P. E. (1995). *Concept phonics*. Farmington, ME: Oxton House.

Fletcher, J. M. (2006). The need for response to intervention models of learning disabilities. *Perspectives, The International Dyslexia Association, 32*(1), 12–15.

Frith, U. (1985). Beneath the surface of developmental dyslexia. In L. Patterson, J. Marshall, & M. Coltheart (Eds.), *Surface dyslexia* (pp. 301–303). London, UK: Erlbaum.

Fuchs, D., & Fuchs, L. (2006). Introduction to response to intervention: What, why, and how valid is it? *Reading Research Quarterly, 41*, 93–99.

Fuchs, L. S., Fuchs, D., Hosp, M. D., & Jenkins, J. (2001). Oral reading fluency as an indicator of reading competence: A theoretical, empirical, and historical analysis. *Scientific Studies of Reading, 5*, 239–259.

Gathercole, S., Willis, C., & Baddeley, A. (1991). Differentiating phonological memory and awareness of rhyme: Reading and vocabulary development in children. *British Journal of Psychology, 82*, 387–406.

German, D. J., & Newman, R. S. (2007). Oral reading skills of children with oral language (word-finding) difficulties. *Reading Psychology*, 28, 397–442.

Gillingham, A., & Stillman, B. (1997). *The Gillingham manual: Remedial training for children with specific disability in reading, writing, and penmanship* (8th ed.). Cambridge, MA: Educators Publishing Service.

Good, R., & Kaminski, R. (Eds.). (2010). *Dynamic indicators of basic early literacy skills next.* Eugene, OR: Institute for the Development of Educational Achievement.

Gosse, C., Hoffman, L., & Invernizzi, M. (2012). Overlap in speech–language and reading services for kindergartners and first graders. *Language, Speech, and Hearing Services in Schools, 43*, 66–80.

Henry, M. (2010). *Unlocking literacy: Effective decoding and spelling instruction* (2nd ed.). Baltimore, MD: Brookes.

Henry, M., & Hook, P. (2006). Multisensory instruction: Then and now. *Perspectives, The International Dyslexia Association, 32*(4), 1–2.

Henry, M., & Redding, N. (2012). Patterns for success in reading and spelling. Austin, TX: PRO-ED.

Hiebert, E. (2005). The effects of text difficulty on second graders' fluency development. *Reading Psychology, 26*, 1–27.

Holliman, A., Wood, C., & Sheehy, K. (2012). A cross-sectional study of prosodic sensitivity and reading difficulties. *Journal of Research in Reading, 35*(1), 32–48.

Hook, P. (2006). Transcription processes related to spelling: Intervention strategies. *Perspectives, The International Dyslexia Association, 32*(2), 19–22.

Hook, P., & Jones, S. (2002). The importance of automaticity and fluency for efficient reading comprehension. *Perspectives, The International Dyslexia Association, 28*(1), 9–14.

Hoover, W., & Gough, P. B. (1990). The simple view of reading. *Reading and Writing, 2*, 127–160.

Hudson, R. F., Lane, H. B., & Pullen, P. C. (2005). Reading fluency assessment and instruction: What, why, and how? *The Reading Teacher, 58*, 702–714.

Individuals With Disabilities Education Improvement Act of 2004, 20 U.S.C. § 1400 *et seq.* (2004).

Institute of Education Sciences (2011). *The nation's report card.* Washington, DC: U.S. Department of Education, Institute of Education Sciences.

Kamhi, A. G., & Catts, H. W. (2012). Language and reading: Convergences and divergences. In A. G. Kamhi & H. W. Catts (Eds.), *Language and reading disabilities* (3rd ed., pp. 1–23). Boston, MA: Pearson.

Kirby, J., Deacon, S., Bowers, P., Izenberg, L., Wade-Woolley, L., & Parrila, R. (2011). Children's morphological awareness and reading ability. *Reading and Writing, 25*, 389–410.

Kuhn, M., Schwanenflugel, P., & Meisinger, E. (2010). Aligning theory and assessment of reading fluency: automaticity, prosody, and definitions of fluency. *Reading Research Quarterly, 45*, 230–251.

Kuhn, M. R., & Stahl, S. A. (2003). Fluency: A review of developmental and remedial practices. *Journal of Educational Psychology*, 95(1), 3–21.

LaBerge, D., & Samuels, S. J. (1974). Toward a theory of automatic information processing in reading. *Cognitive Psychology, 6*, 293–323.

Lesnick, J., George, R., Smithgall, C., & Gwynne, J. (2010). *Reading on grade level in third grade: How is it related to high school performance and college enrollment?* Chicago, IL: Chapin Hall at the University of Chicago.

LeVasseur, V., Macaruso, P., & Shankweiler, D. (2008). Promoting gains in reading fluency: A comparison of three approaches. *Reading and Writing, 21*, 205–230.

Lindamood, P., & Lindamood, P. (2011). *The Lindamood phoneme sequencing program for reading, spelling, and speech* (4th ed.). Austin, TX: PRO-ED.

Lyon, G., Shaywitz, S., & Shaywitz, B. (2003). A definition of dyslexia. *Annals of Dyslexia, 53*, 1–14.

MacGinitie, W., MacGinitie, R., Maria, K., Dreyer, L., & Hughes, K. (2002). *Gates-MacGinitie Reading Test* (4th ed.). Rolling Meadows, IL: Riverside.

Manis, F., & Freedman, L. (2001). The relationship of naming speed to multiple reading measures in disabled and normal readers. In M. Wolf (Ed.), *Dyslexia, fluency and the brain* (pp. 65–92). Timonium, MD: York Press.

Martens, B., Eckert, T., Begeny, J., Lewandowski, L., DiGennaro, F., Montarello, S., Arbolino, L., Reed, D., & Fiese, B. (2007). Effects of a fluency-building program on the reading performance of low-achieving second and third grade students. *Journal of Behavioral Education, 16*, 38–53.

Martin-Chang, S., & Levy, B. (2005). Fluency transfer: Differential gains in reading speed and accuracy following isolated word and context training. *Reading and Writing, 18*, 343–376.

Meyer, M., & Felton, R. (1999). Repeated reading to enhance fluency: Old approaches and new directions. *Annals of Dyslexia, 49*, 283–306.

Miller, J., & Schwanenflugel, P. J. (2008). A longitudinal study of the development of reading prosody as a dimension of oral reading fluency in early elementary school children. *Reading Research Quarterly, 43*, 336–354.

National Association of State Directors of Special Education. (2005). *Response to intervention: policy considerations and implementation*. Alexandria, VT: Author.

National Governors Association Center for Best Practices and Council of Chief State School Officers (2010). *Common Core State Standards for English Language Arts & Literacy in History/Social Studies, Science, and Technical Subjects*. Washington, DC: Author. Retrieved from http://www.corestandards.org

National Reading Panel. (2000). *Teaching children to read: An evidence-based assessment of the scientific research literature on reading and its implications for reading instruction* (NIH Pub. No. 00–4754). Washington, DC: U.S. Government Printing Office. Available at http://www.nationalreadingpanel.org/

Pearson Publishing. (2001). *AIMSweb*. San Antonio, TX: Author.

Pearson Publishing (2012). *Stanford Achievement Test Series* 10th ed. San Antonio, TX: Author.

Rashotte, C. A., & Torgesen, J. K. (1985). Repeated reading and reading fluency in learning disabled children. *Reading Research Quarterly, 20*, 180–188.

Rasinski, T. (1990). Effects of repeated reading and listening-while-reading on reading fluency. *Journal of Educational Research, 83*(3), 147–150.

Robertson, C., & Salter, W. (2007). *Phonological Awareness Test* (2nd ed.). East Moline, IL: LinguiSystems.

Schwanenflugel, P., Hamilton, A., Kuhn, M.,Wisenbaker, J., & Stahl, S. (2004). Becoming a fluent reader: Reading skill and prosodic features in the oral reading of young readers. *Journal of Educational Psychology, 96*, 119–129.

Senechal, M., Ouellette, G., Pagan, S., & Lever, R. (2012). The role of invented spelling on learning to read in low-phoneme-awareness kindergartners: A randomized controlled-trial study. *Reading and Writing, 25*, 917–934.

Share, D. (1995). Phonological recoding and self-teaching: *sine qua non* of reading acquisition. *Cognition, 55*, 151–218.

Share, D., & Stanovich, K. (1995). Cognitive processes in early reading development: Accommodating individual differences into a model of acquisition. *Issues in Education: Contributions from Educational Psychology, 1*(1), 1–57.

Snow, C. E., Burns, M. S., & Griffin, P. (Eds.). (1998). *Preventing reading difficulties in young children.* Washington, DC: National Academy Press.

Snowling, M. J. (2000). *Dyslexia.* Oxford, England: Blackwell.

Spencer, E., Schuele, C., Guillot, K., & Lee, M. (2008). Phonemic awareness skill of speech–language pathologists and other educators. *Language, Speech, and Hearing Services in Schools,* 39, 512–520.

Stackhouse, J., & Wells, B. (1997). How do speech and language problems affect literacy development? In C. Hulme & M. Snowling (Eds.), *Dyslexia: Biology, cognition, and intervention* (pp. 182–211). London: Whurr.

Steere, A., Peck, C., & Kahn, L. (1988). *Solving language difficulties.* Cambridge, MA: Educators Publishing Service.

Tallal, P. (1988). Developmental language disorders. In J. F. Kavanaugh & T. J. Truss, Jr. (Eds.), *Learning disabilities: Proceedings of the national conference* (pp. 181–272). Parkton, MD: York Press.

Telian, N. (2001). *Lively letters.* Stoughton, MA: Telian-Cas Learning Concepts.

Torgesen, J. (2002). The prevention of reading disabilities. *Journal of School Psychology, 40,* 7–26.

Torgesen, J. K. (2006) *A comprehensive K–3 reading assessment plan: Guidance for school leaders.* Portsmouth, NH: RMC Research, Center on Instruction.

Torgesen, J., Alexander, A., Wagner, R., Rashotte, C., Voeller, K., Conway, T., & Rose, E. (2001). Intensive remedial instruction for children with severe reading disabilities: Immediate and long-term outcomes from two instructional approaches. *Journal of Learning Disabilities, 34,* 33–58.

Torgesen, J., Rashotte, C., & Alexander, A. (2001). Principles of fluency instruction in reading: Relationships with established empirical outcomes. In M. Wolf (Ed.), *Dyslexia, fluency, and the brain* (pp. 333–355). Timonium, MD: York Press.

Torgesen, J., Wagner, R., & Rashotte, C. (2011). *Test of Word Reading Efficiency* (2nd ed.). Austin, TX: PRO-ED.

Vellutino, F. R., Scanlon, D. M., Small, S., & Fanuele, D. P. (2006). Response to intervention as a vehicle for distinguishing between children with and without reading disabilities: Evidence for the role of kindergarten and first-grade interventions. *Journal of Learning Disabilities, 38,* 157–169.

Wagner, R. K., Torgesen, J. A., Rashotte, C. A., & Pearson, N. A. (2013). *Comprehensive Test of Phonological Processing* (2nd ed.). Austin, TX: PRO-ED.

Weiss-Kapp, S. (2005). *WKRP: Reading by the rules.* Arlington, MA: Dearborn Academy.

Wiederholt, J., & Bryant, B. (2012). *Gray Oral Reading Tests* (5th ed.). Austin, TX: PRO-ED.

Williams, K. (2001). *Group reading assessment and diagnostic evaluation, level 3.* Circle Pines, MN: American Guidance Services.

Wilson Language Training Corporation. (2010). *Wilson Reading System.* Oxford, MA: Author.

Wolf, M. (1997). A provisional integrative account of phonological and naming-speed deficits in dyslexia: Implications for diagnosis and intervention. In B. Blachman (Ed.), *Foundations of reading acquisition and dyslexia: Implications for early intervention* (pp. 67–92). Mahwah, NJ: Erlbaum.

Wolf, M., & Bowers, P. (1999). The double-deficit hypothesis for the developmental dyslexias. *Journal of Educational Psychology, 91*, 415–438.

Wood, F., Flowers, L., & Grigorenko, E. (2001). On the functional neuroanatomy of fluency or why walking is just as important to reading as talking is. In M. Wolf (Ed.), *Dyslexia, fluency, and the brain* (pp. 235–244). Timonium, MD: York Press.

Woodcock, R. (2011). *Woodcock Reading Mastery Tests* (3rd ed.). San Antonio, TX: Pearson.

Chapter **14**

Spelling and Word Study: A Guide for Language-Based Assessment and Intervention

Julie A. Wolter

Spelling is often considered part of the code aspect of reading and writing. However, spelling, especially the process of learning how to spell new words, draws heavily on multiple language skills. This chapter will explain the language basis for how children learn to spell, how spelling is typically taught, and how spelling challenges exist even for fluent spellers. The chapter will focus on the particular difficulties manifested by children with language impairments and on how a language-based approach can address these spelling difficulties as well as the underlying linguistic weaknesses that also compromise other aspects of communication.

Spelling is a language- or linguistically based skill (Apel & Masterson, 2001; Bear, Invernizzi, Templeton, & Johnston, 2004; Ehri, 2000; Henderson, 1990; Moats, 2009; Treiman, Cassar, & Zukowski, 1994), and the awareness of sounds in words (phonological awareness), knowledge of the spelling patterns in words (orthographic pattern knowledge), understanding of relationships among base words and their inflectional and derivational forms (morphological awareness), all influence not only spelling acquisition but also vocabulary, reading decoding, reading comprehension, and writing development (Berninger, Abbott, Abbott, Graham, & Richards, 2002; Bourassa & Treiman, 2001; Graham & Harris, 2005). In fact, as a production skill, spelling instruction helps also to facilitate reading recognition (Ehri, 1997; Shahar-Yames & Share, 2008). Thus, a developmental treatment approach that incorporates spelling and nurtures these multiple linguistic factors may be an effective way to help children with language impairment to succeed academically.

The Speech–Language Pathologist's Role

Speech–language pathologists (SLPs) may play a unique role in facilitating the acquisition of the language skills related to spelling and reading success. Spelling is often considered part of the code aspect of reading and writing. However, spelling, especially the process of learning to spell new words, draws heavily on multiple language skills. SLPs who bring their language expertise into spelling instruction can mutually reinforce their students' gains in spelling and language.

Many SLPs view spelling as a skill outside of their purview. It can be argued, however, that spelling can be used as a tool to assess and treat language-specific goals. Theoretically, then, it can provide benefits that include an assessment window to determine where language breakdowns occur as well as a functional context in which to prescriptively target linguistic skills such as phonological awareness, morphological awareness, or orthographic pattern knowledge. Moreover, given the SLP's scope of practice, which includes written language (American Speech-Language-Hearing Association, 2001, 2010), and the fact that many children with speech and language impairments struggle with literacy, it is critical that SLPs play an active role facilitating student success in the areas of reading and writing (Fallon & Katz, 2011). Whether or not an SLP chooses to directly target spelling or to indirectly improve this skill through the implementation of language work, it is important for SLPs to know how spelling develops, how to teach it, and how it interacts with language.

The Spelling–Reading and Spelling–Language Links

Spelling and reading are integrally related skills that employ the same foundational language knowledge sources and follow a common developmental process (Ehri, 2000). Early emerging spelling performance is related to early and later literacy success (Apel, Wolter, & Masterson, 2006; Shattil, Share, Levin, 2000; Wolter, Self, & Apel, 2011). In addition, language-based spelling instruction has been found to improve not only spelling but also reading decoding, sight-word reading, and even reading comprehension skills in children with and without language and literacy impairments (Apel & Masterson, 2001; Berninger, Lee, Abbott, & Breznitz, 2011; Kelman & Apel, 2004; Wolter, 2005; Wolter & Dilworth, 2014; Wolter & Green, 2013). Reading instruction, however, does not necessarily result in improved spelling skills. This outcome may be due to the particular demands exerted by spelling, which requires analysis and attention to all the sounds and letters in a word, as opposed to the more general recognition skill of reading, which only requires attention to parts of a word (Shahar-Yames & Share, 2008). For example, many individuals may read the word *catastrophe* but not know how to spell it.

Spelling is linked to more than reading. Contrary to simple code-plus-language distinctions, spelling is a code skill that is based on linguistic knowledge (Apel & Masterson, 2001; Bear et al., 2004; Ehri, 2000; Henderson, 1990; Moats, 2009; Treiman et al., 1994). In learning to spell a new word, the phonemes of the word are matched to letters or letter combinations based on spelling patterns or on orthographic pattern knowledge. The awareness of morphology, which includes knowledge of base words or meaning-based word parts, also may be used to spell words. Eventually, through repeated exposure, mental pictures of the printed word develop and are linked to pronunciation and meaning forms. For fluent spellers, these mental graphemic representations are readily recalled and relied upon. In the following sections, each of these linguistic influences on spelling will be defined and described in more detail.

Phonological Awareness

Phonological awareness is the conscious knowledge of the sound structures of a language. The part of phonological awareness that matters most for spelling in English is phonemic awareness: the understanding that words are composed of phonemes that are separable and manipulable. SLPs have long focused on phonemic awareness because researchers have consistently found this skill to be very closely related to reading and spelling achievement (Catts, Fey, Zhang, & Tomblin, 2001; Ehri et al., 2001).

A reciprocal relationship between phonemic awareness and word reading and spelling exists: knowing that the spoken word "cat" is composed of three sounds helps the child learn to use three letters to spell the word (even if the word is spelled as *kat*), whereas noticing that the written word *plant* has five letters helps a child become aware of the subtle /n/ in the spoken word "plant" (Ukrainetz, 2006; Ukrainetz, Cooney, Dyer, Kysar, & Harris, 2000). Good phonemic awareness, through its contribution to better word recognition and reading fluency, also contributes to better reading comprehension in both early and later grades. An impressive body of research documents the crucial role of phonemic awareness in reading and spelling for children with and without literacy deficits (e.g., Blachman, Ball, Black, & Tangel, 1994; Blachman, Tangel, Ball, Black, & McGraw, 1999; Blachman et al., 2004; Lonigan, Burgess, & Anthony, 2000; Schuele et al., 2008; Storch & Whitehurst, 2002; Vadasy, Sanders, & Peyton, 2006).

Orthographic Pattern Knowledge

Orthographic pattern knowledge involves the translation of sound(s) to letter(s), or phonemes to graphemes, which requires the understanding and use of general spelling rules and patterns (e.g., long- and short-vowel rules) and the ability to write letter sequences that correctly match specific sounds. Just like phonological awareness, it is a rule-based generative process that is part of communication and as such can also be considered a linguistic skill.

Orthographic pattern knowledge involves far more than simple phoneme-grapheme relationships and includes the understanding of the intricacies of legal spelling combinations and patterns. For example, students must learn when /k/ is represented by *ck*, *c*, or *k*. Additional factors involved in orthographic processing include positional constraints on the sequences of graphemes in printed words (e.g., *ck* cannot occur at the beginning of an English word). This knowledge can be explicitly learned through instruction (e.g., a spelling rule such as "*i* before *e* except after *c*") or implicitly learned through exposure. Children with language impairments may not be as savvy as their typically developing peers in implicitly recognizing and applying these patterns in spelling and thus require explicit instruction.

The importance of orthographic pattern knowledge as a significant predictor of children's literacy success is well established. Hammill (2004) analyzed the combined results of three meta-analyses (approximately 450 studies reviewed) and found tasks related to print, which included an awareness of orthographic spelling patterns, to be the best predictors of children's reading and, not surprisingly, spelling success. Moreover, research supports the use of orthographic pattern instruction that focuses on recognizing and discovering spelling patterns across many words instead of memorization of word lists and rote teaching of spelling rules without links to spelling patterns in multiple words. This type of instruction has been found to improve spelling and reading in children who have typical literacy abilities (Abbott, 2001; White, 2005; Williams & Hufnagel, 2005; Williams & Lundstrom, 2007; Williams & Phillips-Birdsong, 2006) and in those who have language or literacy impairments (Apel & Masterson, 2001; Berninger et al., 2002; Berninger, et al., 2008; Graham & Harris, 2005; Kelman & Apel, 2004; Masterson & Crede, 1999).

Mental Graphemic Representations

While orthographic pattern knowledge refers to an understanding of the rules or letter patterns governing a symbol system, mental graphemic representations (MGRs) refer to stored memories of specific words (Apel, 2011; Apel, Wolter, & Masterson, 2012). MGRs, also referred to as mental orthographic images or visual orthographic images in the literature, are stored visual representations of written words in long-term memory. As children are frequently exposed to words in print, they either implicitly store MGRs holistically or make connections between letters or graphemes and corresponding phonemes when sounding out novel words. In the latter process, children gradually develop images of the patterns of graphemes seen in words. Thus MGRs are developed through the direct holistic memory of words (an implicit or explicit process), or through active recognition and storage of sound-to-letter (phonological-to-orthographic) correspondences.

Unlike the indirect routes of accessing orthographic pattern knowledge or sounding out words through phonemic segmentation to spell or read, MGRs may be directly and thus quickly accessed to spell and read. A child who has incomplete (i.e., letters missing in the image) or unclear (also called a fuzzy image) MGRs may still be able to fluently read or recognize words (reading the word *train* with the incomplete MGR of *tra-n*); however, clear and complete MGRs are required to accurately spell words. Although reading provides multiple opportunities to form MGRs, reading alone may not be adequate to develop the clear mental representations required for spelling. That is, an individual may only focus on parts of words, resulting in a "fuzzy" MGR (e.g., storing *tr--n* for *train*). Even fluent spellers may have fuzzy MGRs for infrequent, complex words. In fact, Katz and Frost (2001) found that parts of words that are ambiguous, such as geminates (i.e., doubled letters as in *better*) and schwas (i.e., unstressed vowels such as the *i* in *sensible*), and whose sound can be represented by several choices of letters or letter combinations are less likely to be clearly stored in MGRs. Exposure to incorrect spellings through advertising or texting (and for teachers, through grading student papers) can also affect the integrity of even a good speller's MGRs.

MGRs have linguistic connections. An MGR is only useful if a speller recognizes the collection of letters as a meaningful word. Connections are made in the child's memory between these MGRs and a word's pronunciation and meaning (Ehri, 1992, Share 2004). The larger a child's vocabulary, the better these MGRs can facilitate fluent and accurate word reading and spelling. Researchers have documented the importance of MGR development in early and later accurate spelling and reading success for children with and without language impairments (Apel et al., 2006; Cunningham, 2006; Evans, Williamson, & Pursoo, 2008; Wolter et al., 2011).

Morphological Awareness

Morphological awareness is the understanding that words are comprised of smaller meaningful word parts called morphemes. It includes conscious reflection on and manipulation of morphemes (Carlisle, 2000). When inflectional and derivational morphemes are added to base words, newly derived forms of words are made and meaning is altered. For example, adding the past tense *-ed* to a verb (e.g., *jump* becomes *jumped*) communicates that the action happened in the past, whereas adding *-er* to the end of the verb changes the verb to a noun (e.g., *jump* becomes *jumper*). Morphological awareness includes knowledge of *inflection*, which affixes tense, plurality, or possession to base words (e.g., *walk* to *walked*) as well as *derivational forms*, which change the base word to create a new word and in so doing generally change the grammatical category (e.g., *sad* to *sadness*).

Morphological relationships can also be described as *transparent* or *opaque*. A morphological formation in which the base word retains its pronunciation and spelling is phonologically and orthographically transparent (Stolz & Felman, 1995). The word *quickly*, for example, is phonologically and orthographically transparent, because both the pronunciation and spelling of the base word *quick* remain the same. A morphological formation in which the pronunciation or spelling of the base morpheme changes is considered phonologically or orthographically opaque. For example, the word *length* is phonologically and orthographically opaque, because changes occur in both the spelling and the pronunciation of the base word *long*.

Morphological awareness is related to and likely facilitates a well-developed grammar system, increased vocabulary development, and high reading, spelling, and writing achievement (McCutchen, Green, & Abbott, 2008; Nagy, Berninger, & Abbott, 2006; Schwiebert, Green, & McCutchen, 2002; Wolter, Wood, & D'zatko, 2009). Specifically, knowledge of morphology helps children to spell, decode, and comprehend new words (e.g., Carlisle, 1996, 2000; Elbro & Arnback, 1996). This is not surprising, given that approximately 60% of new words acquired by school-age children are morphologically complex (Anglin, 1993).

Models of Spelling Development

Stage Theory

In a common model of spelling development, children progress through a series of stages in which different facets of word structure are learned (Bear et al., 2004; Ehri, 1992; Henderson, 1990). In stage theory, beginning readers and spellers are largely focused on the phonetic level of written language. Additional information, such as morphology, is not thought to influence children's spelling and reading until relatively late in the process of literacy learning.

In stage theory, children initially are in an *emergent* or *prephonetic* stage of spelling development where they intentionally "write" or scribble in horizontal lines that look different from their scribbled drawings. They may show more print knowledge with strings of letters and letterlike shapes with no letter-sound correspondence. Children may be able to write approximations of their own names in a holistic manner, without knowing the individual letters or their correspondence with sounds.

When they reach the next stage, children become aware of letter names and cue in to the sounds in a letter name (*p* says /pi/ and *r* says /ar/). This *semiphonetic* stage, also known as the *partial-alphabetic* stage, develops in typically developing preschool children who may use a letter to represent a whole word or parts of words (e.g., *PR* for *pear*; *B* for *bead*).

Following the semiphonetic stage is the *phonetic* or *alphabetic* stage, where children become increasingly aware of phoneme-letter correspondence and will attempt to account for all sounds in a word with letters. Here, common mistakes still include using some letter names, such as the syllabic *r* or *l* (e.g., *PAPR* for *paper*, *TABL* for *table*), or providing only one consonant to represent a phoneme cluster (e.g., *SEP* for *step*, *TET* for *tent*). Typically developing kindergarteners are in this stage.

Beginning in first grade, typically developing children enter a *within-word pattern* stage, and begin to apply their knowledge of spelling rules or orthographic pattern knowledge. As children are exposed to print and are taught general spelling rules, they begin to spell using a rule-based system (e.g., including a silent *e* or two vowels to make a long-vowel sound). In the last two stages of spelling development, the *syllable juncture* and *derivational constancy* stages, the awareness of morphology emerges. According to stage theorists such as Henderson (1990) and Schlagal (2001), morphological awareness may not appear in typically developing children until third or fourth grade. In the syllable juncture stage, children develop an awareness of inflectional morphology (e.g., spelling past-tense *-ed* correctly) as well as the ability to apply it. In the last stage, derivational constancy, children begin to apply their knowledge of derivational morphology by combining affixes and base words to accurately spell multimorphemic words (e.g., *prehistoric, magician*).

It should be noted that display of these stages is affected by how children are allowed or encouraged to spell. If children see writing as communication and are encouraged to "use their best guess" in spelling whatever they want to communicate, then all these stages are likely to be seen. In contrast, if children are allowed to write only what they can spell correctly, they may skip the earlier stages. This means they will make fewer spelling errors but carries the risks of both more limited knowledge of orthography and less interest in writing that their knowledge of orthography will be more limited. More importantly, students who are conditioned to write only what they can spell correctly will be much more likely to avoid writing as a mode of expression and learning.

Repertoire Theory

In contrast to stage theory, other researchers suggest that an early influence of multiple sources of linguistic information (phonological awareness, orthographic pattern knowledge, morphological awareness) is involved in spelling development. Researchers have found that beginning spellers are not necessarily limited to a phonetic strategy of progressing through a word from left to right, assigning a letter to each sound they hear (Treiman & Cassar, 1996). Children were able to also incorporate basic morphological knowledge (e.g., applying knowledge of basic inflectional morphology, such as past tense *-ed*) or orthographic pattern knowledge (e.g., employing knowledge of orthographic constraints and not spelling words with a *ck* at the beginning) as early as first grade (Apel & Lawrence, 2011; Treiman et al., 1994; Wolter et al., 2009).

Based on these and other findings, some authors have proposed a *repertoire theory* of spelling development (Masterson & Apel, 2014). The repertoire theory suggests that as children develop, they use a range of linguistic knowledge when spelling, and the degree to which they use this linguistic knowledge in the respective areas of phonological awareness, orthographic pattern knowledge, and morphological awareness changes over time. (See Masterson & Apel, 2014, for full review.) According to this theory, although children may rely more heavily on phonological, orthographic pattern, or morphological knowledge at different phases in their spelling development, all linguistic processes are being tapped into at an early age. This theory does not necessarily discount the aforementioned developmental stage research. Instead it accounts for developmental spellings through a differential linguistic lens, in that the degree to which specific linguistic knowledge is applied varies across time.

In the repertoire developmental model, the term *phases* is used instead of stages because this term better encompasses the idea that there are overlapping knowledge sources. In the *prespelling* phase of spelling development, children may show some knowledge of MGRs or the overall picture of a word in addition to scribble and nonsense letter strings. They may not be able to align phonemes with letters, use spelling rules, or analyze word affixes, but they may write some whole words, such as *mom* or *the.* Children's mastery of writing their own names while able to spell little else is an example of an early MGR.

Next, in the *early spelling* phase of preschool through first grade, children learn to use phonemic awareness and orthographic pattern knowledge along with some rudimentary morphological awareness, such as knowing that plural nouns often end with the letter *s*. In addition, as the spelling of more words becomes familiar, the store of MGRs steadily increases, and fuzzy MGRs become clearer. In the *intermediate* phase (second through third grade in typical spelling) and the advanced phase (third and fourth grade on), good spellers use MGRs to spell known words. To spell unknown words, they rely heavily on their orthographic pattern knowledge and morphological awareness in addition to phonological awareness when appropriate.

The result is that at a single point in time, beginning spellers may spell some words correctly, even complex ones if they are used a lot, while other, less familiar words may be spelled phonetically, semiphonetically, or with memorized morphological chunks. Thus, if following a repertoire developmental theory, teachers will adopt assessment practices that involve examining multiple sources of linguistic breakdowns in spelling. Depending on the spelling errors that a child demonstrates, intervention will focus on one or several areas at one time. The remainder of this chapter will focus on how to assess and provide such linguistically based spelling intervention.

Spelling Assessment

Standardized Measures

Standardized, norm-referenced measures of spelling may be used to determine how a student performs in comparison to her or his peers. Two commonly used measures are the *Test of Written Spelling–Fifth Edition* (Larsen, Hammill, & Moats, 2013) and the *Test of Written Language–Fourth Edition* (Hammill & Larsen, 2009). These tests are a valuable means of documenting students' relative level of performance, on the basis of which students' eligibility for school services is determined. However, these measures are not designed to allow analysis of the underlying language sources of a spelling deficit and provide direction for treatment. In these measures, an all-or-none scoring system is used: accurate spelling is scored as correct and misspelling is scored as incorrect. The scoring system does not incorporate an analytic linguistic consideration of misspellings. Moreover, these tests do not sample a full inventory of words, which is needed to reliably identify the sources of errors.

Prescriptive Linguistic Spelling Assessment

An alternative to standardized measures is that of a prescriptive spelling assessment (Moats, 1995) in which the individual linguistic breakdowns can be identified. The term *prescriptive* refers to the fact that the results of such an assessment can be used to inform or prescribe the linguistic focus for an individualized treatment plan. Apel and Masterson developed a prescriptive spelling assessment that is focused on identifying the underlying linguistic breakdowns in order to direct and determine the linguistic focus for treatment (see Masterson & Apel, 2010, 2014). These researchers developed a commercially available computerized assessment program, the *Spelling Performance Evaluation for Language and Literacy–Second Edition* (SPELL-2; Masterson, Apel, & Wasowicz, 2006). The SPELL-2, which is based on algorithms, will analyze student spellings from a thorough spelling inventory gathered from the student via computer to determine specific linguistic deficits. If a tool such as this is not available, a clinician can perform a prescriptive analysis on a client's dictated spelling sample. The next sections will delineate the steps involved in a prescriptive spelling assessment.

Spelling Sample

The first step in analyzing spelling is to obtain an adequate spelling sample. Grade-level spelling word inventories are available (Bear et al., 2004; Schlagal, 1992) in which a spelling dictation test is provided. In this test, a word is first presented verbally, then used in a sentence, and then repeated. If a published spelling inventory is not readily available, an SLP can create one. Ideally, a spelling inventory should include common words with a sampling of a wide variety of letters in the alphabet and corresponding sounds. It should also include digraphs, which are two letters represented by one sound (e.g., *th*, *ck*), and words that sample the multiple spellings for common sounds (*c* for the /s/ and hard /k/). There should be multiple examples of a variety of age-appropriate orthographic spelling rules (e.g., long/short vowels), and depending on the age of the child, a wide variety of base words and corresponding inflected and derivational forms. The base words and the derived words should include transparent (e.g., *swim* to *swimming*) and opaque (e.g., *five* to *fifth*) relationships. To find grade-appropriate words, a clinician can search the web or consult a spelling book from the classroom. A reference for common spelling rules that can assist in generating a spelling inventory is *Words Their Way* (Bear et al., 2004).

From a contextualized standpoint, one might also analyze the spellings in a written sample provided by the student. An SLP can analyze the spellings found in narrative and expository written samples. Although this reveals how spelling deficits are demonstrated in a functional context, there is a caveat: often children choose to write only the words that they know how to spell, which yields a limited spelling sample (Graham & Harris, 2005). Thus, analysis of written samples can show the functional effects of children's spelling deficits: either many spelling errors or avoidance of many words. However, written sample analysis needs to be accompanied by analysis of a systematic inventory of words to determine the extent and nature of spelling breakdowns. How to determine the nature of the errors will be discussed next.

Phonological Awareness Errors

In general, misspellings should be considered phonological in nature if a spelling error in which not all phonemes are represented by corresponding graphemes is made. A phonological error may be one in which not enough letters are written to represent all sounds (e.g., *HD* for *hand*). Conversely, a spelling in which there are too many letters that do not accurately represent the number of sounds in the word (e.g., *GASKT* for *cat*) would also be considered a phonological error. The student needs practice in isolating and segmenting the phonemes in a word and then representing each with letters.

A common mistake is to believe that if a student writes a letter that does not correspond to a sound (e.g., spelling *CATE* for *gate*), it is because the student does not "hear" the sound correctly. If the SLP suspects the student cannot discriminate phonemes, then a follow-up probe should be provided to determine whether or not a child can differentiate between two sounds given a minimal pair choice (e.g., "Do these words sound the same or different: *cap* and *gap*?"). However, this is unlikely because even children who have articulation errors typically can hear the phonemes accurately. It is much more likely that the student simply does not know what letter or letter combination corresponds with the phoneme, which is then an orthographic pattern error.

Orthographic Pattern Knowledge Errors

A spelling error due to deficits in orthographic pattern knowledge includes any misspelling that violates a spelling rule or letter-sound correspondence. For example, not using two vowels to represent a long vowel (e.g., *TRAN* for *train*) or writing a letter that does not correctly correspond to a sound (e.g., writing *TAT* for *that* where the sound /ð/ is not properly represented with the digraph *th*). If this is the case, then it is an orthographic pattern knowledge error, and the specific letter-sound correspondence or pattern must then be taught (e.g., "every time you hear /g/ then write *G*").

Morphological Awareness Errors

Spelling errors that are morphological in nature can be those that involve the transformation of the base word to the inflected or derived form. Misspellings may be on the affix itself (e.g., *HELPT* for *helped*; *ONDO* for *undo*). Although this misspelling is phonetic and plausible, these errors are considered morphological because the spelling reflects the meaning not the sound. For example, past tense is represented with the letter combination *-ed* regardless of whether it sounds like /t/ (e.g., *popped*), /d/ (e.g., *canned*), or /Ed/ (e.g., *rated*). Another morphological awareness spelling error is one in which the misspelling is due to an incorrect application of a rule for adding the morphological form. For example, in the misspelling *POPING* for *popping*, the error is secondary to the application of a spelling rule regarding the doubling of a consonant in a short-vowel word when adding the inflectional suffix *-ing*.

A morphological spelling error can be one in which the base word is misspelled in the derived form (e.g., *MAJICIAN* for *magician*). In this type of error, the student is likely not using knowledge regarding the base word to write the derived form. This deficit is commonly found in children with language impairments because, in addition to their restricted vocabulary and spelling knowledge, students may be intimidated by derived words, which are often long. As a result, a student may be inclined to guess the spelling based on the first few known letters or to spell the word phonetically instead of applying base-word knowledge. In determining whether or not this type of error is truly morphological in nature, there is one caveat: it is important to document whether or not the student correctly spells the base word in isolation. For example, if the student spells *MAJIC* for the base word *magic* in isolation and then spells *MAJICIAN* for *magician*, then the student is actually using base-word knowledge to inform spelling, but the misspelling reflects an MGR error.

Semantic Errors

One type of meaning-based error that occurs with homophones is a semantic error. Homophones are words that sound alike but are spelled differently (e.g., *there, their, they're*). In semantic errors, the MGR is not linked to the correct meaning. For example, if the student wrote *SHE HAD TO COOKIES*, the spelling *TO* would be a semantic error. Thus, if a misspelling is simply an incorrect application of a homophone (e.g., spelling SOME for SUM), then it is considered a semantic error. Other semantic errors include cases where the pronunciation is not clearly distinguished and correct use requires knowing how the word is used grammatically. For example, even a college student can err by confusing *effect* versus *affect* in written contexts.

Mental Graphemic Representation Errors

In general, a misspelling can be categorized as an MGR error if the spelling is plausible and does not violate any orthographic pattern rules. For example, an MGR misspelling could be phonetically correct (e.g., *kot* for *cot*) and/or include an incorrect application of an orthographic pattern (e.g., *GOTE* for *goat*). Essentially, the error could be inferred as being due to an incorrect or incomplete MGR. These errors are common for the ambiguous parts of a word, such as vowels, where several letters or letter combinations are plausible. For example, the unstressed schwa is word-specific and can be spelled with any vowel letter, and doubled letters in words do not occur consistently. So, for a word like *tarragon*, likely MGR misspellings include *TARIGON*, *TAREGON*, and *TARUGAN*, where the ambiguous phoneme-grapheme relationships are in error. Misspellings can be consistently spelled the same way, which indicates that the MGR is completely but incorrectly formed or that the misspelling may be inconsistently spelled, which indicates there may be an unclear part or parts of the word where the speller is uncertain of which letter to write for that portion of the word.

Taking It All Apart: Systematic Analysis

When analyzing spellings for the aforementioned types of errors, it helps to go about the analysis in a systematic and ordered manner. Box 14.1 shows a decision tree that

Box 14.1. ***Linguistic Analysis of Spellings***

Step 1: Phonological Analysis
Are all sounds accounted for?

If YES, go to Step 2 ← → If NO, Phonological Awareness Error

Step 2: Orthographic Analysis
Within a base word:
Is a correct letter/letter sequence used to represent a sound?
OR
Is a correct spelling pattern being applied?

If YES, go to Step 3 ← → If NO, Orthographic Pattern Knowledge Error

Step 3: Morphological Analysis
Is an affix present, spelled correctly, or its addition to the base word correctly modified?
OR
Does the derived form appear to use the knowledge of the base word or another derived form in its spelling?

If YES, go to Step 4 ← → If NO, Morphological Awareness Error

Step 4: Semantic Analysis
Is the word spelled incorrectly because it is a homophone or a similar-sounding word with a different meaning and spelling?

If YES, Semantic Error ← → If NO, go to STEP 5

Step 5: Mental Graphemic Representation
Is the word spelled phonetically correct?
AND/OR
Does it follow conventional or plausible orthographic rules?

→ If YES, MGR error

Note: A misspelled word may involve more than one type of error.

Note: From *SPELL-2: Spelling Performance Evaluation for Language and Literacy, 2nd ed.*, by J. Masterson, K. Apel, and J. Wasowicz [Computer software]. Evanston, IL: Learning by Design. Copyright by Learning by Design. Adapted with permission.

delineates the systematic self-questioning process needed for a prescriptive analysis (Apel, Masterson, & Niessen, 2004; Masterson, Apel, & Wasowicz, 2006; Masterson & Apel, 2010). This analysis involves noting: (a) the number of sounds represented (phonological awareness), (b) the accuracy of letter representations (orthographic knowledge), (c) the meaning-based components (morphological, semantic knowledge), and finally (d) the plausibility of a spelling (MGR). It is only necessary to continue through the self-questioning process after the error is categorized. Some misspellings may be due to several types of linguistic errors; for these, the analysis should not end until all errors within the spelling have been accounted for. For example, in the misspelling *TRAND* for the word *trained*, both an orthographic pattern knowledge spelling error (i.e., the long vowel *a* is not accurately represented with two vowels) and a morphological awareness spelling error (i.e., the past tense *-ed* is not accurately spelled) exist.

Box 14.2. ***Prescriptive Spelling Analysis Practice Items***

Misspelling	Intended Word	Linguistic Error
pup	pump	
rid	ride	
bare	bear	
peachs	peaches	
cuting	cutting	
carful	careful	
wat	what	
noat	note	
chal	trail	
mugishun	magician	

Box 14.3. ***Prescriptive Spelling Analysis With Answers***

Misspelling	Intended Word	Linguistic Error
pup	pump	PA
rid	ride	OP
bare	bear	SK
peachs	peaches	MA
cuting	cutting	MA
carful	careful	MA (if base word *care* spelled correctly) OP (if base word *care* misspelled *car*)
wat	what	MGR
noat	note	MGR
chal	trail	PA, OP
mugishun	magician	MA (if base word *magic* spelled correctly and suffix -*cian* misspelled) OP (if base word *magic* mispelled *mugis*)

Note: PA = phonological awareness; OP = orthographic pattern knowledge; MA = morphological awareness; SK = semantic knowledge; MGR = mental graphemic representation.

A list of practice words is presented in Box 14.2, followed by the answers in Box 14.3. Before examining Box 14.3, practice analyzing spellings using the decision tree before checking your answers. Box 14.4 presents a written sample from a 12-year-old student, and Box 14.5 shows the subsequent error analysis. It should be noted that, just as in other types of language assessment, determination of the source of errors is not always clear and that clinician judgment may be required. The goal is to identify patterns to be further assessed or better understood during the course of treatment.

Follow-up Assessment

A spelling error analysis that reveals deficits in phonological awareness, orthographic pattern knowledge, and/or morphological awareness may lead to a follow-up assessment. For example, spelling errors due to phonological awareness may warrant further assessment using a standardized measure such as the Elision or Nonword Segmentation subtest from the *Comprehensive Test of Phonological Processing–Second Edition* (Wagner, Torgeson, Rashotte, & Pearson, 2013). If a student's errors are in the area of

Box 14.4. ***Writing Sample for Spelling Error Analysis***

The[1] is an asay[2] abot[3] wether[4] or
not Kids should where[5] anything
they want in school. I don't think
you should where[6] just anything to
School. Here are some resones[7] why.
The load[8] colirs[9] miht[10] desrupd[11] the
class of stodents[12] Hoks in cloths[13]
miht[14] be disrespectfil[15] It miht[16]
Create compotishun[17] between girls
Who like to loke[18] rilly[19] good.
The Kides[20] miht[21] have bad gag[22]
Stuff on there[23] shirts. These
are the resons[24] why I think
you should not where[25] any thing.

Note: This is a written sample from a 10-year-old student in response to the directions to write a persuasive essay for "Why children should or should not just wear anything to school."

orthographic pattern knowledge, depending on how thorough the initial sampling of spelling rules was in the spelling inventory, the clinician may follow up with a more focused dictated spelling test that directly probes a grouping of grade-level spelling rules found in error.

If a pattern of spelling errors resulting from weak morphological awareness were found, the clinician needs to determine whether follow-up testing is needed. One standardized measure of morphology that may have already been administered in the spoken language assessment battery is the Morphological Completion subtest from the *Test of Language Development Primary–Fourth Edition* (Newcomer & Hammill, 2008), which samples inflectional morphology and early developing derivational morphology (e.g., comparatives such as *big* to *bigger*). If the clinician has not administered a standardized morphology measure in spoken language testing or would like to further investigate whether the student has difficulty with inflectional or derivational morphology in transparent versus opaque circumstances, then nonstandard spoken measures may be appropriate. The clinician may use measures such as a production morphological awareness task developed by researchers (Carlisle, 1988, 2000) to probe. In this type of task, the student is provided with a base word (e.g., farm) and then asked to complete

Box 14.5. ***Linguistic Spelling Analysis of Writing Sample***

Error	Misspelling	Word	Linguistic Error
1	the	this	PA (or a grammatical error in text)
2	asay	essay	OP (short *e* spelling); MGR (*s* for *ss*)
3	abot	about	OP (dipthong *ou* spelling)
4	wether	whether	MGR
5, 6, 25	where	wear	SK
7	resones	reasons	OP (if base word spelled *resone*, then schwa spelling error MA (if base word spelled *reson*, then error of adding plural)
8	load	loud	PA
9	colirs	colors	MGR
10, 14, 16, 21	miht	might	OP (long *igh* spelling)
11	disrupd	disrupt	OP (*t* spelling)
12	stodents	students	OP (long *u* vowel spelling)
13	cloths	clothes	OP (long *o* spelling
15	disrespectfil	disrespectful	MA (affix spelling of *ful*)
17	compotis-hun	competition	MA (if base word spelled *compete* and *-tion* suffix spelled)
18	loke	look	OP (*oo* spelling)
19	rilly	really	MGR (may argue MA error because form of word *real*)
20	kides	kids	OP (short *i* spelling)
22	gag	gang	OP (*-ng* cluster spelling)
23	there	their	SK
24	resons	reasons	OP (long *e* spelling)

Note: PA = phonological awareness; OP = orthographic pattern knowledge; MA = morphological awareness; SK = semantic knowledge; MGR = mental graphemic representation.

the sentence using that base word (My uncle is a ______. *farmer*). Word pairs with transparent (e.g., *jump*: "As he crossed the street, Paul ______." *jumped*) and opaque relationships (e.g., *steal*: "Last week, the painting was ______." *stolen*) can then be systematically assessed. Some published measures of morphological awareness assessment can be found in the appendixes of research articles such as Apel and Masterson (2001), Carlisle (1988), and Wolter et al. (2009). If the combination of spoken language testing and written spelling errors reveals a weakness in morphological awareness, then there is ample evidence for targeting morphological awareness in treatment and justification for the importance of spoken language intervention applied to written language standards of spelling in the curriculum.

Multilinguistic Spelling Intervention

Most spelling errors (excluding keyboarding errors) reflect some kind of linguistic issue. Once the aforementioned prescriptive spelling analysis has been completed and the linguistic sources of errors identified, then linguistically focused spelling instruction can be conducted. Explicit, systematic procedures that involve repeated opportunities for students to identify and apply linguistic sources to the spelling of words are called word study instruction.

Research evidence indicates that word study instruction is effective in improving spelling and word reading in children with and without language or literacy impairments (Apel & Masterson, 2001; Berninger, Abbott, Nagy, & Carlisle, 2010; Kelman & Apel, 2004; Masterson & Apel, 2010; Masterson & Crede, 1999; Vadasy et al., 2006; Wolter et al., 2009). For example, phonemic segmenting activities linked to orthographic patterns were found to increase the spelling and reading performance of children with language impairments between 10 and 13 years of age (Apel & Masterson, 2001; Kelman & Apel, 2004; Masterson & Crede, 1999). The addition of a morphological awareness linguistic component to phonological and orthographic pattern-based word study instruction also has been found to facilitate spelling, reading, and vocabulary success (Berninger et al., 2003; Bowers, Kirby, & Deacon, et al., 2010; Nunes, Bryant, & Olsson, 2003). Specific spelling-based word study activities in the areas of phonemic awareness, orthographic pattern knowledge, and morphological awareness can be found in spelling programs such as those by Bear et al. (2004) or Wasowicz, Apel, Masterson, and Whitney (2004).

One component of word study instruction that is important for children with language impairment is the self-discovery component of spelling. Typically children with language impairment are not successful in a classroom with traditional methods of spelling instruction, which often includes the formal teaching of a spelling rule followed by memorization of a spelling list for a test that may or may not follow the spelling rule lesson. A self-discovery model requires students to self-question and to actively seek patterns that may result in possible internalization of spelling rules. A word sort is often the mode of delivery for presenting patterns. In this type of activity, children are presented with note cards that exemplify targeted patterns (e.g., short-vowel *a* words, as in *bat* and *can*, and long-vowel *a* words, as in *bate* and *cane*) and asked to self-discover a pattern by lining words up according to a spelling rule. In addition, self-problem solving may result in noting exceptions to the rule, which may be as important as being able to follow the spelling rule. For example, one commonly taught rule says that when two vowels are paired in the middle of a word, the first one has a long sound and the second one is silent, but this is less than half of the time (Johnston, 2001). However, when students are encouraged to sort words when the pattern is not followed (e.g., *oy*, *oi*, and *au* patterns never follow the rule), they may be able to problem-solve and self-identify a new pattern to apply when the traditional rule is not applicable. By simply teaching the spelling rules without problem solving, these exceptions would be missed.

Therefore, it appears that multilinguistic spelling-based word study instruction fo cused on strengthening students' understanding of the ties among sound, meaning, and print is effective in facilitating spelling and word reading for children with language impairments (cf. Wolter & Squires, 2014). In the following sections, a summary of evidence-based spelling practices and clinical applications will be provided for each linguistic area.

Phonological Awareness

Instruction in the awareness of phonemes has been found to be consistently and significantly related to improved spelling and reading (Ehri et al., 2001). Evidence suggests that a focus at the phoneme level rather than mixing phonemes with supra-phonemic units such as syllables produces stronger effects (Ukrainetz, 2008). Effect sizes were found to be almost twice as great in both spelling and reading for instruction that included linking phonemes to letters than for phoneme-only instruction (Ehri et al., 2001). In addition, researchers have found that explicit and systematic phonemic instruction was found to be effective (Amtmann, Abbott, & Berninger, 2008; Boyer & Ehri, 2011; Ferguson, Currie, Paul, & Topping, 2011; Roberts & Meiring, 2006; Weiser & Mathes, 2011). When compared to control groups, children with and without literacy deficits who received explicit phonemic instruction combined with instruction in phoneme-grapheme correspondence performed significantly better, with robust effect sizes in spelling and reading outcomes (Weiser & Mathes, 2011).

Classroom teachers now regularly address phonemic awareness as part of reading and spelling instruction (Ukrainetz, 2009a; Ukrainetz, Ross, & Harm, 2009). However, students with language impairments will benefit from additional attention to phonemic awareness, especially if it is linked to spelling. Although a preschool focus on rhyming can be helpful in getting young children to attend to the sounds of words, awareness of individual phonemes should be the focus in kindergarten and beyond. This is due to the fact that in English and other alphabetic writing systems, phonemes are what matter. Indeed, the functional context of writing, with its necessity of isolating, segmenting, and blending phonemes to spell words, is ideal for teaching phonemic awareness. Phonemic awareness intervention may include skills such as phoneme isolation (e.g., Say and write the first sound in *bat*), phoneme blending (e.g., Combine /b/, /ae/, /t/ to spell *bat*.), phoneme segmentation (e.g., Segment *bat* to /b/, /ae/, /t/. Now write each sound.), and phoneme deletion (e.g., Spell *bat* without /b/.). In fact, with the exception of the deletion task, all other skills occur naturally as a child is guided in spelling words (e.g., What is

Box 14.6. ***Phonological and Morphological Awareness Spelling Activity***

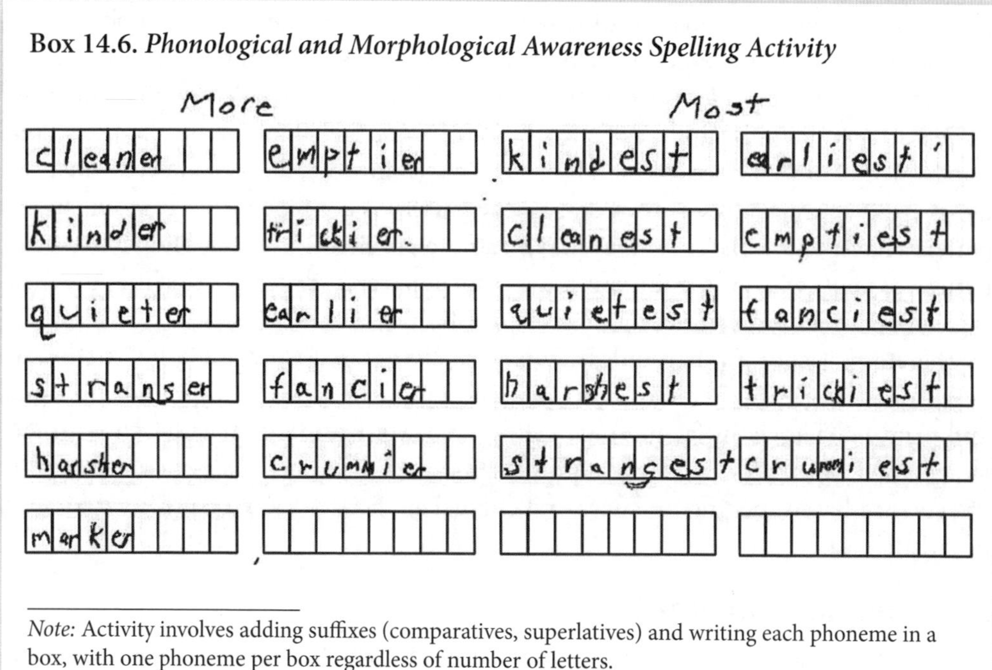

Note: Activity involves adding suffixes (comparatives, superlatives) and writing each phoneme in a box, with one phoneme per box regardless of number of letters.

the first sound in *dog*? Let's say the sounds in *dog*: /d/-/aw/-/g/. Good, spell that. Now, say the sounds you have spelled: /d/-/aw/-/g/. What word do those sounds say?). (See Ukrainetz, 2006, and Chapter 12.)

Phonemic awareness instruction does not require any specialized materials or activities. Common treatment activities include matching pictures by first sound and segmenting children's names. Any phonemic awareness activity can be adapted to spelling intervention by simply including a writing component where the student not only isolates or segments sounds but also writes the corresponding letter or letters. A sample of how phonemic awareness segmenting was integrated into a spelling activity is provided in Box 14.6. The phonemic segmenting component of the activity required the student to segment and identify each sound in a word; the spelling component involved identifying the letter and writing it in its own box to help match the sounds to the letters in the word. The complexities of English orthography, which is addressed next, can be introduced in this activity by putting digraphs into a single box (e.g., *TH-E*).

Orthographic Pattern Knowledge

Research supports orthographic pattern instruction in which students conduct the previously described word sorts to self-discover spelling rules, or orthographic patterns. This method has been found to improve spelling and reading in school-age children with and without language and/or literacy impairments (Abbott, 2001; Apel & Masterson, 2001; Berninger et al., 2002; Berninger, et al., 2008; Graham & Harris, 2005; Kelman & Apel, 2004; Masterson & Crede, 1999; White, 2005; Williams & Hufnagel, 2005; Williams & Lundstrom, 2007; Williams & Phillips-Birdsong, 2006). For example, in two randomized controlled trials, third-grade children with low writing scores (Berninger et al., 2002) and second-grade children with low spelling scores (Graham & Harris, 2005) were explicitly taught phoneme-orthographic correspondences (e.g., different ways to spell /k/, /j/, /z/) and orthographic rules (e.g., short- versus long-vowel rules) through word sort activities. In both studies, students performed significantly better on spelling and reading measures than a control group who did not receive orthographic pattern knowledge word study spelling instruction.

Williams and colleagues (2006, 2007) conducted research that extended orthographic pattern knowledge instruction and documented the benefit of the additional contextualized intervention component of writing. Children as young as first grade initially learned orthographic spelling rules with word sort activity instruction, which was followed by lessons on how to integrate newly learned spellings into their writing composition lessons. The first-grade children who received additional explicit spelling instruction in the context of writing applied their spelling knowledge in their writing activities.

A spelling word sort activity focused on orthographic pattern knowledge might include providing students with note cards bearing spellings of words containing the final phoneme /k/. Students solve the problem of sorting these words into the categories of /k/ spelled with *-ck* when following the short vowel (e.g., *lick*, *rack*, *clock*) and /k/ spelled with *-k* following the long vowel (*like*, *rake*, *cloak*). Through the use of minimal pairs, this activity helps students to meaningfully note the difference in pronunciations of words dictated by their spelling with one vowel (short-vowel sound) versus two vowels (long-vowel sound).

Following the word sort, students should have opportunities to write or spell these words using the newly learned orthographic spelling rule. This may be at the word level by creatively integrating spelling into a game format. One commonly used commercial spelling program that utilizes this word study approach and includes follow-up game ideas is *Words Their Way* (Bear et al., 2004). For example, a *Jeopardy* game could be played with clue categories that vary according to a spelling rule (*-k*, *-ck*) and then students must write the word in order to answer the clue (*The tool used to clean up leaves. What is RAKE?*). The game component provides a motivating context that requires students to use their newly learned knowledge. (See Box 14.7 for an orthographic pattern knowledge activity.) Instruction then moves beyond word-level games to functional writing activities that match the requirements of the school curriculum. For example, the student would be given a list of words that follow the spelling rule learned in the prior spelling activities and asked to incorporate those words, spelled correctly, into a written assignment.

Mental Graphemic Representations

For any speller, the application of MGRs as a strategy becomes increasingly important when the other linguistically based strategies (i.e., phonological awareness, orthographic pattern knowledge, morphological awareness, semantics) do not facilitate the accurate spelling of a word. For example, for the word *love*, the silent *-e* presents a predicament for a child applying a phonological or sounding-out strategy because the *o* is not pronounced consistent with an orthographic pattern of a long *-o*. In this case, the speller is required to use memory or the MGR of the word. Instruction might involve improving those MGRs or helping the student to know when to use an MGR strategy.

Box 14.7. ***Long-o Versus Short-o Spelling Game***

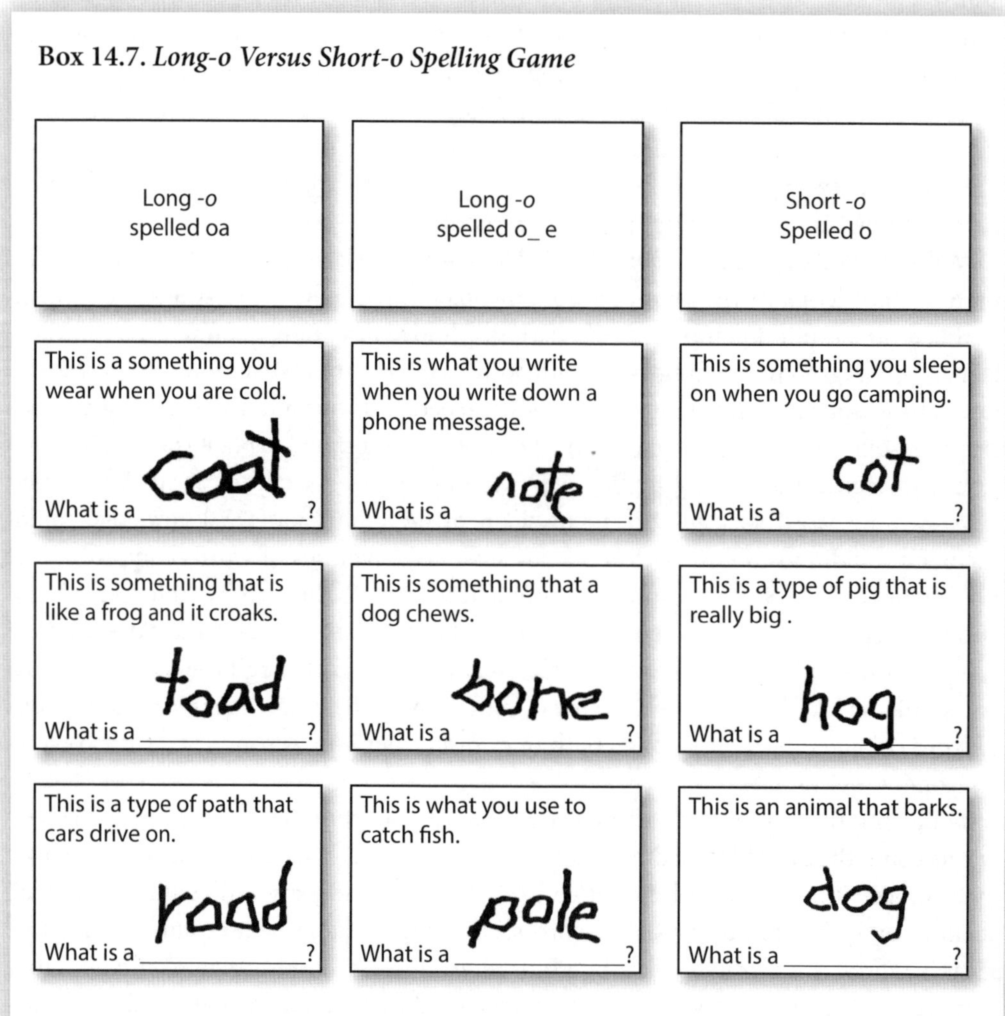

Long -o
spelled oa
Long -o
spelled o_ e
Short -o
Spelled o
This is a something you wear when you are cold.
What is a coat?
This is what you write when you write down a phone message.
What is a note?
This is something you sleep on when you go camping.
What is a cot?
This is something that is like a frog and it croaks.
What is a toad?
This is something that a dog chews.
What is a bone?
This is a type of pig that is really big .
What is a hog?
This is a type of path that cars drive on.
What is a road?
This is what you use to catch fish.
What is a pole?
This is an animal that barks.
What is a dog?

One common component of activities associated with improving MGRs is that of letter and word visualization. Berninger et al. (2011) found that visualization activities, such as backward spelling, improve MGRs (Berninger et al., 2011; Wasowicz et al., 2004). In this activity, the student looks at the printed word, looks away and visualizes the word, then says each letter, starting from the end of the word, and then repeats this routine until the MGR is transformed from a fuzzy to a sharp, detailed image. (Try it and you will see it requires a very solid MGR and a good working memory.) A variation studied by Berninger et al. (2011) is a multistep process for which students: (a) first named the letter of a word, (b) then closed their eyes and pictured the word, (c) then answered questions about the position of certain letters within the word while visualizing the word, and (d) finally opened their eyes to check their MGR against the written word.

Similarly, the *Cover-Copy-Compare* method (Skinner, McLaughlin, & Logan, 1997) was found to improve MGRs (Cates et al., 2007; Erion, Davenport, Rodax, Scholl, & Hardy, 2009). This method refers to a sequential process with these steps: (a) *looking* at a target word, (b) *covering* the word with a note card, and (c) then *copying* the word from memory. After uncovering the word, students then compare the written word to the target word. If discrepancies between the student's spelling and the target word are found, the word is then copied three more times with the correct spelling present.

While the previously described activities help strengthen MGRs, the following analogy method focuses on using an MGR strategy to identify and spell unknown words. The analogy method (Gaskins, Ehri, Cress, O'Hara, & Donnelly, 1996–1997) utilizes the MGRs of known parts of words to facilitate the accurate spellings of similarly spelled words. Unlike word-specific methods, this procedure applies MGRs to groups of words related by rime units (the syllable following the initial phoneme or phoneme cluster). The student is taught to focus on the rime unit of the MGR of a known word (e.g., *L-IGHT*) in order to spell the rime unit part of a word that may not be known (e.g., *FL-IGHT*). This procedure significantly improves spelling and reading in children with and without literacy deficits (Ehri, Satlow, & Gaskins, 2009; Savage, Deault, Daki, Aouad, 2011), although it is more effective when combined with other linguistic-based instruction (phonemic awareness, orthographic pattern knowledge, morphological awareness).

An example of MGR instruction that employs several of these procedures is adapted from *SPELL-Links* (Wasowicz et al., 2004). This procedure begins with having a student write the word in the air, starting with the first letter and progressing to the final letter. The student then "takes a picture of the word." Next, while still visualizing that word, the student spells it backward, starting with the last letter and progressing to the first. The backward spelling component requires the student to focus on every letter within the word, instantiating a clear MGR. MGRs might be targeted for words with common rime units and then, in accordance with the analogy method, the rime unit of one word (e.g., *LOUD*) could be used to consider how to spell unknown words with similar rime units (e.g., *C-LOUD*).

Morphological Awareness Instruction

Recent systematic reviews of morphologically based instruction have revealed morphological awareness to be effective in improving spelling and reading outcomes for students from kindergarten through ninth grade who have a range of abilities (Bowers, Kirby, & Deacon, 2010; Carlisle, 2010; Goodwin & Ahn, 2010; Reed, 2008). Most notably, for children with language impairment or literacy deficits, morphological awareness instruction was found to be particularly beneficial (Bowers et al., 2010; Casalis, Colé, & Sopo, 2004; Goodwin & Ahn, 2010; Wolter, 2005; Wolter & Dilworth, 2014). These studies revealed that effective morphological instruction included not only a content focus but also the when and how to use morphology as a strategy in spelling. These practices addressed the meaning of the word as well as the manipulation of morphemes (i.e., segmenting, blending, and classifying words by their morphological components). As with orthographic pattern knowledge instruction, word study programs, which included self-discovery of patterns (in this case morphological patterns) through word sort activities, were found to be beneficial. An added benefit or outcome from morphological awareness instruction was improvement in vocabulary. That is, instruction that focused on the meaning in morphological units was found to increase students' awareness of taught vocabulary (Templeton, 2004). This instruction resulted in knowledge transfer to learning new vocabulary words not directly taught (Bowers & Kirby, 2010; Wolter & Green, 2013).

Based on this research, morphological awareness intervention should provide opportunities for students to actively reflect on and manipulate meaning through morphological analysis. The goal is to heighten students' awareness of inflectional and derivational morphology by linking meaning between words, identifying relationships, targeting correct reading and spelling of derivations, and/or identifying commonalities among base words and derived forms. Activities include word sorts (e.g., sorting words by prefixes or suffixes), word building (e.g., combining prefixes, base words, and/or suffixes

Box 14.8. *Morphological Awareness "Friends and Family" Sample Word Sort*

to build and spell new words), and instruction on word origins (e.g., meaning of Latin/ Greek roots).

An example of a morphological awareness word sort activity for inflectional morphology might focus on the past-tense *-ed*. Using word lists from *Words Their Way* (Bear et al., 2004) or *SPELL-Links* (Wasowicz et al., 2004), a past-tense *-ed* activity might include comparing or sorting words with the morphological pattern as well as those with a similar phonological pattern (i.e., /d/ in *fanned* versus /d/ in *sand*, /t/ in *messed* versus /t/ in *rest*). This activity demonstrates that, despite different pronunciations, when a meaningful inflectional morpheme is included (past tense), the spelling remains consistent (*-ed*). This type of instruction not only focuses the student on morphological awareness or the meaning component but also simultaneously increases the students' awareness of phonology and orthographic patterns. (See Boxes 14.6 and 14.8 for sample morphological awareness activities.)

The relations between base words and derivational morphology can be made explicit though word sort activities that require students to identify transparent versus opaque relationships. One way to do this is to create a word sort through an analogy of family and friends. The SLP explains that word derivatives, like *family* members, can look and sound similar and be related (transparent relationship: *swim-swimming*) or look and sound dissimilar but still be related (opaque relationship: *divide-division*). Similarly, like *friends*, words can look and sound similar but not be related (nonrelated foils: *luck-cluck*). Thus, words can be related in meaning but look similar or different from each other. Picture cards showing family members or friends, or written cards with the relationships depicted are used as category markers to help students sort the word pairs written on note cards in the corresponding categories. Box 14.8 shows what this word sort might look like. In order to link this exercise to spelling, students write these word pairs in three columns on a worksheet to represent these three categories. This exercise helps students begin to use base-word knowledge to write larger derived words, an important skill given that, as of third grade, 60% of all newly learned words are morphological transparent or opaque derivatives (Anglin, 1993).

Putting It Together: Effective Spelling Intervention

Multilinguistic, Strategic, and Collaborative

As indicated in the respective reviews of the individual linguistic areas, intervention that focuses on multiple linguistic areas in one integrated intervention plan is an effective way of teaching both spelling and language skills. Indeed, in a systematic review of multilinguistic spelling instruction, Wolter (2009) found support for the effectiveness of combining linguistic areas in spelling instruction to improve reading and spelling for children with and without language impairments. In one noteworthy study, Berninger et al. (2003) found that instruction incorporating all linguistic components is beneficial for fourth- through sixth-grade children diagnosed with dyslexia. Berninger et al. compared a group of students who received spelling instruction that focused on morphological awareness in addition to orthographic pattern knowledge and phonological awareness to a comparison group who received the same instruction but without the morphological component. Students in both groups improved in spelling, but those who received the additional morphological awareness component performed significantly better on spelling and reading. Other studies have shown improved reading and spelling as a result of combined phonological, orthographic pattern, and morphological awareness instruction for children with literacy deficits (Vadasy et al., 2006; Wolter, 2005) and language impairments (Apel & Masterson, 2001; Kirk & Gillon, 2009).

This multilinguistic intervention is aimed at improving a student's size and clarity of MGRs, and use of each linguistic skill for spelling. In addition, a necessary component of multilinguistic instruction is teaching when and how to apply each phonological, orthographic, and morphological strategy in communicative activities where the words needed are largely uncontrolled. Self-regulated strategic use of these skills is necessary to become more independent and better spellers and readers in academic contexts. There are several published case studies describing multilinguistic intervention that provide specific examples and details regarding how an SLP might proceed (Apel & Masterson, 2001; Kelman & Apel, 2004; Masterson & Apel, 2010; Masterson & Crede, 1999; Wolter & Dilworth, 2014; Wolter & Green, 2013). In these studies, the general approach is to have the SLP model "think-alouds" that demonstrate how to approach spelling a difficult word and then have the student practice those strategies aloud in communicative writing activities. The SLP scaffolds the student's selection and use of strategies, along with how to check for accuracy of the resultant spelling and how to modify the strategy choice if the spelling is incorrect. A checklist of self-questions related to phonological awareness, orthographic pattern knowledge, and morphological awareness can be used for model and practice in problem solving the spelling of a novel word.

Multilinguistic instruction provides a flexible means for coordinating team intervention based on individual expertise and preference for varying language and literacy areas. For example, the SLP may lead intervention in the area of morphological awareness to address both vocabulary and spelling goals. In parallel, the special educator may focus on orthographic knowledge instruction, and the literacy coach may facilitate spelling-based phonological awareness instruction. As such, literacy success for a student with language impairments is manifested through a unified multidisciplinary team effort.

RISE

In addition to the linguistic considerations discussed throughout this chapter, there are several general principles or elements that should be included in any word study spelling intervention, regardless of the linguistic skill or skills targeted (Box 14.9). Consistent with Ukrainetz's RISE model (see Chapter 2), spelling researchers have consistently found the components of **R**epeated opportunities, **I**ntensity, **S**ystematic support, and **E**xplicit instruction to be critical features of effective spelling instruction (Amtmann, Abbott, & Berninger, 2008; Berninger et al., 2008; Ehri, 2000; Graham & Harris, 2005; Schlagal, 2007; Wanzek et al., 2006).

Box 14.9. *RISE and SPELL for Effective Spelling Intervention*

Repeated opportunities	**S**elf-discovery
Intensity of service delivery	**P**roblem solving
Systematic support	**E**mployment of strategies
Explicit instruction	**L**inks to . . .
	Literacy

Repeated Opportunities

The first element of effective instruction is repeated opportunities. Repetition is especially important in spelling instruction in order to establish clear MGRs (Ehri, 1997; 2000). Indeed, spelling outcomes of students with literacy deficits are significantly improved when multiple practice spelling opportunities are provided (Fulk & Stormont-Spurgin, 1995; McNaughton, Hughes, & Clark, 1994; Wanzek et al., 2006).

Of course, repetition is only valuable if the correct spelling is practiced. In fact, if incorrect spellings are repeatedly reproduced, incorrect MGRs may be established in as few as three exposures (Katz & Frost, 2001). Thus, in addition to practice, immediate feedback regarding accuracy of a spelling is important. Students who were provided immediate, corrective feedback and additional practice after spelling verbally presented words scored higher on spelling measures than students who practiced writing words presented on a sheet and receiving feedback upon completion (Grskovic & Belfiore, 1996).

This need for avoiding exposure to incorrectly spelled words can be a conundrum when students are encouraged to write communicatively. They need to be able to "use their best guesses" for spelling in early drafts in order to maintain their focus on idea generation and sentence composition. One way to help students avoid losing their focus on content is to allow spelling errors in the drafts, but then require them to be their own editors and, with help from an educator, peer, or spell-check software, go back to correct their misspellings—just like real authors do. Then, to correct their faulty or fuzzy MGRs, either during the editing or after the editing is done, students should write the corrected word about five times in isolation and in phrases. The latter option will reveal whether this MGR-correction drill is effective by whether the student can then catch any subsequent appearances of their error later in the paper. If the drill is begun after the editing is complete, then subsequent assignments will need to be checked to determine if the correct MGR has been maintained.

A final note is that, for the MGR-correction exercise to be successful, it is important that the students know the purpose of the exercise. They need to view it as part of the process of learning to spell difficult words, not as a punishment for attempting those words. Otherwise, students may avoid words they are not sure they can spell rather than become better spellers by pushing their limits.

Intensity of Service Delivery

The recommended duration of spelling instruction is 60–75 minutes a week (Graham et al., 2008). In a national survey of spelling practices, however, Graham et al. (2008) reported that approximately 45% of teachers spend considerably less than this on spelling instruction. Just as in other areas of language research (Ukrainetz, 2009b; Warren, Fey, & Yoder, 2007), optimal session length and frequency for children with language impairments are not yet known. When considering patterns of intensity in spelling research, however, it appears that significant spelling and reading outcomes may result from spelling instruction across a wide variety of service delivery models with a wide range of intensities or dosages.

Effective literacy outcomes from linguistically based word study spelling instruction have been achieved through individual therapy conducted for 60 minutes per week for 11 weeks (Kelman & Apel, 2004) and for 60 minutes per day for 2 weeks (Wolter & Dilworth, 2014; Wolter & Green, 2013). Small group instruction was found to be effective in intensive daily service delivery models where instruction was provided in a summer camp for 2 hours per day for 2 weeks (Wolter, 2005). Small group instruction was also found to be effective in dosages ranging from 30 minutes once a week for 8 weeks (Berninger et al., 1999) to 20 minutes triweekly over 16 weeks (Graham & Harris, 2005). Thus, it appears that providing focused spelling instruction in individual or small group settings for a total intensity of 8–20 hours in a variety of schedules can result in positive reading and spelling outcomes for students with language impairments.

Systematic Support

When students are provided with instruction that is systematically introduced in a simple, structured context (e.g., word sorts) with specific targets (e.g., orthographic spelling rule) and interactive scaffolds from the clinician (modeling, redirections), learning is facilitated. The treatment studies reviewed in each of the linguistic instruction sections in this chapter all employed structural and interactive learning supports. The SLP may provide direct instruction or may guide teachers in supporting a particular student in the classroom. Indeed, the classroom teacher may welcome SLP consultation or collaboration: A recent survey of classroom teachers found that 42% of teachers reported making few or no adaptations for weaker spellers (Graham et al., 2008).

Systematic learning support includes selecting and structuring activities to keep students interested, motivated to learn, and actively involved (deGraaff, Bosman, Hasselman, & Verhoeven, 2009). Students need to want to spell correctly and to be motivated to learn to spell better. In a study of spelling and writing instruction with fourth, sixth, seventh and ninth graders with dyslexia, Berninger et al. (2008) found that linguistically based spelling instruction that was integrated into activities described as "hands-on, highly engaging, science problem solving" (p. 116) significantly improved reading, spelling, note taking, and written composition skills. Not only may this learning be motivating and improve students' internal self-monitoring, but from a neurological perspective, Berninger et al. hypothesized that the common brain region activated for activities that require manipulation by hand may improve the neural networks related to phonological tasks, which are considered to be weak in children with dyslexia. Thus, hands-on activities that require active manipulation and entertaining elements (e.g., competitive word sorts, detective themes) or activities that have personal appeal (e.g., spelling dinosaur words) will likely improve student application of learned words in assignments and provide students with an important component to spelling success.

Explicit Instruction

Explicit or direct teaching of spelling is recommended to improve spelling for children of all abilities (Amtmann et al., 2010; Kohnen, Nickels, & Coltheart, 2010), and may be even more important for those children with language impairments who have particular difficulty implicitly learning and applying linguistic strategies. Borrowing from Graham et al.'s (2008) contrastive wording, explicit instruction is essentially an approach in which "spelling-is-*taught*" as opposed to an approach in which "spelling-is-*caught*" (p. 800). That is, in a spelling-is-caught approach, it is expected that children will pick up spelling through passive exposure to print. In this approach, the focus may be on assessing, rather than instructing, and the only attention to spelling may be the memorization that students do at home for the weekly spelling tests. Conversely, an explicit spelling-is-taught approach means that spelling instruction is directly and explicitly provided. Explicit linguistically based instruction, with spelling practice and active reflection on spelling patterns, has been found to be effective in improving literacy success (Amtmann et al., 2008; Kohnen et al., 2010; Schlagel, 2007).

SPELL

Finally, in addition to RISE, four other elements have been linked to effective spelling instruction practices. Referred to as ***SPELL***, these are the need for **S**elf-discovery, **P**roblem solving, **E**mployment of strategies, and contextualized **L**inks to **L**iteracy (Berninger & O'Malley May, 2011; Darch, Eaves, Crowe, Simmons, & Conniff, 2006; Masterson & Apel, 2010; Santa & Hoien, 1999). While these SPELL elements have been mentioned in the previous sections focused on the specific linguistic interventions, they warrant explicit consideration as part of an overall model for effective word study spelling instruction.

Self-Discovery and Problem Solving

A review of the literature on spelling reveals that for many effective, linguistically based, word-study spelling methods, an element of student-facilitated problem solving or self-discovery was included in the instruction (Apel & Masterson, 2001; Bowers et al., 2010; Goodwin, Lipsky, & Ahn, 2012; Wolter, 2009). Bowers et al. noted that the theme of student "detectives" was repeatedly used in the context of effective linguistically based literacy instruction. This problem-solving approach is valuable because, in addition to being a motivating activity, it helps the many children who have deficits in executive functioning as well as language or literacy impairments (Berninger & O'Malley May, 2011). These children are likely to benefit from instruction that requires them to use their executive functioning to problem-solve.

Employment of Strategies

It is important to help facilitate children's knowledge of when and how to apply their newly learned spelling strategies as much as it is to teach the strategies themselves (Graham, 1999; Masterson & Apel, 2010). This is especially important for students with language impairment who may struggle with spelling because they are less effective in systematically applying spelling patterns or because they employ ineffective strategies for spelling words (Darch et al., 2006). Indeed, Darch and colleagues discovered that students who used systematic study and word practice procedures experienced moderate to large effect sizes in spelling outcomes as opposed to those taught in a nonstrategic manner, who did not. Thus, systematic strategy instruction includes introducing strategies in a model that includes teaching students when and how to use this knowledge.

Link to Literacy

It is as important for students with language impairment to have practice learning to spell in the context of writing as it is to have structured spelling exercises. This means not only recognizing spellings in activities like word sorts but also spelling the words by pen or keyboard and applying spelling in the context of compositional writing (Berninger et al., 2008; Graham & Harris, 2005; Kohnen et al., 2010; Santa & Hoien, 1999; Williams & Lundstrom, 2007; Williams & Phillips-Birdsong, 2006). Only recognizing spellings in word sort activities may not be enough to establish clear MGRs for accurate spelling. For example, Santa and Hoien (1999) specifically compared writing versus identification of spelling in instruction, and found that those who were taught word study *and* spelling production in the written mode performed significantly higher on a dictated spelling assessment than those who simply read spellings. Thus, it appears that just conducting activities that focus on spelling is not enough. Instead, a student must have the opportunity to spell words out and ideally also will have opportunities to use these words in authentic writing contexts, such as compositional writing.

Conclusion

In summary, spelling is a linguistically complex skill that requires the processing of phonological, orthographic, morphological, and semantic knowledge sources. Given the linguistic nature of spelling, the SLP can play an important role in the spelling assessment and intervention process. A prescriptive spelling assessment that includes thoughtful linguistic analysis of misspellings provides the SLP with a valuable tool that can be used to identify the source of a literacy deficit. Moreover, this type of analysis will help to direct and inform the linguistically based spelling intervention, which may focus on one or multiple linguistic skills. Multiple linguistic spelling intervention, which focuses systematically on when and how to use linguistic strategies in a problem-solving format in the context of writing, can improve spelling and provide additional attention to language, reading, and executive functioning for children with language impairment.

References

Abbott, M. (2001, October). Effects of traditional versus extended word-study spelling instruction on students' orthographic knowledge. *Reading Online, 5*(3), 1096–1232. Retrieved from http://www.readingonline.org/articles/art_index.asp?HREF=abbott/index.html

American Speech-Language-Hearing Association. (2001). *Roles and responsibilities of speech-language pathologists with respect to reading and writing in children and adolescents: Guidelines and technical report.* Rockville, MD: Author. Retrieved from http://www.asha.org/docs/html/GL2001-00062.html

American Speech-Language-Hearing Association. (2010). *Roles and responsibilities of speech-language pathologists with respect to schools: Guidelines and technical report.* Rockville, MD: Author. Retrieved from http://www.asha.org/docs/html/PI2010-00317.html#sec1.2

Amtmann, D., Abbott, R. D., & Berninger, V. W. (2008). Identifying and predicting classes of response to explicit phonological spelling instruction during independent composing. *Journal of Learning Disabilities, 41*, 218–234.

Anglin, J. (1993). Vocabulary development: A morphological analysis. *Monographs of the Society of Research in Child Development, 58*(10, Serial No. 238).

Apel, K. (2011) The acquisition of mental orthographic representations for reading and spelling development. *Communication Disorders Quarterly, 31*, 42–52.

Apel, K., & Lawrence, J. (2011). Contributions of morphological awareness skills to word-level reading and spelling in first-grade children with and without speech sound disorder. *Journal of Speech, Language, and Hearing Research, 54*, 1312–1327.

Apel, K. & Masterson, J. J. (2001). Theory-guided spelling assessment and intervention: A case study. *Language, Speech, and Hearing Services in Schools, 32*, 182–195.

Apel, K., Masterson, J. J., & Niessen, N. L. (2004). Spelling assessment frameworks. In A. Stone, E. R. Silliman, B. Ehren, & K. Apel (Eds.), *Handbook of language and literacy: Development and disorders* (pp. 644–660). New York, NY: Guilford.

Apel, K., Wolter, J. A., & Masterson, J. J. (2006). Effects of phonotactic and orthotactic probabilities during fast-mapping on five-year-olds' learning to spell. *Developmental Neuropsychology, 29*(1), 21–42.

Apel, K., Wolter, J. A., & Masterson, J. J. (2012). Mental graphemic representations (MGRs). In *Encyclopedia of the sciences of learning* (Vol. 5, pp. 2185–2186). New York: Springer.

Bear, D. R., Invernizzi, M., Templeton, S., & Johnson, F. (2004). *Words their way: Word study learning and teaching phonics, vocabulary, and spelling* (3rd ed.). Upper Saddle River, NJ: Merrill.

Berninger, V. W., Abbott, R. D., Abbott, S. P., Graham, S., & Richards, T. (2002). Writing and reading connections between language by hand and language by eye. *Journal of Learning Disabilities, 35*, 39–56.

Berninger, V. W., Abbott, R. D., Nagy, W., & Carlisle, J. (2010). Growth in phonological, orthographic, and morphological awareness in grades 1 to 6. *Journal of Psycholinguistic Research, 39*, 141–163.

Berninger, V. W., Abbott, R. D., Zook, D., Ogier, S., Lemos-Britton, Z., Brooksher, R. (1999). Early intervention for reading disabilities: Teaching the alphabetic principle in a connectionist framework. *Journal of Learning Disabilities, 32*(6), 491–503.

Berninger, V. W., Lee, Y., Abbott, R. D., & Breznitz, Z. (2011). Teaching children with dyslexia to spell in reading-writers' workshop. *Annals of Dyslexia*, doi: 10.1007/s11881-011-0054-0.

Berninger, V. W., & O'Malley May, M. (2011). Evidence-based diagnosis and treatment for specific learning disabilities involving impairments in written and/or oral language. *Journal of Learning Disabilities, 44*, 167–183.

Berninger, V., Nagy, W., Carlisle, J., Thomson, J., Hoffer, D., Abbott, S., & Johnson, C. (2003). Effective treatment for dyslexics in grades 4 to 6: Behavioral and brain evidence. In B. Forman (Ed.), *Preventing and treating reading disability: Bringing science to scale* (pp. 382–417). Timonium, MD: York Press.

Berninger, V. W., Winn, W. D., Stock, P., Abbott, R. D., Eschen J., Lin, S.-J., & Nagy, W. (2008). Tier 3 specialized writing instruction for students with dyslexia. *Reading and Writing, 21*(1–2), 95–12.

Blachman, B. A., Ball, E. W., Black, R., & Tangel, D. M. (1994). Kindergarten teachers develop phoneme awareness in low-income, inner-city classrooms. *Reading and Writing, 6*, 1–18.

Blachman, B. A., Schatschneider, C., Fletcher, J. M., Francis, D. J., Clonan, S. M., Shaywitz, B. A., & Shaywitz, S. E. (2004). Effects of intensive reading remediation for second and third graders and a one-year follow up. *Journal of Educational Psychology, 96*, 444–461.

Blachman, B. A., Tangel, D. M., Ball, E. W., Black, R., & McGraw, C. K. (1999). Developing phonological awareness and word recognition skills: A two-year intervention with low-income, inner-city students. *Reading and Writing, 11*, 239–273.

Bourassa, D. C., & Treiman, R. (2001). Spelling development and disability: The importance of linguistic factors. *Language, Speech, and Hearing Services in Schools, 32*(3), 172–181.

Bowers, P. N., & Kirby, J. R. (2010). Effects of morphological instruction on vocabulary acquisition. *Reading and Writing, 23*, 515–537.

Bowers, P. N., Kirby, J. R., & Deacon, S. H. (2010). The effects of morphological instruction on literacy skills: A systematic review of the literature. *Review of Educational Research, 80*(2), 144–179.

Boyer, N. & Ehri, L. C. (2011). Contribution of phonemic segmentation instruction with letters and articulation pictures to word reading and spelling in beginners. *Scientific Studies of Reading, 15*, 440–470.

Carlisle, J. F. (1988). Knowledge of derivational morphology and spelling ability in fourth, sixth, and eighth graders. *Applied Psycholinguistics, 9*, 247–266.

Carlisle, J. F. (1996). An exploratory study of morphological errors in children's written stories. *Reading and Writing, 8*, 61–72.

Carlisle, J. F. (2000). Awareness of the structure and meaning of morphologically complex words: Impact on reading. *Reading and Writing, 12*, 169–190.

Carlisle, J. F. (2010). Effects of instruction in morphological awareness on literacy achievement: An integrative review. *Reading Research Quarterly, 45*, 464–487.

Casalis, S., Colé, P., & Sopo, D. (2004). Morphological awareness in developmental dyslexia. *Annals of Dyslexia, 54*, 114–138.

Cates, G. L., Dunne, M., Erkfritz, K. N., Kivisto, A., Lee, N., Wierzbicki, J. (2007). Differential effects of two spelling procedures on acquisition, maintenance, and adaption to reading. *Journal of Behavioral Education, 16*, 71–82.

Catts, H. W., Fey, M. E., Zhang, X., & Tomblin, J. B. (2001). Estimating the risk of future reading difficulties in kindergarten children: A research-based model and its clinical implementation. *Language, Speech, and Hearing Services in Schools, 32*, 38–50.

Cunningham, A. E. (2006). Accounting for children's orthographic learning while reading text: Do children self-teach? *Journal of Experimental Child Psychology, 95*, 56–77.

Darch, C., Eaves, R. C., Crowe, D. A., Simmons, K., & Conniff, A. (2006). Teaching spelling to students with learning disabilities: A comparison of rule-based strategies versus traditional instruction. *Journal of Direct Instruction, 6*(1), 1–16.

deGraaff, S., Bosman, A. M., Hasselman, F., & Verhoeven, L. (2009). Benefits of systematic phonics instruction. *Scientific Studies of Reading, 13*, 318–333.

Ehri, L. C. (1992). Reconceptualizing the development of sight word reading and its relationship to recoding. In P. B. Gough, L. C. Ehri, & R. Treiman (Eds.), *Reading acquisition* (pp. 107–143). Hillside, NJ: Erlbaum.

Ehri, L. C. (1997). Learning to read and learning to spell are one and the same, almost. In C. Perfetti, L. Rieben, & M. Fayol (Eds.), *Learning to spell: Research, theory, and practice across language* (pp. 237–129). Mahwah, NJ: Earlbaum.

Ehri, L. C. (2000). Learning to read and learning to spell: Two sides of a coin. *Topics in Language Disorders, 20*, 19–36.

Ehri, L. C., Nunes, S. R., Willows, D. M., Schuster, B. V., Yaghoub-Zadeh, Z., & Shanahan, T. (2001). Phonemic awareness instruction helps children to learn to read: Evidence from the National Reading Panel's meta-analysis. *Reading Research Quarterly, 36*, 250–287.

Ehri, L. C., Satlow, E., & Gaskins, I. (2009). Grapho-phonemic enrichment strengthens keyword analogy instruction for struggling young readers. *Reading and Writing Quarterly, 25*, 162–191.

Elbro, C., & Arnbak, E. (1996). The role of morpheme recognition and morphological awareness in dyslexia. *Annals of Dyslexia, 46*, 209–240.

Erion, J., Davenport, C., Rodax, N., Scholl, B., & Hardy, J. (2009). Cover-copy-compare and spelling: One versus three repetitions. *Journal of Behavioral Education, 18*, 319–330.

Evans, M. A., Williamson, K., & Pursoo, T. (2008). Preschoolers' attention to print during shared book reading. *Scientific Studies of Reading, 12*, 106–129.

Fallon, K. A., & Katz, L. A. (2011). Providing written language services in the schools: The time is now. *Language, Speech, and Hearing Services in Schools, 42*, 3–17.

Ferguson, N., Currie, L., Paul, M., & Topping, K. (2011). The longitudinal impact of a comprehensive literacy intervention. *Educational Research, 53*(3), 237–256.

Fulk, B. M., & Stormont-Spurgin, M. (1995). Spelling interventions for students with disabilities: A review. *Journal of Special Education, 28*, 488–513.

Gaskins, I. W., Ehri, L. C., Cress, C., O'Hara, C., & Donnelly, K. (1996–1997). Procedures for word learning: Making discoveries about words. *The Reading Teacher, 50*, 312–327.

Goodwin, A. P., & Ahn, S. (2010). A meta-analysis of morphological interventions: Effects on literacy achievement of children with literacy difficulties. *Annals of Dyslexia, 60*, 183–208.

Goodwin, A. P., Lipsky, M., & Ahn, S. (2012). Word detectives: Using units of meaning to support literacy. *The Reading Teacher, 65*(7), 461–470.

Graham, S. (1999). Handwriting and spelling instruction for students with learning disabilities: A review. *Learning Disability Quarterly, 22*(2), 78–98.

Graham, S., & Harris, K. R. (2005). Improving the writing performance of young struggling writers: Theoretical and programmatic research from the center on accelerating student learning. *Journal of Special Education, 39*(1), 19–33.

Graham, S., Murphy, P., Harris, K., Fink-Chorzempa, B., Saddler, S., & Mason, L. (2008). Teaching spelling in primary grades: A national survey of instructional practices and adaptations. *American Educational Research, 4*, 796–825.

Grskovic, J. A., & Belfiore, P. J. (1996). Improving the spelling performance of students with disabilities. *Journal of Behavioral Education, 6*, 343–354.

Hammill, D. (2004). What we know about correlates of reading. *Exceptional Children, 70*, 453–468.

Hammill, D. D., & Larsen, S. C. (2009). *The test of written language* (4th ed.). Austin, TX: PRO-ED.

Henderson, E. H. (1990). *Teaching spelling* (2nd ed.). Boston, MA: Houghton Mifflin.

Johnston, F. R. (2001). Spelling exceptions: Problems or possibilities? *The Reading Teacher, 54*, 372–378.

Katz, L., & Frost, S. J. (2001). Phonology constrains the internal orthographic representation. *Reading and Writing, 14*, 297–332.

Kelman, M. E., & Apel, K. (2004). Effects of a multiple linguistic and prescriptive approach to spelling instruction: A case study. *Communication Disorders Quarterly, 25*(2), 56–66.

Kirk, C. & Gillon, G. T. (2009). Integrated morphological awareness intervention as a tool for improving literacy. *Language, Speech, and Hearing Services in Schools, 40*, 341–351.

Kohnen, S., Nickels, L., & Coltheart, M. (2010). Skill generalisation in teaching spelling to children with learning disabilities. *Australian Journal of Learning Difficulties, 15*(2), 115–129.

Larsen, S. C., Hammill, D. D., & Moats, L. (2013). *Test of written spelling* (5th ed.). Austin, TX: PRO-ED.

Lonigan, C. J., Burgess, S. R., & Anthony, J. L. (2000). Development of emergent literacy and early reading skills in preschool children: Evidence from a latent variable longitudinal study. *Developmental Psychology, 36*, 596–613.

Masterson, J. J., & Apel, K. (2010). Linking characteristics discovered in spelling assessment to intervention goals and methods. *Learning Disability Quarterly, 33*, 185–198.

Masterson, J. J., & Apel, K. (2014). Spelling assessment frameworks. In A. Stone, E. R. Silliman, B. Ehren, & G. Wallach (Eds.), *Handbook of language and literacy: Development and disorders* (2nd ed. pp. 584-601). New York, NY: Guilford.

Masterson, J. J., Apel, K. & Wasowicz, J. (2006). *Spelling performance evaluation for language and literacy* (2nd ed). Evanston, IL: Learning By Design.

Masterson, J. J. & Crede, L. A. (1999). Learning to spell: Implications for assessment and intervention. *Language, Speech, and Hearing Services in Schools, 30*, 243–254.

McCutchen, D., Green, L. & Abbott, R. D. (2008). Children's morphological knowledge: links to literacy. *Reading Psychology, 29*, 289–314.

McNaughton, D., Hughes, C. A., & Clark, K. (1994). Spelling instruction for students with learning disabilities: Implications for research and practice. *Learning Disability Quarterly, 17*, 169–185.

Moats, L. (1995). *Spelling development, disability, and instruction*. Baltimore, MD: York Press.

Moats, L. (2009). Knowledge foundations for teaching reading and spelling. *Reading and Writing, 22*, 379–399.

Nagy, W., Berninger, V. W., & Abbott, R. (2006). Contributions of morphology beyond phonology to literacy outcomes of upper-elementary and middle-school students. *Journal of Educational Psychology, 98*(1), 134–147.

Newcomer, P. L., & Hammill, D. D. (2008). *Test of language development–primary* (4th ed.). Austin, TX: PRO-ED.

Nunes, T., Bryant, P., & Olsson, J. (2003). Learning morphological and phonological spelling rules: An intervention study. *Scientific Studies of Reading, 7*, 289–307.

Reed, D. K. (2008). A synthesis of morphology interventions and effects on reading outcomes for students in grades K–12. *Learning Disabilities Research and Practice, 23*, 36–49.

Roberts, T. A., & Meiring, A. (2006). Teaching phonics in the context of children's literature or spelling: Influences on first-grade reading, spelling, and writing and fifth-grade comprehension. *Journal of Educational Psychology, 98*, 690–713.

Santa, C. M., & Hoien, T. (1999). An assessment of Early Steps: A program for early intervention of reading problems. *Reading Research Quarterly, 34*, 54–79.

Savage, R. S., Deault, L., Daki, J., & Aouad, J. (2011). Orthographic analogies and early reading: Evidence from a multiple clue word paradigm. *Journal of Educational Psychology, 103*, 190–205.

Schlagal, B. (1992). Pattern of orthographic development into the intermediate grades. In S. Templeton & D. Bear (Eds.), *Development of orthographic knowledge and the foundations of literacy: A memorial Fetschrift for Edmund H. Henderson* (pp. 31–52). Hillsdale, NJ: Erlbaum.

Schlagal, B. (2001). Traditional, developmental, and structural language approaches to spelling: Review and recommendations. *Annals of Dyslexia, 51*, 147–176.

Schlagel, B. (2007). Best practices in spelling and handwriting. In S. Graham, C. MacArthur, & J. Fitzgerald (Eds.), *Best practices in writing instruction* (pp. 179–201). New York, NY: Guilford.

Schuele, C. M., Justice, L. M., Cabell, S. Q., Knighton, K., Kingery, B., & Lee, M. W. (2008). Field-based evaluation of two-tiered instruction for enhancing kindergarten phonological awareness. *Early Education and Development, 19*, 726–752.

Schwiebert, C., Green, L. & McCutchen, D. (2002). *The contribution of morphology to reading and spelling*. U.S. Department of Health and Human Services, National Institute of

Child Health and Human Development (NIH Publication No. 50HD33812). Retrieved from ERIC database (ED465986)

Shahar-Yames, D., & Share, D. L. (2008). Spelling as a self-teaching mechanism in orthographic learning. *Journal of Research in Reading, 31*, 22–39.

Share, D. L. (2004). Orthographic learning at a glance: On the time course and development onset of self-teaching. *Journal of Experimental Child Psychology, 87*, 267–298.

Shattil, E., Share, D. L., & Levin, I. (2000). On the contribution of kindergarten writing to Grade 1 literacy: A longitudinal study in Hebrew. *Applied Psycholinguistics, 28*, 1–25.

Skinner, C. H., McLaughlin, T. F., & Logan, P. (1997). Cover, copy, and compare: A self-managed intervention effective across skills, students, and settings. *Journal of Behavioral Education, 7*, 295–306.

Stolz, J. A., & Feldman, L. B. (1995). The role of orthographic and semantic transparency of the base morphemes in morphological processing. In L. B. Feldman (Ed.), *Morphological aspects of language processing* (pp. 109–130). Hillsdale, NJ: Erlbaum.

Storch, S. A., & Whitehurst, G. J. (2002). Oral language and code-related precursors to reading: Evidence from a longitudinal structural model. *Developmental Psychology, 38*, 934–947.

Templeton, S. (2004). The vocabulary-spelling connection: Orthographic development and morphological knowledge at the intermediate grades and beyond. In J. F. Baumann & E. J. Kame'enui (Eds.), *Vocabulary instruction: Research to practice* (pp. 118–138). New York, NY: Guilford.

Treiman, R., & Cassar, M. (1996). Effects of morphology on children's spelling of final consonant clusters. *Journal of Experimental Child Psychology, 63*, 141–170.

Treiman, R., Cassar, M., & Zukowski, A. (1994). What types of linguistic information do children use in spelling? The case of flaps. *Child Development, 65*, 1318–1337.

Ukrainetz, T. A. (2006). Using emergent writing to develop phonemic awareness. In L. M. Justice (Ed.), *Clinical approaches to emergent literacy intervention* (pp. 225–259). San Diego, CA: Plural.

Ukrainetz, T. A. (2008). Phonemic awareness instruction for preschoolers: The evidence for prephonemic versus phonemic tasks. *EBP Briefs, 2*, 47–58.

Ukrainetz, T. A. (2009a). Phonemic awareness: How much is enough within a changing picture of reading instruction? *Topics in Language Disorders, 29*, 344–359.

Ukrainetz, T. A. (2009b). Foreword: How much is enough? The intensity evidence in language intervention. *Topics in Language Disorders, 29*, 291–293.

Ukrainetz, T. A., Cooney, M. H., Dyer, S. K., Kysar, A. J., & Harris, T. J. (2000). An investigation into teaching phonemic awareness through shared reading and writing. *Early Childhood Research Quarterly, 15*, 331–355.

Ukrainetz, T. A., Ross, C. L., & Harm, H. M. (2009). An investigation of treatment scheduling for phonemic awareness with kindergartners at risk for reading difficulties. *Language, Speech, and Hearing Services in Schools, 40*, 86–100.

Vadasy, P. F., Sanders, E. A., & Peyton, J. A. (2006). Code-oriented instruction for kindergarten students at risk for reading difficulties: A randomized field trial with paraeducator implementers. *Journal of Educational Psychology, 98*, 508–528.

Wagner, R. K., Torgeson, J. K., Rashotte, C. A., & Pearson, N. (2013). *Comprehensive Test of Phonological Processing* (2nd ed.). Austin, TX: PRO-ED.

Wanzek, J., Vaughn, S., Wexler, J., Swanson, E., Edmonds, M., & Kim, A.-H. (2006). A synthesis of spelling and reading interventions and their effects on the spelling outcomes of students with LD. *Journal of Learning Disabilities, 39*, 528–543.

Warren, S. F., Fey, M. E., & Yoder, P. J. (2007). Differential treatment intensity research: A missing link to creating optimally effective communication interventions. *Mental Retardation and Developmental Disabilities Research Reviews, 13*, 70–77.

Wasowicz, J., Apel, K., Masterson, J. J., & Whitney, A. (2004) *SPELL-Links to Reading and Writing*. Evanston, IL: Learning By Design.

Weiser, B., & Mathes, P. (2011). Using encoding instruction to improve the reading and spelling performances of elementary students at risk for literacy difficulties: A best-evidence synthesis. *Review of Educational Research, 81*, 170–200.

White, T. G., (2005). Effects of systematic and strategic analogy-based phonics on grade 2 students' word reading and reading comprehension. *Reading Research Quarterly, 40*, 234–255.

Williams, C., & Hufnagel, K. (2005). The impact of word study instruction on kindergarten children's journal writing. *Research in the Teaching of English, 39*, 233–270.

Williams, C., & Lundstrom, R. P. (2007). Strategy instruction during word study and interactive writing activities. *The Reading Teacher, 61*, 204–212.

Williams, C., & Phillips-Birdsong, C. (2006). Word study instruction and second-grade children's independent writing. *Journal of Literacy Research, 38*, 427–465.

Wolter, J. A. (2005). Summary of special interest division 1 student research grant: A multiple linguistic approach to literacy remediation. *Perspectives on Language Learning and Education, 12*(3), 22–25.

Wolter, J. A. (2009). A systematic research review of word study treatment practices for the speech–language pathologist. *Evidence-Based Practice Briefs, 3*, 43–58.

Wolter, J. A., & Dilworth, V. (2014). The effects of a morphological awareness approach to improve language and literacy. *Journal of Learning Disabilities, 47*, 76–85.

Wolter, J. A., & Green, L. (2013). Morphological awareness in early elementary school children with language and literacy deficits: A case study. *Topics in Language Disorders, 47*, 76–85.

Wolter, J. A., Self, T., & Apel, K. (2011). Initial mental graphemic representation acquisition and later literacy achievement in children with language impairment: A longitudinal study. *Journal of Learning Disabilities, 44*, 543–555.

Wolter, J. A., & Squires, K. (2014). Spelling: Instructional and intervention frameworks. In A. Stone, E. R. Silliman, B. Ehren, & G. Wallach., (Eds.), *Handbook of Language and Literacy: Development and Disorders* (2nd ed., pp. 602–615). New York: Guilford.

Wolter, J. A., Wood, A., & D'zatko, K. (2009). The influence of morphological awareness on first-grade children's literacy development. *Language, Speech, and Hearing Services in Schools, 40*, 286–298.

Chapter **15**

Improving Reading Comprehension: More Than Meets the Eye

Teresa A. Ukrainetz

This chapter could be considered the culmination of the preceding chapters, because reading comprehension encompasses language, learning, and processing. Reading comprehension requires the ability to decode the printed word and many of the skills involved in listening comprehension. Even speaking and writing are ways into comprehending texts. More than ever, texts involve multiple modalities and representations: spoken word, printed word, icon, picture, spatial arrangement, and audio signal. At 4 years of age, my niece could not decode print but could independently operate computer games that called on considerable symbol comprehension skills. This chapter builds on the active and strategic engagement theme of Ukrainetz and Ross (2006). Intervention recommendations are built around the contextualized skill and whole-part framework of Chapter 3, with explicit, systematic instruction; purposeful engagement in reading; and application of skills and strategies across learning activities.

What Is Reading Comprehension?

Reading comprehension is "the process of simultaneously extracting and constructing meaning through interaction and involvement with written language" (RAND Reading Study Group [RRSG], 2002, p. xiii) or more simply, "gaining meaning from text." Reading comprehension involves relating words and sentences to one another, relating what is read to what is known, and attending to how the message aligns with the reading purpose. It involves print information, language skills, cognitive strategies, and world knowledge. Academic comprehension involves both *understanding* what is read and *learning* from what is understood.

More and Less Than the Words on the Page

Reading comprehension is complicated partly because it is so difficult to define the borders of an act of comprension (Kamhi, 2012; Snow, 2010; Willingham, 2006). For these two sentences, *Hal dropped a cup of coffee. My rug is a mess*, there is, at minimum, a mental image of a cup of brown liquid dropping from a character's hand onto a carpet. Within this image, there are also inferences about the character's age and gender as well as the physical dimensions of the objects involved. The two sentences are not explicitly linked, but their adjacency implies a causal relation between the events. The word *mess* implies that the carpet owner is particularly aggrieved, suggesting perhaps the unstated modifier of "yet again."

Reading performance can also suggest more comprehension than has actually occurred. Given a paragraph about the statistical procedure of logistic regression, a reader can correctly answer questions about the text, such as, "What does logistic regression do?" by finding the words "predict a discrete outcome," or the statement of the main idea as "use of logistic regression in health sciences" (Willingham, 2006). The reader might be able to determine the main idea, answer questions about the text, and even make some reasonable inferences, with little understanding of what the author is saying about logistic regression.

Neither of these examples have even touched on what a reader does with his or her understanding. As Kamhi (2012) explains, the single scores used in reading assessments can hardly begin to represent a reader's reading comprehension ability or how this ability is manifested in particular situations or even in general academic achievement. Reading comprehension performance needs to be viewed with a wider lens, one that considers the three interrelated and overlapping dimensions of reader, text, and activity (RRSG, 2002; Snow, 2010).

The Reader

Readers come to reading tasks with varying abilities, motivations, expectancies, knowledge, and life experiences. To be successful comprehenders, readers need the ability to fluently recognize printed words as well as sufficient communicative and metalinguistic language skills. But reading comprehension involves much more than decoding and language skills. Cognitive processes include selective and sustained attention, working and long-term memory, critical analytic ability, inferencing, and visualization (RRSG, 2002; Snow, 2010). In addition to these more stable characteristics, there are more dynamic features of individuals that significantly impact how their comprehension abilities will be applied to reading tasks.

Domain knowledge is a major factor in reading comprehension. Tests and measures of reading comprehension are designed with the expectation that, within a general age range, readers have a fairly common store of world knowledge. However, a reader who happens to be particularly familiar with a topic has a huge advantage in understanding new material. For example, high school students judged to be poor readers on general comprehension tests can do as well as good readers on understanding passages about high-knowledge topics, such as baseball or football, even when responses require analysis, synthesis, and inferencing (Recht & Leslie, 1988; Yekovich, Walker, Ogle, & Thompson, 1990).

Related to expertise is interest. Being interested in the topic affects how readers allocate mental resources, how persistently they seek comprehension, how fast they read, and how much they gain from the reading. The powerful effect of interest has been demonstrated across ages, knowledge domains, and subject areas (Hidi, 2001; Oakhill & Petrides, 2007). Even simply the wording of a title attached to a text can influence affective responses, persistence, and ultimately comprehension and recall of the larger passage (Ainley, Hidi, & Berndorff, 2002).

Stimulating situational interest may be particularly important for boys because they seem to show more specific topic interests than girls do and seem to be less successful in academic topics that do not interest them (Ainley, Hillman, & Hidi, 2002; Oakhill & Petrides, 2007). For example, Oakhill and Petrides compared fifth-grade boys and girls on passages they had rated as higher and lower interest: the boys preferred a piece on spiders while the girls preferred a piece about children being evacuated during war. The boys were 60% correct on the high-interest-passage questions and 38% for the low-interest ones. In contrast, the girls performed at about 62% for both high- and low-interest passages.

Attitudes toward reading affect willingness to read, how the reading is approached, and subsequent comprehension (Guthrie, Klauda, & Ho, 2013; Wigfield et al., 2008). This includes enjoyment of reading, the belief that you can succeed, valuing the specific reading activity, and wanting to cooperate with others. Negative attitudes include perceiving the task as too difficult, believing the activity to be irrelevant, and avoiding the task.

The Text

Text means, "the main body of printed or written matter on a page" (Merriam Webster, 1993, p. 1219). A *piece of text* usually means "a paragraph or a passage on a page." *Text* is also shorthand for books written to support didactic instruction (i.e., textbooks). *Text* is sometimes used interchangeably with *discourse*, but in contrast to discourse, *text* does not refer to a whole, coherent, structured communication unit, such as a narrative or an essay. *Text* can be *prose* or *document*, with the former involving sentences connected into paragraphs and passages, and the latter involving noncontinuous words and phrases, such as those in forms, websites, and pamphlets (Kutner, Greenberg, & Baer, 2006). *Text* means "print," but may include models, diagrams, photographs, videos, and other representations of ideas and experiences (Alvermann & Wilson, 2011).

The mental representations that a reader constructs from text will be affected by the wording of the text, the idea units representing the meaning, and the text structure (RRSG, 2002). *Readability*, or ease of reading, is improved by consistent word use, paragraphs with topic sentences, and essays with stated purposes and concluding paragraphs. Headings and bulleted lists are easier to skim than connected text. Elaborate syntax may require close reading but can transmit subtle shades of meaning, such as this sentence from the novel *Emma*: "She was not deceived as to her own skill either as an artist or a musician, but she was not unwilling to have others deceived, or sorry to know her reputation for accomplishment often higher than it deserved" (Austen, 1816/1957, p. 32).

Part of reading comprehension is monitoring and repairing one's own understanding. It also involves learning to determine when comprehension difficulties are due not to the reader but to the text. Students often assume that comprehension difficulties are their fault, when they may be due more to dense, convoluted, or illogical writing, or simply to a mismatch of the writing and the audience. Simple changes in the text, such as adding headings, can significantly improve passage comprehension (Moravcsik & Kintsch, 1993). Display characteristics, such as font size, layout, and graphics, can also affect comprehension.

Text difficulty is hard to determine independent of the reader. For example, the nomenclature of chemistry (e.g, *peroxyacetyl nitrates, aldehyde*) is opaque for most readers but transmits specific information about molecular content, structure, and processes to a chemist. The chemist would have difficulty understanding vague and imprecise lay terminology (e.g., "What does polluted air mean? I need to know the chemicals involved in this smog.").

Text readability can be quantified with procedures such as Fry's formula (Fry, 1977), which calculates a reading grade level based on the average number of syllables and sentences across three 100-word passages. Another measure is the informal *five-finger rule*: more than five errors made while reading aloud a page of text means that it is too difficult (Ukrainetz & Trujillo, 1999). This is a handy guide for young readers at the library shelf. However, domain knowledge, strong interest, and inferential skills can override difficult words. For example, a book on dinosaurs may rate at a ninth-grade level, but much younger dinosaur aficionados can comprehend the text. Perhaps the best guidance, like that for new foods, is: "Try it and see if you like it."

The Activity

A reader comprehends a text at a particular time and place under particular conditions. This entirety is the activity of reading comprehension (RRSG, 2002; Snow, 2010). The reasons and conditions of reading will determine the array of skills and strategies needed for successful comprehension. This harkens back to Chapter 3, where an activity needs to be considered in terms of motivation, purpose, skills, strategies, and conditions. The conditions of an activity are layered, from the immediate reading task to the place of the activity within the lesson, the classroom, and even the reader's cultural community (Silliman & Wilkinson, 1991).

The purpose of reading affects comprehension by determining which elements are foregrounded, how they are grouped, and what ideas should be linked to the text. Readers may recall the exact words, paraphrase or summarize, synthesize the meaning into a larger whole, or infer implied or unintended meanings. The purpose may be externally imposed, such as a class assignment, or internally generated, such as programming a cell phone. The purpose can evolve during the reading, as the reader encounters new information that leads to new questions.

The conditions of the activity affect comprehension. Selecting an answer from multiple-choice questions will show aspects of comprehension that are different from those present in an oral summarization—even knowing how comprehension will be tested will affect how reading occurs. Students who are rewarded for reading the most books are likely to read for speed rather than understanding. In the face of heavy reading loads in college, diligent students who read all their course materials comprehensively and carefully in high school may need to change to their modus operandi to skimming texts and notes, seeking recognition knowledge and prioritizing what should be read.

Beyond the immediate activity are the sociocultural layers of literacy and academic learning. Communities and individuals differ in the types of comprehension acts they value. For those who follow certain literary and religious traditions, literal memory of text is valued above interpretation, whereas for others, recall of the actual words of the original text are less important than interpreting, connecting, or even critiquing the text (Scollon & Scollon, 1988; Snow, 2010). Some families may be accustomed to uncritical acceptance of the published word. Other families routinely question media reports, seek credible sources, and integrate multiple sources into critical interpretations of what they have read and heard.

Development of Reading Comprehension

Reading comprehension does not develop in clear stages, but three general levels of reading comprehension can be differentiated (Shanahan & Shanahan, 2008; Snow, 2010). These are preceded by a very early phase of literacy learning that contributes to the development of both word recognition and reading comprehension. How far students progress depends on formal instruction, literacy experiences, and individual characteristics.

Emergent Literacy

Young children develop from being *nonreaders* or *prereaders* to *readers*, with ability to decode unfamiliar words being the dividing line (if you can read *BLEEG*, you are a reader). However, before this and before the onset of formal instruction, children can know a lot about reading, especially if their early lives are immersed in literacy experiences. They may be able to read some common words, such as their names or *Mom*, through holistic recognition or identifying some letters. Preschoolers are also making sense of familiar sentences and larger units of meaning, and can even "read" some familiar texts (e.g., a birthday message on a card or a favorite storybook). Children's text comprehension develops at this age through shared storybooks, informational books, and discussions about how the world works. This period of time when children begin to figure out how words are represented in print but know a lot about the uses and forms of reading and writing is called *emergent literacy.*

Learning to Read

On the other side of the reading line from emergent literacy is *learning to read.* Learning to read involves both learning how to recognize individual words and learning how to make sense of those words when combined into sentences and paragraphs. Because much of their cognitive resources are consumed by decoding, beginning readers' comprehension of written language is much lower than their comprehension of spoken language. As decoding skills improve, the gap between reading and listening closes so that students can easily understand simple texts delivered through either modality.

The processes of word recognition and text comprehension at this *basic* level of reading are difficult to untangle in connected text reading. If a reader struggles to sound out and recognize individual words, the slow, disjointed reading will hurt comprehension of the sentence and the larger passage. Good decoding skills allow readers to use key words to determine the meaning of sentences and passages. Text comprehension is needed to confirm decoding choices. For example, when a reader attempts to sound out the word *read*, sentence information is needed to make the choice of [*rid*] versus [*rEd*] (*read now* versus *read yesterday*). This entanglement is why the comprehension part of reading is best evaluated through listening tasks, even if the student is a competent decoder (Catts, Adolf, & Weismer, 2006; Gough & Tunmer, 1986). (However, due to the differences in how oral and written discourse are structured, measures designed to be read by the student will not yield valid scores if the passages are delivered orally to the student. Only measures developed for spoken language should be used to obtain norm-referenced listening comprehension scores.)

In the past, children learned their letters, how to write their names, and simple decoding in first grade then progressed into reading simple stories in second grade. With earlier expectations for reading, this pattern has backed up at least a year. Children are now expected to leave kindergarten knowing how to decode simple words. By the end of second grade, students are expected to have basic control of decoding, fluency, and

Box 15.1. ***Learning to Read Expectations for Second Grade in Common Core***

1. Know and apply grade-level phonics and word analysis skills in decoding words, including vowel varieties, two-syllable words, words with affixes, inconsistent but common words, and irregular words.
2. Read on-level text with purpose, understanding, and sufficient accuracy, rate, and expression to support comprehension.
3. Use context to confirm or self-correct word recognition and understanding, rereading as necessary.
4. By the end of the year, read and comprehend literature, including stories, dramas, and poetry, and informational texts, including history/social studies, science, and technical texts in the Grades 2–3 text complexity band independently and proficiently with scaffolding as needed at the high end of the range.
5. Identify, describe, determine, explain, compare, and use content and structure of literature and informational texts.

Note: From NGA-CSSO (2010, pp. 11, 15, 16).

comprehension. Box 15.1 shows the second-grade expectations set in the *Common Core State Standards* (National Governors Association for Best Practices and the Council of Chief State School Officers [NGA-CSSO], 2010).

Reading to Learn

Third-grade students are expected to know how to read proficiently across prose, poetry, and informational text. Further reading experience and instruction will improve word attack skills and comprehension of difficult reading material, but basic reading competence is expected. In this *intermediate* level of comprehension, students shift from primarily learning to read to primarily *reading to learn. Reading to learn* means actively and independently engaging in reading to gain new knowledge and achieve learning goals. Box 15.2 sets out reading expectations for third-grade students, who often falter with this jump in language and cognitive demands, which used to be known as the *fourth-grade slump* (Chall, 1983).

This intermediate level of reading, spanning from third grade to high school, requires general knowledge and reading skills (Shanahan & Shanahan, 2008; Snow, 2010). In later elementary grades, students should be able to maintain their attention to extended discourse, monitor their comprehension, and employ simple repair strategies, such as rereading or asking for help. They learn to recall, paraphrase, and provide the gist of texts. They use inferencing from prior text, context cues, and background knowledge to determine word meaning, link sentence meaning, and understand passages. As they move through the grades, text difficulty increases, and students become better at constructing critical and creative interpretations of text. They engage in an increasing variety of conscious cognitive strategies to monitor, enhance, and repair their comprehension. Eighth grade involves a rather daunting array of expectations (Box 15.3).

Box 15.2. ***Reading to Learn Expectations for Third Grade in Common Core***

Key Ideas and Details

1. Ask and answer questions to demonstrate understanding of a text, referring explicitly to the text as the basis for the answers.
2. Determine the main idea of a text; recount the key details and explain how they support the main idea.
3. Describe characters in a story (e.g., their traits, motivations, or feelings) and explain how their actions contribute to the sequence of events.

Craft and Structure

4. Determine the meaning of words and phrases as they are used in a text, distinguishing literal from nonliteral language.
5. Describe the relationship between historical events, scientific ideas or concepts, or steps in technical procedures in a text, using language pertaining to time, sequence, and cause/effect.
6. Refer to parts of stories, dramas, and poems when writing or speaking about a text, using terms such as chapter, scene, and stanza; describe how each part builds on earlier sections.
7. Determine the meaning of general academic and domain-specific words and phrases in a text relevant to a Grade 3 topic or subject area.

Integration of Knowledge and Ideas

8. Compare and contrast the themes, settings, and plots of stories written by the same author about the same or similar characters (e.g., in books from a series).
9. Compare and contrast important points and key details in two texts on the same topic.

Note: From NGA-CSSO (2010, pp. 12, 14).

There is increasing attention to the types and difficulty of texts that students encounter in the later grades. Since the 1970s, in an effort to promote student interest and independent reading, educators have opted for textbooks and standardized exams that have shorter sentences and simpler wording and thus are less difficult to read (Adams, 2011). Readings were specifically crafted for instructional purposes, or a very limited selection with few topical links between materials within or across grades was used. Writing assignments also became less demanding and emphasized personal meaning, such as stories and memoirs, over formal composition and analytic communication (Tyre, 2012). While these changes increased student interest and helped poor readers succeed, they may have negatively affected higher levels of achievement. Since the early 1990s, although reading scores in the earlier grades have increased or held steady, high school

Box 15.3. ***Reading Comprehension Standards for Eighth Grade in Informational Text***

Key Ideas and Details

1. Cite the textual evidence that most strongly supports an analysis of what the text says explicitly as well as inferences drawn from the text.
2. Determine a central idea of a text and analyze its development and relationship to supporting ideas; provide an objective summary of the text.
3. Analyze how a text makes connections among and distinctions between individuals, ideas, or events (e.g., through comparisons, analogies, or categories).

Craft and Structure

4. Determine the meaning of words and phrases as they are used in a text, including figurative, connotative, and technical meanings.
5. Analyze in detail the structure of a specific paragraph in a text, including the role of particular sentences in developing and refining a key concept.
6. Determine an author's point of view or purpose in a text and analyze how the author acknowledges and responds to conflicting evidence or viewpoints

Integration of Knowledge and Ideas

7. Delineate and evaluate the argument and specific claims in a text, assessing whether the reasoning is sound and the evidence is relevant and sufficient.
8. Analyze a case in which two or more texts provide conflicting information on the same topic and identify where the texts disagree on matters of fact or interpretation.

Note: Excerpted from a larger set in the *Common Core State Standards* (NGA-CSSO, 2010, pp. 36–37).

reading levels have dropped (Adams, 2011; Shanahan & Shanahan, 2008). There is now a call for making texts more difficult, with more information-rich words, subtle grammatical expressions, and challenging concepts, along with a greater emphasis on nonfiction and informational texts. Multimodal formats, thematic links across grades, and explicit instruction in strategic reading are now being promoted to support access to this deeper knowledge (Adams, 2011; Shanahan & Shanahan, 2008; Wilson, 2011).

Disciplinary Reading

The third level of reading is *disciplinary* comprehension. In high school, students are expected to begin to develop the *advanced* comprehension (meaning reading, thinking, talking, and writing) involved in subject areas such as literature, science, math, and history. There is no precise delineation between intermediate and advanced reading, but advanced reading involves texts that many adults would find challenging to understand. Success at this advanced level involves: (a) deep knowledge of the topic, (b) knowing the communication conventions of the discipline, (c) having clear purposes for the reading task, and (d) being in control of the strategies needed to achieve those purposes. This level of reading has a wide range of accomplishment, from a high school student to a professional in that discipline.

Experts in different domains make sense of what they read in different ways (Shanahan & Shanahan, 2008; Wilson, 2011). A novelist and a civil engineer will come away with different understandings of a report of the development of interstate highways. Shanahan and Shanahan had teams of scholars and instructors identify disciplinary approaches to reading and explore ways of teaching those features to high school students. Historians read not so much for chronologies of events but rather for the networks of causal relations among events. They viewed published histories not as factual recounts of events but rather as stories told by particular authors who selected, organized, and interpreted those events through their own sociopolitical lens. In math and chemistry, authors and backstory were less important than specification and accuracy of the procedures used to arrive at the answers. Disciplinary reading is the most specialized and least generalizable of the three levels of reading: a professor of English literature will understand little of a physics paper, and a math teacher will have trouble with an acoustic phonetics text.

Relatively little attention has been paid to helping students achieve this level of literacy. There was an assumption that those students who knew how to read and could read to learn needed instruction in subject area content only. Content area teachers often viewed literacy instruction as being separate from teaching chemistry or history (Wilson, 2011). Lack of training in literacy and the need to get through the curriculum were part of the reason for this error, but there has also been a lack of awareness of discipline-specific ways of reading and how to introduce them to students. However, educators are now dealing with the advanced, disciplinary-specific comprehension and thinking skills that are now expected.

Reading Proficiency in Adults

To better understand what we can reasonably expect for reading achievement of high school graduates, we should look at how well grown-ups read. It would also be informative to know what type and level of reading is actually needed by average working adults but that is beyond what can be addressed in this chapter.

Rates of adult illiteracy in the U.S. and around the world depend greatly on how illiteracy is operationalized. *Illiteracy* can refer to being unable to recognize unfamiliar printed words or write one's own name (Chudgar, 1993; Kamhi, 2009; Kutner, Greenberg, & Baer, 2006). However, the term is typically used to refer to some significant degree of insufficiency in reading comprehension (and sometimes quantitative reasoning and writing). Illiteracy may reference some number of years of schooling or some standard based on the needs of daily life in that society. A reading level that may be sufficient in a developing country may be considered functional illiteracy in a technologically advanced one. The *CIA World FactBook* used completion of five years of schooling as the basis for its 1993 rate of 98% literacy for adult Americans. The same 98% rate for Americans was obtained for a standard of being unable to answer any questions about connected text in English or Spanish (Kutner et al., 2006).

The 2003 National Assessment of Adult Literacy sampled over 19,000 adults in national and state-level assessments in U.S. homes and prisons (Kutner et al., 2006). Prose, document, and numerical literacy were examined across a set of functional daily life tasks. Results showed that, in 2003, 14% of adult Americans had *below basic* reading literacy, which meant they were not able to locate information, make low-level inferences, or integrate easily identifiable pieces of information in short, commonplace texts such as a medication instruction, a jury selection pamphlet, and a television program guide. Of these adults with below basic literacy, 45% had earned a high school degree or GED. Adults seem to drop in literacy performance soon after leaving school: only 5% of 16- to 18-year-olds were below basic, but 25% of those older than 25 years were also. A similar drop over time was obtained in the 1992 survey, suggesting that it was not a matter of poorer education in certain decades but rather a loss of proficiency during adulthood.

At the upper end of the literacy scale, the 2003 NAAL standard of *proficient* involved synthesizing and analyzing complex prose and documents, such as comparing viewpoints in two editorials or interpreting a table about blood pressure, age, and physical activity (Kutner et al., 2006). Less than 5% of adults with high school and GED scored as proficient readers. Less than a third of college graduates scored as proficient. Furthermore, the NAAL standard for proficient seems low compared to the Common Core eighth-grade standards. Whatever the concerns with the "failure" of American education at present, historically the average American adult has never functioned higher than the eighth grade; having a college degree does not assure reading proficiency; and many adults, including high school graduates, are functionally illiterate. Americans may aspire to higher levels of educational achievement, but this is uncharted territory.

Teaching Students to Be Strategic Readers

Multiple reviews of the research have supported increasing students' awareness and optimization of their mental processes to improve comprehension and learning across a range of reading levels and learning abilities (Gersten, Fuchs, Williams, & Baker, 2001; National Reading Panel [NRP], 2000a; RRSG, 2002; Rosenshine & Meister, 1994; Rosenshine, Meister, & Chapman, 1996). Two federal guides to best practices for reading comprehension instruction (Kamil et al., 2008; Shanahan et al., 2010) found consistently strong research evidence for strategy instruction. There are persistent questions about what strategies to teach, how best to teach maintained use of these strategies, and how to combine them with content instruction, but teaching students to read strategically is a key part of effective comprehension instruction.

Reading Comprehension Strategies

There are many useful reading comprehension strategies. Strategies are short-term, general problem-solving mental or observable procedures or *heuristics* that highlight information and guide attentional focus (Rosenshine et al., 1996). A selection of reading strategies organized by time of use is presented in Box 15.4. Prereading acts lead to activation of prior knowledge, prediction of text content, and a plan for reading. During-

Box 15.4. ***Some Comprehension Strategies for Before, During, and After Reading***

Stage	Strategy
Before Reading	Look for organizing concepts across the topics Recall related information and experiences Predict how easy or difficult the reading selection is likely to be Notice the author's purpose Set a purpose for reading: what you want to know or learn Find a reason for interest in the reading
During Reading	Translate ideas into own words Use prior knowledge to make sense of information Compare ideas to personal experience Identify main ideas Notice unfamiliar vocabulary and infer meanings Monitor reading speed Recognize passage structure Note important details Link ideas from part to part Reread parts to link and clarify Notice if the ideas do not fit together Pause to review and consolidate ideas Evaluate the author's purpose or authority Manage time to sustain concentration
After Reading	Review the main idea Summarize the information Ask self what has been learned Decide what is important Try to clarify ambiguous ideas Relate what has been learned to other experiences Evaluate new information in terms of prior knowledge Reread the text that is unclear or fading in mind

reading acts maintain the reader's purpose for reading, highlight important information, help integrate new with known information, and keep the reader alert to lapses in understanding. After-reading acts further integrate new and prior knowledge, and alert the reader to gaps in comprehension.

Reading strategies are generalizable and adaptable across reading situations. Readers select from these strategies to accomplish their goals within specific activities. This selection process itself is a skill; students need to know *when* and *why* to use *what* strategies *how*—essentially to have *strategic control of strategies* (Paris, Lipson, & Wixson, 1983). It is also affected by motivation (e.g., "I know I should write a summary and then compare it to what I read, but I think I understood it pretty well without all that"). Although the word strategy suggests intentional use, proficient readers may automatically and unconsciously employ these helpful actions. To teach students, SLPs can increase their own awareness of strategies by finding a text that is difficult for them and reflecting on their own cognitive processes as they read.

The strategies involved in reading vary with the purpose and conditions of the task. Skimming, careful reading, memorizing, seeking the main idea, or editing all involve different strategies. Memorizing material just long enough to pass a test followed by a "data dump" is very different from becoming engrossed in the reading and gaining enduring understandings. Rather than telling students to "learn it all," teachers can point out what is more and less important in a text and show how to strategically read difficult texts by looking for key sections and critical elements.

Professionals rarely start on page 1 and read every page. They know why they are reading and read accordingly. For example, Bazerman (1985) interviewed and observed seven physicists as they perused journal articles. They were asked to reflect on their reading habits and talk aloud as they read. The scientists discarded as much as 75% of what they initially examined. They considered titles, authors, and abstracts, matching what they read with their research interests and knowledge of the authors' labs. They read selectively within the articles, jumping among parts, looking for specific features or surprising elements. The physicists constantly made judgments about the relative value of a reading versus the time and thought investment. Some articles were set aside for reflection and a second reading, with understanding sometimes coming a while after the reading had ceased.

In contrast to professionals, students show limited monitoring or repair of even basic comprehension. For example, August, Flavell, and Clift (1984) had stronger and weaker fifth graders read stories, some of which were missing a page. The better readers commented more frequently on the missing page or at least showed some awareness with slower reading times and look-backs. However, half the children, regardless of reading level, did not report a problem, and many made unwarranted inferences to fill in the missing information. Garner and Reis (1981), who examined look-back behavior in fourth- to tenth-grade good and poor comprehenders, found a similar lack of text awareness. Test questions were designed to vary in their need for students to look back in the text for answers. While older good comprehenders were more likely to look back for information, many good and poor readers did not look back when necessary.

An essential part of reading is identifying main ideas. To do this, readers must understand what they have read, make judgments about relative importance, and synthesize the information. Skill in identifying the main idea and presenting it in a summary with supporting points improves over the later school years but remains challenging even in college. Brown and Day (1983) investigated the summarization performance of fifth-, seventh-, tenth-grade, and college-age students. The two younger groups tended to delete irrelevant and redundant information and report ideas verbatim in their original sequence. Older students collapsed and combined information across paragraphs, synthesizing and paraphrasing. However, only half of the older students inferred main ideas that were not explicitly stated.

There is a lot involved in strategic reading. Readers must monitor their own comprehension. They must evaluate their understanding of individual words, sentences, and passages. They must maintain an ongoing judgment process as they read, monitoring the construction of meaning and recognizing when they are inferring instead of using stated content and when there is a problem with text, and knowing where to find information. In a review of the developmental literature, Paris, Wasik, and Turner (1991) determined that these skills are only emerging in later elementary school and that, "even 12-year-old good readers do not detect a large number of errors and inconsistencies inserted into meaningful text" (p. 621).

Selecting Reading Strategies to Teach

The National Institute of Child Health and Human Development convened the National Reading Panel to review the research evidence across areas of reading instruction (NRP, 2000a). For teaching reading comprehension, NRP systematically reviewed the controlled research evidence published between 1980 and 1998. The 205 studies investigated instruction from third to eighth grade across a range of reading levels. In addition to the effective teaching procedures of cooperative learning, answering teacher questions, using graphic organizers, and identifying story structure, the NRP identified three types of reading strategies that showed a firm scientific basis: comprehension monitoring (readers being aware of their own understanding of the text), question generation (readers asking themselves questions about about the text), and summarization (readers integrating ideas from the text). The NRP recommended using multiple instructional procedures and reading strategies to improve reading comprehension.

Unfortunately, the NRP (2000a) guidance did little to narrow the strategy selection. These three strategy types comprise many specific instructional possibilities. Almost any strategy can serve as a check on one's comprehension (e.g., "I am having trouble summarizing and answering my own questions, which shows I do not really understand this."). Question generating involves many possible questions used at many different points of reading. A factual question (e.g., "Who is in this story?") is very different from an inferential question (e.g., "What is the author's purpose in giving all this detail?") or an evaluation question (e.g., "Does this author's claim make sense?"). There is so much to summarization that it requires multistep procedures.

Two other reviews of the reading comprehension research (Rosenshine & Meister, 1994; Rosenshine et al., 1996) report that helpful strategies tended to be specific prompts or questions about ideas (e.g., "What is the main idea of this paragraph? What is an example of this idea? What is the difference between this idea and the preceding idea?") and structure (e.g., "What was the problem in this story? Can you tell how the problem was resolved?"). Less beneficial was having students generate their own questions based on their perceptions of what is important or what they think that a teacher might ask. For example, Mason (2004) compared teaching fifth graders to ask themselves nine specific questions, organized into a TWA (Think before reading, While reading, After reading) checklist (Box 15.5) to teaching students to generate their own questions and predictions based on text content, a procedure called reciprocal questioning. For the reciprocal questioning condition, students were provided a chart listing examples of good comprehension questions. Students were systematically and explicitly taught to use both procedures. Results showed that TWA produced significantly better oral summarization of read expository passages.

Box 15.5. ***A Simple Memorable Strategy Format: TWA Checklist***

	When to Think	Strategy	Done?
T	Think before reading	The author's purpose What you know What you want to learn	____ ____ ____
W	While reading think about	Reading speed Linking what you know Rereading parts	____ ____ ____
A	After reading think about	The main idea Summarizing information What you learned	____ ____ ____

Note: Based on Mason (2004) and Mason, Meadan, Hedin, and Corso (2006).

Students raise clarification questions and make predictions based on what they find unclear or think will come next. However, depending on the texts, these may not be very helpful strategies. Rosenshine and Meister (1994) reported that, with informational texts, middle school students can learn to ask questions about material that is unclear to them, but they have trouble finding clarifying answers in the texts. Predicting upcoming information is also problematic because texts are often not linked very coherently. Finally, while graphical support, visual images, and illustrations can be helpful, they can also be distracting and produce smaller treatment effects than language-based strategies do (Sencibaugh, 2007).

How to Teach Comprehension Strategies

There are a variety of effective teaching procedures and supports (Gersten et al., 2001; Rosenshine & Meister, 1994; Rosenshine et al., 1996; RRSG, 2002; Swanson & Hoskyn, 1998; Sencibaugh, 2007). Teaching strategies one at a time as well as using a more flexible multiple strategy format have been found to benefit students ranging in age and abilities in small group and whole class arrangements. Length of program has not been found to be a significant factor: programs of as few as six sessions are no less effective than programs of 20–50 sessions (Rosenshine et al., 1996). Several important components of instruction have been identified across research studies: (a) explicit teacher modeling, (b) practice with feedback, (c) adjustment of support to the learner level, and (d) having students maintain a mindful engagement with the purposes of the reading. In an analysis of intervention research on students with learning disabilities, Swanson and Hoskyn (1998) found that out of 20 instructional components, just three explained virtually all the common variance in outcomes: (a) controlling task difficulty, (b) using small interactive groups, and (c) having students use a specified language or format for strategy questions. One persistent teaching challenge is implementing strategy instruction within "a natural reading context with readers of various levels on reading materials in content areas" (NRP, 2000b, pp. 4–47). Another challenge is knowing how to help students acquire the habit of using the strategy independently. Assessments that reveal strategy use in addition to content acquisition are also needed.

Research studies generally examine only short-term use by students and teachers. For strategy instruction to be effective, teachers need to be at ease teaching it within their content lessons, and students need to be supported in using the strategies in mainstream classrooms. Baker, Gersten, and Scanlon (2002) describe how important it is for teachers to think critically about the content they cover to determine what students need to be successful and to teach with routines and instructional supports that assist students in applying reading strategies and learning techniques successfully. In what Baker et al. call *content enhancement*, the content and learning processes are taught simultaneously, with the teacher stressing how as well as what students should learn.

In addition to specific strategy instruction, struggling students often benefit from a broader focus on self-regulation and executive function. A program that explicitly and systematically does this is self-regulated strategy development (SRSD; Graham & Harris, 1999; Graham, Harris, & Troia, 2000). Self-instruction, goal setting, self-monitoring, and self-reinforcement are addressed along with teaching students specific strategies through a recursive progression of discussion, modeling, memorization, and practice. SRSD is most often applied to writing narrative and expository compositions but has also been found to be effective for reading comprehension (Gersten, Fuchs, Williams, & Bakjer, 2001; Mason et al., 2006). Box 15.6 presents a synthesis of the instructional steps common to many effective instructional programs, including SRSD. Not all the steps listed are needed for all students, but for poor readers, explicit instruction and systematic support are needed all the way into independent classroom use.

The instructor is a critical part of effective strategy instruction. Traditionally, the teacher is a task director who requires, supervises, and evaluates recitations, content recall, and writing activities (Pearson & Fielding, 1991). Improved comprehension outcomes have been obtained when teachers are more interactive, asking questions about text structure, linking text to background knowledge, and engaging students in asking their own questions. Teacher modeling involves demonstrating and sharing thinking processes during purposeful reading so that students see the *when*, *why*, and *how*, not just *what* of reading (Pearson & Fielding, 1991; Willingham, 2006). Effective modeling practices included: (a) modeling how to read before the students start reading, (b) modeling during the student reading, demonstrating at designated stopping points or when students have difficulties, and (c) after the reading ends, discussing and modeling what strategies could have been used more effectively during the reading.

Small collaborative groups provide a more natural context than teacher-student exchanges for students to "think aloud" about their own reading strategies and comprehension processes (Gersten et al., 2001; NRP, 2000a). Students benefit from talking with each other about what they are reading and from embedding strategic questioning into these conversations. Students can take turns being teachers and lead each other in practice sessions. Thinking aloud is an important part of learning strategies, and being

Box 15.6. ***Taking Students From the Idea to Independent Use of Strategic Reading***

Introduction to the Strategies

1. Activate or teach background knowledge
2. Present a few strategies in a simple, memorable format
3. Discuss the strategy goals and how they improve comprehension
4. Model the strategy as a think-aloud during reading

Teaching Strategy Use

5. Have the students memorize the strategy
6. Provide procedural prompts, cue cards, or mnemonics
7. Provide and teach use of a checklist
8. Regulate the difficulty of the material and its match to the target strategies
9. Provide ample practice and require students to use the strategies
10. Guide use with helpful hints, positive support, and corrections
11. Monitor independent performance and provide reminders as needed

Promoting Independent Strategy Use

12. Analyze with the students how independent use is facilitated or impeded
13. Provide further practice with fewer reminders in more natural contexts
14. Connect with the teachers on supporting strategy use within the classroom
15. Periodically check on independent use in the classroom, and reinforce or solve problems as necessary

able to do so with peers is more natural and more effective than thinking aloud to the teacher.

Reciprocal teaching is a multiskill dialogic instruction procedure that involves teaching four reading comprehension strategies (summarize, question, clarify, and predict) by having students pose questions to each other about a reading (Palincsar, 1986; Palincsar & Brown, 1984; Palincsar, Brown, & Martin, 1987). The teacher begins the process by modeling how to think about a passage and then has a student lead the questioning with the teacher's support. Next, this "student-teacher" has a student read the selection aloud while the other students read silently and then asks comprehension questions of the other students, helps them find the answers, and evaluates their answers. The teacher assists the student-teacher in asking the questions and obtaining answers from her or his peers. In the early sessions, the role of the instructor is heavy because students are accustomed to passive reading, and they do not know how to formulate appropriate questions and respond to peers. As the students become accustomed to asking each other the questions and finding the answers in the text, they are expected to begin asking themselves those questions as they read.

Reciprocal teaching across controlled research studies has had considerable success (Rosenshine et al. 1996; Rosenshine & Meister, 1994). However, Rosenshine and colleagues noted that, for both poor readers and many teachers, more scripted procedures with specified language formats are easier to learn and teach. In Ukrainetz and Ross (2006), we promoted reciprocal teaching as particularly well suited to SLP intervention due to the SLPs' small group service delivery, focus on underlying skills over curricular content, and expertise with scaffolding spoken interactions. However, we have also found that we needed to use a more scripted procedure and focus on summarizing and question generating over prediction and clarification. In addition, we give students practice constructing summaries and generating questions before they are placed in the "student teacher" role.

Whose Strategy Is It?

A confusing aspect of strategy instruction is that the word *strategy* is used in two quite different ways in the literature: as the tool of the instructor versus that of the student. (Even NRP [2000a], groups the two together as "comprehension instruction strategies".) In the first case, instructors use strategies such as posing questions to students after reading or putting students in cooperative learning groups to help the student gain better vocabulary, sentence structure, discourse structure, or content knowledge. Students may notice that these are useful procedures, but they are not taught and given practice to use these as their own learning tools. In the second case, students learn to use simple cognitive acts to improve their own comprehension of text before, during, and after reading or listening. Students are explicitly and systematically taught to ask themselves a question, identify a main idea, or repair their comprehension independently and as needed in their own reading.

Many tools or strategies can go both ways. For example, one popular instructional strategy is a graphic organizer that visually groups and links words, concepts, or parts of discourse. SLPs often use graphic organizers to teach language goals. To do this, an SLP constructs these organizers with his or her students, discusses how the parts are linked, and reviews what has been learned, often quite apart from the original text-sharing activity. The SLP then takes progress data on the language or comprehension skills demonstrated by the students. In contrast, for a graphic organizer to be used by a student as a reading comprehension strategy, the SLP teaches a student to quickly sketch out a visual map after reading a passage. The student is given opportunities to practice using the organizer during reading activities, and then guided on employing the organizer in a helpful way in class assignments. Ideally, the SLP will collaborate with a subject area teacher to identify reading opportunities for the student to use the graphic organizer. In this case, the SLP takes progress data on whether the student chooses to use the organizer in reading assignments as well as whether comprehension improves as a result of the use.

The question of strategy ownership is an issue even when the student is taught to use the strategy as a learning tool. Many students stop using their learned strategies as soon as the requirements and reminders are removed (Gersten et al., 2001). For example,

Chan and Cole (1986) taught fairly simple strategies that involved asking themselves and a robot content questions, underlining interesting words, and explaining to the robot why 11-year-olds with reading disabilities would find these words interesting. Posttesting showed, after only four sessions, improved comprehension and recall of stories compared to the results of a condition that controlled for reading time and special attention by having the students reread the story to the robot in case he missed parts the first time. However, the day after the training sessions, when given two more stories with no directions for how to read, none of the students used the explaining and question generating. The underlining with the fluorescent pen showed more maintenance, with two-thirds of the students using it to some degree without direction.

Chan and Cole (1986) also found that not all students need specific reading strategies. The 11-year-olds had been matched to younger typical readers in each condition. The 8-year-old regular education students improved just as much from rereading the passage as from the use of explicit strategy. Simply answering questions about a text and then rereading the text may be enough for some readers to actively process what they are reading and improve their comprehension. This outcome goes to the core of reading strategies and strategic reading. Reading strategies are simply helpful practices that readers need to remember to use. Willingham (2006) compares reading strategies to checking one's work in math: it is easy to do, but it needs to be done and done carefully. Self-question checklists, procedural steps, and training regimens help students apply strategies to their reading, but fundamentally, what matters is their mindful engagement with reading.

Teaching Text Language and Structure

Using reading strategies to monitor and repair comprehension is like checking your answers in math. However, checking your math does not tell you how to fix the errors you find (Willingham, 2006). For text comprehension, students need be careful checkers of their understanding, but they also need to have the language skills, cognitive processes, and domain knowledge to repair their understanding.

Language Skills

A central part of improving text comprehension is developing language skills. The chapters of this book on vocabulary, grammar, and discourse all deal with improving students' language abilities in academically relevant ways. Growth in the breadth and depth of curricular vocabulary, control over complex clausal and expanded phrasal structure, awareness of narrative and expository structure, metalinguistic skills, and understanding of how all these linguistic areas vary by subject area all improve the ability to understand academic texts.

Language intervention involves both spoken and written modalities. Students listen to and talk about written-style sentences and discourse, and refer to books and print to find information. Using both spoken and written modalities to teach academic language expands teaching options. A benefit of printed text is its static nature. Students can see the vocabulary, grammar, and discourse structure of a passage. They can search, revise, and review. At the same time, spoken interactions give the SLP the benefit of hearing and responding to a student's learning as it occurs. In addition to circumventing decoding problems, the SLP can monitor and scaffold the student's meaning making, self-monitoring, and self-correction in a way that having a student read silently or aloud does not afford.

While transfer is expected and capitalized upon, there are differences in the vocabulary and grammar of the two modalities. Formal written language has a much higher density of specific, infrequent vocabulary and propositions (idea units) with more subordination and phrasal elaboration and less redundancy and rephrasing (Kamhi & Catts, 2012; Scott, 1995; see Chapter 8). It can be both more concise and more elaborated than spoken language and is usually better organized. At the same time, written language does not capture the subtleties of communicative emphasis and attitude: punctuation is a poor substitute for timing, stress, facial expression, and gesture.

In the early grades, spoken language intervention without specific attention to print will transfer to understanding of written language (American Speech-Language-Hearing Association, 2010; Kamhi & Catts, 2012). What is termed *language* and *speaking and listening* in the Common Core represents only a small portion of possible language intervention goals. Most of the language expectations are actually embedded in the categories of reading and writing. These goals can be addressed through speaking and listening interactions relating to print and books that allow beginning readers and poor decoders to bypass their reading limitations. Students can develop their linguistic skills, academic concepts, and world knowledge through talking and listening and then apply them to their reading and writing. Close connections with teachers and classroom activities further improve students' application of their improved language skills to educational success.

As students move into the later grades, the focus of intervention changes from developing academic language skills to helping students intentionally and strategically use those skills in particular contexts, which means that rather than focusing only on how to make definitions and sentences out of curricular vocabulary, more attention will be given to teaching students how to notice when they do not understand a word, how to use context to infer the word meaning, and what to do to figure out word meaning when the text is not enough (Kamil et al., 2008). A common syntax goal is learning how to combine simple sentences into complex grammar in written compositions. A reading comprehension goal for students can be to *simplify* grammar. Students can be taken sentence by sentence through a formal written paragraph to restate each in plain English. (I do this with college students on research reports.) The process of chunking, reordering, and rewording words and sentences teaches students to understand the meaning of complex sentences and sets up the foundation for paraphrasing and summarization.

Text Summarization

Finding the main idea and constructing summaries of paragraphs, sections, chapters, and articles are central to academic learning. Teaching summarizing is one of the most effective ways to improve students' reading comprehension (NRP, 2000a). However, many students are not ready to use summarization as a strategy and need explicit instruction in the component elements, beginning simply with identifying main idea statements (Baumann, 1984; Taylor & Beach, 1984; Wong, Wong, Perry, & Sawatsky, 1986).

Wong et al. (1986) investigated teaching seventh graders with learning disabilities to compose well-structured summaries. The procedure used is presented in Box 15.7. This instruction began by presenting a simple paragraph with an explicit topic sentence, such as: "Mr. Brown was getting angry. His face was bright red. His pupils seemed to enlarge in size suddenly. His body began to shake. His voice was becoming louder and louder"

Box 15.7. ***A Multistage Procedure for Teaching Summarization***

Start with the Concept of Main Idea and Details

1. The main idea is the most general statement in the paragraph.
2. The main idea should explicitly explain the general topic.
3. Most of the other sentences should refer to the main idea.
4. The other sentences are details that should elaborate or qualify the main idea.
5. Do those sentences make sense if the main idea sentence is gone?

Composing a Summary

1. Identify and paraphrase the most important sentence in the paragraph.
2. If there is no stated topic sentence, create one from the main idea of the detail sentences.
3. Identify and then ignore redundant, trivial, or irrelevant details.
4. Add the major relevant details to the main idea.
5. Link the summary statements to make a larger unified idea for a section.

Self-Questioning for Summarizing Readings

1. In this paragraph, is there anything I don't understand?
2. In this paragraph, what's the most important sentence (main idea)? I will underline it.
3. I will summarize the paragraph. I will rewrite the main idea sentence and add important details.
4. Now, does my summary statement link up with the subheading?
5. I will review my written summary statements for a whole subsection. Do all my summary statements link up with one another? Do they all link up with the subheading?
6. At the end of this reading section, can I see all the themes here? If yes, let me predict the teacher's test question on this section. If no, let me go back to step 4.

Note: From Wong et al., 1986.

(p. 23). The investigators started instruction at this very simple level because they observed that initially, when their students were told to underline and then paraphrase the main idea of simple paragraphs, they just repeated random sentences from the paragraphs and became frustrated with their own confusion. The instructor illustrated the relationship of main ideas and supporting details with a graphical organizer (Box 15.8). To help students see how the main idea unifies and makes sense of the detail sentences, the instructor covered the main idea sentence box and asked the students whether the other sentences made any sense without the main idea: "Who are the sentences talking

Box 15.8 ***A Graphical Organizer for Main Ideas and Details***

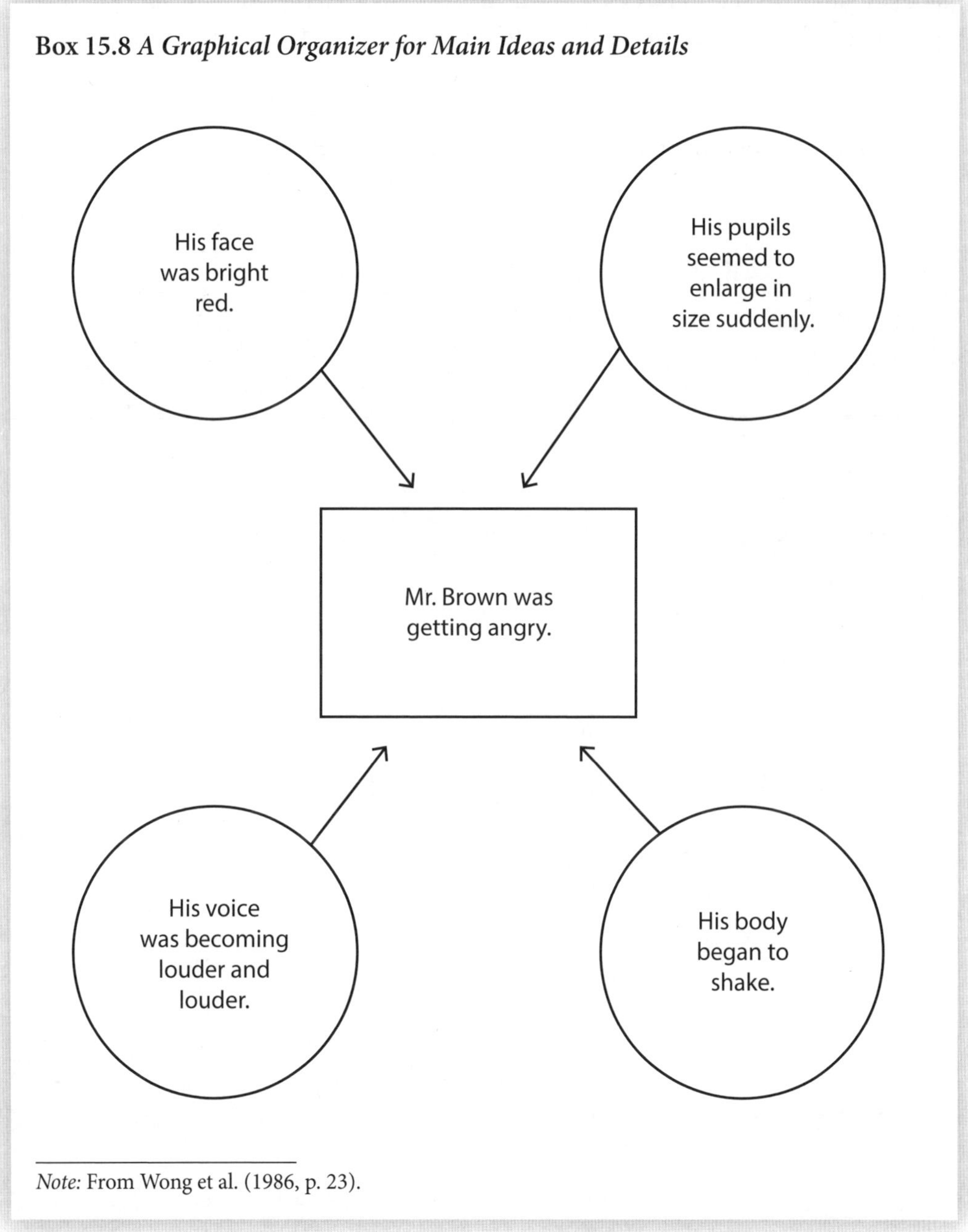

Note: From Wong et al. (1986, p. 23).

about? Whose voice is getting louder? If I came into the room and said those sentences, would I make sense?" The students then practiced on paragraphs with support from a card displaying the main idea rules. The position of the topic sentence in the paragraphs varied, so students had to examine the ideas in the sentences to find the main idea. After students could independently find the main ideas in these paragraphs, paragraphs containing two main ideas and double paragraphs were used.

For the next stage of summarization, using simple paragraphs, Wong et al. (1986) taught the students to locate the main idea sentence first, then rewrite it in their own words, and then add important detail sentences. Students followed a summarization guide similar to the one in Box 15.9. The instructor modeled the thinking process of saying aloud words that came to mind, writing them down, and deciding on the phrasing.

Box 15.9. ***A Summarization Form for a Subject Area Text***

Chapter Title:
Main Section Title:
Subsection Subtitle:
A. Main Idea Sentence(s):
B. Important Details: 1. 2. 3. 4.
C. Summary Sentence:

The paraphrased main idea sentence was written on the summarization form. Wong et al. reported that it took about a month for the students to be able to articulate their thoughts and paraphrase main ideas. When the students could summarize simple paragraphs unaided, the steps were repeated with more complex paragraphs.

The final stage involved the students applying the summarization procedure to their classroom social studies texts using the summarization form and six self-questioning prompts. The students memorized the self-questions to provide themselves with an executive control strategy. The instructor showed how the summarization statements from each paragraph linked up with the textbook subheadings, revealing the themes of the chapter. The instructor then showed the students how to summarize without writing the main idea sentence verbatim but rather by beginning with a paraphrase and how crossing out and revising the paraphrase to find the best wording was part of the process.

In a multiple baseline design across eight middle school students with learning disabilities, Wong et al. (1986) found, after three months of three 30-minute sessions a week, noticeable improvement on summarization elements and recall of social studies passages. Six of the students maintained use one month after the end of instruction and showed substantial transfer to general science texts. However, there was considerable variation in achievement. Two students quickly learned how to summarize and apply the self-questioning procedure to their reading. Those students maintained use and made modifications that indicated ownership of the strategy. Two students showed a lack of motivation, slow learning, and lack of retention. These students showed a fundamental disengagement with academic learning that extended beyond the study.

The foregoing instruction involved paragraphs with explicit main idea statements. Students must also deal with paragraphs that lack topic sentences and even with some that have trivial, redundant, or irrelevant details. The graphical organizer can be used to map details to reveal an unstated main idea. The circles are again used for each detail sentence but without the linking lines. Each sentence is examined for how it relates to the others. When an idea that is common to several detail sentences is determined, that idea is written in the main idea box and linking lines are drawn. Irrelevant detail circles remain isolated. Details are then ranked as major or minor. Redundant details are linked by an equal sign and one of the pair is crossed off. In this way, students learn how to infer a main idea and plan a well-formulated summary.

Summarization can operate on noncontinuous document text as well as on prose text. Students can learn to extract the main idea and supporting details from websites, brochures, and PowerPoint presentations. While discontinuous text is easier to read quickly, it can be difficult to get a coherent sense of the whole from varied fonts, images, headings, bulleted lists, and isolated statements. Thus, students need support to learn to understand this kind of text, too.

Text Structure

Written texts have main ideas and details, but they are also organized into discourse that achieves communicative purposes. Teaching students to identify and map the organization of discourse improves reading comprehension (Gersten et al., 2001; RRSG, 2002). Text structure analysis involves both linguistic and cognitive skills as students construct mental schematic representations of text that interrelate new actions, ideas, and events, and combine all this with prior knowledge. Graphical organizers, also known as concept maps or semantic webs, are helpful for displaying and organizing narrative and expository discourse structure.

Narrative has a characteristic episodic structure that is fairly easy to map using story grammar charts, manipulatives, and visual organizers. Identifying episodic elements, such as complication, motivations, and attempts, and determining how these relate to each other help students understand the stories they hear and read. Story grammar instruction is usually used to help young students compose complete and elaborate episodic narratives (see Chapter 8). It can also be used to help older students with reading comprehension (Crabtree, Alber-Morgan, & Konrad, 2010; Goddard & Sendi, 2008; Nathanson, Crank, Saywitz, & Ruegg, 2007; Idol, 1987; Idol & Croll, 1987). For example, in a multiple baseline across subjects design, Crabtree et al. investigated the use of story grammar mapping for three high school students with learning disabilities. After the students learned how to identify story grammar elements, they were required to stop at predesignated points in their narrative reading and identify story grammar elements by writing them down on a structured guide. Using this procedure rather than having the students simply read stories and answer questions about the content improved story recall and comprehension.

Expository or informational discourse is more difficult to analyze structurally. It is made up of a variety of subgenres that lack characteristic organizations. There is a conventional five-paragraph format to essays, and research papers follow a standard structure, but there is little other definitive structure. A persuasion or opinion essay has a characteristic form that has been taught within SRSD with the mnemonic of DARE (Graham & Harris, 1999; Wong, Butler, Ficzere, & Kuperis, 1996). Unfortunately, while the mnemonic is memorable, its components are not: "**D**etermine your premise, **A**ssemble reasons to support your premise, **R**eject arguments for the other side, and **E**nd with a conclusion" (p. 259). Adding key words (e.g., *I believe, there is evidence, first, in addition, in conclusion*) helps with the comprehension and composition of a persuasive essay (Ukrainetz, 2006).

Graphical organizers are helpful in identifying and understanding discourse structure. For explanations and descriptions, a taxonomic layout of main ideas and categories, subordinate ideas and subcategories, and supporting details is a common display. Procedural discourse can be represented as a sequential flowchart to aid comprehension and recall. Other types of informational discourse involve relations between ideas that are often not set out in a clear, sequential fashion. Analysis of these logically related structures promote deeper understandings of text (Armbruster, Anderson, & Meyer, 1991; Gersten et al., 2001). For example, cause-effect, problem-solution, and compare-contrast information often require students to review, reorganize, and integrate information to answer questions such as: "What are three major obstacles to progress on Israeli-Palestinian peace talks?" and "What does this passage say about the similarities between the concerns of Israelis and Palestinians?" Discourse analysis with graphical supports helps students identify discourse components, separate out essential from nonessential details, decide on the most important concepts, work through the logical relations of a text, and organize and integrate the content into a coherent mental structure.

Armbruster et al. (1991) showed how using a multifaceted discourse structure intervention instead of following standard teacher-led content-focused question-answer activities benefitted the reading comprehension of fourth- and fifth-grade students. In a repeated measures group experimental study, using teacher-directed and cooperative group activities, students analyzed social studies textbook passages using cause-effect, problem-solution, and compare-contrast frames. Results showed better recognition and recall of information for the instructional condition, especially for the fifth graders. Scanlon, Deshler, and Schumaker (1996) showed similar benefits for middle school students with learning disabilities in inclusive lessons taught by history and civics teachers.

Text Preview

Related to discourse structure analysis but operating on an even larger unit of communication is *text preview*, a strategy that involves teaching students how to become familiar with the text organization of their reading materials and to activate their own background knowledge. This is especially important for informational texts, which vary considerably in their organization and their reader friendliness. The preview process can also be applied to electronic sources, so that students learn to notice menus and navigational tools and obtain a sense of what the site is about and its likely value.

Text preview starts by identifying the purpose of reading the chosen material. The student then quickly travels through it to get a sense of the topics covered, the organization, how important points are indicated, and where summaries of the main ideas are located. Some informational texts provide a lot of organizational guidance and others less. The front cover, back cover, and inside cover all provide indicators of the topic and purpose. Chapter titles and section headings show how the material is organized. Knowing that there is an index or glossary will be useful at later points in reading. Interestingly, many science books written for students lack an introduction or even an opening paragraph. Instead, the prose embarks immediately on the first topic, prefaced perhaps with a "Note to Parents" or "Teacher's Guide" that describes the organization and purpose of the book (Ukrainetz & Ross, 2006). Students who understand the components of an informational text and how to preview their assigned or project materials will soon see how much more sense their materials make and how much faster they can get at the information they need. Motivated students are likely to adopt text preview as a regular reading strategy.

A Focus on Content in Comprehension Instruction

Topic expertise is a huge part of success in reading comprehension, exceeding academic aptitude, short-term memory, or reading fluency (Shanahan & Shanahan, 2008; Snow, 2010; Willingham, 2006). However, the rich store of interconnected knowledge that characterizes topic expertise needs more than traditional reading of controlled texts and answering recall questions. Although the Common Core does not specify which topics should be addressed at each grade, a high level of topic knowledge is required to achieve the set standards.

Life experiences are what contribute fundamentally to the funds of knowledge that students draw on for reading comprehension and educational success (Adams, 2011; Neuman, 2006; Willingham, 2007). However, educators only have control over school experiences. One way students can increase the knowledge they need to meet the twelfth-grade expectations of the Common Core is to "stay on topic" over time (p. 33). Staying on topic means that students are supported in reading rigorous texts and developing knowledge by delving deeply into a single broad topic within and across grades. For example, the Common Core lists books that all address the human body in increasingly difficult ways across kindergarten to fifth grade, such as *My Five Senses* by Aliki (1989) in kindergarten, *Under Your Skin* (Manning & Granstrom, 2007), *The Digestive System* (Taylor-Butler, 2008), and *The Amazing Circulatory System* (Burstein, 2009). By staying on topic across multiple texts and time in this way, a student can use what she or he already knows about the topic to facilitate comprehension of the next text. Concepts and language are repeatedly encountered in successively more difficult readings, with each experience building on the prior one (Adams, 2011). SLPs can emulate this on a smaller scale by linking their intervention content to classroom topics and materials and by creating miniature topic worlds by embedding skill treatment in projects and thematic units in the whole-part framework described in Chapter 3.

Building Content Comprehension

Content and strategy instruction both aim to engender active student engagement with reading (McKeown, Beck, & Blake, 2009). The two differ in their relative focus on mental processes versus text ideas. Content instruction is directed at integrating new ideas with existing knowledge in deep and coherent mental representations or schema. Instructional procedures may be teacher directed I-R-E (Initiation-Response-Evaluation) or may involve more beneficial discussion and interactive methods (McKeown et al., 2009).

There are some simple procedures that guide the students to notice text information and help students integrate new learning into existing knowledge. In K-W-L+, anticipation-based reading guides are filled on the basis of what the students **K**now, what they **W**ant to know, and, after the reading, what they have **L**earned (Carr & Ogle, 1987). The final *plus* element refers to categorizing and relating the concepts using graphic organizers. This procedure activates background knowledge, reminds students about the goal of the reading, and then helps them be aware of what was new and integrate it into their existing knowledge.

Raphael (1986) had young students think about the relationship between the text and the reader. Raphael grouped questions as *In the Book*, which can be *Right There* (obvious), or *Think and Search* (putting it together), or *In My Head*, which can be *Author and You* (inferring) or *On My Own* (known without reading). Teaching students the type of questions they are asking and the source of their answers helps them be aware of their own comprehension processes and where their answers are coming from.

In a procedure called Questioning the Author (QtA; Beck, McKeown, Sandora, Kucan, & Worthy, 1996), students seek to understand the text as communication, asking questions like: "What is the author trying to say here? Did the author explain this clearly? How does that connect with what the author already told us?" and "Did the author give us the answer to that?" In QtA, students take turns reading a passage aloud. Reading is stopped and discussion initiated at preselected points, such as when a key character is introduced, an important event has occurred, or reader confusion seems likely. At each stopping point, the teacher asks an open-ended question to foregound an important idea and then follows with a question to elicit additional information about aspects of that idea. Through qualitative analysis of QtA conversations in fourth-grade classrooms, Beck et al. found that teachers gradually increased their emphasis on constructing and extending meaning. Over time, conversations about the readings gradually shifted from teacher-dominated to more student participation, and students increased the number and complexity of their questions and contributions.

McKeown et al. (2009) compared the effects of QtA to a strategy-focused instruction condition and a scripted basal text instruction condition for six classrooms of fifth graders. In the strategy condition, students learned to summarize, predict, draw inferences, generate questions, and monitor comprehension. The three approaches were taught through teacher-directed whole class instruction over the school year. The teacher read aloud while the students followed in their text, stopping at set points in the text for content discussion, strategy practice, or answering questions. Year-end results showed no significant differences across the three approaches for sentence verification, comprehension monitoring, or recognition of better summaries, inferences, and questions. For narrative recall and expository knowledge probes, amount and quality of responses were better for the content condition, even for new texts. For transfer to unlearned material, there was a nonsignificant trend in favor of the content condition.

McKeown et al. (2009) sought the source of this modest but consistent advantage by analyzing the lesson transcripts. For the content condition, the students focused on the text and remembered it, whereas for the strategies condition, the focus was split between strategies and content. The summarizing strategy broke up meaning making because the students had to think about who, what, when, and where and then build these into a summary in contrast to the more integrative and simple content question of "What's going on?" For questioning, students thought about what makes a good question rather than what is important content to be questioned. This strategy instruction was not about consistent use of a few easy strategies, but rather it targeted a large number of strategies, with many requiring extended instruction, all done at the same time as students were trying to learn new content. McKeown et al. recognized some of this learning overload and recommended teaching strategies using short texts unrelated to the main lesson, then introducing them into the content lesson with teacher cognitive modeling as natural opportunities occur. McKeown et al. noted that, in different ways, all three approaches, with their directed discussions of text, encouraged active comprehension and mental knowledge templates that could be applied to other texts. Even the basal condition did better than expected, which might have been due to its delivery with oral reading and discussive question asking.

Teaching Disciplinary Comprehension

Understanding and learning from academic texts involves tailoring strategies and structures to specialized subject areas. The Common Core separates only literature and informational texts, but students need to know the nature of knowledge and how it is communicated across subject areas. High school is only the beginning of disciplinary comprehension, with expertise in specialized areas developing over years of higher education and work experience. However, disciplinary literacy begins here. Different approaches to teaching disciplinary literacy are only just emerging, but there is increasing attention to them (Kamhi, 2012).

Using historical dramas and biographies provides students with emotional and personal connections to events and helps them to see multiple perspectives and connections among those events (Hansen, 2009). Teachers can guide students to read multiple historical texts on a topic and to start learning to "read like historians." Starting in middle school, students can learn how to evaluate, compare, and synthesize across fictional and factual accounts of history and how to determine whether sources are informative or reliable (Van Sledright & Kelly, 1998).

Disciplinary instruction increasingly integrates learning across modalities in purposeful learning activities. Project-based and experiential learning introduces students to the ways that professionals in those disciplines formulate and communicate knowledge. Alvermann and Wilson (2011) describe a middle school unit on soil erosion that involved making connections from outdoor observations not only to their science textbook but also to maps and photographs of the dust bowl in America in the 1930s. Ideas for applying metacognitive processes, comprehension strategies, and language flexibility in science lessons based on Wilson (2008) are presented in Box 15.10.

The SLP can guide students to examine the expository organization of explanations and processes in a particular subject area, and to fit general reading strategies to the discipline. Shanahan and Shanahan (2008) give an example for chemistry in which, instead of summarizing from a main idea and detail format, students fill in a chart of substances, properties, and reactions as they read. For math, disciplinary experts preferred a chart that listed one column as the "big idea," the next as the formal definition, followed by the formula, and then an example. Historians favored a summarization chart of who, what, where, when, how, and why for each event along with a specification of the relationship between events. The relationship between events was much more important than the event features or chronological succession.

The disciplinary experts in Shanahan and Shanahan (2008) considered that customized strategies were not separable from disciplinary learning itself: filling out a structured summarization chart for chemistry is "doing chemistry." This highlights the importance of learning comprehension strategies in the context of the content. In addition, the disciplinary experts considered that supplementary motivational and contextualizing information in textbooks distracted from and obscured the subject matter, making the intended learning more difficult. Shanahan and Shanahan gave the example of a story about lake pollution that focused students on a particular event and its larger

Box 15.10. ***Teaching Multimodal Texts in Science***

Principle	**Specific Applications**
Students should be metacognitive concerning their own comprehension as they make sense of multimodal texts.	• Conduct a think-aloud on a lab or demonstration, modeling wonderings about why a physical reaction happened, and then ask students to do the same.
Students should apply comprehension strategies as they read, view, and listen to multimodal texts.	• In a demonstration or lab, ask students to identify the one or two most important factors that caused the phenomenon to occur and to justify why they chose that factor. • Ask students to connect a demonstration, a written passage, a diagram, or a video clip to another text or to natural phenomena observed in their own lives.
Students should be aware of the affordances and limitations in different representations of scientific content, including their own representations.	• Ask students to demonstrate a scientific concept in three different ways, say which way they thought most clearly conveyed the content, and explain why. • Show students a scientific concept in one mode (e.g., a written paragraph) and ask them to display the content differently (e.g., a diagram or three-dimensional model) and explain why their new representation is better.

Note: From "Moving Beyond the Page in Content Area Literacy: Comprehension Instruction for Multimodal Texts in Science," by A.A. Wilson, 2011, *The Reading Teacher, 62,* p. 153.

environmental aspects and deflected attention from the main lesson on chemical concepts and their abstract hierarchical arrangement.

Putting It All Together: Strategies, Content, and Engagement

Effective reading comprehension instruction is multifaceted. It involves teaching language skills and cognitive strategies for gaining meaning and monitoring comprehension. Having students analyze, synthesize, and transform texts with visual graphical supports improves their understanding of what they read (Gersten et al., 2001; NRP, 2000a; RRSG, 2002; Willingham, 2006). Instructor modeling of thinking processes, cooperative student learning, and connecting strategy instruction to subject matter increase student engagement and enhance learning. Literature discussions, projects, and experiential learning further promote student engagement, acquisition of funds of knowledge, and disciplinary literacy. All of these instructional elements contribute to effective reading comprehension instruction (Box 15.11).

Box 15.11. ***Elements of Effective Reading Comprehension Instruction***

Discourse Structure Activities

1. Explicit attention to text structure and features that indicate how ideas are related
2. Graphical representation of ideas and the relations among ideas
3. Drawing relationships between students' own knowledge and the content of the reading selection
4. Determining and recasting in a summary the most important information
5. Transforming ideas from one form to another

Instructional Arrangements

1. Having students actively involved in their own learning, both through motivated student choice and self-monitoring during reading
2. Instructor modeling of thinking and comprehension processes
3. Students tutoring each other or studying cooperatively
4. Increasing reading of connected text, including sustained silent reading and repeated readings of a single text
5. Connecting strategy instruction to subject matter
6. Employing a diversity of authentic text genres
7. Exposure to quality books, films, and other media and life experiences
8. Assessment of the learning process through observation, think-alouds, and self-reports.

Note: Compiled from RAND Reading Study Group (2002), Paris et al. (1991), Pearson and Fielding (1991), Tierney and Readence (2000), and Willingham (2006).

While no single instructional program can do it all, Concept-Oriented Reading Instruction (CORI; http://www.cori.umd.edu) might come close. CORI is systematically organized around student motivation and engagement, scientific concepts and inquiry skills, and reading strategies taught within content reading with differentiated learning support (Box 15.12). Guthrie et al. (2009) investigated this program in a group comparative design. Six classes of fifth graders received 12 weeks of instruction, 90 minutes a day, with additional instruction for low achievers, that was based on the theme of animal-plant interactions in ecological communities. Their performance was compared to that of three classes of fifth graders who received the same amount of instruction but in disconnected lessons involving decoding and fluency, basal readers, story writing, and independent reading on diverse topics. Results showed greater improvement for the treatment condition in attitude toward learning, reading comprehension, content

Box 15.12. ***Features of Concept-Oriented Reading Instruction***

Motivational and Concept Features	
Choices	Students given some control over texts, subtopics, and writing activities
Relevance	Hands-on activities and connection of texts to theme and experiences
Collaboration	Students collaborate in pairs on strategy selection and practice
Thematic Units	An overarching theme links all the reading and writing activities to promote deep, interconnected knowledge
Success	Students read trade books related to the theme at their level
Diverse Texts	Concepts learned and linked through science, poetry, novel, and legend books
Strategy Instruction	
Word Fix-Ups	Reread, use a picture, chunk it, discuss with a partner, draw it, look it up, read ahead, read aloud
Sentence Fix-Ups	Fix-up strategies applied to confusing sentences
Passage Analysis	Identify main idea versus details and how details link to the main idea
Instructional Features for Low Achievers	
Texts	Informational and narrative trade books at a range of reading levels
Concepts	Fewer concepts taught at a time, with more graphics and less print
Writing	Student charts and reports require less writing
Fluency	Extra guided practice in fluency and decoding skills
Strategies	Fix-up strategies taught at a slower pace with more modeling; taught inferencing conclusions from stated information in text

Note: Based on Guthrie et al. (2009).

knowledge, and word recognition for both typical and low-achieving students. The improvements carried over to subsequent reading and learning activities.

Key elements to this integrated reading program were student motivation and engagement with learning. Guthrie et al. (2013) statistically modeled the relationships among reading instruction, motivation, engagement, and achievement across data from over 1,000 seventh graders in CORI and traditional instruction. The statistical path analysis revealed that in traditional instruction, engagement and achievement were separate outcomes of instruction and motivation. In contrast, CORI showed a cascading and reciprocal positive effect between student interest and educational achievement. Guthrie et al. suggested that not only were the more motivated and confident students more successful but that CORI benefited even the low-achieving students by increasing their confidence in their capacity to succeed as well as their interest in science reading. This improved their performance, which further promoted positive attitudes toward academic learning. This positive attitude toward challenging scientific learning was due, in part, to having tools for success, such as strategy instruction and relevant, accessible texts.

Beyond Instruction to Intervention

Comprehensive reading instruction involves cognitive strategies, language skills, discourse structure awareness, content knowledge, disciplinary literacy, and student motivation and engagement in learning. That is a lot to do. How should the SLP fit into this daunting picture of instruction? Happily, recommendations to coordinate content and strategy instruction within motivating activities accords well with what SLPs can do with their distinctive areas of expertise and service delivery models and fits with a contextualized skill whole-part approach to intervention.

A Contextualized Skill Framework

The main advice is to connect with the classroom. The more SLPs can connect their individualized interventions to the classroom and the curriculum, the more likely that students will apply the knowledge and skills they acquire in treatment to their assignments and exams. SLPs can observe students, examine work artifacts, and collaborate with teachers to identify strategies that make sense within content lessons. For older students, a partnership in selecting goal priorities, materials, and activities will produce the buy-in needed to make real change.

Intervention links to the classroom can be simply thematic, or they can involve classroom reading materials or activities structured like those of the classroom. SLPs can teach skills and strategies by using a student's existing interests and expertise or by using thematic units and projects. Small group instruction allows for motivating peer interactions and modeling. Intervention in disciplinary literacy can involve helping students with features of subject-area texts, like precise word use and logical links in science and metaphorical word use and character perspective in English. SLPs can work with teachers to elicit and support use of the practiced strategies within classroom lessons.

SLPs need to stay therapeutic. Almost any academic activity will provide rich language and learning opportunities, but only a small number of goals can be addressed effectively given the limited contact time of speech–language services. Students need repeated opportunities, intensity, systematic scaffolding, and explicit instruction (RISE) to make changes. SLPs, therefore, should choose a small number of goals that produce noticeable, functional change and help students become more competent and independent learners. For example, teaching older students to notice when they do not understand a word and what to do about it may be more helpful to them than practicing writing definitions and sentences for a small set of new vocabulary.

While classroom connections are critical to intervention success, this does not mean SLPs teach the curricular content. Teachers teach content following a prescriptive curriculum of scope and sequence of knowledge and skills throughout the grades and across subject areas. Teachers can also address underlying skills and strategies, but often, in the face of heavy curricular demands, this attention is fleeting (Ukrainetz & Fresquez, 2003). In contrast, the distinctive contribution of SLPs is that they can teach at a rate and in a manner that enables each student to significantly improve on a few critical linguistic and cognitive skills that support success across content areas.

Text Choices for Comprehension Intervention

Comprehension must operate on something. For text comprehension, that something must form some kind of coherent communicative whole but be short and structured enough to systematically work on the parts. Texts are primarily written prose texts that are read aloud to students, but they can also be electronic noncontinuous texts, diagrams, and graphs.

Printed text provides a critical structural scaffold for comprehension of academic discourse. Listening to passages read aloud and answering questions about them avoids the issue of decoding ability. However, written and spoken discourse are structured differently (Kamhi & Catts, 2012; Scott, 1995), and texts designed for the eye are not well received by the ear. Thus, when working on listening comprehension, SLPs should share the printed text with their students (by showing the text on a screen for a small group or sitting on the same side of the table with an individual student). Even poor decoders are able to locate information better by looking back at the printed page than by depending on recall alone. Underlining and marginalia can help the student focus on the important parts of the text.

Sets of paragraphs and passages from instructional programs provide repeated, equivalent opportunities for learning and practice. There is a reading fluency program called *QuickReads* (Hiebert, 2003) that provides a large collection of history, civics, and science passages at second-, third-, and fourth-grade reading levels. The reading materials consist of sets of controlled-difficulty passages on a single topic, such as "Life in Colonial America," "National Symbols," or "Your Five Senses." The passages could also be modified to provide confusing or missing elements for comprehension momitoring and clarification. Making comprehension monitoring a detective game would further increase student motivation: Oakhill and Petrides (2007) reported that 8- and 9-year-olds improved their comprehension monitoring and subsequent understanding when passages were presented as a game of spotting problems in texts to solve a crime.

Even more effective than using isolated passages and activities is using passages selected from a larger whole to provide better topical coherence and more possibilities for meaningful, purposeful reading. Social studies and science texts or source papers for classroom projects can be used to learn underlying skills and strategies. In doing so, students and SLPs need to keep their focus on strategies, text structure, and language skills, and not get drawn into completing assignments or studying for tests.

If the SLP can provide the texts or articles, then he or she can better control the instruction. Trade books, magazines, and websites can be selected to match classroom topics, individual student interests, or thematic treatment units. A website that reviews mountain bikes or video games provides a motivating context in which to apply language skills or reading strategies. These sources are often heavy on disconnected document text, with pictures, subheadings, bulleted lists, points to ponder, and salient facts. Students need to learn how to sort through and make sense of these discrete information bites just as they do with prose texts.

Students can engage in activities that require purposeful text comprehension. Collections of short pieces of discourse provide an ideal balance between repeated, structured learning opportunities and a meaningful whole. For example, the book *202 Oozing, Bubbling, Dripping, and Bouncing Experiments* (Van Cleave, 1996) provides repeated comprehension opportunities in high-interest, purposeful activities. For each experiment a purpose, materials, sequenced steps, and expected results are specified. While most could be completed within a single treatment session, repeated readings with modeling, guidance, discussion, and review maximize the opportunities for learning and practice. Sandra McKinnis, an SLP in Anchorage, Alaska, recommends manuals and kits for green slime, balloon animals, origami, airplanes, and magic tricks. The completed projects and written compositions are shared at home or in school. One principal put the projects in the school's central display case. As McKinnis said, "What a motivator!"

In Ukrainetz and Ross (2006), we describe embedding text comprehension intervention into an oral debate on a controversial topic and a presentation on a student-selected library research project. Since then, Ross has found that keeping the projects simpler is better for maintaining a therapeutic focus on the intervention goals. Providing the source materials for the student to produce a short PowerPoint presentation with rehearsed spoken statements is sufficient to provide a motivating context and purposeful reading activities.

Strategy Intervention

Strategy intervention has some particular considerations (Box 15.13). The first is that the teaching of particular strategies is not as important as teaching habitual use of strategies and their contribution to students becoming mindful, engaged readers. As Gersten et al. (2001) note, strategies are "crude approximations" (p. 309) of what expert readers occasionally engage in. What matters most is that students get into the habit of asking themselves, "Where does this seem to be going?" and responding with, "I think I missed something. I better reread that part."

Second, SLPs need to be strategic about their strategy instruction. A large number of vague and variable strategies, strategies that require extensive instruction or those that do not produce obvious benefits, will not result in mindful engagement with reading. Choose a few simple strategies that can be easily learned and used. Connect with the classroom to be sure those strategies will work in those contexts. Use a specific format

Box 15.13. ***Text Comprehension Intervention by SLPs***

1. Connect with the classroom to determine the strategy goal.
2. Stay therapeutic with RISE.
3. Be strategic in choosing intervention goals.
4. Be a cognitive model for strategic reading.
5. Teach a few strategies and use consistent, memorable wording.
6. Teach one before, one during, and one after reading strategy.
7. Some strategies need to be taught first as skills.
8. Collect data on the process of use in addition to the product.
9. Help students develop the habit of mindful engagement with reading.
10. Connect with the classroom to determine success on the strategy goal.

and systematic instruction with visual supports. A simple strategy plan is "before, during, after," or BDA, which is similar to Mason's (2004) TWA but is a more transparent mnemonic. For example: (a) *before* reading, ask and answer the question "*What* is this passage about?" by looking at the heading or other topic indicators (b) *during* reading, stop to state one idea per paragraph that relates to the *what*; and (c) *after* reading several paragraphs, restate the main ideas from each paragraph and describe how those ideas link again to *what* this passage is about. To aid recall, idea statements can be underlined in the text or written on a separate sheet. Over repeated opportunities with reminders in advance and checkups during reading, students are likely to begin to develop the habits recommended by NRP (2000) of asking themselves questions, monitoring their comprehension, and summarizing what they have read.

SLPs should teach reading comprehension strategies through cognitive modeling. To be an effective cognitive model, the clinician reviews the reading selection in advance, considering it from a student perspective and checking that it matches the strategies to be demonstrated. Points in the text are planned to model particular strategies (e.g., "This paragraph isn't clear, I will reread it and find the main idea."), demonstrating how to read and think about reading at the same time. Cognitive modeling should be applied not only to preplanned texts but also to more natural situations where students are likely to encounter bumps in the acquisition process.

For strategy instruction, it is particularly important that treatment goals and progress data examine the *process* as well as the *product* of comprehension (Kamhi, 2012). Observing a student's actions during reading, having the student stop and say what he is thinking (called *think-alouds*), or having the student say or show what he did after reading are all ways of getting at the process. The statements, the underlining, SLP notes on prompts required, and other evidence of students' mental processes during intervention can be used as data to show progress toward the goal of strategic reading. These alternate assessment procedures can reveal not only independent strategy use but also how well students understand text and where breakdowns are occurring (Gillam, Fargo, & Robertson, 2009; Wong et al., 1986).

Conclusion

Academic reading and listening comprehension involve active, mindful engagement with meaningful texts. The skills and strategies occur before reading, such as previewing subheadings and looking for organizing concepts; during reading, such as identifying the main idea and rereading for clarification; and after reading, such as reflecting on what has been learned and relating it to prior experiences. Text comprehension also involves vocabulary, grammar, discourse, and metalinguistic skills, all of which vary by subject area, communicative purpose, and modality. Students need to be taught strategies and supported in their pursuit of independent, habitual use to improve text comprehension across modalities and representations. Peer interactions, systematic explicit procedures, cognitive modeling, and connections with the classroom are all vital to helping students become engaged learners who can improve their skills and strategies to achieve educational success.

References

Adams, M. J. (2011). Advancing our students' language and literacy. *American Educator, 34*(4), 3–11, 53.

Ainley, M., Hidi, S., & Berndorff, D. (2002). Interest, learning, and the psychological processes that mediate their relationship. *Journal of Educational Psychology, 94*, 545–561.

Ainley, M., Hillman, K., & Hidi, S. (2002). Gender and interest processes in response to literary texts: Situational and individual interest. *Learning and Instruction, 12*, 411–428.

Aliki. (1989). *My five senses.* New York, NY: Crowell.

Alvermann, D. E. & Wilson, A. A. (2011). Comprehension strategy instruction for multimodal texts in science. *Theory Into Practice, 50*, 116–124.

American Speech-Language-Hearing Association. (2010). *Roles and responsibilities of speech-language pathologists in schools* [Professional issues statement]. Baltimore, MD: Author.

Armbruster, B. B., Anderson, T. H., & Meyer, J. L. (1991). Improving content-area reading using instructional graphics. *Reading Research Quarterly, 26*, 393–416.

August, D. L., Flavell, J. H., & Clift, R. (1984). Comparison of comprehension monitoring of skilled and less skilled readers. *Reading Research Quarterly, 20*, 39–53.

Austen, J. (1816/1957). *Emma.* Boston, MA: Houghton-Mifflin.

Baker, S., Gersten, R., & Scanlon, D. (2002). Procedural facilitators and cognitive strategies: Tools for unraveling the mysteries of comprehension and the writing process, and for providing meaningful access to the general curriculum. *Learning Disabilities Research & Practice, 17*, 65–77.

Baumann, J. F. (1984). Effectiveness of a direct instruction paradigm for teaching main idea comprehension. *Reading Research Quarterly, 20*, 93–108.

Bazerman, C. (1985). Physicists reading physics. *Written Communication, 2*, 3–23.

Beck, I. L., McKeown, M. G., Sandora, C., Kucan, L., & Worthy, J. (1996). Questioning the author: A yearlong classroom implementation to engage students with text. *The Elementary School Journal, 96*, 385–414.

Brown, A. L., & Day, J. D. (1983). Macrorules for summarizing texts: The development of expertise. *Journal of Verbal Learning and Verbal Behavior, 22*, 1–14.

Burstein, J. (2009). *The amazing circulatory system: How does my heart work?* New York, NY: Crabtree.

Carr, E. M., & Ogle, D. M. (1987). K-W-L Plus: A strategy for comprehension and summarization. *Journal of Reading, 30*, 626–631.

Catts, H. W., Adolf, S. M., & Weismer, S. E. (2006). Language deficits in poor comprehenders: The case for the Simple View of Reading. *Journal of Speech, Language, and Hearing Research, 49*, 278–293.

Chall, J. (1983). *Stages of reading development.* New York, NY: McGraw-Hill.

Chan, L. K. S., & Cole, P. G. (1986). The effects of comprehension monitoring training on the reading competence of learning disabled and regular class students. *Remedial and Special Education, 7*, 33–40.

Chudgar, A. (1993). The challenge of universal elementary education in rural India: Can adult literacy play a role? *Comparative Education Review, 53*, 403–433.

Crabtree, T., Alber-Morgan, S. R., & Konrad, M. (2010). The effects of self-monitoring of story elements on the reading comprehension of high school seniors with learning disabilities. *Education and Treatment of Children, 22*, 187–203.

Fry, E. B. (1977). *Elementary reading instruction.* New York, NY: McGraw Hill.

Garner, R., & Reis, R. (1981). Monitoring and resolving comprehension obstacles: An investigation of spontaneous text lookbacks among upper-grade good and poor readers' comprehension. *Reading Research Quarterly, 16*, 569–582.

Gersten, R., Fuchs, L. S., Williams, J. P., & Baker, S. (2001). Teaching reading comprehension strategies to students with learning disabilities: A review of research. *Review of Educational Research, 71*, 279–320.

Gillam, S. L., Fargo, J. D., & Robertson, K. (2009). Comprehension of expository text: Insights gained from think-aloud data. *American Journal of Speech–Language Pathology, 18*, 82–94.

Goddard, Y. L., & Sendi, C. (2008). Effects of self-monitoring on the narrative and expository writing of four fourth-grade students with learning disabilities. *Reading and Writing Quarterly: Overcoming Learning Difficulties, 24*, 408–433.

Gough, P., & Tunmer, W. (1986). Decoding, reading, and reading disability. *Remedial and Special Education, 7*, 6–10.

Graham, S., & Harris, K. R. (1999). Assessment and intervention in overcoming writing difficulties: An illustration from the self-regulated strategy development model. *Language, Speech, and Hearing Services in Schools, 30*, 255–264.

Graham, S., Harris, K. R., & Troia, G. (2000). Self-regulated strategy development revisited: Teaching writing strategies to struggling writers. *Topics in Language Disorders, 20*(4), 1–14.

Guthrie, J. T., Klauda, S. L., & Ho, A. N. (2013). Modeling the relationships among reading instruction, motivation, engagement, and achievement for adolescents. *Reading Research Quarterly, 48*, 9–26.

Guthrie, J. T., McRae, A., Coddington, C. A., Klauda, S. L., Wigfield, A., & Barbosa, P. (2009). Impacts of comprehensive reading instruction on diverse outcomes of low- and high-achieving readers. *Journal of Learning Disabilities, 42*, 195–214.

Hansen, J. (2009). Multiple literacies in the content classroom: High school students' connections to U.S. history. *Journal of Adolescent & Adult Literacy, 52*, 597–606.

Hidi, S. (2001). Interest, reading, and learning: Theoretical and practical considerations. *Educational Psychology Review, 13*, 191–209.

Hiebert, E. H. (2003). *Quickreads: A research-based fluency program.* Parsippany, NJ: Pearson Learning Group.

Idol, L. (1987). Group story mapping: A comprehension strategy for both skilled and unskilled readers. *Journal of Learning Disabilities, 20*, 196–205.

Idol, L., & Croll, V. J. (1987). The effects of training in story mapping procedures on the reading comprehension of poor readers. *Learning Disability Quarterly, 10*, 214–230.

Kamhi, A. (2009). Prologue: The case for the narrow view of reading. *Language, Speech, and Hearing Services in Schools, 40*, 174–178.

Kamhi, A. (2012). Perspectives on assessing and improving reading comprehension. In A. G. Kamhi and H. W. Catts (Eds.), *Language and reading disabilities* (3rd ed., pp. 146–162). Boston, MA: Pearson.

Kamhi, A. G. & Catts, H. W. (2012). Language and reading: Convergences and divergences. In A. G. Kamhi & H. W. Catts (Eds.), *Language and reading disabilities* (3rd ed., pp. 1–23). Boston, MA: Pearson.

Kamil, M. L., Borman, G. D., Dole, J., Kral, C. C., Salinger, T., & Torgesen J. (2008). *Improving adolescent literacy: Effective classroom and intervention practices: A Practice Guide* (NCEE #2008-4027). Washington, DC: Institute of Education Sciences, U.S. Department of Education.

Kutner, M., Greenberg, E., & Baer, J. (2006). *National assessment of adult literacy (NAAL): A first look at the literacy of America's adults in the 21st century* (NCES 2006-470). Washington, DC: National Center for Education Statistics.

Manning, M., & Granstrom, B. (2007). *Under your skin.* Morton Grove, IL: Albert Whitman.

Mason, L. H. (2004). Explicit self-regulated strategy development versus reciprocal questioning: Effects on expository reading comprehension among struggling readers. *Journal of Educational Psychology, 96*, 283–296.

Mason, L. H., Meadan, H., Hedin, L., & Corso, L. (2006). Self-regulated strategy development instruction for expository text comprehension. *Teaching Exceptional Children, 38*, 47–52.

McKeown, M. G., Beck, I. L., & Blake, R. G. K. (2009). Rethinking reading comprehension instruction: A comparison of instruction for strategies and content approaches. *Reading Research Quarterly, 44*, 218–253.

Merriam-Webster. (1993). *Merriam-Webster's Collegiate Dictionary* (10th ed.). Springfield, MA: Author.

Moravcsik, J. E., & Kintsch, W. (1993). Writing quality, reading skills, and domain knowledge as factors in text comprehension. *Canadian Journal of Experimental Psychology, 47*, 360–374.

Nathanson, R., Crank, J. N., Saywitz, K. J., & Ruegg, E. (2007). Enhancing the oral narratives of children with learning disabilities. *Reading and Writing Quarterly, 23*, 315–331.

National Governors Association Center for Best Practices and Council of Chief State School Officers (2010). *Common Core State Standards for English Language Arts & Literacy in History/Social Studies, Science, and Technical Subjects.* Washington, DC: Author. Retrieved from http://www.corestandards.org/

National Reading Panel. (2000a). *Teaching children to read: An evidence-based assessment of the scientific research literature on reading and its implications for reading instruction* (NIH Publication No. 00-4769). Washington, DC: U.S. Department of Health and Human Services, National Institute of Child Health and Human Development. Retrieved from http://www.nationalreadingpanel.org/

National Reading Panel. (2000b). *Teaching children to read: an evidence-based assessment of the scientific research literature on reading and its implications for reading instruction: Reports of the subgroups* (NIH Publication No. 00-4754). Washington, DC: U.S. Department of Health and Human Services, National Institute of Child Health and Human Development.

Neuman, S. B. (2006). How we neglect knowledge—and why. *American Educator, Spring*, 24–27.

Oakhill, J. V., & Petrides, A. (2007). Sex differences in the effects of interest on boys' and girls' reading comprehension. *The British Psychological Society, 98*, 223–235.

Palincsar, A. S. (1986). The role of dialogue in providing scaffolded instruction. *Educational Psychologist, 21*, 73–98.

Palincsar, A. S., & Brown, A. L. (1984). Reciprocal teaching of comprehension-fostering and comprehension-monitoring activities. *Cognition and Instruction, 1*, 117–175.

Palincsar, A. S., Brown, A. L., & Martin, S. M. (1987). Peer interaction in reading comprehension instruction. *Educational Psychologist, 22*, 231–253.

Paris, S. G., Lipson, M., & Wixson, K. (1983). Becoming a strategic reader. *Contemporary Educational Psychology, 8*, 293–316.

Paris, S. G., Wasik, B. A., & Turner, J. C. (1991). The development of strategic readers. In R. Barr, M. L. Kamil, P. B. Mosenthal, & P. D. Pearson (Eds.), *Handbook of reading research* (Vol. II, pp. 609–640). New York, NY: Longman.

Pearson, P. D., & Fielding, L. (1991). Comprehension instruction. In R. Barr, M. L. Kamil, P. B. Mosenthal, & P. D. Pearson (Eds.), *Handbook of reading research* (Vol. II, pp. 815–860). New York, NY: Longman.

RAND Reading Study Group. (2002). *Reading for understanding: Toward a research and development program in reading comprehension.* Santa Monica, CA: RAND. Retrieved from http://www.rand.org/pubs/monograph_reports/MR1465/index.html

Raphael, T. (1986). Teaching question-answer relationships. *The Reading Teacher, 39,* 516–520.

Recht, D. R. & Leslie, L. (1988). Effect of prior knowledge on good and poor readers' memory of text. *Journal of Educational Psychology, 80,* 16–20.

Rosenshine, B., & Meister, C. (1994). Reciprocal teaching: A review of the research. *Review of Educational Research, 64,* 479–530.

Rosenshine, B., Meister, C., & Chapman, S. (1996). Teaching students to generate questions: A review of the intervention studies. *Review of Educational Research, 66,* 181–221.

Scanlon, D., Deshler, D. D., & Schumaker, J. B. (1996). Can a strategy be taught and learned in secondary inclusive classrooms? *Learning Disabilities Research & Practice, 11,* 41–57.

Scollon, R., & Scollon, S. B. K. (1988). *Narrative, literacy, and face in interethnic communication.* Norwood, NJ: Ablex.

Scott, C. M. (1995). A discourse approach to syntax teaching. In D. F. Tibbits (Ed.), *Language intervention: Beyond the primary grades* (pp. 435–463). Austin, TX: PRO-ED.

Sencibaugh, J. M. (2007). Meta-analysis of reading comprehension interventions for students with learning disabilities: Strategies and implications. *Reading Improvement, 44,* 6–22.

Shanahan, T., & Shanahan, C. (2008). Teaching disciplinary literacy to adolescents: Rethinking content-area literacy. *Harvard Educational Review, 78,* 40–59.

Shanahan, T., Callison, K., Carriere, C., Duke, N. K., Pearson, P. D., Schatschneider, C., & Torgesen, J. (2010). *Improving reading comprehension in kindergarten through 3rd grade: A practice guide* (NCEE 2010-4038). Washington, DC: Institute of Education Sciences, U.S. Department of Education.

Silliman, E., & Wilkinson, L. C. (1991). Communicating for learning: Classroom observation and collaboration. Gaithersburg, MD: Aspen.

Snow, C. E. (2010). Reading comprehension; Reading for learning. *International Encyclopedia of Education, 5,* 413–418.

Swanson, H. L. & Hoskyn, M. (1998). Experimental intervention research on students with learning disabilities: A meta-analysis of treatment outcomes. *Review of Educational Research, 68,* 277–321.

Taylor, B. M., & Beach, R. W. (1984). The effects of text structure instruction in middle-grade students' comprehension and production of expository texts. *Reading Research Quarterly, 19,* 134–146.

Taylor-Butler, C. (2008). *The digestive system.* New York, NY: Children's Press.

Tierney, R. J., & Readence, J. E. (2000). *Reading strategies and practices: A compendium.* Boston, MA: Allyn and Bacon.

Tyre, P. (2012, October). The writing revolution. *The Atlantic.* Retrieved from http://www.theatlantic.com/magazine/archive/2012/10/the-writing-revolution/309090/

Ukrainetz, T. A. (2006) The many ways of exposition: A focus on text structure. In T. A. Ukrainetz (Ed.), *Contextualized language intervention: Scaffolding preK–12 literacy achievement* (pp. 246–288). Austin, TX: PRO-ED.

Ukrainetz, T. A., & Fresquez, E. F. (2003). "What isn't language?": A qualitative study of the role of the school speech–language pathologist. *Language, Speech, and Hearing Services in Schools, 34,* 284–298.

Ukrainetz, T. A., & Ross, C. L. (2006). Text comprehension: Facilitating active and strategic engagement. In T. A. Ukrainetz (Ed.), *Contextualized language intervention: Scaffolding preK–12 literacy achievement* (pp. 503–564). Austin, TX: PRO-ED.

Ukrainetz, T. A., & Trujillo, A. (1999). "You know, I just don't know what else you'd do?" Five SLPs' perspectives on children's literature in speech–language intervention. *Contemporary Issues in Communication Sciences and Disorders, 26*, 35–48.

Van Cleave, J. (1996). *202 oozing, bubbling, dripping, and bouncing experiments*. New York, NY: Wiley.

Van Sledright, B. A., & Kelly, C. (1998). Reading American history: The influence of multiple sources on six fifth graders. *The Elementary School Journal, 98*, 239–265.

Wigfield, A., Guthrie, J. T., Perencevich, K. C., Taboada, A., Klauda, S. L., Mcrae, A., & Barbosa, P. (2008). Role of reading engagement in mediating effects of reading comprehension instruction on reading outcomes. *Psychology in the Schools, 45*, 432–445.

Willingham, D. T. (2006). The usefulness of *brief* instruction in reading comprehension strategies. *American Educator, Winter*, 39–50.

Willingham, D. T. (2007). Critical thinking: Why is it so hard to teach? *American Educator, Summer*, 8–19.

Wilson, A. A. (2008). Moving beyond the page in content area literacy: Comprehension instruction for multimodal texts in science. *The Reading Teacher, 62*, 153–156.

Wilson, A. A. (2011). A social semiotics framework for conceptualizing content area literacies. *Journal of Adolescent and Adult Literacy, 54*, 435–444.

Wong, B. Y. L., Butler, D. L., Ficzere, S. A., & Kuperis, S. (1996). Teaching low achievers and students with learning disabilities to plan, write, and revise opinion essays. *Journal of Learning Disabilities, 29*, 197–212.

Wong, B. Y. L., Wong, R., Perry, N., & Sawatsky, D. (1986). The efficacy of a self-questioning summarization strategy for use by underachievers and learning disabled adolescents in social studies. *Learning Disabilities Focus, 2*, 20–35.

Yekovich, F. R., Walker, C. H., Ogle, L. T., & Thompson, M. A. (1990). The influence of domain knowledge on inferencing in low-aptitude individuals. *The Psychology of Learning and Motivation, 25*, 259–278.

Chapter 16

The Final Frontier: High School and College Students With Reading Disorders

Lauren A. Katz & Karen A. Fallon

Children with spoken language disorders become children with written language disabilities. Moreover, most of these children grow up and become adolescents and then adults who face lifelong struggles with reading and, more broadly, learning. In this chapter, we will describe some of the challenges that students with reading difficulties face in high school and beyond as well as the challenges that speech–language pathologists (SLPs) face in working with these students. We will then discuss methods of assessing reading comprehension, with a focus on why *reading to learn* is so difficult for these older students. Finally, we present a framework for reading intervention with older students. We refer to this framework as the Four S's: Skills, Strategies, School, and Student Buy-in. Our focus will be not just on comprehending written information but on *learning* from texts to reach academic success (see W. Kintsch, 1994, 1998; E. Kintsch, 2005). Although there are many challenges in working with this older population, there are also great rewards in turning a *turned-off* student back *on* to learning.

What Becomes of the Older Student?

The research literature supports a solid relationship between language and reading skills (Catts, Fey, Zhang, & Tomblin, 1999; Nation & Snowling, 2004). A prime example of this is phonological awareness and word recognition (Catts et al., 1999): children with deficits in phonological awareness will have a more difficult time learning to read than their peers (National Reading Panel [NRP], 2000; National Institute for Literacy, 2003). Lexical and grammatical skills also account for significant variance in reading outcomes (Catts et al., 1999; Nation & Snowling, 2004; Rescorla, 2005, 2009; Roth, Speece, & Cooper, 2002; Storch & Whitehurst, 2002). Students with strong spoken language skills will be most successful in acquiring literacy skills (Catts, Fey, Zhang, & Tomblin, 2001). Conversely, students with weak spoken language foundations will experience difficulty with written language (Catts, Fey, Tomblin, & Zhang, 2002; Snow, Scarborough, & Burns, 1999), and are likely to fall farther and farther behind (e.g., Catts et al., 2002; Stanovich, 1986).

As children progress through elementary-, middle-, and secondary-school years, they engage in reading and writing activities that become increasingly more challenging (Swanson & Hoskyn, 2001). Linguistically, texts become more difficult: the vocabulary is more infrequent and abstract, and the syntax is more complex. Students must think about what they are reading in more sophisticated ways: they must synthesize information across multiple texts, evaluate the quality or veracity of what they read, and argue positions about information they have read.

As an example, in the state of Michigan's report on Common Core State Standards for Grades 6–12 (Michigan State Board of Education, 2010), students in Grades 6–8 are expected to read and engage with scientific texts in such a way that they can analyze the author's purpose. Once these students move into Grade 9 and beyond, the texts increase in difficulty, as do the expectations. In Grades 9 and 10, students must define questions that the author seeks to address, and in Grades 11 and 12, students are expected to identify any important issues that remain unresolved. For students with language disorders, these increasingly demanding curricular expectations can be insurmountable, particularly without continued intervention.

Rising academic demands in secondary and postsecondary settings paired with persistent language impairment resoundingly indicate the need for more support, not less (Deshler & Hock, 2007; Joffe & Nippold, 2012; Snow & Moje, 2010). With expertise in language, coupled with their attention to students' underlying processes, skills, and strategies (see Ukrainetz & Fresquez, 2003), SLPs are well suited for working with these older students. Unfortunately, older students have been and continue to be an underserved group (Joffe & Nippold, 2012; Larson & McKinley, 1993). An American-Speech-Language-Hearing Association (2006) survey reported that 67% of SLPs practicing in school settings listed pre-elementary or elementary schools as their primary facilities. In comparison, only about 7% reported a high school as their primary facility. These findings suggest that many students are dismissed from SLPs' caseloads once they move into middle and high school. While it is possible that some of these students do receive help through special education or other related services (e.g., reading specialists, instruction in a resource room), intervention services by language experts cease for the vast majority.

So, what happens to these students? Some graduate and even pursue college educations, but many of these individuals continue to struggle academically. In 2002, the Institute for Education Sciences estimated that there were over 200,000 students with learning disabilities (LD) attending colleges and universities across the country. The majority of these students (80%) struggle with reading and writing (e.g., Rath & Royer, 2002; Vogel, 1985). Of particular consequence are data showing that retention rates in college for students with LD are lower than those of their normally achieving peers (Hurst & Smerdon, 2000; Murray, Goldstein, Nourse, & Edgar, 2000; Institute for Education Sciences, 2010). So, just as in high school, college presents trouble for these students.

More broadly, there is extensive evidence showing that individuals with a history of language disorders fair less well in higher education and employment than those without (Clegg, Hollis, Mawhood, & Rutter, 2005; Conti-Ramsden & Durkin, 2012; Felsenfeld, Broen, & McGue, 1994; Johnson, Beitchman, & Brownlie, 2010; Lindsay & Dockrell, 2012). In a 20-year longitudinal study, Johnson et al. found that, compared to typical peers, individuals with a history of language disorders achieved significantly lower scores on language, cognitive, and academic measures; reached significantly lower levels of educational attainment; and worked in occupations that were significantly lower in terms of socioeconomic status. These results warrant interventions that improve educational and vocational success for individuals with language disorders.

Using Models of Reading Comprehension to Guide Clinical Practice

For clinicians, both empirical findings and theoretical models serve as useful guides for knowing what to assess when trying to identify why someone is struggling with reading comprehension. It is well established that reading comprehension is a complex process that involves the coordination and deployment of an array of linguistic, cognitive, and metacognitive skills (see Adams, 1990; Cromley & Azevedo, 2007; Cutting & Scarborough, 2006; Gersten, Fuchs, Williams, & Baker, 2001; Gough & Tunmer, 1986; W. Kintsch, 1994; Perfetti, 1985).

At a very basic level, Gough and Tunmer (1986) proposed that reading comprehension is composed of decoding and linguistic comprehension. In recent years, researchers have explored the underlying specific skills that contribute to successful reading comprehension, some of which change as children grow up. For example, while phonemic awareness has been identified as an important contributor to reading comprehension, its importance decreases over time as other skills (e.g., morphological awareness, background knowledge, language comprehension, vocabulary) contribute more to the reading process (Aarnoutse, van Leeuwe, Voeten, & Oud, 2001; Braze, Tabor, Shankweiler, & Mencl, 2007; Cromley & Azevedo, 2007; Francis, Fletcher, Catts, & Tomblin, 2005; Roth et al., 2002; Storch & Whitehurst, 2002). Therefore, it makes sense to look at models of reading comprehension that are developed specifically with the older student in mind.

Using extensive empirical evidence, Deshler and Hock (2007) presented a theoretical model of reading comprehension for adolescents that illustrates how certain reading (i.e., phonological awareness, decoding, sight word reading, and fluency), language comprehension (i.e., background knowledge, syntax, vocabulary, and text structures), and executive processing skills (i.e., cognitive and metacognitive strategies) work together to bring about successful reading comprehension in this age group. In their Adolescent Reading Model, Deshler and Hock proposed that all three of these skills must be well developed to enable adolescents to successfully comprehend what they are reading as they integrate what they understand from the text with their existing knowledge and apply this newly learned information to novel learning experiences. The Adolescent Reading Model, despite its age-limited label, also serves as a framework for addressing the needs of college students with reading comprehension difficulties who must be even more intentional and autonomous in their reading and studying activities.

Word Reading

Obviously, the ability to read words is a necessary component of reading comprehension (Gough & Tunmer, 1986; Hoover & Gough, 1990). Individuals who struggle with word reading can struggle for different reasons. When learning to read, phonological awareness is critical for helping young readers in their acquisition of the alphabetic code, which is necessary for sounding out words (Bradley & Bryant, 1983; Bryant, MacLean, Bradley, & Crossland, 1990; Liberman, Shankweiler, & Liberman, 1989; Wagner & Torgesen, 1987). Over time and with practice, children move from reliance on the alphabetic code to more efficient word reading processes that are tied to the development of orthographic knowledge (Ehri, 1997). Orthographic knowledge develops as children begin to recognize familiar patterns of letters (which translate into sound) and use these chunks of information (i.e., syllables, prefixes, suffixes, roots) to read words accurately and automatically. Although they may return to using alphabetic strategies when confronted with an unfamiliar word, they no longer rely on the letter-sound strategy to read. Ehri explained that children are able to consolidate their knowledge and increase efficiency by using familiar chunks to read words. Ehri suggested that it is the connection between the orthography and phonology (grapho-phonics) that leads to automatic sight word recognition.

Morphology of written words involves phonology, orthography, semantics, and syntax. For example, consider the word *natural.* Phonological and orthographic abilities will enable a reader to recognize that although the base word of *natural* (i.e., *nature*) is phonologically different from its derivative, its orthographic representation is quite similar. Semantic abilities help readers to make connections between the meaning of *nature* and the meaning of *natural* as well as to apply the meaning of the suffix *-al* (i.e., *relating to*) to make meaning out of the derivative. Finally, syntactic abilities help readers to recognize that the suffix *-al* is adjectival and thus transforms the noun *nature* into an adjective. Thus, morphological processing involves the integration of multiple aspects of language: not surprisingly, it has been found to be important for word reading and even reading achievement (Carlisle & Stone, 2003; Carlisle, Stone, & Katz, 2001; Elbro & Arnbak, 1996; Nagy, Anderson, Schommer, Scott, & Stallman, 1989). Moreover, the importance of morphological knowledge increases as the prevalence of morphologically complex words in texts increases, which begins to happen around the fourth grade (Nagy & Anderson, 1984).

Language Comprehension

Reading comprehension hinges on an individual's language abilities. However, it is difficult to remove the effect of decoding ability from a reading comprehension test. One way of doing this is by assessing language skills through receptive language. Across a variety of age groups, researchers have found performance on spoken language measures to be a significant contributor to reading comprehension (Catts, 1993; Catts et al., 1999; Nation, 2001; Nation & Snowling, 2004; Aaron, Joshi, & Williams, 1999). Language comprehension requires facility with a variety of linguistic skills, and if one or more of these skills are deficient, language comprehension—both spoken and written—can be diminished. For example, research has shown that receptive vocabulary (Freebody & Anderson, 1983; Ouellette, 2006), the ability to derive meaning from context (McKeown, 1985), morphological awareness and knowledge (Carlisle, 1995, 2000; Katz, 2004; Windsor, 2000), syntactic comprehension (Bowey, 1994; Catts, Adlof, & Ellis-Weismer, 2006; Just & Carpenter, 1992; Kamhi & Catts, 1991; Perera, 1984; Tyler & Nagy, 1990), inferential reasoning (W. Kintsch, 1992), and comprehension of nonliteral language (Cain, Oakhill, & Bryant, 2004; Cain, Oakhill, & Lemmon, 2005) are all important contributors to reading comprehension. Moreover, with age comes an increase in one's capacity—as well as the necessity—to handle more linguistically challenging tasks. Form, content, and use are not easily separable; older students must use these skills simultaneously to interpret spoken and written language.

Executive Skills

Metacognitive skills (i.e., thinking about thinking) are here subsumed under executive processing skills, which involve behaviors that enable individuals to monitor and regulate their performance in order to successfully reach their goals (Brown, 1980;

Flavell, 1979). For example, a person engaging in metacognition might recognize that he or she has more trouble understanding expository texts than narrative texts; with this knowledge, the person might *strategically* allocate more time for completing reading assignments for science class than for poetry class. In a discussion of reading strategies, Brown (1980) described them as "... any deliberate planful control of activities that give birth to comprehension" (p. 456). Brown explained that skilled readers are able to proceed through reading activities without much effort; she likened this effortless process to being on "automatic pilot" until some "triggering event" or comprehension failure is detected. It is at this point that readers must slow down and employ "debugging devices" or strategies (e.g., monitoring, reviewing, self-testing) to overcome the comprehension failures. Pressley and Afflerbach (1995) found that skilled adult readers employ metacognitive strategies while reading. For example, they make predictions as they read, they use prior knowledge to support their engagement and understanding of the text, they revise their prior knowledge when they encounter information that conflicts with what they know, they underline important points, and they reread as necessary to make sense of difficult text.

In contrast, children with reading disabilities engage in fewer metacognitive acts during reading than same-age skilled readers do (Brown, 1980; Garner & Kraus, 1981–82; Palincsar & Brown, 1987; Stone & Conca, 1993). Palincsar and Brown (1987) noted that compared to good readers, poor readers do not see reading as a search for meaning, monitor their comprehension, engage in strategies when there is a breakdown in comprehension, or modify their choice of strategy to meet the task demands. Stone and Conca (1993) characterized students with LD as using fewer and less-efficient strategies less often and less well than their normally achieving peers. The lack of attention to comprehension will be exacerbated for students who are weak decoders and who therefore must allocate their attention to decoding.

Assessing Older Students' Comprehension of Written Text

Getting Started

The goal of reading in school is not just to comprehend or take away meaning from written texts (Oakhill, 1995) but also to *learn* from them (see W. Kintsch, 1994, 1998; E. Kintsch, 2005). Difficulties with reading comprehension and learning are very likely to lead to academic struggles even for students without diagnosed disabilities. For the students previously identified as eligible for speech–language services, the SLP will be carrying out assessments in order to identify any progress or changes since the last assessment, identify current language status, and make recommendations for direct intervention or other supports (e.g., accommodations, referrals, home support). For other students, high school or college may be the first time they are referred for a language assessment. These students have coped adequately with academic challenges in elementary grades, but the reading material and expectations of later grades become too much to handle with informal family and educational supports. For these students, apart from determining eligibility for speech–language services, the SLP's most important task is to figure out *why* the student is struggling academically, so that appropriate intervention goals can be developed and implemented or so that the student can be directed to other assistance services.

It is this *why* question that should guide *every* SLP's assessment, making the process of assessing very much like solving a mystery. To understand *why* an older student is struggling with reading comprehension, it is important for the SLP to gather clues or data that, once assembled, help to solve the mystery of *why*. The *why* is not answered by administration of a reading comprehension measure; this kind of measure will only serve to confirm (or call into question) what is already known: the student is having difficulties with reading comprehension. This part of the assessment may be needed for eligibility or for quantifying severity, but it is not, in the end, what will help guide intervention. It is critical that the SLP also assess the underlying skills that are particularly important for reading comprehension and academic success for older students.

Before any testing takes place, the SLP is given a few clues in the reason for referral, the case history, and interview data. Then the SLP must deliberately choose for assessment the specific skills that might help to solve the mystery behind the student's difficulties with reading comprehension. It is often the case that the SLP has only a short amount of time to conduct an in-depth, comprehensive assessment. However, with thoughtful planning and prioritizing, it is possible and necessary for the SLP to quickly recognize, understand, and assess the skills needed for successful comprehension of written text in the high school and college years. In the following four sections, we will first discuss methods for assessing reading comprehension broadly and then discuss methods for assessing specific skills: word reading, spoken language comprehension, and use of metacognitive strategies.

Assessing Reading Comprehension

Assessing the older student's reading comprehension skills is not as straightforward as it may seem. There is a variety of reading comprehension measures available for older students that purport to measure reading comprehension (Box 16.1). However, these measures do so in different ways, and some may not do so at all. Morsy, Kieffer, and Snow (2010) critically reviewed and reported on some of the most commonly used measures of adolescent reading comprehension. They provided objective information and subjective judgments about the strengths and weaknesses of each of nine measures. The main findings about the reading measures were that they contained minimal requirements for critical thought beyond inferencing, little attention to subject area content, and variation in what reading skills were examined (Box 16.2).

In addition, Morsy et al. (2010) drew attention to important factors for deciding which tests make the most sense to use and for interpreting performance on particular tests. First, different aspects of reading comprehension are involved, depending on how the measure is structured. For example, a measure that requires students to

Box 16.1. ***Commonly Used Measures of Reading Comprehension for Older Students***

Name	Reading Comprehension Measure	Other Areas Tested	Age Range	Potential Limitations
Diagnostic Assessments of Reading–Second Edition (Roswell, Chall, Curtis, & Kearns, 2006)	Norm-referenced, individually administered; students silently read expository passage per grade level, answer four multiple-choice inferential questions, retell passage	Print awareness, Phonemic awareness, Word recognition, Reading fluency, Spelling, Reading vocabulary	5 years–Adult	Narrow scope of text types; Only one text per grade; Passages on familiar topics; May not correlate highly with other reading comprehension measures
Gates-MacGinitie Reading Tests–Fourth Edition (MacGinitie, MacGinitie, Maria, Dreyer, & Hughes, 2000)	Norm-referenced, group administered; students silently read passages from multiple genres, answer multiple-choice inferential questions; item analysis identifies comprehension breakdown and ineffective strategy use	Reading vocabulary	5 years–Adult	Multiple-choice questions only; May only be useful for students with good fluency and decoding skills
Gray Oral Reading Tests–Fifth Edition (Wiederholt & Bryant, 2012)	Norm-referenced, individually administered; 16 developmentally sequenced orally read passages, 5 orally presented open-ended questions per passage; students respond orally	Oral reading fluency (rate and accuracy)	6–24 years	Some familiar topics; Easier passages tend to be narratives, more difficult, expository; Some expressive demands
Group Reading Assessment and Diagnostic Evaluation (Williams, 2001)	Norm-referenced, group administered; 5 silently read passages of different genres, multiple-choice inferential questions	Reading vocabulary Listening comprehension	Pre-K–12th grade	Multiple-choice questions only; Passages are at similar readability levels; Few reading passages

Box 16.1. (*continued*)

Name	Reading Comprehension Measure	Other Areas Tested	Age Range	Potential Limitations
Nelson-Denny Reading Test (Brown, Fishco & Hanna, 1993)	Norm-referenced, group administered; 7 silently-read passages in different content areas, multiple-choice explicit and inferential questions	Reading vocabulary, Reading rate	9–16 years and adults	Multiple-choice only; Norms outdated; Passages cover familiar topics
Qualitative Reading Inventory–Fifth Edition (Leslie & Caldwell, 2011)	Criterion-referenced, individually administered; orally or silently read narrative and expository passages, multiple passages per grade; students retell passages, respond orally to explicit and inferential open-ended questions	Single-word reading, Reading fluency (rate and accuracy)	Emergent–high school	No standard scores; Some passages cover familiar topics; Expressive demands
Test of Reading Comprehension–Fourth Edition (Brown, Wiederholt, & Hammill, 2009)	Norm-referenced, individually administered, silently read; single sentences missing two words, choose the best pair to complete each sentence; rearrange misordered sentences into a coherent paragraph; respond to multiple-choice questions about read passages	Reading vocabulary, Silent contextual reading fluency	7–18 years	Some passages cover familiar topics

(continues)

Box 16.1. *(continued)*

Name	Reading Comprehension Measure	Other Areas Tested	Age Range	Potential Limitations
Woodcock-Johnson III Diagnostic Reading Battery (Woodcock, Mather & Schrank, 2004)	Norm-referenced, individually administered; students silently read one to two sentence passages with single word missing; verbally produce single word to complete each item	Word recognition, Reading vocabulary, Reading fluency, Spelling, Phonemic awareness	2–90 years	Passages do not exceed two sentences in length; Lacks authenticity; Expressive spoken demands

read a multiparagraph passage and then to answer a series of multiple-choice questions may provide information that is different from that provided by a measure that requires students to read an incomplete sentence and then supply a missing word that renders the sentence semantically and syntactically sound. It is possible for a student to answer multiple-choice questions with ease but struggle to generate answers. It is also possible for a student to comprehend a single sentence quite well but be unable to distinguish main ideas from details or to identify themes when asked to read a chapter from a textbook for class. It is important for the SLP to examine measures critically and consider the reasons behind a student's performance—good or bad—when drawing conclusions about a student's capacity to understand and learn from a variety of written texts (e.g., narrative, expository, particular content areas, familiar/unfamiliar topics, topics of interest/no interest) with a variety of different purposes (e.g., for pleasure, for main ideas, for a message or moral, for comparison with another text).

Second, some measures may not measure reading comprehension at all. Keenan and Betjemann (2006) examined and found serious problems with the validity of the comprehension component of the *Gray Oral Reading Tests–Third Edition* (which contained the same passages and questions as the later version of the same test, the *Gray Oral Reading Tests–Fourth Edition*) (Wiederholt & Bryant, 1992, 2001). On both the GORT-3 and GORT-4, students are required to orally read passages as well as they can and then respond to a series of multiple-choice questions. Keenan and Betjemann found that performance on this measure was best predicted, not by how well participants read, but by how well the questions could be answered without reading. Participants could answer many of the comprehension questions without actually reading the passages by using their own background knowledge of the topic as well as verbal reasoning skills. Coleman, Lindstrom, Nelson, Lindstrom, and Gregg (2010) found the same problems with

Box 16.2. ***Findings of Adolescent Reading Comprehension Measures***

1. Most of the measures included at least some questions that required the students to draw inferences (e.g., *What is the main idea of the story? How do you think the main character felt at the end of the story? Why do you think that this topic is important?*).
2. None of the measures had questions that required that the students use critical thinking skills beyond those involved in inferencing (e.g., synthesizing information across texts, reflecting on an author's point of view).
3. None of the measures had questions that assessed content area comprehension (e.g., science, history, math).
4. Measures varied in the degree to which they allowed for examination of skills that underlie reading comprehension (e.g., word reading, spoken language comprehension, use of metacognitive strategies).

Note: From Morsy, Kieffer, & Snow (2010).

the validity of the *Nelson-Denny Reading Test* (Brown, Fishco, & Hanna, 1993). In both of these studies, the researchers suggested that reading disorders could go undetected by using either of these measures. This is an important lesson for SLPs to take away: just because a measure is popular and has reasonable psychometric properties (e.g., interrater reliability) does not mean that it is a good measure.

SLPs need to be critical consumers and use research evidence as well as their own experiences and knowledge to guide them in making sound clinical decisions, particularly when working with older students, for whom there is much less published research and fewer standardized assessment measures. SLPs are often left to extrapolate from what exists for younger students, and this requires time and thought. As a follow-up, the GORT-4 was revised in response to the Keenan and Betjemann study and released in 2011 as the GORT-5 (Wiederholt & Bryant, 2012). The most notable change is that the comprehension questions are no longer presented in a multiple-choice format, instead students must generate their own responses to the questions. This format is expected to tap comprehension of read material more than verbal reasoning.

Assessing Word Reading Skills

In this section, recommended methods for assessing word reading skills in older students are presented. We begin this section by underscoring the importance of the individual student's history in judging the extent to which assessing word reading skills makes sense: imagine a student who has been receiving intervention focused on improving his decoding skills for 10 years with negligible progress. Maybe this student's word reading skills are as good as they will get, so further attention to word reading may not be a good use of the SLP's scarce time. Instead, the SLP may want to focus on

Box 16.3. ***Questions to Guide Evaluation of Reading Comprehension Measures***

1. Are there enough multisyllabic and morphologically complex words included on the measure to give a realistic sense of how the student is managing to read words in advanced texts?
2. Could the student be relying on strong visual memory to successfully read the words included on the measure?
3. Does the measure take automaticity into account in calculating the student's score?
4. Do the word reading measures examine word reading in isolation as well as in running text?

examination of spoken language comprehension skills and use of metacognitive reading strategies (e.g., using context clues along with partial decoding, spending more time reading tables and figures, using text-to-speech software). Alternatively, if this student has been receiving intervention that does not target his word reading needs, then focused instruction along with careful assessment in this area is merited. Remember, the assessment should drive intervention, so assess the areas that would make sense to target in therapy.

If an older student is struggling to read words, deficiencies in phonological processing, orthographic knowledge, morphological knowledge, or decoding strategies are the reasons why. It is not enough to identify *if* there is a problem with word reading; *why* there is a problem with word reading is also necessary. Again, it is the *why* that informs intervention. Word reading skills can be assessed in a variety of ways, and there are a number of norm-referenced measures deemed suitable for use with older students. However, these measures are not without limitations. If an older student scores within normal limits on one or more measures of word reading, despite reporting difficulties with word reading, there are a several questions to consider (Box 16.3).

The first question is whether there were enough multisyllabic and morphologically complex words included on the measure to give a realistic sense of how the student is managing to read words in high school or college texts. At this level of education, most of the reading material is discipline-specific, with specialized vocabulary. Second, could the student be relying on strong visual memory to successfully read the words included on the measure? Some students have learned to compensate quite well for their difficulties with word reading; they can read real or familiar words but may run into problems with words they've never seen before (e.g., nonwords, names, foreign words). Another question is whether the measure takes automaticity into account in calculating the student's score. Some students can read words accurately but not very automatically, and on some measures, students are not penalized for effortful or slow decoding. Finally, do the word reading measures examine word reading in isolation as well as in running text? Some students benefit from context clues and therefore show better word reading accuracy at the passage level than with words in isolation. Other students are able to manage reading words in isolation but struggle to read accurately when they have additional demands such as syntax and punctuation with which to contend.

If answers to these questions suggest potential weaknesses not identified by the standardized measure(s) administered, the SLP should use some informal measures to further examine these concerns. For example, if the SLP is concerned that the student might struggle to read the morphologically complex words, a list of such words can be taken from a class text. If the SLP is concerned that the student lacks automaticity despite reasonable accuracy, administering a standardized measure that takes speed into account might make sense. Alternatively, if the SLP does not have access to such a measure, for the read-aloud test passages, latencies (i.e., length and frequency of pauses) and behaviors that suggest problems with automaticity can be documented. In general, further testing and careful reporting (in writing) are particularly important when assessing older students whose difficulties might not be fully captured on standardized measures.

As a supplement to testing, it is important for the SLP to carefully observe and analyze behaviors that point to difficulties not identified by scores on formal measures. Qualitative findings might include observations of the behaviors that students use during reading tasks. Box 16.4 lists a number of questions that can guide observation of these behaviors.

Box 16.4. ***Guiding Questions for Investigating Skills Underlying Word Reading***

1. Does the student skip words without trying?
2. Are the words skipped critical to the meaning of the text?
3. Does the student sound out most of the letters or letter combinations before guessing at the word?
4. Does the student correctly produce the first and final sounds but seem to guess the middle of the word?
5. Does the student use a phonemic, a syllabic, or a morphemic approach?
6. Does the guess make sense without context?
7. Does the student persist until the word makes sense with the context?
8. Does the student appear confident in his or her word reading?
9. Does the student look to the clinician for feedback or clues?
10. What kinds of error patterns is the student demonstrating?
11. Does the student stress the wrong syllables?
12. Does the student omit or inaccurately pronounce words with derivational suffixes?
13. Does the student demonstrate particular problems with morphologically complex words that have phonological shifts (e.g., *natural* versus *cultural*)?

Answers to the questions above can help identify the reasons behind a student's difficulties with word reading. While scores on word reading measures can be useful in identifying a word reading problem, it is also important to consider which underlying word reading skills are likely contributors to the problem (i.e., phonological awareness, letter-sound correspondence, orthographic knowledge, morphological knowledge, or decoding strategies). Identification of the weaknesses that affect word reading is critical for intervention planning.

Assessing Language Comprehension Skills

Knowing that receptive language skills are implicated in reading comprehension means that the SLP and other team members should do their best to thoroughly assess spoken language comprehension in an effort to determine *why* the student might be struggling to understand written texts. Standardized measures of language comprehension for older students do exist; however, for older students, there are important considerations in choosing measures as well as in interpreting scores earned on these measures.

First, written language is more literate in style than spoken language. Literate language includes more infrequent or abstract words, greater use of figurative forms, and more complex syntactic structures, such as passive structures and embedded clauses (Benson, 2009). For the older student, it is important to tap into these literate forms when assessing spoken language comprehension. For example, some measures include items or subtests that examine abstract and nonliteral language. Some measures require students to actually demonstrate skill with deriving meaning from unfamiliar words or phrases. These kinds of tasks require the inferential reasoning needed by older students for reading their academic texts (Just & Carpenter, 1992; W. Kintsch, 1992; Pressley & Afflerbach, 1995).

A second consideration is recognizing that most standardized measures of spoken language comprehension are not normed for students beyond high school. And, even for those that are normed for this age group, many measures are not sensitive to the variations in performance of the older student (for example, a subtest may have a ceiling effect, so that a raw score of 9 out of 10 resulting from a momentary loss of attention is enough to result in a low percentile score). When measures that are normed for or better suited to younger students are used, performance must be interpreted with caution. In these cases, rather than reporting standard scores, SLPs and others should report on proportion of items that were answered incorrectly, types of items that seemed particularly difficult (or not difficult), types of errors made, and behaviors suggestive of difficulties (e.g., frequent requests for repetitions, notable response latencies). SLPs and others may also supplement data from standardized tests with data from informal measures of language comprehension. For example, SLPs can make use of a student's curriculum in designing criterion-referenced measures of receptive vocabulary, inferential reasoning, and comprehension of complex syntactic structures.

Third, most standardized language measures assess individual aspects of language in a decontextualized environment, instead of using more authentic discourse. Narrative and expository measures of language competency can be particularly useful for identifying language disorders in older students who might otherwise go undiagnosed (Cain et al., 2004; Greenhalgh & Strong, 2001; Klecan-Aker & Caraway, 1997; Nippold, 1994). Types of expository discourse, such as persuasion, negotiation, and explanation, are particularly important for high school and college students (Nippold, 1994).

Assessing Metacognitive Skills

Given the role that metacognitive skills play in older students' comprehension of written texts (e.g., Pressley & Afflerbach, 1995), SLPs should examine this area when trying to decipher the reasons *why* a student might be struggling with reading comprehension. Although no norm-referenced measures of metacognitive skills for reading are available, there are criterion-referenced and informal measures that have been used with older students to examine their use of metacognitive strategies for comprehending written texts, such as questionnaires and interviews, think-alouds, and diagnostic therapy.

Questionnaires and Interviews

Metacognitive questionnaires and interviews involve asking readers to respond to questions about their strategy use. For example, Mokhtari and Reichard (2002) developed the *Metacognitive Awareness of Reading Strategies Inventory* (MARSI) for assessing adolescents' reported use of metacognitive strategies when reading academic texts. The 30 items on the inventory are categorized into three types of strategies: (a) global reading strategies (e.g., thinks about what he or she knows to help with understanding, decides what to read carefully and what to ignore), (b) support reading strategies (e.g., takes notes while reading, uses dictionaries and glossaries to help with understanding), and (c) problem-solving strategies (e.g., reads slowly to ensure comprehension, tries to refocus when concentration wanders). Students rate the extent to which they engage in each of the strategies on a 5-point Likert scale. Mokhtari and Reichard caution that though the measure is psychometrically supported, it is a self-report measure, so it does not necessarily reflect what the student *actually* does when reading: students may not be fully aware of their mental acts during reading or they may not remember what they did. There is also a risk that respondents might report strategies that they believe to be useful as opposed to strategies that they actually use.

Think-Alouds

In order to better gauge the extent to which students are *actually* using metacognitive strategies during reading, they can be asked to "think aloud" while reading. The think-aloud method has been used to learn more about the metacognitive strategies that skilled readers use as they use them: readers simply stop periodically and report their thinking as they read (Pressley & Afflerbach, 1995). Think-alouds have also been used as an assessment tool. For example, the *Qualitative Reading Inventory–Fifth Edition* (QRI-5; Leslie & Caldwell, 2011) includes passages at the sixth-grade through high school levels that can be used for think-alouds. Using a script, the SLP first models the process for the student: stopping the reading periodically to summarize, reflect on prior knowledge about the topic, or pose questions that indicate understanding. Following this model, the student reads the passage, stopping where indicated, and reports his or her thinking. While think-aloud measures can uncover the extent to which the student uses metacognitive strategies during reading, there are limitations to this approach as well. For example, if a student's verbalizations are limited, it is difficult to know if he or she lacks metacognitive strategies or if he or she has limited language skills. Limited output during think-alouds may also result when the reader considers the processes trivial or fails to recognize that he or she is using a reading strategy at all (Bereiter & Bird, 1985; Brown, 1980; Pressley & Afflerbach, 1995).

Diagnostic Therapy

Though there are limitations in the methods available for assessing older students' metacognitive strategy use before, during, and after reading, these methods can provide SLPs with some valuable insight into their students' skills in this area. There is tremendous value in continuing to assess older students' metacognitive skills during intervention. For example, graduate clinicians in one of our university language clinics saw a 21-year-old college student who had just been diagnosed with a reading disorder. A comprehensive language evaluation revealed strengths in decoding and metacognitive strategies but significant deficits in spoken language comprehension: below-average skills in deriving word meanings from context and drawing inferences, and a score on nonliteral language comprehension more than three standard deviations below the mean for her age. However, it became obvious after the second session that the student's primary weakness was really in her understanding and use of metacognitive strategies.

During the assessment, this client appeared highly strategic in her reading, but in fact, she only thought that she was (Box 16.5). Through engaging in reading activities with her, we realized that the student was either implementing unnecessary strategies that she was able to successfully check off of her to-do list (e.g., photocopying all of her textbooks, highlighting boldfaced or italicized words, writing boldfaced terms on note cards along with their dictionary definitions) or poorly implementing reasonable strategies (e.g., highlighting almost everything, writing "notes" in the margins that were, in reality, lines of actual text). She had no purpose when reading academic texts other than to use the same three strategies each time: highlight, identify key words, and copy lines of text. The student was not even thinking about what the key words meant in relation to the topic or even to the course in general. It was through continued assessment during intervention that the clinicians were able to identify substantial weaknesses in metacognitive strategy use. This then allowed for development of more appropriate intervention goals.

Assessment of word reading skills, language comprehension skills, and metacognitive strategy skills is important for determining *why* the older student is struggling with reading comprehension. These findings are important for determining next steps that

Box 16.5. *A Case Example of Diagnostic Therapy on Reading Strategies*

Consider Mel, a 21-year-old college student with a diagnosed learning disability and attention-deficit/hyperactivity disorder. Mel was a theater major with an outgoing personality and a motivation to do better in school. She had been an A student in high school, but she was struggling to make Cs in college, and she was frustrated and depressed. Mel's primary difficulties were with reading comprehension. Her word recognition skills and spoken language comprehension skills were quite strong, though she did have some difficulties with abstract vocabulary and complex syntax. Mel reported that her general strategy was to just read the assigned text and check it off her list. She thought that strategy use took too much time away from getting through all of her work. The strategies she knew were "support" strategies, and she couldn't bear adding note-taking, summarizing, or discussing readings to her busy schedule.

During an early intervention session, the clinician focused on teaching Mel to use strategies through working on her understanding of the Russian plays she was required to read for one of her theater classes. The plays were translated into English, but the characters' names were definitely foreign and the style of the writing was different. The hour-long session went something like this:

The clinician asked Mel if she knew what her professor wanted the students to take away from the assigned plays. Mel said that the professor was really interested in the students connecting with the characters in the plays. This was great—the instructor had been explicit about what he wanted, which would become Mel's *purpose* when reading these plays. Mel needed to focus her attention on understanding the characters and remind herself of her purpose *before* reading and *during* reading.

The clinician used the assigned play *The Cherry Orchard* by Anton Chekhov, in order to work through understanding and implementing the right strategies. After about a page of reading aloud, it was clear that much of Mel's effort was allocated toward attempting to decode the names of the Russian characters (e.g., Ranevskaya, Lopakhin).

Accurate decoding is important for comprehension, but these were just character names; correct pronunciation was not going to improve her understanding of them or the play. The clinician quickly devised a strategy for these foreign names: Don't read them! Assign each an easy nickname; maybe call them by the first letter or part of their names (e.g., Ran, Lop). Mel was ecstatic; this idea had never occurred to her. She now had a quick and easy strategy that would make her reading less disrupted and more fluent.

Mel reread what she had just read. This time, her reading was much more fluent, but she was still reading through the text without any obvious focus on her *purpose* to connect with the characters. When Mel stopped at the end of the page, she could say nothing about the setting, characters, or events. So, the clinician talked about investing a bit of time in increasing Mel's engagement with the text through *making predictions* and activating *prior knowledge.*

First, the clinician provided explicit instruction on the *what, why, how,* and *when* of *making predictions.* The clinician explained that *making predictions* was about thinking logically about what Mel might expect based on what information she already had. As an example, before jumping into reading the play, Mel had the title to use to make some predictions through

(continues)

Box 16.5. *(continued)*

self-questioning, "Hmmm. What do I know about cherry orchards? Could the story take place on a cherry orchard? Might some of the characters work or live on the orchard?" By *self-questioning*, Mel started to engage herself with the text, thinking about possibilities, and maybe piquing her own interest in the answers that would be revealed.

Mel also used her *prior knowledge* to help her *make predictions*, such as what she knew about the playwright's other works. In this case, Mel had read one other play by Chekhov, but (like this play) she could not easily recount anything meaningful about it. So, the clinician asked Mel if she had other *prior knowledge* that might help her *make predictions*, such as something about Chekhov himself or the time period in which the play was written. Not surprisingly, Mel really did not know much of anything about either aspect.

In an effort to illustrate the value of using *prior knowledge* and *making predictions* for the purpose of increasing engagement, comprehension, and learning, the clinician suggested intentionally collecting background knowledge. Pressley and Gaskins (2006) suggest that students learn to search for easy-to-understand and easy-to-access background information so that they can enter into the reading with more *prior knowledge* and greater engagement. A quick search on the web revealed that Chekhov often wrote about individuals' futile struggles to maintain their wealth in a changing economy. The clinician modeled how she made sense of this to increase engagement with the text, "Oh, so you are used to having lots of something, but then it's taken away. You know it's not worth the effort to try and get it back because you probably won't. Like if you have lots of chocolate, and then you go on some fitness reality show and it's taken away. Why bother trying to get it back; it's not gonna happen."

At this point, the clinician reviewed the strategies she and Mel had employed in preparation for reading this text. Then, the clinician took the lead, modeling strategic reading. She began by reiterating the *purpose*—to connect with the characters in the story. She *made predictions* using *prior knowledge*, "Based on my quick check on the Internet, Chekhov has a theme to his writing. Maybe this is going to be about wealthy people living on a cherry orchard who are losing their money and are just going to give up." Then, the clinician began reading aloud (abbreviating the characters' names as she read), and stopped after every few lines to *make predictions* based on her *purpose*—learning about the characters. In the margins of the text, she made notes to keep track of the characters' personality traits. These traits were not explicitly stated in the text, so the clinician engaged in self-talk about possible personalities as she read the dialogue. For example, upon waiting at the estate for the landowner to arrive, "Lop" acknowledged his error in oversleeping, recounted memories of the landowner with fondness, and referred to himself as now rich but still a peasant in his "bones." The clinician reflected aloud suggesting that Lop was probably a good person. He admitted his mistakes, spoke well about others, and didn't forget his humble beginnings. She predicted that he would probably lend support to the landowner should any trouble arise in the story. Mel understood what the clinician was doing, was engaged in the process, and even helped contribute her thoughts as they progressed through the pages.

Box 16.5. (*continued*)

The clinician continued to read aloud and model these behaviors with Mel engaged and providing contributions. At the end of the session, the Mel acknowledged that using these strategies in her college reading would be a small investment of time that would be worth it. Mel agreed to try these strategies for the next two weeks and report back.

move directly into intervention—intervention that can make a functional difference in students' lives.

Intervention With Older Students: It's Not Too Late

There is a small but growing database of studies reporting successful intervention outcomes with adolescent and adult clients with reading disabilities. Studies have addressed a range of areas, including word-level reading (e.g., Apel & Swank, 1999; Rickard et al. 2011), inferential reasoning (e.g., Rickard et al., 2011), reading comprehension (e.g., Dreyer & Nel, 2003; Fallon & Carlberg, 2012; Nicaise & Gettinger, 1995), vocabulary (Fallon & Carlberg, 2012; Dreyer & Nel, 2003; Nicaise & Gettinger, 1995), metalinguistic awareness, and syntax (Schiff & Calif, 2004). Progress in improving reading or reading-related skills and strategies were reported in all of these studies. The message from these studies is: it's *not* too late to intervene with adolescents and young adults who struggle with reading. However, the intervention will be challenging, with improvements often slow to emerge and measured in small increments.

Evidence of these small but important gains argues for sustained support for older students struggling with written language (Rath & Royer, 2002; Snow & Moje, 2010). It is important, however, when implementing targeted literacy instruction that expectations be set at the start. Making students and their families aware that the intervention journey will be ongoing, with progress measured in small degrees, can make all the difference in the client's "buy-in" to the therapeutic process. The overriding theme with the older student is not to give up. The concept of sustained support needs to be shared by service providers, the struggling students, and their families. Appropriate expectations and motivation lay the critical building blocks for successful therapeutic outcomes.

Planning Balanced Intervention

Developing and implementing an intervention plan with adolescents and young adults can be an overwhelming prospect. Each student we endeavor to help has capabilities and struggles interwoven with countless cognitive, linguistic, neural, psychosocial, and experiential threads. To understand and appreciate the art in its entirety, it is important

Box 16.6. ***The Four S's of Intervention With Older Students***

1. **Skills**—goals to improve underlying skills in vocabulary, morphology, syntax, inferential reasoning, word-level reading, reading fluency, and knowledge of text structures (Deshler & Hock, 2007; Kamil et al., 2008; Roberts, Torgesen, Boardman, Scammacca, 2008)
2. **Strategies**—goals to improve awareness and use of helpful learning behaviors, including reading strategies and study skills (Ehren, 2007; Kamil et al., 2008)
3. **School**—methods to improve the application of language skills and strategic learning behaviors to content-area learning (Deshler & Hock, 2007; E. Kintsch, 2005; Snow & Moje, 2010)
4. **Student "buy in"**—methods to engage and motivate the student to believe and fully participate in the therapeutic process (Guthrie & Wigfield, 2000; Roberts et al., 2008)

to examine it from both a micro and a macro perspective. An SLP must be familiar not only with each component of the student's profile (e.g., word-level reading skills, language comprehension skills, understanding and use of metacognitive strategies, motivation, self-perceptions), but also with how the components interact and interconnect to form the whole individual (Deshler & Hock, 2007; Roberts, Torgesen, Boardman, & Scammacca, 2008).

That is the challenge for the SLP tasked with helping the older student. The SLP must address the needs of individuals who are deficient in basic spoken and written language skills, yet trying to survive in a language-loaded environment wherein they struggle daily to keep up with increasing academic demands. In addition, older struggling readers are often frustrated, unmotivated, and disengaged as a result of years of coping with their language impairment (Brophy, 2004; Guthrie & Wigfield, 2000; Morgan & Fuchs, 2007). Well-designed interventions aimed at helping older students *read to learn* are individualized, co-constructed with the student, and contain a balance of key instructional components. Moreover, collaboration with general education teachers, special education teachers, reading specialists, and other related service personnel is key so that responsibilities are shared and, therefore, more manageable, For adolescents and young adults, the essential elements of instruction can be divided into the following four categories, the four *S's* of intervention: *skills*, *strategies*, *school*, and *student buy-in* (Box 16.6). The SLP needs to address all four of these components for intervention to be effective with this age group.

Adding the right amount of each of these ingredients is a delicate process that must be driven by assessment data *and* even more importantly, by the students themselves. Listening to students in order to discover their concerns and priorities is essential in deciding how much time and energy will be devoted to each intervention component. For example, if the student is unwilling to engage in word-level activities such as decoding tasks but is very motivated to work on metacognitive strategies, that should be taken into consideration. By understanding and acknowledging the student's priorities, the SLP can increase buy-in and further motivate the student to engage in the slow and difficult process of making significant changes to her or his reading and academic success.

Skills: Improving Underlying Language

Recent research attention in the area of adolescent literacy has resulted in a variety of practice guides, meta-analyses, descriptive papers, and empirical studies that can inform clinical decision making concerning critical language and reading skills (Biancarosa & Snow, 2004; Deshler & Hock, 2007; Kamil et al., 2008; Roberts et al., 2008; Torgesen et al., 2007). With respect to instructional methods, the literature consistently suggests the importance of language intervention being explicit, systematic, and direct (Biancarosa & Snow, 2004; Kamil, 2003; Kamil et al., 2008; Ukrainetz, 2006). Kamil further suggests that intervention with the older struggling student be "reflective" and offer opportunities for repeated practice with targets such as word reading, vocabulary knowledge, and discussions about the meaning of text. The need for collaboration among educational personnel has also been discussed in the adolescent reading literature (Biancarosa & Snow, 2004; Ehren, 2006). Across the reading instruction literature, there is general agreement on methods of instruction and specific intervention targets for adolescents, which are summarized next. One major difference is a modification to the five essential instructional areas reported by NRP (2000), from phonological awareness, phonics, fluency, vocabulary, and comprehension. The latter three areas are maintained, but phonological awareness is dropped as a distinct instructional area and phonics is expanded to what is called "word study".

Word Study and Fluency

With older students it is often the case that they have some decoding skills but not sufficient to be proficient, fluent readers (Biancarosa & Snow, 2004; Edmonds et al., 2009; Roberts et al., 2008). It is important to use assessment and baseline data to first determine word-level reading ability. The key questions to ask are: "Does the student read words at the letter-sound level?" and, "Is the student decoding many single-syllable words successfully but struggling with multisyllabic words?" Most older students can sound out single-syllable words and thus, do not need to go back to the early phonemic awareness and sound-by-sound phonics instruction of kindergarten. Instead, attention should be focused on word-analysis intervention, also called *advanced word study* (Curtis, 2004; Roberts et al., 2008).

Word-study intervention can help struggling readers build word reading skills by teaching them to use a variety of word reading strategies described by Ehri and McCormick (1998). These include mature decoding (i.e., ability to pronounce and blend familiar clusters such as phonograms, prefixes, suffixes), analogizing (i.e., reading by recognizing the similarity between an unknown and known word, such as *chelation/nation*), prediction (i.e., using letters, context, pictures, and cues to make guesses), and sight word reading (using memory to read words that have been read before). Mature readers have well-developed lexicons of sight words and the ability to use all word reading strategies when they encounter unfamiliar words. The goals of instruction are to build sight word vocabularies of words that can be immediately and effortlessly recognized as well as to improve word analysis and word recognition strategies for unfamiliar words (Ehri & McCormick, 1998; Scammacca et al., 2007).

Improved word recognition can also lead to better reading fluency, which is reading accurately, quickly, and with appropriate expression (NRP, 2000). The close connection between fluent reading and good reading comprehension is repeatedly cited in the literature and makes an important case for including word reading in intervention plans (Hawkins, Hale, Sheeley, & Ling, 2011; Kershaw & Schatschneider, 2012; Kuhn & Stahl, 2003; Nation, 2005; Rasinski, 2003; Rasinski et al., 2005; Rasinski, Samuels, Hiebert, Petscher, & Feller, 2011; Tilstra, McMaster, Van den Broek, Kendeou, & Rapp, 2009). Reading text automatically allows the reader to devote cognitive and linguistic resources to higher order processes such as thinking about the meaning of text, making predictions, and activating background knowledge.

Once students reach high school, reading fluency intervention is likely to benefit reading comprehension when reading rate is excessively slow (less than 100 words correct per minute) or below the 25th percentile for second-semester eighth graders (less than or equal to 145 correct words per minute; Rasinski et al., 2005). The use of repeated oral readings has been found to be effective in promoting both reading fluency and reading comprehension in younger students (Devault & Joseph, 2004) as well as in high school students (Hawkins et al., 2011). However, performance-based activities that provide older students with a natural rationale for engaging in repeated readings are recommended (see Rasinski et al., 2005). In addition, for older students, Roberts et al. (2008) suggested combining reading fluency instruction with focused word learning instruction. Repeatedly exposing struggling readers to the same words may have the added benefit of improving word recognition skills.

It is important to note that although the connection between reading fluency and reading comprehension is well reported, research has indicated that improvements in reading rate and accuracy do not always translate into improvements in reading comprehension (Allinder, Dunse, Brunken, & Obermiller-Krolikowski, 2001; Edmonds et al., 2009). Some research indicates that the connection between oral reading fluency and comprehension may be developmental, with the impact of fluency diminishing with age and text complexity (Francis, Fletcher, Catts, & Tomblin, 2004; Paris, Carpenter, Paris, & Hamilton, 2004). So while reading fluency may be important for reading comprehension in the early elementary grades, it becomes less important (compared to other skills) as children grow older and as their texts become more difficult. For adolescents, the importance of factors such as vocabulary knowledge, background knowledge, and world knowledge may trump the need for fluent oral reading (W. Kintsch & E. Kintsch, 2004).

Vocabulary

The ability to decode text does not guarantee understanding (Gough & Tunmer, 1986). Knowing the meanings of words encountered in written text is essential to the reading process and is a repeated recommendation for intervention with students of all ages (Biancarosa & Snow, 2004; Ebbers & Denton, 2008; Kamil et al., 2008; NRP, 2000; Stanovich, 1986). Increasing the number and deepening the students' knowledge of word meanings can be achieved using a variety of methods.

Ebbers and Denton (2008) suggested three vocabulary instruction techniques for older struggling readers: (a) creating a language-rich learning environment that promotes word consciousness, (b) using explicit instruction to directly teach specific words; and (c) teaching students independent word learning strategies involving analysis of the context and word structure (i.e., contextual morphemic analysis). In addition, evidence indicates the importance of using academically relevant texts and providing direct instruction that uses simple definitions, semantic maps, and functional examples (Kim, Vaughn, Wanzek, & Wei, 2004). Finally, it is critical that students have repeated exposures to new words in multiple contexts with extensive opportunities to practice target words using a variety of activities, including discussion, writing, and reading (Kamil et al., 2008).

Reading Comprehension

Taking meaning from text involves "the process of simultaneously extracting and constructing meaning through interaction and involvement with written language" (RAND Reading Study Group, 2002, p. xiii). Two primary approaches to reading comprehension instruction are a content approach and a strategy approach (McKeown, Beck, & Blake, 2009). Instruction that focuses students' attention on what they are reading and that helps them build representations of concepts conveyed in the text is referred to as a *content approach*. A content approach to instruction seeks to engage students in the text itself in order to create mental representations that can be used in combination with prior knowledge to form a deep understanding of the text (Applebee, Langer, Nystrand, & Gamoran, 2003; McKeown, et al., 2009). This focus on the text itself is what distinguishes a content approach from strategy-based instruction, which teaches students to maneuver purposefully and tactically through texts regardless of their content.

The content approach to reading comprehension has been reported to be effective with older students (Allen & Petersen, 2011; Applebee et al., 2003; Mastropieri, Scruggs, & Graetz, 2003; McKeown et al., 2009). Evidence from McKeown et al. dovetails well with recommendations from the Kamil et al. (2008) Adolescent Literacy Practice Guide, which suggests the importance of providing adolescents with opportunities for extensive, guided discussions focused on interpreting the meaning of written text. Specific suggestions for facilitating these discussions include selecting engaging texts, developing stimulating questions, using follow-up questions to extend discussion, and using a discussion protocol or format that students can follow during small group instruction (Kamil et al., 2008). The content approach involves initiating discussion, activating background information, linking concepts, focusing on the author's message, and making inferences. This approach may be particularly effective for facilitating understanding of the specific content addressed in discussions and for improving general language skills (see Beck, McKeown, Sandora, Kucan, & Worthy, 1996).

Strategies: Intentionally Reading to Learn

The Importance of Reading Strategies

In their qualitative study on the roles of school-based SLPs, Ukrainetz and Fresquez (2003) found that SLPs tended to be distinguished (and distinguished themselves) from reading and resource teachers as professionals who teach students strategies that will eventually allow them to become independent learners. One SLP participant remarked that the resource teachers only have time to help students keep up with their academic demands. This is an important point, particularly as it pertains to our work as SLPs who work with older students, we need to focus on preparing these students to be successful for the long term, not just for one assignment or one class. Moreover, for high school students, the clock is ticking; their free access to federally mandated services ends when they graduate. SLPs need to direct their efforts toward making these students into independent learners.

As stated earlier, unlike younger students, older students come to the therapy table with long histories of academic difficulties, language and reading interventions, frustration, and failure. While it may still be reasonable to work on improving specific underlying language skills, these older students need primarily to *learn how to learn*. For older students, much of their learning will come from reading, so they need to be taught how to engage in metacognitive and metalinguistic reading strategies consistently, systematically, and largely independently. Research has shown that older struggling readers can show substantial improvements in their reading comprehension when provided with explicit instruction in the use of metacognitive reading strategies (Edmonds et al., 2009).

Review of Reading Strategies

Strategies are frequently organized into the categories of *prereading* (e.g., activating prior knowledge, setting a purpose for reading), *during reading* (e.g., reading aloud when the text gets difficult, visualizing information), and *postreading* (e.g., formulating main ideas, summarizing). This organizational framework helps students understand *when* certain strategies might be used. Metacognitive strategies can also be grouped by function (i.e., *how* and *why* they are used rather than *when*). For example, as described in the section on assessment, the *Metacognitive Awareness of Reading Strategies Inventory* (MARSI) categorizes 30 strategies into three categories: (a) global strategies, (b) problem-solving strategies, and (c) support strategies (Mokhtari & Reichard, 2002).

Global reading strategies are used for macro-level analysis to determine the author's purpose, main idea, and overall theme(s) of the text. These strategies include previewing the text for headings, key words, layout, and summary. These strategies are effective when used in conjunction with the strategy of activating prior knowledge to help the reader make predictions regarding the content of the text and what is likely to be expected (Houtveen & van de Grift, 2007; Mokhtari & Reichard, 2002).

Problem-solving strategies are used when the text becomes challenging to read. Problem-solving strategies help the student create a plan for navigating through a difficult text in ways that support overall comprehension. These strategies require readers to first recognize when they encounter an unknown word, conflicting information, or comprehension breakdown, and then to utilize appropriate techniques to repair the breakdowns. Problem-solving strategies can include adjusting reading rate, reading out loud, and rereading if necessary (Houtveen & van de Grift, 2007; Mokhtari & Reichard, 2002).

Support reading strategies typically require the use of outside resources, such as taking notes while reading, underlining, paraphrasing, using outside reference materials, and discussing the readings (Mokhtari & Reichard, 2002). Older students may view these as necessary only when they are a part of teacher instructions or assignments. Students need to learn that these are helpful for reading comprehension and retention of information regardless of whether or not they have been explicitly required to use them.

How to Teach Reading Strategies

Older students, like younger students, need explicit instruction and intensive repeated opportunities for guided practice (Ehren, 2007; Faggella-Luby & Deshler, 2008; Mastropieri et al., 2003; Pressley & Gaskins, 2006). However, more so than with younger students, SLPs need to focus on making their older students strategic readers and independent learners who know how to compensate for their deficits across diverse reading tasks and texts (e.g., reading to learn subject content such as that in a history textbook, reading for pleasure such as a popular novel). On their own, older students need to be able to recognize when they are not comprehending adequately and then access and correctly use the right strategies at the right times so that they are learning from reading. To that end, SLPs also need to be problem solvers, identifying the specific underlying difficulties or obstacles that make "reading to learn" a problem for their older students and doing so thoughtfully on a case-by-case basis.

In teaching older students strategies, it is important for SLPs to focus on *what* they are, *why* they are useful, *when* or under what circumstances they should be used, and *how* to use them (see Lenz & Deshler, 2004). Recall our earlier example of the 21-year-old college-student client who reported using many metacognitive reading strategies? As it turned out, the client was not using the right ones at the right times or in the right ways, and she was neither comprehending nor learning. In addition to helping older students to understand *what*, *when*, *why*, and *how* to use reading strategies, an important part of strategy-focused intervention is helping the older student understand that strategic reading is an ongoing process. Over time and with lots of practice, implementation of taught strategies may become less conscious and more automatic, but when faced with a difficult topic or piece of text, a return to conscious selection and implementation of strategies becomes necessary. Finally, as with any intervention, it is valuable for SLPs to regularly evaluate their students' progress with strategy use (Swanson, 1999). However, in so doing, it is essential to examine both process and product. Gains in reading comprehension measures will not necessarily reflect improvement in strategy use; think-alouds, on the other hand, will.

Strategic Use of Reading Resources

In many cases, older students will need to go beyond the written text in order to comprehend it and learn from it. For example, if they do not understand a particular word that is critical to the larger meaning of the text, they might need to use an online or printed dictionary. When a student is lacking prior knowledge on the topic of a given text, he or she needs to know how to gather that knowledge from outside of the text itself. At a basic level, SLPs should make sure that their older students know how to search for and find information in a dictionary and on the web. Additionally, older students should develop shortcuts (e.g., on their "favorites" bar or list) and learn to use helpful search engines and websites to gather information when it is needed. It can be helpful for older students to use child-friendly search engines that are specifically designed to locate easier-to-understand information on a variety of topics (e.g., dibdabdoo.com, dmoz.org, and kidrex.org). Similarly, older students can benefit tremendously from websites that can provide them with easy-to-understand background knowledge that they do not already have. For instance, while the free, web-based encyclopedia Wikipedia (www.wikipedia.org) is helpful, the text can be difficult for older students with reading deficits to process on their own. Simpler information can sometimes be found on websites geared toward children, such as kids.net.au and factmonster.com. Older students might find it worthwhile to purchase a subscription to a children's web-based encyclopedia (e.g., kidsbritannica.com) to have ready access to easy-to-understand information on a variety of topics. Finally, for older students who struggle substantially with decoding/word recognition, text-to-speech software (e.g., readplease.com and naturalreaders.com) can provide them with the opportunity to access and learn from the same texts as their same-age peers. What's more, the SLP can and should incorporate these and other augmentative resources into therapy (e.g., helping older students learn *when* and *how* to gather background knowledge quickly and independently, helping older students learn how to become strategic *readers* even when they are *listening* to texts).

School: Service Delivery Models for High School

As curricular demands intensify in the secondary and postsecondary years, older students with language disorders need intervention that will support their content learning and lead them in the direction of independence. This should involve not only comprehension but also learning from texts (Biancarosa & Snow, 2004; W. Kintsch, 1994; E. Kintsch, 2005). Comprehending from text enables the learner to answer questions about or retell the content from written contexts. This ability conveys whether or not the student perceived and remembered what he or she read. Learning from text is a much deeper process. It requires the reader to draw upon information from the text and use prior knowledge to make inferences (E. Kintsch, 2005). Most important, it enables the reader to use knowledge in novel learning situations, a skill critical for content learning. So, how does the SLP do this?

Focus on Building Academic Independence

Reading to learn is the goal. SLPs need to help their older students reach that goal. In large part, the SLP should provide intervention focused on improvement of students' underlying *skills* and *strategies* the first two *S's* as described in the preceding two sections. However, in doing this, care should be taken to ensure that: (a) students are receiving intervention that makes use of their curricular content, thereby providing greater chances for transfer of the taught skills and strategies, and (b) the SLP is maintaining a therapeutic focus and not taking on the role of a tutor (see Ehren, 2000; Ukrainetz, 1998, 2005, 2006).

Any clinician who has provided intervention to high school or college students has probably faced the difficult challenge of resisting pleas for help with academic assignments. When twelfth-grade student enters your office almost in tears because he has to read and answer questions about a chapter in *Beowulf* by the end of the day, it is very hard to resist the urge to save that student by helping him to read (and understand) the chapter and then answer all of the questions (in writing). As the SLP, you want to help your older students succeed in school, and using their classroom texts and assignments in therapy is a perfectly reasonable approach. However, the SLP's primary concern should always be with helping these students to reach the prescribed intervention goals so that they can become better and more independent learners rather than with achieving immediate improvement in assignments and test grades. The SLP must not only keep this focus but also must convey this message to the high school or college students with whom he or she works. Students need to believe that, despite the lack of immediate benefit, the approach will pay off in the long term with better grades and academic success.

SLPs must be particularly mindful of the years of struggle and failure often experienced by these students. From the start, the SLP and the student should work together to identify and develop short-term functional goals that are coupled with corresponding academic outcomes. For example, the SLP might suggest that if they work on understanding and using three reading strategies over the semester, with progress based on the student's ability to complete question/answer homework for history class in less than 45 minutes and achieve passing scores on weekly history quizzes in two months' time. The SLP can tell the student that, in two months' time, they will revisit the goals together, measure the progress, and decide on the next steps. Hopefully, as students implement their new skills and strategies, they will see improvements in their grades. At the same time, it is reasonable to have students work with academic tutors on their assignments so they can get the immediate academic assistance they need to pass their assignments and tests.

Making Service Delivery in High School a Collaborative Practice

There are a number of benefits that come from the collaborative practices of SLPs, special educators, and classroom teachers when addressing the language needs of students (see Beck & Dennis, 1997; Dodge, 2004; Ehren & Ehren, 2001; Elksnin, 1997; Elksnin & Capilouto, 1994; Nelson et al., 2001; Shaughnessy & Sanger, 2005). More specifically, students benefit by: (a) learning language in their natural environment; (b) receiving the knowledge and skills from a range of expert professionals; (c) receiving services that target all areas of language impairment, including reading and writing; and (d) receiving greater literacy services directly from SLPs when high levels of collaboration occur. Despite the potential value of collaborative service delivery, a recent national survey of school-based SLPs found that regardless of students' grade level, type of disorder, or severity of disorder, they are most likely receiving speech–language services in small groups outside of the classroom setting (Brandel & Loeb, 2011). In this survey, SLPs reported providing their high school students with just 20–30 minutes of intervention per week. Classroom-based services, whether collaborative or not, were not happening, and pullout services were barely happening. Why? While some of this can be due to larger institutional issues and practices, Brandel and Loeb found a significant relationship between SLPs' clinical training experiences in graduate school and their methods of service delivery. SLPs who experienced collaborative intervention at the middle school or high school level during their graduate school program were more likely to use such an approach in their own practice. Unfortunately, less than 10% of the SLPs surveyed reported having experienced such practices, suggesting bad news for older students. Knowing this, it is critical that practicing SLPs, especially those who supervise graduate student clinicians, make concerted efforts to design and build the infrastructure that will support older students' transfer of newly learned reading skills and strategies to the classroom setting.

Students who have difficulties with *reading to learn* require more than what traditional pullout services (e.g., working out of class with the SLP one or two times per week for 30 minutes at a time) provide. These students need frequent, intense, and explicit intervention that includes opportunities for practice across text types as well as corrective feedback (Mastropieri & Scruggs, 1997; Vaughn & Klingner, 2004). This is not to say that pullout services should not be provided to older students but that they are not sufficient. Furthermore, at the secondary level in particular, pullout services can be barriers to learning (see Larson, McKinley, & Boley, 1993). For instance, a student who misses spoken instruction in a class has to make up for that missed information by doing even more *reading to learn*. Scheduling therapy during a study hall, when no lesson is missed, still means that the student will have even more homework to complete at home.

In order to maximize students' chances for success, SLPs must strive to develop solid, collaborative relationships with principals, general education teachers, special education teachers, reading specialists, and the like (see Biancarosa & Snow, 2004; Ehren & Murza, 2010; Larson et al., 1993). In many cases, teachers meet as teams to coordinate instruction, reinforce strategies and techniques, and support content learning across different subject areas. By becoming active, contributing members of these teams, SLPs and teachers can better work together to ensure the coordinated exchange of information that will connect therapeutic activities with classroom learning (Butler, Nelson, Roth, & Paul, 2006; Nippold, 2010).

Collaboration can also come in the form of consultation. As an example, in a recently published randomized control study, an SLP trained secondary school teachers to modify their use of spoken and written language in the classroom to improve learning in their students with language impairments (see Starling, Munro, Togher, & Arciuli, 2012). Through this collaborative relationship, the SLP provided her students with more indirect intervention by helping the teachers learn to integrate therapeutic approaches into their daily instructional practices. In the end, the students in classes with trained teachers showed significant improvements in language comprehension and written expression compared to the students in classrooms with untrained teachers.

Making intervention relevant for older students is critical for motivation (discussed in more detail later) as well as for academic success. By connecting with teachers and spending time in classrooms, SLPs will be more in tune with the linguistic and cognitive demands that their students are experiencing on a daily basis. Furthermore, SLPs can incorporate and reinforce the content that their students are being exposed to in the context of therapy. By keeping in regular contact with special education teachers and reading specialists, these professionals can all work collaboratively to better address each student's needs. Finally, while collaborative models of service delivery are highly advisable, building and maintaining collaborative relationships takes time, effort, and persistence (Ehren & Ehren, 2001; Elksnin & Capilouto, 1994; Fallon & Katz, 2011; Shaughnessy & Sanger, 2005; Staskowski & Zagaiski, 2003). By providing principals, teachers, and other service personnel with a better understanding of the important role that language plays in *reading to learn*, SLPs will increase the likelihood of successful service delivery (Ehren & Murza, 2010).

Serving Students in High School Classrooms

Two very different types of classroom-based intervention also warrant some attention: SLPs providing services to students on their caseloads in general education classrooms and SLPs providing services to students on their caseloads in the *SLPs' own classrooms*.

SLPs sometimes work with their students in their general education classrooms. Sometimes SLPs separate the caseload student(s) from the rest of the class and conduct intervention while the lesson is occurring. The intervention usually involves the topic and materials of the lesson, with specific attention being paid to targeted language skills and learning behaviors. Sometimes SLPs work collaboratively as partners with teachers, providing both students who *are* and *are not* on their caseloads with co-taught lessons that involve a therapeutic emphasis on particular skills. There is evidence that the latter approach, capitalizing on the involvement of student peers, can be effective for promoting the generalization of reading comprehension skills and strategies to the whole class (Biancarosa & Snow, 2004; Mastropieri et al., 2003).

Peer-assisted or peer-mediated learning has been found effective in promoting reading comprehension skills in high school students (e.g., Biancarosa & Snow, 2004; Fuchs, Fuchs, & Kazdan, 1999; Mastropieri et al., 2003). Generally speaking, the model of peer-assisted or peer-mediated learning involves students of varying ability levels working together with direction from a teacher (or SLP) in order to improve a specific academic skill. While this approach is not readily discussed in the speech–language literature, it offers potential value to the SLP providing intervention in reading comprehension to older students in the classroom setting.

In contrast to working in other educators' classrooms, SLPs have successfully taken on the role of teacher in their *own* classrooms comprised exclusively of students on their caseloads (see Throneburg, Calvert, Sturm, Paramboukas, & Paul, 2000; Work, Cline, Ehren, Keiser, & Wujek, 1993). Specifically with adolescents in mind, Larson et al. (1993) proposed that the SLP would *teach* a for-credit course as an alternative means for providing older students with frequent, intense, and explicit intervention that would include opportunities for practice across text types as well as for corrective feedback. By making language intervention a for-credit course, Larson et al. argued that student motivation would be greater and thus likely to result in positive outcomes. Similarly, in their description of four model programs for middle and high school students, Work et al. emphasized the value of making language therapy an elective or required for-credit course. In each of the four programs presented, SLPs taught courses for the students on their caseloads on a daily basis for up to five class periods per day. Skills and strategies were taught and practiced with an aim toward improving students' spoken and written language abilities and learning behaviors.

School: Service Delivery in Postsecondary Settings

The Challenges of Postsecondary Settings

The third *S* of "School" for SLPs is increasingly including working with postsecondary students. At community college and university levels, the role of the SLP in promoting the older student's application of skills and strategies to academic tasks takes a somewhat different form. First, in any given semester, a college student's professors, although small in number, do not come together to meet (regularly or at all) as teachers do in a high school setting. Second, colleges and, even more so, universities are not seen as places for remedial learning. The emphasis is on lecturing rather than on teaching, because college students are expected to be good learners who can succeed independently. Grades are intended to show class ranking as much as degree of acquisition of knowledge and skills. Most instructors, understandably, consider it inappropriate to collaborate with tutors, academic support staff, or SLPs in order to facilitate the language and reading skills of students taking their college courses. That said, college and university faculty, for the most part, believe that students with LDs can be successful in college (Houck, Asselin, Troutman, & Arrington, 1992; Katz & Guarracino, 2010; Murray, Wren, & Keys, 2008) and see college students' efforts to improve their learning skills through intervention as highly commendable (Katz & Guarracino, 2010).

The Hub for College Students Who Need Services

So, where and how do college students with identified or even unidentified LDs find appropriate intervention services? Not all of these college students choose to disclose their disabilities, but for those who do, an office of disability support services (DSS) is generally a student's best option for assistance with transitioning into and meeting with success in college. Personnel in DSS offices serve critical roles: they provide academic counseling, make necessary referrals, and set up appropriate academic accommodations (Lindstrom, 2007; Rath & Royer, 2002). Appropriate accommodations are changes in modality, time, or conditions that do not change the knowledge and skills being taught. These include note taking, permission to record lectures, alternative locations for exams, additional time on exams, or exam readers. While DSS offices all provide these basic services to their students with disabilities and may provide tutoring services, most do not provide therapeutic intervention services. However, DSS plays an important role in helping students find the help they need, even if it is not available within the institution. High school SLPs should encourage their college-bound caseload students to register and consult with DSS, advocate for themselves, and assume greater responsibility for their own learning.

Making College Accessible Through Departments of Speech–Language Pathology

Therapeutic language and reading services for college students through speech clinics are not readily promoted or available, and this does not have to be the case. Currently, there are over 250 accredited graduate programs in speech–language pathology across the United States. These programs have faculty and clinical staff who are experts in language disorders. While they may not have (or believe they have) expertise in written language disorders (see Fallon & Katz, 2011), they have the capacity to become experts. They also have the responsibility to provide their graduate students with training in the area of written language disorders. In addition, on these campuses, there are many college students with (or suspected of having) written language disorders who are underserved, struggling, and often failing in their courses. It is obvious that the opportunities for benefiting both graduate speech pathology students and college students with LDs are great. Two service delivery models that capitalize on the presence of speech–language pathology departments for improving the written language skills of struggling college students are a strategic reading course and in-house reading clinics.

Strategic reading courses offer university students focused, classroom-based instruction on reading skills strategies. Caverly, Nicholson, and Radcliffe (2004) reported on two studies designed to examine the short-term and long-term effects of a one-semester strategic reading course designed for college students who had failed a state-mandated basic-skills reading test (i.e., "developmental students"). Using evidence-based approaches for teaching reading strategies to college students in concert with authentic reading materials, the participants in Caverly et al.'s first study showed significant improvements in comprehension of a college-level textbook chapter, in a standardized reading comprehension test, and in reported use of reading strategies. In addition, qualitative interviews with a subset of the participants suggested that all but one of these students found value in the course, reporting benefits such as being able to apply the reading strategies in subsequent courses, being better studiers, and making better grades. In their second study, Caverly et al. compared the short-term and long-term outcomes (over a fourth-year period) of a group of "developmental students" enrolled in the strategic reading course with another group of "developmental students" who served as controls and were not enrolled in the strategic reading course. The enrolled group showed significantly greater improvements than the control group on a standardized measure of reading comprehension, and the enrolled group's grades in a reading-intensive history course were significantly higher than the control group's grades. The success of this strategic reading course, although not developed or conducted by SLPs, warrants serious consideration from departments of speech–language pathology as an alternative and innovative model of service delivery for college students struggling with spoken and written language disorders.

The second model of service delivery comes from our own teaching and research interests and efforts in addressing the needs of college students with (or suspected of having) written language disorders. With that goal in mind and with the infrastructure in place (i.e., in-house clinics with treatment rooms, observation suites, and recording equipment), each of us developed literacy clinics housed in the speech–language departments at our respective universities. To our knowledge, these clinics were the first of their kind, and they have thrived, together serving over 30 college students with language disorders and reading comprehension deficits. We believe that these clinics have thrived, in large part, for four reasons: (a) easy access, often within walking distance, (b) free or reduced costs, (c) relationships with DSS personnel, and (d) high-quality, evidence-based services. Through our experiences, it has become clear that there is tremendous potential for making service delivery to college students straightforward and widespread, not necessarily on every college and university campus, but at least on the more than 250 campuses with graduate programs in speech–language pathology.

Student Buy-in: Facilitating Motivation and Engagement

Student buy-in is the fourth *S*, but it could be considered the primary *S*: the importance of student buy-in cannot be overstated. Student buy-in involves the belief, on the part of the student, that he or she—with support from the SLP—has the potential to develop the skills and strategies needed to become academically successful. With this belief, also referred to as *self-efficacy*, comes *motivation*; you cannot be motivated to engage in intervention if you do not believe it will make you smarter or more capable (Dickson, Collins, Simmons, & Kame'enui, 1998). Unlike young students with language disorders, older students have struggled for years and years, watched their peers repeatedly excel at tasks that are monumentally difficult for them, and have long given up on themselves (Guthrie & Davis, 2003; Ivey, 1999). Many of these older students have come to attribute their successes to external forces (e.g., an easy test) and their failures to internal forces (e.g., not being smart enough; Borkowski, Weyhing, & Carr, 1988; Yasutake & Bryan, 1995). This sense of helplessness is further complicated by the seemingly infinite and unachievable academic tasks that they are required to complete for school. These older students are generally in survival mode; they do not have the time or the skills to complete what is required of them, much less to engage in tasks that they perceive as irrelevant to their immediate needs. The SLP must find ways to help these students recognize that they are capable of influencing their own academic successes so that they begin to believe in themselves and in the intervention process (Guthrie & Wigfield, 2000). In addition, the SLP has to provide intervention that these students see as relevant to their immediate academic needs. In doing so, however, the SLP has to avoid the pull to respond to the student's pleas for help with a paper that is due first thing tomorrow or even yesterday. In these not-so-uncommon scenarios, maintaining one's role as an SLP and avoiding the lure of becoming a sympathetic tutor often means saying "no," which can be hard.

The SLP's beliefs about the older student's potential for success should be positive and transparent. First, the SLP must believe that he or she can help the student, which sends a message of confidence and positivity to the student and builds an important foundation on which to build trust and a cooperative working relationship. In this process, the SLP must understand that motivation is not a prerequisite for beginning intervention. A lack of motivation in older students will often be a given; the SLP's job is to target improvement in *both* motivation *and* reading comprehension. Even small successes with reading comprehension skills and strategies will beget student motivation, and motivation, in turn, will beget greater engagement and even more successes (Guthrie & Wigfield, 2000). Finally, it is important that the SLP focus on establishing and maintaining a safe and supportive environment. When working with more than one student at a time, the SLP should create a culture wherein the students' strengths and difficulties are openly and respectfully addressed and clinician-student partnership is valued.

When older students can see firsthand that they are making progress in their use of reading comprehension skills and strategies, their motivation to continue to engage in the therapeutic process will increase as well. Therefore, it is critical that SLPs make use of evidence-based intervention approaches and report progress to students on a regular basis. Furthermore, evidence suggests that in order to build and maintain older students' motivation to read, intervention must: (a) provide interesting texts for the students to read, (b) foster student autonomy, (c) increase reading-related social peer interactions, and (d) target interesting content goals for reading (Guthrie & Humenick, 2004; Roberts et al., 2008). Finally, building rapport by listening to the student's concerns and co-constructing an action plan that incorporates language skills, metacognitive strategies, and the application of literacy skills to novel learning situations is essential to helping close the achievement gap and move toward successful academic and vocational outcomes.

Conclusion

As language disorders persist across the lifespan, so does the need to support and provide treatment to students in secondary and postsecondary settings. It is critical that older students receive continued attention and services from SLPs and other relevant players as these students progress through increasingly demanding academic settings. In middle school and high school, SLPs and other educators must work together to provide thoughtful assessments and meaningful intervention services that address the skills and strategies that students need to learn from the texts they read. As students advance into postsecondary settings, responsibility for obtaining help transfers from educators to the individual student. Thus, in the secondary years, students need to be prepared to advocate for themselves, including seeking out personnel in DSS offices. These DSS offices are often a student's link to resources such as academic counselors, university language and reading clinics, tutors, writing labs, academic accommodations, and community service providers.

Assessing and treating reading disorders in older students calls for an understanding of the underlying skills and strategies that make reading comprehension and learning from written texts possible. When providing older students with reading intervention, SLPs can approach treatment using a framework that targets the Four *S*'s: (1) Skills, (2) Strategies, (3) School, and (4) Student Buy-in. It is tremendously important to focus on the comprehension of written texts, not just for the goal of understanding individual texts but also for the much greater goal of *learning* from texts and achieving academic success. Although there are many challenges in working with this older population, there are also great rewards in supporting students whose language needs are so often neglected just when they need help the most.

References

Aarnoutse, C., van Leeuwe, J., Voeten, M., & Oud, H. (2001). Development of decoding, reading comprehension, vocabulary, and spelling during the elementary school years. *Reading and Writing, 14*(1–2) 61–89.

Aaron, P. G., Joshi, R. M., & Williams, K. A. (1999) Not all reading disabilities are alike. *Journal of Learning Disabilities, 32*, 120–127.

Adams, M. J. (1990). *Beginning to read.* Cambridge, MA: MIT Press.

Allen, M. M., & Petersen, D. B. (2011). Reading comprehension: A proposal for a hybrid approach. *Perspectives on Language Learning and Education, 18*, 13–19.

Allinder, R. M., Dunse, L., Brunken, C. D., & Obermiller-Krolikowski, H. J. (2001). Improving fluency in at-risk readers and students with learning disabilities. *Remedial and Special Education, 22*, 48–45.

American Speech-Language-Hearing Association. (2006). *2006 Schools Survey report: Caseload characteristics* [Professional issues statement]. Retrieved from www.asha.org/policy

Apel, K., & Swank, L. K. (1999). Second chances: Improving decoding skills in the older student. *Language, Speech, and Hearing Services in Schools, 30*, 231–242.

Applebee, A. N., Langer, J. A., Nystrand, M., & Gamoran, A. (2003). Discussion-based approaches to developing understanding: Classroom instruction and student performance in middle and high school English. *American Educational Research Journal, 40*, 685–730.

Beck, A. R., & Dennis, M. (1997). Speech–language pathologists' and teachers' perceptions of classroom-based interventions. *Language, Speech, and Hearing Services in Schools, 28*, 146–153.

Beck, I. L., McKeown, M. G., Sandora, C., Kucan, L., & Worthy, J. (1996). Questioning the author: A year-long classroom implementation to engage students with text. *The Elementary School Journal, 96*, 385–414.

Benson, S. E. (2009). Understanding literate language: Developmental and clinical issues. *Contemporary Issues in Communication Sciences and Disorders, 36*, 174–178.

Bereiter, C., & Bird, M. (1985). Use of thinking aloud in identification and teaching of reading comprehension strategies. *Cognition and Instruction, 2*, 131–156.

Biancarosa, G., & Snow, C. (2004). *Reading next: A vision for action and research in middle and high school literacy: A report to Carnegie Corporation of New York.* Washington, DC: Alliance for Excellent Education.

Borkowski, J. G., Weyhing, T. M., & Carr, M. (1988). Effects of attributional retraining on strategy-based reading comprehension in learning disabled students. *Journal of Educational Psychology, 80*, 46–53.

Bowey, J. (1994). Grammatical awareness and learning to read: A critique. In E. Assink (Ed.), *Literacy acquisition and social context* (pp. 122–149). New York, NY: Harvester Wheatsheaf.

Bradley, L., & Bryant, P. E. (1983). Categorizing sounds and learning to read: A causal connection. *Nature, 30*, 419–421.

Brandel, J., & Loeb, D. F. (2011). Program intensity and service delivery models in the schools: SLP survey results. *Language, Speech, and Hearing Services in the Schools, 42*, 461–490.

Braze, D., Tabor, W., Shankweiler, D., & Mencl, W. E. (2007). Speaking up for vocabulary: Reading skill differences in young adults. *Journal of Learning Disabilities, 40*, 226–243.

Brophy, J. (2004). *Motivating students to learn* (2nd ed.). Mahwah, NJ: Erlbaum.

Brown, A. L. (1980). Metacognitive development and reading. In R. J. Spiro, B. Bruce, W. Brewer (Eds.), *Theoretical issues in reading comprehension* (pp. 453–482). Hillsdale, NJ: Erlbaum.

Brown, J. I., Fishco, V. V., & Hanna, G. (1993). *Nelson-Denny Reading Test.* Austin, TX: PRO-ED.

Brown, V. L., Wiederholdt, J. L., & Hammill, D. D. (2009) *Test of Reading Comprehension* (4th ed.) Austin, TX: PRO-ED.

Bryant, P. E., MacLean, M., Bradley, L. L. & Crossland, J. (1990). Rhyme and alliteration, phoneme detection, and learning to read. *Developmental Psychology, 26*, 429–438.

Butler, K., Nelson, N., Roth, F., & Paul, D. (2006). *Partnerships for literacy: Principles and practices.* Hagerstown, MD: Lippincott Williams and Wilkins.

Cain, K., Oakhill, J., & Bryant, P. E. (2004). Children's reading comprehension ability: Concurrent prediction by working memory, verbal ability, and component skills. *Journal of Educational Psychology, 96*, 31–42.

Cain, K., Oakhill, J., & Lemmon, K., (2005). The relation between children's reading comprehension level and their comprehension of idioms. *Journal of Experimental Child Psychology, 90*, 65–87.

Carlisle, J. (1995). Morphological awareness and early reading achievement. In L. Feldman (Ed.), *Morphological aspects of language processing* (pp. 189–209). Hillsdale, NJ: Erlbaum.

Carlisle, J. (2000). Awareness of the structure and meaning of morphologically complex words: Impact on reading. *Reading and Writing, 12*, 169–190.

Carlisle, J. F., & Stone, C. A. (2003). The effects of morphological structure on children's reading of derived words. In E. Assink & D. Santa (Eds.), *Reading complex words: Cross-language studies* (pp. 27–52). New York, NY: Kluwer Academic.

Carlisle, J. F., Stone, C. A., & Katz, L. A. (2001). The effects of phonological transparency on reading derived words. *Annals of Dyslexia, 51*, 249–274.

Catts, H. W. (1993). The relationship between speech–language impairments and reading disabilities. *Journal of Speech and Hearing Research, 36*, 948–958.

Catts, H., Adlof, S., & Ellis-Weismer, S. (2006). Language deficits in poor comprehenders: A case for the simple view of reading. *Journal of Speech, Language, and Hearing Research, 49*, 278–293.

Catts, H. W., Fey, M. E., Tomblin, J. B., & Zhang, X. (2002). A longitudinal investigation of reading outcomes in children with language impairments. *Journal of Speech, Language, and Hearing Research, 45*, 1142–1157.

Catts, H. W., Fey, M. E., Zhang, X., & Tomblin, J. B. (1999). Language basis of reading and reading disabilities: Evidence from a longitudinal investigation. *Scientific Studies of Reading, 3*, 331–361.

Catts, H. W., Fey, M. E., Zhang, X., & Tomblin, J. B. (2001). Estimating the risk of future reading difficulties in kindergarten children: A research-based model and its clinical implementation. *Language, Speech, and Hearing Services in Schools, 32*, 38–50.

Caverly, D. C., Nicholson, S. A., & Radcliffe, R. (2004). The effectiveness of strategic reading instruction for college developmental readers. *Journal of College Reading and Learning, 35*(1), 25–49.

Clegg, J., Hollis, C., Mawhood, L., & Rutter, M. (2005). Developmental language disorders—a follow-up in later adult life: Cognitive, language and psychosocial outcomes. *Journal of Child Psychology and Psychiatry, 46*, 128–149.

Coleman, C., Lindstrom, J., Nelson, J., Lindstrom, W., & Gregg, K. N. (2010). Passageless comprehension on the Nelson-Denny reading test: Well above chance for university students. *Journal of Learning Disability, 43*, 244–249.

Conti-Ramsden, G., & Durkin, K. (2012). Postschool educational and employment experiences of young people with specific language impairment. *Language, Speech, and Hearing Services in Schools, 43*, 507–520.

Cromley, J., & Azevedo, R. (2007). Testing and refining the direct and inferential mediation model of reading comprehension. *Journal of Educational Psychology, 99*, 311–325.

Curtis, M. (2004). Adolescents who struggle with word identification: Research and practice. In T. L. Jetton & J. A. Dole (Eds.), *Adolescent literacy research and practice* (pp. 119–134). New York, NY: Guilford.

Cutting, L., & Scarborough, H. (2006). Prediction of reading comprehension: Relative contributions of word recognition, language proficiency, and other cognitive skills can depend on how comprehension is measured. *Scientific Studies of Reading, 10*, 277–299.

Deshler, D. D., & Hock, M. F. (2007). Adolescent literacy: Where we are, where we need to go. In M. Pressley, A. K. Billman, K. H. Perry, K. E. Reffitt, & J. M. Reynolds (Eds.), *Shaping literacy achievement: Research we have, research we need* (pp. 98–128). New York, NY: Guilford.

Devault, R., & Joseph, L. M. (2004). Repeated readings combined with word boxes phonics technique increases fluency levels of high school students with severe reading delays. *Preventing School Failure, 49*(1), 22–27.

Dickson, S. V., Collins, V. L., Simmons, D. C., & Kame'enui, E. J. (1998). Metacognitive strategies: Research bases. In D. C. Simmons & E. J. Kame'enui (Eds.), *What reading research tells us about children with diverse learning needs* (pp. 295–360). Mahwah, NJ: Erlbaum.

Dodge, E. P. (2004). Communication skills: The foundation for meaningful group intervention in school-based programs. *Topics in Language Disorders, 24*(2), 141–150.

Dreyer, C., & Nel, C. (2003). Teaching reading strategies and reading comprehension within a technology-enhanced learning environment. *System, 31*, 349–365.

Ebbers, S. M., & Denton, C. A. (2008). A root awakening: Vocabulary instruction for older students with reading difficulties. *Learning Disabilities Research and Practice, 23*, 90–102.

Edmonds, M. S., Vaughn, S., Wexler, J., Reutebuch, C., Cable, A., Tackett, K. K., & Schnakenberg, J. W. (2009). A synthesis of reading interventions and effects on reading comprehension outcomes for older struggling readers. *Review of Educational Research, 79*, 262–300.

Ehren, B. J. (2000). Maintaining a therapeutic focus and sharing responsibility for student success: Keys to in-classroom speech–language services. *Language, Speech, and Hearing Services in Schools, 31*, 219–229.

Ehren, B. J. (2006). Partnerships to support reading comprehension for students with language impairment. *Topics in Language Disorders, 26*(1), 41–53.

Ehren, B. J. (2007). Responsiveness to intervention: An opportunity to reinvent speech–language services in schools. *The ASHA Leader, 12*(13), 10–12.

Ehren, B. J., & Ehren, T. C. (2001). New or expanded literacy roles for speech–language pathologists: Making it happen in the schools. *Seminars in Speech and Language, 22*, 234–243.

Ehren, B. J., & Murza, K. (2010). The urgent need to address workforce readiness in adolescent literacy intervention. *Perspectives on Language Learning and Education, 17*(3), 93–99.

Ehri, L. C. (1997). Learning to read and learning to spell are one and the same, almost. In C. A. Perfetti, L. Rieben, & M. Fayol (Eds.), *Learning to spell: Research, theory, and practice across languages* (pp. 237–269). Mahwah, NJ: Erlbaum.

Ehri, L. C., & McCormick, S. (1998). Phases of word learning: Implications for instruction with delayed and disabled readers. *Reading and Writing Quarterly, 14*, 135–164.

Elbro, C., & Arnbak, E. (1996). The role of morpheme recognition and morphological awareness in dyslexia. *Annals of Dyslexia, 46*, 209–240.

Elksnin, L. K. (1997). Collaborative speech and language services for students with learning disabilities. *Journal of Learning Disabilities, 30*(4), 414–426.

Elksnin, L. K., & Capilouto, G. J. (1994). Speech–language pathologists' perceptions of integrated service delivery in school settings. *Language, Speech, and Hearing Services in Schools, 25*, 258–267.

Faggella-Luby, M., & Deshler, D. (2008). Reading comprehension in adolescents with LD: What we know; what we need to learn. *Learning Disabilities Research and Practice, 23*, 70–78.

Fallon, K., & Carlberg, R. (2012). *A hybrid approach to reading comprehension: Intervention with a university student* (Unpublished Master's thesis). Towson University, MD.

Fallon, K. A., & Katz, L. A. (2011). Written-language services in the schools: The time is now. *Language, Speech, and Hearing Services in Schools, 42*(1), 3–17.

Felsenfeld, S., Broen, P. A., & McGue, M. (1994). A 28-year follow-up of adults with a history of moderate phonological disorder: Educational and occupational results. *Journal of Speech and Hearing Research, 37*, 1341–1353.

Flavell, J. H. (1979). Metacognition and cognitive monitoring: A new area of cognitive-developmental inquiry. *American Psychologist, 34*, 906–911.

Francis, D. J., Fletcher, J. M., Catts, H., & Tomblin, B. (2004, September). *Dimensions affecting the assessment of reading comprehension.* Paper presented at PREL Focus on Comprehension Forum, New York, NY.

Francis, D. J., Fletcher, J. M., Catts, H. W., & Tomblin, J. B. (2005). Dimensions affecting the assessment of reading comprehension. In S. G. Paris & S. A. Stahl (Eds.), *Children's reading comprehension and assessment* (pp. 369–394). Mahwah, NJ: Erlbaum.

Freebody, P., & Anderson, R. C. (1983). Effects of vocabulary difficulty, text cohesion, and schema availability on reading comprehension. *Reading Research Quarterly, 18*, 277–294.

Fuchs, L. S., Fuchs, D., & Kazdan, S. (1999). Effects of peer-assisted learning strategies on high-school students with serious reading problems. *Remedial and Special Education, 20*, 309–318.

Garner, R., & Kraus, C. (1981–82). Good and poor comprehender differences in knowing and regulating reading behaviors. *Educational Research Quarterly, 6*, 5–12.

Gersten, R., Fuchs, D., Williams, J. P., & Baker, S. (2001). Teaching reading comprehension strategies to students with learning disabilities: A review of research. *Review of Educational Research, 71*, 279–320.

Greenhalgh, K., & Strong, C. (2001). Literate language features in spoken narratives of children with typical language and children with language impairments. *Language, Speech, and Hearing Services in the Schools, 32*, 114–135.

Gough, P. B., & Tunmer, W. E. (1986). Decoding, reading, and reading disability. *Remedial and Special Education, 7*, 6–10.

Guthrie, J. T., & Davis, M. H. (2003). Motivating struggling readers in middle school through an engagement model of classroom practice. *Reading and Writing Quarterly, 19*, 59–85.

Guthrie, J. T., & Humenick, N. M. (2004) Motivating students to read: Evidence for classroom practices that increase reading motivation and achievement. In P. McCardle & V. Chabra (Eds.), *The voice of evidence in reading research* (pp. 329–354). Baltimore, MD: Brookes.

Guthrie, J. T., & Wigfield, A. (2000). Engagement and motivation in reading. In M. L. Kamil, P. B. Mosenthal, P. D. Pearson, & R. Barr (Eds.), *Handbook of reading research* (Vol. 3; pp. 403–422). Mahwah, NJ: Erlbaum.

Hawkins, R. O., Hale, A., Sheeley, W., & Ling, S. (2011). Repeated reading and vocabulary previewing interventions to improve fluency and comprehension for struggling high school readers. *Psychology in the Schools, 48*(1), 59–77.

Hoover, W. A., & Gough, P. B. (1990). The simple view of reading. *Reading and Writing, 2,* 127–160.

Houck, C. K., Asselin, S. B., Troutman, G. T., & Arrington, J. (1992). Students with learning disabilities at the university environment: A study of faculty perceptions. *Journal of Learning Disabilities, 25,* 678–684.

Houtveen, A., & van de Grift, W. (2007). Effects of metacognitive strategy instruction and instruction time on reading comprehension. *School Effectiveness and School Improvement, 18,* 173–190.

Hurst, D., & Smerdon, B. (2000). Postsecondary students with disabilities: Enrollment, services, and persistence. *Education Statistics Quarterly, 2*(3), 55–58.

Institute for Education Sciences. (2002). *The condition of education 2002* (NCES 2002–025). Washington, DC: U.S. Department of Education, Institute for Education Sciences.

Institute for Education Sciences. (2010). *The condition of education 2010* (NCES 2010-028). Washington, DC: U.S. Department of Education, Institute for Education Sciences.

Ivey, G. (1999). A multicase study in the middle school: Complexities among young adolescent readers. *Reading Research Quarterly, 34,* 172–193.

Joffe, V. L., & Nippold, M. A. (2012). Progress in understanding adolescent language disorders. *Language, Speech, and Hearing Services in Schools, 43,* 438–444.

Johnson, C. J., Beitchman, J. H., & Brownlie, E. B. (2010). Twenty-year follow-up of children with and without speech–language impairments: Family, educational, occupational, and quality of life outcomes. *American Journal of Speech–Language Pathology, 19,* 51–65.

Just, M. A., & Carpenter, P. A. (1992). A capacity theory of comprehension: Individual differences in working memory. *Psychological Review, 98,* 122–149.

Kamhi, A. G., & Catts, H. W. (1991). Language and reading: Convergences, divergences, and development. In A. G. Kamhi & H. W. Catts (Eds.), *Reading disabilities: A developmental language perspective* (pp. 1–34). Boston, MA: Allyn & Bacon.

Kamil, M. L. (2003). *Adolescents and literacy: Reading for the 21st Century.* Washington, DC: Alliance for Excellent Education.

Kamil, M. L., Borman, G. D., Dole, J., Kral, C. C., Salinger, T., & Torgesen, J. (2008). *Improving adolescent literacy: Effective classroom and intervention practices: A Practice Guide* (NCEE #2008-4027). Washington, DC: U.S. Department of Education, Institute of Education Sciences, National Center for Education Evaluation and Regional Assistance.

Katz, L. A. (2004). An investigation of the relationship of morphological awareness to reading comprehension in fourth and sixth graders (Doctoral dissertation, University of Michigan). *Dissertation Abstracts International, 65,* 2138.

Katz, L. A., & Guarracino, S. (2010, November). *Is disclosure of speech–language therapy advantageous for college students?* Poster presented at the American Speech-Language-Hearing Association Convention, Philadelphia, PA.

Keenan, J. M., & Betjemann, R. S. (2006). Comprehending the Gray Oral Reading Tests without reading it: Why comprehension tests should not include passage-independent items. *Scientific Studies of Reading, 10,* 363–380.

Kershaw, S., & Schatschneider, C. (2012). A latent variable approach to the simple view of reading. *Reading and Writing, 25,* 433–464.

Kim, A., Vaughn, S., Wanzek, J., & Wei, S. (2004). Graphic organizers and their effects on the reading comprehension of students with LD. *Journal of Learning Disabilities, 37,* 105–118.

Kintsch, E. (2005). Comprehension theory as a guide for the design of thoughtful questions. *Topics in Language Disorders, 25,* 51–64.

Kintsch, W. (1992). How readers construct situation models for stories: The role of syntactic cues and causal inferences. In A. E. Healy, S. M. Kosslyn, & R. M. Shiffrin (Eds.), *From learning processes to cognitive processes. Essays in honor of William K. Estes* (Vol. 2, pp. 261–278). Hillsdale, NJ: Erlbaum.

Kintsch, W. (1994). Text comprehension, memory, and learning. *American Psychologist, 49,* 294–303.

Kintsch, W. (1998). *Comprehension: A paradigm for cognition.* Cambridge, UK: Cambridge University Press.

Kintsch, W., & Kintsch, E. (2004). Comprehension. In S. G. Paris & S. A. Stahl (Eds.), *Children's reading comprehension and assessment* (pp. 71–92). Mahwah, NJ: Erlbaum.

Klecan-Aker, J. S., & Caraway, T. H. (1997), A study of the relationship of storytelling ability and reading comprehension in fourth- and sixth-grade African-American children. *European Journal of Disorders of Communication, 32,* 110–125.

Kuhn, M. R., & Stahl, S. A. (2003). Fluency: a review of developmental and remedial practices. *Journal of Educational Psychology, 95,* 3–21.

Larson, V. L., & McKinley, N. L. (1993). An introduction. *Language, Speech, and Hearing Services in Schools, 24,* 19–20.

Larson, V. L., McKinley, N. L., & Boley, D. (1993). Service delivery models for adolescents with language disorders. *Language, Speech, and Hearing Services in Schools, 24,* 36–42.

Lenz, B. K., & Deshler, D. D. (2004). Teaching content to all. Evidence-based inclusive practices in middle and secondary schools. Boston, MA: Pearson.

Leslie, L., & Caldwell, J. S. (2011). *Qualitative reading inventory* (5th ed.). Boston, MA: Pearson.

Liberman, I. Y., Shankweiler, D., & Liberman, A. M. (1989). The alphabetic principle and learning to read. In D. Shankweiler & I. Y. Liberman (Eds.), *Phonology and reading disability: Solving the reading puzzle* (pp. 1–33). Ann Arbor: University of Michigan Press.

Lindsay, G. & Dockrell, J. E. (2012). Longitudinal patterns of behavioral, emotional, and social difficulties and self-concept in adolescents with a history of specific language impairment. *Language, Speech, and Hearing Services in Schools, 43,* 445–460.

Lindstrom, J. H. (2007). Determining appropriate accommodations for postsecondary students with reading and written expression disorders. *Special Issue of Learning Disabilities Research & Practice: Postsecondary Learning Disabilities (22)*4, 229–236.

MacGinitie, W. H., MacGinitie, R., Maria, K., Dreyer L. G., & Hughes, K. (2000). *Gates-MacGinitie Reading Tests* (4th ed.). Itasca, IL: Riverside.

Mastropieri, M. A., & Scruggs, T. E. (1997). Best practices in promoting reading comprehension in students with learning disabilities, 1976 to 1996. *Remedial and Special Education, 18,* 197–214.

Mastropieri, M., Scruggs, T., & Graetz, J. (2003). Reading comprehension instruction for secondary students: Challenges for struggling students and teachers. *Learning Disability Quarterly, 26,* 103–116.

McKeown, M. G. (1985). The acquisition of word meaning from context by children of high and low ability. *Reading Research Quarterly, 20,* 482–496.

McKeown, M. G., Beck, I. L., & Blake, R. G. (2009). Rethinking reading comprehension instruction: A comparison of instruction for strategies and content approaches. *Reading Research Quarterly, 44,* 218–253.

Michigan State Board of Education. (2010). *Common core state standards: A crosswalk to the Michigan grade level and high school content expectations* (ELA, social studies, and science). Lansing, MI: Michigan Department of Education.

Mokhtari, K., & Reichard, C. (2002). Assessing students' metacognitive awareness of reading strategies. *Journal of Educational Psychology, 94,* 249–259.

Morgan, P. L., & Fuchs, D. (2007). Is there a bidirectional relationship between children's reading skills and reading motivation? *Exceptional Children, 73,* 165–183.

Morsy, L., Kieffer, M., Snow, C. E. (2010). *Measure for measure: A critical consumers' guide to reading comprehension assessments for adolescents.* New York, NY: Carnegie Corporation of New York.

Murray, C., Goldstein, D. E., Nourse, S., & Edgar, E. (2000). The postsecondary school attendance and completion rates of high school graduates with learning disabilities. *Learning Disabilities Research and Practice, 15,* 119–127.

Murray, C., Wren, C. T., & Keys, C. (2008). University faculty perceptions of students with learning disabilities: Correlates and group differences. *Learning Disability Quarterly, 31,* 95–113.

Nagy, W., & Anderson, R. C. (1984). How many words are there in printed school English? *Reading Research Quarterly, 19,* 304–330.

Nagy, W. E., Anderson, R. C., Schommer, M., Scott, J. A., & Stallman, A. C. (1989). Morphological families in the internal lexicon. *Reading Research Quarterly, 24,* 262–282.

Nation, K. (2001). Reading and language in children: Exposing hidden deficits. *The Psychologist, 14,* 238–242.

Nation, K. (2005). Children's reading comprehension difficulties. In M. J. Snowing & C. Hulme (Eds.), *The science of reading: A handbook* (pp. 248–266). Oxford, UK: Blackwell.

Nation, K., & Snowling, M. (2004). Beyond phonological skills: Broader language skills contribute to the development of reading. *Journal of Research in Reading, 27,* 342–356.

National Institute for Literacy. (2003). *Put reading first: The research building blocks for teaching children to read* (2nd ed.). Jessup, MD: ED Publications.

National Reading Panel. (2000). *Teaching children to read: An evidence-based assessment of the scientific research literature on reading and its implications for reading instruction: Reports of the subgroups* (NIH Publication No. 00-4754). Washington, DC: U.S. Department of Health and Human Services, National Institute of Child Health and Human Development. Retrieved from http://www.nationalreadingpanel.org/

Nelson, N., Catts, H., Ehren, B., Roth, F., Scott, C., & Staskowski, M. (2001). Roles and responsibilities of speech–language pathologists with respect to reading and writing in children and adolescents. *Asha, Supplement 21*, 17–28.

Nicaise, M., & Gettinger, M. (1995). Fostering reading comprehension in college students. *Reading Psychology, 16*, 283–337.

Nippold, M. A. (1994). Persuasive talk in social contexts: Development, assessment, and intervention. *Topics in Language Disorders, 14*(3), 1–12.

Nippold, M. A. (2010). It's not too late to help adolescents succeed in school. *Language, Speech, and Hearing Services in Schools, 41*, 137–138.

Oakhill, J. (1995). Development in reading. In V. Lee & P. DasGupta (Eds.), *Children's cognitive and language development* (pp. 269–299). Oxford, UK: Blackwell.

Ouellette, G. (2006). What's meaning got to do with it: The role of vocabulary in word reading and reading comprehension. *Journal of Educational Psychology, 98*, 554–566.

Palincsar, A. S., & Brown, D. S. (1987). Enhancing instructional time through attention to metacognition. *Journal of Learning Disabilities, 20*, 66–75.

Paris, S. G., Carpenter, R. D., Paris, A. H., & Hamilton, E. E. (2004). Spurious and genuine correlates of children's reading comprehension. In S. G. Paris & S. A. Stahl (Eds.), *Children's reading comprehension and assessment* (pp. 131–160). Mahwah, NJ: Erlbaum.

Perera, K. (1984). *Children's writing and reading: Analyzing classroom reading*. London, UK: Blackwell.

Perfetti, C. A. (1985). *Reading ability*. New York, NY: Oxford University Press.

Pressley, M., & Afflerbach, P. (1995). *Verbal protocols of reading: The nature of constructively responsive reading*. Hillsdale, NJ: Erlbaum.

Pressley, M., & Gaskins, I. W. (2006). Metacognitively competent reading comprehension is constructively responsive reading: How can such reading be developed in students? *Metacognition and Learning, 1*, 99–113.

RAND Reading Study Group. (2002). *Reading for understanding: Toward an R&D program in reading comprehension*. Santa Monica, CA: RAND.

Rasinski, T. V. (2003). *The fluent reader: Oral reading strategies for building word recognition, fluency, and comprehension*. New York, NY: Scholastic.

Rasinski, T. V., Padak, N. D., McKeon, C. A., Wilfong, L. G., Friedauer, J. A., & Heim, P. (2005). Is reading fluency a key for successful high school reading? *Journal of Adolescent and Adult Literacy, 49*(1), 22–27.

Rasinski, T., Samuels, S. J., Hiebert, E., Petscher, Y., & Feller, K. (2011). The relationship between silent reading fluency instructional protocol on students' reading comprehension and achievement in an urban school setting. *Reading Psychology, 32*, 75–97.

Rath, K. A., & Royer, J. M. (2002). The nature and effectiveness of learning disability services for college students. *Educational Psychology Review, 14*, 353–381.

Rescorla, L. (2005). Age 13 language and reading outcomes in late-talking toddlers. *Journal of Speech, Language, and Hearing Research, 48*, 459–472.

Rescorla, L., (2009). Age 17 language and reading outcomes in late-talking toddlers: Support for a dimensional perspective on language delay. *Journal of Speech, Language, and Hearing Research, 52*, 16–30.

Rickard, B. L., Richards, S. A., Katz, L. A., Brackenbury, K., Best, L., & Spencer, R. (2011, November). *Literacy intervention at the college level: A success story*. Poster presented at the American Speech-Language-Hearing Association Convention, San Diego, CA.

Roberts, G., Torgesen, J. K., Boardman, A., & Scammacca, N. (2008). Evidenced-based strategies for reading instruction of older students with learning disabilities. *Learning Disabilities Research and Practice, 23*, 63–69.

Roswell, F. G., Chall, J. S., Curtis, M. E. & Kearns, G. (2006) *Diagnostic Assessments of Reading* (2nd ed.). Austin, TX: PRO-ED.

Roth, F. P., Speece, D. L., & Cooper, D. H. (2002). A longitudinal analysis of the connection between oral language and early reading. *Journal of Educational Research, 95*, 259–272.

Scammacca, N., Roberts, G., Vaughn. S., Edmonds, M., Wexler, J., Reutebuch, C. K., & Torgesen, J. K. (2007). *Interventions for adolescent struggling readers: A meta-analysis with implications for practice*. Portsmouth, NH: RMC Research Corporation, Center on Instruction.

Shaughnessy, A., & Sanger, D. (2005). Kindergarten teachers' perceptions of language and literacy development, speech–language pathologists, and language interventions. *Communication Disorders Quarterly, 26* (2), 67–84.

Schiff, R., & Calif, S. (2004). An academic intervention program for EFL university students with reading disabilities. *Journal of Adolescent and Adult Literacy, 48*(2), 102–113.

Snow, C., & Moje, E. (2010). Why is everyone talking about adolescent literacy? *Phi Delta Kappan, 91*(6), 66–69.

Snow, C. E., Scarborough, H. S., & Burns, M. S. (1999). What speech–language pathologists need to know about early reading. *Topics in Language Disorders, 20*, 48–58.

Stanovich, K. E. (1986). Matthew effects in reading: Some consequences of individual differences in the acquisition of literacy. *Reading Research Quarterly, 21*, 360–380.

Starling, J., Munro, N., Togher, L., & Arciuli, J. (2012). Training secondary school teachers in instructional language modification techniques to support adolescents with language impairment A randomized controlled trial. *Language, Speech, and Hearing Services in Schools, 43*, 474–495.

Staskowski M., & Zagaiski K. (2003) Reaching for the stars: SLPs shine on literacy teams. *Seminars in Speech and Language, 24*(3), 199–213.

Stone, C. A., & Conca, L. (1993). The origin of strategy deficits in children with learning disabilities: Social constructivist perspective. In L. J. Meltzer (Ed.), *Strategy assessment and instruction for students with learning disabilities* (pp. 23–59). Austin: PRO-ED.

Storch, S. A., & Whitehurst, G. J. (2002). Oral language and code-related precursors to reading: Evidence from a longitudinal structural model. *Developmental Psychology, 38*, 934–947.

Swanson, H. L. (1999). Reading research for students with LD: A meta-analysis of intervention outcomes. *Journal of Learning Disabilities, 32*, 504–532.

Swanson, H. L., & Hoskyn, M. (2001). Instructing adolescents with learning disabilities: A component and composite analysis. *Learning Disabilities Research and Practice, 16*, 109–120.

Throneburg, R. N., Calvert, L. K., Sturm, J. J., Paramboukas, A. A., & Paul, P. J. (2000). A comparison of service delivery models: Effects on the curricular vocabulary skills in the school setting. *American Journal of Speech–Language Pathology, 9*, 10–20.

Tilstra, J., McMaster, K., Van den Broek, P., Kendeou, P., & Rapp, D. (2009). Simple but complex: components of the simple view of reading across grade levels. *Journal of Research in Reading, 32*, 383–401.

Torgesen, J. K., Houston, D. D., Rissman, L. M., Vaughn, S., Wexler, J., Francis, D. J., et al. (2007). *Academic literacy instruction for adolescents: A guidance document from the Center on Instruction*. Portsmouth, NH: RMC Research.

Tyler, A., & Nagy, W. E. (1990). Use of derivational morphology during reading. *Cognition, 36*, 17–34.

Ukrainetz, T. A. (1998). Beyond Vygotsky: What Soviet activity theory offers naturalistic language intervention? *Journal of Speech–Language Pathology and Audiology, 22*, 122–133.

Ukrainetz, T. A. (2005). What to work on and how: An examination of the practice of school-age language intervention. *Contemporary Issues in Communication Sciences and Disorders, 32*, 108–119.

Ukrainetz, T. A. (2006). Assessment and intervention within a contextualized skill framework. In. T. A. Ukrainetz (Ed.), *Contextualized language intervention: Scaffolding preK–12 literacy achievement* (pp. 7–58). Austin, TX: PRO-ED.

Ukrainetz, T. A., & Fresquez, E. F. (2003). "What isn't language?": A qualitative study of the role of the school speech–language pathologist. *Language, Speech, and Hearing Services in Schools, 34*, 284–298.

Vaughn, S., & Klingner, J. (2004). Teaching reading comprehension to students with learning disabilities. In C. A. Stone, E. R. Silliman, B. J. Ehren, & K. Apel (Eds.), *Handbook of language and literacy: Development and disorders* (pp. 541–555). New York, NY: Guilford.

Vogel, S. A. (1985). Syntactic complexity in written expression of LD college writers. *Annals of Dyslexia, 35*, 137–157.

Wagner, R. K., & Torgesen, J. K. (1987). The nature of phonological awareness and its causal role in the acquisition of reading skills. *Psychological Bulletin, 101*, 192–212.

Wiederholt, J. L., & Bryant, B. R. (1992). *Gray Oral Reading Tests* (3rd ed.). Austin, TX: PRO-ED.

Wiederholt, J. L. & Bryant, B. R. (2001). *Gray Oral Reading Tests* (4th ed.). Austin, TX: PRO-ED.

Wiederholt, J. L., & Bryant, B. R. (2012). *Gray Oral Reading Tests* (5th ed.). Austin, TX: PRO-ED.

Williams, K. T. (2001). *Group reading assessment and diagnostic evaluation*. New York, NY: Pearson.

Windsor, J. (2000). The role of phonological opacity in reading achievement. *Journal of Speech, Language, and Hearing Research, 43*, 50–61.

Woodcock, R., Mather, N., & Schrank, F. (2004). *Woodcock-Johnson III Diagnostic Reading Battery*. Rolling Meadows, IL: Riverside.

Work, R. S., Cline, J. A., Ehren, B. J., Keiser, D. L., & Wujek, C. (1993). Adolescent language programs. *Language, Speech, and Hearing Services in Schools*, *24*, 43–53.

Yasutake, D., & Bryan, T. (1995). The influence of affect on the achievement and behavior of students with learning disabilities. *Journal of Learning Disabilities*, *28*, 329–334.

Index

About the Editor

Teresa Ukrainetz, Ph.D., S-LP(C), is professor and director of communication disorders at the University of Wyoming. She has a Bachelor's degree in psychology and French from the University of Calgary and a Master's degree in speech–language pathology from the University of British Columbia. Teresa worked as a school speech–language pathologist for several years in British Columbia, Canada, before earning her doctorate in speech–language pathology from the University of Texas at Austin. She enjoys the small town and mountain life of Wyoming, with frequent trips back north of the border. Teresa's research and scholarship address the intersection of skill and context in school-age language intervention. Her publications include assessment validity, treatment efficacy, intervention practices, phonemic awareness, narrative, and the role of the SLP in the schools. Her other language intervention book, *Contextualized Language Intervention: Scaffolding PreK–12 Literacy Achievement*, is also available from PRO-ED.